Fundamentals *of the* CRIMINAL JUSTICE SYSTEM

Second Edition

DONALD A. MACINTOSH

B.A., M.A., LL.B.

MEMBER OF THE ONTARIO BAR

CARSWELL

Thomson Professional Publishing

Canadian Cataloguing in Publication Data

MacIntosh, Donald A., 1952-
    Fundamentals of the criminal justice system

2nd. ed.
Includes bibliographical references and index.
ISBN 0-459-55348-8 (bound) ISBN 0-459-55335-6 (pbk.)

1. Criminal justice, Administration of — Canada.
2. Criminal law — Canada.   I. Title.
KE8809.M25   1995   345.71'05   C95-932145-4
KF9219.M25   1995

© 1995 Thomson Canada Ltd.

The publisher is not engaged in rendering legal, accounting or other professional advice. If legal advice or other expert assistance is required, the services of a competent professional should be sought. The analysis contained herein represents the opinions of the authors and should in no way be construed as being official or unofficial policy of any governmental body.

The paper used in this publication meets the mimimum requirements of American National Standard for Information Sciences - Permanence of Paper for Printed Library Materials, ANSI Z39.48-1984.

CARSWELL
Thomson Professional Publishing

One Corporate Plaza, 2075 Kennedy Road, Scarborough, Ontario M1T 3V4
Customer Service:
Toronto 1-416-609-3800
Elsewhere in Canada/U.S. 1-800-387-5164
Fax 1-416-298-5094

To my late father, Alex J. MacIntosh, Q.C.,
and my loving wife, Geneviève

Preface

This book is intended as an introductory work on criminal law aimed at students who have not previously studied the subject. It is hoped that students will develop an interest in the subject matter which will lead to further study. Because the enactment of the Charter of Rights is working the most profound change in our criminal law in our history, the Charter has been discussed in some detail. An historical analysis of the events leading up to the implementation of the Charter has been avoided because these have been discussed in great detail in other works. Rather, an attempt has been made to show the magnitude of the changes which are occurring as the development of Charter law illustrates the role which judges play in using somewhat general principles to develop a body of jurisprudence.

It is quite clear that the Charter has been capable of a variety of interpretations and, indeed, many commentators thought it would do little more than to codify principles which had long been honoured in our society. Although the decisions of some of the lower courts in the early days of the Charter seemed to confirm such expectations, the Supreme Court of Canada took a much more expansive view of the Charter. In fact, the Charter has transformed Canada's legal system. Parliament no longer has absolute supremacy in the sense that it may pass laws within its own jurisdiction as it sees fit. Subject to the override powers in section 33 of the Charter, Parliament must enact legislation which conforms with the rights and freedoms guaranteed by the Charter. This new judicial power has had more influence on the criminal law than on any other branch of Canadian law, as the Charter has given citizens new protections which were not previously available to those charged with criminal offences. A detailed discussion of the Charter would require a separate book, but an attempt has been made to describe the major changes effected by the courts as a result of the Charter and to give some indication of the possibilities for the future.

This book makes no attempt to state definitively the criminal law in 1995. Rather, an attempt has been made to discuss those aspects of the criminal law which are of the greatest interest and have the widest application. An effort has been made to illustrate the constantly changing nature of criminal law as courts deal with new problems and expand legal principles to accord with the demands of a modern society.

The author has attempted to avoid burdening the reader with technical, legal expressions, using these only when they are essential elements of the principles being discussed. Some introductory legal texts avoid quoting extensively from cases and from statutes, simply summarizing these. In this book deliberate use has been made of quotations so the students can see, at first hand, the kind of reasoning which judges apply in making decisions and thus appreciate the types of problems which the courts are called upon to decide. The actual text of statutes has been used so that students may appreciate that the criminal law is not merely a simple enunciation of what may and may not be done, but rather is often a complex set of rules reflecting the checks and balances which the legislatures deem appropriate. In some cases, the appellate courts of various provinces differ as to the appropriate interpretation of the law and, until these differences are settled by the Supreme Court of Canada, the interpretation of the law may differ from one province to another. Accordingly, decisions are frequently used throughout the work which reflect such differences.

Part of this book is addressed to the needs of the citizen who may at some time or another be involved in the criminal process. In any society it is important that people be aware of their rights and be vigilant in their protection. Hopefully, this book will make some contribution to an understanding of the criminal law and its importance to society. Although many substantive changes have been made in our criminal law, much in the way of reform is still needed. The impetus for such reform can only come from a citizenry aware of its rights and obligations and of the fundamental truth that an attack on the rights and liberties of any one of us is an attack on all.

Acknowledgements

I am indebted to Paul J. Evraire, Q.C., Director of the Toronto Regional Office, Department of Justice, who supported me throughout the revision of this work and generously permitted me to make use of the facilities of the Department of Justice.

I am indebted to D.R.H. Heather, Q.C., editor of Snow's Criminal Code, who has given me valuable suggestions and advice.

No book could be written without the assistance of an able secretary. I have benefitted greatly from the tireless energy of Julie Mouchbahani, who found time to type and retype the manuscript in addition to fulfilling her responsibilities for two busy lawyers.

I have been fortunate to have had the able assistance and encouragement of Bernie Aron, my legal editor, who, as always, has been a pleasure to work with. I am also indebted to production editors Dennis Brennan and Steven Hostetter for their able assistance in improving the manuscript.

I hope that this book fulfills, in some measure, the high expectations of those who have offered me criticism and advice. I am, of course, solely responsible for the shortcomings contained herein.

The views expressed herein are those of the author and do not represent the opinions of the Department of Justice.

Donald A. MacIntosh
Toronto, Ontario

Publisher's Note

The 1985 Revised Statutes of Canada were proclaimed in force on December 12, 1988. This consolidation resulted in changes to the section numbers of the Canadian Criminal Code as well as other federal statutes. General references in the text to section numbers of federal statutes will contain the revised numbering under this recent consolidation.

Where the author refers to the court's interpretation or treatment of a section of a federal statute, and the court was dealing with the statutory provision as numbered under the prior consolidation of the 1970 Revised Statutes of Canada, the section number under the R.S.C. 1970 consolidation will be shown in the text, followed by the corresponding section number under the R.S.C. 1985 consolidation in square brackets.

Table of Contents

Table of Cases

1

Canada's Legal System

1. ORIGINS OF OUR LEGAL SYSTEM

It is not possible to have an understanding of Canadian criminal law without having some knowledge of the history and origins of Canada's legal system, its Constitution, and its court structure. Canada's legal system has been greatly influenced by the development of British common law and by British Parliamentary conventions and traditions. When British settlers came to Canada they brought with them their traditions, conventions and comparable institutions, and these in large part have laid the foundation for our present legal system. The common law of England, which is the foundation for many of our laws and principles, was first brought to Canada when British settlers came to Prince Edward Island, Nova Scotia and New Brunswick. Indeed, the law imported into a settled British colony was both English common law and English statute law, unless, of course, it was deemed unsuitable to the circumstances of the colony.[1] Although Quebec was conquered in 1760, the British system of common law only applied to it for a short time. By 1774, the Quebec Act[2] provided that the pre-conquest civil law would apply to all matters relating to property and civil rights in the province, while English criminal law continued in force.[3]

(a) English Common Law

Under the common law, judges decide cases on the basis of principles which have been set down in previous cases, some of which have been decided years or even centuries before. Under this system cases are decided on the basis

---

[1] P.W. Hogg, *Constitutional Law of Canada*, 2nd ed. (Toronto: Carswell, 1985), at pp. 24-25.
[2] (14 Geo. III), c. 83.
[3] *Supra*, note 1, at p. 27.

of precedent in the sense that judges follow earlier decisions. Thus, in legal circles, it is often said that a judge relied upon precedent in making his decision. The principle of *stare decisis*, which, roughly translated, means to stand by decided matters, is an important part of Canada's legal system. Under this doctrine a lower court is bound to act in accordance with the decision of a precedent which has been handed down by a higher court. Therefore, if the Supreme Court of Canada, as the highest court in the land, decides that drunkenness is not a defence to a particular charge, the lower courts are bound to follow that decision and apply the law so established. Similarly, a provincial criminal court judge is bound to follow the decisions handed down by the Supreme Court in the province where he or she is sitting. A Supreme Court judge will be bound by the decisions of the Court of Appeal for such a jurisdiction.

In applying the doctrine of *stare decisis*, a court will follow the most recent precedent available. The doctrine presupposes that a court is only bound by the precedent which exists within its own jurisdiction and, accordingly, although decisions of courts outside that jurisdiction may have some persuasive value, they are not binding. Canadian courts, which have been influenced by the British common law tradition, do pay special attention to English cases which are considered to be highly persuasive. Cases from other common law countries, such as Australia, are also considered to be of persuasive value, although they are not considered to be as persuasive as the English case law.

Although English case law is not now binding upon Canadian courts, such was not always the case. The British North America Act of 1867,[4] which was Canada's principal constitutional document until the Constitution Act of 1982[5] came into effect, did not establish a Supreme Court. It was not until 1875 that the Supreme Court of Canada was established by Parliament.[6] As the Supreme Court of Canada was not established by the British North America Act (B.N.A. Act), it did not have constitutional status. When Parliament created the Supreme Court of Canada in 1875, appeals to the Judicial Committee of the Privy Council, which for many years was the final appeal court for Canada, the British Commonwealth and British colonies, were retained.[7] Canadian courts had to follow the decisions of the British House of Lords and the Judicial Committee of the Privy Council.[8]

While criminal appeals to the Privy Council were abolished in 1933, it was not until 1949 that civil appeals were abolished and the Supreme Court of Canada finally became the highest court in the land. Thus, English case law has had an enormous influence on the development of Canadian law. Even after the

---

[4] (30 & 31 Vict.), c. 3.
[5] Enacted by the Canada Act, 1982 (U.K.), c. 11, s. 1.
[6] *Supra*, note 1, at p. 4.
[7] *Ibid.*
[8] *Supra*, note 1, at p. 183.

Supreme Court of Canada became the final appellate court, it only gradually ceased to follow Privy Council decisions faithfully and considered itself free to override its own earlier decisions which, of course, were heavily influenced by English decisions.[9]

(b) British North America Act, 1867

The influence of English law on Canadian law is also a direct result of the close ties which Canada has had and continues to have with Britain. Prior to the Constitution Act of 1982, the B.N.A. Act was Canada's principal constitutional document. It was an ordinary statute passed by the British Parliament which created a new Dominion of Canada by uniting the Provinces of Ontario, Quebec, New Brunswick and Nova Scotia and contained a provision providing for the admission of other parts of British North America. The enactment of the B.N.A. Act, unlike the enactment of the American Constitution, did not symbolize a breaking away from Britain and contained no ringing declaration of independence. The framers of the legislation, rather than contemplating any marked separation between Great Britain and Canada, probably contemplated that Canada would continue to remain very closely associated with Britain and this, of course, proved to be the case. Indeed, it was not until the Statute of Westminster was passed in 1931[10] that the Canadian Parliament and legislatures became truly sovereign by gaining the power to repeal British statutes which applied to them.[11]

The B.N.A. Act had a distinctive British character, as there was an unspoken implication that many of the fundamental principles of government did not need to be stated. Great Britain has, for centuries, had an unwritten constitution, unlike the United States whose constitution provides in detail for the legislative, executive and judicial branches of government. The drafters of the B.N.A. Act contemplated that much of Canada's constitution would be based upon the unwritten customs and conventions which had prevailed in Great Britain for many years. The preamble to the Act provides that Canada is to have a constitution "similar in Principle to that of the United Kingdom." That preamble was considered sufficient to establish the rules for some of the most important functions of government. The statement provided the theoretical justification for importing British constitutional principles to supplement the rather sparse framework of the British legal system. The three major doctrines so imported as part of Canadian constitutional law are: (i) responsible government, (ii) Parliamentary supremacy, and (iii) the rule of law.

---

[9] *Ibid.*
[10] (22 & 23 Geo. 5), c. 4.
[11] *Supra*, note 1, at p. 167.

(c) British Legal System

(i) *Responsible government*

The B.N.A. Act did not establish the rules for responsible government, so the working of the system depended on the adherence to established conventions. There are several sections in the B.N.A. Act which state that the executive government of Canada is vested in the Queen and provide that some of the Queen's powers may be exercised by a Governor General or, in the case of a province, by a Lieutenant Governor. Under the Act, the Governor General has the power to appoint members of the Senate, to summon Parliament and to dissolve Parliament. A bill passed by Parliament does not become law until it is presented to the Governor General for the Queen's assent. Under section 55 of the B.N.A. Act, that assent could theoretically be withheld. If the assent is not given within two years from the day on which it is presented to the Governor General for such assent, the bill will not have any force. Under section 56 of the Act, the Queen in Council has power to disallow legislation. If one simply looked at the B.N.A. Act one could conclude that the sovereign had very substantial powers relating to the Government of Canada. In fact, the powers of the sovereign and the Governor General are exercised on the basis of the advice of the government of the day because of the conventions establishing responsible government inherited from the United Kingdom.[12]

The B.N.A. Act, which conferred such significant powers upon the sovereign and the Governor General, does not mention the Prime Minister or the Cabinet or political parties. Section 11 of the Act provides for a Privy Council to be chosen by those summoned from time to time by the Governor General. Section 12 provides that the executive power be vested in the Governor General, acting on the advice of the Privy Council of Canada. Apart from these rather sketchy provisions, the relationship of the executive to Parliament is undefined. Thus, the fundamental principles governing the relationship of Parliament to the executive, composed of the Prime Minister and the Cabinet, were left to be determined by the conventions and traditions governing Parliamentary democracy in Great Britain. A brief review of some of these principles will illustrate the extent to which the drafters of the B.N.A. Act effectively relied on the established conventions which are now fundamental to the form of responsible government enjoyed in Canada.

Under these conventions the Prime Minister and the Cabinet will only hold office so long as they are able to command the majority of support in the House of Commons. Whenever there is a political party holding a majority of the seats it is not difficult for the Prime Minister to maintain the necessary support because, under our system, members of the House of Commons vote according to party lines. If there is no party holding a majority in the House

---

[12] *Supra*, note 1, at pp. 12-14; pp. 18, 19; pp. 191-94.

of Commons, the government may lose the confidence of the House of Commons and may have to resign. In such circumstances, the Prime Minister will normally ask the Governor General to dissolve the House so that an election may be called. Theoretically, the Governor General could refuse to dissolve the House and ask the Leader of the Opposition to form the government. In 1926, the Governor General of Canada, Lord Byng, refused to grant Prime Minister Mackenzie King a dissolution and called upon Mr. Meighen, the Leader of the Conservative Party, to form the government. However, this precipitated a constitutional crisis and no Governor General since then has refused to grant a Prime Minister such a dissolution.[13] Obviously, these practices are fundamental to the system of responsible government, but their observance in Canada is based upon the conventions which Canada has inherited from Great Britain. These obviously are only a few of the fundamental features of responsible government, but they do serve to illustrate that a large part of our constitutional law is based upon conventions and traditions established in Great Britain.

(ii) *Parliamentary supremacy*

Another cardinal feature of our constitutional law is the doctrine of Parliamentary supremacy which, once again, is a concept Canada has inherited from Great Britain. The principle of Parliamentary supremacy, within the British context, means that Parliament can pass whatever legislation it wishes. Indeed, it has sometimes been said that Parliament can do everything but make a man a woman. In Canada, this doctrine is modified somewhat because of the nature of the Canadian federal system by which legislative power is shared between Parliament and the provincial legislatures. Thus, in Canada, the doctrine means that Parliament and the legislatures of the provinces are supreme, so long as the law passed relates to a matter which falls within their legislative jurisdiction established by the B.N.A. Act and does not offend the Charter of Rights and Freedoms.[14] The result of this distribution of powers is that neither Parliament nor the provincial legislatures are supreme in the unqualified British sense, so that Canadian constitutional law is substantially different than its British counterpart where all power is concentrated in the hands of one legislative body.

This substantial difference between the British and Canadian forms of government has made for a very different development of constitutional law in Canada because the validity of a particular piece of legislation will depend upon whether the legislative body passing it was acting within its jurisdiction. There can be a considerable overlapping of legislative power as sometimes there is not a clear division between the two jurisdictions. For example, in the

---

[13] *Supra*, note 1, at p. 210.
[14] Being Part I of the Constitution Act, 1982 [en. by the Canada Act, 1982 (U.K.), c. 11, s. 1].

field of criminal law Parliament has the power to pass criminal law, but the provinces are responsible for its administration. The provinces have jurisdiction over property and local works and undertakings in the province, while Parliament has jurisdiction over trade and commerce. The result of such shared jurisdiction is that legislation may have more than one aspect to it and it is often unclear whether legislation falls within provincial or federal jurisdiction. An example is provided by federal and provincial laws regulating .dangerous driving. The Criminal Code of Canada[15] creates the offence of the dangerous operation of a motor vehicle, vessel or aircraft which falls within the federal criminal law legislative jurisdiction. However, the Supreme Court of Canada has said that the provinces may pass legislation creating provincial offences of driving without due care and attention. Such legislation, which is very similar to the federal offence of dangerous driving, has been held to fall within provincial jurisdiction as legislation regulating the conduct of highway traffic.[16]

Many disputes have arisen about the legislative jurisdiction of Parliament and provincial legislatures and much of the work of the Supreme Court of Canada has related to attempts by one jurisdiction or the other to broaden its power to legislate. The division of powers under the B.N.A. Act has meant that English constitutional law is not as relevant to the Canadian experience as it otherwise would be. Nevertheless, the doctrine of Parliamentary supremacy means that the ultimate authority in the field of law is the appropriate legislative body because it can effectively overrule the decisions of our highest courts. This doctrine is now subject to one major limitation because the Constitution Act of 1982 added the Charter of Rights and Freedoms to the Constitution of Canada. As will be discussed in greater detail in Chapter 3, Effect of the Charter on Criminal Law, this has fundamentally limited the doctrine of Parliamentary supremacy in Canada.

For many years Canadians were dependent on the courts applying conventions developed in England since the enactment of the Magna Carta to place some limitation on the absolute power of legislative bodies. Thus, when in 1937 Alberta passed legislation affecting freedom of the press, some of the Supreme Court judges, in declaring that legislation unconstitutional, resorted to the preamble of the B.N.A. Act.[17] They held that as the B.N.A. Act contemplated a constitution similar to that of the United Kingdom the Parliamentary system must be the subject of free discussion and criticism. Indeed, one Supreme Court judge expressed the view in a later case that Parliament itself could not suppress that free discussion and criticism which was essential to the workings of a parliamentary democracy.[18]

---

[15] R.S.C. 1985, c. C-46, s. 253.
[16] *Supra*, note 1, at p. 418.
[17] *Ref. re Alberta Statutes*, [1938] S.C.R. 100, at 133 and 145, affirmed [1939] A.C. 117 (P.C.).
[18] *Switzman v. Elbling* (1957), 7 D.L.R. (2d) 337, at 371 (S.C.C.).

(iii) *Rule of law*

Another fundamental feature of the Canadian legal system was its acceptance of the principle known as the "rule of law." This principle, developed in Great Britain, was used by the courts to protect the citizen against possible excesses of authority by government officials. In short, it means that the government itself is subject to the law and must operate according to its terms. Courts consistently used this principle to ensure that government officials were kept within the bounds of the law and that any action they undertook was to be pursuant to a law.

Professor A.V. Dicey, in his book, *Introduction to the Study of the Law of the Constitution*,[19] outlined the basic principles of the rules as:

(1) the supremacy of regular law as opposed to the influence of arbitrary power, excluding the existence of arbitrariness, prerogative, or even of wide discretionary authority on the part of the government;

(2) equality before the law, excluding the idea of any exemption of officials or others from the duty of obedience to the law which governs other citizens;

(3) the law of the constitution is not the source but the consequence of the rights of individuals as defined and enforced by the courts.

(d) Statutory Law

Increasingly, the law is the product of a statute rather than the judge-made law which was an essential feature of the common law. In the case of a federal law, a bill is ordinarily introduced in the House of Commons where it is given three readings. On the occasion of the first reading the bill is not debated, as debate takes place on second reading, during which the Minister will inform the House of the purpose of the bill and the bill will be fully debated. In the case of any substantive bill it will ordinarily then be forwarded to a legislative committee for further consideration. At that time the committee will frequently hold public hearings so that criticism and suggestions for amendment may be made. Once the committee makes its report, which may include recommendations for changes, the bill will be reintroduced in the House of Commons and the House must then decide whether or not it will accept it as reported from the committee. The bill is then ready for third reading when the only question is whether or not the bill will be passed. The bill must also be passed by the Senate which follows a procedure very similar to that of the House of Commons. When a bill has been passed both by the House of Commons and the Senate it will then be given Royal Assent.

---

[19] A.V. Dicey, *Introduction to the Study of the Law of the Constitution* (London: MacMillan, 1961), at pp. cxiiv; pp. 183-205.

A somewhat similar procedure regarding the passing of bills is followed by the provincial legislatures. This is the process by which much of our law is now established. Although the common law was capable of being developed, the changing conditions of society often demanded a more rapid response than the judicial process provided. Such a development of the law also permits a substantial public participation which was not a feature of the development of the common law.

Canadian criminal law is statute law. Much of Canadian criminal law has now been codified in the statute entitled "An Act respecting the Criminal Law", which is cited as the Criminal Code. In addition to the Criminal Code there are several other federal statutes which apply to criminal law, such as the Narcotic Control Act,[20] the Food and Drugs Act,[21] the Competition Act,[22] and the Young Offenders Act.[23] The result is that although the Canadian criminal law owes much to the common law, there are now substantial differences between English criminal law and Canadian criminal law, with the result that English precedents are increasingly less useful.

The law pertaining to search and seizure is one example of the substantial differences which are arising between English criminal law and Canadian criminal law. In England, the common law places severe restrictions upon the search and seizure powers of police officers because a search warrant authorizing a search and seizure is considered to be an exception to the age-old legal principle that a man's home is his castle. Thus, under English law, a judge will not issue a search warrant to search someone's residence for evidence relating to the commission of a murder offence.[24] The English position was described by Mr. Justice Martin of the Ontario Court of Appeal in *R. v. Rao*, wherein His Lordship said:

> In England, statutory authority for the granting of search warrants is conferred by particular enactments. In the main, a warrant can be obtained only where there is a reasonable cause for believing that an offence against the relevant Act has been committed. The powers are mainly confined to entry and search for such articles as stolen goods, counterfeit coins and instruments of counterfeiting, forged documents and material intended to be used for forgery of documents, explosives, firearms, dangerous drugs, and the seizure of anything likely to be evidence of an offence under the relevant statute. . . . No statutory authority, is of course, required where the basis of the entry and search is consensual.

> England, however, did not enact general or comprehensive legislation similar to that under the Criminal Code in Canada authorizing the issuing of search warrants to search for and seize property related to crime or affording evidence of crime. In England, for example, there is no authority whereby a police officer investigating a possible murder may obtain a warrant to search private premises

---

[20] R.S.C. 1985, c. N-1.

[21] R.S.C. 1985, c. F-27.

[22] R.S.C. 1985, c. C-34.

[23] R.S.C. 1985, c. Y-1.

[24] *Ghani v. Jones*, [1970] 1 Q.B. 693 (C.A.).

for the body of victim or the murder weapon. . . . The recent British Royal Commission on Criminal Procedure recommended that, for the first time in Britain, the police should be enabled to apply for warrants to search for evidence of crime. . . . The commission recommended that this power should be confined to serious offences and should be subject to certain safeguards.[25]

As will be seen in Chapter 8, Search and Seizure, Canadian police officers have broad powers under the Criminal Code to search premises for evidence relating to the commission of a crime. For example, a justice of the peace may authorize a search warrant where he is satisfied by information upon oath that there is reasonable ground to believe that there is in some place anything which will afford evidence with respect to the commission of an offence against the Criminal Code. Thus, Canadian law is more permissive in this respect than the common law.

It is apparent that British legal traditions have had a profound impact on the development of Canada's legal system, but any discussion of the Canadian legal system would be incomplete without noting that the Canadian legal system has been greatly influenced by French civil law. Indeed, Canada is blessed with two legal systems: the common law system and the civil law system which has been preserved in Quebec. The influence of the civil law tradition, however, is not a particularly appropriate subject for this book because the civil law of Quebec relates to such matters as contracts, wills, real estate and other private law as opposed to criminal law.

2. FEDERALISM AND THE DISTRIBUTION OF POWERS

In a federal state, the central government is supreme within its own jurisdiction and the regional government is supreme within its own jurisdiction. Thus, in the Canadian context, the Parliament of Canada has powers which cannot be altered or affected by the provinces and, similarly, the legislature of a province has powers which cannot be altered by the Parliament of Canada. In a federal state each level of government is "co-ordinate;" thus, one level of government cannot pass laws which would change the powers of the other level of government. Professor Dicey outlines the cardinal features of a federal state as follows:

> (1) two levels of government rule the same land and people, (2) each level has at least one area of action in which it is autonomous, and (3) there is some guarantee (even though merely a statement in the constitution) of the autonomy of each government in its own sphere.[26]

---

[25] (1984), 40 C.R. (3d) 1, at 16 (Ont. C.A.).
[26] Dicey, *supra*, note 19, at pp. 140-43; pp. 151-55.

(a) Federal States and Unitary States

Canada, Australia and the United States are all federal states whose constitutions differ substantially from "unitary" states such as Britain and New Zealand. In a unitary state there are not two co-ordinate levels of government, each passing laws in its own jurisdiction, but rather the power to make laws is concentrated in one central legislative authority. There are municipal governments which have a power to pass laws, but these governments are not independent and their powers may be abolished or otherwise changed by the national legislature.[27] In a federal state, municipalities are also creatures of the provinces and can have their powers abolished or changed by provincial governments. However, in a federal state, the state governments or provincial governments are distinct entities and are not subordinate to the federal or central government.

(b) Division of Powers Under the British North America Act, 1867

Under the B.N.A. Act powers were divided between the federal and provincial governments on the basis of what was thought to be their relative importance. The Fathers of Confederation believed that Canada should have a strong central government with the provinces playing very much the subordinate role. To this end, the powers which were regarded as being the most important powers were given to the federal government and those powers which were regarded as being less important were allocated to the provinces. Eugene Forsey, a renowned constitutional scholar, has stated that the division of powers in the B.N.A. Act is a reflection of Sir John A. Macdonald's desire to have a strong central government.[28]

In Dr. Forsey's view, a strong centralization of power in the hands of the federal government was "a conscious revulsion from (the) U.S. experience."[29] The American founding Fathers had provided that the powers which were not specifically given to the federal government and legislatures were to be reserved for the states. Since the U.S. Constitution gave the federal government a relatively short list of powers, many observers believed that government power would be decentralized and the states would have vast political power.

---

[27] Hogg, *supra*, note 1, at p. 80.
[28] E. Forsey, "In Defence of Macdonald's Constitution" (1976), 3 Dalhousie L.J. 529.
[29] *Ibid.*

(c) Sections 91 and 92 of the B.N.A. Act

It is not within the scope of this book to conduct a detailed analysis of the effect which the division of powers under the B.N.A. Act has had on Canadian constitutional law. However, it is not possible to deal with criminal law issues without having some understanding of the constitutional authority that Parliament and provincial legislatures have in relation to criminal law. The two principal sections of the B.N.A. Act which deal with the division of powers are sections 91 and 92 of the Act. Section 91 gives the federal government exclusive power to pass legislation in relation to the subjects set out in that section, while section 92 gives the provinces the exclusive power to legislate with respect to the subjects listed in that section. For example, section 91 gives the federal government the exclusive power to pass laws in relation to trade and commerce and banking. If a province were to pass legislation in respect of banking, the legislation would be attacked as being beyond provincial jurisdiction. Similarly, Parliament may not pass legislation which deals with a matter exclusively within provincial jurisdiction. As an example, Parliament could not pass a law dealing exclusively with education, which falls within provincial jurisdiction.

(d) Power to Pass Criminal Law

Parliament has been given the exclusive jurisdiction to pass criminal laws. The provinces, on the other hand, have jurisdiction over the administration of justice in the province, including the constitution, maintenance, and organization of provincial courts, both of civil and of criminal jurisdiction, and including procedure in civil matters in those courts.

There is strong evidence that the Fathers of Confederation were seeking to avoid the U.S. experience when they gave Parliament the exclusive power to legislate in the field of criminal law. In the United States, the states have the exclusive power to pass criminal law legislation. As a result, there is no uniform criminal law in the United States and the criminal law frequently varies greatly from one state to another.

Sir John A. Macdonald (who was then the Attorney General of Canada) outlined, during debate in the House of Commons, the reasons why criminal law should fall under federal jurisdiction, saying that:

> The criminal law too — the determination of what is a crime and what is not, and how crime shall be punished — is left to the General Government. This is a matter almost of necessity. It is of great importance that we should have the same criminal law throughout these provinces — that what is a crime in one part of British America, should be a crime in every part — that there should be the same protection of life and property in one as in another.[30]

---

[30] M.A. Lapin and J.S. Patrick (eds.), *Index to Parliamentary Debates on Confederation of the British North America Provinces* (Ottawa: 1951), at pp. 40-41.

He criticized the drafters of the U.S. Constitution for their decision to leave the criminal law power to the individual states saying that:

> It is one of the defects in the United States system, that each separate state has or may have a criminal code of its own — that what may be a capital offence in one state, may be a venial offence, punishable slightly, in another. But under our Constitution we shall have one body of criminal law, based on the criminal law of England, and operating equally throughout British America, so that a British American, belonging to what province he may, going to any other part of the Confederation, knows what his rights are in that respect, and what his punishment will be if an offender against the criminal laws of the land. I think this is one of the most marked instances in which we take advantage of the experience derived from our observations of the defects in the Constitution of the neighbouring Republic.[31]

(e) Provincial Offences

The provinces may create offences, as section 92(15) of the B.N.A. Act enables a province to pass laws providing for penalties, fines and imprisonment to enforce any law on a matter within provincial jurisdiction. Provinces may legislate on property and civil rights within a province, matters of a local or private nature and the licensing of occupations among other matters. Such provincial legislation creating offences will only be valid if it relates to a matter within provincial jurisdiction, such as the use of highways or the sale of liquor. It must secure some objective within a provincial legislative field.

(f) Constitution Act, 1982

In 1982, after much discussion and debate, Canada received a new Constitution by the Canada Act of 1982, called the Constitution Act, 1982, as passed by Britain's Parliament. The Act was proclaimed on April 17, 1982 by Queen Elizabeth. For the first time in its history Canada had a constitution which could be amended without the consent of the United Kingdom Parliament. Until then Canada's Constitution, the B.N.A. Act, 1867, could only be altered by the British Parliament.

The Constitution Act, 1982 consists of seven parts, including the Canadian Charter of Rights and Freedoms contained in Part I and new amending procedures contained in Part V. The B.N.A. Act, which was the principal source of constitutional law and procedure, has been included as item 1 in the Schedule to the Constitution Act, 1982; it establishes the legislative powers of Parliament and the provincial legislatures. Section 52 of the Act provides that the Constitution includes the Canada Act, the Constitution Act of 1982, the B.N.A. Act and amendments passed since 1867, and all further amendments.

---

[31] *Ibid.*, at p. 41.

Accordingly, the law dealing with the distribution of powers in the B.N.A. Act is still relevant in determining the limits to federal or provincial jurisdiction under the Constitution Act.

The inclusion of the existing B.N.A. Act which has been brought forward along with the other constitutional documents contained in the old Constitution has prompted one legal scholar to ask: what is new "about the so-called new Constitution?" In his book, *The Canadian Legal System*, Professor G.L. Gall says that "what is new is, essentially, the Charter of Rights and Freedoms."[32] Professor Gall adds that the made-in-Canada amending formula which allows Canadians to amend their Constitution without the amendments being passed by the Parliament of Westminster is "a second major new aspect of the Constitution."[33] The Charter has already had such a major effect on the Canadian legal system that the Constitution Act, 1982 may be regarded as having created a radically new constitutional system for Canada by imposing limitations on the powers of Parliament and the legislatures. The effect of the Charter of Rights and Freedoms on criminal law will be considered in Chapter 3, Effect of the Charter on Criminal Law.

3. THE COURTS

In Canada, there are both provincial and federal courts. Section 92(14) of the B.N.A. Act gives each province the power to make laws in relation to the administration of justice in the province. It also gives each province the power to maintain provincial courts, both of civil and criminal jurisdiction. The power to regulate criminal procedure, however, is reserved to Parliament by section 91(27). Section 101 of the B.N.A. Act confers on Parliament the power to establish a general court of appeal for Canada and any additional courts for the better administration of the laws of Canada.

(a) Provincial Courts

Generally speaking, the provincial court system is a three-tiered system consisting of (1) the superior court, which includes a Court of Appeal as well as a trial division; (2) the county or district courts; and (3) the inferior courts, which in most provinces are now called "Provincial Courts." Because the provinces have power over the administration of justice in the province, the provincial courts may be given jurisdiction over all applicable law, whether it is federal, provincial or constitutional. The jurisdiction of the courts over criminal matters will be dealt with in some detail later in this book.

---

[32] G.L. Gall, *The Canadian Legal System*, 2nd ed. (Toronto: Carswell, 1983), at p. 55.
[33] *Ibid.*, at p. 55.

Generally, provincial court judges have jurisdiction to hear cases involving breaches of provincial Acts and less serious criminal offences. They also preside over preliminary hearings which are held to determine whether there is sufficient evidence to commit an accused for trial. The bulk of the more serious cases are heard by the district or county courts, although as will be seen later, the most serious cases must be heard by a court of superior jurisdiction. Several provinces have conferred on the provincial court judges the power to hear civil matters where the amounts involved are not large. The most complex civil cases are dealt with by courts of superior jurisdiction, although county and district courts may hear less important civil cases. Some provinces have created special courts to deal with special matters such as criminal law and administrative law. In Ontario, for example, the Divisional Court, which is a court of superior jurisdiction, hears cases involving administrative law, such as whether the Labour Relations Board or Mental Health Review Board has acted in accordance with the law.

The majority of the provinces have now amalgamated county and district courts with the superior court. County courts now exist only in Nova Scotia. Provincial Courts of Appeal have a broad jurisdiction to deal with appeals from all of the inferior courts. There is not a general right of appeal in all cases to the provincial Court of Appeal, however. For example, an appeal in a criminal case which involves a question of mixed law and fact may only be taken with leave of the Court of Appeal. An appellate court does not retry a case, but rather considers whether, in examining the record, the trial judge has erred in applying the law, or has arrived at a factual conclusion which cannot be supported by the weight of evidence.

(b) Federal Courts

The Supreme Court of Canada is the highest court in the land which hears appeals involving criminal and civil law. The Supreme Court of Canada judges are appointed by the federal government in consultation with the Canadian Bar Association. The court consists of nine judges, three of whom have backgrounds in civil law. There are eight justices and one chief justice who serves as the Chief Justice of Canada. In civil matters, a party may only appeal to the Supreme Court of Canada if the Supreme Court of Canada grants leave to do so. Leave may be obtained on questions of law and mixed law and fact. However, leave will not be granted unless the issue is of substantial importance. In criminal cases, an accused whose acquittal on an indictable offence has been set aside by a provincial Court of Appeal has an automatic right to appeal to the Supreme Court of Canada. The Supreme Court of Canada will also hear an appeal in a criminal case where a judge of a provincial Court of Appeal has given a dissenting judgment on a question of law. The Supreme Court also hears appeals in criminal matters where the appeal involves a question of law and leave to appeal has been granted by the Supreme Court. As well, the Supreme Court of Canada may be asked to consider the constitutional validity of federal legislation by way of reference. Overall, the work of the Supreme Court of Canada is becoming increasingly difficult. With the passage of the Canadian Charter of Rights and Freedoms the workload has increased voluminously. Consequently, it is more difficult to obtain leave to appeal, particularly in civil cases.

The Federal Court of Canada is a specialized court which hears cases involving federal law such as tax cases, immigration cases and admiralty cases. The court consists of two levels, the appellate division and the trial division. The bench, which consists of one chief justice, one associate chief justice, and not more than 29 other judges, is appointed by the federal government. The trial division has exclusive jurisdiction to deal with matters of intellectual property, such as copyright, trademark, industrial design and patents. The Federal Court of Appeal hears appeals from the trial division and on questions of law arising from decisions of federal boards and commissions. The court also deals with appeals under specific federal legislation such as the Income Tax Act[34] and the Citizenship Act.[35] Most of the Federal Court, Trial Division's work consists of immigration cases.

---

[34] R.S.C. 1985, c. 1 (5th Supp.).
[35] R.S.C. 1985, c. C-29.

2

Nature and Purpose of Criminal Law

Criminal law is of the utmost importance to society. People rely on it for protection of life and property against those who, left to their own devices, would have little regard for those rights. At its best, criminal law should represent a fair balance between the interests of society in a peaceful society and the rights and freedoms of the individual. At its worst, it can become an instrument of oppression permitting the state to wipe out individual freedom. Thus, the type of criminal law which a country has and the manner in which it is administered will be a reliable indication of whether freedom is cherished there.

Criminal law is also one of the most interesting branches of law, commanding the attention of much of the population as the space given to it by the media so clearly demonstrates. Everyone should have an elementary knowledge of criminal law so that its protection may be invoked if necessary and there will be a general awareness of the obligations which are imposed on everyone by the criminal law. Such a knowledge is particularly important because ignorance of the law is not ordinarily any excuse for a breach of the criminal law.

1. SOURCES OF OUR CRIMINAL LAW

(a) English Common Law

The right to pass criminal laws is vested in Parliament by section 91 of the B.N.A. Act.[1] The source of much of our criminal law, however, is the common law of England and its statute law. When the English colonies in North America were settled, the criminal law of England was the common law (developed over centuries by English courts) and the laws of England were

---

[1] (30 & 31 Vict.), c. 3.

deemed to apply to the colonies. When territory was conquered, as was the case with Quebec, the law then in place was left in force until changed. The colonies had legislatures which had the power to change the criminal law if they wished. Thus, at the time of Confederation, the criminal law of Canada was a mixture of British law, the law prevailing in Quebec in 1763 when the English succeeded, and the laws enacted by the legislatures of Nova Scotia, New Brunswick and Canada.[2] After Confederation, efforts were made to consolidate Canadian criminal law, but as late as 1892 the criminal law of Canada was still an amalgam of the common and statute law of England, the law of the former colonies and some federal laws passed after Confederation.[3]

(b) Criminal Code

In 1892, Parliament enacted the first Criminal Code[4] based on an English draft code, the writings of some respected English writers and Canadian statutory law. This was not, however, a complete code as some existing federal legislation was preserved, and, although it effectively ended the application of British statute law, it did not purport to terminate the application of English common law.[5] Finally, in 1955, a new Criminal Code[6] was enacted which declared that persons could no longer be prosecuted for offences created by common law and the laws in force in the provinces at the time of Confederation.

The present Criminal Code[7] now contains most of the Canadian federal criminal law which applies to the general public, such as offences against the public order, offences against the administration of justice, sexual and moral offences, offences against the person, offences against property, fraudulent transactions, currency offences and conspiracies. But there are a number of federal statutes which create criminal offences. For example, the Competition Act[8] creates a number of criminal offences such as price fixing; the Customs Act[9] creates offences to punish smuggling; the Narcotic Control Act[10] creates offences relating to the sale and use of drugs.

(c) Provincial Offences

Under section 92 of the B.N.A. Act, the provinces have the power to

---

[2] P.W. Hogg, *Constitutional Law of Canada*, 2nd ed. (Toronto: Carswell, 1985), at pp. 26-30.
[3] A.W. Mewett and M. Manning, *Criminal Law*, 2nd ed. (Toronto: Butterworths, 1985), at p. 5.
[4] S.C. 1892, c. 29.
[5] Hansard, Vol. 1 (1892), at pp. 1312-13.
[6] S.C. 1953-54, c. 51.
[7] R.S.C. 1985, c. C-46.
[8] R.S.C. 1985, c. C-34.
[9] R.S.C. 1985, c. 1 (2nd Supp.).
[10] R.S.C. 1985, c. N-1.

impose fines, penalties or imprisonment to enforce any law which they have the jurisdiction to pass. The Act also gives the provinces exclusive jurisdiction to legislate over such matters as property and civil rights, matters of a local or private nature, the licensing of occupations such as the sale of securities, the administration of justice within the province, and municipal institutions. Thus, there are also many provincial laws which create offences. The validity of such provincial laws, however, depends on their enactment serving some purpose related to the matters on which the provinces may legislate. For example, provinces may create offences relating to the use of highways. This is necessary to ensure the proper use of highways. The procedure to be used in the prosecution of provincial offences is not that established by the Criminal Code, but rather the procedures set out in provincial Acts which are based in part on the Criminal Code, but usually contain some provisions appropriate to the provincial offences.

Often there is no clear-cut distinction between federal and provincial criminal jurisdiction and, accordingly, conflicts do arise. Parliament has sometimes used its criminal jurisdiction to trespass, as the courts have found, on provincial jurisdiction; for example, Parliament has attempted to use its power to enact criminal law to regulate the insurance industry.[11] In turn, provinces have attempted to use their power to enact penal sanctions for the purpose of trespassing on federal jurisdiction.[12] Such disputes are beyond the scope of this book. It is important, however, to understand that they do occur and that penal legislation, whether it be federal or provincial, will only be valid if it can be shown that Parliament or the province, in enacting the legislation, was exercising a legislative power assigned to it by the B.N.A. Act.

(d) Constitutional Considerations

It is not always easy to determine whether penal legislation is constitutional, as the powers assigned to Parliament and the provinces are relatively wide and, on occasion, both Parliament and the provinces may have the right to legislate on the same subject. The regulation of highway traffic, for example, is within provincial jurisdiction, but reckless driving may present a danger to the well-being of everyone using the highway. Therefore, both Parliament and provincial legislatures may have the power to legislate to attempt to ensure the safe use of the highways. Obviously, however, it is completely unsatisfactory to have legislation which may conflict. The courts have resolved this problem by holding that if there is such a conflict the federal legislation will prevail and the provincial legislation will be inoperative.[13] Yet courts have allowed provincial and federal penal laws to co-exist even though they appear

---

[11] *Ontario (A.G.) v. Reciprocal Insurers*, [1924] A.C. 328 (P.C.).

[12] *Kent (District of) v. Storgoff* (1962), 38 D.L.R. (2d) 362 (B.C.S.C.).

[13] *Great West Saddlery Co. v. R.*, [1921] 2 A.C. 91 (P.C.).

to cover the same subject. Thus, the Criminal Code provides that everyone is guilty of an offence who is criminally negligent in the operation of a motor vehicle. It also creates the offence of dangerous driving — driving a motor vehicle on a highway in a manner dangerous to the public, having regard to the circumstances. At the same time, most provinces have an offence called "careless driving" or "negligent driving" or "driving without due care and attention." All this legislation has been held to be valid although such legislation imposes penal sanctions; the federal legislation is justifiable because the conduct represents a public danger and the provincial legislation is justifiable because it is an attempt to regulate responsible conduct on highways which are a provincial responsibility.

2. NATURE OF CRIMINAL LAW

(a) Definition

Several writers have attempted to define what constitutes a crime and why society should determine that some actions should be deterred by penal sanctions while others, which frequently can cause serious harm, can only be remedied by private civil actions.

Blackstone, one of the great English legal writers, defined crime as "an act committed or omitted in violation of a public law forbidding or commanding it."[14] This is not very enlightening as the term "public law" can include all law. Blackstone also defined crime as "a violation of the public rights and duties due to the whole community considered as a community."[15] This definition was not considered satisfactory by later commentators as there are acts which could injure a community, yet would not be crimes. If people generally broke contracts, commerce would be impossible and the community would be endangered, but breaches of contract are not treated as crimes. The distinction suggested by Blackstone did not distinguish crimes from civil wrongs even in his day. Thus it was for many years a crime to steal horses, but the killing of horses gave rise only to a civil action for damages. Yet the destruction of horses was more injurious to the community as a whole than was the theft of horses.[16]

It is sometimes suggested that crimes are acts which offend the moral sense of society, although this is clearly not true of all crimes. The leaders of the Rebellion of 1837, which led to responsible government in Quebec and Ontario, were undoubtedly guilty of a crime and yet their actions certainly did not shock the moral sense of the whole society and were later regarded as

---

[14] 4 Blackstone Commentaries 5.
[15] *Ibid.*
[16] C.S. Kenny, *Outlines of Criminal Law* (Cambridge: Cambridge Press, 1947), at p. 6.

initiatives required to achieve self-government.[17] Directors of a bank may, by negligence, ruin a bank, dissipating the savings of depositors and shocking the moral sense of society by their neglect and yet not be guilty of a crime. Obviously, then, not all acts which shock society are crimes.

It has been suggested that crimes may be distinguished from civil wrongs because the state, by its law enforcement agencies, attempts to restrain criminal acts, but it only acts in civil matters when the wrong is done. This distinction is not valid, however, as the courts will act in civil matters to prevent an act which would cause a person irreparable harm by ordering that the act not be done. Others have suggested that the distinction between a crime and a civil wrong is that a crime may be punished. But this distinction does not distinguish criminal law from non-criminal activity because courts do award punitive damages in civil actions when they believe a wrongdoer has acted without any regard for the rights of others as, for example, when one has maliciously defamed another person's reputation. Thus, while punishment is certainly an object of criminal proceedings, it is sometimes an object of civil proceedings as well. After analyzing many of these distinctions C.S. Kenny, a leading authority on English criminal law, concluded that the ultimate distinction between criminal and civil law is that a private person may never release a person from prosecution for a crime whereas a private person could do so in the case of a civil wrong.[18] Only the Crown has the power to determine that a prosecution shall not be pursued and that a criminal shall be pardoned.

A well known English commentator, Glanville Williams, has defined a crime as a legal wrong which may be followed by criminal proceedings that may result in punishment.[19] In a leading Canadian text, two distinguished criminal lawyers have concluded that "the essence of criminal law is its public nature," as a crime is a wrong against the entire community.[20] Obviously, it is very difficult to formulate a definition which will prescribe any guiding principle which will tell one, in advance of legislation, the types of actions which will be considered to be crimes. Rather, we must conclude that a crime is an action declared to be criminal by the state because it concludes that the public interest requires that such activity be restrained. The prevention of it and the sanction of it cannot be left to the persons wronged, but is the responsibility of the community as a whole. One consequence of this is that an act may give rise both to civil and criminal liability. Thus, a person who has assaulted another may be prosecuted and imprisoned because such actions are deemed to be a threat to the community and the person assaulted may, by a civil court action, recover damages for the wrong suffered.

---

[17] D. Creighton, *Dominion of the North* (Toronto: MacMillan Co. of Can., 1953), at pp. 42 and 46.

[18] *Supra*, note 16.

[19] G. Williams, *Criminal Law* (London: Stevens & Sons, 1983), at p. 15.

[20] Mewett and Manning, *supra*, note 3, at pp. 14-15.

(b) Scope

There are still major disagreements about the types of activity which should be restrained by criminal law. For example, a debate has raged for many years as to the rights of consenting adults who commit acts in private which are shocking to large elements of the community. In 1957, a Parliamentary committee recommended that English criminal law be changed by dropping the prohibitions of certain homosexual acts committed in private and by legislating to limit prostitution offences to those which constituted some public harm or nuisance. A great debate resulted, known as the Hart-Devlin Debate.[21] Lord Devlin, on the one hand, argued that criminal law should reflect the views of morality held by the public generally. Professor Hart, on the other hand, argued that criminal law should not be based on such views of morality, but rather should be based on the social harm an act might cause.

In many cases the results of the two views will be the same, as assaults, murders, rapes and robberies would be considered to be crimes under either approach. But, in many other cases, such as sexual acts committed in private by consenting adults, gambling, obscenity or abortion, it may be argued that such acts are not a danger to society although they are morally wrong in the view of large segments of the population. The so-called Hart view was the one adopted by Prime Minister Trudeau when he said that the law had no place in the bedrooms of the nation. Parliament adopted his viewpoint by excluding from criminal law most sexual acts committed in private by consenting adults. The same issue underlies the debate on abortion which has been waged by those favouring and those opposed to abortion clinics, such as the clinics operated by Dr. Henry Morgentaler.

The issue is also important in the judgments which courts make in interpreting the law. Laws are very rarely precise; thus, for example, the definitions of obscenity and gross indecency leave much room for interpretation by the judges, and the result in any particular case may depend to a great extent on the views of the judge about the proper object of criminal law. Courts frequently differ as to what is obscene or grossly indecent. The trend appears to be towards more permissiveness, probably reflecting in part the attitudes of society and in part the view that the blunt instrument of criminal law should be restricted, so far as possible, to actions which can cause real harm to society. The determining factor will always be what Parliament concludes should be restrained by criminal sanctions. If it concludes that the existing law as interpreted by the courts is either too restrictive or is failing to restrain some conduct which is detrimental to the community, the law will be altered subject only to the rights and freedoms guaranteed by the Charter of Rights, which will be discussed in Chapter 3, Effect of the Charter on Criminal Law.

---

[21] Y. Caron, "The Legal Enforcement of Morals and the So-Called Hart-Devlin Controversy" (1969), 15 McGill L.J. 9.

3. PURPOSE OF CRIMINAL LAW

(a) Punishment

Determining the essence of criminal law is an issue that also affects the attitudes of legislators and judges to punishment. If an act is morally wrong, it is easy to understand that punishment should follow. If an act is not morally wrong, by what standard may a person know whether the act is criminal and what right has the state to exact punishment? The doctrine of *mens rea*, which will be examined in detail later, rests on the assumption that an essential feature of a crime is a blameworthy intention. Lord Denning, a leading English jurist, wrote in his outstanding work, *The Changing Law*: "In order that an act should be punishable, it must be morally blameworthy. It must be a sin."[22] However comforting this concept may be to law enforcement officers, not all crimes may be regarded either as sinful or morally wrong.

It is also an assumption of criminal law that people have it in their power to do or not do criminal acts, and that anyone who chooses to do such an act should be fully accountable for the consequences. Once again, this assumption is not always true because if one has the capacity to choose, one must know that a choice is being made to commit a crime. Yet, ignorance of the law is not an excuse and one may legitimately wonder whether every offender who has had sexual relations with a person under the age of 14 knew that it was a crime even if the person consented. Despite Charles Dickens' famous saying, the law is not always an "ass." In reality, it does recognize that it is difficult to assign blame in every situation in that there are varying degrees of wrongfulness. Accordingly, in virtually all cases the law does not prescribe a fixed punishment, but leaves it to the judge to fix a sentence which may vary from an absolute discharge to the maximum sentence possible.

(i) *Moral blameworthiness*

Courts, until recently, often selected a penalty which, in their view, fitted the crime. Under this approach the greatest punishment possible for the offence should only be imposed in the worst conceivable cases and cases of a lesser degree of seriousness should be dealt with by measuring their seriousness against cases calling for the maximum penalty. In other words, the judge should ask himself, "What proportion does the crime before me bear to the greatest possible crime coming under the same name?"[23] This punishment was imposed by the judicial view of the degree of moral blameworthiness and,

---

[22] Lord Denning, *The Changing Law* (London: Stevens & Sons Ltd., 1953), at p. 112.
[23] *R. v. Edwards* (1910), 4 Cr. App. R. 280 (C.C.A.).

accordingly, it may be said that it was imposed because of moral blameworthiness. One English judge, Slipper J., said that he thought it highly desirable
that criminals should be hated and that their punishment should reflect that
hatred.[24] This is an extreme statement which would not be endorsed by modern judges. Nevertheless, retribution does have an influence on the sentence
imposed. If punishment is to be related to justice, it surely must be deserved.
If it is not deserved, then the sentence must be unjust. Appellate courts in considering appeals from sentence consider these factors when concluding that a
sentence should be altered because it is less or more than is deserved.

(ii) *Fitting the crime*

The basic question that must be asked is by what standards is a judge to
determine whether a sentence is deserved? Lord Denning, one of the most distinguished and innovative English judges of his time, stated that the punishment
inflicted for a grave crime shoud adequately reflect the revulsion felt by the
majority of citizens for it. It was his view that it was wrong to consider the
objects of punishment as being a deterrent or reformative or preventative and
nothing else. "The ultimate justification of any punishment is not that it is a
deterrent but that it is the emphatic renunciation by the community of a crime."[25]
Another approach to be used in sentencing is to consider the harm done.
However, this should not be the sole criterion because even in cases where the
harm resulting from crimes is identical, the punishment should not be the
same. For example, there are clearly cases of manslaughter which differ greatly and deserve very different treatment. One death may have resulted from
momentary inattention in driving a car, while another may be the result of a
race on a public highway by two drunken drivers. Yet, measuring the extent
of harm done is obviously a relevant factor. If a man drives recklessly, he is
deserving of punishment in the sense that he is morally blameworthy, but it
would be wrong to impose the same punishment in cases where he had injured
someone as in cases where he had not.

(b) Deterrence

Moral indignation and consideration of the harm done may justify punishment, but they offer little guidance to a judge in deciding what a sentence
should be. In Canada, courts now consider that the objective of criminal law
is to protect the public, and penalties should be determined by considering

---

[24] "Report of the Royal Commission on Capital Punishment" (1953), 4th Session, Cmd. 8932
(H.M.S.O.), at p. 18.
[25] *Ibid.*, at para. 53.

what punishment will serve to further the protection of the public. In *R. v. Morrissette*, Chief Justice Culliton, in giving the judgment of the Court of Appeal of Saskatchewan, stated that "the public can best be protected by the imposition of sentences which punish the offender for the offence committed; that may deter him and others from committing such an offence and that may assist in his reformation and rehabilitation."[26]

If one was solely intent on protecting the public, one could adopt the philosophy in force in England in the Eighteenth century when even the theft of a small amount of money could lead to execution or banishment. Fortunately, such an approach is no longer acceptable in a civilized society, as the principal modern objective is not to remove the offender from society, but to protect the public by deterrence and rehabilitation. Thus, the punishment imposed should deter the offender; the sentence in itself should be a lesson that anti-social activities will lead to very unpleasant results and also will probably lead to a more severe punishment if subsequent offences are committed. The sentence is intended to deter others.

It is very difficult to determine the value of deterrence. Some commentators have concluded that it is impossible to measure the deterrent effect of sentences on potential offenders.[27] Deterrence does depend upon a belief by those deterred that they will be apprehended and convicted and that the unpleasantness and conviction outweigh any possible advantage from the crime. It is not clear that criminals balance these risks as logically as the theory supposes. Yet, courts clearly do impose sentences for deterrent effect, particularly after a rash of crimes occur, as in many cases it is said that it is necessary to make an example of the offender. Thus, in England, after a series of racial riots, nine youths convicted of assault and wounding a black man were sentenced to four years although it was the first offence for each. The Court of Appeal upheld the sentence saying, "The time certainly came for the courts to put down offences such as these with a heavy hand."[28]

(c) Reform of the Offender

More and more, criminologists believe that the interests of society are best served by the reform of the offender and that sentencing should place a great emphasis on this aspect. Courts do, as the *Morissette* case demonstrates, seriously consider this aspect and their willingness to impose suspended sentences, community work and periods of probation are all directed to this end. But it is not, nor is it likely to be, the sole consideration until it can be shown that it affords the best method of securing the interests of society. For the present, considerations of punishment, deterrence and rehabilitation all

---

[26] (1970), 1 C.C.C. (2d) 307, at 311 (Sask. C.A.).

[27] B. Wooton, *Crime and the Criminal Law* (London: Stevens & Sons Ltd., 1963), at p. 101.

[28] *R. v. Hunt*, The Times Newspaper, London: November 26, 1958.

play an important role in the sentencing decision. These are the factors which will determine whether the court will impose a sentence of imprisonment, a fine, a suspended sentence or a period of probation, or grant an absolute or conditional discharge. These punishments will be considered in much greater detail later in this text.

3

Effect of the Charter on Criminal Law

1. INTRODUCTION

Although the effect of the Canadian Charter of Rights and Freedoms[1] on specific aspects of criminal law are examined later in this text, its potential and actual effect may be best understood by examining the extent of its use in criminal cases, the trend of judicial decisions, the application of Charter sections 10, 12, 15 and 24 and some of its possible effects on future legislation.

The enactment of the Charter has led to a veritable flood of litigation, as lawyers have concluded that it has created a series of new rights. By 1985, there had been almost 2,000 reported decisions by our courts dealing with the Charter.[2] In 1984 and 1985, Charter litigants won nine out of 14 Supreme Court of Canada cases, a 64 percent success rate.[3] From 1986 to 1992, the success rate for Charter litigants averaged 23 to 38 percent.[4] The drop in success rates has been attributed by some commentators to a philosophical shift in attitude on the part of some Supreme Court judges as the court heard more Charter cases.[5] Most of the Supreme Court's Charter cases have dealt with the legal rights sections of the Charter—that is sections 7 to 14. A recent study shows that 143 of 195 decisions consisted of decisions dealing with legal rights.[6] The decisions interpreting legal rights deal primarily with criminal law. The most commonly litigated matter is the right under section 7 not to be deprived of "life, liberty or security of the person . . . except in accordance with the principles of fundamental justice." Other cases have involved the right against unreasonable search, the right to counsel, the right to be pre-

---

[1] Being Part I of the Constitution Act, 1982 [en. by the Canada Act, 1982 (U.K.), c. 11, s.1].

[2] F.L. Morton, *Charting the Charter 1982-4, Analytical Analysis* (Calgary: University of Calgary Press, 1976).

[3] F.L. Morton, Peter H. Russell and Troy Riddell, "The Canadian Charter of Rights and Freedoms: A Descriptive Analysis of the First Decade, 1982-1992", (1994).

[4] *Ibid.*

[5] *Ibid.*, at p. 6.

[6] *Ibid.*, at p. 13.

sumed innocent until proven guilty and the right to be tried within a reasonable time.

Some observers believed that the courts would adopt a rather conservative approach towards the interpretation of the Charter, as they had done in the case of the Canadian Bill of Rights,[7] limiting its application to the preservation of rights which were generally considered to exist under our present law. Indeed, the decisions of some of the provincial appellate courts in the first Charter cases tended to confirm this view.[8] However, the work of the Supreme Court in the 14 Charter cases decided by the end of 1985 was a clear indication that a liberal interpretation to the Charter would be taken. In nine of the 14 cases the litigants won. In four of the cases the Crown relied on pre-Charter precedents to support its interpretation of the Charter, but the Supreme Court has indicated quite clearly that it will not be bound by such precedents.[9]

A study of Charter litigation in the Supreme Court during the period 1984-1992 shows that 65 of the first 195 Charter cases were won by the person asserting a breach of his Charter rights. In contrast, the Supreme Court of Canada decided 34 cases under the Bill of Rights between 1960 and 1982. The claimant won only five times.[10] The Supreme Court obviously regards the Charter as being more than just an affirmation of existing rights, but rather a means of ensuring that as society changes and laws are enacted to respond to such changes, citizens may use the Charter to preserve their liberties and prevent overreaching by Parliament and the legislatures.

(a) Scope of the Charter

The Charter consists of 34 sections which are contained within Part I of the Constitution Act, 1982. The preamble to the Charter states that "Canada is founded upon principles that recognize the supremacy of God and the rule of law." Section 1 guarantees the individual rights and freedoms set out in the Charter "subject only to such reasonable limits prescribed by law as can be demonstrably justified in a free and democratic society." Section 32(1) of the Charter indicates to whom the Charter applies:

> (1) This Charter applies
> (a) to the Parliament and Government of Canada in respect of all matters within the authority of Parliament including all matters relating to the Yukon Territory and the North West Territories; and
> (b) to the legislature and government of each province in respect of all matters within the authority of the legislature of each province.

---

[7] R.S.C. 1970, Appendix III.
[8] *Supra*, note 2, at p. 14.
[9] *Ibid.*, at p. 16.
[10] *Supra*, note 3, at p. 5.

The Supreme Court of Canada has held that "the Government of Canada" includes the Cabinet which is obligated to conform to the Charter. In *Operation Dismantle Inc. v. R.*,[11] Chief Justice Dickson, who wrote the majority judgment of the Supreme Court of Canada, held that "the executive branch of the Canadian Government is duty bound to act in accordance with the dictates of the Charter."[12] In this case, in which Operation Dismantle Inc. and other organizations tried to stop the testing of the cruise missile in Canada, government lawyers argued that Cabinet decisions could not be attacked under the Charter.

The Charter cannot be used to regulate disputes between private individuals nor to regulate activities in the private sector. For example, if a private company were to introduce mandatory drug testing of all employees, the employees could not use the Charter to challenge the regulations which would make it mandatory for them to undergo compulsory drug testing. The wording of section 32(1) would seem to suggest that the framers of the Charter did not intend it to apply to private concerns not involving government activity. Of course, there has been conflicting opinion as to whether the Charter may be invoked to regulate activity within the private sector.[13] However, the Supreme Court of Canada has conclusively settled the issue. In *R.W.D.S.U., Loc. 580 v. Dolphin Delivery Ltd.*,[14] Mr. Justice McIntyre held that the Charter does not apply to private litigation.

The enactment of the Charter marked a profound change in the way in which Canada is governed today. Unfortunately, a detailed examination of the Charter and its effect on Canadian laws is beyond this work. However, because the Charter is making the most profound change in Canadian law, and particularly criminal law, since the time of Confederation, it is important for any student of criminal law to appreciate the nature of the change and the potential the Charter has to revolutionize our laws. Broadly speaking, the Charter protects eight different types of rights: fundamental freedoms (section 2); democratic rights (sections 3-5); mobility rights (section 6); legal rights (sections 7-12 and 14); equality rights (sections 15 and 28); language rights (sections 16-22); minority language education rights (section 23) and native rights (section 25).

(b) Rights and Freedoms

The fundamental freedoms guaranteed by section 2 of the Charter are:

---

[11] (1985), 18 D.L.R. (4th) 481 (S.C.C.).

[12] *Ibid.*, at 491.

[13] P.W. Hogg, *Constitutional Law of Canada*, 2nd ed. (Toronto: Carswell, 1985), at p. 674; K. Swinton, "Application of the Canadian Charter of Rights and Freedoms" in *Canadian Charter of Rights and Freedoms*, eds. Tarnopolsky and Beaudoin (Toronto: Carswell, 1982), at p. 41.

[14] [1986] 2 S.C.R. 573.

(*a*) freedom of conscience and religion;
(*b*) freedom of thought, belief, opinion and expression, including freedom of the press and other media of communication;
(*c*) freedom of peaceful assembly; and
(*d*) freedom of association.

The guaranteed rights include the right of citizens to vote in elections and to be qualified for membership in the provincial legislative assemblies and the House of Commons. Section 4 of the Charter states that elections for the House of Commons and legislative assemblies must be held once every five years. (Section 4(2) allows for an extension when war has been declared or there is an "apprehended war.") Section 5 guarantees that Parliament and each legislative assembly will sit once a year. The mobility rights guaranteed to citizens are intended to give them the right to enter and remain in Canada and to move freely throughout Canada to reside and earn their living. The language rights give English and French equivalent status in all the institutions of Parliament and the Government of Canada. They provide the same rights with respect to the English and French languages for the Province of New Brunswick, but at the time the Charter was enacted the other provinces did not agree that English and French should have equal status in their jurisdictions. Agreement was achieved on the principle that minorities of French- or English-speaking people should have the right to be educated in their first language whenever, in any province, the number of children was sufficient to warrant providing such education to them out of public funds. Although no new rights were conferred on native peoples, section 25 preserved all of the existing rights and freedoms of aboriginal peoples.

(i) *Legal rights*

The legal rights and equality rights conferred by the Charter are those which are having, and will likely have, the greatest influence on criminal law. The legal rights stated in sections 7-14 of the Charter provide:

7. Everyone has the right to life, liberty and security of the person and the right not to be deprived thereof except in accordance with the principles of fundamental justice.

8. Everyone has the right to be secure against unreasonable search or seizure.

9. Everyone has the right not to be arbitrarily detained or imprisoned.

10. Everyone has the right on arrest or detention
　(*a*) to be informed promptly of the reasons therefor;
　(*b*) to retain and instruct counsel without delay and to be informed of that right; and
　(*c*) to have the validity of the detention determined by way of *habeas corpus* and to be released if the detention is not lawful.

11. Any person charged with an offence has the right

(*a*) to be informed without unreasonable delay of the specific offence;

(*b*) to be tried within a reasonable time;

(*c*) not to be compelled to be a witness in proceedings against that person in respect of the offence;

(*d*) to be presumed innocent until proven guilty according to law in a fair and public hearing by an independent and impartial tribunal;

(*e*) not to be denied reasonable bail without just cause;

(*f*) except in the case of an offence under military law before a military tribunal, to the benefit of trial by jury where the maximum punishment for the offence is imprisonment for five years or a more severe punishment;

(*g*) not to be found guilty on account of any act or omission unless, at the time of the act or omission, it constituted an offence under Canadian or international law or was criminal according to the general principles of law recognized by the community of nations;

(*h*) if finally acquitted of the offence, not to be tried for it again and, if finally found guilty and punished for the offence, not to be tried or punished for it again; and

(*i*) if found guilty of the offence and if the punishment for the offence has been varied between the time of commission and the time of sentencing, to the benefit of the lesser punishment.

12. Everyone has the right not to be subjected to any cruel and unusual treatment or punishment.

13. A witness who testifies in any proceedings has the right not to have any incriminating evidence so given used to incriminate that witness in any other proceedings, except in a prosecution for perjury or for the giving of contradictory evidence.

14. A party or witness in any proceeding who does not understand or speak the language in which the proceedings are conducted or who is deaf has the right to the assistance of an interpreter.

(ii) *Equality rights*

The equality rights conferred by the Charter provide that every individual is equal before and under the law and has the benefit to the equal protection and equal benefit of the law without discrimination, and, in particular, without discrimination based on race, national or ethnic origin, colour, religion, sex, age or mental or physical disability.

These rights and freedoms are not absolute, as section 1 of the Charter provides that the rights and freedoms are subject only to "such reasonable limits prescribed by law as can be demonstrably justified in a free and democratic society." Also, Parliament or the legislature of a province may declare that legislation shall operate, notwithstanding that it breaches the fundamental freedoms provided by section 2 of the Charter or the legal rights granted by sections 7 to 14 of the Charter. These declarations are effective only for a period of five years, but may be renewed at the end of that period.

(c) Constitutional Interpretation Under the Charter

The Charter radically changed the way in which Canadian courts approached constitutional interpretation. Prior to the passage of the Charter, Parliament and the legislatures of each province were supreme as long as they were acting within their own jurisdiction. Parliamentary supremacy was modified with the passage of the Constitution Act of 1982 and was effectively relegated to the history books. This is because section 52(1) of the Constitution Act provides that:

> (1) The Constitution of Canada is the supreme law of Canada, and any law that is inconsistent with the provisions of the Constitution is, to the extent of the inconsistency, of no force or effect.

The effect of this section is that the Constitution Act, which includes the Charter, can be used to strike down any law which violates any of the rights and freedoms guaranteed by the Charter. With the advent of the Charter, Canadian courts for the first time in history have been given an effective mandate to protect Canadians from laws enacted by Parliament and legislatures of the provinces which violate individual rights and freedoms.

In *Hunter, Director of Investigation & Research, Combines Investigation Branch v. Southam Inc.*[15] Dickson J. (as he then was) said that the Charter must be given a liberal interpretation consistent with its goal of protecting individual rights and freedoms. His Lordship pointed out that the Charter is not intended to serve as an authorization for government action, saying:

> I begin with the obvious. The Canadian Charter of Rights and Freedoms is a purposive document. Its purpose is to guarantee and to protect, within the limits of reason, the enjoyment of the rights and freedoms it enshrines. It is intended to constrain governmental action inconsistent with those rights and freedoms; it is not in itself an authorization for governmental action.[16]

The Supreme Court of Canada has recognized that the Charter gives the courts broad new powers of judicial review. Thus in *R. v. Therens*,[17] Mr. Justice Le Dain stated:

> ... the Charter must be regarded, because of its constitutional character, as a new affirmation of rights and freedoms and of judicial power and responsibility in relation to their protection. This results from s. 52 of the Constitution Act, 1982, which removes any possible doubt or uncertainty as to the general effect which the Charter is to have by providing that it is part of the supreme law of Canada and that any law that is inconsistent with its provisions is to the extent of such inconsistency of no force and effect, and from s. 24 of the Charter, which provides that anyone whose guaranteed rights or freedoms have been infringed or denied

---

[15] (1984), 41 C.R. (3d) 97 (S.C.C.) (hereinafter referred to as *Hunter v. Southam Inc.*).
[16] *Ibid.*, at 111.
[17] (1985), 45 C.R. (3d) 97 (S.C.C.).

may apply to a court of competent jurisdiction to obtain such remedy as the court considers appropriate and just in the circumstances.[18]

(d) Remedies for Infringement

Section 24 of the Charter of Rights and Freedoms provides a remedy for the infringement of the rights and freedoms guaranteed by the Charter. It states that

(1) Anyone whose rights or freedoms, as guaranteed by this Charter, have been infringed or denied, may apply to a court of competent jurisdiction to obtain such remedy as the court considers appropriate and just in the circumstances.

(2) Where, in proceedings under subsection (1), a court concludes that the evidence was obtained in a manner that infringed or denied any rights or freedoms guaranteed by this Charter, the evidence shall be excluded if it is established that, having regard to all the circumstances, the admission of it in the proceedings would bring the administration of justice into disrepute.

Many of the clauses in the Charter were based on principles which were firmly rooted in the common law or, as it was true in some cases, were an expansion of ideas already expressed in the Canadian Bill of Rights. Thus, the Charter's guarantee that everyone has the right not to be arbitrarily detained or imprisoned is not a right which was first recognized when the Charter came into effect, but rather is a well-established common law doctrine which was in existence long before the Criminal Code[19] was passed and was enforced by a writ of *habeas corpus*. Similarly, many of the principles expressed in section 11 of the Charter, which, among other things, guarantees that everyone has the right to be presumed innocent until proven guilty in a fair and public hearing by an independent and impartial tribunal, have been rooted in Canadian case law from the beginning. However, having said this, it must be noted that section 24 of the Charter, which has been called the Canadian equivalent of the American exclusionary rule, is based on concepts which are completely foreign to British and Canadian common law. The principal provision which runs counter to the Canadian common law tradition is found in section 24(2) of the Charter which makes it mandatory for a court to exclude evidence if the court concludes that the evidence was obtained in a manner that infringed any of the rights guaranteed by the Charter, and if the court is satisfied, after considering all the circumstances, that to admit the evidence would bring the administration of justice into disrepute.

---

[18] *Ibid.*, at 121.
[19] R.S.C. 1985, c. C-46.

2. EFFECT OF THE CHARTER ON ADMISSION OF EVIDENCE

(a) Admission of Illegal Evidence at Common Law

Until the Charter of Rights came into effect, Canadian judges were not authorized to exclude relevant evidence which had been illegally obtained. Canadian judges (who were largely influenced by the British common law tradition of admitting evidence which was relevant to the issue of guilt or innocence) were not concerned with whether or not the evidence had been illegally obtained. For example, if police officers conducted an illegal search and seizure, the evidence obtained as a result of that illegal search and seizure could not be excluded on the grounds that its admission would bring the administration of justice into disrepute. Thus, in *R. v. Wray*, the Supreme Court of Canada held that a trial judge did not have the authority to reject relevant evidence on the ground that the admission of the evidence would bring the administration of justice into disrepute. Martland J. stated:

> The issue of law before this court is as to the validity of the principle stated in the reasons of the Court of Appeal of Ontario that a trial judge in a criminal case has a discretion to reject evidence, even of substantial weight, if he considers that its admission would be unjust or unfair to the accused or calculated to bring the administration of justice into disrepute.
>
> . . . .
>
> I am not aware of any judicial authority in this country or in England, which supports the proposition that a trial judge has a discretion to exclude admissible evidence because, in his opinion, its admission would be calculated to bring the administration of justice into disrepute. The test of admissibility of evidence was stated by Lord Goddard in *Kuruma v. The Queen* [1955] A.C. 197 at 203, [1955] 1 All E.R. 236, as follows:
>
>> In their Lordships' opinion the test to be applied on considering whether evidence is admissible is whether it is relevant to the matters in issue. If it is, it is admissible and the court is not concerned with how the evidence was obtained.[20]

His Lordship stated that while a trial judge had a discretion to refuse to allow evidence to be introduced which was not relevant to the accused's guilt or innocence, there was no general discretion to exclude evidence because its admission would bring the administration of justice into disrepute. Accordingly, it is fair to say that section 24 of the Charter of Rights constitutes a marked departure from the common law principle under which judges have no real discretion to exclude illegally-obtained evidence.

---

[20] *R. v. Wray*, [1971] S.C.R. 272 at 287.

(b) Charter Test for Exclusion of Evidence

The phrase "bring the administration of justice into disrepute" is not defined in section 24 of the Charter of Rights. It is, however, a well-established principle of law that, where possible, words in a statute are to be given their ordinary meaning. His Honour, Judge Borins, in *R. v. Samson*,[21] stated that when determining the meaning of the phrase "would bring the administration of justice into disrepute," the word disrepute should be given its ordinary meaning. In the Gage Canadian Dictionary, disrepute is defined as meaning disgrace, discredit, disfavour. In the *R. v. Samson* case, His Honour noted that the phrase "the administration of justice" is not just confined to the courts, but rather refers to laws which govern the investigation and detection of crime. His Honour stated that the phrase suggests there must be the fair, just and impartial upholding of rights and punishment of wrongs according to the rule of law.

It is not possible at this juncture to examine in detail the numerous cases which have considered and applied section 24 of the Charter of Rights and Freedoms. There is a substantial body of law dealing with section 24 of the Charter, some of which will be examined later. However, considering the effect which the Charter has had on criminal law, it is appropriate to examine some of the principles which the courts have applied in interpreting section 24.

There are now several cases from the Supreme Court of Canada and the appellate courts which deal with the exclusion of evidence under section 24(2) of the Charter. In *R. v. Collins*,[22] a majority of the Supreme Court of Canada set down the approach which the lower courts should apply in dealing with the exclusion of evidence under section 24(2) of the Charter. In *Collins*, the Supreme Court for the first time engaged in a detailed analysis of the factors which the lower courts should consider in determining whether evidence should be excluded under section 24(2) because its admission would bring the administration of justice into disrepute. In summary, Lamer J. (as he then was), writing for the court, stated:

1. The accused bears the burden of convincing the court that evidence obtained in breach of a Charter right or freedom should be excluded under s. 24(2).

2. The standard of proof is the civil standard of balance of probabilities rather than the criminal standard of proof beyond a reasonable doubt. The accused must show that it is more probable than not that the admission of the evidence would bring the administration of justice into disrepute.

[The English version reads "would," but the Supreme Court in *Collins* held that the accused is entitled to the benefit of the French version which reads "could." Both the English and French versions of the Charter are, of course, equally authoritative.]

---

[21] (1982), 29 C.R. (3d) 215 at 229 (Ont. Co. Ct.).
[22] (1987), 56 C.R. (3d) 193 (S.C.C.).

3. Section 24(2) is not intended to punish the police for deliberately violating the accused's rights. Rather, s. 24(2) is intended to prevent the administration of justice from being brought into *further disrepute* by admitting the evidence in the proceedings.

4. The judicial system will be brought into further disrepute by the admission of evidence that would make the accused's trial unfair.

5. Further disrepute will also result from judges condoning unacceptable conduct by the investigatory and prosecutorial agencies. [The police, and the Crown Attorney's office.]

6. In deciding whether to exclude evidence under s. 24(2), the courts must consider whether the exclusion of evidence from the proceedings will bring the administration of justice into greater disrepute than if the evidence were admitted.

7. In determining whether to admit or exclude the evidence from the proceedings, the court must also focus on the effect of admission or exclusion of evidence on the long-term repute of the administration of justice.

8. The consideration of the repute of the administration of justice necessarily involves some determination as to the views of the community with respect to whether the admission or exclusion of the evidence would result in greater disrepute to the administration of justice.[23]

The Supreme Court of Canada has held that in deciding whether to admit or exclude evidence, a judge is not to look at public opinion polls in an attempt to determine what the average person thinks should be done. In this regard, Lamer J. said:

Members of the public generally become conscious of the importance of protecting rights and freedoms of accused only when they are in some way brought closer to the system either personally or through the experience of friends or family.

. . . .

The Charter is designed to protect the accused from the majority, so the enforcement of the Charter must not be left to the majority.[24]

In *Collins*, Lamer J. held that since the concept of disrepute involves some consideration of public opinion, a judge should ask himself or herself the following question:

Would the admission of evidence bring the administration of justice into disrepute in the eyes of a reasonable man, dispassionate and fully apprised of the circumstances of the case?[25]

---

[23] *Ibid.*, at 208-209.
[24] *Ibid.*, at 209.
[25] *Ibid.*

Lamer J. stated that although the reasonable person is usually the average person in the community, this will only be the case when the community's mood is reasonable.

In *Collins*, Lamer J. stated that in determining whether to exclude evidence under section 24(2) of the Charter, judges should "consider all the circumstances." In considering all the circumstances as to whether the evidence should be admitted under section 24(2), Lamer J. said that he found it useful to group the factors according to the way in which they affected the repute of the administration of justice.

Lamer J. placed the factors into three categories:

1. those affecting the fairness of the trial;
2. those relating to the seriousness of the violation; and
3. those relating to the effect on the reputation of the administration of justice.[26]

Mr. Justice Lamer stated that the most important factor was the effect which the admission of the evidence would have on the fairness of the trial. Thus, if the admission of the evidence would render the trial unfair, then to admit the evidence would *tend* to bring the administration of justice into disrepute and, accordingly, subject to the consideration of the remaining factors listed above, the evidence should generally be excluded.

In *R. v. Jacoy*,[27] Dickson C.J.C., writing for a majority of the Supreme Court, summarized the *Collins* list of factors for determining whether evidence should be excluded under section 24(2):

> First, the court must consider whether the admission of evidence will affect the fairness of the trial. If this inquiry is answered affirmatively, "the admission of evidence would *tend* to bring the administration of justice into disrepute and, subject to a consideration of the other factors, the evidence generally should be excluded" . . . One of the factors relevant to this determination is the nature of the evidence; if the evidence is real evidence that existed irrespective of the Charter violation, its admission will rarely render the trial unfair.
>
> The second set of factors concerns the seriousness of the violation. Relevant to this group is whether the violation was committed in good faith, whether it was inadvertent or of a merely technical nature, whether it was motivated by urgency or to prevent the loss of evidence, and whether the evidence could have been obtained without a Charter violation.
>
> Finally, the court must look at factors relating to the effect of excluding the evidence. The administration of justice may be brought into disrepute by excluding evidence essential to substantiate the charge where the breach of the Charter was trivial. While this consideration is particularly important where the offence is

---

[26] *Ibid.*, at 211-212.
[27] (1988), 66 C.R. (3d) 336 at 344-345 (S.C.C.).

serious, if the admission of the evidence would result in an unfair trial, the seriousness of the offence would not render the evidence admissible.

In *Collins*, Lamer J. stated that where the accused is "conscripted against himself" by a confession or other self-incriminating evidence, the use of this evidence would make the trial unfair, as the evidence did not exist previous to the violation and its use violates one of the fundamental principles of a fair trial, the right against self-incrimination. His Lordship contrasted self-incriminating evidence such as a confession with real evidence, saying that real evidence existed irrespective of the Charter violation and, thus, its use would rarely render the trial unfair.[28]

Real evidence is the term used to describe physical evidence such as objects found in the accused's possession — i.e., a weapon or drugs. Lamer J.'s statement that the admission of real evidence would rarely render the trial unfair proved to be a powerful disincentive for the lower courts to exclude real evidence. Most of the lower court judges interpreted Lamer J.'s comments about real evidence in *Collins* as a hard and fast rule and would never exclude real evidence under section 24(2) of the Charter.

The distinction between real evidence and other evidence, such as a confession which was conscripted from an accused, was a highly artificial distinction. After all, if the real evidence could not have been found without the use of the accused's statements, it could not be said that the accused's participation had no role to play in the creation of the evidence. In *Thomson Newspapers Ltd. v. Canada (Director of Investigation and Research)*,[29] La Forest J. distinguished between real evidence that could have been found without the use of the accused's compelled statements and independently existing real evidence which would have been found without the use of the accused's compelled testimony. He stated:

> I would first of all note that I do not believe that in drawing this distinction Lamer J. intended to draw a hard-and-fast line between real evidence obtained in breach of the Charter and all other types of evidence that could be so obtained . . . . I think . . . that what Lamer J. had in mind was the much broader distinction between evidence which the accused has been forced *to create* and evidence which he or she has been forced to merely *locate or identify*.
>
> . . . where the effect of a breach of the Charter is merely to locate or identify already existing evidence, the case of the ultimate strength of the Crown's case is not necessarily strengthened in this way. The fact that the evidence already existed means that it could have been discovered anyway.
>
> The one qualification that must be made to the above has to do with the difference between independently-existing evidence that could have been found without compelled testimony and independently-existing evidence that *would* have

---

[28] *Supra*, note 22, at 211.
[29] (1990), 76 C.R. (3d) 129 (S.C.C.).

been found without compelled testimony. As I have acknowledged at several points in these reasons, there will be situations where derivative evidence is so concealed or inaccessible as to be virtually undiscoverable without the assistance of the wrongdoer. For practical purposes, the subsequent use of such evidence would be indistinguishable from the subsequent use of the pre-trial compelled testimony.[30]

Recently in *R. v. Mellenthin*,[31] the Supreme Court of Canada held that in determining whether evidence should be excluded under section 24(2) of the Charter, the fact that the evidence seized by police can be classified as real evidence does not mean that the evidence should not be excluded under section 24(2). In this case, the police had obtained marijuana as a result of an illegal search of a gym bag located in the accused's vehicle. For Mr. Justice Cory, the fact that the evidence was real evidence was not determinative of whether it should be admitted or excluded under section 24(2). In *Mellenthin*, Cory J. quoted from *R. v. Leclair*,[32] a 1989 decision of the Supreme Court where Lamer J. stated:

> . . . the use of any evidence that could not have been obtained but for the participation of the accused in the construction of the evidence for purposes of the trial would tend to render the trial process unfair.[33]

In *Leclair*, the evidence which was sought to be excluded under section 24(2) was not real evidence. Rather, the evidence consisted of evidence relating to the identification of the accused persons as a result of their compelled participation in a police line-up.

The Supreme Court's reliance in *Mellenthin* on Lamer J.'s comments in *Leclair* to justify the exclusion of real evidence under section 24(2) of the Charter indicates that the court has moved away from its initial position in *Collins* that real evidence would rarely be excluded under section 24(2) of the Charter, as such evidence existed independently of the Charter breach and, therefore, its admission into evidence in a proceeding could not be said to render the proceeding unfair.

Before *Mellenthin*, the Supreme Court's judgment in *Collins* was the lead case for determining the factors which should be considered under a section 24(2) application to exclude evidence. The Supreme Court in *Mellenthin* has substantially modified the *Collins* test. It can no longer be said that real evidence should rarely be excluded and the court in *Mellenthin* has held that where the trial has been rendered unfair, this is a sufficient ground for the exclusion of evidence under section 24(2) of the Charter by itself.[34] Thus, once a court has found that a Charter breach has rendered the trial unfair, there is

---

[30] *Ibid.*, at 232-234.
[31] (1992), 16 C.R. (4th) 273 (S.C.C.).
[32] (1989), 67 C.R. (3d) 209 (S.C.C.).
[33] *Ibid.*, at 220-221.
[34] *Supra*, note 31, at 285.

no need to consider the other factors mentioned in *Collins* — namely, the seriousness of the violation and the effect which the admission of the evidence would have on the repute of the administration of justice.

One legal commentator has stated that the Supreme Court's modification of the Collins test for exclusion of evidence under section 24(2) amounts to an automatic exclusionary rule where a lower court judge has determined that to admit the evidence would render the trial unfair.[35] Although the Supreme Court's ruling in *Mellenthin* has modified the *Collins* test, it is likely that the Supreme Court will still consider the third group of factors set out in *Collins* — that is, whether the exclusion of the evidence would bring the administration of justice into disrepute.

In *Collins*, the Supreme Court of Canada held that a decision to exclude evidence on the ground that it could bring the administration of justice into disrepute is a question of law. Thus, it is open to the Crown to appeal a trial judge's exclusion of the evidence under section 24(2). However, the Supreme Court has stated that provincial appellate courts should not interfere with the decision of a trial judge to exclude evidence under section 24(2) of the Charter unless the Court of Appeal is of the view that the trial judge's decision is unreasonable. The fact that the members of the Court of Appeal would not have decided the case in the same way is not sufficient to interfere with the trial judge's exclusion of the evidence. The only question is whether it can be said that the exclusion of evidence under section 24(2) was unreasonable given the facts of the case.

The Supreme Court of Canada has stated on several occasions that it will not lightly interfere with the findings of a provincial appellate court as to whether evidence was properly excluded under section 24(2) of the Charter. The Supreme Court has stated that it is only if the Court of Appeal made an unreasonable finding or applied incorrect legal principles that it will review the court's findings in respect of section 24(2) of the Charter.

3. CHARTER RIGHTS ON ARREST OR DETENTION

(a) Generally

Section 10 of the Charter provides that

Everyone has the right on arrest or detention
(*a*) to be informed promptly of the reasons therefor;
(*b*) to retain and instruct counsel without delay and to be informed of that right; and

---

[35] R.J. Delisle, "Mellenthin: Changing the *Collins* Test" (1993), 16 C.R. (4th) 286.

(*c*) to have the validity of the detention determined by way of *habeas corpus* and to be released if the detention is not lawful.

The magnitude of the change in criminal law effected by the enactment of the Charter is illustrated by the difference between the rights of a person upon arrest or detention prior to and after the enactment of the Charter. Individual rights have been extended because the courts have given a liberal meaning to what constitutes detention, ensuring that a person will have a very early opportunity to take advantage of the rights available. The Charter has also assured individuals of the right to retain counsel promptly and to know forthwith what the reason for the arrest or detention is. In these respects the Charter has significantly altered the pre-Charter position by giving an individual the earliest possible opportunity to have the knowledge and advice required for an adequate defence. The legal meaning of "arrest or detention" and the examination of the "right to counsel" is discussed in detail in Chapter 5, A Person's Rights and Obligations under the Criminal Law.

(b) Reasons for Arrest or Detention

(i) *Pre-Charter requirement*

Prior to the enactment of the Charter, police officers had a discretion as to whether to inform the accused of the reasons for his or her arrest. The general common law rule, developed from a long line of British cases, was that a police officer had a general duty to inform the accused of such reasons, but this was subject to a number of exceptions. In *Christie v. Leachinsky*,[36] a leading British case which has been applied by Canadian courts, the House of Lords held that the general duty of a police officer to advise the accused of such reasons did not apply where the reasons for the arrest must have been obvious, or where it was impractical to inform the person being arrested of such reasons as, for example, the arrest was attended with violence or the person was fleeing. In Canada, section 29(2) of the Criminal Code provides that where an individual is arrested with or without a warrant, the person making the arrest must, where it is feasible to do so, notify the person being arrested of "(*a*) the process or warrant under which he makes the arrest; or (*b*) the reason for the arrest." The Supreme Court of Canada, in *Gamracy v. R.*,[37] held that where a police officer is arresting an accused on the basis of an outstanding warrant which the police officer does not have with him, "the duty of the

---

[36] [1947] A.C. 573 (H.L.).
[37] (1973), 12 C.C.C. (2d) 209 (S.C.C.).

arresting officer is fully discharged by telling the arrested person that the reason for his arrest is the existence of an outstanding warrant therefor."[38]

(ii) "To be informed promptly of the reasons"

Since the Charter has been enacted, it is mandatory that a police officer inform a person who is being detained or arrested as to the reasons for his arrest. The right to be informed promptly of the reasons for one's detention or arrest, which is guaranteed by section 10(a) of the Charter, is based principally on the notion that a person does not have to submit to being arrested unless he knows the reasons for his arrest. Section 10(a) enables a person to properly exercise his right to counsel. In R. v. Black,[39] Madam Justice Wilson, writing for the Supreme Court, stated:

> An individual can exercise his s. 10(b) right in a meaningful way only if he knows the extent of his jeopardy.[40]

In R. v. Greffe,[41] the Supreme Court of Canada restored the accused's acquittal on charges of importing heroin into Canada and possession of a narcotic for the purpose of trafficking after the court concluded that the accused's section 10(a) Charter rights had been violated by Customs officers and the R.C.M.P. In Greffe, the R.C.M.P. had received a "tip" that Greffe, who was returning to Canada from Amsterdam, was expected to be carrying heroin. In this case, the R.C.M.P. officers lied to the accused, saying that he was arrested on outstanding traffic warrants. He was actually arrested on a suspicion of having imported narcotics into Canada. After the accused was arrested, he was taken to a hospital where a doctor conducted a rectal search and removed a condom containing heroin. The evidence in this case was excluded and the acquittal was restored by the Supreme Court of Canada partly on the basis of the breach of the accused's section 10(a) Charter rights. The majority of the court found that the police had wilfully violated the Charter by not advising the accused as to the real reason for his arrest. The majority of the court found that the section 10(a) violation coupled with the section 8 violation of unreasonable search and seizure justified the exclusion of the evidence obtained under section 24(2) of the Charter.

Recently, the Supreme Court of Canada considered whether the failure of the police to advise an accused as to the extent of his jeopardy violated section 10(a) of the Charter. In R. v. Evans,[42] the accused, a youth of borderline

---

[38] *Ibid.*, at 211.
[39] (1989), 70 C.R. (3d) 97 (S.C.C.).
[40] *Ibid.*, at 108.
[41] (1990), 75 C.R. (3d) 257 (S.C.C.).
[42] (1991), 4 C.R. (4th) 144 (S.C.C.).

retardation, was convicted of the first-degree murder of two women. The police originally suspected the accused's brother of having committed the murders but arrested the accused on a charge of trafficking in narcotics, after obtaining some wiretap evidence which established that the accused may have sold marijuana. The accused was arrested, in part, to obtain information from his brother as to the brother's suspected involvement in the murders. When the accused was questioned about his trafficking in marijuana, the police became suspicious that he had been involved in the murder of the women and the focus of their investigation shifted to the accused as the prime murder suspect. Shortly after he was questioned, the accused was advised that he was a suspect in the killings by police in the following terms:

> J.S.: (LONG PAUSE) To traffic marijuana, that was originally why we're here. But now that things have taken quite a change.

> W.E.: Yeah but . . . why are you asking me this? I never killed no one . . . I don't know who did. It's none of my business.[43]

Although the British Columbia Court of Appeal was of the view that the accused's section 10(*a*) Charter rights were violated, the majority of the Supreme Court of Canada held that there was no violation of the accused's right to be informed promptly of the reasons for his arrest. McLachlin J., writing for the court, stated:

> When considering whether there has been a breach of s. 10(*a*) of the Charter, it is the substance of what the accused can reasonably be supposed to have understood, rather than the formalism of the precise words used, which must govern. The question is whether what the accused was told, viewed reasonably in all the circumstances of the case, was sufficient to permit him to make a reasonable decision to decline to submit to arrest, or alternatively, to undermine his right to counsel under s. 10(*b*).[44]

The majority of the Supreme Court found that the accused's response to the officer's statement that while he had been arrested on a marijuana charge things had taken "quite a change" demonstrated that the accused knew that he was now being questioned with respect to the killing of the women. In this case, although the court excluded the accused's statements because of a breach of his right to counsel under section 10(*b*) of the Charter, the court found that the police had complied with the requirements under section 10(*a*) of the Charter.

---

[43] *Ibid.*, at 153.
[44] *Ibid.*, at 160.

4. PROTECTION AGAINST CRUEL AND UNUSUAL PUNISHMENT

One of the more interesting clauses in the Charter of Rights and Freedoms is section 12, which provides that:

Everyone has the right not to be subjected to any cruel and usual treatment or punishment.

The Charter's ringing declaration that "everyone" is protected against cruel and unusual punishment as a right may be contrasted with the weak assertion under section 2(*b*) of the Canadian Bill of Rights that "no law of Canada shall be construed or applied so as to . . . (*b*) impose or authorize the imposition of cruel and unusual treatment or punishment." Section 12 has not been used as frequently as other sections of the Charter, although it has been applied to a broad range of issues. Defence counsels have used section 12 to challenge Canada's abortion legislation, the fingerprinting of young offenders, a court order preventing an accused from hunting, legislation creating a mandatory minimum driving suspension, deportation orders, and legislation providing for the indefinite detention of dangerous offenders.

(a) Capital Punishment

Section 12, which governs one's treatment as well as one's punishment, will undoubtedly receive its major test if the death penalty is restored. The death penalty, or capital punishment, was abolished in 1970 by a one-vote margin in the House of Commons. In *R. v. Miller*,[45] a case decided under the Bill of Rights, the Supreme Court of Canada held that capital punishment did not constitute cruel and unusual punishment. Similarly, the United States Supreme Court has held that the death penalty does not violate the Eighth Amendment's protection against cruel and unusual punishment. The Eighth Amendment of the American Constitution provides that:

Excessive fines [shall not be] imposed, nor cruel and unusual punishments inflicted.

Section 12 of the Charter is much broader than the Eighth Amendment of the American Constitution, which does not provide any protection against cruel and unusual treatment. The difference in wording could be significant, as Canadian courts may give section 12 of the Charter a more expansive treatment than the American courts have accorded to the Eighth Amendment.

---

[45] (1976), 31 C.C.C. (2d) 177 (S.C.C.).

(i) *Free vote and capital punishment*

During the 1984 federal election, Brian Mulroney, who is on record as personally opposing the death penalty, promised to allow a free vote in the House of Commons on the issue of capital punishment if the Conservatives were elected. Mulroney did allow a free vote on capital punishment and in 1987 a resolution supporting the return of capital punishment was defeated. Members on all sides of the House of Commons were free to vote according to their individual consciences rather than according to party lines. While capital punishment has been placed on the back burner for the immediate future, the debate is far from being over. The restoration of the death penalty is a contentious issue in our society and is likely to spark debate well into the next century. Since the majority of Canadians favour the restoration of capital punishment, it is likely that the issue will re-surface in Parliament before the end of this century. If a subsequent Parliament restores capital punishment, the legislation restoring the death penalty will undoubtedly be challenged under the Charter of Rights and Freedoms.

(ii) *Charter challenge*

Many Canadians believe that a restoration of the death penalty will effectively end the debate over capital punishment because once the bill becomes law, Parliament will have spoken and capital punishment will be a *fait accompli*. The reality is otherwise. People who believe that capital punishment will automatically be restored if the death penalty is re-enacted as part of the Criminal Code do not understand the profound impact which the Charter of Rights and Freedoms has had on Canadian society. The Charter has effectively ended Parliamentary supremacy with the result that Parliament will no longer be the complete master of its own house. Historically, federal and provincial governments have been supreme within their own jurisdiction. Parliamentary supremacy meant that the federal or provincial governments could pass whatever legislation they wished, providing that the legislation in question fell within the legislative powers allotted to the federal or provincial governments under the B.N.A. Act.[46] Today, the situation is quite different. Parliament is no longer supreme as legislation which violates the rights and freedoms guaranteed in the Charter will be struck down by the courts. Section 52 of the Charter of Rights and Freedoms provides that the Charter is the supreme law of Canada and, therefore, overrides ordinary legislation. Thus, if the Supreme Court of Canada decided that capital punishment legislation violated section 12 of the Charter, the legislation would not have any effect.

---

[46] (30 & 31 Vict.), c. 3.

Parliament's only recourse would be to resort to section 33 of the Charter which allows Parliament or the legislature of a province to opt out of sections 2 and 7 to 15 of the Charter. Section 33 allows Parliament, or the legislature of a province, to expressly declare that an Act passed by Parliament or the legislature of a province shall operate despite the rights guaranteed by sections 2 and 7 to 15 of the Charter. Thus, Parliament could expressly declare that a law providing for the return of capital punishment would not be affected by the cruel and unusual punishment section of the Charter or by section 7, which states that everyone has the right to life, liberty and security of the person and the right not to be deprived thereof except in accordance with the principles of fundamental justice. The political cost of resorting to section 33, however, will mean that it will rarely be used. Once the section is used, the declaration will only last for a maximum of five years. At the end of five years the government resorting to section 33 must expressly declare once again that the above sections of the Charter do not apply to the legislation in respect of which the declaration is made.

Section 24(1) of the Charter provides that:

> Anyone whose rights or freedoms, as guaranteed by this Charter, have been infringed or denied may apply to a court of competent jursidiction to obtain such remedy as the court considers appropriate and just in the circumstances.

It seems obvious that a prisoner facing execution would argue that capital punishment is cruel and unusual and infringes his rights as guaranteed under section 12 of the Charter. The outcome, of course, is not certain, but the Supreme Court of Canada could, if it chose to, render the political decision academic if it decided capital punishment was cruel and unusual treatment or punishment. Such a ruling would make it extremely difficult for Parliament to risk the political backlash that would ensue if it resorted to section 33 of the Charter.

(iii) *Bill of Rights*

Two Bill of Rights decisions handed down by the Supreme Court of Canada dashed any hopes that civil libertarians had that the Bill of Rights would protect Canadians against the erosion of civil liberties and create new rights. In *R. v. Burnshine*,[47] Mr. Justice Martland, who wrote the majority decision, held that the Bill of Rights did not create new rights, but rather "declared and continued existing rights and freedoms."[48] In *R. v. Miller*[49] a majority of the Supreme Court of Canada held that the Bill of Rights did not create new

---

[47] [1975] 1 S.C.R. 693.

[48] *Ibid.*, at 705.

[49] *Miller, supra*, note 45.

rights but merely recognized rights which had existed before the Bill of Rights was enacted. The Supreme Court of Canada's decisions in *Burnshine* and *Miller* have more than an academic interest; if the Bill simply declared existing rights, then captial punishment, which was legal before the Bill of Rights became law, could not be invalidated by the Bill of Rights. In *R. v. Miller*, the Supreme Court of Canada decided that the death penalty was not cruel and unusual punishment within section 2(*b*) of the Bill of Rights. Ritchie J. stated that:

> Accepting as I do the proposition that s. 2 [of the Bill of Rights] did not create new rights, it cannot be that Parliament intended to create anew the absolute right not to be deprived of life under any circumstances by providing that no law of Canada was to be applied so as "to impose or authorize the imposition of cruel and unusual treatment or punishment". If so construed the section would prevent the infringement of a right which had never existed and would thus run contrary to the purpose for which it was enacted.[50]

It should be noted that whereas section 1 of the Bill of Rights stated that "there have existed and shall continue to exist . . . the following human rights and fundamental freedoms," section 1 of the Canadian Charter of Rights and Freedoms makes no mention of existing rights and freedoms, but rather "guarantees the rights and freedoms set out in it." The different emphasis in wording has already proven to be significant, as the Supreme Court of Canada has recognized that the Charter of Rights creates new rights and freedoms.[51] Thus, if capital punishment were to be reintroduced, supporters of capital punishment would not be able to argue that capital punishment is legal just because the Supreme Court of Canada said so in the *Miller* case. This does not mean that legislation providing for capital punishment would necessarily violate section 12 of the Charter. What it does mean is that the Supreme Court of Canada may, if it chooses, determine that legislation imposing capital punishment is invalid.

(b) Mandatory Sentences

Some offences in the Criminal Code carry a mandatory minimum punishment. When a criminal offence has a minimum sentence, the sentencing judge has no discretion but to give the person convicted at least the minimum sentence. In the past, section 2(*b*) of the Canadian Bill of Rights dealing with "cruel and unusual punishment" was unsuccessfully utilized in challenging the validity of minimum punishments.

---

[50] *Ibid.*, at 196.
[51] *R. v. Big M Drug Mart Ltd.* (1985), 18 C.C.C. (3d) 385 at 423 (S.C.C.).

(i) *Charter challenge to mandatory minimum punishments*

The Charter has provided an opportunity for striking down mandatory minimum punishments. The Supreme Court of Canada's judgment in *R. v. Smith*[52] has been used as the benchmark for challenging the constitutional validity of such punishments under the Criminal Code and other related statutes. The Supreme Court of Canada's landmark ruling gives defence counsel leverage to challenge the constitutionality of mandatory minimum punishments. In *Smith*, the Supreme Court of Canada held that the mandatory minimum penalty of seven years' imprisonment for importing narcotics as set out in section 5(2) of the Narcotic Control Act[53] was cruel and unusual punishment under the Charter. Lamer J., writing for a majority of the court, concluded that this section violated section 12 of the Charter of Rights and was not a reasonable limit as demonstrably justified in a free and democratic society. Section 5 of the Narcotic Control Act provides:

> **5.** (1) Except as authorized by this Act or the regulations, no person shall import into Canada or export from Canada any narcotic.
>
> (2) Every person who contravenes subsection (1) is guilty of an indictable offence and liable to imprisonment for life but not less than seven years.

In *Smith*, the accused pleaded guilty to importing seven and one-half ounces of cocaine into Canada and was sentenced to eight years in a penitentiary. There was evidence at trial that the cocaine, which was imported from Bolivia, was 85 to 90 percent pure and had a street value of between $126,000 and $168,000. The accused appealed his sentence to the British Columbia Court of Appeal. The British Columbia Court of Appeal dismissed the appeal from sentence, holding that section 5(2) of the Narcotic Control Act was constitutional. The accused appealed to the Supreme Court of Canada on the ground that the mandatory minimum sentence violated sections 7, 9 and 12 of the Charter of Rights. Lamer J. stated that because he found that section 5(2) of the Narcotic Control Act violated section 12 of the Charter it was not necessary to consider whether the section also violated sections 7 and 9 of the Charter.

In determining whether a punishment is cruel and unusual under section 12 of the Charter, the test to be applied is "whether the punishment prescribed is so excessive as to outrage standards of decency." In *Smith*, Lamer J. recognized that the state had a right to punish offenders as long as the effect of the punishment was not "grossly disproportionate to what would have been appropriate." Justice Lamer stated:

---

[52] (1987), 58 C.R. (3d) 193 (S.C.C.).
[53] R.S.C. 1985, c. N-1.

One must also measure the effect of the sentence actually imposed. If it is grossly disproportionate to what would have been appropriate, then it infringes s. 12. The effect of the sentence is often a composite of many factors and is not limited to the quantum or duration of the sentence but includes its nature and the conditions under which it is applied. Sometimes by its length alone or by its very nature will the sentence be grossly disproportionate to the purpose sought. Sometimes it will be the result of the combination of factors which, when considered in isolation, would not in and of themselves amount to gross disproportionality. For example, 20 years for a first offence against property would be grossly disproportionate, but so would three months of imprisonment if the prison authorities decide it should be served in solitary confinement. Finally, I should add that some punishments or treatments will always be grossly disproportionate and will always outrage our standards of decency: for example, the infliction of corporal punishment, such as the lash, irrespective of the number of lashes imposed, or, to give examples of treatment, the lobotomization of certain dangerous offenders or the castration of sexual offenders.[54]

The Supreme Court found that the minimum term of imprisonment imposed by section 5(2) of the Narcotic Control Act was grossly disproportionate and thus violated section 12 of the Charter. In so holding Lamer J. stated:

At issue in this appeal is the minimum term of imprisonment provided for by s. 5(2) of the Narcotic Control Act. It thus is not necessary to delimit the scope of the terms "treatment" and "punishment", since they clearly include the imposition by a judge of a term of imprisonment. The minimum seven-year imprisonment fails the proportionality test enunciated above and therefore prima facie infringes the guarantees established by s. 12 of the Charter. The simple fact that s. 5(2) provides for a mandatory term of imprisonment does not by itself lead to this conclusion. A minimum mandatory term of imprisonment is obviously not in and of itself cruel and unusual. The legislature may, in my view, provide for a compulsory term of imprisonment upon conviction for certain offences without infringing the rights protected by s. 12 of the Charter. For example, a long term of penal servitude for he or she who has imported large amounts of heroin for the purpose of trafficking would certainly not contravene s. 12 of the Charter, quite the contrary. However, the seven-year minimum prison term of s. 5(2) is grossly disproportionate when examined in light of the wide net cast by s. 5(1).

As indicated above, the offence of importing enacted by s. 5(1) of the Narcotic Control Act covers numerous substances of varying degrees of dangerousness and totally disregards the quantity of the drug imported. The purpose of a given importation, such as whether it is for personal consumption or for trafficking, and the existence or non-existence of previous convictions or offences of a similar nature or gravity are disregarded as irrelevant. Thus, the law is such that it is inevitable that, in some cases, a verdict of guilt will lead to the imposition of a term of imprisonment which will be grossly disproportionate.

This is what offends s. 12, the certainty, not just the potential. Absent the minimum, the section still has the potential of operating so as to impose cruel and unusual punishment. But that would only occur if and when a judge chose to impose, let us say, seven years or more on the "small offender". Remedy will then

---

[54] *Supra*, note 52, at 236.

flow from s. 24. It is the judge's sentence, but not the section, that is in violation of the Charter. However, the effect of the minimum is to insert the certainty that, in some cases, as of conviction the violation will occur. It is this aspect of certainty that makes the section itself a prima facie violation of s. 12, and the minimum must, subject to s.1, be declared of no force or effect.[55]

Lamer J. found that section 5(2) of the Narcotic Control Act could not be saved by section 1 of the Charter. In so holding, His Lordship concluded that section 5(2) of the Narcotic Control Act was grossly disproportionate to the objective which this section sought to achieve because the section provided for a mandatory seven years' imprisonment for importing narcotics irrespective of the quantity imported. His Lordship stated:

Clearly there is no need to be indiscriminate. We do not need to sentence the small offenders to seven years in prison in order to deter the serious offender. Indeed, the net cast by s. 5(2) for sentencing purposes need not be so wide as that cast by s. 5(1) for conviction purposes. The result sought could be achieved by limiting the imposition of a minimum sentence to the importing of certain quantities, to certain specific narcotics of the schedule, to repeat offenders, or even to a combination of these factors. But the wording of the section in the schedule is much broader. I should add that, in my view, the minimum sentence also creates some problems. In particular, it inserts into the system a reluctance to convict and thus results in acquittals for picayune reasons of accuseds who do not deserve a seven-year sentence, and it gives the Crown an unfair advantage in plea bargaining, as an accused will be more likely to plead guilty to a lesser or included offence. For these reasons, the minimum imprisonment provided for by s. 5(2) breaches s. 12 of the Charter and this breach has not been justified under s.1.[56]

The effect of Lamer J.'s judgment in *Smith* is that the mandatory minimum sentence for importing narcotics under section 5(2) of the Narcotic Control Act has been struck down as violating section 12 of the Charter.

The Supreme Court of Canada's ruling in *Smith* does not mean that all mandatory minimum sentences will be subsequently found to be unconstitutional. It is clear from the court's ruling that the mandatory minimum sentence for importing narcotics was found to be unconstitutional because it was grossly disproportionate to the objective sought to be achieved by the legislation. The section constituted cruel and unusual punishment in that an offender who imported one marijuana cigarette into Canada could receive the same sentence as a person who imported a ton of marijuana. Clearly, the section was grossly disproportionate in that it did not take into account the quantities of the drug imported or consider the personal circumstances of the offender. In *Smith*, Lamer J. pointed out that the seven-year importation penalty did not allow a judge to consider whether the drug was imported for personal consumption or whether it was imported for trafficking, or whether the accused had been convicted of similar offences in the past.

---

[55] *Ibid.*, at 239.
[56] *Ibid.*, at 241-242.

The existence of mandatory minimum sentences runs counter to our entire sentencing philosophy. While the protection of the public is the foremost goal in sentencing an offender for an offence committed, the courts take into consideration individual factors such as rehabilitation of the offender and have not held that the goal protecting the public excludes all other sentencing goals. The effect of a mandatory minimum sentence is that individual sentencing considerations are totally excluded. It does not matter that the offender committed the offence because of a mental illness or a drug or alcohol-induced state because a mandatory minimum sentence does not permit a judge to take into consideration mitigating factors. Such sentencing may also run afoul of section 7 of the Charter of Rights which states that "everyone has the right to life, liberty and security of the person and the right not to be deprived thereof except in accordance with the principles of fundamental justice." An accused who commits an offence for which a mandatory minimum sentence applies may challenge the constitutionality of such sentences under sections 12 and 7 of the Charter. The Supreme Court of Canada's judgment in *Smith* provides the impetus for challenging mandatory minimum sentences under section 12 of the Charter.

It was clear from the Supreme Court of Canada's judgment in *Smith* that not all mandatory minimum sentences would be found to be a violation of section 12 of the Charter. In this regard, Lamer J. stated:

> The test for review under s. 12 of the Charter is one of gross disproportionality, because it is aimed at punishments that are more than merely excessive. We should be careful not to stigmatize every disproportionate or excessive sentence as being a constitutional violation, and should leave to the usual sentencing appeal process the task of reviewing the fitness of a sentence. Section 12 will be infringed only where the sentence is so unfit having regard to the offence and the offender as to be grossly disproportionate.

> In assessing whether a sentence is grossly disproportionate, the court must first consider the gravity of the offence, the personal characteristics of the offender and the particular circumstances of the case in order to determine what range of sentences would have been appropriate to punish, rehabilitate or deter this particular offender or to protect the public from this particular offender.[57]

In *R. v. Luxton*,[58] the majority of the Supreme Court of Canada held that the mandatory minimum penalty for first-degree murder did not contravene section 12 or section 7 of the Charter. In *Luxton*, the accused argued that the combined effect of section 214(5)(e) [now section 231(5)(e)] and section 669(a) [now section 742(a)] of the Criminal Code violated section 12 of the Charter. The accused, who was convicted of first-degree murder, was sentenced to life imprisonment and must serve a minimum of 25 years' imprisonment before being eligible for parole. In this case, the accused argued

---

[57] *Ibid.*, at 235.
[58] (1990), 79 C.R. (3d) 193 (S.C.C.).

that the mandatory minimum penalty prescribed by Parliament amounted to cruel and unusual punishment as it did not permit a judge to consider individual factors when passing a sentence on the accused. Lamer C.J.C., writing for a majority of the court, noted that the mandatory minimum sentence for first-degree murder reflected the fact that murder is a crime which carries with it the highest degree of moral blameworthiness — namely, "subjective foresight of death." In holding that the mandatory minimum sentence for first-degree murder did not violate section 12 of the Charter, Lamer C.J.C. stated:

> The penalty is severe and deservedly so. The minimum 25 years to be served before eligibility for parole reflects society's condemnation of a person who has exploited a position of power and dominance to the gravest extent possible by murdering the person that he or she is forcibly confining. The punishment is not excessive and clearly does not outrage our standards of decency. In my view, it is within the purview of Parliament, in order to meet the objectives of a rational system of sentencing, to treat our most serious crime with an appropriate degree of certainty and severity. I reiterate that even in the case of first degree murder, Parliament has been sensitive to the particular circumstances of each offender through various provisions allowing for the Royal prerogative of mercy, the availability of escorted absences from custody for humanitarian and rehabilitative purposes and for early parole.[59]

Parliament has classified murder as first or second-degree murder depending upon the seriousness of the murder which has been committed. While all murder is serious, some murders are more heinous than others. Murder which is planned and deliberate is classified as first-degree murder and a person can be convicted of first-degree murder if he murders someone while in the course of committing an underlying offence such as sexual assault or forcible confinement. Where a person murders someone in circumstances where the accused is illegally dominating the person by forcibly confining them or sexual assaulting them, Parliament has decided that such murders should be classified as first-degree murders. Thus, if a murder occurs during the course of a sexual assault, the accused will be charged with first-degree murder even if the murder was not planned and deliberate.

In *R. v. Arkell*,[60] the accused argued that the mandatory minimum penalty for first-degree murder violated section 7 of the Charter. The accused contended that the mandatory minimum penalty for first-degree murder was arbitrary and irrational and that Parliament had not properly distinguished between offences which should be classified as first or second-degree murder. Rejecting the accused's contention that the classification scheme was so arbitrary that it violated the principles of fundamental justice under section 7 of the Charter, Lamer C.J.C. stated:

---

[59] *Ibid.*, at 203.
[60] (1990), 79 C.R. (3d) 207 (S.C.C.).

I can find no principle of fundamental justice that prevents Parliament . . . from classifying murders done while committing certain underlying offences as more serious, and thereby attaching more serious penalties to them. In the case of the distinction between first and second degree murder, the difference is a maximum extra 15 years that must be served before one is eligible for parole. This distinction is neither arbitrary nor irrational. The section is based on an organizing principle that treats murders committed while the perpetrator is illegally dominating another person as more serious than other murders. Further, the relationship between the classification and the moral blameworthiness of the offender clearly exists. Section 214 [now s. 231(5)] only comes into play when murder has been proven beyond a reasonable doubt . . . . . this means that the offender has been proven to have had subjective foresight of death. Parliament's decision to treat more seriously murders that have been committed while the offender is exploiting a position of power through illegal domination of the victim accords with the principle that there must be a proportionality between the sentence and the moral blameworthiness of the offender and other considerations such as deterrence and societal condemnation of the acts of the offender.[61]

It is clear from the principles which the Supreme Court of Canada has expressed in *Arkell* and *Luxton* that the mandatory minimum penalty for second-degree murder cannot be said to be a violation of sections 7 or 12 of the Charter. Although mandatory minimum sentences run counter to our individualized sentencing philosophy, the principles of individual and general deterrence justify the imposition of mandatory minimum sentences for first and second-degree murder.

(ii) *The case against mandatory sentences*

The Canadian Sentencing Commission recommended that mandatory minimum sentences be abolished for all offences except murder and treason. In *Smith*, Lamer J. quoted the Commission as stating:

> . . . existing mandatory minimum penalties, with the exception of those prescribed for murder and high treason, serve no purpose that can compensate for the disadvantages resulting from their continued existence.[62]

Although mandatory minimum sentences run counter to our sentencing philosophy, this does not mean that all mandatory minimum sentences will be struck down under the Charter. Generally, courts are reluctant to strike down mandatory minimum sentences as the Supreme Court of Canada's most recent judgment in *R. v. Goltz*[63] clearly indicates. In *Goltz*, the Supreme Court of Canada upheld provincial legislation which provided for a mandatory penalty of seven days' imprisonment for someone who was convicted of driving a

---

[61] *Ibid.*, at 214–215.
[62] *Supra*, note 52, at 242.
[63] (1991), 8 C.R. (4th) 82 (S.C.C.).

motor vehicle while his licence was under suspension. At trial, the accused challenged the constitutionality of section 88(1) of the British Columbia Motor Vehicle Act,[64] arguing that the mandatory penalty of seven days' imprisonment for a first offence constituted cruel and unusual punishment under section 12 of the Charter. The trial court held that the legislation was valid and sentenced the accused to seven days' imprisonment to be served intermittently over a period of consecutive three-day weekends. The accused appealed to the British Columbia Court of Appeal which held that the minimum period of incarceration violated section 12 of the Charter. The Crown successfully appealed to the Supreme Court of Canada.

The court was badly divided as to whether the mandatory minimum seven-day sentence constituted cruel and unusual punishment under section 12. However, in a four to three decision, a bare majority of the court held that the legislation did not violate section 12.

In *Goltz*, the British Columbia Court of Appeal concluded that the minimum sentence of seven days' imprisonment under the British Columbia Motor Vehicle Act breached section 12 of the Charter because it was inevitable that in certain cases to impose a minimum penalty of seven days' imprisonment on someone who was convicted of driving while prohibited from driving would be grossly disproportionate under section 12 of the Charter. In the Supreme Court of Canada, the majority of the court concluded that seven days' imprisonment for knowingly driving while prohibited from driving could not be reasonably compared to seven years' imprisonment for importing one marijuana cigarette, the sentence which an accused was potentially liable to receive based upon the wording of section 5(2) of the Narcotic Control Act as it stood before it was struck down by the Supreme Court of Canada in *Smith*.

In *Goltz*, the majority of the Supreme Court also held that the accused had failed to demonstrate that there were reasonable hypothetical circumstances where the minimum sentence of seven days' imprisonment would be grossly disproportionate to the sentence which an accused should actually receive. Accordingly, the majority of the court concluded that the provisions of the British Columbia Motor Vehicle Act did not outrage the standards of decency under section 12 of the Charter.

In *Goltz*, McLachlin J., writing for the two other judges who dissented, held that in some cases the mandatory minimum penalty of seven days' imprisonment coupled with a $300 fine would be disproportionate and shocking to the Canadian conscience and thus violated section 12 of the Charter.

Under the British Columbia Motor Vehicle Act, an accused who was prohibited from driving and who had moved a motor vehicle with a disabled driver at an accident scene in a freeway to permit other cars backed up for miles to get by would face a mandatory minimum penalty of seven days' imprisonment and a $300 fine. Section 88(1)(c) of the British Columbia

---

[64] R.S.B.C. 1979, c. 288.

Motor Vehicle Act would have permitted such a result. The majority of the British Columbia Court of Appeal and McLachlin J. for the dissenters in the Supreme Court of Canada cited this scenario as an example of a sentence mandated by the impugned provision which would be grossly disproportionate within the meaning of section 12 of the Charter.

The majority reasoning of the Supreme Court of Canada in *Goltz* is most unfortunate. When this case was argued in the Supreme Court of Canada in 1991, British Columbia was the only province which had a mandatory minimum penalty for a first offender who had been convicted of driving while his licence had been under suspension. The majority of the court in Goltz took an unduly restrictive approach to analyzing whether the provincial legislation breached section 12 of the Charter. It is not difficult to imagine a reasonable hypothetical set of circumstances in which the impugned provision would violate section 12 of the Charter. Also, the provision appears to be grossly disproportionate to the objective of the legislation, particularly when one considers that the Criminal Code does not prescribe a mandatory minimum penalty for manslaughter, a much more serious offence than the provincial offence of driving while one is prohibited from driving.

Section 12 has been used to challenge indeterminate sentences where persons have alleged that their continued detention in a penitentiary for an indefinite period of time constituted cruel and unusual punishment. In *Steele v. Mountain Inst.*,[65] the Supreme Court of Canada held that the continued detention of a criminal sexual psychopath violated section 12 of the Charter. In Steele, an inmate who had been confined for the better part of 37 years for attempted rape and other sexual offences brought an application for a writ of *habeas corpus* on the ground that his continued detention violated the section 12 Charter protection against cruel and unusual punishment. In 1953, Steele, then 18 years of age, pleaded guilty to a charge of attempted rape. He was declared to be a "criminal sexual psychopath" pursuant to the dangerous offender provisions in the Criminal Code. Steele was sentenced to five years' imprisonment for the attempted rape and to an indeterminate period of detention after that. At the time of sentencing, Steele was described as being of limited intelligence and physically immature with "the personality development of a nine-year old." Throughout the years, a number of highly qualified psychiatrists recommended that Steele be released and the warden of the institution where he was incarcerated also recommended his release. Although Steele was paroled in 1960, he was convicted of common assault and his parole was revoked. Steele was given a number of temporary passes during the 1970s and '80s but was denied full parole by the National Parole Board.

In holding that Steele's continued detention violated section 12 of the Charter, Cory J., writing for a unanimous Supreme Court of Canada, stated that the evidence presented indicated that the National Parole Board had applied the wrong criteria in assessing whether Steele should be granted

---

[65] (1990), 80 C.R. (3d) 257 (S.C.C.).

parole. The Supreme Court held that the board, in denying parole, had focused on minor breaches of discipline committed by Steele rather than determining whether Steele's release from prison resulted in undue risk to society. Cory J. held that Steele's sentence was grossly disproportionate, having regard to his personal circumstances and the offence that he had committed. In holding that Steele's continued detention violated section 12 of the Charter, Cory J. stated that it will only be "on rare and unique occasions that a court will find a sentence so grossly disproportionate that it violates the provisions of s. 12 of the Charter."[66]

5. TRIAL WITHIN A REASONABLE PERIOD OF TIME

Section 11(*b*) of the Charter states:

> Any person charged with an offence has the right to be tried within a reasonable period of time.

Section 11(*b*) of the Charter represents a profound change in Canadian criminal law. Prior to the enactment of the Charter, there was no constitutional right to have a trial within a reasonable period of time. Although the Criminal Code provides that summary conviction offences must be prosecuted within a six-month time period, there are generally no limitation periods in criminal law. Most accused persons do not want to be tried at all and are certainly loath to receive a speedy trial. Before the Charter was enacted, persons who were concerned about trial delay occasionally argued that an excessive delay in being tried amounted to an abuse of process. Such arguments usually fell on deaf ears. In *Rourke v. The Queen*, a pre-Charter case, the majority of the Supreme Court of Canada stated:

> I cannot find any rule in our criminal law that prosecutions must be instituted promptly and ought not to be permitted to be proceeded with if a delay in instituting them may have caused prejudice to the accused. In fact, no authority was cited to establish the existence of such a principle, which is at variance with the rule that criminal offences generally are not subject to prescription [a limitation period] except in the case of specific offences for which a prescription time has been established by statute. . . .[67]

Section 11(*b*) of the Charter has had a dramatic effect on the prosecution and trial of criminal offences in Ontario. In *R. v. Askov*,[68] the Supreme Court of Canada's landmark decision on unreasonable delay, the court held that a

---

[66] *Ibid.*, at 280.
[67] (1977), 38 C.R.N.S. 268 at 272 (S.C.C.).
[68] (1990), 79 C.R. (3d) 273 (S.C.C.).

delay of 34 months between the laying of charges and trial violated section 11(*b*) of the Charter. In *Askov*, Cory J. held that a delay between six and eight months between committal and trial in the ordinary criminal case "might be deemed to be the outside limit of what is reasonable."[69] The fallout from the *Askov* decision was swift. Courts from across Ontario dismissed thousands of cases. It became customary for many police officers, in writing a note to the file, explaining that the case had been dismissed, to say that the case had been "Askoved."[70]

In Ontario, since the *Askov* decision was handed down in October, 1990, 40,127 charges had been stayed, dismissed or withdrawn up to May 24, 1991, which constituted 14 percent of the charges processed in Ontario. The *Askov* decision resulted in the stay, dismissal or withdrawal of 8,600 impaired driving charges, 6,000 charges of theft under $1,000 and a large number of assault and fraud charges. The decision resulted in more than 500 charges of sexual assault and other sexual offences being stayed and also resulted in more than 1,000 drug-related charges being stayed. The *Askov* decision also led to thousands of parking tickets and over 15,000 other provincial offences being stayed.[71]

A stay of proceedings is equivalent to an acquittal in that it brings the proceedings to an end in favour of the accused. The Crown can appeal from a stay of proceedings as the stay is treated as tantamount to an acquittal. Although a stay of proceedings for an abuse of process is a discretionary remedy, the Supreme Court of Canada before *Askov* held that when an accused has established a violation of section 11(*b*) of the Charter, a stay of proceedings is the minimum remedy to which an accused is entitled.

In *Rahey v. R.*,[72] Lamer J., writing for a majority of the Supreme Court of Canada, in explaining why a stay is the minimum remedy for unreasonable delay, stated:

> . . . if an accused has the constitutional right to be tried within a reasonable time, he has the right not to be tried beyond that point in time, and no court has jurisdiction to try him or order that he be tried in violation of that right. After the passage of an unreasonable period of time, no trial, not even the fairest possible trial, is permissible. To allow a trial to proceed after such a finding would be to participate in a further violation of the Charter.[73]

In *Askov*, as a result of the "systemic" delays inherent in the court system, it had taken 34 months to try the accused on a charge of conspiracy in a case which was routine. There were no complicating factors which could

---

[69] *Ibid.*, at 313.
[70] See Donald MacIntosh, "Askov Trends", (1991) 1 N.J.C.L. 268.
[71] *R. v. Bennett* (1991), 6 C.R. (4th) 22 (Ont. C.A.), affirmed (1992), 74 C.C.C. (3d) 384 (note) (S.C.C.).
[72] (1987), 57 C.R. (3d) 289 (S.C.C.).
[73] *Ibid.*, at 305-306.

explain the inordinate delay which resulted from delays inherent in the system rather than from any delay peculiar to this particular case. The accused, Askov, had been incarcerated for six months and had been subject to restrictive bail conditions. In dealing with the 34-month period of delay in *Askov*, Cory J. had before him a study prepared by Professor Carl Baar, Director of the Judicial Administration Program at Brock University. Professor Baar's study demonstrated that the Peel District, which he called Brampton, had delays which were lengthy when compared with the rest of Ontario, other parts of Canada or the United States. In a much-publicized comment, Cory J. stated that the Peel District was not only the worst district in Canada, "but, so far as the studies indicate, anywhere north of the Rio Grande."[74] Mr. Justice Cory indicated that in resolving the question of whether a delay is inordinately long, it is appropriate to compare the jurisdiction in question to the best comparable jurisdiction in the country.

In *Askov*, the Supreme Court of Canada made it clear the Crown bares the responsibility for bringing the accused to trial. Accordingly, the Crown will be responsible for delay which is caused by systemic or institutional factors such as the failure of a province to provide a sufficient number of judges, courtroom facilities or Crown attorneys. In *Askov*, the Supreme Court of Canada set out four factors which are to taken into account in determining whether there has been an unreasonable delay in bringing the accused to trial. The factors are as follows:

(a) the length of the delay;
(b) explanation for the delay;
    (i)   delays that should be attributable to the Crown;
    (ii) systemic or institutional delays;
    (iii) delays attributable to the accused;
(c) waiver;
(d) prejudice to the accused.[75]

The court stated that all of the above factors are to be balanced against one another in determining whether the Crown has fulfilled its obligation to bring the accused to trial within a reasonable period of time. The court stated that the longer the delay, the more difficult it would be for the Crown to justify it, saying that some delays may be so excessive that they cannot be justified for any reason. Delays attributable to the Crown or officers of the Crown — i.e., the police, weigh in favour of the accused. The court recognized that complex cases require more time for preparation and will, therefore, justify a longer period of delay. The court stated that the Crown will always have the onus of justifying a delay which can be characterized as institutional — that is, a delay resulting from inadequate resources. In determining whether a delay

---

[74] *Supra*, note 68, at 312.
[75] *Ibid.*, at 306-307.

caused by inadequate institutional resources is excessive, the proper approach is to compare the jurisdiction where the delay occurs to the best jurisdiction in the country.

The court held that in determining whether there has been a breach of section 11(*b*), it is proper to consider the direct acts of the accused which contributed to the delay. Thus, if an accused sought an adjournment in order to obtain a new lawyer, the adjournment request would be a factor which is attributable to the accused rather than to the Crown. The court held that although the Crown had the duty to bring the accused to trial within a reasonable period of time, there may be circumstances where the accused has waived his right to a trial within a reasonable period of time. The failure of the accused to complain about not being tried within a timely fashion does not constitute a waiver. The accused will not have waived his right to be tried within a reasonable period of time unless the waiver is explicit. In order for the waiver to be a valid waiver, a court must also be in a position that it can infer from the surrounding circumstances that the accused has understood his right to be tried within a reasonable period of time and the effect of giving up such a right.

The court held that in some cases the delay will be so excessive that there is a "virtually irrebuttable presumption of prejudice to the accused resulting from the passage of time."[76] The court stated that where the Crown can demonstrate that there is no prejudice to the accused which results from the passage of time, the delay may be excused. It also held that the accused may call evidence to show actual prejudice which results from the delay in being tried.

In *Askov*, the delay of 34 months in bringing the accused to trial on a charge of conspiracy to commit extortion and on charges of certain weapons offences was regarded as being so excessive by the Supreme Court of Canada that the accused benefited from the "irrebuttable presumption" that he had been prejudiced by the excessive delay in proceeding with his trial. In this case, the accused was initially detained in custody for six months, and was then released on a $50,000 recognizance and ordered not to communicate with his co-accused.

Askov and his co-accused were charged with conspiracy to commit extortion and various weapons offences, including possession of a weapon for a purpose dangerous to the public peace. In this case, the complainant alleged that he had been requested by Askov to pay a sum of money "for the privilege" of supplying exotic dancers to establishments in the Toronto area. Cory J., writing for the majority of the court, stated that extortion and threatened armed violence "tear at the basic fabric of society" but held that the 34-month delay between committal (the preliminary hearing) and trial was so excessive that a stay of proceedings must be granted. Mr. Justice Cory stated that for the court not to grant a stay of proceedings in light of the excessive delay would

---

[76] *Ibid.*

render meaningless the section 11(*b*) right to be tried within a reasonable period of time.

Prior to the Supreme Court of Canada's landmark decision in *Askov*, the court had been divided as to the nature of the section 11(*b*) guarantee as to whether an accused was required to show that he was actually prejudiced by the Crown's excessive delay in bringing him to trial. Some of the judges believed that the accused was presumed to have suffered prejudice from the moment that he was charged and the prejudice was presumed to increase over time. Actual prejudice was irrelevant when determining whether there had been an unreasonable delay. Other judges took the position that the accused must show actual prejudice resulting from the unreasonable delay.[77]

In *Askov*, Cory J., writing for the majority of the court, attempted to reconcile the differing views that had been previously expressed by various members of the court as to the purpose of section 11(*b*) of the Charter. Cory J. held that section 11(*b*) protected not only the interest of the accused but the interests of society. The *Askov* decision was criticized by some commentators as departing from the traditional view that section 11(*b*) was purely an individual right which protected the accused's interest in being tried within a reasonable period of time without regard to the broader societal interest in bringing accused persons to trial.

In *R. v. Bennett*,[78] the Ontario Court of Appeal rejected the suggestion that the Supreme Court of Canada in *Askov* had established a six to eight-month limitation period for trying cases in the provincial courts. The majority of the Ontario Court of Appeal in *Bennett* stated that the lower court judges had applied the *Askov* decision in a mechanical fashion, saying that the six to eight-month period for trying a case in a provincial court was intended to be a guideline rather than a hard and fast rule as to when cases had to be brought to trial. When *Bennett* was argued in the Ontario Court of Appeal, close to 50,000 charges had been stayed, withdrawn or dismissed by the lower courts as a result of the *Askov* decision. The majority of the Ontario Court of Appeal characterized the fallout from the *Askov* decision as "staggering."[79]

In *R. v. Morin*,[80] the Supreme Court stated that the time period mentioned in *Askov* as being appropriate for the case to come to trial in provincial court was not intended as a limitation, but, rather, as a guideline to judges as to the delay which could be tolerated without violating section 11(*b*) of the Charter. The court in *Morin* went to great lengths to point out that the suggested period of six to eight months between committal and trial was never intended to be applied in mechanical fashion, saying that the *Askov* decision had intended that this only be used as a guideline. In *Morin*, Sopinka J., writing for a majority of the court, retrenched from the position taken by a majority

---

[77] *Mills v. R.* (1986), 52 C.R. (3d) 1 (S.C.C.), *Rahey, supra*, note 72.
[78] *Supra*, note 71, at 30-32.
[79] *Ibid.*, at 27.
[80] (1992), 12 C.R. (4th) 1 (S.C.C.).

of the court in *Askov* that it was appropriate to compare jurisdictions in determining the level of systemic or institutional delay which would be tolerated without resulting in a section 11(*b*) violation. The Supreme Court in *Askov* had held that it was appropriate to compare those jurisdictions with the greatest degree of promptness with those jurisdictions with the longest delays in determining whether a delay which has been caused by a lack of institutional resources is so excessive that it cannot be justified by the Crown.

In *Morin*, a majority of the court stated that comparison with other jurisdictions is to be applied with caution. In *Morin*, the accused who was arrested for impaired driving had asked for the "earliest possible trial date." At trial, the defence counsel brought a motion to stay the charges on the ground of unreasonable delay under section 11(*b*) of the Charter, arguing that the delay of over 14½ months from the date of the accused's arrest until her trial breached a right to be tried within a reasonable period of time. The accused's motion was dismissed and she was subsequently convicted of driving with excess alcohol in her blood (the "over 80" charge). On appeal, the Summary Conviction Appeal Court stayed the "over 80" charge on the ground that the accused had not been tried within a reasonable period of time. The Crown appealed to the Ontario Court of Appeal and the Ontario Court of Appeal restored the conviction. The accused appealed to the Supreme Court of Canada, who dismissed the appeal on the ground that the delay of over 14½ months from arrest to trial did not result in a violation of the accused's section 11(*b*) rights.

In *Morin*, the majority of the Supreme Court of Canada held that an eight to ten-month delay caused by a lack of institutional resources in the provincial courts would not be inappropriate. The eight to ten-month period was to be used as a guideline only.[81] Thus, it would be open to the accused to show that he had been prejudiced by restrictive bail conditions or pre-trial incarceration. The court noted that if the accused is in custody, a shorter period of delay will be tolerated than would otherwise be the case. The accused may lead evidence which establishes that there has been prejudice to his security of the person by virtue of the stress and damage to his reputation which results from an excessively long exposure to a pending criminal charge. The court also held that the Crown could lead evidence to show that the accused had benefited from the delay which had ensued and that he fell into the majority of persons who did not want an early trial date.

In *Morin*, the majority of the Supreme Court was undoubtedly influenced by the number of cases which had been stayed, dismissed or withdrawn in Ontario as a result of the lower court judges' interpretation of the Supreme Court's previous decision in *Askov*. While the *Morin* decision is generally regarded as a retrenchment from the Supreme Court's decision in *Askov*, a careful reading of the *Askov* decision indicates that the court never intended a

---

[81] *Ibid.*, at 19.

six to eight-month time period for proceeding in provincial court to be interpreted as a limitation period.

In *Morin*, a majority of the Supreme Court of Canada reaffirmed its position in *Askov* that systemic delay in bringing the accused to trial as a result of inadequate financial resources will not be tolerated. The court stated that while a lack of institutional resources is one factor which can be taken into consideration in assessing delay under section 11(*b*), the limitation of such resources must be assessed in light of the government's "constitutional obligation to commit sufficient resources to prevent unreasonable delay which distinguishes this obligation from many others that compete for funds within the administration of justice."[82] Although a majority of the court in *Morin* reaffirmed many of the principles expressed in *Askov*, it is clear from the *Morin* decision that the Supreme Court was surprised at the number of cases which had been stayed, withdrawn or dismissed in Ontario as a result of the court's decision in *Askov*. It is also clear that the Supreme Court in *Morin* is prepared to tolerate delays of a longer period in provincial courts than was the case when the court decided *Askov*.

In *Morin*, the Supreme Court of Canada held that section 11(*b*) protects the accused's right to security of the person, right to liberty, and right to a fair trial. The court stated that:

> The right to security of the person is protected in s. 11(*b*) by seeking to minimize the anxiety, concern and stigma of exposure to criminal proceedings. The right to liberty is protected by seeking to minimize exposure to the restrictions on liberty which result from pre-trial incarceration and restrictive bail conditions. The right to a fair trial is protected by attempting to ensure the proceedings take place while evidence is available and fresh.[83]

(a) Pre-charge Delay

Section 11(*b*) of the Charter protects the accused from unreasonable delay which results from the time that the charge is laid until the end of the trial. However, the Supreme Court of Canada has held that section 11(*b*) does not protect the accused against pre-charge delay — that is, the delay in charging the accused with the offence contained in the information or indictment. In *R. v. Kalanj*,[84] McIntyre J., writing for a majority of the court, held that a person is "charged with an offence" under section 11 of the Charter when an information is sworn (a charge is laid) or a direct indictment is preferred against him. McIntyre J. held that section 11(*b*) is intended to deal with the time during which the charge is laid and the trial ends, saying that the word

---

[82] *Ibid.*
[83] *Ibid.*, at 12.
[84] (1989), 70 C.R. (3d) 260 (S.C.C.).

"charge" in section 11 "should not be twisted in an attempt to extend the operation of the section into the pre-charge period."[85]

Subsequent to *Kalanj*, in 1991 the Supreme Court of Canada held that pre-charge delay, which is excessive and has caused actual prejudice to the accused, may constitute a violation of section 7 of the Charter. In *R. v. L. (W.K.)*,[86] the court held that a stay of proceedings may not be entered simply because there has been an excessive delay in proceeding with the charge. In delivering the judgment of the court, Stevenson J. stated:

> Sections 7 and 11(d) of the Charter protect, among other things, an individual's right to a fair trial. The fairness of a trial is not, however, automatically undermined by even a lengthy pre-charge delay. Indeed, a delay may operate to the advantage of the accused, since Crown witnesses may forget or disappear.[87]

In *L. (W.K.)*, the appellant was charged with 17 counts of sexual assault, gross indecency and assault relating to his step-daughter and two daughters. With respect to some of the charges, there was a 30-year delay before the police laid charges. The first assault was alleged to have occurred in 1957 and the last in 1985. Before the trial began, the accused's counsel brought a motion to stay the proceedings on the ground that the excessive period of pre-charge delay violated the accused's sections 7 and 11(*d*) Charter rights. The accused's counsel argued that it was open to the trial judge to stay the proceedings merely based upon the length of time that had passed between when the assaults took place and the charges were laid. The accused did not call any evidence establishing that he had been prejudiced by the pre-charge delay. The trial judge stayed the proceedings under section 24 of the Charter and the Crown appealed to the British Columbia Court of Appeal. The British Columbia Court of Appeal set aside the stay and the accused appealed to the Supreme Court of Canada. In setting aside the stay of proceedings, the Supreme Court of Canada said that delay in reporting sexual abuse is a common phenomenon, noting that the complainant often does not discover that she or he was sexually abused until years later.

The Supreme Court's decision in *L. (W.K.)* means that an accused will be able to rely on section 7 where there has been an excessive pre-charge delay which causes prejudice to the accused's ability to obtain a fair trial. Thus, the accused may call evidence indicating that crucial defence witnesses have disappeared. Delay by itself will not be sufficient for a court to halt proceedings by granting a stay of proceedings.

Since an accused does not have the right to invoke section 11(*b*) of the Charter in support of pre-charge delay, the accused will not have the benefit

---

[85] *Ibid.*, at 273.
[86] (1991), 6 C.R. (4th) 1 (S.C.C.).
[87] *Ibid.*, at 9.

of the presumption of prejudice which exists in cases where there is an excessive delay which is challenged on the basis of section 11(*b*) of the Charter. Under section 7, no presumption of prejudice can be inferred from an excessive delay in proceeding to lay the charge, and the accused will be required to demonstrate actual prejudice to his ability to have a fair trial.

(b) Appellate Delay

A majority of the Supreme Court of Canada has held that section 11(*b*) does not protect an accused person against appellate delay. In *R. v. Potvin*,[88] Sopinka J. held that section 11(*b*) does not apply with respect to the delay in proceeding with an appeal from conviction by the accused and does not apply to the delay where the Crown is appealing the accused's acquittal. Sopinka J. held that the use of the word "tried" in section 11(*b*) of the Charter indicates that the framers of the Charter did not intend the protection against a delay in proceeding to apply to proceedings other than trials. Mr. Justice Sopinka stated that had it been intended that section 11(*b*) apply to a broader class of proceedings, section 11(*b*) would have used language other than the word "tried." Sopinka J. also stated that a convicted person is not a person charged with a criminal offence and concluded that where an accused appeals his conviction, the appeal itself is not government action.

Although a majority of the court held in *Potvin* that section 11(*b*) does not apply to protect an accused against appellate delay, the court stated that section 7 of the Charter can provide a remedy for appellate delay in cases where the accused can demonstrate real prejudice arising from such delay.

It appears that section 7 affords little protection for an accused where there is a delay of appeal proceedings. In *Potvin*, the majority of the court stated that an appeal by the accused would not constitute the required government action (see section 32(2) of the Charter) so as to come within the scope of section 11(*b*). Similar reasoning would apply to section 7.

6. EQUALITY RIGHTS

(a) Generally

Subsection 15(1) of the Charter provides that:

Every individual is equal before and under the law and has the right to the equal protection and equal benefit of the law without discrimination and, in particular,

---

[88] (1993), 23 C.R. (4th) 10 (S.C.C.).

without discrimination based on race, national or ethnic origin, colour, religion, sex, age or mental or physical disability.

Subsection 15(2) of the Charter states that:

> Subsection (1) does not preclude any law, program or activity that has as its object the amelioration of conditions of disadvantaged individuals or groups including those that are disadvantaged because of race, national or ethnic origin, colour, religion, sex, age or mental or physical disability.

When section 15 became part of the Charter of Rights, government officials and legal commentators predicted that the section would provide the thrust for a wide range of constitutional challenges. The federal and provincial governments were sufficiently concerned about the explosive impact of section 15 that the framers of the Charter specifically provided that this section would not become law until April 17, 1985. (See section 32(2) of the Charter of Rights.) In commenting on the likely impact of section 15, J. Gregory Richards and the late Gary J. Smith, two well-known Canadian administrative lawyers, in their book, *Charter of Rights and Administrative Law*, remarked:

> It should be noted that it is under the equal protection clause of the Fourteenth Amendment of the United States Constitution that American courts have engaged in the most searching substantive review of legislation in that country. . . . It is probably under section 15 of the Charter that Canadian courts will have the greatest potential to assume a legislative role.[89]

The Fourteenth Amendment of the American Constitution provides:

> No state shall . . . deny to any person within its jurisdiction the equal protection of the law.

The Fourteenth Amendment of the American Constitution has proven to be a powerful weapon in dealing with the problem of racial discrimination in the United States. For example, in *Strauder v. West Virginia*,[90] the Supreme Court of the United States ruled that a state statute providing that only white male citizens were eligible for jury duty violated the Fourteenth Amendment's guarantee of equal protection because it precluded blacks from serving as jurors and thereby constituted racial discrimination. Section 15 of the Charter is likely to provide the grist for substantially more constitutional challenges than the Fourteenth Amendment of the American Constitution, which does not contain the broad-based guarantees that are found in section 15 of the Charter, including a right to "equal benefit of the law."

---

[89] J.G. Richards and G.J. Smith, *Charter of Rights and Administrative Law 1983-1984* (Toronto: Carswell, 1983), at p. 144.
[90] 100 U.S. 303 (U.S.S.C.) (1879).

The federal and provincial governments expected that section 15 would provide individuals challenging the constitutionality of legislation with a powerful tool with which to work. Consequently, the federal government and the provinces used a three-year period before section 15 became law to review existing laws to determine whether such laws violated the section 15 rights. In this regard, the then Conservative government of Ontario stated in a June 1985 background paper entitled, "Sources for the Interpretation of Equality Rights under the Charter," that the government had "conducted a thorough assessment of its legislation to determine whether it conforms to section 15."[91] The paper pointed out that "a bill amending fifty-eight statutes to bring them into better conformity with the equality rights provisions of the Charter was introduced in the Ontario Legislature on June 11th, 1985."[92]

(b) Sexual Offences

(i) *Impact of the Charter*

Section 7 and section 15 of the Charter have been used to attack the previous wording of section 146(1) of the 1970 Criminal Code which made it unlawful for a male to have sexual intercourse with a female under the age of 14 on the ground that it applied only to males. Section 146(1) of the 1970 Code, prior to the 1987 amendment,[93] specified that:

> Every male who has sexual intercourse with a female person who
> (*a*) is not his wife, and
> (*b*) is under the age of fourteen years,
> whether or not he believes she is fourteen years of age or more, is guilty of an indictable offence and is liable to imprisonment for life.

Previously, section 140 of the 1970 Criminal Code provided that a female under 14 could not consent to sexual intercourse with a male. This section precluded an accused from defending the charge on the basis that a female consented to having sexual intercourse with him. But that consent was a defence to a charge of sexual assault which was the only section under which a female could be charged for having sexual intercourse with a male under the age of 14. The effect of the previous provisions in section 146(1) and section 140 of the 1970 Criminal Code was that an accused who was charged with

---

[91] Government of Ontario, "Sources for the Interpretation of Equality Rights Under the Charter: A Background Paper" (Ministry of the Attorney General of Ontario: June 1985), at p. xi.
[92] *Ibid.*
[93] S.C. 1987, c. 24, s. 2.

having sexual intercourse with a female under 14 years of age would not be able to rely on defences which were available to a female accused facing a sexual assault charge. In other words, section 146(1) of the 1970 Code created an absolute liability offence applicable only to males for which there was no defence once the Crown proved that the accused had had sexual intercourse with a female under 14 years of age. Such an accused would be convicted unless he could convince a court that section 146(1) violated the Charter of Rights.

In the past, persons who had been charged with an offence under the former section 146(1) argued that the section violated the equality of rights clause in the Charter of Rights. The principal argument in this regard was that section 146 of the 1970 Criminal Code discriminated against males on the basis of sex and age. Several judges ruled that section 146(1) of the Code violated the Charter of Rights by discriminating against males on the basis of sex and age. While challenges based on section 15 of the Charter failed, the section was ultimately struck down by the Supreme Court of Canada as violating section 7 of the Charter.

In *R. v. Hess*; *R. v. Nguyen*,[94] the Supreme Court of Canada struck down the old section 146(1) on the basis that it violated the principles of fundamental justice under section 7 of the Charter. Wilson J., writing on behalf of a majority of the court, held that section 146(1) of the Code was an absolute liability offence as the accused's honest but mistaken belief that the female was over 14 years of age was no defence to the charge. Accordingly, a person who had no intention with respect to an essential element of the offence could be sentenced to life imprisonment even though he was "morally innocent" of the offence for which he was charged. Wilson J. held that it is a principle of fundamental justice under section 7 of the Charter that *mens rea* is required for a criminal offence which carries a maximum penalty of life imprisonment. Wilson J. held that the requirement of *mens rea* necessitated that there be a defence of due diligence. Since the existing wording of the statute did not allow for a defence of due diligence, the section violated section 7 of the Charter and could not be justified under section 1.

Before the Supreme Court, it was argued that section 146(1) also violated section 15 of the Charter as it discriminated on the basis of sex as only adult males could be charged under the section. Wilson J. held that section 146(1) did not contravene section 15 of the Charter since the offence under this section involved an act "that as a matter of biological fact only men over a certain age are capable of committing." Section 3(6) of the Criminal Code had defined sexual intercourse as being completed where there was penetration to even the slightest degree. Madam Justice McLachlin, writing for the majority of the court, held that while section 146(1) violated section 15(1) of the Charter, the breach of the Charter was justifiable under section 1.

---

[94] (1990), 79 C.R. (3d) 332 (S.C.C.).

McLachlin J., with whom Gonthier J. concurred, held that the fact that males are singled out by section 146(1) was justified since only males can cause pregnancies.

Because of the judicial pronouncements and mounting pressure to remove discriminatory references from the Criminal Code, Parliament amended the sexual offences part of the Code in 1987. By "An Act to amend the Criminal Code and the Canada Evidence Act (S.C. 1987, c. 24) enacted on June 30, 1987 and proclaimed in force on January 1, 1988, sections 140 and 146 were repealed. The consent provision (section 140) was re-enacted as section 139 [150.1] and provided that, in respect of a complainant under the age of 14 years, it was not a defence that the complainant consented to the activity that formed the subject matter of the charge. Accordingly, consent was not a defence for the specified offences whether the complainant was female or male.

Two new offences, "sexual interference" (section 140 [151]) and "sexual exploitation" (section 146 [153]), were created which replaced those provisions of the Code dealing with sexual intercourse with a female under 14, seduction and sexual intercourse with a step-daughter, foster-daughter or female ward, or female employee. The new offences refer to "every person" and, accordingly, replace the corresponding offences only applicable to male accused. The amendments are reflective of the unprecedented impact of the Charter on criminal offences themselves.

7. REASONABLE LIMITS DEMONSTRABLY JUSTIFIED IN A FREE AND DEMOCRATIC SOCIETY

(a) Generally

The rights and freedoms guaranteed by the Charter of Rights and Freedoms are not absolute. Section 1 of the Charter provides that:

> The *Canadian Charter of Rights and Freedoms* guarantees the rights and freedoms set out in it subject only to such reasonable limits prescribed by law as can be demonstrably justified in a free and democratic society.

The effect of section 1 of the Charter of Rights and Freedoms is that a citizen's rights under the Charter can be limited by law if the limit can be said to be "demonstrably justified in a free and democratic society." If a court decides that a federal or provincial law which violates the Charter is a reasonable limit which can be demonstrably justified in a free and democratic society, the law will not be held to be invalid under the Charter. Section 1 of the Charter is a recognition by the drafters of the Charter that the fundamental rights and freedoms contained in it should be subject to limitations which a court believes are reasonable and demonstrably justified in a democratic society.

(b) Prescribed by Law

When the Charter was first proclaimed, some courts applied section 1 without stating how the section should be interpreted. However, the Supreme Court of Canada has interpreted its broad language. In *Therens*, Justice Le Dain stated that the section 1 requirement that a limit to a Charter right be prescribed by law "is chiefly concerned with the distinction between a limit imposed by law and one that is arbitrary." His Lordship stated:

> The limit will be prescribed by law within the meaning of s. 1 if it is expressly provided for by statute or regulation, or results by necessary implication from the terms of a statute or regulation or from its operating requirements. The limit may also result from the application of a common law rule.[95]

A limit will not be prescribed by law if it results from the actions of officials rather than from the express or implied operation of legislation. In *Therens*, the majority of the Supreme Court of Canada held that a police officer's breach of the accused's right to counsel could not be justified under section 1 as nothing in the legislation justified the denial of counsel. The Supreme Court has consistently followed the approach in *Therens* that a breach of Charter rights by police officers and other state agents is not justifiable under section 1 of the Charter where the legislation contains no express or implied limitation which would justify the breach.

(c) Reasonable Limit Defined

The Charter of Rights does not define what is meant by the words "reasonable limit" and the definition has been left to the courts to develop in decided cases. Black's Law Dictionary defines the word "reasonable" as follows:

> Reasonable: Fair, proper, just, moderate, suitable under the circumstances. Fit and appropriate to the end in view. Having the faculty of reason; rational; governed by reason; under the influence of reason; agreeable to reason. Thinking, speaking, or acting according to the dictates of reason. Not immoderate or excessive, being synonymous with rational, honest, equitable, fair, suitable, moderate, tolerable.[96]

Although a dictionary definition of the word "reasonable" is not a con-

---

[95] *Supra*, note 15, at 126.
[96] Black's Law Dictionary, 5th ed. (St. Paul, Minn.: West Publishing Co., 1979) at p. 1138.

clusive guide to its use and meaning within section 1 of the Charter, some courts have used dictionary definitions as a starting point in determining the meaning of the phrase "reasonable limit."

(d) Justifying Charter Limit

In determining what constitutes a reasonable limit prescribed by law as can be demonstrably justified in a free and democratic society, the courts have not presumed that governments have acted reasonably. Thus, the fact that a statute has existed in statute books for 50 years or more without being challenged does not mean that it is constitutional. There is no presumption of constitutionality under the Charter.

The burden of justifying a Charter breach is on the government as the party seeking to uphold the legislation. The standard of proof is the civil standard, proof by a preponderance of probabilities. Thus, the government must show that it is more likely than not that the limit is reasonable and demonstrably justified in a free and democratic society.

The Supreme Court in *R. v. Oakes*[97] and subsequent cases has made it clear that not all legislative objectives will be of sufficient importance to justify overriding a constitutionally protected right or freedom. Objectives which are trivial will not justify the limitation of a Charter right or freedom. An objective must relate to concerns which are pressing and substantial in a free and democratic society before it will be sufficiently important to warrant overriding Charter rights or freedoms.

(i) *Proportionality test*

In *Oakes*, the Supreme Court of Canada struck down section 8 of the Narcotic Control Act on the ground that it violated the presumption of innocence under section 11(*d*) of the Charter. Dickson C.J.C., who delivered the judgment of the court, held that the section which placed the burden of proof on the accused to prove that he was not in possession of a narcotic for the purposes of trafficking could not be justified as a reasonable limit under section 1 of the Charter. The *Oakes* criteria for determining whether a limit is a reasonable limit under section 1 has been cited in every subsequent Supreme Court of Canada case dealing with section 1 of the Charter. In *Oakes*, the Supreme Court set out the procedure to be followed for determining whether a limit of a Charter right or freedom is demonstrably justified under section 1:

> 1. The objective of the impugned provision must be of sufficient importance to warrant overriding a constitutionally protected right or freedom; it must relate

---

[97] (1986), 50 C.R. (3d) 1 (S.C.C.).

to concerns which are pressing and substantial in a free and democratic society before it can be characterized as sufficiently important.

2. Assuming that a sufficiently important objective has been established, the means chosen to achieve the objective must pass a proportionality test; that is to say they must:

   (a) be "rationally connected" to the objective and not be arbitrary, unfair or based on irrational considerations;

   (b) impair the right or freedom in question as "little as possible"; and

   (c) be such that their effects on the limitation of rights and freedoms are proportional to the objective.[98]

In *Oakes*, the Supreme Court of Canada held that the burden of proof required under section 1 would be commensurate with the occasion. Although the court did not explain what it meant by this phrase, it became apparent in subsequent cases that the court was not prepared to consistently apply the criteria that Parliament or provincial legislatures were required to adopt the least restrictive means of limiting Charter rights. In *R. v. Videoflicks Ltd.*,[99] the Supreme Court of Canada for the first time moved away from the least restrictive means test by holding that the question is whether the impugned legislation infringes a Charter right or freedom as little as reasonably possible. In *Videoflicks Ltd.*, the question was whether Sunday closing legislation enacted by the province of Ontario violated the freedom of religion guarantee in section 2(*a*) of the Charter. In upholding the legislation as a reasonable limit under section 1, Dickson C.J.C. stated that the question was "whether there is some reasonable alternative scheme which would allow the province to achieve its objective with fewer detrimental effects on religious freedom."[100]

More recently, in *R. v. Chaulk*,[101] Lamer C.J.C., writing for a majority of the court, held that Parliament "is not required to search out and to adopt the absolutely least intrusive means of attaining its objective." The Chief Justice further stated that when a court is assessing the alternative means which were available to Parliament or a provincial legislature in enacting the legislation under attack, "it is important to consider whether a less intrusive means would achieve the 'same' objective or would achieve the same objective as effectively."[102]

The Supreme Court of Canada's relaxation of the minimal impairment test in *Oakes* has been criticized by some legal commentators. It has been suggested that the requirement that Parliament restrict a right or freedom as little

---

[98] The test is taken from *R. v. Chaulk* (1990), 2 C.R. (4th) 1 at 27-28 (S.C.C.).

[99] (1986), 55 C.R. (3d) 193 (S.C.C.).

[100] *Ibid.*, at 237.

[101] *Supra*, note 98.

[102] *Ibid.*, at 32.

as reasonably possible is not appropriate for a criminal law setting where the state is the single antagonist of the individual.[103] Although it is recognized that Parliament should have more flexibility in a non-criminal setting where it passes legislation in relation to economic matters and other matters where it has mediated between the conflicting demands of competing interest groups, many commentators believe that a more exacting standard is required where the state uses the full arsenal of its law enforcement powers to prosecute and incarcerate criminal offenders

The Supreme Court of Canada has not accepted the view that the more exacting *Oakes* standard should be applied to criminal cases while the less exacting standard should be applied to non-criminal cases.

---

[103] See Don Stuart, "Will Section 1 Now Save Any Charter Violation? The Chaulk Effectiveness Test is Improper" (1991), 2 C.R. (4th) 107 at 114-115.

4

A Basic Overview of the Criminal Code

1. CLASSIFICATION OF OFFENCES

(a) At Common Law

Under common law, crimes were classified as being either indictable offences or petty offences. Indictable offences were tried by a judge and jury, while petty offences were tried by justices of the peace sitting without a jury. Indictable offences included treasons, felonies and misdemeanors. Felonies consisted of serious crimes such as murder and robbery, while misdemeanors referred to less serious crimes. A felony was punishable by death, whereas a misdemeanor was not.[1] The classification of crimes as felonies or misdemeanors, which continues to exist in the United States, was abolished in Canada by the Stevens' 1892 Criminal Code.[2] In the present Criminal Code,[3] offences are divided into three classifications, consisting of indictable offences, summary conviction offences and hybrid or dual procedure offences.

(b) Under the Criminal Code

Prosecutions are initiated by an information sworn before a justice of the peace alleging that a person has committed a criminal offence, or that there are reasonable and probable grounds for believing such an offence has been committed. If the justice is satisfied that a case has been made out, justifying an appearance in court, he will issue process to bring the person named in the information before the court. If the offence is indictable the named person is

---

[1] Halsbury's Laws of England, 3rd ed., at p. 293 et seq.
[2] The Honourable Roger E. Salhany, *Canadian Criminal Procedure*, 4th ed. (Aurora: Canada Law Book, 1984) at p. 3.
[3] R.S.C. 1985, c. C-46.

known as the accused; if it is a summary conviction matter he is called the defendant.

(i) Indictable offences

Indictable offences cover the most serious crimes such as murder, robbery, kidnapping and treason which are punishable by life imprisonment, as well as some indictable offences which are only punishable by two years' imprisonment. When an accused appears in court charged with an indictable offence, the first formal process, unless the accused waives it, is a preliminary inquiry to determine whether, on the evidence presented, a court could convict. If the presiding justice finds there is such evidence he will commit the accused for trial; if not, the accused will be discharged. The evidence required to commit for trial is not evidence which necessarily would justify a finding of guilt, but merely evidence which could lead to a conviction.

(ii) *Summary conviction offences*

Summary conviction offences are the less serious crimes in the Criminal Code. Section 787(1) of the Code provides that someone who is convicted of an offence punishable by summary conviction may be imprisoned for six months and subject to a fine not exceeding two thousand dollars. The section also gives a trial judge the discretion to order that the accused be sentenced to a period of imprisonment in addition to paying a fine. The offence of failing to act as a lookout as someone is being towed by a motor boat is an example of a summary conviction offence. Section 250(1) of the Code makes it an offence to take someone water skiing without having someone in the boat to watch the water skier. Offences such as disturbing a religious meeting or trespassing on someone's property at night are also offences which are punishable by summary conviction.

The procedure governing summary conviction offences is set out in Part XXVII of the Criminal Code which deals with the rules pertaining to summary conviction trials and appeals. Summary conviction offences include not only those created by the Code but a large number created by other Acts of Parliament. Some of this legislation provides for a greater penalty than those set out in the Criminal Code and thus section 787(1) authorizes a judge to impose a greater punishment than the punishment set out in that section.

(iii) *Hybrid or dual offences*

A hybrid or dual procedure offence is an offence which may be prosecuted by indictment or summary conviction. There are more than 50 hybrid offences in the Criminal Code where the Crown counsel will have to decide whether to proceed summarily or by way of indictment. The Crown makes the choice to proceed summarily or by way of indictment before the accused decides whether or not to plead guilty.

Before the Crown elects whether to proceed summarily, a hybrid offence is treated as an indictable offence. If the Crown does not make any election and the case proceeds in a summary conviction court (a provincial court), the Crown is deemed to have elected to proceed by way of summary conviction. In deciding whether to proceed summarily or by way of indictment Crown counsel will consider factors such as the seriousness of the offence and whether the accused has a long criminal record for similar offences. If the Crown elects to proceed by way of indictment, the penalty upon conviction will be greater than it would be had the Crown proceeded summarily.

The Crown has total discretion as to whether to elect to proceed by indictment or summary conviction. The Supreme Court of Canada has held that prosecutors have a discretion to withdraw a charge, proceed by way of indictment or summary conviction and launch an appeal. The decision as to whether to proceed by way of indictment or summary conviction is part of the broad powers of discretion exercised by prosecutors and cannot be attacked unless the exercise of prosecutorial discretion amounts to an abuse of the court's process.

2. CRIMINAL COURTS

(a) Court Levels

The Criminal Code divides criminal courts into three levels consisting of provincial courts, courts of criminal jurisdiction, and superior courts of criminal jurisdiction. Section 2 of the Criminal Code states that "court of criminal jurisdiction" means

(a) a court of general or quarter sessions of the peace, when presided over by a superior court judge,
(a.1) in the Province of Quebec, the Court of Quebec, the municipal court of Montreal and the municipal court of Quebec,
(b) a provincial court judge or judge acting under Part XIX, and
(c) in the Province of Ontario, the Ontario Court of Justice.

Section 2 provides that "superior court of criminal jurisdiction" means

(a) in the Province of Ontario, the Court of Appeal or the Ontario Court (General Division),
(b) in the Province of Quebec, the Superior Court,
(c) in the Province of Prince Edward Island, the Supreme Court,

(d) in the Provinces of New Brunswick, Manitoba, Saskatchewan and Alberta, the Court of Appeal or the Court of Queen's Bench,

(e) in the Provinces of Nova Scotia, British Columbia and Newfoundland, the Supreme Court or the Court of Appeal,

(f) in the Yukon Territory, the Supreme Court, and

(g) in the Northwest Territories, the Supreme Court.

The provincial courts are courts of criminal jurisdiction, such as the municipal court of Montreal and the municipal court of Quebec are inferior courts whose jurisdiction is limited. The superior courts of criminal jurisdiction such as the Ontario Court (General Division) and the Nova Scotia Supreme Court have jurisdiction to try certain very serious criminal offences, such as murder, which the lower courts are not able to hear.

(b) Jurisdiction Over the Person Charged

Jurisdiction over the person charged refers to the authority which a court has to try an accused for a particular offence. Generally, summary conviction offences will be tried before a provincial court judge having jurisdiction in the territorial division where the offence is alleged to have been committed (section 798). Section 335 of the Criminal Code, which deals with taking a motor vehicle or vessel without consent is an example of a type of offence which would be tried before a provincial court judge. Section 335(1) provides:

> Every one who, without the consent of the owner, takes a motor vehicle or vessel with intent to drive, use, navigate or operate it or cause it to be driven, used, navigated or operated is guilty of an offence punishable on summary conviction.

If an accused person was charged with an offence under section 335 of the Criminal Code, the trial would take place before a provincial court judge. Since the section does not specify the maximum penalty upon conviction, the accused would be liable under the summary conviction offence provisions contained in Part XXVII of the Code to receive a $2,000 fine and six months' imprisonment.

Section 469 provides that every court of criminal jurisdiction has jurisdiction to try an indictable offence other than serious offences such as treason, murder, intimidating Parliament or a legislature, piracy and seditious offences. Section 468 confers on superior courts of criminal jurisdiction the right to try any indictable offence. The result is that the most serious offences may only be tried by a superior court of criminal jurisdiction.

(c) Mode of Trial

(i) Trial by jury

Section 471 of the Criminal Code sets out the general rule that an accused who is charged with an indictable offence is to be tried by a judge and jury. The section reads:

> Except where otherwise expressly provided by law, every accused who is charged with an indictable offence shall be tried by a court composed of a judge and jury.

There are many indictable offences in the Criminal Code which provide that an accused does not have a right to be tried by a jury. Someone who is charged with one of the indictable offences set out in section 553, for example, does not have the right to be tried by a jury, but rather without his or her consent may be tried by a provincial court judge. Under section 553 such offences include:

1. theft, other than theft of cattle,
2. obtaining money or property by false pretenses,
3. unlawful possession of property obtained by crime or unlawful possession of the proceeds of such property,
4. mischief under subsection 430(4), where the mischief does not relate to something which could be classified as a testamentary instrument and the mischief is in relation to property, the value of which does not exceed $5,000,
5. keeping a gaming or betting house,
6. book-making,
7. placing bets for a fee,
8. operating lotteries, or other games of chance,
9. cheating at play,
10. keeping a common bawdy-house, and
11. driving while disqualified.

The absolute jurisdiction of a provincial court judge over section 553 offences does not mean that a provincial court is the only court which has the jurisdiction to try this offence. It is clear from reading sections 468 and 469 of the Code that every court of criminal jurisdiction and every superior court of criminal jurisdiction may try the offences set out in section 553 although normally these are tried by a provincial court judge.

(ii) *Election by accused*

An accused charged with an indictable offence, other than a section 469 or 553 offence, may elect the mode of trial. Thus, he or she can choose to be tried by a provincial court judge without a jury, by a judge with a jury after a preliminary inquiry has been held, or by a judge and jury. Where the accused has an election as to his or her mode of trial, the clerk of the court will read the following words, as stated in section 536(2) to the accused:

> You have the option to elect to be tried by a provincial court judge without a jury and without having had a preliminary inquiry; or you may elect to have a preliminary inquiry and to be tried by a judge without a jury; or you may elect to have a preliminary inquiry and to be tried by a court composed of a judge and jury. If you do not elect now, you shall be deemed to have elected to have a preliminary inquiry and to be tried by a court composed of a judge and jury. How do you elect to be tried?

Where an accused elects to be tried by a judge without a jury after a preliminary inquiry, the accused will usually be tried by a County or District Court judge. In other words, the accused will be tried by a "court of criminal jurisdiction." The accused cannot elect the type of judge who will try the case. This is an administrative decision. The superior courts normally try only the most serious cases leaving those where the accused has an election to be tried by the County and District Courts. If the offence is a particularly serious one, the accused may wish to be tried after having a preliminary inquiry. A preliminary inquiry, as explained earlier, is a hearing to determine whether there is sufficient evidence for the accused to be tried. When a preliminary inquiry is held, the accused's lawyer will be able to question witnesses to determine the weaknesses, if any, in the prosecution's case. A preliminary inquiry is not a trial and therefore an accused cannot be convicted of an offence at such a hearing. The fact that an accused is committed for trial at a preliminary inquiry does not necessarily mean that he or she will be convicted at trial. In certain cases, an accused may wish to be tried by a court comprised of a judge and jury, believing that he or she would be more likely to be acquitted by a jury than by a judge sitting alone.

Where the Criminal Code permits the accused to elect the mode of trial, the accused's election is not absolute, as section 568 permits the Attorney General of a province to require that an accused be tried by a court comprised of a judge and jury, except in cases where the offence is punishable by imprisonment for five years or less. Also, where an accused is jointly charged with another accused, an accused who elects to be tried by a provincial court judge may have his or her election nullified if the co-accused elects to be tried by a judge and jury.

(d) Place of Trial

(i) *Territorial jurisdiction*

The trial will normally be held by a court in the territorial division where the offence is alleged to have occurred. Section 2 of the Criminal Code defines "territorial division" as follows:

> "territorial division" includes any province, county, unicn of counties, township, city, town, parish or other judicial division or place . . .

This effectively means (subject to some specific exceptions set out in the Criminal Code) that an accused must be tried in the county or territory where the offence occurred. The basic rules governing a court's jurisdiction to try someone for a criminal offence are set out in sections 470 and 785(1) of the Criminal Code. Section 470 of the Code provides:

> Subject to this Act, every superior court of criminal jurisdiction and every court of criminal jurisdiction that has power to try an indictable offence is competent to try an accused for that offence
> (a) if the accused is found, is arrested or is in custody within the territorial jurisdiction of the court; or
> (b) if the accused has been ordered to be tried by
>   (i) that court, or
>   (ii) any other court, the jurisdiction of which has by lawful authority been transferred to that court.

The rules governing summary conviction offences are set out in Part XXVII of the Criminal Code. Section 785(1) provides that such matters must be tried by a person who has jurisdiction in the territorial division where the subject matter of the proceedings is alleged to have arisen. The Criminal Code provides that, generally, an accused must be tried in the province where the offence was committed. Section 478(1) of the Code provides:

> Subject to this Act, a court in a province shall not try an offence committed entirely in another province.

Thus, a charge which states that an offence was committed "at Montreal, District of Montreal, Province of Quebec or elsewhere in Canada" is invalid and a court has no jurisdiction to try the offence.[4] The general rule that an offence must be tried in the province where it was committed is subject to some exceptions. For example, section 478(2) of the Criminal Code provides that the owner, publisher or editor of a newspaper charged with publishing a

---

[4] *Nikolai v. R.* (1981), 63 C.C.C. (2d) 165 (Que. S.C.).

defamatory libel may be tried in the province where he or she resides or in the province where the newspaper is printed. Further exceptions to the rule that an accused will be tried in the province where the offence was committed are found in sections 739(1) and 740(1) of the Criminal Code which deal with breaches of probation orders. Section 740(1) of the Code provides that where an accused intentionally fails to abide by a probation order the accused is guilty of a summary conviction offence. This section states that where the offence was committed in one province and the accused is subsequently in another province, he or she may be tried in the province where the arrest took place providing that the Attorney General of such a province consents to the accused being tried there.

(ii) *Concurrent jurisdiction*

Although the general principle is that all crime is local and must be tried in the district where the offence was committed, some offences begin and end in two different territories. For example, someone may be kidnapped in one county and driven to another county before the offender is apprehended by the police. In such circumstances, the courts of both territorial divisions will have concurrent jurisdiction to try the offence. A crime may be committed on board an aircraft, vessel or a vehicle which passes from one territorial division to another. In such a case, several territorial divisions will have jurisdiction to try the offence as section 476 provides that the offence is deemed to have been committed in the territorial jurisdictions through which the vessel passed.

Section 470(*a*) provides that a court will have jurisdiction to try an indictable offence which was committed in another jurisdiction where an accused has been arrested or is being held in custody within the jurisdiction of the court. Section 6(2) of the Code provides that courts do not have jurisdiction to try offences committed outside Canada. This general rule is subject to a number of exceptions. For example, if two people agree to kill someone who is outside Canada, the unlawful agreement is called a conspiracy and the conspirators can be tried in Canada. Furthermore, the Criminal Code makes it an offence for two or more people outside of Canada to enter a conspiracy to commit an indictable offence in Canada and the conspirators may be tried in Canada. The detailed provisions governing conspiracies outside Canada are contained in section 465(1) of the Criminal Code. Section 7 extends jurisdiction to crimes committed on Canadian aircraft and the Canada Shipping Act[5] also does so for crimes committed on Canadian ships. Other exceptions are the offence of treason, the offence of having something in one's possession,

---

[5] R.S.C. 1985, c. S-9.

knowing it was obtained by an act which would have constituted an indictable offence if committed in Canada, and the offence of bringing into Canada property obtained by crime.[6]

3. COMPELLING ATTENDANCE AND INTERIM RELEASE

(a) Compelling Attendance of Accused

When an accused has been charged with a criminal offence, a police officer may compel the accused to appear in court by issuing an appearance notice, promise to appear or summons to appear, or release the accused on his or her own recognizance.

(i) *Appearance notice*

An appearance notice informs the accused of the offence which he or she is supposed to have committed and specifies the date when the accused is required to appear in court. The notice will inform the accused that a failure to appear in court in accordance with an appearance notice is a criminal offence under section 145(5) of the Code. If the accused has been charged with an indictable offence or a hybrid offence, the notice will state that the accused is required to have his or her fingerprints taken in accordance with the Identification of Criminals Act,[7] and will specify the time and place where the accused must go to be fingerprinted. The notice will inform the accused that his or her failure to attend for fingerprinting is a criminal offence by virtue of subsections 145(5) and (6) of the Code.

(ii) *Promise to appear*

A promise to appear is similar to an appearance notice, but in a promise to appear the accused promises to attend court on the date and time specified in the notice and, where applicable, promises to attend the police station specified in the notice to be fingerprinted.

---

[6] *Libman v. R.* (1985), 21 C.C.C. (3d) 206 (S.C.C.).
[7] R.S.C. 1985, c. I-1.

(iii) *Summons to appear*

A summons to appear in court is similar to an appearance notice, except that it is signed by a justice of the peace, or a judge, rather than by a police officer. A summons will order the accused in the name of the Queen to attend court at a given time on a particular day. If the accused is required to attend for fingerprinting, a statement to this effect will be set out in the summons. Where an accused is given an appearance notice, a promise to appear, or is released by a recognizance, he or she will be asked to sign the document. An appearance notice or promise to appear or recognizance is not invalidated because the accused refuses to sign the document.

(iv) *Recognizance*

A recognizance is an acknowledgment to the Crown that the accused will owe a certain amount of money in the event that he or she fails to attend court as required, or go to the police station for fingerprinting if required to do so.

(b) Release From Custody by Police Officer

The scheme of the Criminal Code is to secure the release of persons in all but the most serious cases, unless the public interest dictates that an arrest should be made. Section 496 of the Code authorizes a police officer to issue an appearance notice to someone when he is not arrested where the offence is a section 553 indictable offence, is an offence punishable on summary conviction, or is a dual procedure offence punishable by indictment or summarily. Thus, even where a person is arrested, the scheme of the Code is to have a person released as soon as possible. Section 497(1) of the Code provides:

> (1) Where a peace officer arrests a person without a warrant for
> (a) an indictable offence mentioned in section 553,
> (b) an offence for which the person may be prosecuted by indictment or for which he is punishable on summary conviction, or
> (c) an offence punishable on summary conviction, he shall as soon as practicable,
> (d) release the person from custody with the intention of compelling his appearance by way of summons, or
> (e) issue an appearance notice to the person and thereupon release him, unless
> (f) he believes on reasonable and probable grounds that it is necessary in the public interest, having regard to all the circumstances including the need to
> > (i) establish the identity of the person,
> > (ii) secure or preserve evidence of or relating to the offence, or
> > (iii) prevent the continuation or repetition of the offence or the commission of another offence,

that the person be detained in custody or that the matter of his release from custody be dealt with under another provision of this Part, or
(g) he believes on reasonable and probable grounds that, if the person is released by him from custody, the person will fail to attend in court in order to be dealt with according to law.

If a peace officer arrests someone for an offence committed in another province, the accused can only be released by a justice of the peace in the province where he or she was arrested.

(i) *Officer in charge*

In some cases, an accused may be released by an officer in charge of a police station. Thus, the Code directs the officer in charge of a police station to release the accused if the accused has not been released by the arresting officer and the release of the accused would not be inconsistent with the protection of the public. The Code gives the officer in charge the authority to release an accused where the accused has been arrested without a warrant, or in cases where the accused has been arrested with a warrant. The authority to release an accused who has been arrested without a warrant is set out in section 498 of the Code. This section authorizes the officer in charge of a police station to release an accused detained in custody where the accused is charged with a summary conviction offence such as shoplifting, a section 553 indictable offence such as theft, a dual procedure offence or an offence which is punishable by five years' imprisonment or less. The section directs the officer to release an accused charged with such an offence as soon as practicable by issuing a promise to appear, releasing the accused on his own recognizance or releasing the accused upon issuing a summons. The section provides that the recognizance is not to exceed $500. The officer is not obliged to release an accused where he has reasonable and probable grounds to believe that the accused will fail to attend court, or where he has reasonable and probable grounds to believe that it is not in the public interest that the accused be released. Paragraph 498(1)(i) states that, in considering whether it is in the public interest that the accused be released, the officer must consider all the circumstances including the need to:

(i) establish the identity of the person,
(ii) secure or preserve evidence of or relating to the offence, or
(iii) prevent the continuation or repetition of the offence or the commission of another offence . . . .

(ii) *"Reasonable and probable grounds"*

The term "reasonable and probable grounds" means that the officer must have facts or evidence which would support his or her belief that something was true. The suspicion that something is true is not the same as reasonable and probable grounds. Thus, in *Broughton v. Jackson,* Lord Campbell stated that reasonable and probable grounds does not mean that the officer reasonably suspected, but rather that the person claiming to have reasonable and probable grounds must present "facts which would create a reasonable suspicion in the mind of a reasonable man."[8]

While the officer's opinion forms part of the reasonable and probable grounds, the officer must be able to produce facts which support his or her opinion, so that a court can see that the officer's opinion is based on objective facts. Section 499 confers a similar power in cases where an arrest has been made with a warrant.

(c) Judicial Interim Release

(i) *Appearance before the justice of the peace*

An accused who is not released by a peace officer, or the officer in charge of a police station, will have a judicial interim release hearing or bail hearing. The Code provides that someone who is arrested with or without a warrant must be taken before a justice of the peace within 24 hours of being arrested. Section 503(1) of the Code states:

> (1) A peace officer who arrests a person with or without a warrant or to whom a person is delivered under subsection (3) [494(3)] [arrest by a private citizen] shall cause the person to be detained in custody and, in accordance with the following provisions, to be taken before a justice to be dealt with according to law, namely:
> (a) where a justice is available within a period of twenty-four hours after the person has been arrested by or delivered to the peace officer, the person shall be taken before a justice without unreasonable delay and in any event within that period, and
> (b) where a justice is not available within a period of twenty-four hours after the person has been arrested by or delivered to the peace officer, the person shall be taken before a justice as soon as possible,
> unless at any time before the expiration of the time prescribed in paragraphs (a) or (b) for taking the person before a justice,
> (c) the peace officer or officer in charge releases the person under any other provision of this Part, or
> (d) the peace officer or officer in charge is satisfied that the person should be released from custody, whether unconditionally or under subsection (3) or otherwise conditionally or unconditionally, and so releases him.

---

[8] (1852), 118 E.R. 141 at 144 (H.L.).

A judicial interim release hearing will be held by a justice of the peace or provincial court judge. Before a bail hearing is held the defence counsel and Crown attorney may agree that the accused should be released. If the Crown consents to the accused being released, the Crown attorney will notify the judge that he or she is not opposing the accused's release. The accused can, if the judge agrees, be released without the necessity of going through a full fledged bail hearing. If the Crown does not consent to the accused being released, a bail hearing will be held.

(ii) *Bail hearing*

The principle governing bail hearings is that generally when an accused is charged with an offence other than one of the very serious offences listed in section 469 of the Code, the accused is entitled to be released upon his giving his unconditional undertaking to appear in court on the day of trial. This principle applies unless there is some reason to believe that something more is required to ensure appearance at trial. The accused will not be released upon his unconditional undertaking if the Crown attorney shows cause why the accused should be detained in custody or shows cause why the accused should not be released on his unconditional undertaking. If the Crown prosecutor shows cause why the accused should be detained in custody, the accused will be so detained. If the Crown prosecutor does not show cause why the accused should be detained in custody, but satisfies a judge that the accused should not be released without conditions, a justice or a judge will release the accused upon such conditions or subject to such recognizance as he directs. Section 515(1) states:

> (1) Subject to this section, where an accused who is charged with an offence other than an offence listed in section 469 is taken before a justice the justice shall, unless a plea of guilty by the accused is accepted, order, in respect of that offence, that the accused be released on his giving an undertaking without conditions, unless the prosecutor, having been given a reasonable opportunity to do so, shows cause, in respect of that offence, why the detention of the accused in custody is justified or why an order under any other provision of this section should be made and where the justice makes an order under any other provision of this section, the order shall refer only to the particular offence for which the accused was taken before the justice.

If the justice does not release the accused under subsection 515(1) of the Criminal Code, the provisions of subsections 515(2), (2.1), (2.2) and (3) come into play:

> (2) Where the justice does not make an order under subsection (1), he shall, unless the prosecutor shows cause why the detention of the accused is justified, order that the accused be released
> (*a*) on his giving an undertaking with such conditions as the justice directs;

(*b*) on his entering into a recognizance before the justice, without sureties, in such amount and with such conditions, if any, as the justice directs but without deposit of money or other valuable security;

(*c*) on his entering into a recognizance before the justice with sureties in such amount and with such conditions, if any, as the justice directs but without deposit of money or other valuable security;

(*d*) with the consent of the prosecutor, on his entering into a recognizance before the justice, without sureties, in such amount and with such conditions, if any, as the justice directs and on his depositing with the justice such sum of money or other valuable security as the justice directs, or

(*e*) if the accused is not ordinarily resident in the province in which the accused is in custody or does not ordinarily reside within one hundred kilometres of the place in which he is in custody, on his entering into a recognizance before the justice with or without sureties in such amount and with such conditions, if any, as the justice directs, and on his depositing with the justice such sum of money or other valuable security as the justice directs.

(2.1) Where, pursuant to subsection (2) or any other provision of this Act, a justice, judge or court orders that an accused be released on his entering into a recognizance with sureties, the justice, judge or court may, in the order, name particular persons as sureties.

(2.2) Where, by this Act, the appearance of an accused is required for the purposes of judicial interim release, the appearance shall be by actual physical attendance of the accused but the justice may, where the prosecutor and the accused so agree, allow the accused to appear by means of any suitable telecommunication device, including telephone, that is satisfactory to the justice.

(3) The justice shall not make an order under any of paragraphs (2)(*b*) to (*e*) unless the prosecution shows cause why an order under the immediately preceding paragraph should not be made.

(A) *Showing cause.* Once the court determines that the accused should not be released upon his undertaking without conditions, a justice or a judge shall release the accused upon his giving an undertaking with such conditions as the justice directs, unless the Crown attorney shows cause why the accused should not be so released. If the judge is not satisfied that the accused can be released upon his entering into an undertaking with such conditions as the judge directs, the judge must then consider whether the accused can be released upon his entering into a recognizance without sureties in such amount and with such conditions, if any, as the judge directs. If the judge is not so satisfied, he then considers the remaining parts of section 515(2) in determining whether the accused can be released under those parts. The Code provisions relating to judicial interim release are designed to ensure that people who are charged with criminal offences are released in the least restrictive manner possible unless a prosecutor, having been given a reasonable opportunity to do so, shows cause why a person who is the subject of a bail hearing should not be released or only released upon strict conditions.

(B) *Test for detention.* The test for determining whether an accused should be detained in custody is set out in section 515(10) of the Criminal Code which states:

(10) For the purposes of this section, the detention of an accused in custody is justified only on either of the following grounds:

(*a*) on the primary ground that his detention is necessary to ensure his attendance in court in order to be dealt with according to law; and

(*b*) on the secondary ground (the applicability of which shall be determined only in the event that and after it is determined that his detention is not justified on the primary ground referred to in paragraph (*a*)) that his detention is necessary in the public interest or for the protection or safety of the public, having regard to all the circumstances including any substantial likelihood that the accused will, if he is released from custody, commit a criminal offence or an interference with the administration of justice.

The Supreme Court of Canada has struck down the words "public interest" in section 515(10)(*b*), holding that the words violate section 11(*e*) of the Charter as the term public interest authorizes pre-trial detention in terms that are vague and imprecise. In *R. v. Morales*,[9] a majority of the court held that the term public interest creates no criteria for detention, saying that the term violates section 11(*e*) of the Charter as it authorizes detention without just cause.

(C) *Evidence at hearing.* Section 518 provides that a justice holding a judicial interim release hearing may make such inquiries, either on oath or otherwise, concerning the accused as he considers desirable. In such a proceeding the accused may not be examined or cross-examined by the justice or any other person, except counsel for the accused, as to the offence with which he has been charged. The prosecutor may lead evidence to show:

1. that the accused has previously been convicted of a criminal offence,
2. that he has been charged with some other criminal offence,
3. that he has committed an offence under section 145 by escaping from lawful custody; or by failing to attend court when released from custody, or
4. the circumstances of the offence, particularly as they related to the probability of conviction.

Evidence may be received which was obtained as a result of a wire tap authorized under the provisions of the Code. The strict rules of evidence do not apply, as the justice or judge may take into consideration any relevant matters agreed upon by the prosecutor and the accused, or his counsel. He may also base his decision upon evidence considered credible or trustworthy by him.

Section 517 provides that the justice may and shall, upon application by the accused, direct that the evidence taken, the information given and the reasons, if any, given by the justice in a proceeding shall not be published before such time as the trial is ended or the accused discharged. Such a ban on publication has been held not to be an infringement of freedom of expression as guaranteed by the Charter.

---

[9] (1992), 77 C.C.C. (3d) 91 at 99-103 (S.C.C.).

(D) *Burden on accused.* Where an accused is charged with one of the serious offences listed in section 469 he may not be released other than by a judge of or a judge presiding in a superior court of criminal jurisdiction. In such a case, section 522(2) provides that an accused shall be detained unless the accused, having been given a reasonable opportunity to do so, shows cause why his detention in custody is not justified. The burden also rests on an accused under the provisions of section 515(6) in a number of other cases where an accused is charged

> (a) with an indictable offence, other than an offence listed in section 469, that is alleged to have been committed while he was at large after being released in respect of another indictable offence . . .
> (b) with an indictable offence, other than an offence listed in section 469 and is not ordinarily resident in Canada,
> (c) with an offence under any of subsections 145(2) to (5) that is alleged to have been committed while he was at large after being released in respect of another offence . . . or
> (d) with having committed an offence under section 4 or 5 of the Narcotic Control Act or the offence of conspiring to commit an offence under section 4 or 5 of that Act . . . .

In *Morales,*[10] the Supreme Court held that the requirement in section 515(6)(a) that the accused show cause why his detention is not justified does not violate sections 7, 9, 11(d) or 11(e) of the Charter.

(iii) *Bail review*

An accused who is detained in custody, or is released on certain conditions, may have the order of the justice reviewed by a judge under the provisions of section 520. At such a hearing the judge will consider the record of proceedings before the justice and any additional evidence which may be presented by the accused or the Crown. The reviewing judge will not set aside the initial order simply on the basis that he or she would not have come to the same conclusion as the justice. On such a hearing the accused, if he is to succeed, must show that his detention is not justified. When an accused has been released, the Crown prosecutor may at any time before trial apply to a judge for a review of the order made by the justice. Section 525 provides that where an accused has been charged with an indictable offence, other than an offence listed in section 469, and has been held in custody for a period of 90 days, the person having custody of the accused shall apply to a judge to fix a date for hearing to determine whether he should be released from custody. A similar provision applies in the case of summary conviction offences, but the time for such action is 30 days, rather than 90. This section does not apply where the

---

[10] *Ibid.*

accused has applied unsuccessfully for a review of the detention, as in that case his remedy is to apply under section 520 for a further review.

4. CITIZEN'S RIGHT OF ARREST

(a) Generally

A private citizen may make a citizen's arrest providing that he or she complies with the requirements set out in the Criminal Code. Section 494 of the Criminal Code is the principal arrest authority for someone other than a peace officer. This section states:

(1) Any one may arrest without warrant
    (*a*) a person whom he finds committing an indictable offence, or
    (*b*) a person who, on reasonable and probable grounds, he believes
        (i) has committed a criminal offence, and
        (ii) is escaping from and freshly pursued by persons who have lawful authority to arrest that person.

(2) Any one who is
    (*a*) the owner or a person in lawful possession of property, or
    (*b*) a person authorized by the owner or by a person in lawful possession of property,
may arrest without warrant a person whom he finds committing a criminal offence on or in relation to that property.

(3) Any one other than a peace officer who arrests a person without warrant shall forthwith deliver the person to a peace officer.

A private person's powers of arrest are much more limited than that of a peace officer. A peace officer has the authority to arrest someone whom he has reasonable and probable grounds to believe has committed, or is about to commit, an indictable offence, but a private person has no such arrest power. Section 494(1)(*b*) could be relied upon in a case where a private citizen has reasonable and probable grounds to believe that a criminal who just robbed a store is escaping from and is being freshly pursued by a police officer.

(b) Authority to Arrest

A citizen making such an arrest must have reasonable and probable grounds to believe that the person being arrested has committed a criminal offence and is escaping from and being freshly pursued by a police officer. A citizen making an arrest must have sufficient knowledge to distinguish between a criminal offence and a provincial offence and to know what a criminal offence is, as his powers of arrest are limited. The Criminal Code creates three categories of offences: indictable offences, summary conviction offences and hybrid or dual procedure offences which may be prosecuted at the election of the Crown by way of indictment or by summary conviction. A person who makes a citizen's arrest under section 494(1)(*a*) must have knowledge as to which offences are indictable offences and which offences are provincial offences, as the arrest may only be made if the offence is an indictable one. Section 24 of the Interpretation Act[11] provides that hybrid or dual procedure offences are deemed to be indictable offences until the Crown exercises its option in court of electing to proceed by summary conviction. This means that a citizen who arrests someone for committing an indictable offence under section 494(1)(*b*) will be protected if the Crown subsequently proceeds summarily. However, someone who makes a citizen's arrest under section 494 of the Criminal Code will be liable for false arrest if the offence for which the arrest is made turns out to be a provincial offence.

Section 494(1)(*b*) of the Code gives a person making a citizen's arrest the power to arrest in some cases someone who has committed a criminal offence. Since a criminal offence can only be created by the federal government, a private citizen has no authority under section 494 to arrest someone who commits a provincial offence. Thus, if a private citizen sees a police officer chasing someone who has committed a provincial offence, such as speeding, the citizen would not have the authority to make a citizen's arrest pursuant to section 494 of the Code. Section 494(2) provides that the owner or occupier of property may arrest someone whom he finds committing a criminal offence on or in relation to that property. This section also authorizes someone who is an agent or employee of the owner or occupier of the property to arrest someone whom he finds committing a criminal offence on or in relation to that property when authorized by the owner or lawful occupier to do so. The section would authorize a store manager, for example, to arrest someone whom he caught stealing store merchandise and would also justify an arrest where the person placed under arrest had been found breaking a window or committing another criminal offence in relation to property under the manager's supervision. Thus, a citizen making an arrest must have some knowledge of the nature of offences and should certainly not attempt an arrest if uncertain of his right.

(c) Breach of Peace

Section 30 of the Criminal Code authorizes a private citizen who witnesses a breach of the peace to detain a person who breaches the peace until the police arrive and to use force to prevent the continuation of a breach of the

---

[11] R.S.C. 1985, c. I-21.

peace in the circumstances set out in that section. The Code does not define the term breach of the peace. Although there is no common agreement as to what constitutes a breach of the peace, Glanville Williams, a famous English law professor, has stated that, under English law it is confined to an act done which either harms a person or one done in his presence which harms his property or is likely to cause such harm.[12] Section 30 of the Criminal Code states:

> Every one who witnesses a breach of the peace is justified in interfering to prevent the continuance or renewal thereof and may detain any person who commits or is about to join in or to renew the breach of the peace, for the purpose of giving him into the custody of a peace officer, if he uses no more force than is reasonably necessary to prevent the continuance or renewal of the breach of the peace or than is reasonably proportioned to the danger to be apprehended from the continuance or renewal of the breach of the peace.

(d) Assisting a Peace Officer

Section 31 of the Code authorizes a private citizen to assist a police officer in arresting someone for a breach of the peace. This section states:

> (1) Every peace officer who witnesses a breach of the peace and every one who lawfully assists him is justified in arresting any person whom he finds committing the breach of the peace or who, on reasonable and probable grounds, the peace officer believes is about to join in or renew the breach of the peace.

> (2) Every peace officer is justified in receiving into custody any person who is given into his charge as having been a party to a breach of the peace by one who has, or who on reasonable and probable grounds he believes has, witnessed the breach of the peace.

(e) Use of Force

Sections 25 and 27 of the Criminal Code protect a private citizen who is lawfully authorized to use force from being charged with a criminal offence for using reasonable force to arrest someone. Someone who assists a peace officer in arresting a suspect or uses force to prevent the commission of an offence, as authorized by section 27, must use reasonable force and will be liable for any excessive force used in arresting that person. Section 26 of the Criminal Code states:

> Every one who is authorized by law to use force is criminally responsible for any

---

[12] G. Williams, *Textbook of Criminal Law* (London: Stevens & Sons, 1983).

excess thereof according to the nature and quality of the act that constitutes the excess.

The result is that someone who uses excessive force will be criminally responsible for the use of the excessive force and liable to criminal prosecution. Thus, someone who uses excessive force could be charged with an assault or one of the more serious offences in the Criminal Code, depending upon the circumstances of the particular case. If excessive force is used, the consequence may be very serious, as the Supreme Court of Canada has held that in such circumstances a qualified defence of self defence does not exist.

5

A Person's Rights and Obligations Under the Criminal Law

1. RIGHT TO BE PRESUMED INNOCENT

The presumption of innocence, which is the cornerstone of our criminal justice system, has long been a feature of British and Canadian common law. Indeed, the presumption of innocence has been dubbed the golden thread of English criminal law. The classic statement outlining the presumption of innocence is found in Viscount Sankey's judgment in *Woolmington v. D.P.P.*,[1] an English House of Lords decision. Viscount Sankey stated:

> Throughout the web of the English Criminal Law one golden thread is always to be seen, that it is the duty of the prosecution to prove the prisoner's guilt subject to what I have already said as to the defence of insanity and subject also to any statutory exception. If, at the end of and on the whole of the case, there is a reasonable doubt, created by the evidence given by either the prosecution or the prisoner . . . prosecution has not made out the case and the prisoner is entitled to an acquittal. No matter what the charge or where the trial . . . the prosecution must prove the guilt of the prisoner as part of the common law of England and no attempt to whittle it down can be entertained.[2]

The *Woolmington* case, although decided in 1935, continues to be the leading explanation of the burden of proof in a criminal case. The onus is normally on the Crown to prove all the elements of the offence committed beyond a reasonable doubt. There is normally no onus upon the accused to prove anything. If a judge or jury has a reasonable doubt on all the evidence, including a defence raised, the accused is entitled to be acquitted. The existence of a reasonable doubt may result in conviction of a lesser offence. Thus, on a charge of first degree murder if a jury has a reasonable doubt that

---

[1] [1935] A.C. 462 (H.L.).
[2] *Ibid.*, at 481.

the accused was, because of drunkenness, incapable of forming the specific intent required to commit first degree murder, a jury will acquit the accused of first degree murder and bring in a verdict of manslaughter.

In *R. v. Oakes*, Chief Justice Dickson eloquently described the purpose of the presumption of innocence, stating:

> The presumption of innocence protects the fundamental liberty and human dignity of any and every person accused by the state of criminal conduct. An individual charged with a criminal offence faces grave social and personal consequences, including potential loss of physical liberty, subjection to social stigma and ostracism from the community, as well as other social, psychological and economic harms. In light of the gravity of these consequences, the presumption of innocence is crucial. It ensures that, until the state proves an accused's guilt beyond all reasonable doubt, he or she is innocent. This is essential in a society committed to fairness and social justice. The presumption of innocence confirms our faith in humankind; it reflects our belief that individuals are decent and law-abiding members of the community until proven otherwise.[3]

The presumption of innocence, which does not exist in much of the world, has been entrenched in section 11(*d*) of the Charter. Section 11 states:

> 11. Any person charged with an offence has the right
> (*d*) to be presumed innocent until proven guilty according to law in a fair and public hearing by an independent and impartial tribunal.

The presumption of innocence ensures that the Crown has the legal or persuasive burden of proving the accused's guilt beyond a reasonable doubt. In *Dubois v. R.*,[4] Lamer J., writing for a majority of the Supreme Court of Canada, stated:

> Section 11(*d*) imposes upon the Crown the burden of proving the accused's guilt beyond a reasonable doubt as well as that of making out the case against the accused before he or she need respond, either by testifying or calling other evidence.[5]

(a) Statutory Exceptions

In *Woolmington*, Viscount Sankey stated that Parliament can provide for statutory exceptions to the presumption of innocence. When there is a statutory exception to the presumption of innocence the accused either bears the burden of proving that he or she did not commit the offence, or bears the burden of presenting evidence to rebut a statutory presumption as to some

---

[3] (1986), 50 C.R. (3d) 1 at 15 (S.C.C.).
[4] (1985), 48 C.R. (3d) 193 (S.C.C.).
[5] *Ibid.*, at 215.

element of the offence. Section 8 of the Narcotic Control Act[6] provides an example of a statutory exception to the presumption of innocence. This section forced an accused who was charged with possession for the purpose of trafficking to prove that he did not possess the narcotic for that purpose. Section 8 stated:

> . . . the court shall make a finding as to whether or not the accused contravened subsection 3(1) and, if the court finds that the accused did not contravene subsection 3(1), the accused shall be acquitted but, if the court finds that the accused contravened subsection 3(1), the accused shall be given an opportunity of establishing that he was not in possession of the narcotic for the purpose of trafficking and, thereafter, the prosecutor shall be given an opportunity of adducing evidence to establish the contrary.
>
> (3) After compliance with subsection (2), in the case of finding a contravention by the accused of subsection 3(1),
>
> (*a*) if the accused establishes that he was not in possession of the narcotic for the purpose of trafficking, the accused shall be acquitted of the offence as charged but shall be convicted of an offence under section 3 and sentenced accordingly; or
>
> (*b*) if the accused fails to establish that he was not in possession of the narcotic for the purpose of trafficking, the accused shall be convicted of the offence as charged and sentenced accordingly.

Seven provincial appellate courts struck down section 8 of the Narcotic Control Act on the ground that it violated the presumption of innocence guarantee contained in section 11(*d*) of the Charter.

In *R. v. Cook*,[7] Mr. Justice Hart, writing for the Nova Scotia Court of Appeal, held that section 8 of the Narcotic Control Act violated the presumption of innocence guarantee:

> Section 8 . . . is a piece of legislation that attempts to relieve the Crown of its normal burden of proof by use of what is known as a reverse onus. Different types of reverse onus have been known to the law and proof of a case with the aid of a reverse onus can, in my opinion, fall into the wording of s. 11(*d*) of the Charter as being proof "according to law". . . to be acceptable. These reverse onus provisions must not be arbitrary and there must be a relationship between the facts proved and the conclusions to be drawn. I know of no justification, however, for holding that it would be "according to law" to allow use of a reverse onus clause which permitted the Crown the assistance of a provision which relieved it from calling any probative evidence to establish one of the essential elements of an offence. This is what s. 8 of the Narcotic Control Act purports to do and I would therefore find it unconstitutional.[8]

Section 8 of the Narcotic Control Act was struck down by the Supreme

---

[6] R.S.C. 1985, c. N-1.
[7] (1983), 147 D.L.R. (3d) 687 (N.S.C.A.)
[8] *Ibid.*, at 703.

Court of Canada in *Oakes* on the ground that the section violated section 11(*d*) of the Charter. Chief Justice Dickson stated:

> In general one must, I think, conclude that a provision which requires an accused to prove on a balance of probabilities the existence of a presumed fact [in this case that he was in possession of a narcotic for the purpose of trafficking] which is an important element of the offence in question violates the presumption of innocence in s. 11(*d*). If an accused bears the burden of disproving on a balance of probabilities an essential element of an offence, it would be possible for a conviction to occur despite the existence of a reasonable doubt. This would arise if the accused adduced sufficient evidence to raise a reasonable doubt as to his or her innocence but did not convince the jury on a balance of probabilities that the presumed fact was untrue.

> To return to s. 8 of the Narcotic Control Act, I am in no doubt whatsoever that it violates s. 11(*d*) of the Charter by requiring the accused to prove on a balance of probabilities that he was not in possession of the narcotic for the purpose of trafficking. Mr. Oakes is compelled by s. 8 to prove that he is *not* guilty of the offence of trafficking. He is thus denied his right to be presumed innocent and subjected to the potential penalty of life imprisonment unless he can rebut the presumption. This is radically and fundamentally inconsistent with the societal values of human dignity and liberty which we espouse, and is directly contrary to the presumption of innocence enshrined in s. 11(*d*).[9]

In *Oakes*, the Supreme Court held that a provision that requires an accused to prove an element of the offence on the balance of probabilities infringes the presumption of innocence guaranteed by section 11(*d*) of the Charter, as the accused could be convicted despite the existence of a reasonable doubt as to his guilt. In *R. v. Whyte*,[10] the Supreme Court held that the protection of section 11(*d*) of the Charter applied to any factor which affected the ultimate verdict of guilt or innocence whether the factor could be characterized as an element of the offence or a defence.

In *R. v. Chaulk*,[11] the Supreme Court of Canada held that the presumption of sanity in section 16(4) of the Criminal Code violated the presumption of innocence in section 11(*d*) of the Charter and was a reasonable limit as demonstrably justified in a free and democratic society under section 1 of the Charter. Section 16 of the Criminal Code provided:

> **16.** (1) No person shall be convicted of an offence in respect of an act or omission on his part while that person was insane.
> (2) For the purposes of this section, a person is insane when the person is in a state of natural imbecility or has disease of the mind to an extent that renders the person incapable of appreciating the nature and quality of an act or omission or of knowing that an act or omission is wrong.
> (3) A person who has specific delusions, but is in other respects sane, shall not be

---

[9] *Supra*, note 3 at 25, 27.
[10] (1988), 64 C.R. (3d) 123 (S.C.C.).
[11] (1990), 2 C.R. (4th) 1 (S.C.C.).

acquitted on the ground of insanity unless the delusions caused that person to believe in the existence of a state of things that, if it existed, would have justified or excused the act or omission of that person.

(4) Everyone shall, until the contrary is proved, be presumed to be and to have been sane.

In holding that the presumption of sanity contained in section 16(4) of the Code violated section 11(*d*) of the Charter, Lamer C.J.C., stated:

> If an accused is found to have been insane at the time of the offence, he will *not* be found guilty; thus the "fact" of insanity precludes a verdict of guilty. Whether the claim of insanity is characterized as a denial of mens rea, an excusing defence or, more generally, as an exemption based on criminal incapacity, the fact remains that sanity is essential for guilt. Section 16(4) allows a factor which is essential for guilt to be *presumed*, rather than proven by the Crown beyond a reasonable doubt. Moreover, it requires an accused to disprove sanity (or prove insanity) on the balance of probabilities; it therefore violates the presumption of innocence because it permits a conviction in spite of a reasonable doubt in the mind of the trier of fact as to the guilt of the accused.
>
> . . . Thus, in enacting s. 16(4), Parliament has not designated any basic "fact" which, when established, removes all possibility of reasonable doubt as to lack of insanity (and therefore removes all reasonable doubt as to guilt). Parliament has simply reversed the onus on a factor which is essential for guilt. If an accused cannot discharge the persuasive burden with respect to his insanity, [prove his insanity on the balance of probabilities] the trier of fact may well be obliged to convict the accused despite the existence of a reasonable doubt as to sanity and, therefore, as to guilt.[12]

Although the court found that the presumption of sanity violated section 11(*d*) of the Charter, the court found that the validation passed the section 1 test as a reasonable limitation on the presumption of innocence. The court concluded that the presumption of sanity was intended to avoid placing on the Crown "the impossibly onerous burden of disproving insanity." The court found that Parliament had chosen from a range of means which impair the presumption of innocence guarantee contained in the Charter as little as reasonably possible.

The former section 16 has been replaced by the defence of mental disorder. The new wording of this section is found in Chapter 12, Defences.

(b) Evidentiary Burdens and Legal Burden

The Criminal Code contains several sections which place an evidentiary burden on the accused to rebut some presumption which has been created. Section 348 of the Criminal Code, which deals with breaking and entering, is an example of one of many sections which creates an evidentiary burden.

---

[12] *Ibid.*, at 24-25.

Section 348(1) of the Code provides that someone who breaks and enters a place with intent to commit an indictable offence therein, or breaks out of a place after committing an indictable offence therein, is guilty of an indictable offence. Section 348(2) of the Code creates an evidentiary presumption in favour of the Crown:

> (2) For the purposes of proceedings under this section, evidence that an accused
> (a) broke and entered a place or attempted to break and enter a place is, in the absence of any evidence to the contrary, proof that he broke and entered the place or attempted to do so, as the case may be, with intent to commit an indictable offence therein; or
> (b) broke out of a place is, in the absence of any evidence to the contrary, proof that he broke out after
>   (i) committing an indictable offence therein, or
>   (ii) entering with intent to commit an indictable offence therein.

Thus the accused is forced to rebut the presumption by some evidence. For practical purposes, this means that an accused is usually forced to take the stand and give evidence as to his intent when he broke into the dwelling-house. The presumption that the accused broke into the dwelling-house with the intent of committing an indictable offence therein is called an evidentiary presumption; it forces the accused to adduce evidence to the contrary. When credible evidence is adduced tending to negative the existence of the intent, the burden will be on the Crown to prove it. If the accused does not adduce evidence to the contrary which rebuts the presumption, the Crown will usually have sufficient evidence to convict the accused. If the presumption is not rebutted, the Crown will still have to prove the other essential elements in its case. However, assuming that it is able to do this, the accused will be convicted. Thus, for example, in the case of someone who is charged with breaking and entering with intent under section 348(1) of the Code, if the accused was not able to rebut the presumption, the Crown would only have to prove that the accused broke into the house in order to obtain a conviction.

Section 348(1) creates two elements of the offence of breaking and entering with intent; firstly, that the accused broke into the dwelling-house, and, secondly, that he did so with the intent to commit an indictable offence therein. Thus, once the Crown proves that the accused broke into a dwelling-house, the accused will, because of the evidentiary burden, be called upon to adduce evidence to contradict the presumption. The evidence required need only be an explanation which might reasonably be true and create a reasonable doubt of which the accused would be given the benefit.

Section 354 of the Criminal Code, which makes it an offence to possess property obtained by crime, is another example of a section which places an evidentiary burden upon the accused. Section 354(1) states:

> (1) Every one commits an offence who has in his possession any property or thing or any proceeds of any property or thing knowing that all or part of the property or thing or of the proceeds was obtained by or derived directly or indirectly from

(*a*) the commission in Canada of an offence punishable by indictment; or
(*b*) an act or omission anywhere that, if it had occurred in Canada, would have constituted an offence punishable by indictment.

The procedure for prosecuting someone charged with unlawful possession of a motor vehicle or motor vehicle parts is set out in section 354(2) of the Criminal Code:

(2) In proceedings in respect of an offence under subsection (1), evidence that a person has in his possession a motor vehicle the vehicle identification number of which has been wholly or partially removed or obliterated or a part of a motor vehicle being a part bearing a vehicle identification number that has been wholly or partially removed or obliterated is, in the absence of any evidence to the contrary, proof that the motor vehicle or part, as the case may be, was obtained, and that such person had the motor vehicle or part as the case may be, in his possession knowing that it was obtained,

(*a*) by the commission in Canada of an offence punishable by indictment; or
(*b*) by an act or omission anywhere that, if it had occurred in Canada, would have constituted an offence punishable by indictment.

This section creates two presumptions, in the absence of evidence to the contrary. Firstly, the section creates a presumption that a motor vehicle or part with an obliterated identification number has been obtained by the commission of an indictable offence; and secondly, that the person in possession of such a motor vehicle or part had possession knowing that the motor vehicle or part was obtained by the commission of an indictable offence.

In *Boyle v R.*,[13] the Ontario Court of Appeal held that the presumption of guilty knowledge created by section 312(2) [354(2)] of the Criminal Code was unconstitutional as violating the accused's right to be presumed innocent until proven guilty. The section provides that the presumption discussed earlier operates "in the absence of any evidence to the contrary" which means that the accused must present evidence which casts doubt upon the presumption. The Ontario Court of Appeal held that section 312(2) [354(2)] violated section 11(*d*) of the Charter, saying that possession of property which was stolen at some point in time does not mean that the accused had knowledge that the property was stolen. Mr. Justice Martin said:

The presumption of guilty knowledge that arises under s. 312(2) [354(2)] upon proof of possession of a motor vehicle the vehicle identification number of which has been removed or obliterated is not restricted to the possession of such a vehicle by persons of a particular class, such as dealers, who may reasonably be presumed to be knowledgeable with respect to the location of vehicle identification numbers and to be alive to the desirability of making an examination to ascertain whether there has been an obliteration of the vehicle identification number or numbers. The presumption of guilty knowledge applies alike to the knowledgeable and the unsophisticated, upon proof that the accused was found in the possession of a motor vehicle the vehicle identification number of which has

---

[13] (1983), 35 C.R. (3d) 34 (Ont. C.A.).

been removed or obliterated. Further, the presumption of guilty knowledge under s. 312(2) is not confined to cases where there is evidence that the motor vehicle has been *recently* stolen or was *recently* obtained by the commission of some other indictable offence.

Parliament by s. 312(1) has made guilty knowledge an essential element of the offence created by that subsection. Upon proof beyond a reasonable doubt of the basic facts giving rise to the presumption, the jury, in the absence of evidence to the contrary, is required by Parliament to find that the accused had the necessary guilty knowledge, even though there is not probative evidence that the accused in fact had such knowledge. In my view, such a requirement contravenes the accused's right under s. 11(*d*) of the Charter to be presumed innocent until proven guilty according to law. Any qualification of that right that may be covered by the words "according to law" in s. 11(*d*) is, under s. 1 of the Charter, subject only to such reasonable limits prescribed by law as can be demonstrably justified in a free and democratic society. A limitation of that right which is arbitrary, and hence unreasonable, is constitutionally invalid. . . .

In my view, no legitimate state interest is served by the creation of legislative presumptions which are arbitrary or capricious with respect to the existence of constituent elements of a crime which are of the essence of the offence.[14]

Thus, it was his view that the facts giving rise to the presumption did not support an inference of guilty knowledge.

Under criminal law there is a presumption that someone who is found to be in possession of recently stolen goods knew that the goods were obtained by the commission of an indictable offence. The presumption that the property is stolen is a factual presumption and is not a presumption of law. The presumption that the property is stolen is one which does not have to be drawn, but which may be drawn if the accused's possession is not explained or the accused offers an explanation which is not reasonable and is not accepted by the judge or the jury. In *Boyle*, the Ontario Court of Appeal distinguished between a presumption which exists when one is found in possession of recently stolen property and the presumption as set out in section 312(2) [354(2)] of the Criminal Code. The presumption in 312(2) [354(2)] of the Code that a person found in possession of a motor vehicle part with an obliterated or partially obliterated serial number had knowledge that the motor vehicle or part was stolen, is a mandatory presumption. The presumption that someone who is in possession of recently stolen property knew the property was stolen is a permissive presumption which means that the judge or jury is not obligated to infer that the property was stolen. It apparently is the mandatory nature of the presumption which rendered it unconstitutional.

In *Boyle*, Mr. Justice Martin made it clear that not all evidentiary burdens violate the Charter. He indicated that, for example, in a murder prosecution the accused has a burden to put forward sufficient evidence of self-defence,

---

[14] *Ibid.*, at 60-61.

automatism, provocation or drunkenness to require the judge to submit the defences for the jury's consideration.

Mr. Justice Martin's analysis assumed that evidence of the accused's proposed defence did not emerge from the testimony of witnesses called by the Crown. If the testimony called by the Crown supported a defence put forward by the accused, the accused could elect to call no evidence and simply rely on the evidence presented by the Crown.

The Ontario Court of Appeal's decision in *Boyle* is not binding on other provincial appellate courts. However, the Ontario Court of Appeal's decision in *Boyle* is persuasive authority and other provincial appellate courts would probably choose to follow it.

2. POLICE QUESTIONING

(a) General Rule

A police officer has an absolute right to question someone he or she suspects has committed a criminal offence. However, a police officer cannot compel a person to answer his questions.

The common law right of the citizen to refuse to answer police questions has been summarized by Lord Parker in the classic English case, *Rice v. Connolly*:[15]

> It seems to me quite clear that although every citizen has a moral duty or, if you like, a social duty to assist the police, there is no legal duty to that effect, and indeed the whole basis of the common law is that right of the individual to refuse to answer questions put to him by persons in authority and, a refusal to accompany those in authority to any particular place, short, of course, of an arrest.[16]

Rice v. Connolly has been applied by several Canadian courts and approved by the Supreme Court of Canada in *Moore v. R.*[17] and *Dedman v. R.*[18]

A good explanation of the common law right to remain silent is found in *R. v. Esposito* where Martin J.A., writing for the Ontario Court of Appeal, stated:

> The right of a suspect or an accused to remain silent is deeply rooted in our legal tradition. The right operates both at the investigative stage of the criminal process and at the trial stage. In Canada, save in certain circumstances, a suspect is free

---

[15] [1966] 2 All E.R. 649 (H.L.).
[16] *Ibid.*, at 652.
[17] (1979), 43 C.C.C. (2d) 83 (S.C.C.).
[18] (1985), 46 C.R. (3d) 193 (S.C.C.).

to answer or not to answer questions by the police. We say that he has a right to remain silent because there is no legal obligation upon him to speak . . . .

A police officer, when he is endeavouring to discover whether or by whom an offence has been committed, is entitled to question any person, whether suspected or not, from whom he thinks that useful information can be obtained. Although a police officer is entitled to question any person in order to obtain information with respect to a suspected offence, he as a general rule has no power to compel the person questioned to answer. Moreover, he has no power to detain a person for questioning, and if the person questioned declines to answer the police officer must allow him to proceed on his way unless he arrests him on reasonable and probable grounds.[19]

The common law pre-trial right to remain silent has now acquired constitutional status as a result of the Supreme Court of Canada's landmark decision in *R. v. Hebert.*[20] In *Hebert*, the Supreme Court of Canada unanimously held that the common law pre-trial right to remain silent is constitutionally protected under section 7 of the Charter as a principle of fundamental justice in circumstances where the person being questioned by the police is detained. In *Hebert*, the Supreme Court was considering whether a statement made by a detainee to an undercover police officer violated the accused's right to remain silent under section 7 of the Charter. Madam Justice McLachlin, who delivered the judgment of the court, expressed the right to remain silent as follows:

The essence of the right to silence is that the suspect be given a choice: the right is quite simply the freedom to choose — the freedom to speak to the authorities, on the one hand, and the freedom to refuse to make a statement to them, on the other hand.[21]

In *Hebert*, an undercover police officer posing as a cellmate of the accused actively solicited information from the accused. The information was solicited from the accused by means of a trick — that is, the use of the under-cover officer after the accused had told the police that he did not wish to speak to them. The court found that in such circumstances, the use of the undercover officer to actively elicit information from the accused breached the accused's section 7 right to remain silent. McLachlin J. described the right as follows:

The common law rules relating to the right to silence suggest that the scope of the right in the pre-trial detention periods must be based on the fundamental concept of the suspect's right to choose whether to speak to the authorities or remain silent. Any doubt on the question is resolved by consideration of related rights protected by the Charter, by the Charter's approach to the question of improperly-obtained evidence, and by the fundamental purpose of the right to silence and

---

[19] (1985), 49 C.R. (3d) 193 at 200-201 (Ont. C.A.).
[20] (1990), 77 C.R. (3d) 145 (S.C.C.).
[21] *Ibid.*, at 190.

related procedural guarantees. In keeping with the approach inaugurated by the Charter, our courts must adopt an approach to pre-trial interrogation which emphasizes the right of the detained person to make a meaningful choice and permits the rejection of statements which have been obtained unfairly in circumstances that violate that right of choice.

The right to choose whether or not to speak to the authorities is defined objectively rather than subjectively. The basic requirement that the suspect possess an operating mind has a subjective element. But, this established, the focus under the Charter shifts to the conduct of the authorities vis-à-vis the suspect. Was the suspect accorded the right to consult counsel? Was there other police conduct which effectively and unfairly deprived the suspect of the right to choose whether to speak to the authorities or not?[22]

The requirement that the suspect have "an operating mind" necessitates that "the accused possess a limited degree of cognitive ability to understand what he or she is saying and to comprehend that the evidence may be used in proceedings against the accused."[23] The "operating mind" test does not require that the accused be capable of making a good or wise choice or a choice that is in his or her interest.

The new constitutional right to remain silent expressed by the court in *Hebert* is not an absolute right. Madam Justice McLachlin set out four limits to the right:

1. The police may question the accused after the accused has retained counsel without counsel being present. Police persuasion, short of denying the suspect the right to choose or depriving him of an operating mind, does not breach the right to silence.
2. The right to remain silent only applies where a person is detained.
3. The right to silence is not breached by voluntary statements made to cellmates provided that a cellmate is not acting as an informer, police agent or is actually an undercover police officer.
4. The right to remain silent will not be violated in circumstances where the police merely observe the suspect and take no steps to actively elicit information in violation of the suspect's choice to remain silent.[24]

In *Hebert*, the court held that the constitutional right to remain silent did not extend to protect a person against police tricks which were used to elicit statements during pre-detention investigations. In so holding, the court noted that a person who is not detained does not have a Charter right to retain and instruct counsel without delay. The court distinguished questioning which takes place during a pre-detention investigation from that which takes place when a person is detained, saying:

---

[22] *Ibid.*, at 186-187.
[23] *R. v. Whittle* (1994), 32 C.R. (4th) 1 at 20 (S.C.C.).
[24] *Supra*, note 20, at 188-189.

> In an undercover operation prior to detention, the individual from whom infor-
> mation is sought is not in the control of the state. There is no need to protect him
> from the greater power of the state. After detention, the situation is quite differ-
> ent: the state takes control and assumes the responsibility of ensuring that the
> detainee's rights are respected.[25]

Subsequent to *Hebert*, situations have arisen where the police have used a friend to elicit information from the accused as to the crime which the accused was alleged to have committed. In *R. v. Broyles*,[26] a 16-year-old accused was convicted of the second-degree murder of his grandmother. The evidence in the case was circumstantial. The accused was initially arrested for fraud and advised of his right to counsel. He asked the police to contact a lawyer and was given an opportunity by the police to call a lawyer. The police advised him that he was not obliged to say anything but questioned him on three occasions that evening with respect to the death of his grandmother. The police arranged for a friend to visit the accused while he was in custody; the friend wore a body-pack recording device which was provided to him by the police. Although Broyles did not admit to his friend that he killed his grand-mother, he admitted that he knew she was dead the day that she went missing.

Broyles was convicted at trial before a judge and jury of second-degree murder. The Alberta Court of Appeal dismissed the accused's appeal, reject-ing his argument that his right to remain silent had been infringed under section 7 of the Charter. The Supreme Court of Canada overturned the judg-ment of the Alberta Court of Appeal, holding that the accused's section 7 right to remain silent had been infringed. The court held that as a result of a breach of the accused's right to remain silent the incriminating statement obtained from the accused should have been excluded from evidence pursuant to sec-tion 24(2) of the Charter and, thus, the court ordered that Broyles be retried.

In *Hebert*, since the accused's cellmate was an undercover police officer, there was no question that the cellmate was a state agent and, thus, the case dealt with the nature and scope of the section 7 right to remain silent. In *Broyles*, the court considered the circumstances in which a person who is not a police officer or prison official would be regarded as a state agent for pur-poses of the section 7 inquiry into whether the accused's right to remain silent has been breached. In *Broyles*, the person who was alleged to be a state agent was a friend of the appellant who had been asked by the police to visit the appellant. The Supreme Court stated that it was not self-evident as to whether or not the manner in which the friend conducted his conversation with the appellant infringed the appellant's right to remain silent under section 7 of the Charter. In *Broyles*, the court set out a test for determining whether a person is acting as an agent of the state and whether the state agent has subverted the accused's section 7 right to remain silent. Iacobucci J., who delivered the judgment of the court, stated:

---

[25] *Ibid.*, at 189.

[26] (1991), 9 C.R. (4th) 1 (S.C.C.).

It is clear from *Hebert* . . . that the purpose of the right to silence is to prevent the use of state power to subvert the right of an accused to choose whether or not to speak to the authorities. Where the informer who allegedly acted to subvert the right to silence of the accused is not obviously a state agent, the analysis will necessarily focus not only on the relationship between the informer and the accused, but also on the relationship between the informer and the state. The right to silence will only be infringed where it was the informer who caused the accused to make the statement, and where the informer was acting as an agent of the state at the time the accused made the statement. Accordingly, two distinct inquiries are required. First, as a threshold question, was the evidence obtained by an agent of the state? Second, was the evidence elicited? Only if the answer to both questions is in the affirmative will there be a violation of the right to silence in s. 7.

. . . one should remember that the purpose of the right to silence is to limit the use of the coercive power of the state to force an individual to incriminate himself or herself; it is not to prevent individuals from incriminating themselves per se. Accordingly, if the person to whom the impugned remarks is made is not an agent of the state, there will be no violation of the right to silence.

In some cases, it will be clear that the person to whom the statements were made was an agent of the state. For example, if the statements were made to a police officer or to a prison official, whether in uniform or in plain clothes, there can be no question that the statements were made to an agent of the state. In other cases, it will be less clear. Where the statements are made to an informer, as in the case at bar, it may be arguable whether or not the coercive power of the state was brought to bear on the suspect in obtaining the statement from him or her.

In determining whether or not the informer is a state agent, it is appropriate to focus on the effect of the relationship between the informer and the authorities on the particular exchange or contact with the accused. A relationship between the informer and the state is relevant for the purposes of s. 7 only if it affects the circumstances surrounding the making of the impugned statement. A relationship between the informer and the authorities which develops after the statement is made, or which in no way affects the exchange between the informer and the accused, will not make the informer a state agent for the purposes of the exchange in question. Only if the relationship between the informer and the state is such that the exchange between the informer and the accused is materially different from what it would have been had there been no such relationship should the informer be considered a state agent for the purposes of the exchange. I would accordingly adopt the following simple test: would the exchange between the accused and the informer have taken place, in the form and manner in which it did take place, but for the intervention of the state or its agents?

If this test is applied to a conversation between a police officer and a suspect in custody, it is clear that the conversation would not have taken place but for the intervention of the officer. If it is applied to a conversation with a cellmate who has no contact with the authorities until after the conversation is concluded, it is equally clear that the actions of the authorities had no effect on the conversation, and that there would be no violation of the s. 7 right to silence. If, however, the cellmate spoke with the authorities before the conversation took place, then the question will be whether the conversation would have occurred or would have taken the same course had the cellmate had no contact with the authorities.

106 / Fundamentals of the Criminal Justice System

> I would add that there may be circumstances in which the authorities encourage informers to elicit statements without there being a pre-existing relationship between the authorities and individual informers. For example, the authorities may provide an incentive for the elicitation of incriminating statements by making it known that they will pay for such information or that they will charge the informer with a less serious offence. The question in such cases will be the same: would the exchange between the informer and the accused have taken place but for the inducements of the authorities?

> Even if the evidence in question was acquired by an agent of the state, it will only have been acquired in violation of s. 7 if the manner in which it was acquired infringed the suspect's right to choose to remain silent. In general, there will be no violation of the suspect's right to silence if the suspect volunteers the information, knowing he or she is talking to an agent of the state.[27]

In *Broyles*, the Supreme Court held that, in determining whether a state agent has actively elicited information from the accused, the courts must consider whether all the circumstances between the state agent and the accused suggest that the statements made by the accused would not have been made but for the conduct of the state agent. In making this determination the court should consider whether the exchange between the accused and the state agent can be characterized as similar to an interrogation and whether the state agent exploited any special characteristics of the relationship to extract a statement. The court also held that it is proper to consider whether there was a relationship of trust between the state agent and the accused and whether the accused was vulnerable to the state agent. A further consideration is whether the state agent manipulated the accused to bring about a mental state in which the accused was more likely to talk. The court stated that the above-listed factors are not an exhaustive list of the factors that should be considered in determining whether a state agent actively solicited the information or statement.

In *Broyles*, the Supreme Court concluded that the appellant's friend, Ritter, was an agent of the state during his conversation with the appellant. The court stated that it was clear that the meeting was set up by the police and that Ritter was able to have an "open visit" with the appellant which was only made possible because of the intervention by the police. Moreover, the police had instructed Ritter to elicit information about the death of the appellant's grandmother. The court found that Ritter attempted to undermine the appellant's confidence in his lawyer's advice to remain silent. The conversation between Ritter and the appellant in this regard was as follows:

JAMES: Well like I talked to my lawyer and what not and he told me not to say anything to anybody else.

TODD: Why? What good is it gonna do you man?

---

27 *Ibid.*, at 11-13.

JAMES: Hey I don't know what he has planned to do and whatnot.

TODD: Well you better talk to him. Cause sounds like he's trying to screw you around. That's what he's doing. Well what good is it gonna do you to spend twenty five years [sic] in jail for something you didn't do cause your lawyer tells you not to say anything.

JAMES: No like he, he has all the information and whatnot. But he doesn't want me to talking [sic] to the crown about it yet. Not until we get up there in, like the courtroom and whatnot. And on the record . . .

TODD: Well I don't see why he's [i.e; the appellant's lawyer] not doing anything then. But he's the one getting paid the bucks.

JAMES: Yeah. Plenty I think too.

TODD: That's why he's not doing nothing.

JAMES: Like when my social worker ever comes down here and what not I'm gonna tell her that bla, bla, bla, To get Pringle . . Instead of Hannington [sic].

TODD: That's who you got now. Hannington [sic] . . . I think Pringle's a much better lawyer."[28]

The common law right to remain silent, which has now been accorded a constitutional status by the Supreme Court of Canada as a result of the court's decisions in *Hebert* and *Broyles*, will not prevent police officers or other state agents from questioning persons who they suspect have committed criminal offences. The Supreme Court has been careful to restrict the parameters of the right to remain silent to cases where the person being questioned is actually detained so as to be entitled to counsel under section 10(*b*) of the Charter. In restricting the constitutional right to remain silent to situations where a person is detained, the Supreme Court has attempted to strike a balance between the right of the police to question anyone who they suspect has committed a criminal offence and the right of a detainee to remain silent in the face of police questioning. Although the Supreme Court of Canada has held that the common law right to remain silent has a constitutional status as a principle of fundamental justice under section 7 of the Charter, the common law right to remain silent will still be relevant. The common law right to remain silent applies whether or not a person being questioned is detained by the police. Accordingly, a person who is not detained by the police will still be protected under the law against questioning which takes place during pre-detention investigations. Thus, a person who is not detained may invoke his right to remain silent in the face of questioning by the police.

---

[28] *Ibid.*, at 17.

(i) *Police line-up*

There is no obligation upon anyone to participate in a police line-up. In some cases, the police may ask a person who they suspect has committed a criminal offence to participate in a line-up held by the police. A person will be asked to participate in a police line-up in cases where there are eyewitnesses who could possibly identify the person who committed the crime. In *R. v. Leclair*,[29] the Supreme Court of Canada stated that identification evidence obtained through a properly held police line-up is "usually strong evidence susceptible of influencing trial deliberations."[30]

In *Leclair*, the Supreme Court of Canada held that while the police may wish to hold a line-up as soon as possible, the concern that the line-up be held promptly must generally give way to the right of the suspect to retain counsel. In this case, the court held that since there is no legal obligation to participate in a line-up, defence counsel have an important role to play in advising a client as to whether he should voluntarily participate in a line-up.

There is no clear answer in every case as to whether someone should voluntarily participate in a police line-up. Much will depend upon where the line-up is held and the similarities of the other persons in the line-up to the accused. An accused should not participate in a line-up where others in the line-up are obviously older than himself. Counsel may advise the accused to obtain pictures of others in the line-up before deciding whether to participate in such a line-up. A suspect or an accused may wish to participate in a line-up where it is clear to him that the proposed line-up will be well run. If the suspect does not participate in the proposed line-up, the suspect's lawyer will be unable to attack the Crown's case on the ground that the police did not hold a proper line-up. In a leading case where the accused attacked the failure of the police to hold a proper line-up, the Crown led reply evidence that the accused had failed to participate in the line-up. This evidence was subsequently held by the Supreme Court of Canada to have been admissible.[31] A person who is asked by the police to participate in a line-up should insist on speaking to legal counsel before agreeing to participate.

(ii) *Polygraph test*

The police will sometimes ask a suspect to undergo a polygraph examination. The polygraph test, commonly referred to as the lie detector test, is used by the police as a device to obtain a confession from a suspect or an accused. There is no legal obligation to undergo a polygraph examination.

---

[29] (1989), 67 C.R. (3d) 209 (S.C.C.).
[30] *Ibid.*, at 218.
[31] *Marcoux v. R.* (1975), 29 C.R.N.S. 211 (S.C.C.).

Polygraph tests are used by the police to eliminate suspects or to obtain a confession from an accused. If an accused fails a polygraph test, the police will confront the accused with his failure to pass the test and proceed to question the accused as to the circumstances surrounding the offence. The test thus becomes "a confession-inducing instrument."[32] The results of a polygraph examination are inadmissible in a court of law and, accordingly, given all of the above, a person who is asked to undertake a polygraph examination should refuse to do so.

(iii) *Bodily substances*

A person is not legally obligated to provide a hair, saliva, semen or urine sample. The police may wish to obtain such a sample for DNA analysis. The federal government recently enacted legislation amending the Criminal Code to allow a police officer to obtain a search warrant for DNA analysis. The enacted legislation, which received Royal Assent on July 13, 1995 covers serious offences such as murder, manslaughter, robbery, kidnapping, and sexual assault. Once a judge authorizes the issuance of a search warrant for a DNA sample, a person would be obliged to provide such a sample.

(iv) *Handwriting samples*

An accused has no legal obligation to provide the police with a sample of his handwriting. The only exception to the general rule is where the accused is released on his giving an undertaking or entering into a recognizance. In such circumstances, the accused will be required to sign his name in order to give effect to the undertaking or recognizance. Experienced defence counsel believe that an accused who is being released on the basis of an undertaking or recognizance should print his name rather than sign it.[33]

(b) Duty to Assist the Police

The common law right of the citizen to remain silent in the face of police questioning cannot be asserted where a statute imposes a duty to answer questions or otherwise cooperate with the police. A person who does not comply with a police officer's lawful request to perform a statutory duty will usually be charged with obstructing a peace officer in execution of his duty. The

---

[32] *R. v. Amyot* (1990), 78 C.R. (3d) 129 (Que. C.A.); *Béland v. R.* (1987), 60 C.R. (3d) 1 (S.C.C.).
[33] Steven Skurka, "When the Telephone Rings: Advising the Arrested Client" (1991-1992) 34 C.L.Q. 349 at 358.

Criminal Code makes it an offence to wilfully obstruct a peace officer in the execution of his duty. Section 129 of the Criminal Code states:

> **129.** Every one who
> (a) resists or wilfully obstructs a public officer or peace officer in the execution of his duty or any person lawfully acting in aid of such an officer;
> (b) omits, without reasonable excuse, to assist a public officer or peace officer in the execution of his duty in arresting a person or in preserving the peace, after having reasonable notice that he is required to do so. . .
> is guilty of
> (d) an indictable offence and liable to imprisonment for a term not exceeding two years, or
> (e) an offence punishable on summary conviction.

There are no hard and fast rules as to what constitutes obstructing a peace officer in the execution of his duty. What constitutes an obstruction will depend upon the facts in any given case. If there is no legal duty to assist the police, a person who refuses to cooperate with the police cannot be convicted of obstructing a peace officer in the execution of his duty. At common law the citizen is not required to assist the police. However, the citizen's rights and obligations are based upon statute as well as common law and certain statutes may require a citizen to provide the police with information.

(i) *Criminal Code*

(A) Breath sample. The police can demand that a person provide a sample of his breath where the police have reasonable and probable grounds to believe that the person has committed a drinking and driving offence. The grounds for demanding the sample are set out in section 254(3)(a) of the Criminal Code. A sample may be demanded where the police have reasonable and probable grounds to believe that a person operated a motor vehicle, vessel, aircraft or railway equipment while his ability to operate the vehicle, etc. was impaired by alcohol or a drug. A person who, without reasonable excuse, refuses to provide a breath sample would be charged with failing to comply with a breathalyzer demand when prosecuted under the relevant provisions of the Criminal Code. The courts have taken a very narrow view as to what constitutes a reasonable excuse within the meaning of section 254(5) of the Criminal Code.

A person who is asked to comply with a breathalyzer demand is entitled to consult legal counsel before complying with the demand. In *R. v. Therens*,[34] the Supreme Court of Canada held that when the police made a breathalyzer demand to a motorist who was not under detention, the motorist was detained

---

[34] (1985), 45 C.R. (3d) 97 (S.C.C.).

within the meaning of section 10(*b*) of the Charter and was entitled to retain and instruct counsel without delay. Consultation with a lawyer about whether to take a breathalyzer test will result in the client being advised to take the test, as the refusal to comply with a breathalyzer demand will constitute an offence under the Criminal Code.

(B) Blood samples. A police officer may, in certain circumstances set out in the Criminal Code, require that a person provide a blood sample. Section 254(3) of the Criminal Code provides that where a police officer has reasonable and probable grounds to believe that by reason of any physical condition of the person the person may be incapable of providing a sample of his breath or that it would be impracticable to obtain a sample of his breath, the officer may demand that the person provide such blood samples as are necessary to determine the concentration of alcohol in the person's blood. Pursuant to section 254(3), the officer must have reasonable and probable grounds for believing that a person is committing or within the preceding two hours has committed as a result of consumption of alcohol an offence under section 253 of the Criminal Code. The Criminal Code provides that blood samples may only be taken under the direction of a qualified medical practitioner and in circumstances where the medical practitioner is satisfied that the taking of the samples would not endanger the life or health of the person.

(C) Fingerprints. A person who is arrested and charged with a hybrid or indictable offence is required to provide his fingerprints under the Identification of Criminals Act.[35] A hybrid or dual procedure offence is deemed to be indictable until the Crown elects to proceed by way of summary conviction and, thus, an accused who was charged with such an offence is required to appear for fingerprinting. In *Beare v. R.*,[36] the Supreme Court of Canada upheld the provisions of the Identification of Criminals Act which authorized mandatory fingerprinting for persons charged with an indictable or hybrid offence. Under the Identification of Criminals Act, a police officer has a discretion as to whether to require the accused to appear for fingerprinting.

With the exception of the few statutory exceptions discussed above, there is ordinarily no legal duty upon a person to answer police questions. Someone who is suspected of a criminal office cannot be charged with obstructing a peace officer in execution of his duty simply because the person refuses to answer police questions. A case in point is *R. v. Guthrie*,[37] a 1982 decision of the Alberta Court of Appeal. The accused was charged that she "did unlawfully and wilfully obstruct W. Gentle, a Peace Officer, in the execution of his duty contrary to paragraph (a) of s. 118 [129] of the Criminal Code." The accused, who was seen in the shadows of the Calgary City Police grounds,

---

[35] R.S.C. 1985, c. I-1.
[36] (1988), 66 C.R. (3d) 97 (S.C.C.).
[37] (1982), 69 C.C.C. (2d) 216 (Alta. C.A.).

was arrested for obstructing a peace officer in execution of his duty after she refused to say what she was doing in the police parking lot and refused to identify herself. The trial judge concluded that the peace officer was in execution of his duty and was enforcing the law when he requested that the accused identify herself.

There was evidence that the police were concerned by the accused walking in the parking lot because several police officers had had their private vehicles broken into in a series of earlier break-ins. There was no suggestion that the accused was involved in any of the break-ins. In overturning the conviction, McClung J.A. adopted the principles expressed in *Rice v. Connolly*,[38] saying that there was no duty upon the accused to answer police questions and cited the accused's common law right to remain silent when questioned by the police as support of her refusal. In holding that the accused did not obstruct a peace officer in execution of his duty, McClung J.A. stated that the accused had not violated the provisions of a statute such as refusing to answer questions which were required to be answered by a provincial or federal statute and that, accordingly, the demand was unjustified.

The police do have the power to require identification in certain circumstances. The majority of the Supreme Court of Canada in *Moore v. R.*[39] held that the police have the power to require a person to identify himself when a person is observed committing an offence. The rationale for the decision was that the information was needed so that the constable could avoid the necessity of an arrest, which he would have been compelled to make if the accused did not identify himself so that a summons could be issued. In *Moore*, the accused was arrested for the summary conviction offence of proceeding against a red light. In *Moore*, the court made it clear that while there is no general duty to cooperate with the police, it viewed the situation differently where the police actually saw someone committing a criminal offence. In such a case, the police can demand identification.

(ii) *Provincial legislation*

If a peace officer requests a British Columbia motor vehicle driver to produce identification, the driver is compelled to do so and could, if he or she refused to produce such identification, be charged with an offence under the Motor Vehicle Act. Similar legislation exists across Canada so that, for example, an Ontario motorist who refuses to identify himself when requested to do so by a peace officer can be charged under the provisions of the Highway Traffic Act. A motorist who refuses to identify himself when requested to do

---

[38] *Supra*, note 15.
[39] *Supra*, note 17.

so by a peace officer can be convicted of obstructing the peace officer in execution of his duty.

3. RIGHTS WHEN DETAINED OR ARRESTED

(a) Arrest and Detention — The Canadian and American Positions Compared

The U.S. Supreme Court's famous ruling in *Miranda v. Arizona*[40] has been immortalized by American television so that many Canadians may assume their rights on detention or arrest are the same in Canada as they are in the United States. However, the law is substantially different. Under the Miranda rules an accused taken into custody must be informed of the following rights:

1. his right to remain silent;
2. his right to be represented by an attorney and to have the attorney present during questioning;
3. his right if he cannot afford to hire an attorney to have one appointed before being questioned by the police; and
4. the police are required to warn the accused that any statements which he makes can be used against him in a court of law.

In Canada, someone who is detained or arrested has the right to be told the reasons for his detention and arrest or to be informed of his or her right to retain or instruct counsel without delay. This right is guaranteed by section 10 of the Charter which states:

> **10.** Everyone has the right on arrest or detention
> (*a*) to be informed promptly of the reasons therefor;
> (*b*) to retain and instruct counsel without delay and to be informed of that right;

In addition to the rights quoted above, the Supreme Court of Canada has now held that a police officer is required to provide a detainee or a person placed under arrest with information concerning the existence and availability of legal aid and duty counsel. In Canada, if an accused cannot afford to hire a lawyer, he may seek assistance from a government-run clinic, or apply for legal aid. In provinces where an accused has a right to hire a private lawyer on obtaining a legal aid certificate, he will have to satisfy the legal aid authorities that he qualifies for legal aid. In some jurisdictions, such aid is not available unless the accused can satisfy the legal aid officials that a conviction will result in a jail term or loss of employment.

---

[40] 384 U.S. 436 (U.S.S.C., 1966).

In each province in Canada, there exists a system of duty counsel whereby adults and young persons who cannot afford a lawyer are provided with temporary advice and assistance. In provinces where there exists a 24-hour duty counsel toll-free number, such as in Ontario, the police must advise all detainees of the existence of the 24-hour duty counsel service as part of the standard section 10(b) right to counsel which they administer to someone who is detained or arrested.[41]

The Supreme Court held in *R. v. Prosper*[42] that where no 24-hour counsel system exists, as is the case in Nova Scotia and Prince Edward Island and parts of the Yukon and Northwest Territories, a detainee must on detention be advised of his right to apply for legal aid under the applicable provincial or territorial legal aid plan.

Section 10(b) confers a much more limited right to counsel than the right conferred by the United States Supreme Court's landmark decision in *Miranda* because an accused is not given an absolute right to have counsel appointed for him by the state.[43] Recently, the Supreme Court of Canada has held that section 10(b) of the Charter does not require a province or territory to establish a 24-hour toll-free telephone number where detainees may obtain free legal advice from duty counsel. In *Prosper*, the issue was whether the section 10(b) Charter right to retain and instruct counsel without delay imposed a constitutional obligation upon governments to provide free and immediate legal advice upon request to detainees and persons who had been arrested by the police. In *Prosper*, the Chief Justice held that section 10(b) of the Charter does not in express terms constitutionalize the right to free and immediate legal advice upon detention, saying that the right to retain and instruct counsel without delay and to be informed of that right is simply not the same thing as a universal right to free 24-hour preliminary legal advice. In holding that the right to counsel under section 10(b) of the Charter did not impose a positive obligation upon governments to provide immediate free legal advice to detainees, the Chief Justice noted that the framers of the Charter had specifically rejected a proposed amendment which would have added the following clause to what is now section 10 of the Charter:

(d) If without sufficient means to pay for counsel and if the interests of justice so require, to be provided with counsel.[44]

---

[41] *R. v. Brydges* (1990), 74 C.R. (3d) 129 at 146-149 (S.C.C.); *R. v. Bartle* (1994), 33 C.R. (4th) 1 at 23 (S.C.C.).

[42] *R. v. Prosper* (1994), 33 C.R. (4th) 85 at 102 (S.C.C.).

[43] If a judge concludes that the accused cannot have a fair trial without being represented by a lawyer, the accused has a constitutional right under section 7 of the Charter to be provided with counsel at the state's expense if he cannot afford to hire a lawyer. See *R. v. Rowbotham* (1988), 63 C.R. (3d) 113 at 174-177 (Ont. C.A.).

[44] *Supra*, note 42, at 106-107.

The right to remain silent, which as a common law right has now been further protected by sections 7, 11(c) and 13 of the Charter of Rights, is somewhat limited when compared to the U.S. rule. In Canada, once an accused elects to give testimony the accused forfeits the right to remain silent and to refuse to give evidence which may be incriminating.[45] Under the U.S. rule, an accused, in giving evidence, may refuse to give evidence which tends to incriminate him.

The Miranda rule requires that a police officer inform an accused of his or her right to remain silent. In Canada, there is no constitutional requirement that the police so inform an accused, although it is common practice for police officers to do so.[46] It is also common practice to advise an accused that any statement made by the accused may be given as evidence in a court of law. There are special rules pertaining to young offenders which require a young person to be advised that there is no obligation to make any statement and that if a statement is made it may be introduced at the trial.

In one respect the rights conferred by the Charter are superior to those afforded by U.S. law. In the landmark decision of *Therens*, the Supreme Court of Canada held that one does not have to be placed under compulsory physical restraint to be detained, saying that a detention can be effected by psychological means. Accordingly, one who is so detained has the right to retain and instruct counsel without delay. In *Miranda*, the court held that the warnings should be given "when an individual is taken into custody or otherwise deprived of his freedom by the authorities in any significant way and is subject to questioning."[47] The scope of this decision was substantially restricted by subsequent decisions of the U.S. Supreme Court. In *Berkemer v. McCarty*, the court held that the Miranda warnings should be given "as soon as a suspect's freedom of action is curtailed to a degree associated with formal arrest."[48] In that case it was held that an accused had not been detained when stopped for questioning, although the evidence showed that the police officer had decided to arrest him when he stopped the car and requested him to perform a number of tests. The evidence established that when the officer made this decision, the suspect was not, subsequent to that decision, free to leave the scene. The decision of the Supreme Court of Canada in *Therens* appears to be a much more realistic approach. If the rights conferred by the Charter and by the Miranda rules are to be fully accorded to the person being detained, that person should be entitled to them when he reasonably believes that he is not free to refuse to comply with directions given by the police.

---

[45] *R. v. S. (R.J.)* (1995), 36 C.R. (4th) 1 (S.C.C.).

[46] *R. v. Van Den Meerssche* (1989), 74 C.R. (3d) 161 (B.C.C.A.); The Supreme Court's ruling in *Hebert* imposes no requirement on police to inform a detainee of his common-law and constitutional right to remain silent.

[47] Supra, note 40, at 1630.

[48] 104 S. Ct. 3138 (U.S.S.C., 1984), at 3150.

(b) "Arrest or Detention"

It is very important to know what constitutes an arrest and what constitutes a detention, as the rights under section 10 of the Charter arise only upon arrest or detention. The Criminal Code does not define the word "arrest" and does not set out what steps must be taken to effect a proper arrest. In *R. v. Whitfield*,[49] the Supreme Court of Canada stated:

> The correct proposition of law is stated in 10 Hals., 3rd ed., p. 342 in these terms:
>
>> MEANING OF ARREST. Arrest consists of the actual seizure or touching of a person's body with a view to his detention. The mere pronouncing of words of arrest is not an arrest, unless the person sought to be arrested submits to the process and goes with the arresting officer.[50]

In holding that an arrest consists of a seizing or touching of a person with a view to detention, Judson J. adopted the proposition put forward in the English "case of *Nicholl v. Darley* where it was said that . . . 'the slightest touch is an arrest'."[51] His Lordship said that this long-established rule probably came about so as to avoid unnecessary violence.

If a person only had the right to obtain the advice of a lawyer upon arrest, the value of the right might be greatly diminished because the police could question people before they placed them under arrest. Accordingly, there would be the clear possibility that a person could fail to assert the rights available because of a lack of awareness of his rights to obtain such advice before discussing any matter with the police. Section 2 of the Bill of Rights[52] which was the federal statute that was the forerunner to the Charter, provided that:

> . . . no law of Canada shall be construed or applied so as to
>
> . . . .
>
> (c) deprive a person who has been arrested or detained
>
> . . . .
>
> (ii) of the right to retain and instruct counsel without delay. . . .

It is obvious that the drafters of the Bill believed that one could be detained without being placed under arrest. Thus, in *R. v. MacDonald*,[53] Macdonald J.A., giving the judgment for the majority of the Nova Scotia Court of Appeal, stated that:

---

[49] [1970] S.C.R. 46.
[50] *Ibid.*, at 48.
[51] *Ibid.*, at 49.
[52] R.S.C. 1985, App. III.
[53] (1974), 22 C.C.C. (2d) 350 (N.S.C.A.).

Parliament in using the words "arrested" or "detained" in section 2(c) of the Canadian Bill of Rights contemplated different situations because although arrest includes detention, detention does not necessarily include arrest.[54]

This view accorded with that of Ritchie J., who delivered the judgment of the Supreme Court of Canada in *Chromiak v. R.*[55] The accused refused to provide a breath sample for a roadside screening device, saying that he wanted his lawyer present before he took any steps. After refusing to take the test the accused was charged with impaired driving, but was allowed to leave after he signed a promise to appear in court. He was convicted of failing to provide a breath sample. This conviction was ultimately appealed to the Supreme Court of Canada on the ground that he had been detained by the police officer and, accordingly, had been effectively denied the right to counsel given by the Bill of Rights. As the Supreme Court of Canada had already held, in *Brownridge v. R.*,[56] that anyone who was under arrest had a right to speak to a lawyer without delay, the denial of an accused's right to speak to a lawyer if he was detained would, under existing law, give the accused a reasonable excuse for refusing to take the test.

The vital question in the *Chromiak* case was whether the right to counsel arose before an accused was restrained or touched by the police; the court had to determine whether a person ordered to do something by a police officer was effectively detained. Ritchie J. held the following:

> It appears to me to be obvious that the word "detention" does not necessarily include arrest, but the words "detained" and "detention," as they are used in section 2(c) of the Bill of Rights, in my opinion connote some form of compulsory restraint. . . ."[57]

The case had a significance which went far beyond the impaired driving context because the Supreme Court of Canada's narrow definition of the word "detention" meant that only people who were arrested or physically restrained had the right to speak to a lawyer. Thus, people, upon being questioned by police, could frequently have their rights compromised because they did not have the benefit of legal advice. The ruling of the Supreme Court failed to recognize that a person subject to a demand or direction by a police officer in most circumstances would not really believe that he or she was free to seek advice before complying with an order.

In *Therens*, the Supreme Court of Canada held that someone may be detained without being placed under compulsory physical restraint. Le Dain J.,

---

[54] *Ibid.*, at 356.
[55] (1979), 12 C.R. (3d) 300 (S.C.C.).
[56] [1972] S.C.R. 926.
[57] *Supra*, note 55, at 307.

whose definition of the word "detention" was adopted by the other members of the court, stated:

> The purpose of s.10 of the Charter is to ensure that in certain situations a person is made aware of the right to counsel. . . .[58]

(c) Detention Defined

(i) *Under the Charter*

In *Therens*, the Supreme Court of Canada overturned its previous decision in *Chromiak v. R.* by holding that a person does not have to be held in custody to be detained:

> In determining the meaning that should be given to the word "detention" in s. 10 of the Charter it is necessary to consider the purpose of the section.
>
> . . . .
>
> The purpose of s. 10 of the Charter is to ensure that in certain situations a person is made aware of the right to counsel and is permitted to retain and instruct counsel without delay. The situations specified in s. 10 — arrest and detention — are obviously not the only ones in which a person may reasonably require the assistance of counsel, but they are situations in which the restraint of liberty might otherwise effectively prevent access to counsel or induce a person to assume that he or she is unable to retain and instruct counsel. In its use of the word "detention", s. 10 of the Charter is directed to a restraint of liberty other than arrest in which a person may reasonably require the assistance of counsel but might be prevented or impeded from retaining and instructing counsel without delay but for the constitutional guarantee.
>
> In addition to the case of deprivation of liberty by physical constraint, there is in my opinion a detention within s.10 of the Charter when a police officer or other agent of the state assumes control over the movement of a person by a demand or direction which may have significant legal consequence and which prevents or impedes access to counsel.
>
> In *Chromiak* this court held the detention connotes "some form of compulsory constraint." There can be no doubt that there must be some form of compulsion or coercion to constitute an interference with liberty or freedom of action that amounts to a detention within the meaning of s. 10 of the Charter. The issue, as I see it, is whether it may also be a compulsion of a psychological or mental nature which inhibits the will as effectively as the application, or threat of application, of physical force. The issue is whether a person who is the subject of a demand or direction by a police officer or other agent of the state may reasonably regard himself or herself as free to refuse to comply.
>
> . . . .

---

[58] *Supra*, note 34, at 123.

In my opinion, it is not realistic, as a general rule, to regard compliance with a demand or direction by a police officer as truly voluntary, in the sense that the citizen feels that he or she has the choice to obey or not, even where there is in fact a lack of statutory or common law authority for the demand or direction and therefore an absence of criminal liability for failure to comply with it. Most citizens are not aware of the precise legal limits of police authority. Rather than risk the application of physical force or prosecution for wilful obstruction, the reasonable person is likely to err on the side of caution, assume lawful authority and comply with the demand. The element of psychological compulsion, in the form of a reasonable perception of suspension of freedom of choice, is enough to make the restraint of liberty involuntary. Detention may be effected without the application or threat of application of physical restraint if the person concerned submits or acquiesces in the deprivation of liberty and reasonably believes that the choice to do otherwise does not exist.[59]

In *Therens*, Mr. Justice Lamer of the Supreme Court of Canada set out the requirements which a police officer or other agent of the state must fulfill in order to comply with section 10(*b*) of the Charter:

In my view, s. 10(*b*) requires at least that the authorities inform the detainee of his rights, not prevent him in any way from exercising them and, where a detainee is required to provide evidence which may be incriminating and refusal to comply is punishable as a criminal offence, . . . s. 10(*b*) also imposes a duty not to call upon the detainee to provide that evidence without first informing him of his s. 10(*b*) rights and providing him with a reasonable opportunity and time to retain and instruct counsel. Failure to abide by that duty will lead to the obtainment of evidence in a manner which infringes or denies the detainee's s.10(*b*) rights.[60]

(ii) *The importance of the Therens case*

The Supreme Court of Canada's judgment in *Therens* marks a watershed in Canadian criminal law. One no longer has to be physically constrained in order to be entitled to retain and instruct counsel without delay. The decision compels police officers and other agents of the state to be vigilant in ensuring that someone who is detained is fully informed of his or her right to retain and instruct counsel without delay. The Charter provides a remedy for someone whose rights have been infringed. Section 24 of the Charter states:

24. (1) Anyone whose rights or freedoms, as guaranteed by this Charter, have been infringed or denied may apply to a court of competent jurisdiction to obtain such remedies as the court considers appropriate and just in the circumstances.

(2) Where, in proceedings under subsection (1), a court concludes that evidence was obtained in a manner that infringed or denied any rights or freedoms guaranteed by this Charter, the evidence shall be excluded if it is estab-

---

[59] *Ibid.*, at 123-126.
[60] *Ibid.*, at 110.

lished that, having regard to all the circumstances, the admission of it in the proceedings would bring the administration of justice into disrepute.

The courts have held that the onus is on the person whose rights have been infringed to establish that the evidence, if admitted, would bring the administration of justice into disrepute.

In *Therens*, the Supreme Court of Canada upheld the accused's acquittal on the charge of driving a motor vehicle with a blood-alcohol level which exceeded 80 mg. The court held that the accused had his right to counsel infringed, as he was not advised of his right to retain and instruct counsel without delay before giving a breathalyzer sample. The court decided that to admit the breathalyzer certificate would bring the administration of justice into disrepute. Le Dain J. stated:

> In my opinion, the right to counsel is of such fundamental importance that its denial in a criminal law context must prima facie discredit the administration of justice.[61]

The Supreme Court's ruling in *Therens* has forced police officers and other agents of the state to carefully examine the circumstances under which a citizen must be instructed as to his or her right to retain counsel. They are now required to consider whether a person who is questioned on the street, in a police station or in his own home, is detained within the meaning of section 10 of the Charter of Rights. A person may be questioned without necessarily being detained. Whether someone is detained will depend upon whether a court believes that the test for detention set down in *Therens* has been met. In considering whether someone has been detained, so as to be entitled to legal counsel, a court will examine all the circumstances including the place and manner in which the person was questioned. If someone voluntarily cooperates with the police the court will probably find that the person has not been detained, unless there is evidence presented which establishes that the detainee believed that he or she was legally obligated to cooperate with the police and was not free to refuse, or that there was the psychological restraint discussed by Justice Le Dain.

Since the *Therens* decision there have been many cases which have considered the content and application of section 10 of the Charter of Rights. It is not possible to review all the case law which has developed in this area, but an examination of cases relating to detention at home and at a police station will illustrate some of the important issues which have arisen.

---

[61] *Ibid.*, at 133.

(d) What Constitutes "Detention"

(i) *Detention at home*

In *R. v. Esposito*,[62] the Ontario Court of Appeal had to determine whether an accused's right to counsel was infringed because he was not advised of his right to retain and instruct counsel without delay before he was questioned at his home. Police officers attended at the accused's home to question him regarding the fraudulent use of a bank credit card. When the police attended at the accused's residence, the accused was a suspect, police officers having discovered that 18 invoices for gasoline purchases were made at the gas station where Esposito worked as a station attendant. The accused was convicted and subsequently appealed his conviction to the Ontario Court of Appeal. The appeal raised the issue as to whether the accused was detained within the meaning of section 10(*b*) of the Charter when he was questioned at his home. The accused was not advised of his right to retain and instruct counsel without delay before being questioned. When the accused was questioned, he made incriminating statements which aided the Crown in proving its case. The Ontario Court of Appeal held that the suspect was not detained when he was questioned at his home and, accordingly, the police officers were not obligated to inform him as to his right to retain and instruct counsel without delay.

In holding that the accused was not detained when questioned at his home, Martin J.A. noted that the accused was questioned when his parents were there, and stated that the questioning prior to the accused being arrested was not "hostile or coarse in nature." His Lordship stated that the arresting officer was not asked whether the accused would have been permitted to leave or otherwise terminate the questioning and the arresting officer testified that he had no grounds for arresting the accused prior to the accused's admission that he had signed the invoices:

> There is no evidence . . . that the appellant actually believed that his freedom was restrained and, in my view, the circumstances would not lead him reasonably to believe that his freedom had been restrained. There was no evidence that the appellant was subject to a demand or direction with which he might reasonably believe he was required to comply. Unless all questioning of a suspect by a police officer, in the absence of a warning that the suspect is free to leave and is entitled to refuse to answer, constitutes a detention under s. 10(*b*) of the Charter, the questioning of the appellant in his home . . . in the circumstances, did not constitute such a detention. In my view, the appellant was not detained within the meaning of s. 10(*b*) of the Charter when he gave the incriminating answers at his home. . . .[63]

---

[62] (1986), 24 C.C.C. (3d) 88 (Ont. C.A.). Leave to appeal to S.C.C. refused (1986), 53 O.R. (2d) 356n.

[63] *Ibid.*, at 101.

The Supreme Court of Canada held in *Therens* that a person's belief that he is detained as a result of a police officer's demand or direction must be a reasonable belief. Thus, while someone may believe that he is detained if a court holds that such a belief is an unreasonable one, the right to counsel will not arise. In assessing whether someone is detained, a court will consider all the surrounding circumstances including the accused's evidence and the evidence given by the arresting officer or officers.

More recently, in *R. v. Siemens*,[64] the Manitoba Court of Appeal overturned the accused's murder conviction and ordered a new trial having found that the questioning of the accused by the police at the police station violated the accused's right to counsel. The court held that the accused should have been advised of his right to counsel at his home when the police required the accused to accompany them to the police station. In this case, the police had gone to the accused's home after the accused had placed two 911 telephone calls to report that his wife had stabbed herself. In this case, Helper J.A., who delivered the majority judgment of the court, held that the police gave the accused no choice but to accompany them to the police station. The court noted that the investigating officer had told the accused in a polite but aggressive manner that he wished to discuss the day's events with the accused at the police station. The accused was not asked whether he wished to accompany the police or whether he wished to go to the hospital where his wife had been taken. The court stated that the words used were: "Okay Robert, we'd like to discuss it with you further at the police station."

The court found that in light of the intention of the police to interrogate the accused at the police station, the police had assumed control over the accused's movements, saying that they had detained him when they placed him in the rear of the police cruiser and were then obligated to inform him of his right to counsel before he was questioned further. In this case, the accused testified at trial on the *voire dire* that he felt threatened by the police, and that he believed that he had no choice but to accompany the officers to the police station. At the police station, when the accused was in the interview room, he stated that he was about to change his story and speak the truth. The police did not advise the accused of his section 10(*b*) right to counsel and caution him that he was not required to say anything in response to questioning by the police. In *Siemens*, when the police failed to advise the accused of his right to counsel and questioned him without advising him of his right to remain silent, the accused admitted that he had stabbed his wife whereupon he was arrested and charged with murder.

While the accused was convicted at trial, the Manitoba Court of Appeal held that his right to counsel had been violated, saying that his confession should have been excluded under section 24(2) of the Charter. Helper J.A. stated:

---

[64] (1994), 88 C.C.C. (3d) 544 (Man. C.A.).

The police cannot defeat the intent of the Charter by interrogating a suspect to the point of self-incrimination and then relying upon a forthcoming confession to argue the evidence would have been available in any event. No one can speculate what this accused might have said or done at the time of his detention had he been advised of his right to counsel or his right to remain silent.[65]

In *Esposito*, the accused testified but did not state that he thought he was compelled to answer the officer's questions or was not free to stop the interview. In such circumstances, the court did not have evidence before it which would have enabled it to reasonably conclude that the accused was subject to a demand or direction and, thus, detained within the meaning of section 10(*b*) of the Charter. In *Siemens*, there was evidence which would enable the court to reasonably conclude that the accused was detained at his home from the moment that the police made a demand that he accompany them to the police station.

(ii) *Police station detention*

An issue which will arise with some frequency is whether someone who is questioned at a police station is detained within the meaning of section 10(*b*) of the Charter.

A person can be questioned at the police station by the police without being detained so as to be entitled to retain and instruct counsel without delay within the meaning of section 10(*b*) of the Charter. If a person is not the subject of a demand or direction by the police and voluntarily accompanies the officers to the police station, it is unlikely that the person would be detained within the meaning of the *Therens* definition of detention. The courts have developed a test for determining whether or not a person who is questioned at a police station by the police is detained. In *R. v. Moran*,[66] Martin J.A., who delivered the judgment of the Ontario Court of Appeal, set out factors which the courts should consider in determining whether someone who is questioned by the police at a police station is detained. Martin J.A. stated that the court should consider the following:

1. the precise language used by the police in requesting that the person who subsequently becomes an accused to come to the police station;
2. whether the accused was escorted to the police station by the police or came himself in response to a police request;
3. whether the accused left at the end of the interview or was arrested by the police;
4. the stage of the investigation, that is, whether the investigation was part of a general investigation of a crime or possible crime or whether the police

---

[65] *Ibid*, at 556.
[66] (1987), 36 C.C.C. (3d) 225 (Ont. C.A.).

had already determined that a crime had been committed and that the accused was a suspect and whether the questioning was conducted in order to obtain an incriminating statement from the accused;

5. whether the police had reasonable and probable grounds to believe that the accused had committed the crime being investigated;

6. whether the questions were questions of a general nature designed to obtain information or whether the accused was confronted with evidence suggesting his guilt;

7. the accused's subjective belief that he is detained is not decisive as the issue was whether the accused *reasonably* believed that he was detained. Personal circumstances relating to the accused, such as low intelligence, emotional disturbance, youth and lack of sophistication are circumstances to be considered in determining whether the accused had a subjective belief that he was detained.[67]

Martin J.A. stated that the factors listed above are not an exhaustive list of the factors that a court should consider in determining whether someone who is asked to come to the police station by the police is detained for purposes of being advised of his section 10(*b*) right to counsel under the Charter.

In subsequent cases, the Ontario Court of Appeal and other provincial appellate courts have applied the test set out by Mr. Justice Martin in *Moran*. In *R. v. Voss*,[68] the majority of the Ontario Court of Appeal held that the accused's section 10(*b*) right to counsel had been violated by the police who questioned the accused at the police station and his home for 4 1/2 hours without advising him of his right to counsel. In *Voss*, the accused had testified that he felt threatened and did not believe that he had a choice of leaving the police station. As a result of the breach of the accused's right to counsel, incriminating statements made by the accused were excluded by the Ontario Court of Appeal, who overturned the accused's conviction for manslaughter and ordered a new trial.

In *R. v. Yorke*,[69] the Ontario Court of Appeal held that the accused was not detained when he was questioned by the police at the police station. In that case, the cross-examination of the accused showed that he had answered the questions put by the police because of his belief that the failure to do so would cast suspicion upon him and that he was "in a dilemma and tried to fake the officers out." In *Yorke*, there was no evidence which established that the accused had a low level of intelligence, was suffering from an emotional disturbance or was generally unsophisticated. In short, there was no evidence which would objectively demonstrate that the accused's belief that he was detained was a reasonable one.

---

[67] *Ibid.*, at 258-259.
[68] (1989), 71 C.R. (3d) 178 (Ont. C.A.).
[69] (1990), 54 C.C.C. (3d) 321 at 329 (Ont. C.A.).

The fact that the police do not demand that a person accompany them to the police station for questioning will not necessarily mean that the person was not detained. In *R. v. Soares*,[70] the Ontario Court of Appeal held that a request by a police officer to come to the police station may reasonably be construed by the person to whom the request is made as a demand or direction. The court stated that in determining whether a request to come to the police station is in fact a demand or direction, all the circumstances must be considered.

Although whether a person who is asked to come to the police station is detained will depend upon factors such as the language used by the police officer and whether the person is wanted for general questioning in relation to a possible crime or is a person who is considered to be the suspect in the case, it is clear that where a person does not believe that he is detained, there can be no detention under section 10(*b*) of the Charter. In *R. v. Hawkins*,[71] the Supreme Court of Canada overturned a decision of the Newfoundland Court of Appeal that the accused was detained where there was no demand or direction by the police that the accused accompany them to the police station and the accused lacked any subjective belief that he was detained when he went to the police station. In *Hawkins*, the Newfoundland Court of Appeal had set aside the accused's conviction for sexual assault, holding that his right to counsel under section 10(*b*) of the Charter was infringed when he was asked by the police to come to the police station to answer questions. The police requested an interview from the accused and he was given a choice as to where the interview could be held. There was no indication that the accused was given the alternative of no interview. The accused agreed to be interviewed and went to the police station.

At trial, the accused testified that he never got the impression that the complaint was a serious one and the majority of the Court of Appeal concluded that the accused did not have a subjective belief that he was under detention. Nevertheless, the majority of the court held that a person who is questioned by the police may be detained in circumstances where the person does not have a subjective feeling of compulsion to answer police questions or to accompany the police to the police station. This decision by the majority of the Court of Appeal was a marked departure from the test set out by the Supreme Court of Canada in *Therens*.

(iii) *Detention by questioning on the street*

Whether someone who is questioned on the street is detained will depend upon the circumstances in each particular case. In *R. v. Grafe*, the Ontario

---

[70] (1987), 34 C.C.C. (3d) 403 (Ont. C.A.).
[71] (1992), 14 C.R. (4th) 286 (Nfld. C.A.), reversed (1993), 20 C.R. (4th) 55 at 56 (S.C.C.).

Court of Appeal held that a person who is questioned on the street by a police officer was not detained for purposes of section 10(*b*) of the Charter, saying that "the Charter does not seek to insulate all members of society from all contact with constituted authority no matter how trivial the contact may be."[72] In this case, the person who was questioned was not required to sit in the back of a police car and was allowed to leave the scene after answering some questions which were of short duration.

In *R. v. Lawrence*,[73] the Ontario Court of Appeal held that an accused who had been convicted on a charge of breaking and entering a dwelling house was not detained when she was first questioned by the police on the street in the vicinity of the place where the break-in had occurred. In this case, the police had seen the accused riding her bicycle on a sidewalk a few houses away from where the break-in had occurred. While the accused did not fit the description provided, the investigating police officer decided to question her. Although the evidence established that the police officer had blocked the path of the accused's bicycle with his car, the court held that the accused was not detained, saying that there was no evidence that the accused felt compelled to remain at the police officer's cruiser. In *Lawrence*, the Court of Appeal held that the investigation was not centred on the accused when she was first questioned by the police. The court concluded that it was not until the accused had lied to the police and a search of her knapsack revealed suspicious articles that the focus of the investigation changed. (The accused had consented to the search of her knapsack.) The court held that the accused was detained when the officer's suspicions focused on her and she was requested to sit in a police cruiser.

There is a tension in the case law between the right of a person to be left alone and to remain silent in the face of police questioning and the right of the police to question anyone whom they believe has information about a criminal offence. It will be recalled that although the courts have said that there is a moral duty to assist the police, there is generally no legal duty to assist the police. The courts have attempted to reconcile this conflict in the law by restricting the circumstances in which a person can reasonably be said to be detained. The philosophy of the courts is expressed by Tarnopolsky J.A., writing for the Ontario Court of Appeal in *Lawrence*:

> . . . in all the circumstances Constable Dankert would probably have been considered at least naive, if not negligent, if he had not tried to ask her some questions. That was his duty: to investigate a reported offence and, to this end, to try to ask questions of anyone who might seem to be a possible source of such information. However, if a police officer who questions a person who might appear suspicious must always provide s. 10(b) warnings, there would be far more detentions and arrests than our society would tolerate. [74]

---

[72] (1987), 60 C.R. (3d) 242 at 249 (Ont. C.A.).

[73] (1990), 80 C.R. (3d) 289 (Ont. C.A.).

[74] *Ibid.*, at 295.

(e) Right to Counsel

Police officers have a right to question someone who is suspected of committing a criminal offence or someone who has been arrested and charged with a criminal offence. However, as has been noted earlier in this chapter, the accused has a right to remain silent. Thus, the accused may refuse to answer police questions. An accused who is knowledgeable about his rights will almost certainly insist on speaking to a lawyer before answering police questions. Police officers who ignore the accused's assertion of his right to remain silent do so at their peril. Thus, where a police officer questions an accused, ignoring the accused's insistence on speaking to a lawyer before answering police questions, the court may find that the officer has breached the accused's right to counsel under the Charter and exclude any evidence so obtained.

(i) *Effect of continued questioning*

Several Ontario cases illustrate the arguments which can be made against continued questioning. In *R. v. Manninen*,[75] the Ontario Court of Appeal held that the accused's right to counsel was breached when police officers continued to question him despite his insistence that he had nothing to say until speaking with a lawyer. The court excluded incriminating statements because it found that police officers had deliberately violated his rights under the Charter by continuing to question him after he insisted that he had nothing to say until he had spoken with his lawyer. At trial, the accused was convicted of armed robbery and use of a firearm and received sentences totalling four years. The Court of Appeal ordered a new trial, saying that evidence obtained as a result of a deliberate violation of the accused's right should have been excluded from his trial.

This decision was upheld by the unanimous judgment of the Supreme Court of Canada, given by Lamer J.[76] The court held that the police must provide the detainee with a reasonable opportunity to exercise the right to retain and instruct counsel without delay. This includes the duty to offer the accused the use of a telephone. In the absence of any urgency requiring the police to proceed with their questioning forthwith, this right is treated as an absolute right. The purpose of the right is not only that the accused be informed of his rights, but equally to obtain advice as to how to exercise these rights. Thus, the accused should not have been questioned until he had had the opportunity to obtain advice. Also, the mere fact that the accused had answered questions

[75] (1983), 8 C.C.C. (3d) 193 (Ont. C.A.).
[76] (1987), 58 C.R. (3d) 97 (S.C.C.).

should not be held to constitute an implicit waiver of his rights. There may be an implicit waiver, but the standard required to show this will be very high.

The court held that the admission of evidence in the circumstances would bring the administration of justice into disrepute as the violation was a very serious one, committed when there were no circumstances of urgency. The court held that the use of such evidence obtained following a denial of the right to counsel will generally go to the fairness of the trial and, thus, will generally bring the administration of justice into disrepute. Even though the accused's guilt was clearly established by his statements to the police, this could not justify the admission of the evidence in light of the seriousness of the violation.

In *R. v. Nyiri*,[77] the Ontario Court of Appeal held that the accused's right to counsel had been infringed when she was questioned by the police after she had been arrested but before she had an opportunity to speak to a lawyer. In *Nyiri*, the accused was arrested and was advised of her right to retain and instruct counsel without delay. The accused's common law husband advised the police in the accused's presence that he would obtain a lawyer on behalf of the accused. The police had begun to question the accused as soon as the accused was in the police car heading for the police station. The accused indicated to the officer that she did not want to answer his questions. The Ontario Court of Appeal found that the arresting officer knew that it was likely that a lawyer would be retained on the accused's behalf and that the lawyer would be contacting the accused at the police station to advise her of her rights. The court found that the accused's right to counsel under section 10(*b*) of the Charter was infringed, saying that there were no circumstances of urgency and that the police were not acting in good faith in questioning the accused without advising her of her right to retain counsel. The court held that all of the accused's statements prior to her consultations with her lawyer should have been excluded from evidence under section 24(2) of the Charter. Given all of the circumstances of the case, the court set aside the conviction and ordered a new trial.

In *R. v. Bain*,[78] the Supreme Court of Canada held that the accused's right to counsel had been infringed where the police continued to question the accused in circumstances when the accused had, in effect, asserted a right to contact counsel. In this case, the accused's father had made it clear to the investigating officer that he had retained a lawyer on behalf of the accused. The accused's lawyer phoned the police station but did not ask to speak to the accused. The accused asked the investigating officer if his father had called and was told, accurately, that he had not. The officer did not tell the accused that a lawyer had been retained on his behalf, believing that he was not legally required to do so. The trial judge held that the officer's failure to advise the

---

[77] (1990), 49 C.R.R. 166 at 168 (Ont. C.A.).
[78] (1992), 10 C.R. (4th) 257 (S.C.C.).

accused that the lawyer had called breached the accused's right to counsel. The trial judge stated that "once the accused had retained counsel to the knowledge of the police officers, it was not open to them to deal with him as if he had not done so."[79]

The Ontario Court of Appeal held that the trial judge had erred in holding that the accused's right to counsel had been breached, saying that the trial judge had erred in law in requiring the police to do more than answer Bain's question as to whether his father had called. The Court of Appeal held that once Bain was advised of his section 10(*b*) right to retain counsel without delay, the police were not required to provide the accused with any additional information. The Supreme Court of Canada disagreed, holding that the accused's section 10(*b*) right to retain and instruct counsel had been infringed by the police. Stevenson J., writing on behalf of the court, stated:

> The Court of Appeal found error in fixing the police with the responsibility of doing more than answering literally the appellant's question whether his father had called. That question had to be addressed in the context of the evidence. Given the circumstances, a literal response was misleading, because the obvious intent of that inquiry was to further the objective of communicating with counsel. It was tantamount to an assertion by the appellant that he wanted counsel, and in those circumstances, the answer was an evasion which the officers used to continue the questioning in the face of that assertion. The trial judge had the advantage of assessing that inquiry and response in the particular circumstances, and did not err in law in excluding the subsequent statements.[80]

In *Nyiri* and *Bain*, questioning by the police subverted the detainee's right to counsel which resulted in the court's ultimate conclusion that there had been a breach of section 10(*b*) of the Charter. In *Nyiri*, the police subverted the accused's right to counsel by questioning her against her wishes before she had been accorded a reasonable opportunity to retain and instruct counsel. In *Bain*, the accused had, in effect, asserted his right to counsel and the police had continued questioning him, ignoring his desire to communicate with a lawyer.

Section 10(*b*) of the Charter is not intended to insulate a detainee against all contact with the police. Once a detainee has requested a lawyer and the police have given the detainee a reasonable opportunity to retain counsel without delay and have ceased questioning the detainee until he has had an opportunity to retain counsel, they may proceed to question the detainee. Thus, in *R. v. Hicks*,[81] Lacourcière J.A., writing for the Ontario Court of Appeal, stated:

> The right to remain silent does not preclude appropriate police questions. The police have the right and duty to ask appropriate questions; provided constitu-

---

[79] *R. v. Bain* (1988), 68 C.R. (3d) 50 at 57 (Ont. C.A.).
[80] *Supra*, note 78, at 288.
[81] (1988), 64 C.R. (3d) 68 (Ont. C.A.), affirmed (1990), 73 C.R. (3d) 204 (S.C.C.).

tional rights have not been infringed, the answers given are admissible in a criminal prosecution if they are proven beyond a reasonable doubt to have been voluntary in the traditional sense . . . .[82]

In *R. v. Greig*,[83] the Ontario High Court of Justice held that the accused had a right to receive continuing legal advice from a lawyer, saying that in most cases the police should take reasonable steps to provide defence counsel with "reasonable notice" of their intention to interview the accused. The view expressed by Dupont J. was not accepted by the Ontario Court of Appeal and has not been adopted by the Courts of Appeal in Manitoba, Nova Scotia or Newfoundland.[84] Thus, for example, in *R. v. Cuff*,[85] the Newfoundland Court of Appeal held that an accused does not have to be advised of his right to retain and instruct counsel on every occasion that he is questioned. Goodridge C.J.N., who delivered the judgment of the court, stated:

> The effect of these cases is that there is no continuing obligation to advise a suspect of his right to retain and instruct counsel. That constitutional obligation is discharged when the suspect is so advised when he is arrested. (In some cases, such as *Clarkson* where the suspect was intoxicated, it may be necessary to advise the detainee upon detention and again, later, of the right to retain and instruct counsel.) More importantly, however, for the purpose of this case, once counsel has been retained and instructed there is no reason why the police should not question the suspect. It is part of the process of criminal investigation. The ethical code which requires in civil cases that persons represented by counsel should communicate only through counsel has no relevance in that process. It is not a deprivation of the right to retain and instruct counsel.
>
> In this particular case, the appellant was advised of his right to retain and instruct counsel and in fact did retain and instruct counsel. What those instructions may have been is not of course known to the court but it is clear that consequent upon these instructions the appellant was advised to make no statements to the police. On several occasions subsequently, the appellant contacted and presumably further instructed counsel and very probably was continually advised to make no statements.
>
> By his statements it is evident that the appellant was clearly aware of his right to counsel and on occasion availed of that right. He made repeated references to it. On one occasion he said he would talk if his lawyer was present. On another occasion he said "Don't write that down. My lawyer told me not to say that."

---

[82] *Ibid.*, at 80.

[83] (1987), 56 C.R. (3d) 229 (Ont. S.C.).

[84] *R. v. Hicks* (1988), 64 C.R. (3d) 68, affirmed (1990), 73 C.R. (3d) 204 (S.C.C.); *R. v. J.(J.T.)* (1988), 40 C.C.C. (3d) 97 (Man. C.A.), reversed in part (1990), 59 C.C.C. (3d) 1 (S.C.C.); *R. v. Logan* (1988), 67 O.R. (2d) 87 (Ont. C.A.), affirmed on other grounds (1990), 58 C.C.C. (3d) 391 (S.C.C.).

[85] (1989), 49 C.C.C. (3d) 65 (Nfld. C.A.).

The appellant, although advised to say nothing, proved to be a compulsive talker who spoke willingly to the police over extended periods in the two months following his arrest.

. . . .

Where a person has been arrested and advised of his right to retain and instruct counsel and has either waived that right or has retained and instructed counsel, he may be questioned by the police in the absence of counsel.[86]

(ii) *Violation of right to consult counsel*

The Supreme Court of Canada has held that where a person is a suspect for a new and more serious crime than was the case when the person was first questioned by the police, the police must reinform the detainee of his right to retain and instruct counsel without delay. In *R. v. Evans*,[87] McLachlin J., who delivered the judgment of the court, stated:

> . . . there is a duty on the police to advise the accused of his or her right to counsel a second time when new circumstances arise indicating that the accused is a suspect for a different, more serious crime than was the case at the time of the first warning. This is because the accused's decision as to whether to obtain a lawyer may well be affected by the seriousness of the charge he or she faces . . . . I add that to hold otherwise leaves open the possibility of police manipulation, whereby the police — hoping to question a suspect in a serious crime without the suspect's lawyer present — bring in the suspect on a relatively minor offence, one for which a person may not consider it necessary to have a lawyer immediately present, in order to question him or her on the more serious crime.

> I should not be taken as suggesting that the police, in the course of an exploratory investigation, must reiterate the right to counsel every time that the investigation touches on a different offence. I do, however, affirm that . . . the police must restate the accused's right to counsel when there is a fundamental and discrete change in the purpose of the investigation, one involving a different and unrelated offence or a significantly more serious offence than that contemplated at the time of the warning.[88]

In *R. v. Borden*,[89] the Supreme Court of Canada held that the accused's right to counsel was infringed when the police failed to inform him that they were gathering information for an offence other than the offence for which he had been given his right to counsel. In this case, the police had informed the accused that they were questioning him in relation to a sexual assault which had occurred at a motel. The accused denied committing the sexual assault

---

[86] *Ibid.*, at 71-73.
[87] (1991), 4 C.R. (4th) 144 (S.C.C.).
[88] *Ibid.*, at 163.
[89] (1994), 92 C.C.C. (3d) 404 at 419-420 (S.C.C.).

and after obtaining legal advice agreed to provide a blood sample to the police. (The accused had been told by his lawyer not to tell the police anything other than his name.) Before consenting to give the blood sample, the accused was not advised that the police wanted the sample principally to determine whether he had committed a sexual assault on an elderly woman in her home. After the blood sample was analyzed, the accused was charged with sexual assault in relation to the woman who had been assaulted at her home. At trial, as a result of DNA analysis, the accused was convicted of sexual assault and sentenced to six years' imprisonment. The accused appealed to the Nova Scotia Court of Appeal which allowed the appeal and set aside the conviction. The majority of the court found that the accused's section 10(*a*) and (*b*) Charter rights had been infringed as well as his right to be secure against unreasonable search and seizure. The majority of the Court of Appeal excluded the results of the DNA analysis, finding that its admission would bring the administration of justice into disrepute.

The Supreme Court held that in this case the police did not tell the accused that they were investigating any offence other than the one for which he had been arrested. The court held that when the nature of the police investigation expanded, the accused should have been reinformed of his right to retain a lawyer. In *Borden*, the failure of the police to properly inform the accused of the offence for which he was being investigated for, coupled with their failure to restate his right to counsel when the nature of their investigations expanded, resulted in the court finding that the Nova Scotia Court of Appeal had properly excluded the DNA evidence.

(iii) *Waiver of right to counsel*

The Supreme Court of Canada in *Clarkson v. R.*[90] has made it very clear that any waiver of the right to counsel must not only be voluntary, but be premised on a true appreciation of the consequences of giving up that right. In *Clarkson*, the accused was very intoxicated when charged with her husband's murder; she was given the usual caution and advised of her right to counsel. She said there was no point in having counsel and made several very damaging statements while drunk and very emotional. There has always been a difference in our courts about the exclusion of statements. One line of reasoning is that they are admissible so long as they are truthful and the accused comprehended what he or she was saying, while the other required the accused to comprehend the consequences of making the admission.

In giving the judgment of the Supreme Court in *Clarkson*, Wilson J. said that the right to counsel and the terms of its waiver might provide an acceptable alternative approach to the problem. She said that section 10(*b*) was

---

[90] (1986), 50 C.R. (3d) 289 (S.C.C.).

aimed at fostering adjudicative fairness. Thus, any "waiver of this right by an accused must be carefully considered and that the accused's awareness of the consequences of what he or she was saying is crucial."[91] In her view such a waiver must be made with eyes wide open. She approved of a number of U.S. authorities holding that there is a presumption against a valid waiver where the accused is not perceived to be capable of comprehending its full implications. She concluded that any waiver must be premised on a true appreciation of the consequences. The evidence, she decided, could not be admitted as the police had blatantly violated the accused's rights as they had disregarded her aunt's requests that she should have counsel when time permitted this and their efforts appeared to be directed at getting a statement before she was sober. In the light of this decision, the police and the courts must be sure an accused understands the consequences of a waiver of the right to counsel if it is to be valid.

(iv) *Delay in affording right to counsel*

(A) *Earliest opportunity.* In *R. v. Dombrowski*,[92] the Saskatchewan Court of Appeal held that the accused's right to counsel had been infringed, the accused not having been allowed to telephone his lawyer at the earliest opportunity. The accused was convicted of theft of batteries, contrary to section 294(1)(*b*) [334(1)(*b*)] of the Criminal Code. Counsel for the accused argued, among other things, that the trial judge should have excluded from evidence statements made after the section 10(*b*) Charter right to retain and instruct counsel without delay was infringed. The accused was arrested after a search of his home revealed three stolen batteries. The police, acting under the authority of a search warrant, arrested the accused for theft and advised him of his right to retain and instruct counsel. The officers told the accused that he would be permitted to retain counsel as soon as they reached the Royal Canadian Mounted Police office in Swift Current. Before attending at the police station Constable Moat and Dombrowski went to the repair shop where the accused worked so that the accused could lock up his tools. When the accused and the constable approached the back door of the repair shop, the constable cautioned the accused as follows:

> I warned Mr. Dombrowski by saying that he need not say anything. He had nothing to hope from any promise or favour and nothing to fear from any threat; however, anything you do say may be used as evidence.[93]

---

[91] *Ibid.*, at 302.
[92] (1985), 18 C.C.C. (3d) 164 (Sask. C.A.).
[93] *Ibid.*, at 168.

The court held that he should have been permitted to telephone a lawyer at his place of work. Tallis J.A. stated:

> After carefully considering the record in this case, we are of the opinion that the appellant's rights under s. 10(*b*) of the Charter were denied or violated. At the time of arrest, the police officers advised that he had the right to retain and instruct counsel (the words "without delay" were not added or used) and that he would be given an opportunity just as soon as they returned to the police detachment office. In the circumstances of this case, we draw the clear inference that the appellant intended to contact counsel and understood that he would be allowed to telephone for counsel from the police detachment but not before. This is demonstrated by his conduct upon arrival at the detachment. When the police officers endeavoured to take a written statement upon arrival at the detachment, the appellant immediately endeavoured to contact counsel and any further discussion with the officers was postponed until he made a further attempt after lunch. There is no evidence that a written statement was ever obtained. We conclude that the appellant did obtain advice from counsel at the first opportunity that was available to him.
>
> . . . .
>
> The basic right to counsel under s. 10(*b*) of the Charter is now part of the supreme law of Canada and must be respected by the courts if it is to have any meaning for the average citizen. This right must also be respected and taken seriously by law enforcement officers. In this case, the arresting officers had no right to limit the appellant's opportunity to contact counsel until they returned to the detachment office. With the availability of a telephone at the business premises of Co-op Implements, there was no justification for limiting or delaying the opportunity. We appreciate that regard must be had to the circumstances of each case but in this case we hold that the incriminating evidence should be excluded under s. 24(2) of the Charter. To hold otherwise would whittle away the right afforded to every citizen under s. 10(*b*). The admission of the oral statements would, in the circumstances of this case, bring the administration of justice into disrepute.[94]

The Saskatchewan Court of Appeal's decision in *Dombrowski* indicates that the courts will not allow the accused's Charter right to retain and instruct counsel without delay to be given or withheld at the whim of law enforcement officials.

(B) *Reasonable opportunity.* The Supreme Court of Canada has held that in addition to informing detainees of their rights under section 10(*b*) of the Charter, the police must give the person detained who wants counsel a reasonable opportunity to exercise the right to retain and instruct counsel without delay. The court has held that the police must not question the detainee until the detainee has had a reasonable opportunity to retain and instruct counsel. What constitutes a reasonable opportunity will depend upon all the circumstances of the case including whether the police had sufficient time to afford the detainee a reasonable opportunity to obtain counsel before

---

[94] *Ibid.*, at 171-172.

the detainee made incriminating statements to the police. Thus, where a murder suspect makes a voluntary statement to the police three minutes after being taken to the police station, the courts have found that there was no violation of the detainee's right to counsel. In *R. v. Yaeck*,[95] the Ontario Court of Appeal held that the accused's section 10(*b*) rights were not violated where the accused's first statement was made well before the police officers had a reasonable opportunity to assist him in obtaining legal counsel.

The Supreme Court of Canada has held that if a detainee is not reasonably diligent in the exercise of his rights, the police are not bound to accord the detainee a reasonable opportunity to retain and instruct counsel. Also, in such circumstances the police can continue to question the detainee and do not have to cease all questioning until the detainee has been given a reasonable opportunity to retain counsel. In *Leclair*,[96] the Supreme Court of Canada held that an accused or detainee has a right to choose his or her own counsel and it is only if counsel cannot be available within a reasonable time that the detainee should be expected to call another lawyer.

Although the Supreme Court of Canada's judgment in *Tremblay* indicates that a detainee must be reasonably diligent in exercising his right to counsel, the Supreme Court of Canada has held that the availability of duty counsel services in the place where the person is being detained may affect what constitutes reasonable diligence in exercising the detainee's right to retain and instruct counsel under section 10(*b*) of the Charter. In *Prosper*, the Supreme Court of Canada held that the non-existence of duty counsel services must be taken into consideration in determining what constitutes a reasonable opportunity to consult counsel. The court stated that the absence of duty counsel extends the period in which a detainee will have been found to be duly diligent in exercising his right to counsel. The court held that the reasonable opportunity provided to detainees in places where duty counsel does not exist (Nova Scotia, Prince Edward Island, parts of the Yukon and Northwest Territories) might extend to when the legal aid office opens, when a private lawyer willing to provide free summary advice can be reached, or when the detainee is brought before a justice of the peace for bail purposes and his needs can be properly assessed and accommodated. The court stated that the fact that evidence may cease to be available as a result of a long delay is a factor to be considered in determining what is a reasonable opportunity.[97]

(C) *The one phone call myth.* A reasonable opportunity to obtain counsel does not mean that the detainee or an accused is limited to one phone call.

---

[95] (1991), 10 C.R. (4th) 1 at 15 (Ont. C.A.), leave to appeal to S.C.C. refused (1992), 71 C.C.C. (3d) vii (note) (S.C.C.).

[96] (1989), 67 C.R. (3d) 209 at 216 (S.C.C.); *Tremblay v. R.* (1987), 60 C.R. (3d) 59 at 62 (S.C.C.).

[97] *Supra*, note 42, at 108-109.

In *R. v. Louttit*,[98] a pre-Charter case, Freedman C.J.M., writing for the Manitoba Court of Appeal, stated that the "one phone call rule is a fiction propagated by Hollywood." The Manitoba Court of Appeal's decision in this regard was adopted by the Ontario Court of Appeal in *R. v. Pavel*.[99] The court held that where the police advised an accused of his section 10(*b*) right to retain counsel and told him that he had the right to make only one telephone call, the accused's section 10(*b*) right to counsel had been infringed. In this case, the one telephone call which the accused made was unsuccessful and the accused did not attempt to contact counsel again as he believed the police officer's statement that he was only entitled to one telephone call.

(v) *What comes after reading one's right to counsel?*

Most police officers are issued a card which contains a summary of an accused's rights on arrest or detention. When an accused is detained or arrested, the officer reads the Charter rights from this card. After the police officer informs an accused as to his or her Charter rights, the officer will usually advise the accused of his or her common law right to remain silent.

Most police forces caution an accused that anything said to the police may be used in evidence at the accused's trial. The standard police warning that the accused is not obliged to say anything to the police is read to facilitate the Crown being able to introduce any incriminating oral or written statement made in the presence of a police officer. Any statement implicating an accused in a crime made in the presence of a police officer or other person in authority can only be introduced at the accused's trial if the Crown satisfies the trial judge that the statement was freely and voluntarily made. The words "free and voluntary" in legal terms mean that the accused's confession must be free from hope of advantage and must not be motivated by fear or oppression. A confession which is not free and voluntary will not be admitted into evidence.

Several years ago, it was believed that a confession could not be introduced into evidence unless the confession was preceded by a caution to the accused that anything said could be introduced into evidence at his trial. It is now clearly established that the absence of a caution or warning does not mean that the confession is not free and voluntary. The converse is also true. In other words, the reading of a caution or warning does not automatically make a confession free and voluntary. However, the absence of a police caution or warning that the accused has the right to remain silent is one factor to be considered in determining whether an accused's statement is admissible. The standard police caution given is usually worded as follows:

---

[98] (1974), 21 C.C.C. (2d) 84 at 86 (Man. C.A.).
[99] (1989), 74 C.R. (3d) 195 at 210 (Ont. C.A.).

Caution to Charged Person

You are charged, or will be charged. . . . Do you wish to say anything in answer to the charge? You are not obliged to say anything unless you wish to do so, but whatever you say may be given in evidence.

Secondary Caution to Charged Person

If you have spoken to any police officer or to anyone with authority, or if any such person has spoken to you in connection with this case, I want it clearly understood that I do not want it to influence you in making any statement.

Section 10 of the Charter has introduced a new factor as any statement made after a waiver of the right to counsel must be made with a clear appreciation of the consequences. In view of the decision of Wilson J. in *Clarkson*, the police must be sure that a person has such an appreciation; this rule will clearly be enforced stringently in cases where a person has limited capacity and also where there is no urgency to engage in questioning.

(vi) *Right to privacy*

There is case law which suggests that the right to retain and instruct counsel without delay under the Charter gives rise to a right to speak to one's counsel in private. In *R. v. Jackson*,[100] the Ontario Court of Appeal held that an accused does not have to specifically ask to speak to his lawyer in private in order to have the right to consult counsel in private. The court held that if the accused speaks to his lawyer, having been informed of his right to do so, he is entitled to speak to his lawyer in private, saying that the right to retain and instruct counsel will have been infringed if, in fact, the accused or detainee is not afforded privacy during his conversation. The court in *Jackson* stated that although it is advisable that the police advise a detainee of his right to consult with counsel in private, the police are not constitutionally required to advise a detainee of his right to retain and instruct counsel in private.

However, in *Jackson*, the Ontario Court of Appeal held that where the circumstances are such that the detainee reasonably believes that he does not have a right to retain and instruct counsel in private and such circumstances are known or ought to be known to the police officer who was advising the detainee of his rights, the officer has a duty to advise the detainee that he has a right to consult counsel in private.

The Nova Scotia Court of Appeal has held that the right to privacy is intrinsic in the right to counsel under the Charter of Rights and Freedoms. In *Le Page v. R.*,[101] Jones J.A. stated:

---

[100] (1993), 25 C.R. (4th) 265 at 272-273, 275 (Ont. C.A.),
[101] (1986), 54 C.R. (3d) 37 (N.S.C.A.).

Even to obtain the minimal advice by means of a telephone, a person detained or arrested must be free to discuss the circumstances of his detention with counsel. If he cannot do so for fear of making admissions in the presence of the police, then obviously his right to instruct counsel has been limited. In such circumstances the right under the Charter has been violated.[102]

In *R. v. Playford*,[103] which predated the Ontario Court of Appeal's decision in *Jackson*, the court excluded the accused's confession in a murder case because police officers violated the accused's right to privacy and did not give him a reasonable opportunity to consult a lawyer. In *Playford*, the Court of Appeal overturned the accused's first degree murder conviction, holding that the trial judge had erred in law admitting the confession.

4. PROTECTION AGAINST ARBITRARY DETENTION OR IMPRISONMENT

The Charter protects people from arbitrary detention or imprisonment. Section 9 of the Charter states: "Everyone has the right not to be arbitrarily detained or imprisoned." The Charter's guarantee against arbitrary detention or imprisonment, however, is not new, as the Canadian Bill of Rights contained a somewhat similar section. Section 2(*a*) of the Canadian Bill of Rights provided:

> Every law of Canada shall, unless it is expressly declared by an Act of the Parliament of Canada that it shall operate notwithstanding the Canadian Bill of Rights, be so construed and applied as not to abrogate, abridge or infringe or to authorize the abrogation, abridgment or infringement of any of the rights or freedoms herein recognized and declared, and in particular, no law of Canada shall be construed or applied so as to

> (*a*) authorize or effect the arbitrary detention and imprisonment of any person.

(a) Arbitrary Defined

Mr. Justice Arnup, of the Ontario Court of Appeal, discussed the meaning of the word "arbitrary" in *Levitz v. Ryan*,[104] a 1972 decision of the Ontario Court of Appeal:

---

[102] *Ibid.*, at 377.
[103] (1987), 61 C.R. (3d) 101 at 117, 129 (Ont. C.A.).
[104] (1972), 9 C.C.C. (2d) 182 (Ont. C.A.).

It seems to me that no matter where I turn for assistance on the meaning of the word "arbitrary," whether to case law or to dictionaries, I inevitably reach the conclusion that s. 10 does not authorize an "arbitrary detention." To be "arbitrary" in this context means to be unreasonable or capricious. As it was put in the *Nebbia* case . . . there is a relationship between "due process" and "arbitrary" laws. In *Isbrandtsen Co. Inc. v. United States* (1951), 96 F. Supp. 883 at p. 889, Frank, J., said:

> . . . arbitrary conduct means unreasoned or unreasonable conduct, i.e. without reference to an adequate determining principle or standard.[105]

Professor Walter Tarnopolsky points out that the key word, "arbitrary," has unfortunately not received much judicial consideration. His resort to the reported cases in which the meaning of that word has been determined, in other contexts, led him to the conclusion that:

> . . . the proscription here is against detention, imprisonment or exile without specific authorization under existing law. And further, that a law giving power to detain, imprison or exile, cannot grant such a power to be exercised "unreasonably" or "without reasonable cause".[106]

In *Jamieson v. R.*,[107] Durand J., of the Quebec Superior Court, defined the word "arbitrary" in the following terms:

> "Arbitrary" means (Dictionnaire Petit Robert (1981)): "that which is not bound by the observance of rules . . . that which depends on the caprice or whim of someone."[108]

The Ontario Court of Appeal's decision in *R. v. Duguay*,[109] is a good example of the type of case where section 9 of the Charter has been successfully invoked. The court held that where a police officer arrests someone without having reasonable and probable grounds to make the arrest and where there is no reason to believe that such grounds existed, the arrest will constitute an arbitrary detention. The accused were arrested and charged with breaking and entering a Windsor, Ontario residence. The evidence indicated that the victim had noticed the accused in a neighbour's backyard before he left his house on the night of the break-in. There was evidence that one of the three young persons charged asked the victim whether he always put his dog in the garage. After the break-in the police were contacted and in the course of their investigation made arrangements with the owner of the neighbouring house to have the three accused attend back at the premises. When they

---

[105] *Ibid.*, at 189.

[106] W.S. Tarnopolsky, *The Canadian Bill of Rights*, 2nd ed. (Toronto: McClelland & Stewart, 1975), at 235.

[107] (1982), 70 C.C.C. (2d) 430 (Que. S.C.).

[108] *Ibid.*, at 439.

[109] (1985), 45 C.R. (3d) 140 (Ont. C.A.).

arrived they were put in the back of a police cruiser and arrested. The accused gave inculpatory statements when questioned by police.

The officers admitted the accused were arrested "to determine whether they actually did it or not." The trial judge rejected the officers' testimony that they had reasonable and probable grounds to believe that the accused had committed an indictable offence, saying that he could not "for one moment, accept that two police officers of 19 and 20 years' experience can swear that they honestly believe that." After noting that one of the detectives admitted that they arrested the accused to determine whether they actually committed the offence, the trial judge held that the arrest was for the police officers "a means of conducting their investigation" and that the arrest was illegal as the accused had been arbitrarily detained. In upholding the trial judge's ruling, MacKinnon A.C.J. said:

> It cannot be that every unlawful arrest necessarily falls within the words "arbitrarily detained." The grounds upon which an arrest was made may fall "just short" of constituting reasonable and probable cause. The person making the arrest may honestly, though mistakenly, believe that reasonable and probable grounds for the arrest exist and there may be some basis for that belief. In those circumstances, the arrest though subsequently found to be unlawful, could not be said to be capricious or arbitrary. On the other hand, the entire absence of reasonable and probable grounds for the arrest could support an inference that no reasonable person could have genuinely believed that such grounds existed. In such cases, the conclusion would be that the person arrested was arbitrarily detained. Between these two ends of the spectrum, shading from white to grey to black, the issue of whether an accused was arbitrarily detained will depend, basically, on two considerations: first, the particular facts of the case; and secondly, the view taken by the court with respect to the extent of the departure from the standard of reasonable and probable grounds and the honesty of the belief and basis for the belief in the existence of reasonable and probable grounds on the part of the person making the arrest.
>
> In my view, on the facts as found by the trial judge, the arrest or detention was arbitrary, being for quite an improper purpose, namely, to assist in the investigation. This conclusion does not minimize the significance or importance of an experienced detective's "hunch" or intuition. Such "hunch" must, however, have some reasonable basis. It cannot be used as a defence and explanation, without examination for irrational and high-handed actions.[110]

The Crown's appeal to the Supreme Court of Canada on the exclusion of evidence under section 24(2) of the Charter was dismissed by the court.[111]

---

[110] *Ibid.*, at 147-148.
[111] (1989), 67 C.R. (3d) 252 (S.C.C.).

(b) Where Violation of Criminal Code

Where a specific section of the Criminal Code provides that an accused must be brought before a justice of the peace for a judicial interim release hearing and the accused is not brought before the justice of the peace for such a hearing, the accused will have been arbitrarily detained. Thus, in *Marshall v. R.*,[112] Osborne J., of the Ontario High Court of Justice, held that where an accused was denied an identity hearing as required by section 454(2) [503(3)] of the Criminal Code, he was arbitrarily detained. The Criminal Code contains a section which provides that an accused who was alleged to have committed an indictable offence outside the province in which he was arrested shall, within the time period specified, be taken before a justice of the peace for a hearing to determine whether there are reasonable grounds to believe he is the person charged. In *Marshall*, Osborne J. held that the accused had been arbitrarily imprisoned because he was not brought before a justice of the peace as required to determine whether he was the same person for whose arrest police had an out-of-province warrant. After concluding that Mr. Marshall had been arbitrarily imprisoned, Osborne J. held that the Crown should be forced to pay Marshall's legal costs as this was the appropriate relief to which Marshall was entitled under section 24(1) of the Charter.

5. REASONABLE BAIL

The Criminal Code provisions pertaining to judicial interim release or bail have been discussed in Chapter 4, A Basic Overview of the Criminal Code. The Charter does not guarantee that everyone will be released upon bail; it does guarantee that an accused will be entitled to receive reasonable bail. Section 11(*e*) of the Charter states: "Any person charged with an offence has the right . . . (*e*) not to be denied reasonable bail without just cause."

6. CONFESSIONS

(a) Classic Test for Admission as Evidence

In criminal cases statements made by the accused to persons in authority are very frequently the principal, and sometimes the only, evidence implicat-

---

[112] (1984), 13 C.C.C. (3d) 73 (Ont. H.C.).

ing the accused. Such statements made out of court by the accused may only be admitted into evidence if the prosecution shows that the statement was made freely and voluntarily. The rule as to voluntariness which is generally accepted in Canada is one established by the Privy Council in *Ibrahim v. R.*[113] In that case Lord Sumner said:

> It has long been established as a positive rule of English criminal law, that no statement made by an accused is admissible in evidence against him unless it is shewn by the prosecution to have been a voluntary statement, in the sense that it has not been obtained from him either by fear of prejudice or hope of advantage exercised or held out by a person in authority.[114]

The rule had its origin in the fear that evidence would be obtained by actual torture or violence. Many Canadian cases have examined the meaning of voluntariness. Despite this there are still questions as to whether the *Ibrahim* rule is exhaustive. Thus, in *Horvath v. R.*,[115] two Supreme Court judges said it was not enough to show a statement had not been induced by any hope of advantage or fear of prejudice. It was their view that a statement could be held not to be voluntary if it was induced by some other motive or some other reason. In the *Horvath* case, Beetz J. rejected a statement made to a police officer because the police officer had induced a state of hypnosis with the result that a statement was made.[116] Clearly this statement was not made of the accused's own free will.

One interesting case is a decision of the Supreme Court of Canada in *Rothman v. R.*[117] In that case the accused was placed in a cell with an undercover police officer. After he had been cautioned by a police officer and had expressly refused to make a statement, an undercover police officer was placed in a cell with him and denied that he was a "narc." Subsequently, the accused made a statement to the officer. The statement was found to be voluntarily given, but Mr. Justice Estey, in a strong dissent, said that a statement must be volunteered by the speaker in the sense that it is a product of his conscious will. It was his view that where the speaker had refused to give a statement to the authorities it could only be a voluntary one if it was established that he was aware that his statement was being volunteered to a person in authority. Lamer J., in the same case, took the view that the deception by the police officer as to his identity was not sufficiently offensive to the administration of justice that the statement should be excluded. Estey J. believed that this was a calculated subversion of the accused's right to remain silent which brought the administration of justice into disrepute. Martland J., who gave the majority judgment, said:

---

[113] [1914] A.C. 599 (P.C.).
[114] *Ibid.*, at 609.
[115] (1979), 7 C.R. (3d) 97 (S.C.C.).
[116] *Ibid.*, at 118.
[117] (1981), 20 C.R. (3d) 97 (S.C.C.).

. . . in determining the admissibility of a confession to a person in authority, the court is not immediately concerned with the truth or reliability of a statement made by the accused, but with the question as to whether the statement he has made is free and voluntary, within the stated rules, and whether the confession was the utterance of an operating mind.[118]

He held that the statement was admissible as the mind of the accused was not affected by the police and there had not been any coercion or persuasion. Today, as a result of the Supreme Court of Canada's judgment in *Hebert* and *Broyles*,[119] *Rothman* is not definitive as to whether a statement made by an accused to an undercover police officer posing as a cellmate is admissible in evidence.

A confession will not be admitted if it was induced by threats or promises by a person in authority. Obviously a confession will not be considered to be voluntary if it was induced by actual violence.[120] In England, it has been expressly recognized that if a statement is obtained in an oppressive manner it will not be admissible even if it has not been obtained by threats or inducements.[121]

(b) Rationale for Confession Rule

The rationale for the rule on involuntary confessions is based in part on the lack of reliability of such statements. There was a time when it was not uncommon for great pressure, including torture, to be applied to extract a statement. Another reason for the rule is the common law principle that a person is not obliged to give a statement to the police.[122] It has also been suggested that the rule is necessary to protect the integrity of the criminal justice system because if involuntary statements were to be admitted it could tempt persons in authority to use improper means to extract them.

The Crown must establish the accuracy of the statement made. Accordingly, much greater credence is given to written statements than to verbal statements.[123] Much difficulty can be avoided by having a statement recorded. If a statement is to be admitted the Crown must show the accused had the capacity to make the statement.[124]

---

[118] *Ibid.*, at 144.

[119] *R. v. Herbert, supra*, note 20; *R. v. Broyles, supra*, note 26.

[120] *R. v. Young* (1984), 12 W.C.B. 335 (Ont. Dist. Ct.).

[121] P.K. McWilliams, *Canadian Criminal Evidence*, 2nd ed. (Aurora: Canada Law Book, 1984), at pp. 446-447; *R. v. Owen* (1983), 4 C.C.C. (3d) 538 (N.S.C.A.).

[122] *Ibid.*; *Rice v. Connolly*, [1966] 2 Q.B. 414 at 419 (H.L.); *Moore v. R.* (1978), 43 C.C.C. (2d) 83 (S.C.C.).

[123] McWilliams, *supra*, note 121, at 483.

[124] *R. v. Albrecht* (1966), 1 C.C.C. (2d) 281 (N.B.C.A.).

In determining whether a statement is given voluntarily, a court will have regard to the individual accused. The court will examine whether some particular characteristic will make the accused more likely to be susceptible to threats and inducements.[125] However, an accused's timidity will not make a statement inadmissible unless there are external circumstances brought about by the conduct of the police that can be said to cast doubt on the voluntariness of the statement.[126]

There are special rules as to the confessions of young people. The Young Offenders Act provides that a young person must be given an explanation in language appropriate to his age and understanding that:

(i) the young person is under no obligation to give a statement,

(ii) any statement given by him may be used as evidence in proceedings against him,

(iii) the young person has the right to consult another person in accordance with paragraph (c), and

(iv) any statement made by the young person is required to be made in the presence of the person consulted, unless the young person desires otherwise.[127]

A person in authority means anyone who has authority or control over the accused or the proceedings or prosecution against him.[128] The test appears to be a subjective one. If the accused believes the person taking the statement is a person in authority, then the person taking the statement will be deemed as such. Thus, in the case of *R. v. Downey*,[129] where an accused, on being taken to a householder who he had been alleged to have robbed, perceived that person to be an agent of the police and one in authority, the Nova Scotia Court of Appeal ruled that the householder was such a person. If the accused makes a statement to a person he does not believe to be a person in authority, the statement will be admissible even if the person was actually a person in authority. Accordingly, where police officers conceal their identity and pose as prisoners they have been held not to be persons in authority. Employers, complainants, informants, the police, prosecutors and magistrates have all been held to be persons in authority.

---

[125] *R. v. Thauvette* (1938), 70 C.C.C. 364 (Ont. S.C.).

[126] McWilliams, *supra*, note 121, at pp. 461-465.

[127] R.S.C. 1985, c. Y-1, s. 56(2)(*b*).

[128] *R. v. Todd* (1901), 4 C.C.C. 514 at 526 (Man. K.B.); *Deokenanan v. R.*, [1969] 1 A.C. 20 at 32-33; McWilliams, *supra*, note 121, at 468.

[129] (1976), 32 C.C.C. (2d) 511 (N.S.C.A.).

(c) The Use of False Affidavits

The development of strict rules governing procedures which may be used in obtaining confessions does not mean that police officers will refrain from using tricks to obtain confessions. In *R. v. Allen (No. 3)*,[130] the accused, Allen, was charged with first degree murder of a Toronto lawyer, Bruce Lorenz. Allen and the victim's wife, Lauralee Lorenz, were jointly charged with the first degree murder of Bruce Lorenz. Two of the investigating officers drew up an affidavit purporting to be signed by Lauralee Lorenz in which Mrs. Lorenz implicated Gordon Allen in the murder of her husband. The affidavit was false. The officers had concocted the false affidavit and forged Lauralee Lorenz's signature to the affidavit. The affidavit was designed to entice Gordon Allen into making incriminating statements. The artifice worked, as Allen gave incriminating statements to the police. However, Allen's lawyer, Edward L. Greenspan, was successful in having such statements ruled inadmissible. The tactics used were not proper and Allen and Lorenz were subsequently acquitted of murder. The officers were subsequently convicted of a criminal offence.

In *Allen*, the accused, Gordon Allen, having read over the false affidavit purporting to be sworn by Lauralee Lorenz said: "I didn't think she'd turn on me." Goodman J. of the Ontario High Court of Justice ruled that the statements made by Allen subsequent to his being shown the false affidavit were inadmissible. In so holding, His Lordship stated:

> In my opinion, the presentation of the concocted affidavit constituted a form of coercion equally as effective as a threat or promise in inducing the accused to make a statement.[131]

---

[130] (1979), 46 C.C.C. (2d) 553 (Ont. H.C.).
[131] *Ibid.*, at 565.

6

The Role of the Police

Police officers are governed by statute as well as by common law. At common law, police officers are given broad powers to keep the peace, protect property, and otherwise prevent crime. In addition, they are given specific statutory authority to prevent crimes. Each province has a statute which sets out the duties and responsibilities of police officers. Police officers are given broad powers of arrest and search and seizure under both common law and statutes. They are entrusted with great responsibility in performing their functions and are called upon to apply the laws in a practical setting.

Each police department has detailed rules and regulations which must be followed. When investigating offences, police are called upon to exercise discretion in deciding whether to lay a charge. Once an officer decides to charge someone with committing an offence, the officer has to decide which offence the accused should be charged with. In some cases this will be obvious, but the facts may support a charge under more than one section of the Criminal Code[1] and then the officer will be required to consider what offences an accused should be charged with. If an officer has doubt as to what charge should be laid and the offence is a serious charge, the officer may consult with a Crown attorney for assistance in laying the charge and in drafting the charge. However, the officer is the front line individual who usually decides which charge to lay.

1. POLICE POWER

(a) Statutory Power

The duties and responsibilities of police officers are set out in federal and provincial statutes. Many of the duties which are expressed in legislation, such as the Royal Canadian Mounted Police Act,[2] have evolved from British

---

[1] R.S.C. 1985, c. C-46.

[2] R.S.C. 1985, c. R-10.

common law. Although most of a police officer's responsibilities are contained in statutes, the police are still affected by the common law which governs their duties (except where the common law has been overruled by a statute). At common law, a police officer has a duty to preserve and maintain the peace, prevent crime and protect life and property.[3] The enforcement of the Criminal Code is a provincial responsibility; some provinces use the R.C.M.P. to provide police services, while others have a provincial police force. Each province has its own Police Act which governs police forces in that province.

The duties of a Royal Canadian Mounted Police Officer are expressed in section 18 of the Royal Canadian Mounted Police Act, which states

> **18**. It is the duty of members who are peace officers, subject to the orders of the Commissioner,
>
> (*a*) to perform all duties that are assigned to peace officers in relation to the preservation of the peace, the prevention of crime and of offences against the laws of Canada and the laws in force in any province in which they may be employed, and the apprehension of criminals and offenders and others who may be lawfully taken into custody;
>
> (*b*) to execute all warrants and perform all duties and services in relation thereto, that may, under this Act or the laws of Canada or the laws in force in any province, be lawfully executed and performed by peace officers;
>
> (*c*) to perform all duties that may be lawfully performed by peace officers in relation to the escort and conveyance of convicts and other persons in custody to or from any courts, places of punishment or confinement, asylums or other places; and
>
> (*d*) to perform such other duties and functions as are prescribed by the Governor in Council or the Commissioner.

In Ontario, municipal and provincial police officers are governed by the Police Services Act,[4] which states the duties and responsibilities of provincial police officers. The Act states that police officers have the following duties:

> **42**. (1) The duties of a police officer include,
>
> (*a*) preserving the peace;
>
> (*b*) preventing crimes and other offences and providing assistance and encouragement to other persons in their prevention;
>
> (*c*) assisting victims of crime;
>
> (*d*) apprehending criminals and other offenders and others who may lawfully be taken into custody;
>
> (*e*) laying charges, prosecuting and participating in prosecutions;
>
> (*f*) executing warrants that are to be executed by police officers and performing related duties;
>
> (*g*) performing the lawful duties that the chief of police assigns;
>
> (*h*) in the case of a municipal police force and in the case of an agreement under section 10 (agreement for provision of police services by O.P.P.), enforcing municipal by-laws;

---

[3] *R. v. Dedman* (1985), 46 C.R. (3d) 193 (S.C.C.).
[4] R.S.O. 1990, c. P.15.

Subsections 42(2) and (3) of the Act provide that a police officer has the authority to act throughout Ontario and has the powers and duties ascribed to a constable at common law. Similar legislation is found in other provinces.

(b) The View of the Courts

The duties expressed by the Royal Canadian Mounted Police Act and the Ontario Police Services Act, to preserve the peace, are very general, but the courts have been reluctant to give a detailed formulation of a police officer's duties, preferring instead to state the duties as each case comes before them. The position of Canadian courts is reflected in the Ontario Court of Appeal's decision in *Schacht v. R.*,[5] wherein Schroeder J.A. stated:

> Police forces exist in municipal, provincial, and federal jurisdictions to exercise powers designed to promote the order, safety, health, morals, and general welfare of society. It is not only impossible but inadvisable to frame a definition which will set definite limits to the powers and duties of police officers appointed to carry out the powers of the state in relation to individuals who come within its jurisdiction and protection. The duties imposed on them by statute are by no means exhaustive. It is infinitely better that the courts should decide as each case arises whether, having regard to the necessities of the case and the safeguards required in the public interest, the police are under a legal duty in the particular circumstances.[6]

2. POWER OF ARREST

(a) General

Criminal law falls under federal jurisdiction and although some provincial statutes, such as Liquor Licence Acts, contain arrest provisions, a police officer's powers of arrest are primarily found in the Criminal Code. The two principal sections dealing with arrest are sections 494 and 495. Section 494, which is considered later, confers a power of arrest on all persons in special circumstances. Section 495 makes the following provisions:

> **495.** (1) A peace officer may arrest without warrant
> (*a*) a person who has committed an indictable offence or who, on reasonable grounds, he believes has committed or is about to commit an indictable offence,
> (*b*) a person whom he finds committing a criminal offence, or
> (*c*) a person in respect of whom he has reasonable grounds to believe that a warrant of arrest or committal, in any form set out in Part XXVIII in relation thereto, is in force within the territorial jurisdiction in which the person is found.

---

[5] (1973), 30 D.L.R. (3d) 641 (Ont. C.A.).
[6] *Ibid.*, at 646.

The term "peace officer" encompasses a broader group of individuals than just a police officer, as is evident in the definition of a peace officer contained in section 2 of the Code:

> "peace officer" includes
> (*a*) a mayor, warden, reeve, sheriff, deputy sheriff, sheriff's officer and justice of the peace,
> (*b*) a member of the Correctional Service of Canada who is designated as a peace officer pursuant to the *Penitentiary Act*, and a warden, deputy warden, instructor, keeper, jailer, guard and any other officer or permanent employee of a prison other than a penitentiary as defined in the *Penitentiary Act*,
> (*c*) a police officer, police constable, bailiff, constable, or other person employed for the preservation and maintenance of the public peace or for the service or execution of civil process,
> (d) an officer or a person having the powers of a customs or excise officer when performing any duty in the administration of the *Customs Act* . . . or the *Excise Act*,
> (*e*) a person appointed or designated as a fishery officer under the *Fisheries Act* when performing any of his duties or functions pursuant to that Act,
> (*f*) the pilot in command of an aircraft
>> (i) registered in Canada under regulations made under the *Aeronautics Act*, or
>> (ii) leased without crew and operated by a person who is qualified under regulations made under the *Aeronautics Act* to be registered as owner of an aircraft registered in Canada under those regulations, while the aircraft is in flight, and
> (*g*) officers and non-commissioned members of the Canadian Forces who are
>> (i) appointed for the purposes of section 156 of the *National Defence Act*, or
>> (ii) employed on duties that the Governor in Council, in regulations made under the *National Defence Act* for the purposes of this paragraph, has prescribed to be of such a kind as to necessitate that the officers and non-commissioned members performing them have the powers of peace officers;

The effect of section 2 of the Criminal Code is that, technically speaking, someone who is a mayor, or other municipal officer, could make an arrest under section 495 of the Criminal Code. Practically speaking, the arrest powers are usually only exercised by police officers. An understanding of the arrest powers would not be possible without knowledge of what constitutes an arrest. The Criminal Code does not define the term "arrest" and the legal definition is found in the common law. The Supreme Court of Canada defined arrest in *R. v. Whitfield*,[7] where Judson J. stated as follows:

> The correct proposition of law is stated in 10 Hals, 3rd ed., p. 342, in these terms:
> . . . Arrest consists of the actual seizure or touching of a person's body with a view to his detention. The mere pronouncing of words of arrest is not an arrest, unless the person sought to be arrested submits to the process and goes with the arresting officer. An arrest may be made either with or without a warrant.[8]

---

[7] [1970] S.C.R. 46.
[8] *Ibid.*, at 48.

Section 495 gives a power of arrest for indictable offences including those which may be proceeded with by summary conviction. Some indictable offences are punishable by indictment or on summary conviction at the election of the Crown prosecutor. Such an offence is known as a hybrid or dual procedure offence. Impaired driving is an example of a hybrid or dual procedure offence.

(b) Reasonable and Probable Grounds

The Criminal Code does not define the words "reasonable and probable grounds," and, as with the term "arrest," the meaning of the term must be found in the case law. The classic definition of the words "reasonable and probable grounds" is contained in the British case, *Hicks v. Faulkner*,[9] where Hawkins J. stated as follows:

> Now I should define reasonable and probable cause to be an honest belief in the guilt of the accused based upon a full conviction, founded upon reasonable grounds, of the existence of a state of circumstances, which, assuming them to be true, would reasonably lead any ordinarily prudent and cautious man, placed in the position of the accuser, to the conclusion that the person charged was probably guilty of the crime imputed. There must be: first, an honest belief of the accuser in the guilt of the accused; secondly, such belief must be based on an honest conviction of the existence of the circumstances which lead the accuser to that conclusion; thirdly, such secondly-mentioned belief must be based upon reasonable grounds; by this I mean such grounds as would lead any fairly cautious man . . . . so to believe; fourthly, the circumstances so believed and relied on by the accuser must be such as to amount to reasonable grounds for the belief in the guilt of the accused.[10]

In *R. v. Storrey*,[11] the Supreme Court of Canada held that the requirement of reasonable and probable grounds necessitates that the police officer subjectively have reasonable and probable grounds on which to base the arrest and, in addition, there must be an objective basis for the reasonable and probable grounds. An objective basis will exist if a reasonable person placed in the position of the police officer would have believed that the police officer had reasonable and probable grounds for arresting the accused. The court held that the police are not required to establish more than reasonable and probable grounds in order to make an arrest, saying that the police are not required to establish a *prima facie* case for conviction. Thus, reasonable and probable grounds may be based on hearsay and other evidence which would not be admissible in court.

---

[9] (1881), 8 Q.B.D. 167 (D.C.), affirmed (1882), 46 L.T. 130 (C.A.).
[10] *Ibid*. D.C., at 171.
[11] (1990), 75 C.R. (3d) 1 (S.C.C.).

In *Storrey*, Cory J. explained the rationale for requiring a police officer to have reasonable and probable grounds before arresting someone. He stated:

> Section 450(1) [495(1)] makes it clear that the police were required to have reasonable and probable grounds to believe that the appellant had committed the offence of aggravated assault before they could arrest him. Without such an important protection, even the most democratic society could all too easily fall prey to the abuses and excesses of a police state. In order to safeguard the liberty of citizens, the Criminal Code requires the police, when attempting to obtain a warrant for an arrest, to demonstrate to a judicial officer that they have reasonable and probable grounds to believe that the person to be arrested has committed the offence. In the case of an arrest made without a warrant, it is even more important for the police to demonstrate that they have those same reasonable and probable grounds upon which they base the arrest.
>
> The importance of this requirement to citizens of a democracy is self-evident. Yet society also needs protection from crime. This need requires that there be a reasonable balance achieved between the individual's right to liberty and the need for society to be protected from crime. Thus the police need not establish more than reasonable and probable grounds for an arrest.[12]

The courts have held that in deciding whether reasonable and probable grounds exist to arrest, a peace officer must consider any information which is relevant. Thus, a police officer cannot simply ignore information which does not incriminate the accused and must consider information which casts doubt on the guilt of the accused.[13] A peace officer who arrests someone must have reasonable and probable grounds to believe that the accused committed the offence that he was arrested for. A peace officer cannot justify an improper arrest on the basis that the officer had reasonable and probable grounds to believe that the accused committed an offence for which the accused was not arrested.[14]

(c) Arrest Without Warrant

Section 495(1)(*a*) authorizes a peace officer to arrest someone who has committed an indictable offence. The officer does not have to see the person commit the offence in order to justify the arrest. However, it is required that the Crown show that the person placed under arrest committed the indictable offence with which he was charged.

A peace officer can also arrest someone if he has reasonable and probable grounds to believe that an indictable offence has been committed. Section

---

[12] *Ibid.*, at 8.
[13] *Chartier v. Quebec (A.G.)* (1970), 104 D.L.R. (3d) 321 (S.C.C.).
[14] R.E. Salhany, *Canadian Criminal Procedure*, 4th ed. (Aurora: Canada Law Book, 1984), at p. 47.

495(1)(*a*) of the Criminal Code states that a peace officer may arrest without warrant a person who, on reasonable and probable grounds, he believes has committed or is about to commit an indictable offence. A peace officer arresting someone under this section will not be liable for false arrest if the person placed under arrest did not actually commit the offence. It is sufficient if the officer has reasonable and probable grounds to believe that the person being arrested has committed or is about to commit an indictable offence. For example, if a peace officer sees someone prying open a window at the back of a house, the officer may well have reasonable and probable grounds to believe that that person is about to commit the indictable offence of breaking and entering.

Section 495(1)(*b*) of the Criminal Code states that a peace officer may arrest without warrant a person whom he finds committing a criminal offence. The Supreme Court of Canada has held that the words, "finds committing," deal with a situation in which the peace officer finds someone committing a criminal offence. In *R. v. Biron*,[15] Martland J. stated:

> Paragraph (b) applies in relation to any criminal offence and it deals with the situation in which the peace officer himself finds an offence being committed. His power to arrest is based upon his own observation. Because it is based on his own discovery of an offence actually being committed there is no reason to refer to a belief based upon reasonable and probable grounds.[16]

(d) Arrest on Outstanding Warrant

A peace officer may arrest someone whom he has reasonable and probable grounds to believe is wanted on an outstanding warrant. Section 495(1)(*c*) of the Criminal Code states that a peace officer may arrest without warrant "a person in respect of whom he has reasonable and probable grounds to believe that a warrant of arrest or committal . . . is in force within the territorial jurisdiction in which the person is found." A peace officer who has reasonable and probable grounds to believe that a warrant has been issued for the arrest of an accused, will not be liable for false arrest if the warrant is subsequently found to be illegal. He, in common with all others executing an act related to the administration of justice, will be protected by section 25 of the Criminal Code:

> **25.** (1) Every one who is required or authorized by law to do anything in the administration or enforcement of the law
> (*a*) as a private person,
> (*b*) as a peace officer or public officer,
> (*c*) in aid of a peace officer or public officer, or

---

[15] (1975), 30 C.R.N.S. 109 (S.C.C.).
[16] *Ibid.*, at 114.

(*d*) by virtue of his office,
is, if he acts on reasonable grounds, justified in doing what he is required or authorized to do and in using as much force as is necessary for that purpose.

(2) Where a person is required or authorized by law to execute a process or to carry out a sentence, that person or any person who assists him is, if that person acts in good faith, justified in executing the process or in carrying out the sentence notwithstanding that the process or sentence is defective or that it was issued or imposed without jurisdiction or in excess of jurisdiction.

(e) Breach of the Peace

A peace officer may arrest someone for breaching the peace. Section 31 of the Criminal Code states that:

31. (1) Every peace officer who witnesses a breach of the peace and every one who lawfully assists the peace officer is justified in arresting any person whom he finds committing the breach of the peace or who, on reasonable and probable grounds, the peace officer believes is about to join in or renew the breach of the peace.

(2) Every peace officer is justified in receiving into custody any person who is given into his charge as having been a party to a breach of the peace by one who has, or who on reasonable and probable grounds he believes has, witnessed the breach of the peace.

There is not much authority as to what constitutes a breach of the peace. The well-known English criminal law professor, Glanville Williams, has defined a breach of the peace in his article, "Arrest for Breach of the Peace," as follows:

Apart from arrest for felony . . . the only power of arrest at common law is in respect of breach of the peace. Anybody may arrest for a breach of the peace committed in his presence or reasonably feared by him, provided that the arrest is made with sufficient promptitude.

The expression "breach of the peace" seems clearer than it is and there is a surprising lack of authoritative definition of what one would suppose to be a fundamental concept in criminal law. Of course, "breach of the peace", as a technical expression has a narrower meaning than the breach of the Queen's peace which is supposed to underlie every crime . . . . The most flagrant instance of a breach of the peace is a riot . . . . The same is true of an unlawful assembly which has not yet become riot. So also a fight between two or more persons is a breach of the peace. . . . There may be a breach of the peace without any general disorder.[17]

---

[17] G. Williams, "Arrest for Breach of the Peace" (1954), Crim. L. Rev. 578.

(f) Arrest for Breach of Summons, etc.

The bail provisions or judicial interim release provisions have already been discussed in Chapter 4, A Basic Overview of the Criminal Code. A person may also be released upon a promise to appear, an appearance notice, summons or recognizance or may be released as a result of the show cause or judicial interim release hearing. A justice of the peace who has reasonable and probable grounds to believe an accused has violated a summons, appearance notice, promise to appear, undertaking or recognizance, may issue a warrant for the arrest of the accused. In addition, a peace officer who has reasonable and probable grounds to believe that an accused has violated a promise to appear, appearance notice, summons, undertaking or recognizance, may arrest the accused without a warrant. The provisions authorizing the arrest of the accused on a promise to appear, etc., are set out in section 524 of the Criminal Code. Section 524 provides as follows:

> **524.** (1) Where a justice is satisfied that there are reasonable and probable grounds to believe that an accused
> (a) has contravened or is about to contravene any summons, appearance notice, promise to appear, undertaking or recognizance that was issued or given to him or entered into by him, or
> (b) has committed an indictable offence after any summons, appearance notice, promise to appear, undertaking or recognizance was issued or given to him or entered into by him,
> he may issue a warrant for the arrest of the accused.
> (2) Notwithstanding anything in this Act, a peace officer who believes on reasonable grounds that an accused
> (a) has contravened or is about to contravene any summons, appearance notice, promise to appear, undertaking or recognizance that was issued or given to him or entered into by him, or
> (b) has committed an indictable offence after any summons, appearance notice, promise to appear, undertaking or recognizance was issued or given to him or entered into by him,
> may arrest the accused without warrant.

(g) Entering Private Property to Make an Arrest

If a peace officer finds someone committing a criminal offence, or has reasonable and probable grounds to believe that someone has committed or is about to commit an indictable offence, can the peace officer, acting without a warrant, enter private property to make the arrest?

The Criminal Code does not indicate whether a peace officer may enter private property to make an arrest. The Supreme Court of Canada has held that resort must be had to the common law to determine a peace officer's power to effect an arrest on private property. In *Eccles v. Bourque*,[18] the court

---

[18] (1974), 19 C.C.C. (2d) 129 (S.C.C.).

held that a criminal may not take refuge in his home or in someone else's home. Accordingly, a peace officer has the right to forcibly enter someone's home to make an arrest where the officer has reasonable and probable grounds to believe that the person wanted for committing a criminal offence is on the premises. In holding that a peace officer may enter private property to arrest a fugitive, without the consent of the homeowner, Dickson J. stated:

> For these principles we go back to vintage common law . . . in which the princi-
> ple, so firmly entrenched in our jurisprudence, that every man's house is his
> castle, was expressed in these words . . . "That the house of every one is to him
> as his castle and fortress, as well for his defence against injury and violence, as
> for his repose . . .". That, then, is the basic principle, as important today as in
> Biblical Times . . . or in the 17th century. But there are occasions when the inter-
> est of a private individual in the security of his house must yield to the public
> interest, when the public at large has an interest in the process to be executed. The
> criminal is not immune from arrest in his own home nor in the home of one of his
> friends.

. . . .

> The *Criminal Code* empowers a justice, on proper grounds being shown, to issue
> a warrant authorizing the search for things but there is no power to issue a war-
> rant to search for persons. Counsel for Mr. Eccles advanced the argument that if
> a fugitive was in the home of a friend a police officer could not enter to arrest
> unless the homeowner gave consent. I cannot agree that this properly expresses
> the position in law. If that be right, a fugitive could obtain permanent sanctuary
> merely by residing with a friend. I know of no place that gives a criminal fugitive
> sanctuary from arrest.

. . . .

> I would wish to make it clear, however, that there is no question of an unrestricted
> right to enter in search of a fugitive. Entry can be made against the will of the
> householder only if (a) there are reasonable and probable grounds for the belief
> that the person sought is within the premises; and (b) proper announcement is
> made prior to entry.

> . . . in the execution of criminal process the test is whether there are reasonable
> and probable grounds for acting. If so, the entry does not become unlawful if the
> fugitive is not found on the premises. The entry of the police is legal or illegal
> from the moment of entry and does not change the character from the result. . . .
> If the police officer has reasonable and probable cause to believe that the person
> named in the warrant for arrest is in the home of a stranger he has the right, after
> proper demand, to enter the home forcibly, to search and to arrest.

. . . .

> Except in exigent circumstances, the police officers must make an announcement
> prior to entry. There are compelling considerations for this. An unexpected intru-
> sion of a man's property can give rise to violent incidents. It is in the interests of
> the personal safety of the householder and the police as well as respect for the

privacy of the individual that the law requires, prior to entrance for search or arrest, that a police officer identify himself and request admittance. No precise form of words is necessary. . . . The traditional demand was "Open in the name of the King." In the ordinary case police officers, before forcing entry, should give (i) notice of presence by knocking or ringing the doorbell, (ii) notice of authority, by identifying themselves as law enforcement officers and (iii) notice of purpose, by stating a lawful reason for entry. Minimally they should request admission and have admission denied although it is recognized that there will be occasions on which, for example, to save someone within the premises from death or injury or to prevent destruction of evidence or if in hot pursuit, notice may not be required.[19]

In the more recent case of *R. v. Landry*,[20] the Supreme Court reaffirmed the principles stated in the *Eccles* decision, saying that *Eccles* is not limited to circumstances where a peace officer has a warrant for the arrest of an accused so that a peace officer acting without a warrant may forcibly enter a dwelling-house to make an arrest. In *Landry*, Chief Justice Dickson stated the reasons for permitting a peace officer to forcibly enter someone's premises to search for a suspect without a warrant. The Chief Justice stated:

Crime is often committed adjacent to residential premises. When a police officer witnesses a crime or appears on the scene shortly thereafter, his ability to apprehend the offender should not be capable of being fooled by an offender ducking into a nearby house or apartment building. Our society is more urban, more mobile, and more anonymous than ever before. If a police officer is forced to obtain an arrest warrant before entering a residence, he will have to attempt to obtain the name of the offender from neighbours. In many cases the offender may have slipped into someone else's dwelling and the neighbours will be unable to supply this information. In other cases the offender may indeed have taken refuge in his own dwelling, but the neighbours may not know him. Even if the police officer is fortunate enough to obtain the offender's name, he will have to seek a justice of the peace to execute an arrest warrant. Valuable time — and probably the offender — will be lost because, when the police officer finally returns with this warrant, the offender will have sought refuge elsewhere.

These serious limitations against effective police work and public protection must be balanced against the intrusiveness of arresting a person in a house or apartment. This intrusiveness is carefully delineated and restricted by the requirement of reasonable and probable grounds for the belief that the person sought is within the premises, and the requirements of notice of presence, notice of authority and notice of purpose. These requirements minimize the invasiveness of arrest in a dwelling and permit the offender to maintain his dignity and privacy by walking to the doorway and surrendering himself.

. . . .

I am unable . . . to fathom how a warrant for arrest can be perceived as a solution to the question of police authority to trespass incidental to arrest. The warrant is

---

[19] *Ibid.*, at 131-134.
[20] [1986] 1 S.C.R. 145 (S.C.C.).

a judicial authorization to arrest and contains no express power of trespass. The justice of the peace must be given evidence as to the reasonable and probable grounds for making an arrest, but hears no evidence as to the likelihood or otherwise that the offender can be found at any particular location. There is no good reason, therefore, why the presence or absence of a warrant of arrest should have any bearing on the right to make an arrest in one particular place or another.[21]

Thus, the fundamental question is whether a peace officer entering someone's premises to make an arrest is in execution of his or her duty. Chief Justice Dickson stated that a peace officer making an arrest in the circumstances described above is in execution of his or her duty "for the purposes of s. 450(1)(a) [495(1)(a)] of the *Criminal Code* if the criteria of that section and the standards enunciated in *Eccles v. Bourque* have been satisfied."[22] His Lordship held that, in determining whether a peace officer is in execution of his or her duty, the following questions should be asked:

1. Is the offence in question indictable?
2. Has the person who is the subject of arrest committed the offence in question or does the peace officer, on reasonable and probable grounds, believe he or she has committed or is about to commit the offence in question?
3. Are there reasonable and probable grounds for the belief that the person sought is within the premises?
4. Was proper announcement made before entry?

An affirmative answer to all these questions will mean that the arrest was lawful.[23]

Accordingly, a peace officer seeking to enter premises to arrest someone can forcibly enter if the officer has reasonable and probable grounds to believe that the accused committed, or is about to commit, an indictable offence, and is in the premises, and makes proper announcement before forcibly entering the premises.

3. SEARCH AND SEIZURE

(a) Statutory Authority

A peace officer has statutory authority to search and seize objects which have been used in the commission of a criminal offence or which will afford evidence with respect to a criminal offence. A peace officer's principal

---

[21] *Ibid.*, at 161-162.
[22] *Ibid.*, at 164.
[23] *Ibid.*, at 165.

powers of search and seizure are found in section 487 of the Criminal Code. This section authorizes a justice of the peace to issue a search warrant in circumstances where a peace officer has reasonable grounds to believe

> that there is in a building, receptacle or place
> (*a*) anything on or in respect of which any offence against this Act or any other Act of Parliament has been or is suspected to have been committed,
> (*b*) anything that there is reasonable ground to believe will afford evidence with respect to the commission of an offence against this Act or any other Act of Parliament or
> (*c*) anything that there is reasonable ground to believe is intended to be used for the purpose of committing an offence against the person for which a person may be arrested without warrant. . . .

Where a justice of the peace is satisfied that the grounds for issuing a warrant, as described above, have been met, the justice may issue a warrant authorizing the peace officer "to search the building, receptacle or place for any such thing and to seize it . . . and bring the thing seized before . . . the justice."

The term "search" is defined in *Black's Law Dictionary*, 5th ed., as:

> An examination of a man's house or other buildings or premises, or of his person, or of his vehicle, aircraft, etc., with a view to the discovery of contraband or illicit or stolen property, or some evidence of guilt to be used in the prosecution . . . for some crime or offense with which he is charged.[24]

(b) Drug Searches

Before 1985, a police officer searching a dwelling-house for drugs was required to obtain a search warrant under the Narcotic Control Act; the Criminal Code did not authorize a police officer to search a dwelling-house for drugs. In 1985, section 443(1) [s. 487] of the Criminal Code was amended to include the words "or any other Act of Parliament." In *R. v. Grant*,[25] the Supreme Court of Canada held that the addition of the words *or any other Act of Parliament* to section 487 of the Criminal Code left no doubt that a police officer could use a Criminal Code search warrant under this section to search a dwelling-house for drugs. The police now have a choice of obtaining a warrant under section 12 of the Narcotic Control Act or under section 487 of the Criminal Code. However, where the police search a dwelling-house for drugs, pursuant to the provisions of the Criminal Code, they will be bound by the Criminal Code's more limited powers of search and seizure. A discussion of the differences between a Narcotic Control Act warrant and a search warrant issued under section 487 of the Criminal Code is contained in Chapter 8, Search and Seizure.

---

[24] *Black's Law Dictionary*, 5th ed. (St. Paul, Minn.: West Publishing Co., 1979), at p. 1211.
[25] (1993), 24 C.R. (4th) 1, at 24 (S.C.C.).

(c) Searching a Person

(i) *Generally*

A Criminal Code search warrant does not authorize a police officer to search a person and in general a police officer has no power to search someone who is not under arrest. Thus, a police officer's power to search only arises once an accused has been arrested. In other words, the officer's power to search is said to arise as an incident of arrest, which means following the arrest. This general rule is subject to two exceptions, the first of which is contained in the provisions of section 101 of the Criminal Code, which authorizes a peace officer to search someone whom he believes has committed an offence in relation to weapons, such as carrying a prohibited weapon or restricted weapon. This section, in effect, authorizes a peace officer who, on reasonable grounds, believes someone is carrying a restricted or prohibited weapon, to search that person prior to the person being placed under arrest. The second exception to the rule is found in section 11 of the Narcotic Control Act, which authorizes a peace officer to search someone found in the premises being searched.

The general rule pertaining to search and seizure has been expressed by Mr. Justice Martin of the Ontario Court of Appeal in *R. v. Rao*:

> At common law there is no power to search premises without a warrant (or with a warrant except for stolen goods) save as incident to a lawful arrest. After making a lawful arrest, an officer has the right to search the person arrested and take from his person any property which he reasonably believes is connected with the offence charged, or which may be used as evidence against the person arrested on the charge, or any weapon or instrument that might enable the arrested person to commit an act of violence or effect his escape: see *Gottschalk v. Hutton* (1921), 36 C.C.C. 298 at pp. 301-2, 66 D.L.R. 499 at pp. 502-3, [1922] 1 W.W.R. 59 (Alta. S.C.A.D.); *Dillon v. O'Brien and Davis* (1887), 16 Cox C.C. 245. The power to search the person of the arrestee has generally been considered to extend to the premises where he is arrested and which are under his control: see the *Report of the Canadian Committee on Corrections* (1969), at p. 62; Leigh, *Police Powers in England and Wales*, at p. 51. Thus, where a person has been arrested in his house, it seems that his house may be searched for evidence of the crime with which he is charged: see *Ghani v. Jones*, supra, at pp. 1165-6.[26]

(ii) *Searching premises under person's control*

Mr. Justice Martin suggests that a peace officer who searches someone as an incident of arrest may search the premises under the accused's control.

---

[26] (1984), 40 C.R. (3d) 1 at 19 (Ont. C.A.).

His Lordship states that "where a person has been arrested in his house, it seems that his house may be searched for evidence of the crime with which he is charged"[27] and quotes a British case, *Ghani v. Jones*,[28] in support of this proposition. There have not been many Canadian cases which have considered a peace officer's power to search the premises of the person placed under arrest. Despite Martin J.A.'s view that the power to search someone as an incident of arrest extends to the premises where that person is arrested, it is not clear that a peace officer has the power to search as an incident of arrest the premises where the person is arrested.

There are few Canadian cases which consider this issue and it is not clear what area may be searched pursuant to a peace officer's power to search someone as an incident of arrest. In the United States, the Supreme Court of the United States has held that police officers searching someone as an incident of arrest cannot search the accused's house, but can only search the immediate area within the accused's reach. Although the law is unclear in Canada, the better view appears to be that a peace officer is only entitled to search the immediate area where the arrest took place. A search of someone's home is regarded as an invasion of privacy, which is why the courts have not permitted someone's home to be searched without a warrant.

(iii) *Reasons for searching person*

Historically, the justification for searching someone as an incident of arrest was to obtain weapons that may have been used in the commission of an offence, or to prevent the destruction of property which was used to commit an offence. A peace officer placing someone under arrest should be, and is, entitled to search the person for weapons and for property which may have been used in the commission of the offence. This seems reasonable as in any civilized society an accused cannot be allowed to threaten a peace officer with a weapon or destroy property which is related to the offence. A peace officer who searches the accused person will be able to discover weapons or evidence related to the commission of an offence and someone who is placed under arrest will not be able to hide a weapon or destroy evidence related to the offence which he or she is alleged to have committed. Once an accused has been arrested and searched following the arrest the immediate threat that the accused would threaten a peace officer with a weapon or destroy evidence is no longer present. If a peace officer believes that evidence relating to the commission of the offence is not on the accused's person but elsewhere in the house, the officer should obtain the appropriate search warrant and the officer's ground for so believing should be canvassed by a justice of the peace. In

---

[27] *Ibid.*
[28] [1970] 1 Q.B. 693 (C.A.).

other words, a search as an incident of arrest should not be used as a pretext to justify warrantless searches and seizure when the law may be enforced by obtaining a warrant.

(iv) *Consent searches*

A peace officer who does not have legal authority to search someone or something may nevertheless conduct a search and seizure if the officer has the person's consent to do so. Thus, if a peace officer does not have a warrant to search a house, but the owner of the house consents to the house being searched, the search of the house would not constitute an improper search. A court may question the consent given if there is evidence that a person consenting to being searched was detained or did not realize that he or she could refuse such consent.

4. LIMITS ON POLICE POWERS

(a) Detention

If a person is detained or arrested, a police officer must advise the person of the reasons for his detention or arrest and of his right to retain and instruct counsel without delay. In addition, the person must be given a reasonable opportunity to retain counsel and must be advised as to the existence of legal aid or duty counsel in the area in which he resides.

It will be a question of fact as to whether someone being questioned by the police is detained. It is not within the scope of this chapter, however, to discuss the circumstances under which section 10 can come into play, as a detailed discussion of section 10 is contained in Chapter 5, A Person's Rights and Obligations Under the Criminal Law. For purposes of this chapter, it is sufficient to note that a police officer's powers to detain are not absolute.

(b) Arrest Jurisdiction of a Peace Officer

A peace officer does not have unlimited power to arrest, as the officer's power is limited by statute and common law. Thus, for example, a municipal police officer does not have province-wide authority and is not entitled to arrest someone who is found in another municipality. In *R. v. Stewart*,[29] the

---

[29] (1982), 66 C.C.C. (2d) 481 (N.B.C.A.).

New Brunswick Court of Appeal held that a peace officer appointed by the City of Saint John did not have the legal authority to arrest someone who was found in a territorial area covered by the R.C.M.P. In *Stewart*, a Saint John police detective was told by his superior officer that the appellant was wanted on an outstanding warrant. The officer, who was informed that the appellant was in the territorial jurisdiction of the R.C.M.P., was instructed to arrest the accused. The accused was convicted of escaping from lawful custody while under arrest. The trial judge held that the accused's arrest was justified on the basis of section 495 of the Criminal Code and section 12 of the New Brunswick Police Act.[30] Section 495(1)(*c*) of the Criminal Code provides:

> **495**. (1) A peace officer may arrest without warrant
>
> . . . .
>
> (*c*) a person in respect of whom he has reasonable grounds to believe that a warrant of arrest or committal, in any form set out in Part XXVIII in relation thereto, is in force within the territorial jurisdiction in which the person is found.

Section 12 of the New Brunswick Police Act states:

> **12**. (1) Each police officer appointed under this Act . . . shall discharge his responsibility
>
> . . . .
>
> (*h*) in the case of a police officer appointed for a municipality or region, . . .
> (iii) when he is investigating a matter that arose wholly or partially within, or is pursuing a person fleeing from a municipality or region for which he was appointed, throughout the Province. . . .

Mr. Justice La Forest rejected the trial judge's rationale, saying:

> If the contention advanced by the respondent [i.e., the Crown] were accepted, it would mean that the territorial limitations imposed on peace officers could be overridden by the simple device of a superior officer instructing a peace officer to arrest someone outside his jurisdiction. These territorial limitations were, no doubt, provided for to ensure that peace officers were, with certain exceptions, limited in exercising their powers to the area over which those who appointed them have responsibility. This ensures political as well as judicial scrutiny over those given power to restrict the liberty of the individual.
>
> Reference is made to s. 12 . . . of the *Police Act*. That section, of course, confers no further power on a peace officer. It merely imposes duties on him when he exercises powers otherwise given to him to act outside his territorial jurisdiction.

---

[30] S.N.B. 1977, c. P-9.2.

Finally, the fact that Detective Desmond was accompanied by an officer who might lawfully have made the arrest makes no difference. The arrest was not made by that officer.[31]

In *Stewart*, the New Brunswick Court of Appeal suggested that the New Brunswick Police Act authorized a municipal police officer to arrest someone outside his or her jurisdiction if the officer was in hot pursuit of a fleeing suspect. The "hot pursuit" issue raised by the New Brunswick Court of Appeal has been settled by the Supreme Court of Canada in *Roberge v. R.*[32] Lamer J. held that a police officer who chases a fleeing suspect from one province into another province is justified in arresting the suspect providing that the officer had lawful authority to arrest the suspect:

> I would . . . find that as a matter of law a peace officer who had lawful authority to arrest a person under s. 450 in one province and is pursuing that person retains . . . his status of a peace officer in another province inasmuch as the pursuit had commenced lawfully in his jurisdiction and as long as such pursuit is fresh.

> I would add one reservation.

> The police officer should endeavour to contact the local peace officers as soon as is possible, even during the pursuit, circumstances permitting. Once the local authorities have taken over the pursuit, he ceases to be a peace officer and becomes then a person assisting peace officers under s. 449(1)(*b*). . . .[33]

(c) Lack of Reasonable and Probable Grounds for Arrest

A peace officer can be sued for false arrest if the officer makes an illegal arrest, but an officer who arrests the wrong person will not be liable for false arrest if the officer acted on reasonable and probable grounds. In such circumstances, the officer is protected by section 25 of the Criminal Code (see earlier discussion of section 25 in this chapter).

(d) Use of Force in Execution of Duty

Section 25 does provide that such a person is not justified in using force intended or likely to cause death or grievous bodily harm unless he believes, on reasonable grounds, that it is necessary to preserve himself or someone under his protection from death or harm. He may use as much force as is necessary to prevent a person being arrested from fleeing unless the escape can

---

[31] *Supra*, note 29, at 484.
[32] (1983), 33 C.R. (3d) 289 (S.C.C.).
[33] *Ibid.*, at 307.

be prevented in a less violent manner. Thus, police officers are not entitled to apply a throat hold in an arrest for a drug offence unless there are reasonable and probable grounds for believing the person being arrested is a drug user and has drugs in his mouth.[34] Each case will depend on its own facts as to whether such reasonable and probable grounds were present. It should be noted that the right to use force applies not only in the case of an arrest, but to any situation where someone has a duty to enforce the law.

Subject to the restrictions about reasonable grounds and the use of excess force, a peace officer who arrests an accused for committing a criminal offence or for committing an indictable offence may use reasonable force to arrest the accused. A peace officer who has reasonable and probable grounds to believe that an accused apparently committed an assault is justified in using reasonable force to arrest the accused. In making the arrest, the peace officer must be acting in execution of his or her duty. If the officer uses excessive force in arresting someone, the officer will not be in execution of his or her duty and will be liable for the excessive force used. Section 26 of the Criminal Code provides that:

> Every one who is authorized by law to use force is criminally responsible for any excess thereof according to the nature and quality of the Act that constitutes the excess.

This section makes a peace officer criminally responsible for any excessive use of force so that an officer who used excessive force in arresting someone could be convicted of assault under the Criminal Code. An officer who uses excessive force in making an arrest may, depending upon the circumstances of the case, be charged with one of the more serious offences in the Criminal Code. Thus, in *R. v. O'Donnell; R. v. Cluett*,[35] a Nova Scotia police constable was convicted of manslaughter after a jury concluded that he had used excessive force in assaulting a citizen who was suspected of having committed a criminal offence. An officer is not entitled to use force in making an investigation only.[36]

(e) Arrest of Wrong Person

Section 28 of the Criminal Code deals with a situation where a peace officer arrests the wrong person:

28. (1) Where a person who is authorized to execute a warrant to arrest believes,

---

[34] *Scott v. R.* (1974), 20 C.C.C. (2d) 65 (Fed. T.D.), affirmed (1975), 24 C.C.C. (2d) 261 (Fed. C.A.).

[35] (1982), 3 C.C.C. (3d) 333 (N.S.C.A.).

[36] *Ibid.*, at 347.

in good faith and on reasonable grounds, that the person whom he arrests is the person named in the warrant, he is protected from criminal responsibility in respect thereof to the same extent as if that person were the person named in the warrant.

(2) Where a person is authorized to execute a warrant to arrest,

(*a*) every one who, being called upon to assist him, believes that the person in whose arrest he is called on to assist is the person named in the warrant, and

(*b*) every keeper of a prison who is required to receive and detain a person who he believes has been arrested under the warrant,

is protected from criminal responsibility in respect thereof to the same extent as if that person were the person named in the warrant.

This section protects a peace officer or someone assisting him from criminal responsibility, such as being charged with assault if force is applied in arresting a person believed to have committed a criminal offence. As with section 25, this section presupposes that a peace officer or person assisting the officer believes in good faith and on reasonable grounds that the person arrested is the person named in the warrant. If an officer does not have reasonable grounds to believe that the person arrested is the person named in the warrant he will not be protected from criminal responsibility.

(f) Use of Force in Investigating an Offence

It is well-established in law that a peace officer may question anyone who is suspected of committing a criminal offence. However, generally speaking, there is no obligation on a citizen to answer police questions and a police officer is not entitled to detain the citizen for questioning. In this respect, the powers of a peace officer are limited, as was recognized by Martin J.A. in *R. v. Dedman*,[37] a judgment of the Ontario Court of Appeal:

> In carrying out their general duties, the police have limited powers, and they are entitled to interfere with the liberty and property of the citizen only where such interference is authorized by law. It is, of course, a constitutional principle that the citizen has a right not to be subjected to imprisonment, arrest or physical restraint that is not justified by law, and every invasion of the property of the citizen is a trespass unless legally justified. . . . [w]hen a police officer is trying to discover whether, or by whom, an offence has been committed, he is entitled to question any person, whether suspected or not, from whom he thinks useful information may be obtained. Although a police officer is entitled to question any person in order to obtain information with respect to a suspected offence, he has no lawful power to compel the person questioned to answer. Moreover, a police officer has no right to detain a person for questioning or for further investigation. No one is entitled to impose any physical restraint upon the citizen except as authorized by law, and this principle applies as much to police officers as to anyone else. Although a police officer may approach a person on the street and ask

---

[37] (1981), 59 C.C.C. (2d) 97 (Ont. C.A.).

him questions, if the person refuses to answer the police officer must allow him to proceed on his way, unless, of course, the officer arrests him on a specific charge or arrests him pursuant to s. 450 of the Code where the officer has reasonable and probable grounds to believe that he is about to commit an indictable offence. . . .[38]

The Ontario Court of Appeal's decision in *Dedman* was applied by the Nova Scotia Court of Appeal in *R. v. O'Donnell; R. v. Cluett.*[39]

(g) Use of Force to Prevent Crime

A peace officer is entitled to use force to prevent the commission of an offence. Section 27 of the Criminal Code states:

> **27.** Every one is justified in using as much force as is reasonably necessary
>   (*a*) to prevent the commission of an offence
>   (i) for which, if it were committed, the person who committed it might be arrested without warrant, and
>   (ii) it would be likely to cause immediate and serious injury to the person or property of anyone, or
>   (*b*) to prevent anything being done that, on reasonable grounds he believes would, if it were done, be an offence mentioned in paragraph (*a*).

5. STATEMENTS AND THE POLICE

(a) Duty to Assist the Police

In a famous English case, *Rice v. Connolly,*[40] Lord Parker C.J. stated that although every citizen has a moral duty or a social duty to assist the police there is no legal duty to assist the police. His Lordship pointed out that the right to silence is one of the foremost principles of our common law system. (The right to silence has been extensively discussed elsewhere in this book; see Chapter 5, A Person's Rights and Obligations under the Criminal Law.)

While it is generally a good idea to cooperate with the police, different considerations come into play when someone is a suspect in a case or is charged with a criminal offence. If a person is a suspect in a criminal case anything said to the police may result in charges being laid and a statement subsequently being introduced at the suspect's trial. If someone is innocent of any wrongdoing, it is usually advisable to cooperate with the police officer so

---

[38] *Ibid.*, at 108-109.
[39] *Supra*, note 35, reversed on other grounds (1985), 21 C.C.C. (3d) 318 (S.C.C.).
[40] [1966] 2 All E.R. 649 (H.L.).

that the matter may be cleared up. If a person has committed a criminal offence, he or she should avoid giving any statement to the police about that offence. Police officers have the right to question anyone whom they suspect has committed a criminal offence. However, a suspect can invoke his or her right to silence and refuse to say anything until legal advice has been obtained.

While there is no duty at common law to identify oneself to a police officer or answer the officer's questions, several provincial statutes make it mandatory to produce identification when requested to do so by the police. Thus, for example, it is an offence under the Highway Traffic Act of Ontario for a motorist to refuse to produce a licence when requested to do so by a police officer. Similar statutes exist in other provinces. However, once a driver has identified himself to police he is not required to answer questions about his driving. He can invoke his common law and section 7 Charter right to remain silent.

(b) Giving Information to the Police

A police officer who suspects someone has committed a criminal offence will be gathering evidence to prove that such is the case. A police officer will usually be very anxious to obtain some incriminating statement from a suspect. As a professional investigator, the police officer realizes the usefulness of an incriminating statement freely and voluntarily given. The police are skillful and clever investigators and will often use various stratagems designed to get an accused to make a statement. The police may say that they have a lot of evidence against the accused and that the accused may wish to give his or her side of what happened. The officers may be exaggerating the evidence against the accused. They may be bluffing when they say that they could prove their case without the accused's statement. Accordingly, a person should invoke his or her right to silence and obtain a lawyer. In such circumstances, the police officer should be regarded as an adversary who is attempting to gather sufficient evidence for the Crown to obtain a conviction in court.

(c) Police Strategies

Police officers sometimes use tricks in order to get a suspect to give a statement to the police. In the famous *Evelyn Dick* case,[41] Evelyn Dick was charged with the murder of John Dick. Evelyn Dick was convicted of murder and appealed her conviction to the Ontario Court of Appeal. The Court of Appeal overturned Dick's conviction and ordered a new trial. Evelyn Dick had originally been arrested on a vagrancy charge. The vagrancy arrest had

---

[41] *R. v. Dick* (1947), 87 C.C.C. 101 (Ont. C.A.).

been a pretext to gather information which would implicate Dick in the murder of her husband, John Dick. Police officers questioned Dick about the murder of John Dick without giving her a caution in relation to the murder charge. It was not until she was later arrested for murder that a caution was given. The court held that the statements made in reference to the vagrancy charge should not have been admitted at Dick's murder trial. The improper admission of these statements was one of the main reasons why a new trial was granted. In overturning Dick's conviction, Chief Justice Robertson stated:

> It seems to me to be an abuse of the process of the criminal law to use the purely formal charge of a trifling offence upon which there is no intention to proceed, as a cover for putting the person charged under arrest, and obtaining from that person incriminating statements, not in relation to the charge laid and made the subject of the caution, but in relation to a more serious and altogether different offence.[42]

Chief Justice Robertson held that any statements which were taken before a proper caution was administered and any statements taken before a murder charge was laid were improperly admitted at Dick's trial.

(i) *Procedures in the Fifties*

Police procedure in the 1940's and 1950's was much different than it is today. Some police officers believed that an accused should be isolated from friends, relatives (not to mention lawyers) so that a statement or confession could be obtained as quickly as possible. This point has been noted by the Honourable Roger E. Salhany in his book, *The Police Manual of Arrest, Seizure and Interrogation*:

> It was not long ago that many police officers believed that once a person was arrested, he could be held incommunicado and interrogated until a confession was obtained. In a leading textbook written in the early 1950's by two members of the Chicago Police Scientific Crime Detection Library, Fred E. Inbau and John E. Reid, entitled *Lie Detection and Criminal Interrogation*, it was suggested that arrested persons should be immediately isolated from family and friends so that they could be interrogated effectively.[43]

The methods recommended by Inbau and Reid were used by some police officers in Canada as well. Judge Salhany points out that the use of such methods was emphatically denounced by the Canadian judiciary. Thus, in *Koechlin v. Waugh*,[44] Mr. Justice Laidlaw, writing for the Ontario Court of Appeal, stated:

---

[42] *Ibid.*, at 113-114.

[43] R.E. Salhany, *The Police Manual of Arrest, Seizure and Interrogation*, 3rd ed. (Toronto: Carswell, 1986), at p. 29.

[44] (1957), 118 C.C.C. 24 (Ont. C.A.).

A person in custody should never be denied his right to communicate with his relatives at the earliest reasonable opportunity so that he may avail himself of their advice and assistance. That right ought to be recognized and given effect in all cases, and care should be exercised by police authorities to see that it is not wholly disregarded.[45]

(ii) *Effect of the Charter*

Tactics such as arresting an accused on one charge as a pretext for questioning him on a more serious charge and keeping an accused incommunicado from friends and relatives (and lawyers) until a confession is obtained will result in statements obtained being ruled inadmissible. Section 10(*a*) of the Charter states that everyone has a right on arrest or detention to be informed promptly of the reasons therefor. The failure to so advise an accused will call into question the lawfulness of the arrest and may result in statements obtained as a result of the breach being excluded from the accused's trial. Such is also the case with the right to counsel. Under Section 10(*b*) of the Charter everyone has a right on arrest or detention to retain and instruct counsel without delay and to be informed of that right. The failure to advise an accused as to her right to retain and instruct counsel without delay will, as has been seen in this book, usually result in the exclusion of evidence obtained as a result of such a breach. As a result of the Charter, a police officer who engages in the tactics employed in the *Dick* case will run a substantial risk of having any statements or confession obtained ruled inadmissible.

(iii) *Giving opportunity to consult counsel*

Under section 10(*b*) of the Charter, a police officer has a duty to advise an accused of his or her right, on detention or arrest, to retain and instruct counsel without delay. Section 10(*b*) of the Charter imposes two additional duties upon police officers where a person indicates that he wishes to speak to a lawyer:

1. The police must provide the detainee with a reasonable opportunity to exercise the right to retain and instruct counsel without delay.
2. The police must cease questioning or otherwise attempting to elicit evidence from the person being questioned until that person has had a reasonable opportunity to retain and instruct counsel.[46]

---

[45] *Ibid.*, at 29.
[46] See *R. v. Manninen* (1987), 58 C.R. (3d) 97 at 103-105 (S.C.C.); *R. v. Prosper* (1994), 33 C.R. (4th) 85 at 108 (S.C.C.).

In *Manninen*, Justice Lamer stated:

> In my view . . . the right to counsel was clearly infringed in this case. The respondent clearly asserted his right to remain silent and his desire to consult his lawyer. There was a telephone immediately at hand in the office, which the officers used for their own purposes. It was not necessary for the respondent to make an express request to use the telephone. The duty to facilitate contact with counsel included the duty to offer the respondent the use of the telephone. Of course, there may be circumstances in which it is particularly urgent that the police continue with an investigation before it is possible to facilitate a detainee's communication with counsel. There was no urgency in the circumstances surrounding the offences in this case.
>
> Further, s. 10(*b*) imposes on the police the duty to cease questioning or otherwise attempting to elicit evidence from the detainee until he has had a reasonable opportunity to retain and instruct counsel. The purpose of the right to counsel is to allow the detainee not only to be informed of his rights and obligations under the law but, equally if not more important, to obtain advice as to how to exercise those rights. In this case, the police officers correctly informed the respondent of his right to remain silent and the main function of counsel would be to confirm the existence of that right and then to advise him as to how to exercise it. For the right to counsel to be effective, the detainee must have access to this advice before he is questioned or otherwise required to provide evidence.
>
> . . . .
>
> This aspect of the respondent's right to counsel was clearly infringed in the circumstances of this case. Immediately after the respondent's clear assertion of his right to remain silent and his desire to consult his lawyer, the police officer commenced his questioning as if the respondent had expressed no such desire. Again, there may be circumstances in which it is particularly urgent that the police proceed with their questioning of the detainee before providing him with a reasonable opportunity to retain and instruct counsel, but there was no such urgency in this case.[47]

The Crown argued that the accused had waived or given up his right to counsel by answering questions posed by the police. Justice Lamer rejected this argument, saying:

> While a person may implicitly waive his rights under s. 10(*b*), the standard will be very high. . . . In my view, the respondent's conduct did not constitute an implied waiver of his right to counsel. It seems that he did not intend to waive his right, as he clearly asserted it at the beginning and at the end of the questioning. Rather, the form of the questioning was such as to elicit involuntary answers. The police officer asked two innocuous questions followed by a baiting question which lead the respondent to incriminate himself. In addition, where a detainee has positively asserted his desire to exercise his right to counsel and the police have ignored his request and have proceeded to question him, he is likely to feel that his right has no effect and that he must answer. Finally, the respondent had the right not to be asked questions, and he must not be held to have implicitly

---

[47] *Ibid*, at 104.

waived that right simply because he answered the questions. Otherwise, the right not to be asked questions would exist only where the detainee refused to answer and thus where there is no need for any remedy or exclusionary rule.

For these reasons, I would conclude that the respondent's rights under s. 10(*b*) were infringed.[48]

---

[48] *Ibid.*, at 105-106.The Supreme Court of Canada's judgment in *Manninen* was recently applied in *R. v. Leclair* (1989), 67 C.R. (3d) 209 (S.C.C.). In *Leclair*, the court held that the police had breached section 10(*b*) of the Charter by forcing the accused to participate in a line-up before they had received a reasonable opportunity to retain counsel. The court noted that there is no legal obligation to participate in a line-up and held that the identification line-up evidence should have been excluded under section 24(2).

7

The Role of the Lawyer

1. THE ROLE OF DEFENCE COUNSEL

(a) General Duty

A defence counsel has a duty to represent a client to the best of his or her ability. As an advocate, defence counsel has a duty to put forward every argument on behalf of the client that will assist the client's cause. It is not up to the defence counsel to pass upon the guilt or innocence of the client. A client who confesses his or her guilt to defence counsel is still entitled to be defended to the best of counsel's ability. The confession of guilt, however, places certain restrictions upon defence counsel. If a client tells his lawyer that he committed the crime the lawyer is restricted in the kind of evidence he or she may call. In such circumstances, a lawyer cannot suggest an alibi. However, defence counsel is entitled to put the Crown to the strict proof of the offence which the client is charged with committing and can rely upon recognized legal technicalities or defences.

In 1969, the Law Society of Upper Canada held special lectures which dealt with defending a criminal case.[1] At these lectures several prominent defence counsel appeared and answered questions concerning the duties of a defence lawyer. The late Joseph Sedgwick, Q.C., a well-known Ontario criminal lawyer, dealt with the question as to whether a defence lawyer can defend a client when the client has admitted his guilt to the lawyer. The question was posed by the then Chief Justice of the Supreme Court of Ontario, Chief Justice Gale:

> Chief Justice Gale: Thank you. Let's pass on to the second question. What is the position of counsel when defending a client who has admitted his guilt?

> 1. What restrictions does this place upon the conduct of the trial by counsel?

---

[1] *Defending A Criminal Case, Special Lectures of the Law Society of Upper Canada* (Toronto: Richard De Boo Ltd., 1969).

2. Assume that counsel has explained the limitations which the client's admission imposes on counsel and the client agrees to permit counsel to defend him in accordance with these limitations but during the trial he insists upon giving evidence and gets into the witness box.

Mr. Sedgwick, would you take this on?

Mr. Sedgwick: Yes sir. Probably the question precisely as it is put is a little too broad but I take it to mean — has counsel the right to defend one whom he knows or believes to be guilty?

The question is, as to a client who has admitted his guilt. Guilt is a question of mixed law and fact. Some years ago I was retained to defend a man who, being harassed beyond all endurance by the woman with whom he was living, surrendered himself to the police, telling them that while he had gone through a form of marriage with the lady, he had thereby committed bigamy as he was already married. He signed a full confession and the police obligingly charged him and locked him up. He languished in jail for a few weeks and began to feel sorry for himself and got in touch with some relatives who retained me to defend him. His voluntary confession was, of course, complete and damaging but when I went over the facts with him I learned that he had been separated from his first wife for some 10 years before the second, and supposedly bigamous, marriage and that during all that time he had no news of wife number one. Although it turned out that she was still alive and living somewhere in the United States, under Section 240 of the Code he had outlasted his seven years and was not guilty. That defence prevailed and the gentleman was acquitted of the charge of bigamy to which he had not only been willing but anxious to plead guilty.

Chief Justice Gale: Did the end result cause him to be happy?

Mr. Sedgwick: Oh, it was the happiest result ever. He got rid of both women. Well, I cite that personal experience to point out what I have said that the client who admits his guilt may only be saying that he did something and in law he may not be guilty of any offence, or at least he may not be guilty of the offence with which he is charged. However, assuming that the guilt of the accused seems reasonably clear, counsel is still entitled to put forward any defence available. As for instance such legal or technical defences as may go to the form of the indictment, limitations, etc. He may not, however, put forward a lying defence, such as an alibi. Nor a fortiori may he put forward any defence that goes to prove that some person other than the accused is the guilty party. This he must explain to his client so that he will not misunderstand the ethical limitations to which counsel is subject, and he should get the client's concurrence to the proposed course of conduct.

As to the second part of the question, Mr. Martin has dealt with that in part. The accused has the right to give evidence and counsel has no right to prevent him although he may and, of course, should give his opinion as to the wisdom of that course.[2]

---

[2] *Ibid.*, at 287.

The noted Harvard law professor and criminal defence attorney, Alan M. Dershowitz, in his book, *The Best Defence*, characterized the duty of the defence lawyer in saying: "The criminal lawyer's job, for the most part, is to represent the guilty, and — if possible — to get them off."[3] This must be accomplished within the rules just discussed. The Law Society of Upper Canada, which is the governing body regulating lawyers who practise law in Ontario, has enacted rules which set out a lawyer's duty and responsibility to clients.

(b) Proper Professional Conduct

The Law Society of Upper Canada's Rules of Professional Conduct are set out in the Law Society's *Professional Conduct Handbook*. The handbook contains 26 rules which regulate a lawyer's conduct with clients, members of the profession and the tribunal before whom he or she is appearing. The rules are followed by commentaries which deal in a more specific manner with the ethical problems which lawyers encounter in the practice of law. Some of the rules are directly relevant to the practice of criminal law. Rule 10 deals with the lawyer's role as an advocate. This rule states:

> When acting as an advocate the lawyer, while treating the tribunal with courtesy and respect, must represent the client resolutely and honourably within the limits of the law.

Commentary 2 of Rule 10 deals directly with the proper ethical conduct which is to be expected from an advocate. This commentary states:

> 2. The lawyer has a duty to the client to raise fearlessly every issue, advance every argument, and ask every question, however distasteful, which the lawyer thinks will help the client's case and to endeavour to obtain for the client the benefit of every remedy and defence authorized by law. The lawyer must discharge this duty by fair and honourable means, without illegality and in a manner consistent with the lawyer's duty to treat the tribunal with candour, fairness, courtesy and respect.

The lawyer must not, for example:

> (a) abuse the process of the tribunal by instituting or prosecuting proceedings which, although legal in themselves, are clearly motivated by malice on the part of the client and are brought solely for the purpose of injuring the other party;

> (b) knowingly assist or permit the client to do anything which the lawyer considers to be dishonest or dishonourable;

. . . .

---

[3] A.M. Dershowitz, *The Best Defence* (New York: Random House, 1982), p. 117.

(e) knowingly attempt to deceive a tribunal or influence the course of justice by offering false evidence, misstating facts or law, presenting or relying upon a false or deceptive affidavit, suppressing what ought to be disclosed, or otherwise assisting in any fraud, crime or illegal conduct;

(f) knowingly misstate the contents of a document, the testimony of a witness, the substance of an argument or the provisions of a statute or like authority;

(g) knowingly assert something for which there is no reasonable basis in evidence, or the admissibility of which must first be established;

(h) deliberately refrain from informing the tribunal of any pertinent authority which the lawyer considers to be directly on point and which has not been mentioned by an opponent;

(i) dissuade a material witness from giving evidence, or advise such a witness to be absent;

(j) knowingly permit a witness to be presented in a false or misleading way, or to impersonate another;

(k) needlessly abuse, hector, or harass a witness;

(l) needlessly inconvenience a witness.

The ethical standards of behaviour set out in Commentary 2 apply to all lawyers who are acting as advocates, whether such lawyers are appearing before a court, administrative tribunal or other body.

(i) *Rules applicable to defence counsel*

There are rules which apply specifically to defence counsel. Commentary 10 sets out the duties of defence counsel in a criminal case. This commentary makes it clear that a lawyer's duty is to raise every possible defence and technicality allowed by law on behalf of his or her client. In addition, Commentary 10 unequivocally states that it is not the defence lawyer's duty to make an ethical judgment about the guilt or innocence of his client. Such a judgment should be left to the trier of fact — namely, the judge or jury. Commentary 10 leaves no doubt that a lawyer may continue to act for a client who has confessed his guilt to the lawyer. This commentary states:

10. When defending an accused person the lawyer's duty is to protect the client as far as possible from being convicted except by a tribunal of competent jurisdiction and upon legal evidence sufficient to support a conviction for the offence with which the client is charged. Accordingly, and notwithstanding the lawyer's private opinion as to credibility or merits, the lawyer may properly rely upon any

evidence or defences including so-called technicalities not known to be false or fraudulent.

Commentary 10 recognizes that there is a distinct difference between factual guilt and legal guilt. A person may have committed a crime but not be guilty of the offence charged because the Crown has not proven its case or the accused has a good technical defence. The notion fostered by television shows and movies that defence lawyers only represent innocent clients, and that it is somehow unethical for a lawyer to defend a client who has confessed his or her guilt to the lawyer, is clearly dispelled by Commentary 10. A similar rule exists in the Canadian Bar Association's Code of Professional Conduct. While the Law Society of Upper Canada's rules recognize that it is justifiable for a lawyer to raise technical defences on behalf of a guilty client, the rules recognize that in cases where a client has confessed his or her guilt to the lawyer such a confession imposes restrictions upon the lawyer's conduct of the defence. The Law Society of Upper Canada's *Professional Conduct Handbook* deals with this situation in Rule 10, Commentary 11:

> 11. Admissions made by the accused to the lawyer may impose strict limitations on the conduct of the defence, and the accused should be made aware of this. For example, if the accused clearly admits to the lawyer the factual and mental elements necessary to constitute the offence, the lawyer, if convinced that the admissions are true and voluntary, may properly take objection to the jurisdiction of the court, or to the form of the indictment, or to the admissibility or sufficiency of the evidence, but must not suggest that some other person committed the offence, or call any evidence which, by reason of the admissions, the lawyer believes to be false. Nor may the lawyer set up an affirmative case inconsistent with such admissions, for example, by calling evidence in support of an alibi intended to show that the accused could not have done, or in fact had not done, the act. Such admissions will also impose a limit upon the extent to which the lawyer may attack the evidence for the prosecution. The lawyer is entitled to test the evidence given by each individual witness for the prosecution and argue that the evidence taken as a whole is insufficient to amount to proof that the accused is guilty of the offence charged, but the lawyer should go no further than that.

(ii) *Defence counsel as officer of the court*

Implicit in the Law Society's Rules of Professional Conduct quoted above is the concept that defence counsel is an officer of the court. As an officer of the court the lawyer has a duty to be scrupulously fair with the court and not to mislead the court. A lawyer who deliberately misleads the court on matters of law or on the facts of the case will be violating his or her position as an officer of the court in addition to breaching the Law Society's Rules of Professional Conduct. In many jurisdictions there is specific legislation which makes a lawyer an officer of the court. Thus, for example, in Ontario, section

29 of the Law Society Act[4] states: "Every member is an officer of every court of record in Ontario."

The lawyer's role as an officer of the court is inconsistent with the view of some members of the public that the defence counsel is nothing but a mouthpiece for his or her client. An advocate's duty was eloquently stated in the Irish case of *R. v. O'Connell*[5] by Mr. Justice Crampton, who categorically rejected the mouthpiece perception of lawyers saying:

> Another doctrine broached by another eminent Counsel I cannot pass by without a comment. That learned Counsel described the Advocate as the mere mouthpiece of his client; he told us that the speech of the Counsel was to be taken as that of the client; and thence seemed to conclude that the client only was answerable for its language and sentiments.

> Such, I do conceive, is not the office of an Advocate. His office is a higher one. To consider him in that light is to degrade him. I would say of him as I would say of a member of the House of Commons — he is a representative, but not a delegate. He gives to his client the benefit of his learning, his talents and his judgment; but all through he never forgets what he owes to himself and to others. He will not knowingly misstate the law — he will not wilfully misstate the facts, though it be to gain the cause for his client. He will ever bear in mind that if he be the Advocate of an individual, and retained and remunerated (often inadequately) for his valuable services, yet he has a prior and perpetual retainer on behalf of truth and justice; and there is no Crown or other license which in any case, or for any party or purpose, can discharge him from that primary and paramount retainer.[6]

(iii) *Solicitor-client privilege*

Aside from the general duty to present the best case for the client, a lawyer has a duty to respect the client's confidences. At common law, there is a solicitor-client privilege which attaches to conversations between a lawyer and his or her client when the client has consulted a lawyer. The privilege is a broad one and covers written correspondence as well as oral conversations. A conversation or written correspondence which is privileged is not admissible at the accused's trial. A solicitor-client privilege only extends to communications which are made for the purpose of obtaining legal advice in respect of the matter on which the client has consulted a lawyer.

For example, if a client is charged with murder and consults a lawyer for advice with respect to the murder charge, anything which the client says to the lawyer will fall under solicitor-client privilege and therefore, cannot be divulged by the lawyer. The privilege will not, however, cover conversations

---

[4] R.S.O. 1990, c. L.8.

[5] (1844), 7 Irish L.R. 261.

[6] *Ibid.*, at 313.

which take place about a matter upon which the lawyer has not been consulted to give legal advice. Accordingly, if a lawyer has been asked to give legal advice in respect of a murder charge or an anticipated murder charge, and the client discusses a robbery, the conversation concerning the robbery will not be privileged unless the lawyer is asked to give legal advice in respect of that matter as well.

The philosophy behind the solicitor-client privilege is that the privilege is essential if a client is to entrust a lawyer with the complete details surrounding his case. It has long been thought that clients would not willingly discuss their affairs with lawyers unless the client was sure that such discussion was privileged. The privilege permits a full and frank disclosure by the client. The privilege is the client's and the lawyer cannot waive or give up the privilege without express permission. A good statement of the rationale for solicitor-client privilege is found in *Anderson v. Bank of British Columbia*,[7] wherein Jessel M.R., of the English Court of Appeal, stated:

> . . . it is absolutely necessary that a man, in order to prosecute his rights or to defend himself . . . should have recourse to . . . lawyers, and . . . equally necessary . . . that he should be able to place unrestricted and unbounded confidence in the professional agent, and that the communications he so makes to him should be kept secret, unless with his consent (for it is his privilege, and not the privilege of the confidential agent). . . .[8]

The Law Society of Upper Canada's Rules of Professional Conduct make it clear that lawyers are duty bound to respect solicitor-client privilege. Rule 4 states:

> The lawyer has a duty to hold in strict confidence all information concerning the business and affairs of the client acquired in the course of the professional relationship, and should not divulge any such information unless expressly or impliedly authorized by the client or required by law to do so.

The Canadian Bar Association has a similar rule governing confidential information. The rules governing solicitor-client privilege can give rise to interesting situations. Suppose that a client is released upon bail after having signed a $2,000 recognizance and agreed to remain within the jurisdiction. If the client leaves the country he will be in breach of his recognizance and may be charged with a criminal offence arising out of the failure to comply with the terms of his recognizance. The client advises his lawyer that he intends to flee the country. As an officer of the court, does the lawyer have a duty to inform the authorities that his client intends to flee the jurisdiction in breach of his recognizance? This question was posed at the special lectures held by the Law Society of Upper Canada by the then Chief Justice of the Supreme Court of Ontario, Chief Justice Gale, to Joseph Sedgwick, Q.C.:

---

[7] (1876), 2 Ch. D. 644.
[8] *Ibid.*, at 649.

Chief Justice Gale: I have a slightly different twist . . . suppose a client for whom you are acting says he is going to take to flight. What would your position be in that situation Mr. Sedgwick?

Mr. Sedgwick: You know I had never thought of it. But what business of mine is it if he leaves the country? If he has been charged with the offence then I assume that he is on bail and if he wants to skip his bail that will be his business. I certainly would not advise him to do so. On the contrary, I would urge him not to and would point out to him that in all likelihood he will be apprehended and his position made much worse by his flight, nevertheless I can't handcuff him to me to keep him in the country and if he leaves the country it will be his business to go and that of the police to catch him wherever he is.

Chief Justice Gale: Do you have any duty to tell the authorities that he is about to take off?

Mr. Sedgwick: No, none whatever. The communication to me is confidential.[9]

(iv) *Duty in relation to incriminating evidence*

A variation of the above occurs when a client arrives at a lawyer's office and deposits incriminating evidence. Suppose that a client attends at his lawyer's office and after confessing to murdering someone deposits the murder weapon with the lawyer. The lawyer must not assist the client in destroying incriminating evidence. If the lawyer gives such assistance, the lawyer will be an accessory after the fact in that he would have assisted the client in getting rid of incriminating evidence. As an officer of the court, a lawyer must be careful in ensuring that he or she does not assist a client in destroying incriminating evidence. Such assistance would violate the law as well as the Rules of Professional Conduct. Chief Justice Gale considered this situation when he posed the following question to Mr. Joseph Sedgwick:

Chief Justice Gale: . . . Counsel is informed by his secretary that there is a man in the waiting room who wishes to see him about a matter of great urgency. The man informs counsel that he wishes to retain counsel to defend him on a murder charge. He expects to be arrested shortly, and then without any warning he produces a gun and puts it on counsel's desk and says, "This is the gun I shot him with." What does counsel do? I suppose what he should do is drop through the floor.

Mr. Sedgwick: Certainly it is not an easy question to answer. Counsel is, of course, an officer of the court and as such he owes a duty to the court and certainly he owes a duty not to conceal or destroy very important evidence and also if he aids in concealing or destroying evidence he may very well put himself in jeopardy as an accessory after the fact under Section 23 of the Code which applies

---

[9] *Defending A Criminal Case, supra*, note 1, at p. 312.

to persons, and lawyers, I suppose, are persons; what the visitor may tell counsel, that is the statement "This is the gun I shot him with", is a privileged communication, but the gun, the physical object, is a piece of evidence and as to it different consideration may well apply. For myself I'd be strongly inclined to hand it back without any advice as to what he should do with it. But if he wouldn't take it or if he ran away before the lawyer could collect his senses and that might well happen, then I think the lawyer should consider handling the gun with great care so as not to either leave any fingerprints on it or obliterate any that might be there and then deliver it to the police or preferably, I think, to the Crown attorney saying merely that a person whose name he cannot divulge left the gun in his office. And then if the man is later arrested and charged with murder, in view of the difficult position of the first lawyer, he should of course decline the defence if it is offered to him. And then if he is subpoenaed as a witness it will be for the trial judge to decide the extent of his privilege as counsel, particularly with relation to the delivery of the gun.[10]

(v) *Pleading client guilty*

It is improper for a client to plead guilty in order to obtain a more lenient sentence. By pleading guilty the client is admitting all the elements of the offence and a client who is innocent should be pleading not guilty. If a client advises his lawyer that he did not commit the crime with which he is charged and intends to plead guilty because he believes he will be treated more leniently, the lawyer is placed in a difficult position. The decision as to how to plead is ultimately the client's. However, having been advised as to the client's innocence the lawyer should not assist a client in pleading to an offence which the client insists he did not commit. To advise the client to plead guilty in such circumstances would be unethical. This point was dealt with in the Law Society of Upper Canada's special lectures on *Defending a Criminal Case* as well. G. Arthur Martin, who was a leading member of the defence bar in Ontario at the time, and is now a retired judge of the Ontario Court of Appeal, dealt with this issue from the defence lawyer's perspective. Chief Justice Gale, the then Chief Justice of Ontario, questioned Mr. Martin as follows:

> Chief Justice Gale: . . . What is the position of counsel where his client has informed him that he is not guilty but he wishes to plead guilty (a) because he thinks he will get a lighter sentence and (b) because he wishes to avoid incriminating his brother. What's your view of that, Mr. Martin?

> Mr. Martin: To permit a client to plead guilty who is innocent and who informs you that he is innocent is really in the nature of a fraud on the administration of justice, and is improper.

---

[10] *Ibid.*, at pp. 311-312.

Sometimes, however, a client will assert his innocence as a sort of face saving device, although a careful investigation, or the evidence adduced at the preliminary hearing makes this position completely untenable, and then he will instruct you that he wishes to plead guilty in order to receive a lighter sentence although he is not guilty. There is a temptation under these circumstances, perhaps, to follow the client's instructions and not take his formal protestations of innocence very seriously.

I think, however, that so long as the client persists in maintaining his innocence after you have confronted him with the evidence against him, and have explained the relevant law, that it is preferable not to represent him for the purpose of entering a plea of guilty.[11]

(c) Canadian Bar Association Rules

The Canadian Bar Association's Code of Professional Conduct contains wording which is substantially similar to the Rules of Professional Conduct set out by the Law Society of Upper Canada; thus, for example, the Canadian Bar Association has adopted Rule 10, Commentary 11 of the Law Society of Upper Canada Rules, which appears as Rule IX, Commentary 11, under the heading "Duty of Defence Counsel."

2. ROLE OF CROWN COUNSEL

(a) Generally

The role of Crown counsel has been eloquently summarized by Mr. Justice Rand in a 1955 judgment of the Supreme Court of Canada wherein His Lordship stated:

It cannot be over-emphasized that the purpose of the criminal prosecution is not to obtain a conviction; it is to lay before a jury what the Crown considers to be credible evidence relevant to what is alleged to be a crime. Counsel have a duty to see that all available legal proof of the facts is presented: it should be done firmly and pressed to its legitimate strength, but it must also be done fairly. The role of the prosecutor excludes any notion of winning or losing; his function is a matter of public duty than which in civil life there can be none charged with greater personal responsibility. It is to be efficiently performed with an ingrained sense of dignity, the seriousness and the justness of judicial proceedings.[12]

In *R. v. Logiacco*,[13] the Ontario Court of Appeal stated:

---

[11] *Ibid.*, at p. 318.
[12] *Boucher v. R.* (1955), 20 C.R. 1 at 8 (S.C.C.).
[13] (1984), 11 C.C.C. (3d) 374 (Ont. C.A.).

It has been said before but perhaps it should be repeated that the role of the Crown Attorney in the adminstration of justice is of critical importance to the courts and to the community. The Crown prosecutor must proceed courageously in the face of threats and attempts at intimidation. He must see that all matters deserving of prosecution are brought to trial and prosecuted with diligence and dispatch. He must be industrious to ensure that all the arduous preparation has been completed before the matter is brought before the court. He must be of absolute integrity, above all suspicion of unfair compromise or favouritism. The Crown prosecutor must be a symbol of fairness, prompt to make all reasonable disclosures and yet scrupulous in attention to the welfare and safety of witnesses. Much is expected of the Crown prosecutor by the courts. The community looks upon the Crown prosecutor as a symbol of authority and as a spokesman for the community in criminal matters.

In the vast majority of cases, the trust to the public is well placed. Generally, the agents of the Crown carry out their duties in an exemplary manner. They personify the virtues required of their office and perform their onerous obligations in a dedicated and skilful manner that reflects great credit on their profession and office.[14]

(b) Crown Counsel vs. American District Attorney

In Canada, the role of the Crown prosecutor is distinctly different from that of an American District Attorney. The Crown prosecutor, unlike the local District Attorney in most of the American states, is not an elected official and is appointed by the government in power. Thus, Crown attorneys do not run on law and order election platforms and are expected to be independent of public pressure and pressure from the police. The Crown attorney is not an agent of the police and unlike his American counterpart does not have an investigatory staff which attends at the scene of the crime and assists the police in conducting an investigation. The Crown attorney is expected to present all the relevant facts which shed light upon the offence with which the accused is charged to the trial judge or the jury, as the case may be.

The Law Society of Upper Canada's Rules of Professional Conduct and the Canadian Bar Association's Code of Professional Conduct state that the Crown prosecutor should give the accused full disclosure of all the relevant facts and witnesses known to the Crown. The Canadian Bar Association's Code of Professional Conduct states that this should be done whether such disclosure produces facts which tend "toward guilt or innocence." In a similar vein, W.B. Common, Q.C., the former director of public prosecutions for the Province of Ontario, in an address before the joint committee of the Senate and House of Commons on capital and corporal punishment, stated:

---

[14] *Ibid.*, at 378-379.

I might say for those members of the Committee who are unfamiliar with the procedure at a trial — and I am not going into technical matters — it will suffice to say this: that in all of the cases not only in capital cases but usually in all criminal cases there is complete disclosure by the prosecution of its case to the defence. To use a colloquialism, there are no "fast ones" pulled by the Crown. The defence does not have to disclose its case to the Crown. We do not ask for a complete and full disclosure of the case. If there are statements by witnesses, statements of accused, the witness is supplied with copies, they know exactly what our case is and there is nothing hidden or kept back or suppressed so that the accused person is taken by surprise at a trial by springing a surprise witness on him. In other words, I again emphasize the fact that every safeguard is provided by the Crown to ensure that an accused person, not only in capital cases but in every case receives and is assured of a fair and legal trial.[15]

(c) Disclosure of Evidence to the Defence

Mr. Common's address contained the lofty statement that "usually in all criminal cases there is complete disclosure by the prosecution of its case to the defence." Defence lawyers and legal historians will have to judge for themselves whether Mr. Common's statement accurately reflected the situation in Canada in 1955 when the address was given. Whatever the position in 1955, such lofty claims could not be made in the 1970's and 80's.

(i) *Lack of full disclosure*

The *Criminal Code* of Canada does not contain a requirement that the Crown disclose all the evidence which it plans to introduce at trial and there is no legislation which imposes such a requirement on Crown counsel. Although for many years provincial Attorneys General issued guidelines to Crown attorneys advising them as to the kinds of material that should be disclosed to defence counsel before trial, the guidelines were not legally enforceable and the quality of disclosure varied from province to province and from jurisdiction to jurisdiction within a province.

The Nova Scotia policy directive on disclosure, which was issued in 1986, stated, in part, that "the Crown shall make full disclosure of its case to the accused, or counsel for the accused."[16] Unfortunately, the policy was not what it appeared to be. In this regard, the *Royal Commission on the Donald Marshall Junior, Prosecution Report* states:

---

[15] W.B. Common, Q.C., quoted in L. Martin, G. Arthur, Q.C., "Preliminary Hearings" in *Law Society of Upper Canada Special Lectures on Evidence*, 1955, p. 3.

[16] *Royal Commission on the Donald Marshall Junior Prosecution*, Volume 6, at p. 148.

The opening paragraph of the original policy statement was one of the widest and most generous statements of disclosure to be found among its provincial counterparts. However, the initial principle of openness was effectively gutted by exception 3 which would justify limiting or withholding disclosure where "it is felt that disclosure would be contrary to the interest of justice". Such an open-ended exception provided virtually no guidance for Crown prosecutors and potentially risked nullification of any principle of full disclosure.[17]

Dalhousie Law School Professor, A. Wayne MacKay, has attacked the "ex gratia basis" on which most pre-trial disclosure was based. In his article, "The Influence of the Prosecutor: Plea bargaining, Stays of Proceedings, Controlling the Process," MacKay states:

> . . . . thus, pre-trial disclosure is just one of the favours dispensed by the Crown as part of their reciprocal relations with certain defence counsel. In return defence counsel are expected to cooperate by producing a certain number of guilty pleas and not abuse the information disclosed to them.
>
> Disclosure on this basis is simply unacceptable. A client may be prejudiced because he has a defence lawyer who has either not been admitted or specifically excluded from this cozy network for exchanging favours. Indeed if a defence lawyer takes too adversarial a stance and is unwilling to cooperate, the price of ostracism may be high for both the lawyer and his client. To the extent that this practice is allowed to continue it fuels the fires of criticism. The adversary structure becomes no more than a myth and the only real outsider in the process is the accused. Full disclosure of the Crown's case should be the right of the accused and not a privilege to be dispensed at will.[18]

Professor MacKay's opinion is supported by the Law Reform Commission of Canada's 1984 Report, "Disclosure by the Prosecution" where the Commission stated:

> It cannot be said that Canadian criminal law enforces a policy of pre-trial disclosure by the prosecution. Apart from specific and limited requirements currently prescribed by law, pre-trial disclosure in Canada is characteristically an informal process, predicated upon the Crown's discretion in the management of its case. To the extent that it exists, pre-trial disclosure is subject to the vagaries of regional practice, plea bargaining and personal relations among members of the Criminal Bar; for these reasons alone it defies systematic analysis as an integral feature of Canadian criminal procedure.[19]

---

[17] *Ibid.,* at pp. 56-57.

[18] A.W. MacKay, "The Influence of the Prosecutor: Plea Bargaining, Stays of Proceedings, Controlling the Process" in S. Oxner, *Criminal Justice: Proceedings of the 1981 Canadian Institute for the Administration of Justice Conference on Criminal Justice* (Toronto: Carswell, 1981) p. 69 at 72.

[19] Cited in the *Royal Commission on the Donald Marshall Junior Prosecution, supra,* note 16, at p. 241.

The Crown's failure to make full disclosure of its case to the defence impedes the accused's right to make full answer and defence to the charge and may lead to the wrongful imprisonment of an innocent person. The classic Canadian case of a person who was wrongfully convicted on the basis of perjured testimony is that of Donald Marshall Junior. Donald Marshall Junior was imprisoned for 11 years for a murder that he did not commit largely as a result of the perjured testimony given by three Crown witnesses who claimed to have seen Marshall stab the victim, Sandy Seale.

Maynard Chant told Detective John MacIntyre, the Sydney Police Chief who was in charge of the investigation, that he had seen two men stab Sandy Seale. John Pratico stated that he had seen two men running from the direction of the railroad tracks where the stabbing took place. Pratico and Chant were intimidated by Detective MacIntyre into falsely implicating Donald Marshall in the murder of Sandy Seale. The Royal Commission on the Donald Marshal Junior prosecution found that Detective MacIntyre "had extracted these false statements" from Pratico and Chant and had threatened them with perjury if they changed their statements.[20]

The Commission concluded that the false statements "played a significant role in Marshall's wrongful conviction."[21]

Prior inconsistent statements given by Pratico and Chant were not disclosed by the Crown to Donald Marshall's defence counsel. The Marshall Commission found that the Crown counsel who prosecuted Donald Marshall, the late Donald MacNeil, had a practice of disclosing information to defence counsel only if they asked for the information. If counsel failed to ask for the information, MacNeil did not bother disclosing it.[22]

The Marshall Commission concluded that if the Crown had disclosed the previous inconsistent statements made by the witnesses to Donald Marshall's defence counsel, counsel "could have used them to raise at least a reasonable doubt about Marshall's guilt in the minds of the jury."[23] "Both before and after trial, the Crown's failure to disclose information to Marshall's counsel contributed to his conviction and continued imprisonment."[24]

The Crown's failure to disclose crucial evidence in the Donald Marshall case was not unique to the *Marshall* case. In Nova Scotia, disclosure of evidence to defence counsel depended upon whether defence counsel had good relations with the Crown Attorney's office. In this regard, the Honourable Judge Felix Cacchione, a former defence counsel, testified before the Marshall Commission that "full disclosure doesn't really exist as Mr. Giffin (former Attorney General of Nova Scotia) is saying it should exist or does exist." Judge Cacchione stated that "disclosure depended on how well defence

---

[20] *Supra*, note 16, at p. 63.
[21] *Ibid.*, Vol. 1, at p. 55.
[22] *Ibid.*, at p. 72.
[23] *Ibid.*, at p. 72.
[24] *Ibid.*, at p. 238.

counsel got along with the Crown as opposed to a positive obligation on the Crown to disclose."[25]

Canadian courts have consistently taken the position that disclosure of evidence to the defence is to be encouraged but there was no general obligation on the part of Crown counsel to fully disclose the Crown's case. In some cases, judges took the position that disclosure of the Crown's case to the defence depended upon whether it could be said that there was an "air of reality" to the defence which defence counsel intended to use.

The lack of disclosure given to defence counsel in the Donald Marshall case is not unique to Nova Scotia; there have been other cases where defence lawyers have not been apprised of crucial evidence which would assist their clients. In *Cunliffe v. Law Society of B.C.*,[26] the British Columbia Court of Appeal confirmed the Law Society of British Columbia's finding that a Crown counsel was guilty of professional misconduct by failing to disclose crucial evidence in a murder trial which would have given the accused an opportunity to raise a defensive alibi.

In *Cunliffe*, the appellants, Bledsoe and Cunliffe, who were in charge of prosecuting the murder charge, had suppressed important alibi evidence by not advising defence counsel as to the existence of such evidence. The appellant, Bledsoe, knew prior to trial that there were witnesses who could have provided the accused with an alibi defence. Mr. Bledsoe, who at the time was in charge of the case, did not inform defence counsel as to the existence of such witnesses and proceeded to trial without disclosing this information to the accused's lawyer. During the trial, the defence lawyer found out that Crown counsel had suppressed evidence which was favourable to the accused and made a motion to the trial judge for an adjournment. Although counsel's application for an adjournment was not granted, counsel was successful in obtaining an order from the court directing the Crown to provide statements of all alibi witnesses to defence counsel. The Crown was also directed to call alibi witnesses to the stand so that they might be cross-examined by defence counsel.

After the accused was acquitted of the murder charge, his lawyer lodged a complaint against Bledsoe and Cunliffe to the Discipline Committee of the Law Society of British Columbia. The Law Society subsequently found the appellants guilty of professional misconduct. In reference to the appellant Bledsoe, the court held that the Law Society's finding that he was guilty of conduct unbecoming a barrister and professional misconduct was justified. The appellant Bledsoe had originally prosecuted the accused for murder and the appellant Cunliffe took over the case when the new trial was granted after the original judge declared a mistrial. When Cunliffe took over the case, he was not advised by the previous Crown counsel, Bledsoe, that the Crown had

---

[25] *Ibid.*, at p. 58.
[26] (1984), 40 C.R. (3d) 67 (B.C.C.A.).

not disclosed the existence of the alibi evidence to defence counsel. In upholding the findings of the Law Society that the appellant, Bledsoe, was guilty of professional misconduct, Hinkson J.A. stated:

> Upon the basis of the findings of fact made by the Discipline Committee it is clear that Mr. Bledsoe failed in his duty to advise Mr. Ritchie in a timely manner of the existence of additional Thursday witnesses once he learned of Mr. Ritchie's ignorance of such witnesses. Mr. Bledsoe was clearly in breach of his duty because he never informed Mr. Ritchie that such witnesses existed. Upon becoming aware that Mr. Ritchie was ignorant that such witnesses existed, Mr. Bledsoe's first decision was to postpone performing his duty until the weekend, when he could consult senior counsel. When the mistrial occurred he then decided to leave it to the prosecutor who would take the second trial to inform Mr. Ritchie. By the time he instructed Mr. Cunliffe on 16th December 1977 he was clearly in breach of his duty but he could have remedied that breach by informing Mr. Cunliffe that Mr. Ritchie was unaware of the existence of the additional Thursday witnesses. Mr. Bledsoe failed to do so therefore he never performed his duty as Crown counsel.
>
> It is extremely important to the proper administration of justice that Crown counsel be aware of and fulfill their duty to be fair. Therefore I would dismiss the appeal of Mr. Bledsoe.[27]

The British Columbia Court of Appeal overturned the Law Society's finding that the appellant, Cunliffe, was guilty of conduct unbecoming of a member of the Society and of professional misconduct; it held that the appellant, Cunliffe, complied with the directions of the court once he had been advised that defence counsel was not aware of the alibi evidence and that in a criminal case Crown counsel has a discretion as to which witnesses to call. In *Cunliffe*, the British Columbia Court stated that the Law Society of British Columbia erred in concluding that Cunliffe should have called the additional alibi witnesses to the stand as part of the Crown's case, saying that he did not exercise his discretion unfairly by not calling such witnesses. The court noted that the trial judge could have called the alibi witnesses and allowed them to be cross-examined by Crown counsel and defence counsel.

In reference to disclosure by the Crown, the Marshall Commission stated that "anything less than complete disclosure by the Crown falls short of decency and fair play."[28] The Commission stated:

> If the integrity of the judicial system in criminal law is to be maintained, we must eliminate those anachronistic and out-moded procedures which breed contempt for the law and which, if left unchecked, will continue to impede the administration of justice. An obligation on the Crown to make full disclosure to the defence is the foundation upon which a fair and efficient system of administration of criminal justice can be built and maintained.[29]

---

[27] *Ibid.*, at 78.

[28] *Supra*, note 16, Vol. 1, at p. 238.

[29] *Ibid.*, at p. 242.

The Commission believed that decisions regarding disclosure of information to the defence should not be left to the whim of Crown counsel or the judge presiding at the accused's trial and called for federal legislation requiring the Crown to disclose all information known to the Crown that may be useful to the accused.[30] Despite the Commission's calls for federal legislation dealing with disclosure, the federal government ignored the Marshall Commission's recommendations; it was not until the Supreme Court of Canada handed down its landmark decision in *R. v. Stinchcombe*[31] that the accused became entitled to the full disclosure which the Marshall Commission had recommended.

(ii) *In Stinchcombe*

Traditionally, many Crown counsel had resisted full disclosure to the defence on the basis that disclosure of information would allow the defence to tailor its evidence to conform with the evidence which was in the Crown's possession. It was also suggested that disclosure of certain information would put at risk the safety of some Crown witnesses. In *Stinchcombe*, the Supreme Court of Canada unanimously held that the Crown has a duty to disclose all relevant evidence to the defence where the accused is charged with an indictable offence. Sopinka J., writing for the court, gave short shrift to the arguments against disclosure, saying:

> It is difficult to justify the position which clings to the notion that the Crown has no legal duty to disclose all relevant information. The arguments against the existence of such a duty are groundless while those in favour are, in my view, overwhelming. The suggestion that the duty should be reciprocal may deserve consideration by this court in the future but is not a valid reason for absolving the Crown of its duty.
>
> .... the fruits of the investigation which are in the possession of counsel for the Crown are not the property of the Crown for use in securing a conviction but the property of the public to be used to ensure that justice is done. In contrast, the defence has no obligation to assist the prosecution and is entitled to assume a purely adversarial role toward the prosecution. The absence of a duty to disclose can, therefore, be justified as being consistent with this role.[32]

Sopinka J. stated that those who feared that disclosure would permit the defence to tailor its evidence for the proposed testimony of Crown witnesses ignored the fact that in civil cases where there is full disclosure of all evidence, there is a possibility that witnesses may change their testimony to conform with a previous statement given. Sopinka J. stated that there is noth-

---

[30] *Ibid.*

[31] (1991), 8 C.R. (4th) 277 (S.C.C.).

[32] *Ibid.*, at 283.

ing wrong with a witness refreshing his or her memory from a previous document or statement given. He stated that although in certain cases there may need to be special measures taken to protect the identity of informers or witnesses, this did not justify the refusal of the Crown to disclose the identity of witnesses. It is evident from *Stinchcombe* that the court believed that in most cases the disclosure of the names of witnesses to the defence would not endanger the safety of such witnesses.

In ordering disclosure of all relevant evidence to the defence, the court was cognizant of the accused's ability to make full answer and defence to the charge and of the miscarriage of justice which had been occasioned by the wrongful conviction of Donald Marshall Junior. The court noted that the Crown's failure to disclose the prior inconsistent statements made by Crown witnesses was an important contributing factor to his wrongful conviction.

In *Stinchcombe*, although the Supreme Court held that there is a continuing duty on Crown counsel to disclose all relevant information to the defence, the court stated that the Crown need not produce information which is irrelevant and the Crown can withhold the identity of persons who have as informers given information to the police.[33] The court also stated that Crown counsel have a discretion as to the timing of disclosure, noting that in some cases early disclosure of information may hinder the completion of an investigation. The discretion exercised by Crown counsel is reviewable by the trial judge. Since the court held that disclosure of all relevant information is the general rule, the Crown must justify any refusal to disclose relevant information.

In *R. v. Durette*,[34] a case decided subsequently to *Stinchcombe*, the Supreme Court held that the section 7 Charter guarantee of the right to make full answer and defence necessitates that as a general rule the Crown is required to provide the accused with all relevant information in its possession. The court stated that the Crown may justify non-disclosure of information in certain cases "by showing that the public interest in non-disclosure outweighs the accused's interest in disclosure."[35]

While *Stinchcombe* dealt with disclosure of evidence in the context of an indictable offence, the courts will apply similar principles to the summary conviction setting. Consequently, the Crown will be required in summary conviction cases to disclose all relevant evidence to the defence.

3. GUARANTEE OF COUNSEL

Section 650(3) of the Criminal Code states:

---

[33] *Ibid.*, at 287-288.
[34] (1994), 28 C.R. (4th) 1 (S.C.C.).
[35] *Ibid.*, at 20.

An accused is entitled, after the close of the case for the prosecution, to make full answer and defence personally or by counsel.

The Sixth Amendment of the United States Constitution states:

In all criminal prosecutions, the accused shall enjoy the right . . . to have the Assistance of Counsel for his defence.

Although the Charter does not contain an express guarantee of state-funded counsel, the Ontario Court of Appeal has held that in cases not falling within provincial legal aid plans where the representation of the accused is essential to a fair trial, section 7 and section 11(*d*) of the Charter require that the accused be provided with funded counsel if he wishes counsel but cannot afford to pay for a lawyer. In *R. v. Rowbotham*,[36] the Ontario Court of Appeal held that a trial judge may stay proceedings against the accused until the accused receives the required funding to hire counsel.

(a) Effective Assistance of Counsel

A number of courts have recently held that the accused has a right to the effective assistance of counsel at trial. In *R. v. Silvini*,[37] the Ontario Court of Appeal held that the right of an accused to make full answer and defence to a charge under section 7 of the Charter includes the right to receive effective assistance of counsel. In *Silvini*, and subsequent cases, the Ontario Court of Appeal has held that where an accused argues that a new trial should be granted by reason of ineffective assistance of counsel, the accused must not only show that counsel's assistance was ineffective, but must demonstrate that counsel's errors where so deficient that the accused has been deprived of a fair trial.

In *R. v. Brigham*,[38] the Quebec Court of Appeal granted the accused a new trial, holding that his counsel did not have the required skill and confidence necessary to conduct his defence. In this case, counsel for the accused was warned by a psychiatrist that the accused's mental condition might deteriorate during the trial so that he would no longer be considered fit to stand trial. The accused, who was charged with first degree murder, had insisted on testifying at his trial. The accused's counsel refused to call him to the stand to testify because of his deteriorating mental condition and did not inform the court as to the accused's deteriorating state of mind. The majority of the Court of Appeal held that counsel was under a duty to inform the court of the

---

[36] (1988), 63 C.R. (3d) 113 at 173 (Ont. C.A.).
[37] (1991), 9 C.R. (4th) 233 at 245-246 (Ont. C.A.).
[38] (1992), 18 C.R. (4th) 309 at 310 (Que. C.A.).

accused's deteriorating mental condition and to suggest that the court re-examine whether the accused was fit to stand trial in light of his deteriorating mental condition. The court overturned the accused's conviction for first degree murder and ordered a new trial based upon the majority's finding that the accused's counsel did not provide effective assistance of counsel at trial.

The courts will not lightly grant a new trial because of ineffective assistance of counsel. In *R. v. Sarson*,[39] the Nova Scotia Court of Appeal held that in order to establish that the accused (appellant) has received ineffective assistance of counsel, the accused must convince the court that (i) defence counsel was not competent and (ii) there is a reasonable probability that but for counsel's unprofessional errors, the results of the trial would have been different. Although several courts have now determined that there is a constitutional right under section 7 and section 11(*d*) of the Charter to the effective assistance of counsel, the courts will be loath to second guess tactical decisions made by counsel. In this regard, the Ontario Court of Appeal in *R. v. Lomage*[40] has stated that it is not the function of an appellate court to play the role of a "Monday morning quarterback" when determining whether an accused has received the effective assistance of counsel.

The section 7 Charter right to effective assistance of counsel is a welcome development. In the United States, accused persons have long been entitled to a constitutional right to the effective assistance of counsel. Furthermore, in England, which does not have a written constitution, a conviction will be set aside where there is a "lurking doubt that the appellant might have suffered some injustice as a result of flagrantly incompetent advocacy."[41] Although there are not many cases where an accused has received ineffective assistance of counsel, this is of no consolation to an accused who has been convicted as a result of counsel's incompetence.

The Marshall Commission found that the failure of defence counsel to obtain crucial statements made by Crown witnesses contributed to Donald Marshall's conviction. The Commission concluded that Donald Marshall Junior "did not get the professional service to which any accused is entitled." The Commission stated:

> Had defence counsel taken even the most rudimentary steps an accused should be entitled to expect from his or her counsel, it is difficult to believe Marshall would have been convicted."[42]

---

[39] (1992); 77 C.C.C. (3d) 233 at 238 (N.S. C.A.).
[40] (1991), 2 O.R. (3d) 621 at 630 (Ont. C.A.).
[41] *R. v. Swain*, [1988] Crim. L.R. 109 (C.A.); *R. v. Ensor* (1989), 89 Cr.App.R. 139 (C.A.).
[42] *Supra*, note 16, Vol. 1, at p. 77. The Commission concluded that Marshall's defence lawyers were skilled lawyers, saying that race played a role in the "totally inadequate defence" provided to Marshall.

8

Search and Seizure

1. SEARCH WARRANT

(a) Introduction

The law pertaining to search and seizure is complex and multi-faceted. In Canada, the state's power of search and seizure is derived from common law and statute law. Although the Criminal Code[1] is the source of much of our search and seizure law, there are several federal and provincial statutes apart from the Criminal Code which contain search and seizure powers. Statutes such as the Competition Act[2] and the Narcotic Control Act[3] contain sections which authorize search and seizure. However, not all search and seizure law is codified in statute and many of the principles pertaining to search and seizure are derived from British common law. Under common law, a man's home was his castle, and except for the very limited purpose of searching for stolen property, the king's officers were not permitted to search someone's home without his permission.

The age-old common law principle that a man's home was his castle dates back to 1604 in *Semayne's* case where the court expressed this principle in the following words: "that the house of everyone is to him as his castle a fortress, as well for his defence against injury and violence, as for his repose . . . ."[4] Search warrants developed because there was generally no right to search a man's home without his permission and even today there is no common law authority to search someone's home without the permission of the owner or occupier.[5] The principles expressed in *Semayne's* case continue to guide us today so that if a court finds a search warrant is invalid a civil action

---

[1] R.S.C. 1985, c. C-46.
[2] R.S.C. 1985, c. C-34.
[3] R.S.C. 1985, c. N-1.
[4] *Semayne's Case* (1604), 77 E.R. 194.
[5] J.A. Fontana, *The Law of Search and Seizure in Canada*, 2nd ed. (Toronto: Butterworths, 1984), p. 2. See also the 3rd edition at pp. 1-8.

can be brought against a person who searches the premises. Furthermore, the material seized under an invalid search warrant may not be admissible at the accused's trial.

(b) Search Warrant Defined

The Chief Justice of Canada, Brian Dickson, defined the term search warrant in *Nova Scotia (Attorney General) v. MacIntyre*:

> A search warrant may be broadly defined as an order issued by a Justice under statutory powers, authorizing a named person to enter a specified place to search for and seize specified property which will afford evidence of the actual or intended commission of a crime. A warrant may issue upon a sworn information and proof of reasonable grounds for its issuance. The property seized must be carried before the justice who issued the warrant to be dealt with by him according to law.

> Search warrants are part of the investigative pre-trial process of the criminal law, often employed early in the investigation and before the identity of all of the suspects is known. Parliament, in furtherance of the public interest in effective investigation and prosecution of crime, and through the enactment of section 443 of the Code, has legalized what would otherwise be an illegal entry of premises and illegal seizure of property.[6]

(c) Prerequisites to Obtaining a Search Warrant

(i) *Criminal Code requirements*

The requirements which must be fulfilled before a search warrant is issued are set out in section 487(1) of the Criminal Code:

> **487.** (1) A justice who is satisfied by information upon oath . . . that there are reasonable grounds to believe that there is in a building, receptacle or place
> (*a*) anything on or in respect of which any offence against this Act or any other Act of Parliament has been or is suspected to have been committed,
> (*b*) anything that there are reasonable grounds to believe will afford evidence with respect to the commission of an offence, or will reveal the whereabouts of a person who is believed to have committed an offence, against this Act or any other Act of Parliament, or
> (*c*) anything that there are reasonable grounds to believe is intended to be used for the purpose of committing any offence, against the person for which a person may be arrested without warrant,

---

[6] (1982), 65 C.C.C. (2d) 129 at 141 (S.C.C.).

may, at any time issue a warrant under his hand authorizing the person named therein or a peace officer,

(*d*) to search the building, receptacle or place for any such thing and to seize it, and

(*e*) subject to any other Act of Parliament, to, as soon as practicable, bring the thing seized before, or make a report in respect thereof to, the justice or some other justice for the same territorial division in accordance with section 489.1.

(ii) *Information upon oath*

In order to obtain a search warrant it is necessary that an informant swear an information upon oath before a justice of the peace. The information must fulfill the requirements stated in Form 1 of the Criminal Code. The informant must describe the things to be searched for and set out the offence in respect of which the search is to be conducted. The informant must state that he has reasonable and probable grounds for believing that the items to be searched for are in the building where the search is to take place. The justice of the peace must be apprised as to what constitutes the reasonable and probable grounds. An information which does not state such grounds for the informant's belief that the items are to be found on the premises to be searched will not be valid. In most cases, the informant is a police officer who swears out an information based upon his personal knowledge or information that he has received from a confidential source. A warrant will not be issued simply because a police officer has reasonable and probable grounds to believe that there is in the place being searched something which will afford evidence of the commission of an offence. Issuing a search warrant is a judicial act and the justice of the peace must be satisfied that the requirements of section 487 have been met.[7]

(iii) *Justice of the peace must act judicially*

The offence must be described in the warrant itself or in the information attached to the warrant. There must be sufficient detail about the person whose premises are being searched so that the person is able to know the nature of the offence and the object of the search.[8] If the warrant does not contain sufficient detail to describe the premises being searched, it will be quashed as being invalid. The justice of the peace must also be satisfied that there are reasonable and probable grounds for believing that there is in a place something which will afford evidence with respect to the commission of an

---

[7] *R. v. Moore* (1922), 37 C.C.C. 72 (Alta. C.A.).

[8] *Borden & Elliot v. R.* (1975), 30 C.C.C. (2d) 337 at 347 (Ont. C.A.); *PSI Mind Development Institute Ltd. v. R.* (1977), 37 C.C.C. (2d) 263 at 268 (Ont. H.C.).

offence. Only then can he be said to be acting judicially. Thus, if a justice of the peace neglects to read the search warrant or the information upon which the warrant is based, he cannot be said to have acted judicially and a civil suit may be brought against him for negligence.

In *R. v. Gray*,[9] drugs obtained pursuant to a search warrant were excluded under section 24(2) of the Charter as the justice of the peace in issuing the warrant had not acted as an independent judicial officer but, rather, as an arm of the police. In *Gray*, there was evidence that members of the Winnipeg Police Department would have a justice of the peace review the information to obtain a warrant to see whether the information was properly worded. In some cases, the justice would dictate the wording of the information in order to make sure that the information was worded in a manner which was acceptable to him. In this case, the Manitoba Court of Appeal held that a practice whereby justices of the peace assisted in preparing the information to obtain a search warrant was a serious breach of the accused's section 8 Charter right to be secure against unreasonable search and seizure. The court held that the justice of the peace who had issued the warrant to search a dwelling-house for narcotics had acted "as if she were an adjunct of the police investigation rather than as a neutral and detached assessor of the evidence advanced in favour of the granting of a warrant."[10] In holding that section 8 of the Charter had been violated and that the evidence should have been excluded from the accused's trial under section 24(2), Scott C.J.M., writing for a majority of the court, stated:

> In my opinion the impugned practice disclosed by the evidence resulted in the failure of the judicial officer to properly exercise her detached independent function. Where direction is given by a judicial officer respecting the contents of the information to obtain on a material point going to the merits of the application, he/she simply becomes an agent or arm of the police. It is not proper for the police to present a judicial officer with an unsigned or incomplete information to obtain and, after receiving inappropriate direction with respect not only to the technical language but also the substance of the document, to then swear it in its altered form before the same judicial officer.
>
> It is of course open to a magistrate hearing an application for a warrant and considering the evidence presented to identify deficiencies and to reconsider the application when these deficiencies have been remedied by the police. But that was not what took place in this case.[11]

The requirement to act judicially does not mean that there must be sufficient evidence for a justice of the peace to conclude that the accused will be found guilty of the offence charged. The test which the justice must apply has

---

[9] (1993), 22 C.R. (4th) 114 (Man. C.A.).
[10] *Ibid.*, at 122.
[11] *Ibid.*, at 122-123.

been set out by the British Columbia Court of Appeal in *B.X. Dev. Inc. v. R.*,[12] where Bull J.A. adopted the test laid down by the trial judge, saying:

> It is not the duty of the Justice to adjudicate upon the adequacy of . . . evidence as proof of the commission of the alleged offence. . . . It is enough for him to be satisfied that there is a connection or link between the documents to be sought and the offence as alleged.[13]

Clearly, the justice of the peace or judge has a large discretion as to whether to issue a search warrant.

(d) The Role of Police Officers

The task of preparing a search warrant and the information which the warrant is based upon usually falls to one of the police officers who is investigating the case. Most search warrants which are issued are based upon personal knowledge of the police officers investigating the case or upon information which a police officer has received from a confidential informant. In most cases, a justice of the peace will issue a search warrant based upon the sworn information of a police officer appearing before him. Accordingly, a police officer appearing before a justice of the peace plays an important role in the search warrant process.

The information which the officer provides to the justice of the peace must be accurate and there must be sufficient information for the justice of the peace to authorize a search and seizure. While in certain cases the police officer may consult a Crown attorney before preparing the wording of the information, informations are usually prepared by police officers. The wording of the search warrant and the information is important because an improperly worded warrant or information may lead to the quashing of the warrant. If the warrant is quashed, the search will have been rendered illegal.

Once the search warrant is issued the police officer authorized to conduct the search is responsible for execution of the warrant. This means that the police officer authorized to conduct the search will be responsible for entering the premises searched and seizing the items named in the warrant. Having seized the items named in the warrant, the officer must then take the goods before a justice of the peace in the territorial division in which the warrant was issued.[14]

A defective search warrant or information which is not properly worded

---

[12] (1976), 31 C.C.C. (2d) 14 (B.C.C.A.).
[13] *Ibid.*, at 20.
[14] Fontana, *supra*, note 5, at pp. 84-89.

could lead to a successful Charter[15] application to exclude the evidence obtained from the accused's trial.

In *R. v. Genest*,[16] substantial defects in a search warrant ultimately contributed to the Supreme Court of Canada's decision to exclude the evidence under section 24 of the Charter. The accused, Genest, was charged with possession of illegal weapons and illegal possession of a restricted weapon after the search turned up three weapons. The search of the accused's house was conducted under the Narcotic Control Act because the police had expected to find drugs. The defective search warrant was partially responsible for the trial judge's decision to exclude the evidence obtained from the accused's trial. The trial judge held that the search violated section 8 of the Charter and, after considering all the facts in the case, ruled that the admission of the evidence would bring the administration of justice into disrepute.

The accused's acquittal was overturned by the Quebec Court of Appeal and the accused appealed as of right to the Supreme Court of Canada, and the accused's acquittal was restored. In the Supreme Court of Canada, the Crown was forced to concede that the search violated section 8 of the Charter and the only question was whether the evidence obtained in the search should have been admitted or excluded from evidence at the trial.

The *Genest* case provides a textbook illustration of how not to prepare a search warrant. The warrant in *Genest* did not name the police officer who was to conduct the search as is required by section 10(2) [12] of the Narcotic Control Act. The warrant was also defective in that it did not state the items to be searched for, or the hours when the search was to be conducted.

The Crown (respondent in the case) argued in the Supreme Court of Canada that the defects in the search warrant were technical, saying that the evidence obtained in the search should not have been excluded at trial because of a technical error. Chief Justice Dickson, who delivered the judgment of the court, disagreed, saying that the defects were sufficiently serious that they should be considered when determining whether the evidence should be admitted. His Lordship said:

> I do not agree that the defects in the warrant can be described as simply technical. The major defect was that the warrant did not name the officer who was to execute the warrant, as required by section 10(2) of the Narcotic Control Act. That requirement is an important one. It is a special condition for drug searches of dwelling-houses. It is not found in the general Criminal Code search provisions. To ignore this special Parliamentary directive for searches of dwellings is not merely a technical defect. Parliament has stated searches of dwellings for drugs are special. The complete absence of times of execution or a listing of objects to be searched for is a further indication of the worthlessness of the warrant in this case. I think it could be said that the Justice of the Peace issued a fish-

---

[15] Canadian Charter of Rights and Freedoms (being Part I of the Constitution Act, 1982 [en. by the Canada Act, 1982 (U.K.), c. 11, s. 1]).

[16] (1989), 67 C.R. (3d) 224 (S.C.C.).

ing licence, not a search warrant. The power to search a dwelling-house under a section 10(2) warrant is significantly broader than the search power granted by a warrant under section 443 [now section 487] of the Criminal Code, as several courts have noted. A narcotic search warrant can be executed at any time, unlike a Criminal Code warrant which normally must be executed during the day . . . . The naming requirement has been consistently interpreted by the courts as an important part of the search warrant provisions of the Narcotic Control Act, emphasizing the seriousness of a search of a dwelling-house and the extent of the powers granted by the warrant.

. . . .

The naming requirement ensures that there is at least one officer who is responsible for the search, who must be personally present and must supervise the search. Because of the greater infringement of the individual's interests caused by the extensive power to search a dwelling-house, some officer must be accountable for the way the search is carried out. The courts have consistently held that a failure to name the officer in a section 10(2) warrant means that the warrant is invalid. . . .[17]

Chief Justice Dickson criticized the police officers who prepared the search warrant saying:

While it is not to be expected that police officers be versed in the minutiae of the law concerning search warrants, they should be aware of those requirements that the courts have held to be essential for the validity of the warrant. The naming requirement of section 10(2) is one such requirement. In addition, a police officer should be put on his guard by a warrant that contains as many blank spaces as the one in this case. Common sense suggests that if a form is used, it should be properly filled out, especially when the form itself states that certain details are to be inserted in the blanks. . . . The defects in the search warrant were serious and the police officers should have noticed them. I do not think the respondent can argue that the police error was inadvertent. The warrant is defective on its face, whether it was issued under the Narcotic Control Act or the Criminal Code.[18]

(e) The Plain View Doctrine

The plain view doctrine is an exception to the search warrant requirement which normally exists in criminal law. The courts have held that police officers may seize items which are not mentioned in a search warrant when the items being seized are in the plain view of a police officer. The doctrine only applies if a police officer is legally authorized to search the premises. The doctrine does not apply unless the police officer discovered the evidence inadvertently. In other words, if the officer knows in advance the location of

---

[17] *Ibid.*, at 245-247.
[18] *Ibid.*, at 247.

certain evidence and relies on the plain view doctrine to camouflage his real intention, the doctrine will not be applied. Finally, evidence will not be admissible under the plain view doctrine unless it is apparent to the police that the items observed were evidence of a crime or otherwise subject to search and seizure.[19]

2. PARTICULAR KINDS OF SEARCHES

(a) Search by a Private Citizen

In Canada, a private citizen may make a citizen's arrest in the limited circumstances set out by section 494 of the Code. A private citizen who makes a citizen's arrest can search the person arrested as an incident of arrest. The search can be for weapons or property which has been used in the commission of an offence. A private citizen's right to search the person being arrested as an incident of arrest is not absolute and must meet the standard of reasonableness as set out in section 8 of the Charter. In *R. v. Lerke,*[20] Laycraft C.J.A., writing for the Alberta Court of Appeal, stated:

> Where the search is not for weapons, but only to seize or preserve property connected to the offence, different considerations apply. The urgency present in the search for weapons would not ordinarily be present in those cases. Often the triviality of the offence charge or the improbability, in the circumstances, that any evidence will be uncovered or will be destroyed even if the search is delayed, will mean that [sic] search by a citizen would not be a reasonable search. Both the *Petty Trespass Act* and section 449 of the *Criminal Code* contemplate that the offender will be turned over to persons in authority without delay. That being the case, it will be rare that the citizen making an arrest will need to search for evidentiary purposes only. The course of wisdom and the requirement that the search be reasonable will usually dictate that the search for evidence be left until the person arrested is turned over to authority.[21]

The decision of the Alberta Court of Appeal in *Lerke* is consistent with the limited arrest powers which an ordinary citizen has under the Criminal Code. It is not surprising that a private citizen making a citizen's arrest has a more limited search and seizure power than a police officer who, unlike a private citizen, has a statutory duty to maintain the public peace.

---

[19] *R. v. Ruiz* (1991), 10 C.R. (4th) 34 at 41 (N.B.C.A.).
[20] (1986), 49 C.R. (3d) 324 (Alta. C.A.).
[21] *Ibid.*, at 335-336.

(b) Search by Peace Officer

(i) *Criminal Code*

A search may only be conducted as an incident of arrest. There is no general power in the Criminal Code to search someone who has not been placed under arrest. The power to search as an incident of arrest is found in the common law. The principal power for obtaining a search warrant is found in section 487 of the Criminal Code. This section does not authorize a police officer to apply for a warrant to search someone whom the officer suspects of committing a criminal offence. Section 101 of the Code gives a police officer a broad power to search a person for weapons. Apart from section 101, there is no authority in the Criminal Code to search a person.

(ii) *Under federal statutes*

The Narcotic Control Act authorizes a peace officer to search someone who is found in a place which is being searched under the authority of section 10 of the Act. Section 10 authorizes a peace officer to conduct a warrantless search of any place other than dwelling-houses. The section authorizes a peace officer acting under the authority of a warrant to search a dwelling-house where the officer has reasonable grounds for believing that there is a narcotic in respect of which an offence under the Narcotic Control Act has been committed. Section 11 states that a peace officer "may search any person found in a place entered pursuant to section 10 and may seize and, from a place so entered, take away any narcotic found therein, anything therein in which the peace officer reasonably suspects a narcotic is contained or concealed, or any other thing by means of or in respect of which that officer believes on reasonable grounds an offence under this Act has been committed . . . " A similar provision is contained in section 42 of the Food and Drugs Act.[22]

(iii) *At common law*

At common law, a peace officer has a limited authority to search someone as an incident of arrest. Historically, the common law power to search a person as an incident of arrest was limited to circumstances where the officer believed the person placed under arrest was carrying a weapon or where it was

---

[22] R.S.C. 1985, c. F-27.

necessary to preserve evidence relating to the commission of an offence. Under common law, the right of search and seizure was regarded as an extraordinary remedy. It was believed that a person had a reasonable expectation of privacy and that very clear grounds should exist before a search was authorized.

Unless the police are in the possession of a warrant or some other specific authority, they have no right to enter private premises and remain there against the occupier's wishes; where they do, the occupier may regard them as trespassers and use whatever force may be necessary to remove them.[23]

In *R. v. Rao*,[24] Martin J.A. of the Ontario Court of Appeal stated:

> At common law there is no power to search premises without a warrant (or with a warrant except for stolen goods) save as an incident to a lawful arrest. After making a lawful arrest, an officer has the right to search the person arrested and take from this person any property which he reasonably believes is connected with the offence charged, or which may be used as evidence against the person arrested on the charge, or any weapon or instrument that might enable the arrested person to commit an act of violence or effect his escape . . . . The power to search the person of the arrestee has generally been considered to extend to the premises where he is arrested and which are under his control . . . . [25]

The courts have not been willing to place many restrictions on a police officer's right to search a person as an incident of arrest. Generally, the courts have taken the position that a police officer is not required to have reasonable grounds for searching a person being arrested. Accordingly, the officer is not required to have reasonable grounds for believing that weapons or evidence will be found as a result of the search of the arrestee's person.[26]

In *Cloutier v. Langlois*,[27] the Supreme Court of Canada confirmed the view of the lower courts that a police officer is not required to have reasonable and probable grounds for searching a person where the search is conducted as an incident of arrest. However, the court has not given the police an unlimited power to search as an incident of arrest. The court has laid down guidelines which the police must follow in conducting such searches. Madam Justice L'Heureux-Dubé J., writing for the court, stated that the search must be conducted for a valid objective, such as the discovery of a weapon or something that may be used as evidence against the accused. If the purpose of the search was to intimidate or pressure the accused in order to obtain a confession, the search will be improper. Her Ladyship held that the search must not be conducted in an abusive fashion and stated that the police have a discretion as to whether to search at all.

---

[23] *Entick v. Carrington* (1765), 19 State Tr. 1029; today the force used to evict would have to be reasonable.

[24] (1984), 40 C.R. (3d) 1 (Ont. C.A.).

[25] *Ibid.*, at 19.

[26] *R. v. Morrison* (1987), 58 C.R. (3d) 63 at 68 (Ont. C.A.).

[27] (1990), 74 C.R. (3d) 316 (S.C.C.).

The Supreme Court of Canada's decision in *Cloutier* was confined to the common law power of the police to search an arrestee's person as an incident of arrest. The case did not deal with the circumstances in which a search of an arrestee's person may violate section 8 of the Charter. In this case, neither party raised section 8 of the Charter and so the court was not called upon to decide whether the absence of reasonable grounds for a search of the arrestee would infringe any section of the Charter. Although the Supreme Court of Canada would probably find that the Charter does not require that a police officer have reasonable grounds for searching a person being arrested, the Alberta Court of Appeal in *R. v. Lerke* has held that "the right to search on arrest is not automatic; it must be a reasonable search."[28] This means that a search following an arrest must meet the test of reasonableness under section 8 of the Charter.

Although most searches which occur as an incident of arrest are conducted following the accused's arrest, the phrase "incident of arrest" does not preclude a police officer from searching the accused prior to his arrest. In *R. v. Charlton*,[29] the British Columbia Court of Appeal stated:

> A search may occur before or after formal arrest as long as the grounds for the arrest exist prior to the search. Furthermore, property from the accused may be seized where the search is made several hours after the initial arrest where the accused is still in detention. Thus, in *R. v. Miller*, the Ontario Court of Appeal found that a search which was conducted 18 hours after the accused's arrest while the accused was still in detention did not violate section 8 of the Charter. In this regard, the Court held that the search was properly conducted as an incident of the accused's arrest.[30]

The courts have held that the police have the power to search the immediate area surrounding the accused as part of a search conducted as an incident of the accused's arrest. Thus, the police are entitled to search an accused and the car driven by him which is in the immediate surrounding area as an incident of the accused's lawful arrest.[31]

In *R. v. Debot*,[32] the Ontario Court of Appeal held that "the search of a person in Canada, save as an incident to a valid arrest, must be justified by statutory authority." Apart from federal statutes such as the Narcotic Control Act and the Food and Drugs Act, search and seizure powers may be found in many provincial statutes such as liquor laws.

---

[28] (1986), 49 C.R. (3d) 324 at 334-335 (Alta. C.A.).

[29] *R. v. Charlton*, June 22, 1992, Vancouver C.A. 013773 (B.C.C.A.); 16 W.C.B. (2d) 423.

[30] *R. v. Miller* (1987), 38 C.C.C. (3d) 252 at 262-263 (Ont. C.A.).

[31] *R. v. Speid* (1991), 8 C.R.R. (2d) 383 (Ont.C.A.); leave to appeal to S.C.C. refused 55 O.A.C. 391 (note).

[32] (1986), 54 C.R. (3d) 120 (Ont. C.A.).

(c) Search for Weapons

Section 101 of the Criminal Code authorizes a police officer to conduct a warrantless search of a person, vehicle, place or premises, other than a dwelling-house, where the officer has reasonable and probable grounds to believe that someone is committing or has committed an offence relating to the possession of prohibited or restricted weapons, firearms or ammunition.

A provincial court judge has the power to issue a search warrant authorizing a peace officer to search and seize an offensive weapon, ammunition or explosives. The judge must be satisfied that there are reasonable grounds for believing that it is not in the interests of the safety of the person whose premises are being searched for him to have possession of a weapon. A warrant may also be issued when someone else may be in danger.

(d) Search for Drugs

There are several distinct differences between search warrants issued under the Criminal Code and search warrants issued under the Narcotic Control Act. These differences have been outlined by Michael R. Dambrot, a senior lawyer of the Department of Justice, in his article "Search and Seizure." The differences are as follows:

1. The Narcotic Control Act search warrant must name the police officer who is executing the warrant; there is no such requirement in the Criminal Code.

2. A Criminal Code warrant may relate to a search for anything that is intended to be used to commit an offence. The Narcotic Control Act has no such provision.

3. A Criminal Code warrant may be issued to permit a search for evidence of an offence. A Narcotic Control Act warrant authorizes the seizure of such evidence, but a warrant may only be issued in the first instance if there are reasonable grounds to believe that there is a narcotic in a place.

4. A Criminal Code warrant may be issued in relation to any building, receptacle or place. A Narcotic Control Act warrant may only be issued in respect of a dwelling house.

5. A Criminal Code warrant requires that the things seized be brought before a justice. . . . A Narcotic Control Act warrant has no such requirement. . . .

6. A peace officer executing a Narcotic Control Act search warrant, unlike a Criminal Code warrant, is specifically empowered to break open doors, windows, locks, fasteners, floors, walls, ceilings, compartments, plumbing fixtures, boxes and containers for the purpose of his search. . . .

7. A peace officer executing a Narcotic Control Act search warrant may, as a result of section 10(1)(b) [11], search any person found in the place he is

searching. A peace officer executing a Criminal Code search warrant may only keep persons present under "reasonable surveillance."[33]

(e) Search by Customs Officials

Customs officials may search someone who enters Canada provided that the official has reasonable cause to believe that the person being searched is carrying prohibited goods. The authority for such a search is contained in section 98 of the Customs Act.[34] Before such a search can be undertaken, a person may require the officer to take him before a senior customs officer to determine if there are reasonable grounds for a search. In *R. v. Simmons*,[35] the Ontario Court of Appeal held that it is not unreasonable for customs officials to search someone whom they suspect is bringing contraband into Canada, saying that such a search would not violate section 8 of the Charter.

The Ontario Court of Appeal's decision in *Simmons* was upheld by the Supreme Court of Canada which ruled that a warrantless search of someone bringing goods into Canada did not violate section 8 of the Charter. The Supreme Court noted that the warrantless search provisions of the Customs Act did not meet the standards laid down in *Hunter v. Southam Inc.*[36] where the Supreme Court held that a search warrant is usually a pre-requisite of a valid search and seizure. However, the court said that persons entering Canada had a lower expectation of privacy than someone who is normally the subject of a search.

In *Simmons*,[37] the Supreme Court of Canada considered sections 143 and 144 of the former Customs Act (R.S.C. 1970, c. C-40). Both sections authorized a search of a person on reasonable cause, a lower standard than the standard for searches applied in *Hunter v. Southam Inc.* (which is discussed later in this chapter).

Sections 143 and 144 have been replaced by sections 98 and 99 of the present Customs Act. Section 98 authorizes the search of a person where an officer believes on reasonable grounds that the person entering the country has, on his person, goods prohibited by the Customs Act.

Section 99 of the Customs Act contains detailed provisions which authorize customs officers to search someone's luggage or other property where the officers have reasonable grounds to believe that the property being searched contains property which is prohibited under the Customs Act. It should be noted that a peace officer, as defined by section 2 of the Criminal Code, includes a customs officer and thus a customs officer has the same powers of arrest as a peace officer.

---

[33] M.R. Dambrot, "Search and Seizure" in Law Society of Upper Canada Bar Admission Course Materials, *Criminal Procedure, 1986-1987* (Toronto: Carswell, 1986), p. 28.
[34] R.S.C. 1985, c. 1 (2nd Supp.), s. 98.
[35] (1984), 11 C.C.C. (3d) 193 (Ont. C.A.), affirmed (1988), 66 C.R. (3d) 297 (S.C.C.).
[36] (1984), 41 C.R. (3d) 97 (S.C.C.).
[37] (1988), 66 C.R. (3d) 297 (S.C.C.).

3. SECTION 8 OF CHARTER OF RIGHTS

(a) Pre-Charter Position

Prior to the enactment of the Charter, Canadians had very inadequate protection against an unreasonable search and seizure. If police officers entered a house on the basis of a search warrant which was subsequently found to be illegal, the evidence obtained as a result could still be admitted as evidence. The Supreme Court of Canada held in *R. v. Wray*,[38] a 1970 decision of the court, that illegally obtained evidence was admissible, saying that under common law a judge had no discretion to exclude evidence because its admission would bring the administration of justice into disrepute. Thus, if a police officer searched a dwelling-house without a warrant, the evidence obtained, even if it was illegally obtained, would still be admissible. The lack of protection afforded Canadians against unreasonable search and seizure was in marked contrast to the protection afforded by the Fourth Amendment of the U.S. Constitution. The Fourth Amendment of the U.S. Constitution states:

> The right of the people to be secure in their persons, houses, papers, and effects, against unreasonable searches and seizures, shall not be violated, and no warrants shall issue, but upon probable cause, supported by oath or affirmation, and particularly describing the place to be searched, and the persons or things to be seized.

(b) Early Interpretation

When the Charter was enacted in 1982, it contained a clause which protects Canadians against unreasonable search and seizure. Section 8 of the Charter states:

> Everyone has the right to be secure against unreasonable search or seizure.

After the Charter was proclaimed, the courts were treading cautiously in interpreting it and it was not uncommon for judges to hold that the Charter had not transformed the law. The comments of Justice Zuber of the Ontario Court of Appeal typified the sentiments of many judges in the early Charter cases. In *R. v. Altseimer*,[39] Mr. Justice Zuber, who was considering whether an accused witness stopped for a vehicle check had been arbitrarily detained contrary to section 9 of the Charter, stated that the Charter did not "intend a transformation of our legal system or the paralysis of law enforcement." This caution was particularly evident in cases dealing with search and seizure.

---

[38] [1971] S.C.R. 272 at 287.
[39] (1982) 1 C.C.C. (3d) 7 at 13 (Ont. C.A.).

Many courts held that the absence of a search warrant did not necessarily make a search and seizure unreasonable. They took the position that as long as the police officers executing the search had reasonable and probable grounds for making the search they did not need to obtain a search warrant.[40] The courts' initial rulings were undoubtedly based in part upon an awareness that many statutes authorized police officers and other officials to search private premises without obtaining a search warrant. In *R. v. Rao*, the Ontario Court of Appeal noted that the Law Reform Commission of Canada calculated that there are 82 federal statutes which empower designated officials to conduct warrantless searches of premises.[41] Provincial statutes also give provincial officials the power to search premises without obtaining a search warrant. Thus, the warrantless search has wide acceptance in Canada.

In England, which does not have an entrenched constitution giving any protection against unreasonable search, the search of private premises without a warrant is confined to emergency situations. Even in emergency situations a government official cannot search private premises without a warrant unless he or she has obtained the authorization of a senior official.[42] Before the Charter was proclaimed, then, Canadians had fewer protections against having their premises searched without a warrant than their counterparts in England and the United States. To this extent, Canadians were not as free as Englishmen or Americans.

(c) Presumption Against Warrantless Searches

The situation has changed dramatically. It is now a well-recognized principle of Canadian search and seizure law that searches conducted without the authorization of a search warrant are presumed to be unreasonable and must be justified on strict grounds. In *R. v. Rao*, the Ontario Court of Appeal held that section 10(1)(*a*) [10] of the Narcotic Control Act was, to the extent that it authorized the search of an office without a search warrant, unconstitutional as being in violation of section 8 of the Charter.[43] In so holding, the court noted that the absence of a search warrant will be an important factor in determining the reasonableness of a search of premises. The evidence established that the police officers, acting on the basis of information received from a confidential informant, arrested the accused after they found several vials of hashish oil in his business premises. A search, which was not authorized by a search warrant, was conducted under the authority of the Narcotic Control

---

[40] R.E. Salhany, *The Origin of Rights* (Toronto: Carswell, 1986), p. 82.
[41] *Supra*, note 24, at 21.
[42] *Ibid.*, at 22.
[43] *Ibid.*, at 35-36.

Act. The court held that the search was improper and that the admission of the evidence obtained as a result of the search and seizure would bring the administration of justice into disrepute. Martin J.A., who delivered the judgment of the court, stated:

> The legitimate expectation of privacy in one's home or office is one of the most valued rights of the individual afforded protection by a democratic society. As Lamer J., speaking for the Supreme Court of Canada, said in *Descôteaux v. Mierzwinski*, . . . "Searches are an exception to the oldest and most fundamental principles of the common law, and as such the power to search should be strictly controlled."

> The requirement of a warrant provides a safeguard against an intrusion at the discretion of a police officer, and is designed to ensure that the justification for the intrusion will be determined in advance by an impartial judicial officer, rather than left for determination by the officer making the search.

> . . . .

> In my view, the warrantless search of a person's office requires justification in order to meet the constitutional standard of reasonableness secured by s. 8 of the Charter, and statutory provisions authorizing such warrantless searches are subject to challenge under the Charter. The justification for a warrantless search may be found in the existence of circumstances which make it impracticable to obtain a warrant. . . . The individual's reasonable expectation of privacy must, of course, be balanced against the public interest in effective law enforcement. However, where no circumstances exist which make the obtaining of a warrant impracticable and when the obtaining of a warrant would not impede effective law enforcement, a warrantless search of an office of fixed location (except as an incident of a lawful arrest) cannot be justified and does not meet the constitutional standard of reasonableness prescribed by s. 8 of the Charter.[44]

Mr. Justice Martin did not believe that a warrantless search and seizure could never be justified:

> I have, for the reasons I have set forth, concluded that the search of an office without a warrant where the obtaining of a warrant is not impracticable, is unreasonable and, to that extent, s. 10(1)(*a*) is of no force or effect. On the other hand, the search of an office without a warrant in circumstances where it is not practicable to obtain a warrant may be entirely reasonable. Further, a warrantless search of vehicles, vessels or aircraft, which may move quickly away, may be reasonable where there are reasonable grounds for believing that such contains a narcotic.[45]

In *Rao*, Mr. Justice Martin did not completely strike down section 10(1)(*a*) [10] of the Narcotic Control Act. His Lordship simply held that section 10 was inoperative to the extent that it authorized a warrantless search and seizure in circumstances where a warrant could be obtained.

---

[44] *Ibid.*, at 31-33.
[45] *Ibid.*, at 35.

(d) The Importance of *Hunter v. Southam Inc.*

Since the Ontario Court of Appeal handed down its decision in *Rao*, the Supreme Court of Canada delivered a landmark decision in *Hunter v. Southam Inc.*,[46] where it held that there is a presumption that a warrantless search is unreasonable as being in violation of section 8 of the Charter. In so holding, the court allowed for exceptions such as where there is evidence that it was not feasible to obtain a search warrant. Chief Justice Dickson, who delivered the majority judgment for the Supreme Court, held that where it is feasible to obtain a search warrant, the obtaining of a search warrant "is a pre-condition for a valid search and seizure." In *Southam*, which is one of the most important Charter decisions handed down by the Supreme Court of Canada, Chief Justice Dickson stated that the starting point for interpreting the Charter is to determine what purpose the specific Charter guarantee was meant to serve. The effect of Chief Justice Dickson's "purposive" approach to Charter interpretation can be seen when one examines the court's ruling in respect of section 8 of the Charter:

I begin with the obvious. The Canadian Charter of Rights and Freedoms is a purposive document. Its purpose is to guarantee and to protect, within the limits of reason, the enjoyment of the rights and freedoms it enshrines. It is intended to constrain governmental action inconsistent with those rights and freedoms; it is not in itself an authorization for governmental action. In the present case this means . . . that in guaranteeing the right to be secure from unreasonable searches and seizures s. 8 acts as a limitation on whatever powers of search and seizure the federal or provincial government already and otherwise possess. It does not in itself confer any powers, even of "reasonable" search and seizure, on these governments. This leads, in my view, to the further conclusion that an assessment of the constitutionality of a search and seizure, or of a statute authorizing a search or seizure, must focus on its "reasonable" or "unreasonable" impact on the subject of the search or the seizure, and not simply on its rationality in furthering some valid government objective.

If the issue to be resolved in assessing the constitutionality of searches under s. 10 were whether *in fact* the governmental interest in carrying out a given search outweighed that of the individual in resisting the governmental intrusion upon his privacy, then it would be appropriate to determine the balance of the competing interests *after* the search had been conducted. Such . . . analysis would, however, be seriously at odds with the purpose of s. 8. That purpose is, as I have said, to protect individuals from unjustified state intrusions upon their privacy. That purpose requires a means of *preventing* unjustified searches before they happen, not simply of determining, after the fact, whether they ought to have occurred in the first place. This, in my view, can be accomplished only by a system of *prior authorization*, not one of subsequent validation.

A requirement of prior authorization, usually in the form of a valid warrant, has been a consistent prerequisite for a valid search and seizure both at common law

---

[46] (1984), 41 C.R. (3d) 97 (S.C.C.).

and under most statutes. Such a requirement puts the onus on the state to demonstrate the superiority of its interest to that of the individual. As such it accords with the apparent intention of the Charter to prefer, where feasible, the right of the individual to be free from state interference to the interests of the state in advancing its purposes through such interference.

I recognize that it may not be reasonable in every instance to insist on prior authorization in order to validate governmental intrusions upon individuals' expectations of privacy. Nevertheless, where it is feasible to obtain prior authorization, I would hold that such authorization is a precondition for a valid search and seizure.[47]

The *Southam* case has been used as the benchmark for interpreting section 8 of the Charter. In holding that there is a presumption that warrantless searches violate section 8 of the Charter, the Supreme Court of Canada called into question the constitutionality of many federal and provincial statutes which authorize a warrantless search and seizure. The onus will be upon the government to justify such searches.

The decision in *Southam* is also important because the court makes it clear that the Charter is not an authorization for government activity and that it is not appropriate for a court to make legislation conform with the Charter by reading into it requirements that would make it conform with the requirements of the Charter. Before the Charter came into effect, the courts when faced with cases involving a constitutional challenge to legislation, where possible, interpreted such legislation as being within the constitutional authority of the government which passed it. The courts developed a doctrine known as the "reading down" doctrine which they applied to constitutional cases. With this doctrine the courts would interpret challenged legislation so that it conformed with the division of powers in the B.N.A. Act.[48] The Supreme Court of Canada's decision in *McKay v. R.*[49] illustrates this reasoning. In *McKay*, the Supreme Court of Canada held that a law which prohibited the erection of unauthorized signs could not have been intended to intrude on federal jurisdiction over elections and, accordingly, "read down" the legislation so that it did not apply to such election signs.

In *Southam*, the appellant, who was the Director of Investigation under the Combines Investigation Branch, argued that the court should read down the legislation so that it conformed with the Charter. Dickson J. (as he then was) rejected the argument, saying:

While the courts are guardians of the Constitution and of individuals' rights under it, it is the legislature's responsibility to enact legislation that embodies appropriate safeguards to comply with the Constitution's requirements. It should not fall

[47] *Ibid.*, at 114-115.
[48] 1867 (30 & 31 Vict.), c. 3.
[49] [1965] S.C.R. 798.

to the courts to fill in the details that will render legislative lacunae constitutional. Without appropriate safeguards, legislation authorizing search and seizure is inconsistent with s. 8 of the Charter. As I have said, any law inconsistent with the provisions of the Constitution is, to the extent of the inconsistency, of no force or effect.[50]

In *R. v. Noble*,[51] the Ontario Court of Appeal held that sections of the Narcotic Control Act and Food and Drugs Act, which authorize a police officer armed with a writ of assistance to conduct a warrantless search of someone's premises, were unconstitutional. In *Noble*, Martin J.A., who delivered the judgment of the court, held that section 10(1)(*a*) [10] of the Narcotic Control Act and section 37(1)(*a*) [42(1)] of the Food and Drugs Act were, to the extent that they authorized warrantless searches by means of a writ of assistance, unconstitutional as being in violation of section 8 of the Charter. A writ of assistance gives the person holding the writ the authority to search someone's premises without a warrant. Writs of assistance are issued under the Food and Drugs Act, the Narcotic Control Act, the Customs Act and the Excise Act.[52] The writ confers the broadest possible power upon the police officer or customs agent as it allows that person to conduct a warrantless search of premises at any time without having to justify the search to independent authorities, such as a justice of the peace. The writ continues in force for years and, in the case of writs issued under the Narcotic Control Act and the Food and Drugs Act, the policy of the Royal Canadian Mounted Police is for the writ to be surrendered when the officer retires from the force.

In *Noble*, Mr. Justice Martin held that the conferring of such broadly based powers did not meet the Charter test of reasonableness and therefore could not be reconciled with the Supreme Court of Canada's judgment in *Southam*.[53] The decision in *Noble* that writs of assistance are unconstitutional as being an unreasonable search and seizure is contrary to the holding of the British Columbia Court of Appeal in *R. v. Hamill*.[54] In *Hamill*, the British Columbia Court of Appeal held that section 10(1)(*a*) [10] of the Narcotic Control Act was not inconsistent with section 8 of the Charter.

(e) Abolition of Writs of Assistance

Writs of assistance which were authorized by the Narcotic Control Act, Food and Drugs Act, the Excise Act and the Customs Act have been abolished

---

[50] *Supra*, note 46, at 121.
[51] (1984), 16 C.C.C. (3d) 146 (Ont. C.A.).
[52] R.S.C. 1985, c. E-14.
[53] (1984), 41 C.R. (3d) 97 (S.C.C.).
[54] (1984), 14 C.C.C. (3d) 338 (B.C.C.A.), affirmed (1987), 33 C.C.C. (3d) 110 (S.C.C.).

by the Criminal Law Amendment Act, 1985.[55] The abolition of writs of assistance is an admission by the federal government that legislation permitting the holder of a writ of assistance to search a dwelling-house or other premises without a search warrant is unconstitutional as being in violation of section 8 of the Charter. The Law Reform Commission of Canada recommended that the federal government abolish writs of assistance, saying that "the powers exercised under writs of assistance are patently unconstitutional."[56] It is noteworthy that the Commission's recommendations which were released in its 1983 report were ignored and it was not until several courts struck down the writs as being unconstitutional that the federal government repealed the legislation. There is little doubt that the writs would still be in existence were it not for the Charter of Rights.

The Supreme Court of Canada subsequently upheld the decision in *Hamill*. It was conceded on appeal by the Crown that the provision authorizing the use of writs of assistance was not valid. However, the Supreme Court of Canada applied the principles it had adopted in *Collins v. R.*,[57] holding that the admission of the evidence would not bring the administration of justice into disrepute and that the admission of the evidence did not affect the fairness of the trial. The police acted in good faith believing writs of assistance were legal. A new trial was ordered. The court held that at such a trial there should be an inquiry as to the reasonableness of the search.

The Supreme Court of Canada reached a similar conclusion in *Sieben v. R.*[58] where the actions of the police were reasonable and their only mistake was in relying on an illegal writ of assistance. Thus, illegally obtained evidence will not always be excluded on the grounds that its admission would bring the administration of justice into disrepute.

(f) Burden of Showing Infringement of Charter Right

In *Collins*,[59] the Supreme Court of Canada held that the burden of persuading a court that Charter rights or freedoms have been infringed must be discharged by the person asserting the breach. The standard of persuasion is the civil one based on a balance of probabilities. There is a presumption that a warrantless search is unreasonable. Thus, once it is shown that a search was a warrantless one the Crown must establish, on a balance of probabilities, that it was reasonable. A search will be reasonable if it is authorized by law, if the

---

[55] S.C. 1985, c. 19.
[56] Law Reform Commission of Canada, *Report on Writs of Assistance and Telewarrants* Report 19 (Ottawa: Minister of Supply & Services, 1983), p. 30.
[57] (1987), 56 C.R. (3d) 193 (S.C.C.).
[58] (1987), 56 C.R. (3d) 225 (S.C.C.).
[59] *Supra*, note 57, at 205.

law itself is reasonable and if the manner in which the search was carried out was reasonable.

(g) Effect of Illegal Searches

Some courts have concluded that an illegal search or seizure is not always unreasonable while other courts have taken the position that illegal searches are necessarily unreasonable. In *R. v. Heisler*,[60] the Alberta Court of Appeal held that a search could be illegal and yet reasonable under the Charter. In so holding, Lieberman J.A., who delivered the judgment of the court, stated:

> We are all of the view that it does not follow that because a search is illegal it must therefore be unreasonable.[61]

The Ontario Court of Appeal has also suggested that a search which is not authorized by law does not always mean that the search is unreasonable under section 8 of the Charter. In *R. v. Benz*,[62] MacKinnon A.C.J., who wrote the judgment of the court, stated:

> . . . every illegality, however minor or technical and peripheral or remote, does not thereupon, of necessity, render such search unreasonable. . . . The section, of course, speaks of unreasonable search and seizure, not of illegal search and seizure. . . .[63]

In *R. v. Dyment*,[64] the Prince Edward Island Court of Appeal stated:

> It would appear to be much more logical to hold that all illegal searches are also unreasonable than to hold some illegal searches as being reasonable. However, this need not be determined at this time.[65]

The Supreme Court of Canada has now held that an illegal search is unreasonable. In *Collins*, Lamer J. stated "without such evidence [of reasonable grounds], it is clear that the trial judge was correct in concluding that the search was unreasonable because unlawful and carried out with unnecessary violence."[66]

---

[60] (1984), 11 C.C.C. (3d) 475 (Alta. C.A.).

[61] *Ibid.*, at 477.

[62] (1986), 51 C.R. (3d) 363 (Ont. C.A.).

[63] *Ibid.*, at 377.

[64] (1986), 49 C.R. (3d) 338 (P.E.I.C.A.).

[65] *Ibid.*, at 346.

[66] *Supra*, note 57, at 207.

4. SPECIFIC SEARCHES

(a) Search of a Hotel Room

Under section 8 of the Charter, the key question in determining whether a police officer or other agent of the state may conduct a warrantless search or seizure is whether a person has a reasonable expectation of privacy. If a person does not have a reasonable expectation of privacy, the activities in question will not be protected under section 8 of the Charter. The Supreme Court of Canada has held that a person has a reasonable expectation of privacy in a hotel room, saying that a hotel room is really one's "home away from home." In *R. v. Wong*,[67] the Supreme Court held that the Ontario Court of Appeal had erred in concluding that the accused could not have a reasonable expectation of privacy in his hotel room by virtue of the fact that he was using the hotel room for the purposes of illegal activity. La Forest J., writing for a majority of the court, held that whether a person has a reasonable expectation of privacy cannot depend upon whether the person who was subject to unauthorized video surveillance is engaged in illegal activity because such a result "would inevitably be to adopt the system of subsequent validation for searches."[68] La Forest J. noted that the Supreme Court's seminal decision in *Hunter v. Southam* attempted to protect persons against a subsequent validation of an improper search and seizure by providing that where feasible a search must be judicially authorized by a justice of the peace or a judge in order to be valid under section 8 of the Charter.

In *Wong*, La Forest J. did not exclude the evidence under section 24(2) of the Charter, holding that the police had acted according to what they believed was required of them under the law. Most of the police investigation in *Wong* was completed before the Supreme Court released its seminal decision in *Southam*, and before the Supreme Court had held that electronic surveillance constituted a search under section 8 of the Charter. Accordingly, if a police officer conducted a warrantless search of a hotel room today, different considerations would apply in determining whether the evidence should be excluded under section 24(2).

(b) Search of an Automobile

A search of an automobile raises different considerations than a search of a home or office. A person who drives an automobile has a lower expectation of privacy than a home owner or person whose hotel room is searched. In

---

[67] (1990), 1 C.R. (4th) 1 (S.C.C.).
[68] *Ibid.*, at 12.

most cases, a search of a vehicle will be conducted without a search warrant. Since a vehicle can move quickly away, it will not normally be feasible to obtain a search warrant.

There is divided authority as to whether a warrantless search of an automobile is justified on the basis that it may move quickly away. In *R. v. McComber*,[69] the Ontario Court of Appeal held that the warrantless search of vehicles, which may move quickly, may be reasonable where there are reasonable grounds for believing that the vehicle contains contraband. In holding that the warrantless search and seizure of a motor vehicle did not violate section 8, the Ontario Court of Appeal relied upon Martin J.A.'s judgment in *DeBot* where Martin J.A., for the court, stated:

> In *R. v. Rao*, this court held that the search of an office where it was not impracticable to obtain a warrant was unreasonable and contravened s. 8 of the Charter. In *Hunter v. Southam Inc.*, *supra*, the Supreme Court held that a warrantless search was prima facie unreasonable but a prior authorization was not required where it was not feasible to obtain one. The Supreme Court in that case was not dealing with a search of an automobile.

> As pointed out in *R. v. Rao*, the Supreme Court of the United States has developed a number of exceptions to the warrant requirement of the Fourth Amendment, one of which is the exception for automobiles because of their mobility. In *R. v. Rao*, the court said . . . that "a warrantless search of vehicles, vessels or aircrafts, which may move quickly away, may be reasonable where there are reasonable grounds for believing that such contains a narcotic."[70]

The British Columbia Court of Appeal has held that there is no "automobile exception" which permits a police officer to conduct a warrantless search of an automobile on the grounds that such vehicles may move away quickly. In *R. v. Klimchuk*,[71] the court held that the power to conduct a warrantless search of a vehicle must either be authorized by statute or must be found at common law as a search conducted incident to a lawful arrest. Since there is divided authority this issue will have to be resolved by the Supreme Court of Canada. Most courts outside of Ontario and British Columbia would probably follow the reasoning of the Ontario Court of Appeal.

Since driving is a licensed activity, not all contact with a police officer will constitute a search under section 8 of the Charter. In this regard, the Supreme Court of Canada has held that if police officers demand that a driver produce his ownership and insurance, it cannot be characterized as a search under the Charter.[72]

The Supreme Court of Canada has held that police officers are entitled to randomly stop cars without reasonable and probable grounds as part of a

---

[69] (1988), 66 C.R. (3d) 142 (Ont. C.A.).
[70] *Supra*, note 32, at 135-136.
[71] (1991), 8 C.R. (3d) 327 (B.C.C.A.).
[72] *R. v. Hufsky* (1988), 63 C.R. (3d) 14 (S.C.C.).

R.I.D.E. program ("Reduce Impaired Driving Everywhere"). The Supreme Court has also held that a visual inspection of a car by the police can be carried out as an incident to a check-stop program without violating section 8 of the Charter. However, in *R. v. Mellenthin*,[73] the Supreme Court held that "random stop programs must not be turned into a means of conducting either an unfounded general inquisition or an unreasonable search." The court stated:

> A check stop does not and cannot constitute a general search warrant for searching every vehicle, driver and passenger that is pulled over. Unless there are reasonable and probable grounds for conducting the search, or drugs, alcohol or weapons are in plain view in the interior of the vehicle, the evidence flowing from such a search should not be admitted.[74]

A police officer can conduct a warrantless search of a motor vehicle if he is relying upon section 10 of the Narcotic Control Act or section 42 of the Food and Drugs Act. Section 10 of the Narcotic Control Act authorizes a peace officer to search any place in which the officer believes on reasonable grounds that there is a narcotic by means of or in respect of which an offence under the Narcotic Control Act has been committed. An automobile is considered a place within the meaning of section 10 of the Narcotic Control Act and section 42 of the Food and Drugs Act. Although a police officer relying on section 10 of the Narcotic Control Act may conduct a warrantless search of an automobile, such a search may still be attacked as being unreasonable under section 8 of the Charter.

The Supreme Court of Canada's holding in *Collins* that a search will be reasonable if it is authorized by law and if the law itself is reasonable raises the question as to whether a statute authorizing a warrantless search of an automobile is reasonable. If the accused alleged that a statute authorizing the warrantless search of an automobile was unreasonable under section 8, the Crown would bear the burden of demonstrating that the statute which authorized the warrantless search and seizure did not violate section 8 of the Charter.

(c) Blood Samples

The Criminal Code contains provisions which authorize a police officer to demand that a person provide a blood sample where the officer has reasonable and probable grounds to believe that the person is committing or has committed within the preceding two hours the offence of operating a motor vehicle or vessel, aircraft or railway equipment when the person was impaired

---

[73] (1992), 16 C.R. (4th) 273 (S.C.C.).
[74] *Ibid.*, at 284.

and has reasonable and probable grounds to believe that by reason of any physical condition of the person, the person in incapable of providing a sample of his breath. Sections 253 and 254 are relevant. Section 253 states:

> **253.** Every one commits an offence who operates a motor vehicle or vessel or operates or assists in the operation of an aircraft or of railway equipment or has the care or control of a motor vehicle, vessel, aircraft or railway equipment, whether it is in motion or not
> (*a*) while the person's ability to operate the vehicle, vessel, aircraft or railway equipment is impaired by alcohol or a drug; or
> (*b*) having consumed alcohol in such a quantity that the concentration in the person's blood exceeds eighty milligrams of alcohol in one hundred millilitres of blood.

Section 254(3) states:

> (3) Where a peace officer believes on reasonable and probable grounds that a person is committing, or any time within the preceding two hours has committed, as a result of the consumption of alcohol, an offence under section 253, the peace officer may, by demand made to that person forthwith or as soon as practicable, require that person to provide then or as soon thereafter as is practicable
> (*a*) such samples of the person's breath as in the opinion of a qualified technician, or
> (*b*) where the peace officer has reasonable and probable grounds to believe that, by reason of any physical condition of the person,
>   (i) the person may be incapable of providing a sample of his breath,
>   (ii) it would be impracticable to obtain a sample of his breath, such samples of the person's blood, under the conditions referred to subsection (4), as in the opinion of the qualified medical practitioner or qualified technician taking the samples
> are necessary to enable proper analysis to be made in order to determine the concentration, if any, of alcohol in the person's blood, and to accompany the peace officer for the purpose of enabling such samples to be taken.

Subsections 254(4) and (5) state:

> (4) Samples of blood may only be taken from a person pursuant to a demand made by a peace officer under subsection (3) if the samples are taken by or under the direction of a qualified medical practitioner and the qualified medical practitioner is satisfied that the taking of those samples would not endanger the life or health of the person.
> (5) Everyone commits an offence who, without reasonable excuse, fails or refuses to comply with a demand made to him by a peace officer under this section.

Section 256 of the Code enables a police officer to apply to a justice of the peace for a search warrant authorizing the officer to require a qualified medical doctor to take or cause to be taken by a qualified technician a blood sample so as to determine the concentration of alcohol in a person's blood. The section applies where the justice is satisfied on information on oath that there are reasonable grounds to believe that a person has within the preceding four hours committed an offence under section 253 and the person was involved in an accident resulting in the death of another person or in bodily harm to himself or herself or to any other person. In addition, the qualified medical practitioner must be of the opinion that by reason of any physical or mental condition of the person that resulted from the consumption of alcohol, the accident or any other occurrence related to or resulting from the accident, the person is unable to consent to the taking of samples of his blood and the taking of samples of blood from the person would not endanger the life or health of the person. Section 257 of the Criminal Code provides that a doctor or qualified technician will not be guilty of an offence by reason of his refusal to take a sample of blood from a person for purposes of section 256. The section also protects a doctor who takes a blood sample and a technician who acts under the doctor's direction from criminal or civil liability for anything which is necessarily done with reasonable care and skill in the taking of the sample of blood.

The Supreme Court of Canada has held that a doctor who takes a blood sample illegally at the behest of the police is acting as a government agent and his actions are subject to the Charter. The Supreme Court has held that a blood sample may not be taken from a hospital patient by a doctor acting on behalf of the police without the consent of the patient unless the police have a search warrant. The taking of a blood sample without the patient's consent violates section 8 of the Charter. In *R. v. Dyment*,[75] La Forest J. stated:

> . . . the sense of privacy transcends the physical. The dignity of the human being is equally seriously violated when use is made of bodily substances taken by others for medical purposes in a manner that does not respect that limitation. In my view, the trust and confidence of the public in the adminstration of medical facilities would be seriously taxed if an easy and informal flow of information, and particularly of bodily substances, from hospitals to the police, were allowed.[76]

In *R. v. Dersch*,[77] the Supreme Court held that the accused's section 8 right to be secure against unreasonable search or seizure was violated when police officers obtained a blood sample and other medical information from the accused's doctor without the accused's consent. In overturning the accused's conviction for criminal negligence causing death and criminal negligence causing bodily harm, the court held that the warrantless seizure of the accused's blood violated section 8 of the Charter. Major J. stated:

> . . . the appellant had a reasonable expectation of privacy in respect of the information revealed to the police by Dr. Gilbert. The obtaining of that information by

---

[75] (1988), 66 C.R. (3d) 348 (S.C.C.).
[76] *Ibid.*, at 368.
[77] (1993), 25 C.R. (4th) 88 (S.C.C.).

the police in the circumstances of this case is analogous to a search or a seizure within the meaning of s. 8 of the *Charter.*

The information at issue was obtained from Dr. Gilbert without a search warrant, rendering the search by the police prima facie unreasonable . . . . The respondent [Crown] has not satisfied the burden of rebutting this presumption of unreasonableness. It has not been demonstrated that there is any basis in statute or under the common law for this search and/or seizure. Nor was there any emergency in the sense of the evidence being in danger of being destroyed if the time were taken to obtain a search warrant.

. . . .

The net result of the *Charter* violation by police, in the particular circumstances of this case, was to take advantage of the improper conduct by his [the accused's] doctors in taking the blood sample contrary to the specific instructions of the patient. When this factor is considered together with the seriousness of the Charter violation by police and the importance of guarding against a free exchange of information between health care professionals and police, in my view, the impugned evidence should be excluded by application of s. 24(2) of the *Charter.*

In the absence of the evidence of the appellant's blood alcohol level, there is no evidence sufficient to sustain convictions on the charges of causing death and bodily harm by having the care and control of a motor vehicle while impaired by alcohol or a drug (the "care and control charges"). Those charges are dismissed.

While there remains evidence to support charges of causing death and bodily harm by criminal negligence (the "criminal negligence charges"), this is not an appropriate case in which to apply the curative provision of s. 686(1)(b)(iii) of the Criminal Code. In the result, a new trial is directed on criminal negligence charges.[78]

The Supreme Court of Canada's decision in *Dersch* is not surprising. In *R. v. Pohoretsky*, Lamer J. (as he then was), for the court, said " . . . a violation of the sanctity of a person's body is much more serious than that of his office or even of his home."[79]

(d) Electronic Surveillance

A police officer or other agent of the state cannot secretly record the conversations of a person who is suspected of committing a criminal offence. The Criminal Code provides that the police must always obtain a judge's authorization before engaging in electronic surveillance. The Code contains stringent requirements for obtaining a judge's authorization. A judge must be satisfied that the police have tried other investigative methods and that such

---

[78] *Ibid.*, at 95-96.
[79] (1987), 58 C.R. (3d) 113 at 116 (S.C.C.).

methods have failed or would be unlikely to succeed. The judge must also be satisfied that it would be in the best interest of the administration of justice to grant the authorization. The Supreme Court of Canada has held that the requirement that a judge be satisfied that the authorization is in the best interest of the administration of justice necessitates that the authorizing judge be convinced that there are reasonable grounds to believe that an offence has been or is being committed and that the authorization which is sought will provide evidence of the offence.

In *Duarte v. R.*,[80] the Supreme Court of Canada held that, in general, surreptitious electronic surveillance of a person by an agent of the state will violate section 8 of the Charter. La Forest J., writing for the majority of the court, stated:

> The rationale for regulating the power of the state to record communications that their originator expects will not be intercepted by anyone other than the person intended by the originator to receive it . . . has nothing to do with protecting individuals from the threat that their interlocutors will divulge communications that are meant to be private. No set of laws can immunize us from that risk. Rather, the regulation of electronic surveillance protects us from a risk of a different order, i.e., not the risk that someone will repeat our words, but the much more insidious danger inherent in allowing the state, in its unfettered discretion, to record and transmit our words.

> The reason for this protection is the realization that, if the state were free, at its sole discretion, to make permanent electronic recordings of our private communications, there will be no meaningful residuum to our right to live our lives free from surveillance. The very efficacy of electronic surveillance is such that it has the potential, if left unregulated, to annihilate any expectation that our communications will remain private. A society which exposed us, at the whim of the state, to the risk of having a permanent electronic recording made of our words every time we opened our mouths might be superbly equipped to fight crime, but would be one in which privacy no longer had any meaning. As Douglas J., dissenting in *U.S. v. White*, . . . put it "electronic surveillance is the greatest leveler of human privacy ever known." If the state may arbitrarily record and transmit our private communications, it is no longer possible to strike an appropriate balance between the right of the individual to be left alone and the right of the state to intrude on privacy in the furtherance of its goals, notably the need to investigate and combat crime.[81]

(e) Search on Suspicion

A police officer has no right to search a person on suspicion alone. The law, in this regard, is accurately summarized by the Nova Scotia Court of Appeal in *R. v. Stevens*,[82] wherein Mr. Justice Hart stated:

---

[80] (1990), 74 C.R. (3d) 281 (S.C.C.).

[81] *Ibid.*, at 290-291.

[82] (1983), 35 C.R. (3d) 1 (N.S.C.A.).

In my opinion, no police officer has the right to search any person upon suspicion alone. He must have reasonable and probable grounds for believing that the suspect is committing or has committed an offence and must seek his justification under the *Criminal Code* provisions relating to lawful arrest or some other special statutory authorization. If the police officer searches on suspicion alone he has committed an illegal act and one that, in my view, would be within the meaning of "unreasonable" in s. 8 of the Charter.[83]

In *Stevens*, the accused was walking down a street when he was approached by a police officer and asked to empty his pockets. The search, which was conducted without the accused's consent, turned up a packet of drugs. The officer testified that he was suspicious that Stevens was carrying drugs because when he spoke to Stevens and asked him whether he was still selling drugs, Stevens replied that yes he was. The officer testified that until he found narcotics in Stevens' jacket pocket, he had no reason for placing Stevens under arrest.

(f) Consent to Search

A search that otherwise would be unreasonable may be reasonable under section 8 of the Charter if an accused consents to being searched.

In *R. v. Wills*,[84] Doherty J.A., writing for the Ontario Court of Appeal, held:

When one consents to the police taking something that they otherwise have no right to take, one relinquishes one's right to be left alone by the state and removes the reasonableness barrier imposed by s. 8 of the *Charter*. The force of the consent given must be commensurate with the significant effect which it produces.[85]

In *R. v. Borden*,[86] the Supreme Court of Canada approved the Ontario Court of Appeal's ruling in *Wills*. However, in *Borden*, Iacobucci J. stated that before a consent to search can be effective, the person waiving his right to be secure against unreasonable search must have sufficient meaningful information to make an informed choice as to whether or not to give up the right. The court held that the accused's consent to a DNA sample was not valid, as the accused was not told that the police were intending to use his blood for a different investigation than the one for which he was detained.[87]

---

[83] *Ibid.*, at 11.
[84] (1992), 12 C.R. (4th) 58 (Ont. C.A.).
[85] *Ibid.*, at 72.
[86] (1994), 92 C.C.C. (3d) 404 (S.C.C.).
[87] *Ibid.*, at 417.

9

Criminal Offences

1. NATURE AND ELEMENTS OF AN OFFENCE

(a) Actus reus

(i) *Definition*

Every crime requires an *actus reus*, or, what is sometimes called, the guilty act. In many cases the Criminal Code[1] specifically defines the guilty act — as, for example, the act of breaking, which is an essential element of the crime of breaking and entering with intent — while in other cases the Code does not define the act — as, for example, in the case of sexual assault. It may include the state of mind of another, as in the case of assault where the force must be applied without the consent of the person assaulted. If the conduct of the accused does not include an *actus reus*, a criminal offence may not be committed. Accordingly, in the case of *R. v. Kissick*, wherein a girl leapt from a car mistakenly believing that she was about to be assaulted and was then injured in the result, the accused was acquitted.[2]

A person will only commit an *actus reus* if he has the willpower to commit the act. In *R. v. King*,[3] the accused was acquitted by the Supreme Court of Canada when, as a result of a sedative injected by his dentist, he drove his car into another vehicle. Taschereau J. said that "there must be a willpower to do an act whether the accused knew or not that it was prohibited by law."[4] The requirement is that a person must direct his mind to what he is doing and not that he appreciates the consequences of the act as the consequences are irrelevant for this purpose.

---

[1] R.S.C. 1985, c. C-46.
[2] (1937), 69 C.C.C. 403 (Man. Police Ct.).
[3] [1962] S.C.R. 746.
[4] *Ibid.*, at 749.

The situation must be one where a person has a chance to act or not act. Hence, in the case of *Hill v. R.*,[5] when an accused was charged with leaving the scene of an accident and argued that there was not an *actus reus* because she did not know that an accident had taken place, Dickson J., who gave the judgment in the Supreme Court of Canada, held that the accused was only ignorant of the result of the damage and that the *actus reus* was found in her leaving the scene without informing herself of the damage. The *actus reus* may be a passive act — as, for example, where the offence is being found in a bawdy-house — it may also be an omission, as the Code specifically makes many omissions crimes, such as a failure to exercise reasonable care when dealing with explosives.

(ii) *Voluntary conduct*

An essential element of an offence is some voluntary conduct by the accused. If a person is standing on a subway platform and is pushed, resulting in the person standing ahead of him falling onto the track, no crime is committed by the person who involuntarily pushed the other person onto the track. Accordingly, the *actus reus* requires a person to do something which involves a conscious decision; this is something different than *mens rea* which will be considered later and which requires a desire to achieve certain consequences or a knowledge that certain consequences will follow.

(iii) *Omission*

If a person is suddenly rendered unconscious while driving a car, there cannot be a conviction for dangerous driving because there is no conscious decision to drive in a dangerous manner. On the other hand, there may be an *actus reus* where a person omits to do something specifically required by the Criminal Code, such as neglecting to obtain assistance in childbirth; in such cases the omission is made the offence. Thus, in *R. v. Dalke*, a son was convicted of manslaughter when he admitted his father to his home and then the father died because of a lack of food and care.[6]

In the case of omission, however, there must be a "will" directed to the failure to act. In *R. v. Sidney*,[7] the accused was acquitted on a charge of failing to supply "necessaries" where he failed to check on the safety of his wife and son and his wife left the home of her own free will. In this instance,

---

[5] (1973), 14 C.C.C. (2d) 505 (S.C.C.).
[6] (1915), 25 C.C.C. 98 (Man. C.A.).
[7] (1912), 20 C.C.C. 376 (Sask. S.C.).

there was nothing to indicate that she would expose herself or her son to danger. Accordingly, the accused had no duty to act and the necessary will to omit to do an act required by law was missing.

(iv) *Causation*

Complicated causation problems can sometimes arise in determining the *actus reus*. Thus, in a manslaughter case it must be established that the accused actually caused the death. There may be a considerable time lapse between the accused's act and the death, as for example where a victim is injured as a result of reckless driving and dies some weeks later. There may also be an intervening act, such as improper medical treatment, or even a further accident involving the victim as he is being driven to hospital.[8] An intervening act may break the chain of causation. In *R. v. Jordan,*[9] the accused was acquitted because, although he had injured the deceased, the deceased died as a result of being given an antibiotic to which he was allergic. In that case it was held that the act of the accused had ceased to be significant as the wounds were practically healed.

The intervening cause, if it is to be judged the effective cause, must be one which is of such overwhelming importance that the initial cause is merely part of the history of the event and cannot be regarded as a contributing cause. The question is whether the original cause continues to be an effective element up to the completion of the *actus reus*. For example, the injuries caused by an aggravated assault may be a contributing factor to a death, although the treatment given may also have contributed. The distinction between a contributing and non-contributing cause is often a difficult one to make, but in each case the question is whether the original cause was an effective cause of the event. In *Smithers v. R.,*[10] Dickson J. dealt with an appeal to the Supreme Court of Canada regarding a situation wherein the deceased had been kicked and death was caused in part by a malfunctioning epiglottis. In that case he held that all the Crown had to prove was that the kick was the contributing cause, in the sense that its effect was more than trivial.

One may cause the death of another person simply by abandoning him. In *Bradley v. R.,*[11] for example, the accused, who after a fight left the victim unconscious and before leaving him removed his coat with the result that the

---

[8] *Smithers v. R.* (1977), 34 C.C.C. (2d) 427 (S.C.C.); *R. v. Munro* (1983), 36 C.R. (3d) 193 (Ont. C.A.).

[9] [1956] Crim. L.R. 700 (C.C.A.).

[10] *Supra*, note 8.

[11] [1956] S.C.R. 723.

victim died, was convicted of murder. If a victim dies as a result of fleeing from someone engaged in an illegal act and is then killed by an automobile, such a person will be held to have caused the death. In *R. v. Munro*,[12] the Ontario Court of Appeal upheld the conviction of murder where the accused, while attempting to commit a robbery, shot a police officer and held him as a hostage for an hour. The officer later died in the hospital of internal haemorrhaging. The court upheld the conviction because death was accelerated by the forceful confinement of the officer, although it was only indirectly caused by the use of the firearm.

The *actus reus* may not be the immediate cause of death, but may result in an accused being held criminally responsible. In *Graves v. R.*,[13] the Supreme Court of Canada concluded that the accused could be held criminally responsible where the victim wounded himself. In that case, the accused had been drinking and shouting in front of the victim's premises. The victim went into his house, loaded his gun, came out to the veranda and asked the accused to depart. Instead of departing, the accused rushed the victim and, as a result of the victim using the gun as a club, the gun went off wounding the victim.

(b) *Mens Rea*

Apart from crimes of strict and absolute liability, which are dealt with later, a guilty mind or *mens rea* is an essential part of the crime which must be established by the Crown. *Mens rea* differs from the mental element in the *actus reus*, involving as it does an intent, knowledge of the consequences of the act forming the *actus reus*, negligence or wilful blindness. In *R. v. Tolson*,[14] Stephen J., a famous English criminal jurist, indicated that the mental element in a crime could differ widely if, as in the case of murder, it involved malice or,

> . . . in the case of theft, an intention to steal; . . . in the case of receiving stolen goods, knowledge that the goods were stolen. In some cases it denotes mere inattention. For instance, in the case of manslaughter by negligence it may mean forgetting to notice a signal.
>
> . . . .
>
> The principle involved appears . . . to amount to no more than this. The full definition of every crime contains expressly or by implication a proposition as to a state of mind. Therefore, if the mental element of any conduct alleged to be a

---

[12] *Supra*, note 8.
[13] (1913), 47 S.C.R. 568.
[14] (1889), 23 Q.B.D. 168.

crime is proved to have been absent in any given case, the crime so defined is not committed. . . .[15]

The required state of mind consists of an intention to cause the *actus reus* of the crime or a knowledge that the conduct may cause the prohibited act. *Mens rea* does not depend on knowledge that the act is illegal, as ignorance of the law is generally not a defence. Some crimes are crimes of "general" intent requiring only an intention of the kind just described, while others, by definition, require some more specific intent. In some cases, the mental element does not require an actual intention to commit the *actus reus* but will be provided by recklessness or negligence, as is the case with criminal negligence.

(i) *Different mental elements*

The necessary intention may be an actual desire to accomplish an objective, as when a person sets out to kill another. It may also be committing an act knowing that it may have a certain result, although not desiring the result — for example, firing a gun to warn someone without any intention to wound, but actually wounding. The necessary mental element may be supplied by recklessness and also by negligence; thus, a person need not have any deliberate intention to commit the act which is a crime.

Problems arise in determining whether the necessary mental element exists where an act is committed under duress. The Supreme Court of Canada, in *Paquette v. R.*,[16] allowed an appeal on the ground of duress where Paquette had been convicted of murder. The conviction was based on the fact that he had formed an intention to commit a robbery with a number of others and a person was killed while the robbery was being committed. Martland J., who wrote the judgment of the Supreme Court of Canada, stated that as Paquette had been threatened with death if he did not participate, he acted under duress, thus negating the necessary intent. Accordingly, in cases of duress, an accused is entitled to an acquittal if he did not desire to effect the common purpose. The mental element, as all other elements in an offence, must be proven by the Crown and if reasonable doubt exists, the accused must be acquitted.

In some cases, the Criminal Code specifies that knowledge is the requisite mental element of an offence, as, for example, receiving stolen property and knowing it to be stolen or "knowingly or wilfully doing an act contributing to the delinquency of a child." In *R. v. Rees*,[17] the Supreme Court of Canada held that the accused must know of the elements necessary to consti-

---

[15] *Ibid.*, at 185-187.
[16] [1962] S.C.R. 746.
[17] [1956] S.C.R. 640.

tute the offence for a conviction to be sustained. In that case, the court held that it must be established that the accused knew the child with whom he had had intercourse with was under 18, as well as knowing that he had had sexual intercourse. In *R. v. McLeod*,[18] the Crown failed to prove a charge of assaulting a police officer because the accused did not know that the person assaulted was a police officer.

(ii) *Negligence or recklessness*

There are a number of offences where the mental element required is neither the intention to achieve a certain result nor the knowledge that certain consequences will probably follow an act or that certain conditions exist, but rather that negligence or recklessness is expressly identified as the requisite mental element. The various offences relating to criminal negligence, which will be considered specifically later, are examples of this. Some offences require that an act be done wilfully, but section 429(1) provides that

> Every one who causes the occurrence of an event by doing an act or by omitting to do an act that it is his duty to do, knowing that the act or omission will probably cause the occurrence of the event and being reckless whether the event occurs or not, shall be deemed. . . .wilfully to have caused the occurrence of the event.

There has been difficulty in determining the nature of the negligence which may constitute *mens rea*. One type of negligence may be described as wanton; i.e., a person recognizes the risks involved in his actions but proceeds in spite of them. A second type is recklessness, where the accused does not necessarily foresee the results but his conduct is such as to increase these risks materially. If *mens rea* consist of recklessness, then that appears to be inconsistent with the idea that a crime must be accompanied by some thought process, as one can hardly have *mens rea* in this sense if one fails to think. If recklessness may constitute *mens rea*, then the state of mind required need only be reprehensible in the sense that the actor is utterly failing to consider the consequences of his acts. Section 219 of the Code in defining criminal negligence requires a showing of wanton or reckless disregard for the lives or safety of others. The Supreme Court of Canada has held that in prosecutions under section 219 it is not necessary to show advertent negligence in that deliberation is not a necessary ingredient of the offence.[19] In some cases, the Code does not indicate that recklessness is an element of the offence and then questions arise as to whether the necessary state of mind may be satisfied by something less than actual subjective knowledge or intention.

---

[18] (1954), 111 C.C.C. 106 (B.C.C.A.).
[19] *R. v. Baker*, [1929] S.C.R. 354; *R. v. Arthurs*, [1974] S.C.R. 287.

The element of *mens rea* may be established by inference; one is assumed to intend the natural consequence of one's act and a jury is entitled to conclude that where what an accused did had a probable consequence, it was something which he intended. Using this standard, recklessness in a situation where the probable consequence of the recklessness would result in the commission of a criminal act, will presumably be held to constitute the necessary *mens rea*. As indicated above, the *mens rea* is ordinarily established by the accused's state of mind and, thus, is subject to a subjective test. However, there are cases where the Code imposes an objective test.

Generally speaking, there is a presumption that *mens rea* is a necessary element of criminal offences, but there are offences created by statutes which are not subject to such a presumption. Whether the presumption exists in the case of legislation depends upon the words of the statute and the subject matter of the legislation.[20] As will be seen in the discussion of strict liability offences, the Charter has effectively placed limitations on the ability of Parliament and legislatures to enact such legislation.

(iii) *Transferred mens rea*

The issue of transferred *mens rea* arises in cases where an accused believes in a mistaken set of facts. If the mistake is one which, if true, would have made his act legal, he should be acquitted, but if the mistake would merely have involved him in a different crime, a question arises whether the *mens rea* can be effectively transferred. Thus, if a person intended to sell L.S.D., but in fact was selling marijuana, is the *mens rea* applicable to the offence of selling marijuana? The courts have held that the mistake must be one which, if true, would have rendered the act innocent.[21]

In *R. v. Blondin*,[22] the Supreme Court of Canada held that an accused could be convicted for importing heroin although he believed it was a different narcotic; a similar result was reached by the court in *R. v. Kundeus*.[23] The result is that *mens rea* can be effectively transferred and that a mistake only avails if it is one which, if true, would have rendered the accused's act an innocent one. The result is rather peculiar, as Laskin C.J.C. pointed out in the *Kundeus* case, because the fundamental principle is that the *actus reus* and the *mens rea* must relate to the same offence which is clearly not so when *mens rea* is transferred.[24]

---

[20] *R. v. Pierce Fisheries Ltd.* (1970), 12 C.R.N.S. 272 (S.C.C.).
[21] *R. v. Watch* (1983), 37 C.R. (3d) 374 (B.C.S.C.); *R. v. Ladue*, [1965] 4 C.C.C. 264 (Y.T.C.A.);
R. v. McAuslane, [1968] 1 O.R. 209 (C.A.).
[22] [1970] 2 C.C.C. (2d) 118 (S.C.C.).
[23] [1976] 2 S.C.R. 272.
[24] *Ibid.*

(iv) *Wilful blindness*

The Crown may also prove the required mental element by showing that the accused who committed the offence acted with wilful blindness towards the facts which comprised the offence. Wilful blindness occurs where a person, having been put on notice of the need to ask questions, refrains from doing so because he does not want to know the truth. The doctrine is sometimes used in possession of stolen property cases to prove that the accused bought property which he knew was stolen.

(c) Strict and Absolute Liability

(i) *Public welfare offences*

Parliament and the legislatures have created a large number of offences which exclude *mens rea* and which may be said to be administrative or public welfare offences. Such offences include measures designed to protect society against pollution, improper trading practices, protection of animals, the sale of unsafe drugs and a very wide range of legislation dealing with the public welfare. Persons committing such offences are liable, whether they did or did not intend the consequences of their acts.

The Supreme Court of Canada in *R. v. Sault Ste. Marie (City)*[25] dealt with a pollution case holding that *mens rea* was not required. Dickson J., speaking for the court, held that there were three categories of offences: (a) offences in which *mens rea* must be proven by the Crown, either as an inference from the type of act committed or by additional evidence; (b) offences where the doing of the prohibited act *prima facie* proves the offence leaving it open to the accused to avoid conviction by proving he took reasonable care (in such cases the accused will have a defence not only if he took all reasonable care to prevent the act, but if he reasonably believed in a mistaken set of facts which, if true, would make the act an innocent one — such offences are offences of strict liability); and, (c) absolute liability offences, which are those offences where it is not open to the accused to exonerate himself by showing he was free from fault. Public welfare offences, such as pollution offences, fall *prima facie* into the secondary category; they will only be offences requiring *mens rea* if the legislation requires wilfulness, intention or knowledge. In such cases the Crown does not need to prove *mens rea*, but the question of culpability may be raised by the accused, who will be acquitted if, on the balance of probabilities, he proves due diligence or a mistaken set of facts, which, if

---

[25] (1978), 3 C.R. (3d) 30 (S.C.C.).

true, would render his act innocent. Thus, a person charged with a pollution-type offence may be acquitted if he proves that he took all reasonable care employing the best anti-pollution devices, but pollution occurred because, despite this, the power failed causing the device not to operate. Offences of absolute liability are those where the legislation clearly shows that guilt is established merely by showing the commission of the prohibited act; in such cases defences such as due diligence are not open to the accused.[26]

The problem of determining whether a particular offence falls into one of these categories is an easy one when the legislation deals with the issue specifically. In other cases, the question will be resolved by the court determining whether the legislature, on a matter such as health, safety and public welfare, is attempting to cast on the individual a burden of conducting his affairs so that the general welfare will not be prejudiced.

Courts have held that the omission of language which indicated a *mens rea* requirement is some indication that the legislature meant to exclude it. In *R. v. V. K. Mason Construction Ltd.*, it was held that strict liability offences usually fall into three categories of offences: (a) public welfare offences; (b) acts which constitute a public nuisance; and (c) criminal proceedings which are really "a summary mode of enforcing a civil right."[27] In *R. v. Pierce Fisheries Ltd.*,[28] the accused was convicted of purchasing undersized lobsters. The legislation is intended to protect lobsters from being depleted. The Supreme Court of Canada held that *mens rea* was not required, saying that the regulation did not contain words such as "knowingly," "wilfully," or "with intent," which would suggest that *mens rea* is an essential element of the offence. The court also noted that the offence of selling undersized lobsters did not carry with it the social stigma which attaches to persons who are convicted of "true criminal offences," such as possession of narcotics.[29] Courts have generally concluded that *mens rea* is a necessary element of all offences by which imprisonment or any severe penalty is imposed. Summary conviction offences — other than those which may be classified as true criminal offences — and offences created by public welfare legislation have been treated generally as strict liability rather than absolute liability offences.

It follows from the *Sault Ste. Marie*[30] judgment that an offence normally will only be held to be one of absolute liability if the court finds that the legislature clearly intended this result. There is, however, some difficulty in deciding in some cases whether the offence is one of strict or absolute liability. In *Strasser v. Roberge*,[31] the Supreme Court of Canada illustrated the

---

[26] *Ibid.*, at 40, 54.
[27] [1968], 1 O.R. 399 at 404 (H.C.).
[28] *Supra*, note 21.
[29] *Supra*, note 21, at 278.
[30] *Supra*, note 25.
[31] (1979), 50 C.C.C. (2d) 129 (S.C.C.).

difficulty when it held that the offence of participating in an unlawful strike did not require *mens rea*. A bare majority of the Supreme Court so found saying that an offence was not automatically removed from the strict liability category to the *mens rea* category merely because the statute put the accused's state of mind in issue. A minority held that when the statute provided for a mental element, *mens rea* must have been intended to be an essential part of the offence. However, where the legislature has expressly referred to intention, recklessness or wilfulness, courts generally classify the offence as a *mens rea* offence and absolute liability offences are only recognized in most cases where the legislature makes its intention clear. The reason for this judicial approach is that it is in keeping with our criminal law traditions to impose punishment only where there is fault.

(ii) *The effect of the Charter*[32]

The Charter has had a marked effect on the right of legislatures to impose absolute liability. The Supreme Court of Canada, in *Reference re s. 94(2) of the Motor Vehicle Act*,[33] has effectively limited absolute liability offences to cases where there is no possibility of imprisonment or even probation. The legislation under review created an absolute liability offence. The legislation provided that a person who drove a motor vehicle while prohibited from driving received a mandatory sentence of seven days' imprisonment. Lamer J., who gave the majority judgment, held that a law that has the potential to convict a person who has not really done anything wrong offends the principle of fundamental justice violating one's right to liberty under section 7 of the Charter, if imprisonment is available as a penalty. He held that a law enacting an absolute liability offence will violate section 7 of the Charter only if, and to the extent that, it has the potential of depriving one of life, liberty or security of the person. Obviously imprisonment (including probation orders) deprives persons of their liberty.

In *Re B.C. Motor Vehicle Act*, Lamer J. concluded that it was in the interest of society that bad drivers be kept off the road, but that this did not constitute a reasonable limit of Charter rights which could be justified in a free and democratic society.

In *Re B.C. Motor Vehicle Act*, the Supreme Court of Canada did not decide what level of fault is constitutionally required for every offence. Thus, for example, the court did not decide whether negligence was the minimum level of fault which was required for a criminal offence. *In R. v. Wholesale Travel Group Inc.*,[34] the Supreme Court of Canada unanimously affirmed its

---

[32] Being Part I of the Constitution Act, 1982 [en. by the Canada Act, 1982 (U.K.), c. 11, s.1].
[33] (1986), 23 C.C.C. (3d) 289 (S.C.C.).
[34] (1991), 8 C.R. (4th) 145 (S.C.C.).

earlier ruling in *Re B.C. Motor Vehicle Act* that a penal law which imposes absolute liability where imprisonment is available as a penalty will violate section 7 of the Charter, since the imposition of absolute liability permits the morally innocent to be convicted. In *Wholesale Travel*, and subsequently in *R. v. Ellis-Don Ltd.*,[35] the Supreme Court held that in cases where imprisonment is available as a penalty, section 7 of the Charter requires the minimal mental state of negligence before the accused may be convicted of the offence.

In *Wholesale Travel*, the accused corporation, a travel agency, was charged with misleading advertising contrary to the Competition Act. Since the offence was a non-criminal offence, some members of the court believed that the standard of fault required (negligence) was less in the regulatory context than it would have been had the corporation or its officers been charged with a "true" criminal offence. The court was divided on the issue of whether the minimal level of fault required depends upon whether the offence may be classified as a regulatory offence, such as misleading advertising, or a true criminal offence — that is, one of the offences which may be prosecuted under the Criminal Code or Narcotic Control Act. Nevertheless, the court's decision in *Wholesale Travel* conclusively establishes that negligence is the minimum level of fault required for an offence which carries a potential penalty of imprisonment upon conviction. It is clear from the Supreme Court's decisions in *Wholesale Travel* and *Ellis-Don* that the mental element required for the commission of an offence will depend upon the nature of the offence, the stigma attached to the offence, and the penalty upon conviction. The Supreme Court of Canada has held that for certain Criminal Code offences such as murder, a minimum level of fault is constitutionally required so that an accused cannot be convicted unless the Crown proves beyond a reasonable doubt that the accused had the required minimum mental element when he committed the offence. The mental element required will be considered later in this chapter.

2. PARTIES TO AN OFFENCE

(a) Generally

A person who assists someone who commits a criminal offence may be held equally liable for the offence under the "parties to offence" provisions of the Code. For example, if two people plan to rob a bank and one person robs the bank while the other person drives the getaway car, the person driving the car can be convicted of robbery even though he did not set foot in the bank.

---

[35] (1992), 71 C.C.C. (3d) 63 (S.C.C.).

If the Crown can establish that the person driving the getaway car knew of his companion's intention to rob the bank and assisted him by driving the car he may be convicted as a party to the offence of robbery by virtue of section 21 of the Criminal Code, which states:

> **21.** (1) Every one is a party to an offence who
> (*a*) actually commits it;
> (*b*) does or omits to do anything for the purpose of aiding any person to commit it; or
> (*c*) abets any person in committing it.
> (2) Where two or more persons form an intention in common to carry out an unlawful purpose and to assist each other therein and any one of them, in carrying out the common purpose, commits an offence, each of them who knew or ought to have known that the commission of the offence would be a probable consequence of carrying out the common purpose is a party to that offence.

(b) Aiding and Abetting

In *R. v. Hoggan*,[36] the Alberta Court of Appeal dealt with aiding and abetting the commission of an offence, saying that:

> There are two things that must be proved before an accused can be convicted of being a party by aiding and abetting. It must first be proved that he had knowledge that the principal intended to commit the offence and that the accused aided and abetted him. Where there is no knowledge that an offence is to be committed, the presence of an accused at the scene of the crime cannot be a circumstance which would be evidence of aiding and abetting.[37]

The decision of the Alberta Court of Appeal in *Hoggan* was adopted by the Supreme Court of Canada in *Dunlop v. R.*[38]

In *Desmond v. R.*,[39] the Nova Scotia Court of Appeal held that the trial judge had erred in convicting an accused of robbery, saying that there was no evidence that the accused was a party to the offence of robbery. In that case, the accused, Desmond, was convicted of robbery on the basis of section 21 of the Criminal Code and sentenced to two years' imprisonment. Desmond's co-accused, Robert Lawrence, robbed a grocery store at gun point. The accused, Desmond, who drove the getaway car, testified that he did not know that Lawrence intended to rob the store until after he had done so. When Lawrence robbed the store, the accused, Desmond, drove him to a location four or five miles from the scene of the robbery. Lawrence subsequently left the car and

---

[36] (1966), 47 C.R. 256 (Alta. C.A.).
[37] *Ibid.*, at 260.
[38] (1979), 8 C.R. (3d) 349 (S.C.C.).
[39] (1981), 22 C.R. (3d) 393 (N.S.C.A.).

entered the woods. He was captured and charged and convicted of robbery. Desmond was also convicted of robbery on the basis that he was a party. The trial judge accepted Desmond's testimony that he did not know that the robbery would be committed until after Lawrence had robbed the store, but nevertheless convicted Desmond of the offence of robbery on the basis of section 21 of the Code. The trial judge stated:

> There's no question in my mind that after the accused Desmond had knowledge of the robbery, he still made some kind of at least a tentative agreement to assist the other person involved, Lawrence, in getting away from the locus of the robbery, and to me this is assisting. . . .This is aiding and abetting escaping from the robbery and to me that makes him just as guilty as the man who originally pulled off the robbery. I find the accused guilty as charged.[40]

The accused's conviction was overturned by the Nova Scotia Court of Appeal. MacDonald J.A. held that the trial judge had erred in holding that Desmond was a party to the offence of robbery under section 21 of the Code. MacDonald J.A. stated:

> In our opinion, the appellant could have been charged possibly as an accessory after the fact under s. 23 . . . of the Criminal Code in that on his own evidence he assisted Mr. Lawrence to escape after the robbery.

> On the finding of the trial judge he did not, however, aid and abet Mr. Lawrence in the actual robbery and hence is not a party thereto under s. 21(1) of the Code. Furthermore, the evidence does not establish a common intention to rob between the appellant and Mr. Lawrence that could inculpate Mr. Desmond under s. 21(2) of the Criminal Code.

> It follows, therefore, that, based on the trial judge's acceptance of Mr. Desmond's evidence as to when he became aware of the robbery, it is our opinion that the respondent's guilt on the robbery charge has not been established.[41]

The Supreme Court of Canada has held that someone may not be convicted of aiding and abetting in the commission of acts if he does not know that such acts may be intended. In *Dunlop*, Dickson J. (as he then was) stated:

> Presence at the commission of an offence can be evidence of aiding and abetting if accompanied by other factors, such as prior knowledge of the principal offender's intention to commit the offence, or attendance for the purpose of encouragement. There was no evidence that while the crime was being committed either of the accused rendered aid, assistance, or encouragement to the rape of [B.R.]. There was no evidence of any positive act or omission to facilitate the

---

[40] *Ibid.*, at 394.
[41] *Ibid.*, at 395.

unlawful purpose. One can infer that the two accused knew that a party was to be held and that their presence at the dump was not accidental or in the nature of casual passers-by, but that is not sufficient. A person cannot properly be convicted of aiding or abetting in the commission of acts which he does not know may be or are intended. . . . One must be able to infer that the accused had prior knowledge that an offence of the type committed was planned, i.e., that their presence was with knowledge of the intended rape.[42]

The word "abet" has been defined in *R. v. Rhyno*,[43] a decision of the Nova Scotia Supreme Court, as follows:

The word "abet" has pretty well phased out of use in popular language. It survives in criminal law. In the Oxford Dictionary "abet" is defined as meaning "to encourage, countenance, uphold or support — now used only in a bad sense." That is, one abets another in committing a crime, but does not "abet" him in performing good works. Stroud's Judicial Dictionary defines the words "aid or abet" together. They mean "encourage, instigate" and include the giving of active assistance.[44]

In *R. v. Mammolita*,[45] the Ontario Court of Appeal concisely set out the requirements for proving that someone aided or abetted the commission of an offence under section 21 of the Code. Howland C.J. stated:

In order to incur a liability as an aider or abettor;

(i) there must be an act or omission of assistance or encouragement;
(ii) the act must be done or the omission take place with the knowledge that the crime will be or is being committed;
(iii) the act must be done or the omission take place for the purpose (i.e., with the intention) of assisting or encouraging the perpetrator in the commission of the crime.[46]

In *R. v. Barr*,[47] the Ontario Court of Appeal held that evidence which merely shows that what the accused did had the effect of aiding is not sufficient to make the accused a party to an offence under section 21 of the Code. Rather, the evidence must show that what the accused did, or omitted to do, was for the purpose of aiding someone else to commit the offence.

(c) Common Intention

Section 21(2) of the Criminal Code has a much different scope than section 21(1) of the Code. Section 21(2) deals with a situation where two or more

---

[42] *Supra*, note 38, at 367.
[43] (1945), 83 C.C.C. 186 (N.S.S.C.).
[44] *Ibid.*, at 189.
[45] (1983), 9 C.C.C. (3d) 85 (Ont. C.A.).
[46] *Ibid.*, at 90.
[47] (1975), 23 C.C.C. (2d) 116 (Ont. C.A.).

persons form an intention in common to commit an offence and to assist each other in carrying out the unlawful purpose.

In *R. v. Miller*,[48] Robertson J.A., writing for the British Columbia Court of Appeal, dealt with the meaning of section 21(2) of the Code, saying:

> That deals primarily with a case where A and B form an intention in common to carry out an unlawful purpose and in carrying out that purpose one of them commits an offence. It does not appear to me to be directed to a case where A and B form an intention to commit a particular crime and in carrying out their intent do commit that crime. The latter type of case is covered by s. 21(1).[49]

In *R. v. Howard*,[50] the Ontario Court of Appeal held that section 21(2) of the Criminal Code is not applicable where the parties do precisely what they intended to do. The scope of section 21(2) of the Criminal Code has been dealt with by the Saskatchewan Court of Appeal in *R. v. Maier*,[51] where Culliton C.J. stated:

> In order to justify a conviction pursuant to s. 21(2), certain essential ingredients must be established by the Crown. These ingredients, in my view, were clearly and correctly stated by Richards, J.A., in *R. v. Leblanc*, 9 C.C.C. 47, 6 C.R. 275. . . . While in that case the learned Judge was considering s. 69(2) of the 1927 Code, that section in no material way differs from s. 21(2) of the present Code. At p. 50 Richards, J.A., said:
>
> > The conditions essential to conviction under s. 69(2) of an offence not actually committed by a person are (1) that a common intention should be formed by the accused and another or others; (2) that the intention should be to prosecute an unlawful purpose and to assist each other therein; and (3) that the crime with which the accused is charged should be one which was or should have been known to him to be a probable consequence of carrying out the unlawful purpose. . . . .[52]

The Ontario Court of Appeal's ruling in *Howard*, that section 21(2) of the Criminal Code does not apply where the unlawful purpose is to commit the offence with which the accused was actually charged, has not been followed by a majority of the British Columbia Court of Appeal in *R. v. Simpson*.[53]

The Criminal Code makes it an offence to offer a comfort or assistance to someone whom one knows has committed a criminal offence. Section 23 states:

---

[48] (1975), 24 C.C.C. (2d) 401 (B.C.C.A.), affirmed (1976), 31 C.C.C. (2d) 177 (S.C.C.).

[49] *Ibid.*, at 440.

[50] (1983), 3 C.C.C. (3d) 399 (Ont. C.A.).

[51] [1968] 2 C.C.C. 328 (Sask. C.A.).

[52] *Ibid.*, at 330.

[53] (1983), 6 C.C.C. (3d) 516 (B.C.C.A.).

23. (1) An accessory after the fact to an offence is one who, knowing that a person has been a party to the offence, receives, comforts or assists that person for the purpose of enabling that person to escape.

(2) No married person whose spouse has been a party to an offence is an accessory after the fact to that offence by receiving, comforting or assisting the spouse for the purpose of enabling the spouse to escape.

There are many examples which could be given of what constitutes assistance. One such example would be the giving of information as to the location of a police roadblock if such information is given so as to assist the criminal to escape the police.

A survey of various Criminal Code offences will be given in this chapter with the exception of motor vehicle offences and drug offences, which are dealt with in their own separate chapters. Motor vehicle offences are covered in Chapter 10, while drug offences are covered in Chapter 11.

3. OFFENCES CAUSING DEATH

(a) Homicide

Homicide is the causing of the death of a human being. Culpable homicide may be murder or manslaughter or infanticide. Culpable homicide is committed by a person when the death of a human being is caused by him:

(*a*) by means of an unlawful act,
(*b*) by criminal negligence,
(*c*) by causing that human being, by threats or fear of violence or by deception, to do anything that causes his death, or
(*d*) by wilfully frightening that human being, in the case of a child or sick person.[54]

Ordinarily it is easy to determine when a person has died, but it is not so easy to determine when the life of an infant begins. The debate about abortion illustrates the different views which may be held on this question. Section 223(1) of the Code provides that a child becomes a human being when it has completely proceeded in a living state from the body of its mother whether or not it has breath, has independent circulation or the navel string is severed. Section 223(2) provides that a person commits homicide when he causes injury to a child before or during birth which causes the death of the child after the child became a human being. Section 238(1) creates a separate offence for causing the death in the act of birth of any child that has not

---

[54] Criminal Code, s. 222(5).

become a human being in circumstances in which it would have been culpable homicide if the child had been a human being. This offence is not committed if the death of the unborn child was necessitated by an act done in good faith to save the life of the mother.

(i) *Causation*

It may sometimes not be easy to show what caused the death of a person. In *R. v. Kitching*,[55] the accused argued that doctors had caused the death of a person and not he, because they removed the victim's kidney when they detected no signs of life. The Manitoba Court of Appeal held that the accused clearly caused the death. O'Sullivan J.A. stated that even if the actions of the doctors were the operative cause of death, which they were not in this case, "that would not exonerate the accused unless the evidence left a reasonable doubt that the accused's actions also constituted an operative cause of the deceased's death."[56]

In *Smithers*, the victim was kicked in the stomach by the accused and died as a result of a malfunctioning epiglottis. Dickson J., who gave the judgment of the Supreme Court of Canada, stated:

> . . . the kick was at least a contributing cause of death outside the *de minimis* range, and that is all that the Crown was required to establish.
>
> . . . .
>
> It is a well-recognized principle that one who assaults another must take his victim as he finds him.[57]

An accused cannot be excused simply because the victim was subject to some peculiar disease which caused the victim to die when people not affected by the disease would not have died.

Section 227 of the Criminal Code requires death to occur within a year and one day of the event by which the accused is alleged to have caused the death of the victim, if a culpable homicide is to be established. Section 226 provides that where a person causes bodily injury to another which results in death, he causes death despite the fact that the effect of the bodily injury is only to accelerate death from a disease or disorder arising from another cause.

Section 225 provides that where a person causes a bodily injury to another that is, of itself, of a dangerous nature and from which death results,

---

[55] (1976), 32 C.C.C. (2d) 159 (Man. C.A.).
[56] *Ibid.*, at 175.
[57] *Supra*, note 8, at 435-437.

he causes the death of that person, though the immediate cause of death is proper or improper treatment that is applied in good faith. The improper treatment of a stab wound which resulted in death has been held not to relieve the stabber of responsibility for the death. If a person by negligent driving runs down another and leaves him on the street where he is robbed and killed by others, the motorist will not be guilty of culpable homicide, unless the injury caused by the hit and run driver was a cause of death. In each case it must be determined whether the first injury results in death despite the intervening act; this will depend on whether the first injury was an operative factor in the death.

Section 222(5)(*a*) provides that culpable homicide will result when a death is caused by means of an unlawful act. The meaning of the term unlawful act is not precise because there are a number of acts prohibited by law which have been held not to be unlawful in the sense required. Thus, the sale of wood alcohol, which was prohibited by liquor control laws, was held not to be an unlawful act which would support a manslaughter charge.[58] It appears that for an act to be unlawful within the meaning of section 222 it must either be a criminal one or at least an act which is prohibited because its commission represents a danger to the public.

(ii) Culpable homicide

(A) *Means to cause death*. A culpable homicide that constitutes murder must fall within sections 229 or 230 of the Code. Section 229 provides that culpable homicide is murder

> (*a*) where the person who causes the death of a human being
> (i) means to cause his death, or
> (ii) means to cause him bodily harm that he knows is likely to cause his death, and is reckless whether death ensues or not;
> (*b*) where a person, meaning to cause death to a human being or meaning to cause him bodily harm that he knows is likely to cause his death, and being reckless whether death ensues or not, by accident or mistake causes death to another human being, notwithstanding that he does not mean to cause death or bodily harm to that human being; or
> (*c*) where a person, for an unlawful object, does anything he knows or ought to know is likely to cause death, and thereby causes death to a human being, notwithstanding that he desires to effect his object without causing death or bodily harm to any human being.

If a person commits culpable homicide and has the objective described in section 229, he is guilty of murder. The simplest case is where the accused means to cause death. A more complex type of murder occurs when the

---

[58] *R. v. D'Angelo* (1927), 48 C.C.C. 127 (Ont. C.A.).

accused meant to cause bodily harm and knew it was likely to cause death and was reckless whether it did or not. In such a case, the accused would be reckless if he foresaw the likelihood of death and did nothing to avoid it, or persisted in his acts and thereby increased the risk of death. The elements of desire and recklessness are subjective and ordinarily must be inferred from the conduct of the accused. Section 229(*b*) deals with a case where a person having the requisite intention to commit murder kills the wrong person. In such a case, a homicide is murder. Section 229(*c*) deals with a more complex situation, as it requires the showing of an unlawful object. Section 229(*c*) of the Code requires that the accused commit some act which is intended to produce some further unlawful object or purpose beyond the act which resulted in death. Thus, if a person commits arson and someone is killed as a result, the arsonist may be guilty of murder if he knew the fire was likely to cause death.[59]

In 1990, the Supreme Court of Canada held that a conviction for murder cannot be based upon a mental element which is less than subjective foresight of death or bodily harm that the accused knows is likely to cause death. Thus, the words "ought to know," which are found in section 229(*c*) of the Criminal Code, have been found to be unconstitutional.[60]

(B) *Causes death in commission of offences*. The second type of murder is the act of causing death during the commission of a number of offences if the offences were committed with an intention other than an intention to kill. This section applies whether or not the person knows that death is likely to be caused to any human being. Section 230 provides that culpable homicide is murder where a person causes death while committing or attempting to commit such crimes as high treason, sabotage, piratical acts, hijacking, escape from prison, assaulting a police officer, sexual assault, aggravated sexual assault, kidnapping, robbery, breaking and entering or arson where

(*a*) he means to cause bodily harm for the purpose of
   (i) facilitating the commission of the offence, or
   (ii) facilitating his flight after committing or attempting to commit the offence, and death ensues from the bodily harm;
(*b*) he administers a stupefying or overpowering thing for a purpose mentioned in paragraph (a), and death ensues therefrom;
(*c*) he wilfully stops, by any means, the breath of a human being for a purpose mentioned in paragraph (a), and the death ensues therefrom; or
(*d*) he uses a weapon or has it upon his person
   (i) during or at the time he commits or attempts to commit the offence, or
   (ii) during or at the time of his flight after committing or attempting to commit the offence,
and death ensues as a consequence.

---

[59] *R. v. Tennant* (1975), 31 C.R.N.S. 1 (Ont. C.A.).
[60] *R. v. Martineau* (1990), 79 C.R. (3d) 129 at 138 (S.C.C.); *R. v. Sit* (1991), 9 C.R. (4th) 126 at 130-131 (S.C.C.).

In R. v. *Martineau*,[61] a majority of the Supreme Court of Canada struck down section 213(*a*) [230(*a*)] of the Criminal Code, holding that the principles of fundamental justice require that a murder conviction be based upon proof of subjective foresight of death or proof that the accused chose to inflict bodily harm that he knew was likely to cause death. Lamer C.J.C., writing for a majority of the court, held that the words "whether or not the person means to cause death to any human being and whether or not he knows that death is likely to be caused to any human being," which are contained in the introductory paragraph of section 230, violated section 7 of the Charter and could not be justified as a reasonable limit under section 1 of the Charter. As a result, Lamer C.J.C. struck down all of section 230, holding that section 213 [230] violated section 7 of the Charter. Lamer C.J.C. stated:

> A conviction for murder carries with it the most severe stigma and punishment of any crime in our society. The principles of fundamental justice require, because of the special nature of the stigma attached to a conviction for murder, and the available penalties, a mens rea reflecting the particular nature of that crime. The effect of s. 213 [230] is to violate the principle that punishment must be proportionate to the moral blameworthiness of the offender, or as Professor Hart puts it in Punishment and Responsibility (1968), at p. 162, the fundamental principle of a morally-based system of law that those causing harm intentionally be punished more severely than those causing harm unintentionally. The rationale underlying the principle that subjective foresight of death is required before a person is labelled and punished as a murderer is linked to the more general principle that criminal liability for a particular result is not justified except where the actor possesses a culpable mental state in respect of that result . . . . In my view, in a free and democratic society that values the autonomy and free will of the individual, the stigma and punishment attaching to the most serious of crimes, murder, should be reserved for those who choose to intentionally cause death or who choose to inflict bodily harm that they know is likely to cause death. The essential role of requiring subjective foresight of death in the context of murder is to maintain a proportionality between the stigma and punishment attached to a murder conviction and the moral blameworthiness of the offender. Murder has long been recognized as the "worst" and most heinous of peace time crimes. It is, therefore, essential that to satisfy the principles of fundamental justice, the stigma and punishment attaching to a murder conviction must be reserved for those who either intend to cause death or who intend to cause bodily harm that they know will likely cause death.[62]

Under section 230(*d*), if a weapon is used or the accused has a weapon at the time mentioned and death ensues, a murder is committed. If a person has a weapon and is fleeing from a robbery and, by accident, the weapon is discharged killing a bystander, the killing will be murder even if the accused did not intend to injure anyone.

Parliament repealed section 230(*d*) of the Criminal Code in 1991. The section had been struck down by the Supreme Court of Canada in 1987 as

[61] *Ibid.*
[62] *Ibid.*, at 138-139.

being in contravention of sections 7 and 11(*d*) of the Charter. Section 230(*d*) of the Criminal Code was substantially different from the other murder sections contained in the Code because it did not require that the accused intend to cause death or have any knowledge that death is likely to result from the commission of an offence. The offence was complete when the Crown proved that the accused armed with a weapon committed, or attempted to commit, one of the offences named in the section, such as kidnapping, forcible confinement, robbery, or breaking and entering. The effect of section 230(*d*) of the Code has long been criticized by academic writers and commentators. In *R. v. Vaillancourt*,[63] the Supreme Court of Canada struck down section 213(d), the forerunner of section 230(*d*) of the Criminal Code.

In *Vaillancourt*, Lamer J. held that before an accused can be convicted of an offence a judge or jury must be satisfied beyond a reasonable doubt of the existence of all the essential elements of the offence. His Lordship stated that the essential elements of the offence included not only those set out by the legislature in the section creating the offence, but also those required by section 7 of the Charter. In *Vaillancourt*, the Supreme Court did not deal with whether the principles of fundamental justice under section 7 required that the Crown prove that the accused intended to kill his victim or intended to cause bodily harm that he knew was likely to cause death. Thus, the court did not decide whether the principles of fundamental justice required that the Crown establish subjective foresight of death. Section 213(*d*) did not even require that the Crown prove "objective foreseeability" — that is, that the accused ought to have known that death was likely to ensue. As we have seen in this chapter, since its pivotal decision in *Vaillancourt*, the Supreme Court of Canada has now held in *Martineau* that where the accused intended to cause death, the minimal mental requirement is subjective foresight of death. In *Vaillancourt*, the accused was convicted of second degree murder by reason of sections 21(2) and 213(*d*) [230(*d*)] of the Criminal Code. The accused appealed his conviction to the Quebec Court of Appeal which upheld the conviction. The accused then appealed further to the Supreme Court of Canada which allowed the appeal and ordered a new trial.

The accused and his accomplice had formed a common intention to rob a pool hall. The accused's accomplice was armed with a gun. In the course of the robbery, the accused's accomplice shot and killed one of the pool hall patrons. The accomplice escaped and was never apprehended. At trial, the accused was convicted of being a party to the offence of second degree murder, pursuant to sections 21 and 213(*d*) [230(*d*)] of the Criminal Code. The accused testified that he was certain that his companion's gun was not loaded. He also testified that he and his accomplice had agreed to commit the robbery armed only with knives. The accused stated that when the accomplice arrived armed with a gun the accused insisted that the gun be unloaded. The accomplice took three bullets from the gun and gave them to the accused. The

---

[63] (1987), 60 C.R. (3d) 289 (S.C.C.).

accused's glove containing the three bullets was found by the police at the pool hall. When the case reached the Supreme Court of Canada, the accused challenged the constitutional validity of section 213(*d*) [230(*d*)] of the Code. Lamer J., who gave the judgment of the court, noted that section 213(*d*) [230(*d*)] of the Code allows an accused to be convicted without proof that the accused knew that death was likely, or ought to have known that death was likely to result from the commission of the acts set out in the section.

Lamer J. stated that section 213(*d*) [230(*d*)] is drafted so as to eliminate the need for the Crown to prove that the accused had what his Lordship termed "objective foreseeability" — that is, that the accused ought to have known that death was likely to ensue. In *Vaillancourt*, Lamer J. held that sections 7 and 11(*d*) of the Charter can be infringed where the definition of an offence does not include an essential element "which is required under s. 7 [of the Charter]."

> ... what offends the presumption of innocence is the fact that an accused may be convicted despite the existence of a reasonable doubt on an essential element of the offence, and I do not think that it matters whether this results from the existence of a reverse onus provision or from the elimination of the need to prove an essential element.[64]

Lamer J. held that objective foreseeability is an essential element of the offence under section 213(*d*) [230(*d*)] of the Criminal Code, saying that "it is a principle of fundamental justice that, absent proof beyond a reasonable doubt of at least objective foreseeability, there surely cannot be a murder conviction."[65] In so holding, he said:

> To varying degrees it can be said that in almost any case a jury satisfied beyond a reasonable doubt that an accused has done one of the prohibited acts described in subss. (*a*) to (*d*) [i.e., in section 213] will be satisfied beyond a reasonable doubt that the accused ought to have known that death was likely to be caused. But not always. Indeed, as a first example, drunkenness would under certain circumstances leave the jury in doubt in that regard. The rule as regards the effect of drunkenness on objective foreseeability was unanimously laid down by this court in *R. v. Vasil* . . ., a murder prosecution under s. 212(*c*). This court addressed the issue at some length and then summarized its conclusion as follows, per Lamer J. . . .:
>> (5) Whilst the test under [s.] 212(*c*) is objective and the behaviour of the accused is to be measured by that of the reasonable man, such a test must nevertheless be applied having regard, not to the knowledge a reasonable man would have had of the surrounding circumstances that allegedly made the accused's conduct dangerous to life, but to the knowledge the accused had of those circumstances;
>> (6) As a result, drunkenness, though not relevant in the determination of what a reasonable man, with the knowledge the accused had of those

---

[64] *Ibid.*, at 327.
[65] *Ibid.*, at 326.

circumstances, would have anticipated, is relevant in the determination of the knowledge which the accused had of those circumstances.

It is clear to me that under s. 213 as drafted, there will be cases where the effect of drunkenness on an accused's knowledge of the circumstances would leave a jury with a reasonable doubt as to whether the accused ought to have known of the likelihood of death ensuing even though it has been proven beyond a reasonable doubt that the accused actually did one of the acts described under subss. (*a*) to (*d*).

A second example, . . . is the accused who is brought into s. 213 not as a principal but through the operation of s. 21(2) of the Criminal Code. . . . It is clear that an accused can be convicted of murder under the combined operation of ss. 21(2) and 213 in circumstances where the death was not objectively foreseeable. As s. 21(2) requires proof of objective foreseeability, the culprit, in my view, must be s. 213.

These two examples suffice, in my view, for one to conclude that notwithstanding proof beyond a reasonable doubt of the matters set forth in subss. (*a*) to (*d*), a jury could reasonably be left in doubt as regards objective foreseeability of the likelihood that death be caused. In other words, s. 213 will catch an accused who performs one of the acts in subss. (*a*) to (*d*) and thereby causes a death but who otherwise would have been acquitted of murder because he did not foresee and could not reasonably have foreseen that death would be likely to result. For that reason, s. 213 prima facie violates ss. 7 and 11(*d*). . . . This takes us to s. 1 for the second phase of the constitutional inquiry.[66]

Having found that section 213(*d*) [230(*d*)] of the Criminal Code *prima facie* violated sections 7 and 11(*d*) of the Charter, Lamer J. considered whether the section could be justified as a reasonable limitation within the meaning of section 1 of the Charter. It will be recalled that section 1 of the Charter states:

The *Canadian Charter of Rights and Freedoms* guarantees the rights and freedoms set out in it subject only to such reasonable limits prescribed by law as can be demonstrably justified in a free and democratic society.

Lamer J. held that section 213(*d*) [230(*d*)] of the Code could not be saved by section 1 of the Charter. In considering that section 213(*d*) [230(*d*)] of the Code was not a reasonable limit demonstrably justified in a democratic society, His Lordship stated:

It is not necessary to convict of murder persons who did not intend to foresee the death and who could not even have foreseen the death in order to deter others from using or carrying weapons. If Parliament wishes to deter the use or carrying of weapons, it should punish the use or carrying of weapons. A good example of this is the minimum imprisonment for using a firearm in the commission of an indictable offence under s. 83 of the Criminal Code. In any event, the conviction

---

[66] *Ibid.*, at 328-330.

for manslaughter which would result instead of a conviction for murder is punishable by from a day in jail to confinement for life in a penitentiary. Very stiff sentences when weapons are involved in the commission of the crime of manslaughter would sufficiently deter the use or carrying of weapons in the commission of crimes. But stigmatizing the crime as murder unnecessarily impairs the Charter right.

In my view, therefore, s. 213(*d*) is not saved by s. 1.[67]

A good definition of the difference between subjective and objective *mens rea* is contained in *R. v. Creighton*,[68] a judgment of the Supreme Court of Canada. In *Creighton*, McLachlin J., writing for a majority of the court, stated:

Subjective mens rea requires that the accused have intended the consequences of his or her acts, or that knowing of the probable consequences of those acts, the accused has proceeded recklessly in the face of the risk. The requisite intent or knowledge may be inferred directly from what the accused said or says about his or her mental state, or indirectly from the act and its circumstances. Even in the latter case, however, it is concerned with "what was actually going on in the mind of this particular accused at the time in question": L'Heureux-Dubé, J. in *R. v. Martineau* . . . .

Objective mens rea, on the other hand, is not concerned with what the accused intended or knew. Rather, the mental fault lies in failure to direct the mind to a risk which the reasonable person would have appreciated. Objective mens rea is not concerned with what was actually in the accused's mind but with what should have been there, had the accused proceeded reasonably.[69]

The Supreme Court of Canada has considered the concept of recklessness in the leading case of *R. v. Sansregret*[70] where the court stated:

[recklessness] is found in the attitude of one who, aware that there is danger that his conduct could bring about the result prohibited by the criminal law, nevertheless persists, despite the risk. It is, in other words, the conduct of one who sees the risk and who takes the chance.[71]

The Supreme Court of Canada has considered the meaning of section 229(*a*)(ii) of the Criminal Code which states that culpable homicide is murder where the person who causes the death of a human being means to cause him bodily harm that he knows is likely to cause his death, and is reckless whether death ensues or not. In *R. v. Nygaard*,[72] the Supreme Court set out the mental element required under section 229(*a*)(ii), saying:

---

[67] *Ibid.*, at 330-331.
[68] (1993), 23 C.R. (4th) 189 (S.C.C.).
[69] *Ibid.*, at 208-209.
[70] [1985] 1 S.C.R. 570.
[71] *Ibid.*, at 582.
[72] (1989), 72 C.R. (3d) 257 (S.C.C.).

The essential element is that of intending to cause bodily harm of such a grave and serious nature that the accused knew that it was likely to result in the death of the victim. The aspect of recklessness is almost an afterthought insofar as the basic intent is concerned.[73]

In *R. v. Cooper*,[74] the Supreme Court of Canada held that in order to convict for murder under section 229(*a*)(ii), the Crown must prove a subjective intent to cause bodily harm and the subjective knowledge that the bodily harm is of such a nature that it is likely to result in death. The court stated that it is only when these two elements of intent are established that an accused can be properly convicted of murder under this section.

(C) *A person who aids or abets the commission of a murder.* A person may be convicted of first or second degree murder if the person is a party to the offence of murder. Thus, if a person aids or abets a murder, the person is on the basis of section 21 of the Criminal Code as guilty of the offence of murder as the person who actually committed the murder. The Criminal Code provisions dealing with aiding and abetting have been discussed earlier in this chapter. In cases where a person is a party to the offence of first or second degree murder, the Supreme Court of Canada has held that the required intent that the aider or abettor must have in order to be convicted of the murder must be the same as that required of the person who actually commits the murder. If the intent of the aiding party is not sufficient to warrant a murder conviction, then the party may still be convicted of manslaughter if the unlawful act which was aided or abetted is one that he knows is likely to cause some harm short of death.[75]

A person who forms a common intention with another person to commit murder can be convicted as a party to the offence of murder under section 21(2) of the Criminal Code. In *R. v. Logan*,[76] the Supreme Court held that the words "ought to know" — that is, the objective component of section 21(2), violated the principles of fundamental justice under section 7 of the Charter in cases where an accused was charged with murder. The court held that the severe stigma attached to a murder conviction coupled with the *mens rea* requirement of subjective foresight of death necessitated the court's finding that in murder cases the Crown could not rely upon the words "ought to have known" to convict an accused under section 21(2) of the Code. Subsequently, in *R. v. Sit*,[77] the Supreme Court affirmed its earlier decision in *Logan*, holding that section 21(2) of the Code violated sections 7 and 11(*d*) of the Charter

---

[73] *Ibid.*, at 277.

[74] (1993), 18 C.R. (4th) 1 at 8 (S.C.C.).

[75] *R. v. Kirkness* (1990), 1 C.R. (4th) 91 at 102 (S.C.C.).

[76] (1990), 79 C.R. (3d) 169 at 178 (S.C.C.).

[77] *Supra*, note 60.

with respect to those offences for which subjective foresight is a constitutional requirement. In *Logan* and *Sit*, the Supreme Court held that only certain Criminal Code offences constitutionally required a minimum level of *mens rea*. Accordingly, the principles of fundamental justice under section 7 of the Charter do not require subjective foreseeability except in those "very few offences" where the stigma associated with conviction and the penalty prescribed is such that subjective foresight is the minimal mental element which is constitutionally required.[78]

(iii) *Classification of murder*

Under section 231, a murder is classified as either first degree murder or second degree murder. First degree murder occurs when one of the following elements is present:

1. The killing is planned and deliberate.
2. Money or other consideration is paid for the killing or arranging for the killing.
3. A police officer, prison employee or similar officer is killed.
4. The killing occurs while committing or attempting to commit a hijacking of an airplane, sexual assault, sexual assault with a weapon, threats to a third party or causing bodily harm, aggravated sexual assault, kidnapping and forcible confinement, or hostage-taking.

"Planned and deliberate" murder does not simply mean "intentional"; an accused cannot be convicted of murder unless his act was intentional. The term "planned and deliberate" has been held by the Supreme Court of Canada to require a considered, "not impulsive" act. In *Aalders v. R.*,[79] the Supreme Court of Canada held that planning and deliberation are separate concepts, both of which must be proven by the Crown beyond a reasonable doubt in any case where the Crown alleges that the murder was planned.

A person may have the intention of killing someone but because of a mental illness, drunkenness, or other condition be incapable of planning a murder. If the murder is not planned, and is not otherwise murder in the first degree by virtue of the identity of the victim or the nature of the offence, the murder will be second degree.[80]

---

[78] In addition to murder, the Supreme Court has required subjective *mens rea* for attempted murder, war crimes, crimes against humanity, theft, and for those crimes where an accessory is required by the Charter to possess the same level of subjective intent as the principal. This list is taken from Don Stuart, *Canadian Criminal Law*, 3rd ed. (Toronto: Carswell, 1995), p. 187.
[79] (1993), 21 C.R. (4th) 141 at 162 (S.C.C.).
[80] Criminal Code, s. 231(7).

The penalty for first degree murder or second degree murder is life imprisonment, but a conviction of first degree murder is subject to a minimum term of 25 years' imprisonment without parole; a conviction for second degree murder requires a minimum term of 10 years without eligibility for parole, or such longer period, up to 25 years, as may be imposed by the judge.

(b) Manslaughter

(i) *Types of manslaughter*

Section 234 provides that culpable homicide which is not murder or infanticide is manslaughter. Manslaughter may be either voluntary or involuntary. Thus, a person who kills another while driving a car may have caused death by criminal negligence and therefore committed a culpable homicide, although he did not intend to injure anyone; such a manslaughter is involuntary. In contrast a person may kill another intending to do so but may have a defence of provocation making the killing manslaughter rather than one of murder; such a case is involuntary manslaughter. Subsections 232(1) and (2) provide that

> (1) Culpable homicide that otherwise would be murder may be reduced to manslaughter if the person who committed it did so in the heat of passion caused by sudden provocation.
> (2) A wrongful act or insult that is of such a nature as to be sufficient to deprive an ordinary person of the power of self-control is provocation . . . if the accused acted on it on the sudden and before there was time for his passion to cool.

The Supreme Court of Canada has decided that provocation must be such as to deprive a reasonable man of his self-control.[81] (This defence is further discussed in Chapter 12, Defences.)

(ii) *Reduction of murder to manslaughter*

As pointed out earlier, all culpable homicides which are not murder or infanticide constitute manslaughter. Accordingly, drunkenness may result in a finding that a person was incapable of the planning and deliberation requisite for murder and thus result in a conviction of manslaughter.[82] Automatism

---

[81] *R. v. Taylor*, [1947] S.C.R. 462 (S.C.C.); *R. v. Manchuk*, [1938] S.C.R. 18.
[82] *R. v. Mitchell*, [1964] S.C.R. 471 (S.C.C.); *R. v. Fyfe*, [1968] 1 C.C.C. 295 (B.C.C.A.).

induced by voluntary intoxication will also reduce a charge of murder to manslaughter.[83]

Manslaughter is a crime requiring *mens rea*.[84] It may be established by showing that the accused committed a prohibited act such as criminal negligence. In *R. v. Mac*,[85] the Alberta Court of Appeal held that the jury may convict a person of manslaughter if satisfied beyond a reasonable doubt that he caused the death of another by an unlawful act or by criminal negligence. *Mens rea* was established by proof that the accused did the prohibited act, even though he had no specific intent to cause death.[86]

(c) Criminal Negligence

Section 219(1) of the Criminal Code provides that

(1) Everyone is criminally negligent who
  (*a*) in doing anything, or
  (*b*) in omitting to do anything that it is his duty to do
shows wanton or reckless disregard for the lives or safety of other persons.

"Duty" is defined to mean a duty imposed by law. There are several offences for which criminal negligence is an essential element. Thus, manslaughter can be committed by criminal negligence; it is an offence to cause bodily harm by criminal negligence (s. 220), and to drive a motor vehicle in a criminally negligent manner (s. 221). Section 220 provides that anyone who causes death by criminal negligence is subject to life imprisonment.

Negligence in criminal law is something more than civil negligence, which occurs when someone who has a duty of care and can foresee that the failure to exercise care may cause harm to others, may be held liable for damages. For criminal negligence to be proven, it must be shown that there was a wanton or reckless disregard for the safety of others. Wanton indicates that the risk had been foreseen, but that the accused chose to act regardless of the risk, while the term reckless covers the situation where the accused may not have foreseen the exact risk, but acted in a manner which indicated that he was unconcerned about such matters. In each case, it is the probable, and not the actual, result of the accused's conduct which must be assessed in determining whether elements of wantonness or recklessness existed.[87] It is quite clear that

---

[83] *Swietlinski v. R.* (1980), 18 C.R. (3d) 231 (S.C.C.); *R. v. Tripodi*, [1955] S.C.R. 438.

[84] The *mens rea* for manslaughter is objective foreseeability of the risk of bodily harm which is not trivial or transitory. There is no constitutional requirement of foreseeability of the risk of death. See *R. v. Creighton* (1993), 23 C.R. (4th) 189 at 199, 238 (S.C.C.).

[85] (1975), 29 C.R.N.S. 270 (Alta. C.A.).

[86] *Ibid.*

[87] *R. v. Louks* (1957), 40 M.P.R. 143 (N.S.C.A.).

the Crown must prove more than a breach of civil law. Thus, a breach of the highway traffic legislation by itself is not sufficient to establish the wanton or reckless disregard element.[88]

In *Leblanc v. R.*,[89] the Supreme Court of Canada considered the case of a pilot who, as a joke, flew over a group of men and killed one of them. Mr. Justice de Grandpré, who gave the majority judgment, held that the Crown in such a case was required to prove:

(*a*) the breach of duty imposed by law, and
(*b*) that the breach showed a wanton or reckless disregard for the lives and safety of other people.[90]

He found that the element of wantonness or recklessness could be established by showing that the accused had acted in a similar manner on other occasions.

The Supreme Court has recently considered the mental element required for criminal negligence. In *R. v. Waite*,[91] the court considered criminal negligence involving the operation of a motor vehicle whereas in *R. v. Tutton*[92] the court dealt with criminal negligence arising out of the failure of parents to provide proper medical treatment for their child. In each case there were three separate judgments and no clear opinion emerged from the cases as to whether criminal negligence required subjective or objective *mens rea.*

Although members of the court disagreed as to whether criminal negligence required subjective or objective *mens rea*, the court agreed that it is an error to instruct the jury that the prosecution must prove that the accused deliberately or wilfully assumed the risk. Accordingly, in a case where the accused is charged with criminal negligence in the operation of a motor vehicle, the Crown does not have to prove that the accused deliberately and wilfully assumed the risk in the manner in which he was driving.

In *R. v. Anderson*,[93] the Supreme Court subsequently held that whether one uses the subjective or objective approach to the accused's state of mind, the fundamental question is whether the accused's conduct constituted a marked departure from the norm. In *Anderson*, Sopinka J., writing for the court, held that as the risk of harm increases, the easier it is to conclude that a reasonably prudent person would have foreseen the consequences and thus it is easier to conclude that the accused must have foreseen the consequences. His Lordship said that as the risk of harm increases the less of a difference there is between the subjective and objective approaches to the accused's mental state.

---

[88] *R. v. Titchner*, [1961] O.R. 606 (Ont. C.A.).
[89] [1977] 1 S.C.R. 339.
[90] *Ibid.*, at 356.
[91] (1989), 69 C.R. (3d) 323 (S.C.C.).
[92] (1989), 69 C.R. (3d) 289 (S.C.C.).
[93] (1990), 75 C.R. (3d) 50 (S.C.C.).

If an accused testifies that he gave no thought to the risk, he can still be convicted of criminal negligence. In *Tutton*, Wilson J. stated:

> Conduct which shows a wanton or reckless disregard for the lives and safety of others will by its nature constitute prima facie evidence of the mental element, and in the absence of some evidence that casts doubt on the normal degree of mental awareness, proof of the act and reference to what a reasonable person in the circumstances must have realized will lead to a conclusion that the accused was aware of the risk or wilfully blind to the risk.[94]

4. NON-FATAL OFFENCES AGAINST THE PERSON

(a) Assaults Generally

Common assault was a crime at common law which could be committed by physical violence or by display of force causing an apprehension of violence. The Code now provides for a variety of assault crimes including simple assaults, assault with a weapon, assault causing bodily harm, aggravated assault, assault with intent, assault of police and a variety of sexual assaults. Section 265 provides:

> (1) A person commits an assault when
> (*a*) without the consent of another person, he applies force intentionally to that other person, directly or indirectly;
> (*b*) he attempts or threatens, by an act or gesture, to apply force to another person, if he has, or causes that other person to believe on reasonable grounds that he has, present ability to effect his purpose; or
> (*c*) while openly wearing or carrying a weapon or an imitation thereof, he accosts or impedes another person or begs.
> (2) This section applies to all forms of assault, including sexual assault, sexual assault with a weapon, threats to a third party or causing bodily harm and aggravated sexual assault.

Under paragraph (1)(*a*) the assault may be committed both directly and indirectly; for example, if the accused forced another person to strike the victim, he could be convicted.

(i) *Absence of consent*

The prosecution must prove the absence of a consent by the victim to the application of force. However, section 265 provides that a consent to any assault is ineffective if obtained by the application of force to the complainant

---

[94] *Supra*, note 92, at 316.

or to a person other than the complainant, by threats or fear of the application of force to any person by fraud or by the exercise of authority. It has been held that consent may be obtained by inducements, such as an offer of payment for sexual intercourse.[95] If an accused alleges that he believed that the complainant did give consent, a judge, if satisfied there is sufficient evidence of consent, shall instruct the jury that in reviewing the evidence relating to such belief it must consider the presence or absence of reasonable grounds for that belief (s. 265(4)). A question of consent sometimes arises in assault cases arising out of a game. In such cases, the consent to be effective must be freely given with an appreciation of all the risks and the force used must not go beyond the consent given.[96]

(ii) *Threats*

Under section 265(1)(*b*) an assault may occur without the application of force by the attempted or threatened use of force if the accused causes the victim to believe reasonably that the accused has the present ability to apply such force. It may be that the force cannot really be applied, but if the victim reasonably believes that it can, the offence will be committed. A reasonable apprehension may be established even though if one knew all of the facts the victim's apprehension may have been unjustified, as for example, when an unloaded gun is brandished.[97] Section 265(1)(*c*) creates the offence of armed begging. In such a case the weapon need not be real or produced so long as it is openly worn or carried at the time the accused accosts or impedes the victim or begs.

(iii) *Mens rea*

Mens rea is an essential element of an assault, and so an accidental touching or some reflex application of force will not create criminal liability. But if the accused intended to strike one person and strikes another, the necessary intent will be established.[98] The necessary *mens rea* is established under section 265(1)(*a*) where the force was either applied intentionally or recklessly.[99] Similarly, in any other types of assault it is sufficient to show that the accused intended the act or was reckless whether it occurred or not.

---

[95] *R. v. Arnold*, [1947] O.R 147 (C.A.).

[96] The courts have held that one cannot consent to the infliction of bodily harm which is not minor. See *R. v. McIntosh* (1991), 64 C.C.C. (3d) 294 (N.S.C.A.).

[97] *London v. D.P.P*, [1976] Crim. L.R. 921.

[98] *R. v. Deakin* (1974), 16 C.C.C. (2d) 1 (Man. C.A.).

[99] *R. v. Abraham* (1974), 30 C.C.C. (2d) 332 (Que. C.A.).

(iv) *Specific defence*

Section 43 of the Code provides that a teacher, parent or a person standing in the place of a parent may use force in correcting a child if the force does not exceed what is reasonable in the circumstances. What is reasonable is a question of fact in each case.[100] The accused may have a defence to an assault if the accused honestly, even if mistakenly, believed that the victim was consenting to the criminal conduct. The Supreme Court of Canada, in *Pappajohn v. R.*, held that where an accused alleges he believed the victim consented, a judge, if satisfied that there is sufficient evidence which if believed by a jury would justify an acquittal, shall instruct the jury to consider whether there was a reasonable ground for such a belief.[101] In that case the Supreme Court found that the real question in cases involving consent was whether the accused himself had an honest belief, and that it is improper to consider that the test is an objective one determined by what a reasonable man would think. Of course, if the evidence of mistake as to consent appears to be based on unreasonable grounds, a jury is very unlikely to credit it. (The defence of self-defence and defence of property are discussed in Chapter 12, Defences.)

(b) Assault with a Weapon

Section 267(1) provides:

(1) Every one who, in committing an assault
    (*a*) carries, uses or threatens to use a weapon or an imitation thereof, or
    (*b*) causes bodily harm to the complainant
is guilty of an indictable offence and is liable to imprisonment for a term not exceeding ten years.

"Bodily harm" means "any hurt or injury to the complainant that interferes with his or her health or comfort and that is more than merely transient or trifling in nature." The offence may be committed, although the weapon is not used. Indeed, it is arguable that it may be committed by a threat to use a weapon, although the accused didn't have a weapon. It has been held that a weapon may be carried for the purposes of the section if it is in an automobile of which the accused had care and control.[102] Of course, the prosecution must establish that the accused committed an assault. A weapon may also have been used, although it was not discharged. In *Rowe v. R.*,[103] Kerwin J., on

---

[100] *Campeau v. R.* (1951), 103 C.C.C. 355 (Que. K.B.).
[101] (1980), 14 C.R. (3d) 243 at 267 (S.C.C.).
[102] *R. v. Hanabury* (1970), 1 C.C.C. (2d) 438 (P.E.I.S.C.).
[103] [1951] S.C.R. 713.

behalf of the majority in the Supreme Court of Canada, held that if a person pulled out a gun and held it in his hand, such an action constituted a use.

If a person is charged with the offence of an assault with a weapon and the Crown only proves that an assault occurred, the accused may be convicted of a simple assault, as it is a lesser offence which is included in the more serious charge. Section 662 of the Code provides that a count in an indictment is divisible and where the offence charged includes the commission of another offence, the accused may be convicted of the included offence or of an attempt to commit an offence so included. Thus, in a case where the evidence does not prove first degree murder, but proves second degree murder or an attempt to commit second degree murder, the jury may find the accused not guilty of first degree murder but guilty of second degree murder or such an attempt.

(c) Assault Causing Bodily Harm

Section 267 creates the offence of an assault causing bodily harm. Section 269 provides that

> Every one who unlawfully causes bodily harm to any person is guilty of
> (a) an indictable offence and is liable to imprisonment for a term not exceeding ten years; or
> (b) an offence punishable on summary conviction and liable to imprisonment for a term not exceeding eighteen months.

The victim in such a case must suffer a hurt or injury that interferes with his health or comfort and is more than merely transient or trifling in nature; it has been held, for example, that repeated face slapping resulting in a swollen face and bleeding nose constitutes bodily harm. It appears that the Crown need not prove physical harm, but may also succeed by establishing psychological harm.[104] A causal connection between the victim's harm and the accused's act is an essential element of the offence. Under section 267(1)(b) the prosecution must show that there was an assault and bodily harm, while under section 269 it is only necessary to show that there was an unlawful act or omission and bodily harm. A person charged with assault with a weapon or assault causing bodily harm may be convicted of simple assault if the weapon or bodily harm element of the offence is not proved.

---

[104] *R. v. Petrovic* (1984), 13 C.C.C. (3d) 416 (Ont. C.A.).

(d) Aggravated Assault

Section 268 provides:

(1) Every one commits an aggravated assault who wounds, maims, disfigures or endangers the life of the complainant.
(2) Every one who commits an aggravated assault is guilty of an indictable offence and is liable to imprisonment for a term not exceeding fourteen years.

The *actus reus* or external circumstances of the crime are proved by showing the accused has wounded, maimed, disfigured or endangered the life of the victim. This is a much more serious offence than other assault offences, being punishable by imprisonment for 14 years. The term "maims" means to deprive a person of the use of some member of the body, to mutilate or to cripple. The term "disfigures" means to do an injury so as to mark the figure or appearance, to deform or to deface. The offence based on wounding, maiming or disfiguring requires bodily harm to be inflicted on the victim. But bodily harm is not a necessary element of the offence of endangering the life of someone; thus a person may issue a threat causing someone to flee over a railway track as a train approaches with the result that the person's life is in danger.

Mens rea is a necessary element of this offence. In *R. v. George*,[105] Fauteux J. said that where a specific intent is required, it is necessary to establish that the act was done for the purpose of securing some result other than the commission of the act. An act requiring only a general intent may be the product of an undeliberated act of passion while a specific intent must show some perception and deliberation. The offence under section 266 does not require anything more than a general intent established by the commission of the act. Offences which require a specific intent are those where the definition of the offence expressly or impliedly requires a mental element beyond that which flows from the doing of the act.[106]

If the Crown fails to prove this offence, the accused may be found guilty of assault, assault causing bodily harm or attempted aggravated assault if the factual proof warrants such a finding, as they all may be considered to be included offences.

---

[105] [1960] S.C.R. 871.
[106] *R v. Slaughenwhite (No. 2)* (1905), 9 C.C.C. 173 (S.C.C.).

5. OFFENCES AGAINST PROPERTY

(a) Theft

Section 322 provides:

(1) Every one commits theft who fraudulently and without colour of right takes, or fraudulently and without colour of right converts to his use or to the use of another person, anything, whether animate or inanimate, with intent,

> (a) to deprive, temporarily or absolutely, the owner of it, or a person who has a special property or interest in it, of the thing or of his property or interest in it;
> (b) to pledge it or deposit it as security;
> (c) to part with it under a condition with respect to its return that the person who parts with it may be unable to perform; or
> (d) to deal with it in such a manner that it cannot be restored in the condition in which it was at the time it was taken or converted.

(2) A person commits theft when, with intent to steal anything, he moves it or causes it to move or to be moved, or begins to cause it to become movable.

(3) A taking or conversion of anything may be fraudulent notwithstanding that it is effected without secrecy or attempt at concealment.

. . . .

There are a number of offences against property which have a certain similarity — *i.e.*, theft, fraud or false pretenses — but in theft the owner seldom intends to part with his property, while in fraud and false pretenses the owner parts with the property with his full consent, but the consent is one obtained by deceit, falsehood or other fraudulent means or some type of false representation.

In *R. v. Myles*,[107] the accused was charged with theft of auto parts and were acquitted because there was no evidence that the parts had been removed from the car pool where they were situate. The British Columbia Court of Appeal, however, reversed the decision because regardless of who had removed them originally, the movement of the parts from a road to the accused's vehicle was theft. In *R. v. Johnson*,[108] a banker deposited $6,000 into the accused's account which the accused retained. The Manitoba Court of Appeal held that the accused's act in so retaining the money and converting it to his own use was theft. Thus, the wrongful use of money given one for a particular purpose and used for another is theft.[109] Section 330 specifically provides that a person commits theft when he receives anything on terms requiring him to account for it or to pay it to someone else and does not do so.

---

[107] (1946), 62 B.C.R. 392 (B.C.C.A.).
[108] (1978), 42 C.C.C. (2d) 249 (Man. C.A.).
[109] *R. v. Lowden* (1981), 59 C.C.C. (2d) 1 (Alta. C.A.).

(i) *Different kinds of theft*

The removal of goods from one part of the store to another without removing them from the store may constitute theft as the evidence may indicate an intention to commit a theft.[110] The offence can only be a theft of the thing; accordingly, one cannot steal a ride on a bus. Moreover, theft will not be committed if the owner has abandoned the property intending to give up the property in the thing.[111]

Section 326 of the Code specifically provides that it is an offence to steal electricity or to use fraudulently any telecommunication facility or service. Hence, if someone finds a method of using a long distance service, he may be prosecuted successfully upon showing that the obtaining of the service was intentional and deliberate and with the knowledge that the service was not freely available to the accused. This section does not, however, criminalize the mere interception of an unpaid signal. Thus, when an accused, in attempting to correct his cable reception, altered it so that he was able to receive pay T.V., he was acquitted.

Section 332(4) provides that property may be converted even though it is not in the possession of the owner. To do so, there must be an act which is inconsistent with the rights of the owner. Accordingly, if someone borrows a book and writes his own name in it, the act of writing his name in the book will constitute conversion.[112]

Section 332 provides that theft is committed where a person receives money or valuable security under a direction requiring him to apply it or the proceeds to a specific purpose or to a specific person and fraudulently, contrary to the direction, fails to do. Subsection 332(2) provides that it is not theft where the accused receives such money in circumstances where it would ordinarily give rise to a debtor-creditor relationship, unless the direction was in writing. It appears that the switching of price tags so that one buys a product for a cheaper price, is a false pretence but not a theft, because the store owner has consented to handing over the property.[113] Thus, when a person switched expensive goods to a box with a cheaper price ticket, the proper charge was one of obtaining by false pretences, but not theft as the property was taken with the consent of the owner.[114]

[110] *R. v. R.D.* (1985), 18 C.C.C. (3d) 36 (Alta. Prov. Ct.).

[111] *Williams v. Phillips* (1956), 41 Cr. App. R. 5 (C.C.A.).

[112] *R. v. Thomas* (1953), 37 Cr. App. R. 169 (C.C.A.).

[113] *R. v. Dawood* (1976), 27 C.C.C. (2d) 300 (Alta. C.A.).

[114] *R. v. Malhotra* (1975), 28 C.C.C. (2d) 551 (Ont. Prov. Ct.).

(ii) *Elements of the offence*

The offence may only be committed if the taking or converting is done (a) fraudulently, (b) without colour of right, and (c) with one of the intents described in section 322(1). If an accused took something without the owner's consent, he does not have any colour of right, but if he took it honestly, believing the owner would have consented to it if the owner had been there, then he may not be acting fraudulently. In *R. v. Howson*, Laskin J.A. said

> Although it may be doubtful . . . whether apart from special situations, the term "fraudulent" adds anything to the phrase "without colour of right", it is enough to say that it merely emphasizes the intentional character of the offence. . . ."[115]

If an accused honestly believes he is entitled to take property, as where a storekeeper repossesses goods for which he has not been paid, the act is not theft because he will not be acting fraudulently and without colour of right. Hence, a person who keeps a car beyond the lease period believing she is entitled to do so is not guilty of theft.

In *Hewson v. R.*[116] the Supreme Court of Canada held that a trial judge was correct in instructing a jury that the reasonableness of a belief when objectively considered does not necessarily destroy the honesty of the belief, but unreasonableness may be considered along with other evidence in determining whether the Crown has established these articles were taken without colour of right. In that case, a garage operator who took a car to a parking compound refused to release it believing he was entitled to so refuse until the parking charges were paid. The belief was mistaken, but he was acquitted because it was considered that he had an honest belief that he was entitled to retain the car.

Once the elements of fraud and without colour of right are established, an essential element of the offence is to establish that the act was done with one of the intents set out in section 322. The intent is clear when one takes something intending to deprive the owner of it permanently. Problems can arise when the intent is only to deprive the owner temporarily, as a person may intend to take something temporarily and return it before the owner requires it — in that case a person would not have the necessary intent to deprive the owner even temporarily.[117] If, for example, an accused left a gas station without paying because he was in a hurry and was not waited upon promptly, he could be acquitted because the Crown might well fail to prove that he had any intention to deprive the owner of the property. *In R. v. Wyman*[118] the accused, who was a bookkeeper, inserted in a group of cheques to be signed by the

---

[115] [1966] 2 O.R. 63 at 78 (C.A.).
[116] [1979] 2 S.C.R. 82.
[117] *R. v. Ballantyne* (1982), 37 O.R. (2d) 794 (Ont. C.A.).
[118] (1977), 8 A.R. 73 (Alta. C.A.).

manager two cheques payable to her which the manager mistakenly signed. The bookkeeper was convicted of theft, as she had intended to deprive the employer of the proceeds of the cheques.

One usually thinks of theft as a deprivation of property from its owner. Section 322 refers not only to the owner but to a person who has "a special property or interest" in the article. The purpose of section 322 is to protect the possession of property. Section 328 specifically provides that a person may be guilty of theft, although the property is taken

> (*a*) by the owner of it from a person who has a special property or interest in it [i.e., a pawn broker];
> (*b*) by a person who has a special property or interest in it from the owner of it;
> (*c*) by a lessee of it from his reversioner;
> (*d*) by one of several joint owners, tenants in common or partners of or in it from the other persons who have an interest in it;

> . . . .

The term, "special property or interest", refers to a property right including a right to possession of the things stolen.[119] It has been held that although gas is put in one's car, indicating an intent to transfer property, the gas station has a special interest in the gas until paid.[120] The purpose of this section is to ensure that disputes as to the title of property are settled in accordance with the law and not by someone taking the law into his own hands.

Section 322(1)(*b*) deals with situations where the accused may not intend to deprive the owner of the property, as where one might take silver or a car to pledge them intending to return the property to the owner. This would be a theft under paragraph (*b*) although the necessary intent to deprive the owner might preclude a conviction under paragraph (*a*). Similarly, the offences created by paragraphs (*c*) and (*d*) cover cases where the intent to deprive the owner of the property may not be established but nevertheless, the accused has done something which would prevent him from returning the property.

(iii) *Doctrine of recent possession*

The proof of the taking may be established by what is known as the doctrine of recent possession. The Supreme Court of Canada held in *R. v. Newton* [121] that when an accused was in possession of stolen goods and no explanation was given, the jury should be instructed that evidence of such possession standing alone raises a *prima facie* case on which a guilty verdict may be

---

[119] *R. v. Schoburn*, [1962] S.C.R. 215.
[120] *R. v. Pratt* (1983), 26 Sask. R. 268 (Sask. Q.B.).
[121] [1976] 3 W.W.R. 199 (S.C.C.).

entered. In *R. v. Riggs*,[122] the accused was convicted of theft after he was seen near the scene of the crime throwing a bag from a car and was found in possession of stolen goods. The term recent is a relative one, as the possession of stolen property has been established as long as eight and one-half months after the theft.[123] But the Supreme Court of Canada found that an appeal should be allowed in a case where the accused was convicted, having been found in possession at a time when the theft could have occurred more than a year before. It was held that a jury might reasonably have acquitted had it been properly instructed as to what could be considered "recent."[124]

(b) Robbery

Robbery is essentially theft with violence. Section 343 of the Code provides:

> **343.** Every one commits robbery who
>   (*a*) steals, and for the purpose of extorting whatever is stolen or to prevent or overcome resistance to the stealing, uses violence or threats of violence to a person or property;
>   (*b*) steals from any person and, at the time he steals or immediately before or immediately thereafter, wounds, beats, strikes or uses any personal violence to that person;
>   (*c*) assaults any person with intent to steal from him; or
>   (*d*) steals from any person while armed with an offensive weapon or imitation thereof.

(i) *Elements of the offence*

Stealing is defined by section 2 of the Code to mean to commit theft and thus it is necessary for the prosecution in a robbery case to show the intent essential for theft. An honest belief that an accused had a right to property will constitute a defence to a robbery charge.[125] The violence required by section 343 is violence which is criminally culpable. In *R. v. Lieberman*,[126] Mr. Justice Jessup of the Ontario Court of Appeal held, "I think the violence so especially condemned by Parliament in section 288 [343] must be taken to be criminally culpable violence and not violence justified as self-defence."[127] It is not necessary that the violence be used to accomplish or further the theft.

---

[122] (1984), 64 N.S.R. (2d) 134 (C.A.).
[123] *R. v. Killan* (1973), 12 C.C.C. (2d) 114 (B.C.C.A.).
[124] *R. v. Saieva* (1982), 68 C.C.C. (2d) 97 (S.C.C.).
[125] *Supra*, note 116.
[126] [1970] 3 O.R. 407 (C.A.).
[127] *Ibid.*, at 416.

The purpose for which the personal violence is used is immaterial, provided it accompanies the act of stealing or immediately precedes it or follows it.[128] However, the violence contemplated requires proof of more than a mere assault. The mere nudge of the victim was held by the Ontario Court of Appeal in *R. v. Lew*[129] to be insufficient to justify a conviction.

If a person threatens violence, the offence of robbery will be committed. In *R. v. Katrensky*,[130] where an accused went to a bank and gave the teller a bag saying "empty your till," it was held that the teller acted under a threat of violence and that accordingly, the offence of robbery had been committed. It is clear that an actual threat need not be made, but it will be sufficient if the act of the accused leads to a state of fear or apprehension, as in *R. v. McDonald*[131] where the accused without showing a weapon said "this is a holdup" while wearing a hallowe'en mask.

The violence required for a conviction under subsection 343(*a*) need not be used to obtain the article stolen, but may be only used to prevent resistance and any force intended to do so will be violence within the meaning of this section.[132] The violence required for conviction under subsection 343(*b*) is more than a mere assault. Thus a nudge, as noted earlier, would not be sufficient, although its use could be an assault[133] which could be sufficient to justify a conviction of robbery if it was applied with intent to steal. It is not necessary to show that the accused intended to use a weapon to sustain a conviction under subsection 343(*d*). The Quebec Court of Appeal held that an accused may be convicted, even though his only intention in having a gun at the site of the theft was to impersonate a bank guard.[134]

The violence required by subsection 343(*d*) need not be for the purpose of effecting the theft, provided it accompanies it or immediately follows it or precedes it. However, there must be some proximity between the time of the theft and the violence. Accordingly, in *R. v. Burden*, where a person stole a wallet and violence was used when the accused was pursued, the Ontario Court of Appeal held that, as the violence was "immediately afterwards" it was related to the theft and there should be a conviction.[135] It seems that if the theft and the violence are part of a continuous chain of events, a robbery conviction will result.

[128] *R. v. Downer* (1978), 40 C.C.C. (2d) 532 (Ont. C.A.); *R. v. Lew* (1978), 40 C.C.C. (2d) 140 (Ont. C.A.).
[129] *Ibid.*
[130] (1975), 24 C.C.C. (2d) 350 (B.C. Prov. Ct.).
[131] (1981), 64 C.C.C. (2d) 415 (Man. C.A.).
[132] *R. v. Trudel* (1984), 12 C.C.C. (3d) 342 (Que. C.A.).
[133] *R. v. Lew, supra,* note 128.
[134] *Tremblay v. Quebec (A.G.)* (1984), 43 C.R. (3d) 92 (Que. C.A.).
[135] (1973), 11 C.C.C. (2d) 491 (Ont. C.A.).

(ii) *Punishment*

The punishment for robbery is life imprisonment. The sentence imposed will depend in most cases on the extent to which violence has been used. A suspended sentence may be imposed where the violence is minimal and the accused does not have a previous record. Where the violence is serious, as in the case of *R. v. Miller* where the victim was left a "living vegetable" following a beating, the Manitoba Court of Appeal imposed a sentence of 15 years.[136] In *R. v. Kempton*, the Alberta Court of Appeal upheld a sentence equivalent of life imprisonment where an accused was convicted of 16 charges of armed robbery by imposing consecutive sentences totalling more than 200 years.[137]

(c) Breaking and Entering

Section 348 provides:

(1) Every one who
  (*a*) breaks and enters a place with intent to commit an indictable offence therein,
  (*b*) breaks and enters a place and commits an indictable offence therein, or
  (*c*) breaks out of a place after
    (i) committing an indictable offence therein, or
    (ii) entering the place with intent to commit an indictable offence therein,

. . . .

is guilty of an indictable offence.

The punishment for such an offence is imprisonment for life if the offence is committed in relation to a dwelling-house, or to imprisonment for 14 years if the offence is committed elsewhere. Subsection (2) provides that evidence that an accused broke and entered a place or attempted to break and enter a place is, in the absence of evidence to the contrary, proof that he broke and entered a place or attempted to, as the case may be, with intent to commit an indictable offence therein. A similar provision applies where a person breaks out of a place. A place includes a dwelling-house, a building or a structure, or any part thereof, railway vehicle, a vessel, an aircraft, a trailer, a pen or enclosure where fur bearing animals are kept for breeding or commercial purposes (s. 348(3)). A dwelling-house means the whole or part of a building or struc-

---

[136] (1972), 8 C.C.C. (2d) 97 (Man. C.A.).
[137] (1980), 53 C.C.C. (2d) 176 (Alta. C.A.).

ture kept or occupied as a permanent or temporary residence. Thus, a mobile home used as a residence is a dwelling-house.

(i) *Elements of the offence*

"Break" is defined by section 321 as meaning "(*a*) to break any part, internal or external, of (*b*) to open any thing that is used or intended to be used to close or to cover an internal or external opening." A person enters as soon as any part of his body or any part of an instrument that he uses is within anything that is being entered. Section 350(*b*) provides:

> (*b*) a person shall be deemed to have broken and entered if
> > (i) he obtained entrance by a threat or artifice or by collusion with a person within, or
> > (ii) he entered without lawful justification or excuse, the proof of which lies on him, by a permanent or temporary opening.

"Artifice" is a manoeuvre or stratagem such as sneaking into premises behind someone entering lawfully.[138] Entering through a door opened sufficiently wide to allow the accused to enter a building was held by the Ontario Court of Appeal not to constitute breaking.[139] The Supreme Court of Canada subsequently held that this decision was wrong, as such an entry was deemed by section 350(*b*) to be breaking and entering as the accused entered without justification.[140] If a person enters a house by an open window, but then opens the door to gain access he will have committed breaking and entering because he has opened something intended to cover an internal opening. An enclosed area surrounded by a fence has been held to be a place.[141] Section 350 includes as breaking and entering, an entrance by collusion, but if an owner tries to trap a person and by doing something to encourage or to induce entry, the owner may be held to have consented. Thus, the Supreme Court of Canada held in the *Lemieux v. R.* that where police induced an entry, the entry should be deemed to have been done with consent and the accused should be acquitted.[142]

Mens rea is an essential element of the offence but the intent required differs depending on the subsection under which the charge is laid. A charge under paragraph 348(1)(*a*) requires a specific intent to commit an indictable offence. However, it would appear that under paragraphs (*b*) and (*c*)(i) only a general intent need be proved. Where a specific intent is required then it must be proven beyond a reasonable doubt, but proof may be supplied by showing circumstances, warranting an inference of guilt.[143]

---

[138] *R. v. Leger* (1976), 31 C.C.C. (2d) 413 (Ont. C.A.).

[139] *R. v. Jewell* (1974), 28 C.R.N.S. 331 (Ont. C.A.).

[140] *Johnson v. R.* (1977), 34 C.C.C. (2d) 12 (S.C.C.).

[141] *R. v. Desjatnik* (1981), 64 C.C.C. (2d) 408 (Que. S.P.).

[142] [1967] S.C.R. 492.

[143] Criminal Code, ss. 348(2), 349(2).

(ii) *Presumption of intent*

Section 348(2) provides that once it is proven that an accused broke and entered a place, then, in the absence of evidence to the contrary, the fact of such breaking is proof he intended to commit an indictable offence. This does not place the onus on the accused to establish that he did not have such an intent, but only imposes an obligation to adduce some evidence to the contrary. Thus, once juveniles gave evidence denying the intent to commit an indictable offence, although they had broken into a house, the onus was on the Crown to prove intent.[144] The evidence to the contrary required to displace the presumption contained in section 348(2) is simply evidence which is sufficient to raise in the mind of the trier of fact a reasonable doubt.[145] The onus, of course, remains on the Crown throughout to show that on the whole of the evidence the Crown has proved its case beyond a reasonable doubt. Evidence of the prior ingestion of alcohol or drugs is evidence to the contrary, as it tends to negative the existence of the requisite intent. In *R. v. Johnnie*, the British Columbia Court of Appeal held that if a person was so drunk that he could not form the specific intent to commit an indictable offence, he could not be convicted of breaking and entering with intent to commit such an offence.[146] Where an accused broke into a cottage, slept there, took nothing and left, the Supreme Court of Canada held that the circumstances negatived any specific intent to commit an indictable offence.[147] Where the evidence did not permit one to identify which of several offences the accused intended to commit, and one was a summary conviction offence, the Ontario Court of Appeal held the accused must be acquitted as the requisite specific intent was not shown.[148] But if an accused breaks into a house and commits an assault there, he may be convicted of an offence under section 348(1)(*b*), as it is not necessary under that section to show any specific intent to commit an indictable offence.

(iii) *Lesser offence*

Section 349 provides for the lesser offence of being unlawfully in a dwelling-house:

(1) Every one who without lawful excuse, the proof of which lies on him, enters or is in a dwelling-house with intent to commit an indictable offence therein is guilty of an indictable offence and liable to imprisonment for a term not exceeding ten years.

. . . .

[144] *R. v. E.R.* (1977), 34 C.C.C. (2d) 249 (B.C. Prov. Ct.).
[145] *R. v. Proudlock* (1978), 5 C.R. (3d) 21 (S.C.C.).
[146] (1975), 30 C.R.N.S. 202 (B.C.C.A.).
[147] *R. v. Bernard*, [1980] 1 S.C.R. 593.
[148] *R. v. Garlow* (1982), 10 C.C.C. (3d) 575 (Ont. C.A.).

There is a presumption under this section that if an accused has entered a dwelling-house without lawful excuse he is, in the absence of any evidence to the contrary, deemed to have been there with intent to commit an indictable offence. The principles applicable to section 348 as to evidence to the contrary and the onus on the Crown to prove intent are also applicable to this section. There does appear to be a question whether placing the burden of proof of an essential part of an offence on an accused offends the presumption of innocence Charter right. This is a much different requirement than placing a burden on an accused to introduce "evidence to the contrary," as that does not shift the burden to prove an essential fact from the Crown to the accused.

6. OFFENCES RELATING TO PEACE OFFICERS IN THE EXERCISE OF THEIR POWERS

(a) Scope of Powers

Peace officers are given broad powers by the Criminal Code, including the power to arrest without warrant and the power to issue an appearance notice requiring one to appear in court. In addition, at common law, the duties of the police include the prevention of crime, the detection and apprehension of criminals, keeping evidence safely for presentation in court, the prevention of breaches of the peace, the enforcement of statutes and by-laws and the preservation of human life.[149] Police officers are also given powers by provincial legislation. The term "peace officer" is defined by section 2 of the Code to include sheriffs, justices of the peace, wardens, prison employees, bailiffs, customs officers, officers of the armed forces and pilots of aircraft as well as any person employed for the preservation and maintenance of the public peace and for the service or execution of civil process. Thus, the Code confers on a substantial body of persons what are commonly thought of as police powers, and contains a number of powers designed to ensure that such persons are able to carry out their duties without interference.

(b) Assaulting a Peace Officer

Section 270 makes it an offence to assault a public officer or police officer engaged in the execution of his duty, or a person acting in aid of such an officer. It also makes it an offence to assault a person with intent to resist or prevent the lawful arrest or detention of the person charged or any other person. It is also an offence to assault a person who is engaged in the lawful execution of a process against lands or goods or to do so with intent to rescue

---

[149] *R. v. Waterfield*, [1964] 1 Q.B. 164; *Johansen v. R.; Daniluk v. R.* (1947), 3 C.R. 508 (S.C.C.); *R. v. Dietrich* (1978), 39 C.C.C. (2d) 361 (B.C.S.C.).

anything taken under such lawful process. This is an offence which may be punishable as an indictable offence with imprisonment for a term up to five years, or on summary conviction.

(c) Obstructing a Peace Officer

Section 129 provides:

129. Everyone who
    (*a*) resists or wilfully obstructs a public officer or peace officer in the execution of his duty or any person lawfully acting in aid of such an officer,
    (*b*) omits, without reasonable excuse, to assist a public officer or peace officer in the execution of his duty in arresting a person or in preserving the peace, after having reasonable notice that he is required to do so, or
    (*c*) resists or wilfully obstructs any person in the lawful execution of a process against lands or goods or in making a lawful distress or seizure,
is guilty of
    (*d*) an indictable offence and liable to imprisonment for a term not exceeding two years, or
    (*e*) an offence punishable on summary conviction.

(i) *In execution of duty*

The broad powers given to police and public officers and the provisions of the Code designed to protect them in the exercise of their duties must be reconciled with the rights of citizens and, accordingly, police powers are construed strictly.[150] Laskin J. in *R. v. Biron* said there was an overriding principle "upon which our criminal law is based, namely, the right of an individual to be left alone, to be free of public or private restraint, save as the law provides otherwise."[151] Thus, a conviction for obstructing police may only be made if the officer is in execution of his duty and has not exceeded the power conferred upon him, and the necessary *mens rea* is established. The courts in such cases ascertain whether there has been a *prima facie* unlawful interference with a person's liberty or property and then determine whether the interference was within the duties of an officer; if it is not, the person accused must be acquitted.[152] A police officer is not acting "in the execution of his duty" merely because he is on duty. The question is not whether the officer was on duty, but whether he was executing some duty at the time of the obstruction. The Crown has the onus of establishing the facts showing that the officer in question was acting in the execution of his duties.[153]

When the police cordoned off an area when Premier Kosygin of the

---

[150] *R. v. Biron* (1975), 30 C.R.N.S. 109 (S.C.C.).
[151] *Ibid.*, at 124.
[152] *R. v. Knowlton* (1973), 21 C.R.N.S. 344 (S.C.C.).
[153] *R. v. Middleton*, [1969] 4 C.C.C. 197 (Ont. C.A.); *R. v. King* (1949), 9 C.R. 34 (Ont. C.A.).

U.S.S.R. was visiting Edmonton and a citizen insisted on his right to enter the area to take pictures, pushing constables to do so, he was convicted of obstruction. The court held that the police were acting within their powers to preserve peace, order and public safety which had been conferred on them by provincial statute.[154] It is irrelevant, however, that the officer believes he was acting within the scope of his duties if he was not.[155] Hence, where a person refuses to identify himself on the demand of police, he cannot be convicted of obstruction because the police do not have the power to require an answer, unless that power is specifically given to them, as is the case under the provisions of the provincial Highway Traffic Acts.[156]

A police officer must be exercising his powers for a proper purpose to be within the execution of his duty. Where a policeman stopped a car, using his powers under the Highway Traffic Act for a purpose unconnected with that legislation, he was held not to be acting within the execution of his duty.[157] The power must also be exercised properly if the officer is to be within the execution of his duty. Where a police officer, when it was feasible to do so, failed to advise a person of the reasons for arrest it was held that the officer was not acting in the execution of his duty.[158]

(ii) *"Obstructing"*

The obstruction under section 129 need not be physical. Where the accused defied a properly given police order to disperse he was convicted of obstructing the police in the execution of their duty.[159] When a person deliberately lied to police, with intent to mislead the police, a conviction of obstructing police was sustained.[160] A person being arrested has a right to know the reason, but an observer who demands such information and impedes the police may be convicted of obstruction.[161] A person may be convicted if he interferes with the police by warning others of a police investigation or trap. Hence, where a person on skid row warned others of the presence of a police officer engaged in arresting beggars the court found that the person giving such warning was guilty of obstruction.[162]

An offence may be committed although the police are not prevented from carrying out their duty. It is the purpose of the act, rather than the result,

---

[154] *R. v. Knowlton, supra*, note 152.
[155] *Koechlin v. Wagh* (1957), 118 C.C.C. 24 (Ont. C.A.).
[156] *Rice v. Connolly*, [1966] 2 All E.R. 649 (H.L.); *R. v. Carroll* (1959), 31 C.R. 315 (Ont. C.A.).
[157] *R. v. Slipp* (1970), 1 C.C.C. (2d) 275 (N.B.C.A.).
[158] *R. v. Acker*, [1970] 4 C.C.C. 269 (N.S.C.A.); see also Chapter 5, A Person's Rights and Obligations Under the Criminal Law.
[159] *R. v. Watkins* (1972), 7 C.C.C. (2d) 513 (Ont. Prov. Ct.).
[160] *R. v. Lawson* (1973), 22 C.R.N.S. 215 (Ont. Prov. Ct.).
[161] *Saunders v. R.* (1977), 38 C.R.N.S. 33 (N.S.C.A.).
[162] *R. v. Westlie* (1971), 2 C.C.C. (2d) 315 (B.C.C.A.).

which constitutes the offence.[163] If a person is requested to aid a police officer in arresting another he may be convicted of the offence of obstructing police even though the person being arrested is one of his own family. In *R. v. Foster* the court held that it was not sufficient for a father to counsel his son to accompany police. He should have lent physical assistance if the mental counselling did not have the appropriate result.[164]

Liability will only arise under section 129(*a*) on a charge of wilfully obstructing a police officer if there is "resistance" or "wilfull obstruction". A mere challenge of authority or non-cooperation does not constitute resistance as there must be some force applied by the accused against the policeman.[165] However, although wilful obstruction requires some unreasonable interference, it does not require the use of force. The threat of force or the incitement of force would constitute wilful obstruction.[166] Criticism or demanding an explanation of the conduct of police, however, will not constitute wilful obstruction unless the accused has been intemperate, unduly persistent or unreasonable.[167]

In a prosecution under section 270 of assaulting a public officer it must be established that the accused knew the public officer was an officer to justify a conviction.[168] This is an essential element of the offence of assaulting a public officer or peace officer, or obstructing such an officer as the necessary *mens rea* may not be established otherwise.[169]

While it has not been possible to discuss many other offences found in the Criminal Code, in a book of this size, the approach taken by our courts in the illustrated offences can be applied in interpreting other offences.

---

[163] *R. v. Tortolano* (1975), 28 C.C.C. (2d) 562 (Ont. C.A.).
[164] (1981), 65 C.C.C. (2d) 388 (Alta. Q.B.).
[165] *R. v. Long*, [1970] 1 C.C.C. 313 (B.C.C.A.).
[166] *R. v. MacPherson* (1977), 24 N.S.R. (2d) 102 (C.A.).
[167] *R. v. Brousseau*, [1969] Que. Q.B. 452.
[168] *R. v. Vlcko* (1972), 10 C.C.C. (2d) 139 (Ont. C.A.); *R. v. McLeod* (1954), 111 C.C.C. 106 (B.C.C.A.).
[169] *R. v. McLeod*, *ibid.*

10

Motor Vehicle Offences

1. CAMPAIGN AGAINST DRINKING AND DRIVING

Motor vehicle law is one area of the law which affects a broad spectrum of the public. Anyone who operates a car on a street or highway is subject to provincial and federal motor vehicle legislation. Each province has enacted provincial motor vehicle legislation which regulates driving on streets and highways. Such legislation covers areas such as licences and rules of the road, including the rate of speed at which vehicles may travel. Parliament has passed legislation which makes it a criminal offence to operate a motor vehicle, vessel or aircraft while one's ability to operate the vehicle, etc. is impaired by alcohol or a drug. The offence which is commonly known as impaired driving is one of many motor vehicle offences contained in the Criminal Code.[1]

In the last 30 years, there has been an increase in the number of people who are driving while impaired by alcohol. The increase in impaired driving has prompted much public debate. Provincial and federal politicians have come under public pressure to take steps to reduce impaired driving. While legislation governing driving falls under federal jurisdiction as part of the criminal law, the provinces are responsible for licensing drivers and thus someone who is convicted of impaired driving will face suspension under provincial motor vehicle legislation. Section 259(1) of the Criminal Code provides for a minimum three-month suspension for impaired driving. In Ontario, public pressure for increased penalties for impaired drivers led to the government imposing a one-year licence suspension which takes effect when someone is convicted of impaired driving under sections 253 of the Criminal Code.

Police forces have established spot check programs to reduce impaired driving. A spot check program enables a police officer to stop a motor vehicle at random even though the officer has no grounds to believe that the motorist has committed a criminal offence prior to being stopped. Police

---

[1] R.S.C. 1985, c. C-46.

forces across Canada believe that spot check programs are an effective tool in their war against impaired driving. The police point to statistics which show that a large number of accidents are caused by impaired driving, saying that motorists will continue to drive while impaired as long as they believe that there is little possibility of being stopped by the police.

The Metropolitan Toronto Police Force has operated a year-round spot check program since 1977 and has asked the Ontario government for increased funding for its spot check program. Sergeant Don Colburne of Metro's community program unit has been quoted in the Toronto Star as saying, "Until we can convince people they're going to get caught and face severe penalties, impaired driving will continue to be a problem."[2] The appellate courts are also emphasizing the need for tougher sentences to combat impaired driving. Thus, for example, in R. v. McVeigh,[3] MacKinnon A.C.J., of the Ontario Court of Appeal, said that the sentences for motor vehicle offences involving alcohol should be increased.

Statistics show that public concern about impaired driving is well placed. In R. v. Jacobs,[4] Laycraft J.A. of the Alberta Court of Appeal said that "in 1980 a person was killed on Alberta streets and highways on the average every 13 hours and 40 minutes." His Lordship noted that "in accidents where fatalities occurred, 19.3% of the drivers, approximately one in five, had been drinking or were impaired."[5] A recent Statistics Canada study shows that alchohol is a contributing factor in 43 percent of the motor vehicle accidents which caused injury and death. The figures show that alchohol was a contributing factor in some 17, 630 deaths between 1983 and 1981; approximately 1,675,000 individual injured between 1983 and 1991; about 1,414 additional deaths (including drivers, passengers, cyclists and pedestrians in 1992; 327,660 days of in-hospital medical treatment in 1987; and 5,160,000 days of lost activity and employment in 1987.[6]

There is evidence that spot check programs reduce impaired driving. In the municipality of Peel, which includes Brampton, Peel Regional police have operated a year-round R.I.D.E. program since 1986. Figures gathered by Peel Regional police show that in 1986, accidents involving alcohol declined by 27 percent for 1986, and by 32 percent in 1987.[7]

The province of Ontario has instituted a year-round R.I.D.E. program. The program, which came into effect on April 14, 1988, is operated by the Ontario Provincial Police. The program is, no doubt, partly in response to studies done by the Ontario Provincial Police which show that impaired dri-

---

[2] H. Stancu, "Year-Round Ride Begins" The Toronto Star (14 April 1988), A2.
[3] (1985), 22 C.C.C. (3d) 145 (Ont. C.A.).
[4] (1982), 70 C.C.C. (2d) 569 (Alta. C.A.).
[5] Ibid., at 574.
[6] The Statistics Canada figures are quoted from Cory J.'s judgment in R. v. Bernshaw (1995), 35 C.R. (4th) 201 at 214-215 (S.C.C.).
[7] H. Stancu, supra, note 2.

ving is as great a problem in the summer as at the Christmas and New Year's period when the majority of spot checks have been done.[8]

There are a number of offences relating to motor vehicles, such as impaired driving, impaired driving causing bodily harm or death, dangerous driving, dangerous operation causing death or bodily harm, failure to stop at the scene of an accident, and taking a motor vehicle without consent and refusal to provide a breathalyzer sample. A discussion of some of these is beyond the scope of this work and, accordingly, it is intended only to discuss the more common offences relating to motor vehicles.

2. ROADSIDE SCREENING AND SPOT CHECKS

(a) Police Powers

Police officers have the authority to demand that someone who is suspected of being impaired take a roadside breathalyzer test by means of an approved screening device. While someone who fails the roadside test will not be charged with a criminal offence, the person failing the test will be asked to take a breathalyzer test. Section 254(2) of the Criminal Code provides the authority for the roadside screening test:

> (2) Where a peace officer reasonably suspects that a person who is operating a motor vehicle or vessel or operating or assisting in the operation of an aircraft or who has the care or control of a motor vehicle, vessel or aircraft, whether it is in motion or not, has alcohol in his body, the peace officer may, by demand made to that person, require that person to provide forthwith such a sample of his breath as in the opinion of the peace officer is necessary to enable a proper analysis of his breath to be made by means of an approved screening device and, where necessary, to accompany the peace officer for the purpose of enabling such a sample of his breath to be taken.

Someone who refuses to take a roadside breathalyzer test will be charged with failing or refusing to comply with the roadside breathalyzer demand. If the Crown intends to introduce results of a roadside test, the Crown must show that the samples of the accused's breath were given into an approved instrument.[9]

The Supreme Court of Canada has held that police officers have the right to randomly stop someone as part of a spot check to determine whether the person is driving while impaired. In *Dedman v. R.*,[10] the Supreme Court of

---

[8] H. Stancu, *supra*, note 2.

[9] *R. v. Moore* (1981), 63 C.C.C. (2d) 135 (B.C.C.A.), leave to appeal to S.C.C. refused (1981), 41 N.R. 104 (S.C.C.).

Canada held that police officers have the authority to stop vehicles at random as part of a well-publicized spot check program. In *Dedman*, the Supreme Court of Canada considered whether a police officer had acted unlawfully in stopping a motorist when the officer did not have reasonable and probable grounds to suspect that the motorist had been driving a motor vehicle while impaired by alcohol or a drug. The accused was stopped solely because of a random vehicle stop program known as the R.I.D.E. program. The accused had been convicted of failing or refusing without reasonable excuse to comply with the breathalyzer demand. The R.I.D.E. program involved police officers being in a location where they believed there had been a high rate of impaired driving and requesting vehicles to stop at random. Once the vehicles were stopped, drivers were asked to produce their licences and the police officers were instructed to ask for proof of insurance and told to observe the driver's physical condition, then drivers might be asked to take a roadside test.

The issues raised by this case were fundamentally important because if the R.I.D.E. program was illegal, similar programs across Canada would be equally invalid. The Supreme Court of Canada held that while there was no statutory authority for the R.I.D.E. program, a random stop of motor vehicles could be justified on the basis of a police officer's common law duty to prevent crime and protect life and property. In so holding, Mr. Justice Le Dain, who wrote the majority judgment of the court, stated:

> It has been held that at common law the principal duties of police officers are the preservation of the peace, the prevention of crime, and the protection of life and property, from which is derived the duty to control traffic on the public roads.[11]

Thus, his lordship held that random stops fall within the general duties of a police officer:

> I do not think there can be any doubt that it [the random stop] fell within the general scope of the duties of a police officer to prevent crime and to protect life and property by the control of traffic. These are the very objects of the R.I.D.E. program, which is a measure to improve the deterrence and detection of impaired driving, a notorious cause of injury and death.

> . . . .

> Because of the seriousness of the problem of impaired driving, there can be no doubt about the importance and necessity of a program to improve the deterrence of it. The right to circulate on the highway free from unreasonable interference is an important one, but it is . . . a licensed activity subject to regulation and control in the interest of safety. The objectionable nature of a random stop is chiefly that it is made on a purely arbitrary basis, without any grounds for suspicion or belief

[10] (1985), 46 C.R. (3d) 193 (S.C.C.).

[11] *Ibid.*, at 218.

that the particular driver has committed or is committing an offence. It is this aspect of the random stop that makes it capable of producing unpleasant psychological effects for the innocent driver. These effects, however, would tend to be minimized by the well-publicized nature of the program, which is a necessary feature of its deterrent purpose. Moreover, the stop would be of relatively short duration and of slight inconvenience. Weighing these factors, I am of the opinion that, having regard to the importance of the public purpose served, the random stop as a police action necessary to the carrying out of that purpose was not an unreasonable interference with the right to circulate on the public highway.[12]

(b) Well-publicized Programs

Section 9 of the Canadian Charter of Rights and Freedoms[13] provides:

9. Everyone has the right not to be arbitrarily detained or imprisoned.

In *R. v. Hufsky*,[14] the Supreme Court of Canada held that a motorist who is randomly stopped pursuant to a spot check program is detained within the meaning of section 9 of the Charter. The court held that provincial legislation which authorized the random stopping of drivers based on no criteria violated section 9 of the Charter, saying that the selection of drivers was in the absolute discretion of the police officer who directed the driver to pull over. The court held that discretion is arbitrary if there are no criteria, express or implied, which govern its exercise. Although the court found that the accused was arbitrarily detained under section 9 of the Charter, the procedure authorized by section 189*a*(1) of the Highway Traffic Act of Ontario was a reasonable limit prescribed by law that was demonstrably justified in a free and democratic society. In upholding the legislation under section 1 of the Charter, the court was heavily influenced by section 1 evidence led by the Crown which demonstrated the difficulty of detecting impaired driving by observation and the need to increase the perceived risk of detection in order to reduce impaired driving.

In this case, the Crown introduced 10 volumes of section 1 material which consisted of legislation in other provinces, provincial government reports containing statistical analysis of motor vehicle accidents, motor vehicle offences, suspension of drivers licences and claims on the motor vehicle accident claims fund. The court stated that the Crown's evidence demonstrated the relative importance of licence suspension and the effective enforcement of it, the relatively higher proportion of unlicensed and

---

[12] *Ibid.*, at 220-221.
[13] Being Part I of the Constitution Act, 1982 [en. by the Canada Act, 1982 (U.K.), c. 11, s. 1].
[14] (1988), 63 C.R. (3d) 14 (S.C.C.).

uninsured drivers, by comparison with the number of licensed and insured drivers, involved in motor vehicle accidents resulting in death and personal injury and the relative importance of motor vehicle offences, including driving without a licence or driving while under suspension or without insurance, which cannot be detected by observation.

In *Hufsky*, Le Dain J., who delivered the judgment of the court, in upholding provincial legislation authorizing a random stop of a motor vehicle, stated:

> . . . I am of the opinion that the limit imposed by s. 189a (1) of the Highway Traffic Act on the right not to be arbitrarily detained guaranteed by s. 9 of the Charter is a reasonable one that is demonstrably justified in a free and democratic society. The nature and degree of the intrusion of a random stop for the purposes of the spot check procedure in the present case, remembering that the driving of a motor vehicle is a licensed activity subject to regulation and control in the interest of safety, is proportionate to the purpose to be served. . . . . As for publicity, which was referred to in *Dedman*, in connection with common law authority for a random stop for the purposes contemplated by the R.I.D.E. program, I think it may be taken now that the public is well aware of random stop authority because of both its frequent and widespread exercise and its recognition by legislatures.[15]

In *R. v. Ladouceur*,[16] the Supreme Court of Canada upheld the constitutional validity of random stops where the stops are not part of a R.I.D.E. type program but are authorized by provincial legislation or permitted at common law. The court stated that although such stops result in arbitrary detention of the motorist contrary to section 9 of the Charter, the stop is a reasonable limit within the meaning of section 1 of the Charter in circumstances where the stop is to check the driver's licence and insurance, the driver's sobriety or to determine whether the motor vehicle is mechanically fit.

(c) Right to Counsel

Section 254(2) is the section which authorizes police officers to use an approved screening device. The Supreme Court of Canada, in *Thomsen v. R.*,[17] held that a person required to take a roadside test pursuant to section 234.1(1) [254(2)] was detained, but that he was not entitled to retain counsel before taking the test. The court concluded that the obligation imposed by section 234.1(1) [254(2)] to take such a test forthwith precluded the right to retain counsel. It found that such a limit was a reasonable one which could be demonstrably justified in a free and democratic society.

The court applied the test in *R. v. Oakes*[18] (discussed in Chapter 3, Effect

---

[15] *Ibid.*, at 25-26.
[16] (1990), 77 C.R. (3d) 110 (S.C.C.).
[17] (1988), 63 C.R. (3d) 1 (S.C.C.).
[18] (1986), 50 C.R. (3d) 1 (S.C.C.).

of the Charter on Criminal Law) concluding that roadside breath testing was desirable, resulting as it did in the detection of impaired driving and the perceived risk of detection by impaired drivers. It found that in these circumstances the limitation on the right to counsel was a reasonable restriction under section 1 of the Charter.

3. IMPAIRED DRIVING

Section 253 of the Criminal Code provides:

253. Everyone commits an offence who operates a motor vehicle or vessel or operates or assists in the operation of an aircraft or of railway equipment or has the care or control of a motor vehicle, vessel, aircraft or railway equipment, whether it is in motion or not,

(*a*) while the person's ability to operate the vehicle, vessel, aircraft or railway equipment is impaired by alcohol or a drug; or

(*b*) having consumed alcohol in such a quantity that the concentration in the person's blood exceeds eighty milligrams of alcohol in one hundred millilitres of blood.

(a) Elements of Offence

(i) *Operating motor vehicle or having care and control*

Section 253 of the Criminal Code creates two separate offences: (1) operating a motor vehicle, etc., while one's ability to do so is impaired by alcohol or a drug, and (2) operating or having care and control of a motor vehicle having a blood-alcohol content which exceeds 80 mg of alcohol in 100 ml of blood. Section 214 of the Code defines the word "operate" as follows:

"operate"

(*a*) means, in respect of a motor vehicle, to drive the vehicle,

(*b*) includes, in respect of a vessel or an aircraft, to navigate the vessel or aircraft.

An accused who is charged with a section 253 offence may be convicted if the Crown establishes that the accused operated the vehicle in the circumstances described above, or had care or control of the vehicle in such circumstances. Thus, the Crown does not have to prove that an accused drove the motor vehicle for the accused to be convicted. The Supreme Court of Canada has outlined the differences between impaired driving and having care and control of a motor vehicle while one's ability to drive is impaired. In *R. v. Toews*,[19] McIntyre J. stated:

---

[19] (1985), 47 C.R. (3d) 213 (S.C.C.).

... it must be observed that the Criminal Code in s. 234(1) [now section 253] creates two separate offences. The first is driving a motor vehicle while the ability to drive is impaired by alcohol or a drug, and the second is having care or control of a motor vehicle, whether it is in motion or not, while the ability to drive is impaired by alcohol or a drug. It follows then that when s. 234(1) provides for this second offence — that of having care or control — its words must refer to an element of care or control other than that of driving. For this reason it is clear . . . that proof of an intent to drive — that is, to set the vehicle in motion — is not an essential element of proof in a charge of having care or control.[20]

In *Ford v. R.*,[21] Mr. Justice Ritchie stated:

Care or control may be exercised . . . where an accused performs some act or series of acts involving the use of the car, its fittings or equipment . . . whereby the vehicle may unintentionally be set in motion creating the danger the section is designed to prevent.[22]

Further, in *Toews*, McIntyre J. stated that care and control meant that:

. . . acts of care or control, short of driving, are acts which involve some use of the car or its fittings and equipment, or some course of conduct associated with the vehicle which would involve a risk of putting the vehicle in motion so that it could become dangerous.[23]

In *Toews*, the accused was charged with having care or control of an automobile while his ability to drive was impaired by alcohol or a drug. He was found lying across the front seat of his truck with his head resting on the passenger's side of the truck. The accused had his legs in a sleeping bag under the steering wheel when the police discovered him. McIntyre J. stated that the accused did not occupy the driver's seat, was unconscious and clearly not in control. His Lordship stated that although the key was in the ignition of the truck there was no direct evidence that the accused had placed the key in the ignition and the accused's use of a sleeping bag would support his statement that he was merely using the vehicle as a place to sleep.

There was no evidence that the accused, Toews, had done something which could have set the truck in motion. If the accused had had the motor running he would have undoubtedly been found to have had care or control over the vehicle. This is evident from the decision of the Saskatchewan Court of Queen's Bench in *R. v. Johnson*.[24] Johnson was charged with having care or control of a motor vehicle after having consumed alcohol in a quantity which exceeded 80 mg in 100 ml of blood. Although the accused argued that he did

---

[20] *Ibid.*, at 217.
[21] (1982), 65 C.C.C. (2d) 392 (S.C.C.).
[22] *Ibid.*, at 399.
[23] *Supra*, note 19, at 220.
[24] (1985), 37 M.V.R. 122 (Sask. Q.B.).

not have the care or control of the vehicle because he was asleep, Matheson J. held that the accused had such care or control, saying:

> In this instance, the respondent [the accused] not only occupied the seat ordinarily occupied by the driver of a motor vehicle . . . he had also engaged in acts, short of driving, which involved the use of his automobile or its fittings and equipment, thereby creating the risk that the automobile could be put in motion and become dangerous. Not only was the ignition key on, the motor was running. Merely because the accused was asleep when apprehended is not of sufficient significance in this instance to avoid the conclusion that the respondent had engaged in sufficient acts to create the risk of the dangers sought to be prohibited.[25]

(ii) *Mens rea and actus reus*

The *mens rea* and *actus reus* required for a conviction has been set out by the Supreme Court of Canada in *Toews*, wherein McIntyre J. stated:

> The mens rea for driving while impaired is the intent to drive a motor vehicle after the voluntary consumption of alcohol or a drug. . . . The actus reus is the act of driving where the voluntary consumption of alcohol or a drug has impaired the ability to drive.[26]

(b) Proving the Offence

(i) *Breathalyzer test or blood sample*

(A) *General provisions.* In most cases, someone who has been charged with an offence under section 253 of the Criminal Code will have been given a breathalyzer test by a qualified breathalyzer technician. The breathalyzer test, which is usually administered at the police station, measures the concentration of alcohol in the accused's blood. If the test results show that the accused had a blood-alcohol content exceeding 80 mg, the accused will be charged with committing an offence under section 253. In administering the breathalyzer test, the qualified breathalyzer technician uses an instrument which has been approved as being suitable "to receive and make a chemical analysis" from a sample of the accused's breath under the Criminal Code. The breathalyzer instrument used in Canada is a Borkenstein breathalyzer.

Section 254(3) of the Criminal Code authorizes a police officer to demand that someone take a breathalyzer test:

---

[25] *Ibid.*, at 126.
[26] *Supra*, note 19, at 218.

(3) Where a peace officer believes on reasonable and probable grounds that a person is committing, or at any time in the preceding two hours has committed, as a result of the consumption of alcohol, an offence under section 253, he may, by demand made to that person forthwith or as soon as practicable, require him to provide then or as soon thereafter as is practicable

(a) such samples of his breath as in the opinion of a qualified technician . . .

are necessary to enable proper analysis to be made in order to determine the concentration, if any, of alcohol in the person's blood and to accompany the peace officer for the purpose of enabling such samples to be taken.

Subsections 254(3) and (4) provide that a blood sample may be taken from a person where the person is incapable of providing a sample of his or her breath, or in circumstances where it would be impractical to obtain a sample of a person's breath:

. . . .

(b) where the peace officer has reasonable and probable grounds to believe that, by reason of any physical condition of the person,
(i) the person may be incapable of providing a sample of his breath, or
(ii) it would be impracticable to obtain a sample of his breath,
such samples of the person's blood, under the conditions referred to in subsection (4), as in the opinion of the qualified medical practitioner or qualified technician taking the samples
are necessary to enable proper analysis to be made in order to determine the concentration, if any, of alcohol in the person's blood, and to accompany the peace officer for the purpose of enabling such samples to be taken.

(4) Samples of blood may only be taken from a person pursuant to a demand made by a peace officer under subsection (3) if the samples are taken by or under the direction of a qualified medical practitioner and the qualified medical practitioner is satisfied that the taking of such samples would not endanger the life or health of the person.

Usually, when someone is charged with committing an offence under section 253, Crown counsel will prove results of a breathalyzer test or blood test indicating that the accused's blood-alcohol content exceeds 80 mg. The proof of such results, if left unchallenged by the defence lawyer, will usually lead to a conviction.

If such a test shows that the person had a blood-alcohol reading which exceeded 80 mg of alcohol in 100 ml of blood, such a person will be charged with either (a) operating a motor vehicle, etc., or having care or control of the vehicle while his ability to operate the vehicle is impaired by alcohol or a drug, or (b) operating a vehicle or having care or control over a vehicle having a blood-alcohol content exceeding 80 mg of alcohol contrary to section 253(b) of the Criminal Code. In both cases, the Crown will introduce the breathalyzer reading to show that the accused committed an offence under section 253. If the accused is charged with operating a vehicle or having care or control of a vehicle under section 253(a) while impaired, the breathalyzer reading will be a strong indication that the accused committed an offence. If the judge accepts the breathalyzer reading, the accused will probably be convicted.

(B) *Reasonable and probable grounds for demand.* Section 254(3) of the Criminal Code states that before taking a breathalyzer a police officer must have reasonable and probable grounds to believe that the person being asked to take the test had, within the preceding two hours, committed an offence under section 253 of the Code. Accordingly, the prosecution will have to introduce evidence as to a police officer's reasonable and probable grounds for demanding that the accused take a breathalyzer test. Usually, the police officer provides such evidence by stating that the accused exhibited the classical signs of impairment — for example, slurred speech, bloodshot eyes, and a strong odour of alcohol on his or her breath.

(ii) *Signs of impairment*

Evidence as to the accused's blood-alcohol content, however, is not essential for the Crown to prove that an accused committed an offence under section 253 in the Criminal Code. In some cases, there is no evidence as to the accused's blood-alcohol content and the Crown will have to lead evidence which would allow a judge to draw an inference that the accused was impaired. Usually, such evidence consists of observations of people as to the accused's appearance. The classic test as to the factors which a court considers in deciding whether to draw an inference that the accused was impaired has been stated in *R. v. McKenzie*,[27] by the then Chief Justice of the District Court of Alberta:

> The effect of alcohol is subjective before it is objective and there may be dangerous impairment even though there are no objective symptoms of intoxication. However, for the practical purposes of a criminal trial, we must, at the present time, depend largely on objective symptoms.

> There appears to be no single test of observation of impairment of control of faculties, standing alone, which is sufficiently conclusive. There should be consideration of a combination of several tests and observations such as general conduct, smell of the breath, character of speech, manner of walking, turning sharply, sitting down and rising, picking up objects, reaction of the pupils of the eyes, character of the breathing.

> If a combination of several tests and observation shows a marked departure from what is usually considered as the normal, it seems a reasonable conclusion that the driver is intoxicated with consequent impairment of control of faculties and therefore his ability to drive is impaired.[28]

---

[27] (1955), 14 W.W.R. 500 (Alta. Dist. Ct.).

[28] *Ibid.*, at 502. See also *R. v. Andres*, [1979] 2 W.W.R. 249 (Sask. C.A.).

Sometimes a police officer will test the accused's faculties by asking that the accused walk in a straight line or perform other coordination tests.

Parliament has not specified the criteria for determining what constitutes impaired driving and thus the courts had to fashion an appropriate test. Some courts have held that for an accused to be convicted of impaired driving, the Crown must prove that driving represents a marked departure from the ordinary standard of driving. In *R. v. Smith*,[29] the Alberta Court of Appeal adopted the "marked departure from the norm" test, saying that if Parliament wanted to specify that any degree of impairment accompanying the operation of a motor vehicle could constitute impaired driving, it should have said so specifically. The approach taken by the Alberta Court of Appeal in *Smith* was not followed by other provincial appellate courts. The British Columbia Court of Appeal, the Prince Edward Island Court of Appeal and the Ontario Court of Appeal all rejected the marked departure test.[30]

In *R. v. Stellato*, the Ontario Court of Appeal held that where a person drives while his ability to do so is impaired by alcohol or drugs, he is guilty of an offence irrespective of whether his ability to drive is greatly or slightly impaired. The court stated that as the Criminal Code does not set out any special test for determining impairment, the standard of proof is neither more nor less than that required for any other criminal offence. In response to the Alberta Court of Appeal's suggestion that had Parliament intended to prohibit any impairment, however slight, it could have done so, the Ontario Court of Appeal stated that had Parliament intended to outlaw impaired driving only where accompanied by a marked departure from the norm, it also could have done so. The Ontario Court of Appeal's decision in *Stellato* was upheld by the Supreme Court of Canada. The Supreme Court adopted the reasons given by Mr. Justice Labrosse, who delivered the judgment of the Ontario Court of Appeal.[31]

In some cases, the officer will have observed the accused's driving and the driving itself coupled with the accused's appearance will constitute the reasonable and probable grounds for making the breathalyzer demand under section 254(3). The requirement that the officer have reasonable and probable grounds for making a breathalyzer demand necessitates that the officer subjectively have an honest belief that the accused has committed the offence and that there are objectively reasonable grounds for the officer's belief.[32] It is essential that reasonable and probable grounds exist before a motorist is required to take the screening test. Although a person who fails the test cannot be convicted of a criminal offence, failure of the test may result in a

[29] (1992), 13 C.R. (4th) 125 (Alta. C.A.).
[30] *R. v. Bruhjell* (September 8, 1986), Doc. Vancouver, C.A. 00416 (B.C.C.A.); [1986] B.C.W.L.D. 4105; *R. v. Campbell* (1991), 26 M.V.R. (2d) 319 (P.E.I.C.A.); *R. v. Stellato* (1993), 18 C.R. (4th) 127 (Ont. C.A.).
[31] (1994), 31 C.R. (4th) 60 (S.C.C.).
[32] *Bernshaw, supra*, note 6, at 225.

motorist being required to take a breathalyzer test under section 254(3) of the Criminal Code.

(iii) *Presumption of care or control*

If an accused occupies the driver's seat of a motor vehicle, the judge may infer that the accused exercised care or control over the motor vehicle. Section 258 (1)(*a*) of the Criminal Code authorizes the judge to so infer.

> **258.** (1) In any proceedings . . . in respect of an offence committed under section 253 . . .
>
> (*a*) where it is proved that the accused occupied the seat or position ordinarily occupied by a person who operates a motor vehicle, vessel or aircraft or who assists in the operation of an aircraft, the accused shall be deemed to have had the care or control of the vehicle, vessel or aircraft, as the case may be, unless he establishes that he did not occupy that seat or position for the purpose of setting the vehicle, vessel or aircraft in motion or assisting in the operation of the aircraft, as the case may be;

If an accused is found in the driver's seat of a motor vehicle, the accused will have to rebut this presumption. It will be recalled that the Supreme Court of Canada held, in *Toews*,[33] that the *mens rea* required in such a case is the intent to exercise care or control over the motor vehicle having voluntarily consumed alcohol or drugs. Accordingly, the prosecution will only succeed if, on all the evidence, the court concludes the accused had the necessary intent. Thus, in *R. v. King*,[34] an accused who was actually impaired was acquitted because he honestly believed the effects of a drug administered by a dentist had ceased. But an intention to drive is not an element of the care or control offence. If the accused performs some act involving the use of the car or equipment by which the car may be unintentionally set in motion, the necessary *mens rea* is established.

(iv) *Breathalyzer certificate*

Not every breathalyzer certificate is admitted into evidence. Before introducing a breathalyzer certificate the Crown attorney must show that the certificate has been properly obtained and was prepared in accordance with the principles set out in the Criminal Code. A breathalyzer certificate will not have been properly obtained if the police officer did not have jurisdiction to demand that the accused provide a breath sample. The officer's jurisdiction will not be a factor if the officer has province-wide jurisdiction. However, a

---

[33] *Supra*, note 19.
[34] [1962] S.C.R. 746.

municipal police officer will only have the authority to demand an accused provide a breath sample within the territorial jurisdiction of the officer.[35] The demand must be made by a peace officer as defined in section 2 of the Criminal Code. In *R. v. Polchies*,[36] it was held that a breathalyzer demand made by a member of the New Brunswick highway patrol was a peace officer.

If a peace officer does not find the accused committing an offence under section 253, the officer must be able to state that he or she had reasonable and probable grounds to believe that the accused committed an offence within the preceding two hours. Otherwise, the officer is not entitled to demand a sample of the accused's breath under section 254(3) of the Criminal Code.

(c) Reasonable and Probable Grounds

A peace officer must have reasonable and probable grounds to believe that the accused committed an offence under section 253 of the Criminal Code. These grounds will exist where the officer acts in good faith upon facts pointing to the commission of an offence. The reasonable and probable grounds may be based on hearsay, but the evidence must be evidence which a court could accept as being truthful. Thus, a peace officer may rely on what he has been told by a person who observed erratic driving by the accused.

In *Rilling v. R.*,[37] a majority of the Supreme Court of Canada held that a certificate could be admitted although the peace officer did not have reasonable and probable grounds. The majority found that an accused could not be convicted of refusing a test as required by the Code, but that the certificate was admissible when the accused complied with the demand. The minority held that such a certificate was not obtained as required by the Code on reasonable and probable grounds and must be rejected.

Although *Rilling* was decided prior to the Charter, several provincial appellate courts have held that where breath samples have been obtained without reasonable and probable grounds for the demand, the evidence should only be excluded if the accused demonstrates that its admission would bring the administration of justice into disrepute.[38]

In *Bernshaw*, the Supreme Court of Canada held that section 8 of the Charter requires that a police officer have reasonable and probable grounds for demanding a breathalyzer sample under section 254(3) of the Criminal Code. The court stated that the existence of reasonable and probable grounds

---

[35] *R. v. Soucy* (1975), 23 C.C.C. (2d) 561 (N.B.C.A.); *R. v. Arsenault* (1980), 55 C.C.C. (2d) 38 (N.B.C.A.).

[36] (1981), 35 N.B.R. (2d) 185 (Q.B.).

[37] (1975), 24 C.C.C. (2d) 81 (S.C.C.).

[38] *R. v. Leneal* (1990), 68 Man. R. (2d) 127 (C.A.); *R. v. McNulty* (1991), 35 M.V.R. (2d) 27 (Ont. C.A.); *R. v. Linttell* (1991), 64 C.C.C. (3d) 507 (Alta. C.A.); *R. v. Langdon* (1992), 74 C.C.C. (3d) 570 (Nfld. C.A.).

is a precondition to a lawful search and seizure under section 8 of the Charter. The court held that a police officer may consider a "fail" result on a screening test along with other factors which would indicate impairment in forming his opinion that reasonable and probable grounds exist for the suspect to take a breathalyzer test. The majority of the court held that where a police officer has reason for believing that if the suspect takes the test immediately, the test would yield a faulty result, such as where the accused had consumed alcohol within 15 minutes prior to the test, the police must wait an adequate period of time to ensure that any mouth alcohol will not affect the test results. The court stated that in such circumstances the police officer's knowledge that the test may be unreliable negates the officer's subjective belief that reasonable and probable grounds exist and that an offence has been committed under section 253 of the Criminal Code.[39]

The manufacturer of the breathalyzer equipment states that where the police have reason to believe that a person has recently consumed alcoholic beverages, the police should wait 20 minutes before administering the breathalyzer test to minimize the possibility that mouth alcohol could adversely affect the breathalyzer test results.

The power of a police officer to demand that an accused accompany him or her to a police station for the purpose of taking a breath sample or a blood sample is not absolute. The officer may not arrest an accused in order to force the accused to give a breath sample.[40]

(d) Samples "taken as soon as practicable"

(i) *Generally*

The Crown must lead evidence to show that the breathalyzer test was administered by a qualified breathalyzer technician on a breathalyzer machine which has been approved by the Attorney General of Canada. In addition, there must be evidence that the test was administered as soon as practicable. Section 258(1) of the Criminal Code provides that two breathalyzer samples must be taken from the accused and that the first sample must be taken not later than two hours after the offence is alleged to have been committed. The section also states that there must be a minimum of 15 minutes between the time breath samples are taken. While a short delay in taking a breathalyzer sample will not result in any breathalyzer sample being inadmissible, the Crown must account for substantial delays of time which would suggest that the samples were not taken as soon as practicable.

---

[39] *Supra*, note 6, at 229.
[40] *R. v. Kells,* [1973] 3 W.W.R. 216 (B.C.S.C.).

(ii) *Taking of blood samples*

For many years, there was no specific authority which authorized a peace officer to demand that an accused take a blood test instead of taking a breathalyzer test. Recently, the Criminal Code was amended to authorize the taking of a blood sample from an accused in certain limited circumstances set out in section 256. The taking of such a sample may be authorized by a warrant issued by a justice of the peace. The justice must be satisfied that there are reasonable grounds to believe a person committed an offence under section 253 and was involved in an accident where someone was killed or injured. He also must be satisfied that a qualified medical practitioner was of the opinion that the person suspected of impaired driving is not physically or mentally able, by reason of alcohol consumption or injuries sustained in a motor vehicle accident, to consent to the taking of a blood sample. The justice must be satisfied that taking the sample would not endanger such a person.

This section may only be used in cases where, for example, the accused is unconscious when a peace officer arrives at the scene where the offence is alleged to have been committed. In normal circumstances where an accused is capable of giving his or her consent to the taking of a blood sample, the peace officer will request that the person give a blood sample. The officer's authority for demanding that an accused provide a sample of his or her blood is contained in section 254(3)(*b*) of the Criminal Code, the provisions of which were set out earlier in this chapter.

Section 257 of the Criminal Code provides that no qualified medical practitioner shall be charged with a criminal offence by reason of his or her refusal to take a blood sample from an accused in the circumstances described in the section. Furthermore, the medical practitioner is protected from any criminal or civil liability, where a blood sample is taken. If section 257 were not in the Criminal Code, an accused could sue a medical practitioner for assault in circumstances where a sample had been taken without consent. In law, the least touching of a person without that person's consent is regarded as an assault and is a tort for which the person being assaulted can recover damages by means of a civil suit.

4. DEFENCES TO IMPAIRED DRIVING

(a) Failure to Prove the Offence

If the Crown fails to prove an essential element of the offence, the accused will be acquitted. Thus, if the Crown's case rests on evidence that the accused drove the motor vehicle, there must be evidence indicating that the accused before the court is the person who drove the motor vehicle. Similarly, if the Crown alleges that the accused had care or control over the motor vehicle, the Crown must prove that the accused had the care or control of such a vehicle. If the Crown fails to establish care or control, the accused will be acquitted. This burden is reduced by the provision which deems a person to have care and control in the absence of an explanation by the accused.

(b) Challenging the Breathalyzer

Where breathalyzer evidence is essential to prove that the accused committed an offence, the accused will be acquitted where the court refuses to admit the breathalyzer evidence. Thus, if an accused is charged with operating a motor vehicle, or having care or control of a motor vehicle, having consumed alcohol in such a quantity that his blood-alcohol content exceeds 80 mg per 100 ml of blood, the Crown will need the certificate evidence to prove the elements of the offence and must establish that the requirements for such a test have been met. If the accused successfully raises a technical objection to the admissibility of the certificate, the Crown's case will fail. The British Columbia Court of Appeal's decision in *R. v. Taylor*[41] illustrates a case where the accused successfully challenged the admissibility of the breathalyzer. Lambert J.A. held that the certificate was not admissible because the solution used in the breathalyzer machine was not properly identified and, accordingly, the accused would not have been able to have an independent chemical analysis done of the characteristics of the solution.[42] Thus, the defence should ensure that the Crown has met all the essential technical requirements.

(c) Attacking the Breathalyzer Readings

Section 258(1)(c) provides that in the absence of "evidence to the contrary" the breathalyzer reading taken in accordance with the Code's requirements is proof of the alcohol level. Evidence which challenges the accuracy of the breathalyzer certificate is called evidence to the contrary. If an accused leads evidence that the breathalyzer machine is not working properly, such evidence, if accepted by the trial judge, constitutes evidence to the contrary. Also, if there is evidence which suggests that the breathalyzer operator did not follow the standard procedures required for operating the machine, this evidence will cast doubt on the validity of the breathalyzer readings and this could be evidence to the contrary. As well, expert evidence which suggests that the accused's blood-alcohol level at the time of driving would not have exceeded the legal limit is evidence to the contrary which, if accepted by the trial judge, rebuts the presumption in section 258(1)(c).

---

[41] (1985), 38 M.V.R. 263 (B.C.C.A.).
[42] *Ibid.*, at 273-274.

Expert evidence which casts doubt on the accused's blood-alcohol reading usually consists of evidence to the effect that the test performed by the expert showed that the accused's blood-alcohol reading would not have been in excess of the legal limit when the driving occurred. This type of evidence is usually led in a borderline case where the accused's blood-alcohol reading does not exceed the legal limit by very much. In other cases, the breathalyzer evidence is likely to be conclusive in the absence of faulty equipment or faulty administration of the test.

(d) Right to Counsel

If an accused's right to counsel has been denied, the accused may have a defence to an impaired driving charge. Section 10 of the Charter of Rights makes it mandatory that someone who is detained or arrested be informed of his or her right to obtain counsel. The accused's right to counsel is considered later in this chapter.

5. PUNISHMENT FOR IMPAIRED DRIVING

(a) Generally

Section 255 of the Criminal Code sets out the punishment for impaired driving which varies depending upon whether the accused has been convicted of impaired driving or impaired driving causing bodily harm or death.

Everyone who commits an offence under sections 253 or 254 — i.e., impaired driving, excess alcohol and failure to take the required test — is guilty of an indictable offence or an offence punishable on summary conviction. The minimum punishments are (1) for a first offence, a fine of not less than $300; (2) for a second offence, imprisonment for not less than 14 days; and (3) for each subsequent offence, to imprisonment for not less than 90 days. Where the offence is prosecuted by indictment, imprisonment for a term not exceeding five years may be imposed and where the offence is punishable on summary conviction, a term not exceeding six months may be imposed. Where a person commits the offence of driving while impaired or having care or control while impaired and causes bodily harm to any other person, such person is liable to imprisonment for a term not exceeding 10 years. If the accused causes the death of another person, he is guilty of an indictable offence and is liable to imprisonment for a term not exceeding 14 years.

(b) Availability of Conditional Discharge

The punishment for impaired driving varies across Canada depending upon whether the accused is entitled to obtain a conditional discharge. Section 255(5) of the Code provides that in certain circumstances an accused may receive a conditional discharge. However, despite the fact that the Criminal Code provisions are supposed to be uniform across Canada, this provision has not been brought into effect by all provinces. Section 255(5) provides as follows:

> . . . a court may, instead of convicting a person for an offence committed under section 253, after hearing medical or other evidence, if it considers that the person is in need of curative treatment in relation to his consumption of alcohol or drugs and that it would not be contrary to the public interest, by order direct that the person be discharged under section 736 on the conditions prescribed in a probation order, including a condition respecting the person's attendance for curative treatment in relation to his consumption of alcohol or drugs.

This section has only been brought into effect in Alberta, Manitoba, New Brunswick, Nova Scotia, the Northwest Territories, Prince Edward Island, Saskatchewan and the Yukon Territory. In provinces where the section has been brought into effect, an accused who is granted a conditional discharge will be in a much better position than someone in a province where a conditional discharge is not available; a conditional discharge means that if the accused complies with the conditions set out in the probation order the accused does not have a criminal record.

6. DANGEROUS OPERATION OF A MOTOR VEHICLE

Section 249 of the Criminal Code makes it an offence to operate a motor vehicle in a manner that is dangerous to the public:

> **249.** (1) Every one commits an offence who operates
> (*a*) a motor vehicle in a manner that is dangerous to the public, having regard to all the circumstances, including the nature, condition and use of the place at which the motor vehicle is being operated and the amount of traffic that at the time is or might reasonably be expected to be on that place;
>
> . . . .
>
> (2) Every one who commits an offence under subsection (1)
> (*a*) is guilty of an indictable offence and liable to imprisonment for a term not exceeding five years; or
> (*b*) is guilty of an offence punishable on summary conviction.

(3) Every one who commits an offence under subsection (1) and thereby causes bodily harm to any other person is guilty of an indictable offence and liable to imprisonment for a term not exceeding ten years.

(4) Every one who commits an offence under subsection (1) and thereby causes the death of any other person is guilty of an indictable offence and liable to imprisonment for a term not exceeding fourteen years.

(a) Elements of Offence

The necessary elements of the offence have been set out in *R. v. Beaudoin*,[43] a decision of the Ontario Court of Appeal. Kelly J.A. held that to convict an accused of dangerous driving the Crown must establish beyond a reasonable doubt:

1. that the lives or safety of others were endangered by the defendant's driving, and
2. that such jeopardizing resulted from the driver's departure from the standard of care that a prudent driver would have exercised having regard to what actually were or might reasonably have been expected to be the condition, nature or use of the place where he was driving (including the amount of traffic thereon).[44]

In order to discharge the onus upon it, the Crown must adduce evidence from which the jury (or a judge) could reasonably infer that the driving was dangerous within the meaning attributed to that word by this section. Once the Crown has done so, while there is no obligation on the accused to disprove the allegation, if he does not offer some explanation and none emerges from the evidence which can reasonably account for his conduct and at the same time absolve him from criminal responsibility, he runs the risk of being convicted. In *R. v. Mueller*,[45] the Ontario Court of Appeal held that the offence could be committed although no member of the public was present. Rather it is sufficient to show that the public might reasonably be expected to be there.

The Ontario Court of Appeal has held that in order to obtain a conviction for dangerous driving, the Crown does not have to establish that an accused's driving was deliberate in the sense of being considered and not impulsive. In *R. v. Sharp*,[46] Morden J.A., who wrote the judgment of the court, set out the mental elements required for criminal negligence and dangerous driving:

Both criminal negligence and dangerous driving are offences which require fault, in the sense of a blameworthy state of mind, to be proven, but in each case (assuming the criminal negligence to involve driving) it is open to a jury [or a judge] to find the required fault in the nature of the accused's driving if, objectively viewed, it amounts to that which is defined in the statute. A jury should not

---

[43] [1973] 3 O.R. 1 (C.A.).
[44] *Ibid.*, at 5.
[45] (1975), 32 C.R.N.S. 188 (Ont. C.A.).
[46] (1984), 39 C.R. (3d) 367 (Ont. C.A.).

find fault, and hence that the accused is guilty, if there is an explanation which arises from the evidence that would account for the deviant conduct in a manner which would negative the element of fault. A cause resulting from circumstances beyond the accused's control, for example, the sudden malfunction of the steering mechanism, would afford such an explanation.[47]

(b) Momentary Loss of Concentration

In the *Sharp* case, the court considered whether someone who had a momentary lapse of concentration could be convicted of dangerous driving and refused to accept the general proposition that a momentary lapse of concentration would, in all cases, provide a defence. Mr. Justice Morden adopted the reasoning of Martin J.A. in *R. v. Lowe*:[48]

> . . . whether a momentary lapse would involve such a departure must also be determined by all the circumstances, including the nature of the lapse, the nature and condition of the highway or other place and the amount of traffic that is at the time or might reasonably be expected to be on such place.[49]

If the dangerous driving resulted from a mechanical failure, such as failure of the steering mechanism, the accused would have a defence to the charge. It would also appear that a sudden distracting event, such as a bird entering the car, a bee sting, or buzzing by an aircraft, might provide an excuse. It will be up to a judge to determine, in any given case, whether the accused's explanation is reasonable or not.

7. FAILURE TO STOP AT SCENE OF ACCIDENT

(a) Criminal Code

The Criminal Code makes it an offence to fail to stop at the scene of an accident with intent to escape liability:

> **252.** Every person who has the care, charge or control of a vehicle . . . that is involved in an accident with
> (*a*) another person,
> (*b*) a vehicle, vessel or aircraft, or
> (*c*) in the case of a vehicle, cattle in the charge of another person,
> and with intent to escape civil or criminal liability fails to stop the vehicle . . . give his or her name and address and, where any person has been

---

[47] *Ibid.*, at 376.
[48] (1974), 21 C.C.C. (2d) 193 (Ont. C.A.).
[49] *Ibid.*, at 198.

injured or appears to require assistance, offer assistance, is guilty of an indictable offence and liable to imprisonment for a term not exceeding five years or is guilty of an offence punishable on summary conviction.

(2) In proceedings under subsection (1), evidence that an accused failed to stop his vehicle . . . offer assistance where any person has been injured or appears to require assistance and give his name and address is, in the absence of evidence to the contrary, proof of an intent to escape civil or criminal liability.

Lamer J., who wrote the judgment of the Supreme Court of Canada in *R. v. Roche*,[50] held that despite the presumption, the onus remained on the Crown to prove the case beyond a reasonable doubt. The presumption merely assists the Crown in establishing evidence of intent.

(b) Provincial Laws

Most provinces have laws which require the driver of a motor vehicle to stop when signalled or requested to do so by a police officer. Such laws, unlike the Criminal Code, do not require any intent to escape liability. A breach of the section is an offence, and if the court is satisfied that the person wilfully continued to avoid police while a police officer gave chase, the driver's licence, in the case of the Ontario legislation, may be suspended for a period of three years in addition to any other period of suspension imposed.

(c) Evidence to the Contrary

What constitutes evidence to the contrary will depend on the circumstances in any particular case. However, *R. v. Whitty*,[51] a decision of the Newfoundland Court of Appeal, and *R. v. Smaggus*,[52] a decision of the Nova Scotia Court of Appeal, illustrate the kind of circumstances which have been accepted as evidence to the contrary. *Whitty* stands for the proposition that evidence of the accused's inability to form the intent to escape civil or criminal liability will be regarded as evidence to the contrary within the meaning of this section. In the *Whitty* case, Gushue J.A. stated that in determining whether an accused intended to escape civil or criminal liability under this section, the court must apply a subjective test — that is to say, the court must try to determine what was in the mind of the accused when he or she left the scene of the accident. In applying this test Gushue J.A. stated:

There is no doubt but that the respondent was driving in a dangerous manner, but this is not the offence with which he was charged. In my view, the Magistrate did

[50] (1983), 3 C.C.C. (3d) 193 (S.C.C.).

[51] (1977), 12 Nfld. & P.E.I.R. 361 (Nfld. C.A.).

[52] (1973), 5 N.S.R. (2d) 409 (C.A.).

not err in finding that there was evidence to the contrary to rebut the guilty intent within the meaning of Section 233(3) [now section 252(1)]. In the first place, it is clear that the test of the defendant's state of mind at the time of the accident is a subjective, not an objective one, and therefore the Magistrate was entitled to accept the respondent's version as being evidence to the contrary to disprove the guilty intent. He had also before him the following additional facts: Firstly, the respondent was of extremely low mentality, and therefore his capability to form this intent was obviously questionable. Secondly, Whitty was a resident of the area and it seems extremely likely that he could have hoped to avoid liability by fleeing the scene of the accident. Thirdly, despite the fact that he lived in the area and was familiar with it, he drove away from the scene and down a road which had no exit and from which there was no escape. In my view, all of this indicates lack of guilty intent which was sufficient to allow the learned Magistrate to find as he did.[53]

In *R. v. Smaggus*, the Nova Scotia Court of Appeal overturned the accused's conviction of failing to stop at the scene of an accident, holding that evidence that the accused reported the accident the next day was evidence to the contrary of intent.[54]

8. OPERATING MOTOR VEHICLE WHILE LICENCE SUSPENDED

The Criminal Code makes it an offence to operate a motor vehicle when one's licence is suspended. Section 259(4) provides:

(4) Every one who operates a motor vehicle . . . in Canada while he is disqualified from doing so
(a) is guilty of an indictable offence and liable to imprisonment for a term not exceeding two years; or
(b) is guilty of an offence punishable on summary conviction.

The disqualification refers to a suspension of one's licence by a province. The Supreme Court of Canada has held in *R. v. Prue*[55] that section 238(3) [259(4)] is an offence which requires *mens rea* holding that the Crown must prove not only that the accused's licence was suspended, but that the accused drove a motor vehicle knowing that his or her licence had been suspended.

9. TAKING MOTOR VEHICLE WITHOUT CONSENT

Section 335(1) of the Criminal Code makes it an offence to take a motor vehicle without the consent of the owner:

---

[53] *Whitty, supra*, note 51, at 368-369.
[54] *Supra*, note 52, at 413.
[55] (1979), 8 C.R. (3d) 68 (S.C.C.).

335. (1) Every one who, without the consent of the owner, takes a motor vehicle or vessel with intent to drive, use, navigate or operate it or cause it to be driven, used, navigated or operated is guilty of an offence punishable on summary conviction.

In order to obtain a conviction under this section the Crown will be required to establish that an accused took the vehicle without the owner's consent and the accused took the vehicle with the intention to operate it or cause it to be used or operated. Accordingly, where there is evidence that the owner consented to the operation of the vehicle, the accused cannot be convicted of committing an offence under this section. There is a distinction between this offence and theft of a vehicle as it may be committed although one does not intend to deprive the owner of the property but merely to joy ride and return it.[56]

10. IMPACT OF THE CHARTER

(a) Section 10

The Charter of Rights has had a great impact upon the prosecution and defence of motor offences. Section 10 of the Charter of Rights provides:

10. Everyone has the right on arrest or detention
(*a*) to be informed promptly of the reasons therefor;
(*b*) to retain and instruct counsel without delay and to be informed of that right; and
(*c*) to have the validity of the detention determined by way of *habeas corpus* and to be released if the detention is not lawful.

Before the Charter of Rights came into effect, someone who was asked to take a breathalyzer test by a police officer was not deemed to be detained, and while an accused had a right under common law to insist on speaking to a lawyer before taking a breathalyzer test, there was no obligation upon a police officer to inform an accused of his or her right to retain and instruct counsel. Accordingly, if an accused did not insist upon speaking to a lawyer before taking a breathalyzer test, there was no duty upon the police officers to ensure that the accused understood his or her legal right to retain counsel.

In *R. v. Therens*,[57] the Supreme Court of Canada held that someone requested to take a breathalzyer test is detained within the meaning of section 10(*b*) of the Charter and is entitled to retain and instruct counsel without delay. The significance of the *Therens* case is that a person no longer has to

---

[56] *R. v. Wilkins* (1964), 44 C.R. 375 (Ont. C.A.).
[57] (1985), 45 C.R. (3d) 97 (S.C.C.).

be under compulsory physical restraint to have the right to speak to a lawyer without delay. In *Therens*, the Supreme Court for the first time recognized that an accused may be detained when the accused believes that he or she is not free to disobey an order of a peace officer. Mr. Justice Le Dain held that a person may be psychologically detained in circumstances where the citizen believes that he or she is not free to disobey a demand or a direction of a police officer.

In *Therens*, Mr. Justice Le Dain stated that he did not regard the accused's compliance with the breathalyzer demand of a police officer as voluntary because most citizens are not aware of the precise limits of a police officer's power and comply with the demand or direction by a police officer to avoid being prosecuted for obstructing police. In the *Therens* case, the breathalyzer certificate was excluded because the Supreme Court held that the accused's right to counsel had been infringed. In excluding the certificate the majority of the court held that the accused, who was taken to the police station without being placed under arrest, was detained within the meaning of section 10 of the Charter and that the police had flagrantly violated his right to retain and instruct counsel. Accordingly, the denial of one's right to counsel generally will result in the exclusion of the breathalyzer evidence and will, where the Crown's case depends upon the accused's blood-alcohol reading set out in the breathalyzer certificate, result in the accused being acquitted.

It will be recalled that someone who is asked to take a roadside screening test is not entitled to retain and instruct counsel. Although as a result of amendments to the section, the section no longer contains a reference to the word "roadside", such tests are usually administered in the roadside setting. The word "roadside" was deleted from section 254 when the section was expanded to allow a police officer to test someone whom the officer reasonably suspects is operating a motor vehicle, vessel, aircraft or railway equipment. The Criminal Law Amendment Act, 1985 deleted the word "roadside" from section 254 of the Criminal Code. In *Thomsen*,[58] the Supreme Court of Canada held that the right to counsel did not exist during the "roadside screening" test, saying that the denial of the right to counsel was a reasonable limit under section 1 of the Charter. The provincial courts of appeal have not accepted arguments by defence counsel that the deletion of the word "roadside" from the Criminal Code meant that the Supreme Court of Canada's restriction on the right to counsel in *Thomsen* no longer applies. Several provincial courts of appeal have held that the thrust of the "roadside screening" scheme is that the breathalyzer samples be provided "forthwith," saying that the deletion of the word "roadside" does not change the Supreme Court of Canada's rationale for denying a person his right to counsel when such a demand is made.[59]

---

[58] *Supra*, note 17.

[59] *R. v. Yuskow* (1989), 73 C.R. (3d) 159 (Alta. C.A.); *R. v. Redding* (1988), 83 N.S.R. (2d) 306 (N.S.C.A.); *R. v. Bacon* (1990), 60 C.C.C. (3d) 446 (Sask. C.A.).

The courts have held that a person who is given a screening test and asked to undergo a physical coordination test is detained under section 10(*b*) of the Charter but is not entitled to retain and instruct counsel without delay. In *R. v. Saunders*,[60] the Ontario Court of Appeal held that the provisions of the Highway Traffic Act, which impliedly authorized a police officer to require that a motorist perform a coordination test, constituted a reasonable limit for purposes of section 1 of the Charter. In so holding, the court stated that the physical coordination test causes slight inconvenience to the driver and does not subject the driver to criminal charges.

(b) Reasonable Opportunity to Obtain Counsel

The Supreme Court of Canada has held that section 10(*b*) of the Charter requires that the detainee be given a reasonable opportunity to retain counsel. In *R. v. Manninen*, Lamer J. said that "the detainee is in the control of the police and he cannot exercise his right to counsel unless the police provide him with a reasonable opportunity to do so."[61] Thus, if a person who is detained requests a lawyer, he must be given a reasonable opportunity to contact counsel and the police must refrain from questioning him until he has had a reasonable opportunity to reach his lawyer. The Supreme Court's decision in *Manninen*, which was discussed in detail in Chapter 5, does not mean that evidence will automatically be excluded where the accused has not been given a reasonable opportunity to obtain counsel.

In *Tremblay v. R.*,[62] the accused's right to counsel was violated in that the accused was not given a reasonable opportunity to retain counsel. At trial, the accused was convicted of operating a motor vehicle with a blood-alcohol content exceeding 80 mg. The accused's conviction was overturned by a District Court judge and the Crown appealed to the Ontario Court of Appeal. The Ontario Court of Appeal restored the accused's conviction and the accused appealed to the Supreme Court of Canada. The Supreme Court of Canada held that the accused had been denied a reasonable opportunity to obtain counsel, but refused to exclude the evidence obtained, saying that the accused's conduct had provoked the infringement of his rights. The accused had been verbally abusive to one police officer and had told another officer that he would use violence if his handcuffs were removed. Lamer J., who delivered the judgment of the Supreme Court of Canada, stated:

> From the moment the accused was intercepted on the road to the moment he was asked to give the first sample of breath, his behaviour was violent, vulgar and obnoxious. A reading of the record and the findings of fact below satisfy me that,

---

[60] (1988), 63 C.R. (3d) 37 at 47 (Ont. C.A.).

[61] (1987), 58 C.R. (3d) 97 at 103 (S.C.C.).

[62] (1987), 60 C.R. (3d) 59 (S.C.C.).

while the police, following the request for counsel, did not, as they must, afford the accused a reasonable opportunity to contact a lawyer through his wife before calling upon him to give a breath sample, their haste in the matter was provoked by the accused's behaviour. Indeed, throughout this encounter with the police the accused, as was found by the trial judge as a matter of fact, "was deliberately attempting to make the investigation difficult" and "was actively obstructing it". As testified to by a police officer, it appeared to the police that the accused was stalling when he was given the telephone to contact a lawyer.

. . . .

While the police's hastiness does not change the fact that the detainee's right to counsel was violated, the reasons therefor make it understandable and relevant when one addresses the s. 24(2) issue. In my view the admission of the evidence obtained would not, having regard to all of the circumstances, bring the administration of justice into disrepute.[63]

The Supreme Court of Canada has held that the availability of duty counsel services in the place where the person is detained may affect what constitutes reasonable diligence in exercising the detainee's right to retain and instruct counsel under section 10(*b*) of the Charter.[64] A fuller discussion of this issue may be found in Chapter 5, A Person's Rights and Obligations under the Criminal Law.

(c) Technical Breaches of the Charter

The Charter of Rights does not provide for the automatic exclusion of evidence and the courts will not exclude evidence where the infringement of a Charter right is insignificant. Thus, in *R. v. Frazer*,[65] the Alberta Court of Appeal overturned an accused's acquittal of driving with a blood-alcohol content exceeding 80 mg, holding that if the accused's right to counsel had been infringed, the infringement was technical and insignificant. In this case, the trial judge refused to admit the breathalzyer certificate because the accused had not been informed of his right to retain counsel before he took the breathalyzer test. The trial judge refused to admit the evidence even though the accused was afforded an opportunity to contact a lawyer at the police station and spoke with someone on the telephone for half an hour before taking the breathalyzer test.

The Alberta Court of Appeal held that the breathalyzer evidence should not have been excluded and allowed the Crown's appeal. In holding that the evidence should not have been excluded, Hetherington J.A. stated:

---

[63] *Ibid.*, at 62.
[64] *R. v. Prosper* (1994), 33 C.R. (4th) 85 at 108-109 (S.C.C.).
[65] (1986), 41 M.V.R. 271 (Alta. C.A.).

Assuming without deciding that there was an infringement of the respondent's right under s.10(*b*) of the Charter to be informed of his right to retain and instruct counsel without delay, the infringement was technical and insignificant. Section 24(2) of the Charter reads as follows:

> 24. (2) Where . . . a court concludes that evidence was obtained in a manner that infringed or denied any rights or freedoms guaranteed by this Charter, the evidence shall be excluded if it is established that, having regard to all the circumstances, the admission of it in the proceedings would bring the administration of justice into disrepute.

This is not a rule of automatic exclusion. . . . Where evidence is obtained in a manner which infringes a right guaranteed by the Charter, that evidence can only be excluded if it is established that in the circumstances the admission of it would bring the administration of justice into disrepute. Since the infringement in this case, if there was one, was technical and insignificant, it is our view that the admission of the certificate in evidence would not have brought the administration of justice into disrepute.[66]

This ruling seems sensible because the accused was not really prejudiced by the failure of the police to read him his right to retain and instruct counsel as there was evidence that he asked to contact a lawyer and was permitted to do so at the police station.

---

[66] *Ibid.*, at 273.

11

Drug Offences

The Narcotic Control Act and the Food and Drugs Act prohibit the possession, trafficking, possession for the purpose of trafficking and importing of some types of drugs.[1] Legislation relating to drugs was first enacted in 1908 largely as a result of an investigation by W.L. Mackenzie King, who later became Prime Minister of Canada, into riots in Vancouver arising from the hostility towards Chinese workers.[2] Over the years the legislation was expanded to cover cocaine, morphine, heroin, codeine, cannabis, hashish and marijuana. As a result of the increasing use of chemical drugs, such as LSD, in 1962 the Food and Drugs Act was amended to prohibit the possession and trafficking of drugs such as LSD and thalidomide. The prohibited drugs under both pieces of legislation are set out in regulations and include opium, cannabis and many chemical substances.

1. POSSESSION OF A NARCOTIC

Section 3(1) of the Narcotic Control Act prohibits the possession of narcotics:

3. (1) Except as authorized by this Act or the regulations, no person shall have a narcotic in his possession.

Many narcotics are not readily identified except by a skilled analyst. In a prosecution, the Crown has the burden of establishing that the substance to which the charge relates is a narcotic. If an analyst was required to appear as a witness in every case, proceedings could be delayed without any benefit to the accused. Accordingly, section 9 of the Narcotic Control Act and section 35(1) of the Food and Drugs Act provide that a certificate of an analyst stating that

---

[1] R.S.C. 1985, c. N-1; R.S.C. 1985, c. F-27.

[2] B. MacFarlane, *Drug Offences in Canada,* 2nd ed. (Aurora: Canada Law Book, 1986), p. 22, *et seq.*

he has analyzed a substance and giving the result of the analysis is admissible in evidence.

(a) Certificate of Analysis

The usual practice in prosecutions is to have an analyst take the substance alleged to be a narcotic and test it to determine if it is an illegal narcotic. After conducting tests to determine the nature of the substance, the analyst will prepare a certificate of analysis which will be used at the accused's trial to prove that the substance is a prohibited narcotic or a drug restricted or controlled under the Food and Drugs Act. An accused must be given reasonable notice that the prosecutor intends to introduce the certificate at the accused's trial and a copy of the certificate must be given to the accused together with the notice that the certificate will be used at trial.

Section 9 of the Narcotic Control Act and section 35(1) of the Food and Drugs Act require that an accused be served with a certificate of analysis so that he or she may hire an expert to dispute the findings of the drug analyst. The accused may require that the analyst appear at the trial so that he may be cross-examined. If the analyst's findings are not successfully disputed, the certificate of analysis is evidence that the substance tested by the drug analyst was a prohibited drug.

Section 9(1) of the Narcotic Control Act states:

> **9.** (1) Subject to this section, a certificate purporting to be signed by an analyst stating that he has analyzed or examined a substance and stating the result of the analysis or examination is admissible in evidence in any prosecution . . . and, in the absence of evidence to the contrary, is proof of the statements contained in the certificate without proof of the signature or the official character of the person appearing to have signed the certificate.

The effect of section 9 was considered by the Ontario Court of Appeal in *R. v. Welsh*[3] where Martin J.A. stated:

> In our view, s. 9 makes the certificate, in the absence of evidence to the contrary, proof of the statements contained in the certificate, relative to the identification of the substance, which the certificate states was analyzed.[4]

In *Oliver v. R.*,[5] Lamer J., who wrote the judgment of the Supreme Court of Canada, defined "evidence to the contrary" as follows:

> "Evidence to the contrary" is any evidence which tends to put in doubt the probative [relevant] value Parliament has legislatively conferred upon the statements

---

[3] (1975), 24 C.C.C. (2d) 382 (Ont. C.A.).
[4] *Ibid.*, at 385.
[5] (1984), 24 C.R. (3d) 1 (S.C.C.).

contained in a s. 9 certificate. This evidence may be in regard to the analyst himself, his qualifications, integrity, or in regard of the procedures he followed to draw his conclusions. Section 9 has been enacted to dispense with the calling of experts to testify in cases where the nature of the suspect substance was not really in issue. . . .

"Evidence to the contrary", as regards an analyst's conclusions set out in a certificate, as those words are used in section 9, is any evidence upon which a finder of fact could as a matter of law rest a reasonable doubt as to that analyst's conclusions had he testified as an expert witness in court.[6]

(b) Requirement of Possession

A prosecutor in a prosecution for possession of a prohibited narcotic must prove that the accused had possession of an illegal narcotic. While the certificate of analysis will prove that the substance which the police have confiscated was a narcotic, it does not prove that an accused had such possession. Evidence that an accused handled a drug, by itself, will not be sufficient to prove that the accused was in possession of the drug. Section 4(3) of the Criminal Code,[7] which defines what constitutes possession under criminal law, creates two kinds of possession: personal possession and what has been called constructive possession. Constructive possession occurs where someone is holding an object for someone else, or where a person has it in any place for the use and benefit of the person or another. For example, if Mr. Smith buys drugs, and with the knowledge and consent of Miss Jones, keeps the drugs at Miss Jones' apartment, Mr. Smith will be said to have constructive possession of the drugs because section 4(3) of the Criminal Code provides that one may be said to be in possession of something without having it in his or her physical possession.

(i) *Personal possession*

In *R. v. Hess (No. 1)*,[8] Mr. Justice O'Halloran of the British Columbia Court of Appeal held that in cases of personal possession of the Crown must establish the following:

> To constitute "possession" within the meaning of the criminal law it is my judgment, that where as here there is manual handling of a thing, it [i.e., the manual handling] must be co-existent with knowledge of what the thing is, and

---

[6] *Ibid.*, at 10.
[7] R.S.C. 1985, c. C-46.
[8] (1948), 94 C.C.C. 48 (B.C.C.A.).

both these elements must be co-existent with some act of control (outside public duty).[9]

In *R. v. Hess*, a girl took a parcel to her mother which she and two of her friends had found near a sign post on a Vancouver street. The mother suspected that the parcel contained narcotics and telephoned the police. The police took the parcel back where it was found and waited for someone to retrieve it. The accused Hess, who was arrested while trying to retrieve the parcel, was charged with possession of narcotics. O'Halloran J.A. found that an accused could not be convicted of possessing an illegal substance unless there was evidence which indicated that the accused knew what the substance was and had some measure of control over it:

> If knowledge of what the thing is were not an essential element, then we would have the ridiculous result that the children who found the parcel in the first place and brought it home to the mother, would by that act alone be automatically guilty of possession under s. 4(1)(*d*). . . . Even with knowledge of what the thing is, if some act of control (outside public duty) is not essential, then we would have the equally ridiculous result that the little girl's mother who received the parcel of drugs and telephoned the police, would be automatically guilty of possession under s. 4(1)(*d*). . . .

> I cannot satisfy myself that Parliament intended "possession" in s. 4 to be interpreted in a way to produce the foregoing absurd results, by eliminating the elements of knowledge and some act of control (outside public duty), and thus making manual handling simpliciter [i.e., simple manual handling] a crime. . . .

> If words employed in a statute seem to achieve that result it is a strong ground for concluding that Parliament did not intend the words should be construed in the sense which brings that about.[10]

The Supreme Court of Canada adopted the British Columbia Court of Appeal's definition of possession in *Beaver v. R.*[11] In *Beaver v. R.*, the Supreme Court of Canada had to decide whether an accused who was in possession of a package which he believed contained milk sugar could be convicted of heroin possession. The principal issue in the case was whether the Crown must establish that the accused knew the substance in his possession was an illegal substance. The Supreme Court of Canada held that an accused cannot be convicted of possessing an illegal substance unless the Crown can show that the accused knew that the substance was illegal. Mr. Justice Cartwright stated:

> Has X possession of heroin when he has in his hand or in his pocket or in his cupboard a package which in fact contains heroin but which he obviously believes contains only baking soda? In my opinion that question must be answered in the negative. The essence of the crime is the possession of the for-

---

[9] *Ibid.*, at 50-52.
[10] *Ibid.*, at 51-52.
[11] (1957), 118 C.C.C. 129 (S.C.C.).

bidden substance and in a criminal case there is in law no possession without knowledge of the character of the forbidden substance. Just as in *R. v. Ashwell* (1885), 16 Q.B.D. 190, the accused did not in law have possession of the complainant's sovereign so long as he honestly believed it to be a shilling, so in my illustration X did not have possession of heroin so long as he honestly believed the package to contain baking soda.[12]

The court's ruling is consistent with the cardinal criminal law principle that *mens rea* is, subject to Parliament's deliberate and clear creation of offences which do not require *mens rea*, an essential feature of every criminal offence.

(ii) *Constructive possession*

The law dealing with proof of possession under the Criminal Code is best summarized in *R. v. Moore*[13] in the decision of Gerein J., of the Saskatchewan Court of Queen's Bench. In *Moore*, Gerein J. explained the different factual situations covered by section 3(4) [4(3)] of the Criminal Code, saying:

The first situation is that of personal possession where, for example, a person has a substance in his hand or in his pocket (s. 3(4)(a)). The second situation is where a person does not have the substance on his person but rather the substance is physically held or is in the custody of another person for the first person's benefit (s. 3(4)(a)(i)). The third situation is where a person does not have the substance on his person, nor does he have the substance in another person's custody, but rather he has the substance in some place for the benefit of himself or another person (s. 3(4)(a)(ii)). The fourth situation is where several people have possession of a common substance (s. 3(4)(b)).

It is noted that the last provision reads " where one of two or more persons . . . has anything in his custody or possession . . ." In my opinion the effect of these words is that if several persons are to be found to be in possession of one common substance, then at least one of them must be in possession of that substance within the meaning of s. 3(4)(a). In the absence of such a person there is no person's possession or custody to whom the requisite knowledge and consent of the other persons could relate.

In short, the Criminal Code provides initially that a person is in the possession of a substance where he personally is holding the substance. The Criminal Code then goes on to deal with the situations where there is no such physical holding and states that even in the absence of such physical holding or handling a person or persons may still be in possession of the substance.

What then is the law where you do not have a physical handling but you have the situations contemplated by s. 3(4)(a)(i)(ii)? In my opinion, in such situations the Crown must prove that the accused had knowledge of the nature of the substance and some control over the substance.

. . . It seems to me that if knowledge and control are essential when a person physically holds the substance then the fact that some other person is actually

12 *Ibid.*, at 139-140.
13 (1983), 24 Sask. R. 199 (Sask. Q.B.).

holding the substance should not remove the necessity for knowledge and control being present in the prime person.[14]

(iii) *Control*

The courts have held that one cannot have possession of something within the meaning of section 4(3) of the Criminal Code unless one has some measure of control over the object in question. In *R. v. Lombardo*,[15] an Ontario County Court judge stated that "An essential element of possession is control and the attempt to exclude others from possession."[16] In the *Lombardo* case, His Honour Judge Moore defined control as: "to exercise directing, guiding or restraining power over something."[17]

The courts have decided that there must be an intent to control something before an accused can be said to exercise control over an object. Thus, in *R. v. Christie*, Mr. Justice Hughes stated:

> In my opinion, there can be circumstances which do not constitute possession even where there is a right of control with knowledge of the presence and character of the thing alleged to be possessed, where guilt should not be inferred, as where it appears there is no intent to exercise control over it. An example of this situation is where a person finds a package on his doorstep and upon opening it discovers it contains narcotics. Assuming he has done nothing further to indicate an intention to exercise control over it, he had not, in my opinion, the possession contemplated by the *Criminal Code*. Nor do I think such a person who manually handles it for the sole purpose of destroying it or reporting it to the police has committed the offence of possession.[18]

(iv) *The "hot potato" cases*

Possession under the Criminal Code excludes a hasty handling of something where there is clearly no intention to exercise control over the object. In *R. v. Vance*, the Ontario Court of Appeal ruled that to establish possession under the Criminal Code the Crown must demonstrate "that an accused was knowingly in control of something in circumstances which show that he was assenting to being in control of it. . . ."[19] In this case, the police were in hot pursuit of the accused, Vance, when Vance unexpectedly passed a bottle containing phencyclidine (PCP) to the accused, Nichols. There was no

---

[14] *Ibid.*, at 201.
[15] (1967), 3 C.R.N.S. 19 (Ont. Co. Ct.).
[16] *Ibid.*, at 21.
[17] *Ibid.*, at 21.
[18] (1978), 41 C.C.C. (2d) 282 at 287 (N.B.C.A.).
[19] (1977), 2 W.C.B. 23 (Ont. C.A.) (summary only). See unreported judgment, File no. 393/77 at p. 4.

evidence that Vance and Nichols had agreed that Nichols would take the PCP if they were followed by the police. At trial, Mr. Nichols was convicted of unlawfully having in his possession a narcotic, to wit, phencyclidine (PCP) for the purpose of trafficking. Nichols appealed his conviction to the Ontario Court of Appeal which overturned his conviction. In his reasons for judgment, Brooke J.A., who delivered the judgment of the Court of Appeal, stated that while the accused suspected that he had been given a narcotic, "the time during which he had . . . (the drugs) in his hands, was hardly time for the making of a conscious decision to accept them so that one could find he had possession of them in law."[20] Mr. Justice Brooke added that, ". . . the evidence fell short of satisfying the onus on the Crown and proving that this appellant accepted the drugs, and that he assented to being in control of them."[21]

If the Crown did not have to prove that an accused intended to exercise some measure of control over a substance, an accused could be convicted of possession of a narcotic in a "hot potato" type of case where drugs were thrown into the accused's lap by someone fleeing from the police. In the *Vance* case, the accused, Nichols, would have been convicted of possession were it not for the need to prove that he consciously exercised some measure of control over the drugs. It could be argued that Nichols had the requisite knowledge and consent to establish possession under section 3(4) [4(3)] of the Criminal Code. The Crown could probably establish that the accused knew that he was being given an illegal substance and it could be argued that he consented to possession of the narcotic when he took if from his co-accused. Thus, if it were not for the need to establish that an accused must consciously consent to being in control of an illegal substance, someone could be convicted of possession simply because he or she had momentarily handled an illegal substance.

(c) Specific Defences

(i) *Lack of knowledge*

If an accused is charged with possession of a narcotic and the Crown cannot establish the required elements of possession under section 4(3) of the Criminal Code, the accused will have a defence. In most cases, the Crown will be able to show that an accused had possession of the drug. Where an accused is searched and the police find an illegal drug, the accused can hardly argue that he or she did not have possession of the drug. The required elements of knowledge, consent and control can generally be satisfied by finding the drug on the accused's person. If someone planted the drug without the accused's knowledge, possession could not be established. If drugs had not been planted, then the accused, practically speaking, will not be in a position to argue that

---

[20] *Ibid.* (393/77).
[21] *Ibid.* (393/77).

he or she did not have possession of the drugs. However, if drugs are found on the kitchen counter in an apartment occupied by several people, the Crown may not be able to prove that the accused is in sole or joint possession of the drugs because it may not be able to show the necessary elements of consent and knowledge.

(ii) *De minimis non curat lex*

The phrase *de minimis non curat lex* is a Latin phrase which means that the law will not concern itself with trifles. The reasoning behind the *de minimis non curat lex* principle is set out in a case called *The "Reward"*:

> The Court is not bound to a strictness at once harsh and pedantic in the application of statutes. The law permits the qualification implied in the ancient maxim De minimis non curat lex — Where there are irregularities of very slight consequence, it does not intend that the infliction of penalties should be inflexibly severe. If the deviation were a mere trifle, which, if continued in practice, would weigh little or nothing on the public interest, it might properly be overlooked.[22]

The *de minimis* defence has been used in drug cases where a minute quantity of drugs were found in the accused's possession. The defence has been used in several cases where the drugs found could not be measured or seen except under a microscope. One such case is *R. v. Ling*,[23] a judgment of the Alberta Supreme Court. The accused, Ling, was arrested and charged with unlawfully having in his possession a drug, to wit, Diacetyl-morphine Hydrochloride, contrary to the provisions of the Opium and Narcotic Drug Act.[24] The accused, who was in the company of known drug traffickers, was arrested in a hotel room after police conducted a search of the room. After searching the accused, the officers took the lint, fluff and dust found in the accused's pants' pockets to be analyzed by a drug analyst. The analyst testified that he found traces of heroin in the dust and stated that the heroin, which could not be seen except under a microscope, was useless and could not be used by anyone. In acquitting the accused, Boyd McBride J. stated:

> On the facts here . . . the submission that the accused illegally had possession of heroin as contemplated by the Act . . . is asking the Court to carry findings to an absurdity. Indeed to me it is so artificial and divorced from reality as to border almost on the fantastic. I cannot bring myself to the view here, that there was illegal possession of heroin in the contemplation of Parliament, in what otherwise were empty pockets. If Parliament had so intended it would have been a simple matter to have said so explicitly in the Act, as, for example, by a definition of pos-

---

[22] (1818), 2 Dods, 1482 at 1484.
[23] (1954), 109 C.C.C. 306 (Alta. S.C.).
[24] R.S.C. 1952, c. 201.

session broad enought to include scientific traces as we have here. . . . the maxim
de minimis non curat lex applies in criminal law as in civil. . . .[25]

The *de minimis* defence has created much controversy and some courts
refuse to acknowledge that the defence exists. In *R. v. Lis*,[26] Mr. Justice
Montgomery of the Ontario High Court of Justice held that the principle of *de
minimis non curat lex* is not a defence to a criminal charge. The law dealing
with the *de minimis* defence is in a state of flux. There is disagreement among
judges as to when the defence applies, if it applies at all. Some judges believe
that someone who is charged under the Narcotic Control Act or the Food and
Drugs Act cannot be convicted of possessing an illegal substance unless there
is evidence that the drug was in a usable quantity. In some cases, judges have
acquitted an accused on the ground that the accused was found to be in possession of such a small quantity of drugs that the drug could not be used in
any form. In other cases, judges have refused to accept the argument that the
Crown must prove that the accused had possession of a usable quantity of
drugs. Thus, in *R. v. McLeod*,[27] the British Columbia Court of Appeal ruled
that in a drug prosecution the Crown was not required to prove that an accused
had possession of a usable quantity of drugs. The result is that one cannot be
certain that the defence will be accepted and the issue will not be resolved
until there is a definitive judgment by the Supreme Court of Canada.
However, the possession of a minute quantity may result in the Crown failing
to show that the accused lacked the requisite knowledge of or control over the
drug.[28]

2. TRAFFICKING IN A NARCOTIC

Section 4(1) of the Narcotic Control Act states:

No person shall traffic in a narcotic or any substance represented or held by the
person to be a narcotic.

The Narcotic Control Act defines the word "traffic" as follows:

"traffic" means

(*a*) to manufacture, sell, give, administer, transport, send, deliver or distribute, or
(*b*) to offer to do anything mentioned in paragraph (*a*) otherwise than under the
authority of this Act, or the regulations.

---

[25] *Supra*, note 23, at 310.
[26] (1984), 16 C.C.C. (3d) 382 (Ont. H.C.).
[27] (1955), 111 C.C.C. 137 (B.C.C.A.); see also *R. v. Quigley* (1954), 111 C.C.C. 81 (Alta. C.A.).
[28] *R. v. Overvold* (1972), 9 C.C.C. (2d) 517 (N.W.T. Magistrate's Ct.); *R. v. McBurney* (1974), 15
C.C.C. (2d) 361 (B.C.S.C.), affirmed (1975), 24 C.C.C. (2d) 44 (B.C.C.A.).

(a) What Constitutes "Trafficking"

Many of the words contained in the definition of "trafficking" in the Narcotic Control Act are self-explanatory. Words such as sell, give, send, deliver and distribute are not technical words and the courts have given them their ordinary meaning. In *R. v. Harrington*, the British Columbia Court of Appeal stated:

> In the definition of "traffic", s. 2 of the Act, the word "transport" is associated with the words "manufacture, sell, give, administer, send, deliver and distribute". Six, if not all of these words, imply something more extensive than a use for the actor's own purposes. When one uses the word "sell", "give", "administer", "send", "deliver" or "distribute", he does not contemplate a transaction involving one person alone, but a transaction involving two or more persons.[29]

(i) *Aiding and abetting*

The Supreme Court of Canada has held that a person who offers to deliver, sell or trade in drugs is guilty of trafficking under section 4(2) of the Narcotic Control Act. In *Poitras v. R.*,[30] Dickson J. said that someone who does something to assist a drug trafficker is equally as guilty of trafficking as the trafficker:

> Section 21(1) of the *Criminal Code* provides that anyone who does or omits to do anything for the purpose of aiding any person to commit an offence or abets any person in committing it is a party to the offence. It follows that anyone who sells or delivers hashish or offers to do so, or does anything for the purpose of aiding another person to do so, is guilty of an offence.[31]

In *R. v. Taylor*, Carrothers J.A., of the British Columbia Court of Appeal, stated that the essence of a trafficking charge is "possession plus the intent or purpose of physically making the . . . (substance) available to others, regardless of ownership."[32] In *Taylor*, Carrothers J.A. said that trafficking under the Narcotic Control Act does not refer to ownership of drugs and consequently one may be convicted of trafficking although the person to whom he or she delivers the drugs has a part ownership in the drugs being delivered:

> . . . one can "give", "deliver" or "distribute" an object to another or others regardless of whether that object is owned by the one, another or others or all or none of them. Here there was ample evidence, including the testimony of the appellant, that the appellant's purpose in bringing the hashish to his home on the

---

[29] [1964] 1 C.C.C. 189, at 195 (B.C.C.A.).
[30] [1974] S.C.R. 649 (S.C.C.).
[31] *Ibid.*, at 651.
[32] (1974), 17 C.C.C. (2d) 36 at 41 (B.C.C.A.).

day in question was to "give", "deliver" or "distribute" it to some or all of the others, as well as to take some for his own use.

... The simple fact that it was economic for the purchase price to be collected in advance from the potential users of the narcotic and a bulk purchase made, thereby vesting in such users some claim to ownership and title and even a deemed joint possession by them, does not alter the nature of the physical act of giving, delivering or distributing the narcotic to another or others, which in itself constitutes the offence.[33]

(ii) *Transporting*

It is clear from the definition of "traffic" in the Narcotic Control Act (discussed at the beginning of this section) that if one sells drugs or distributes drugs to another person, one will have committed the offence of trafficking. However, what if instead of selling drugs to someone else, an accused transports drugs in his car from one area to another? If drugs are transported or carried from one location to another without being sold or otherwise distributed to anyone is this transport of drugs trafficking? Several courts have considered whether the word "transport" means simply to carry something from one place to another, or whether transport as used in the Narcotic Control Act suggests something more than that.

In *Turcotte v. R.*,[34] it was held that someone who carried drugs from one place to another did not transport the drugs so as to be guilty of trafficking under the Narcotic Control Act. Dutil J.S.P. said that the word "transport" could not be given its ordinary dictionary definition, but rather must be interpreted within the context of the other words contained in the definition of "traffic". His Honour referred to the words of Justice Bird in *R. v. Harrington*:

> These considerations impel me to the view that the word "transport" in the definition of "traffic" is not meant in the sense of mere conveying or carrying or moving from one place to another, but in the sense of doing so to promote the distribution of the narcotic to another. In my opinion there must be something more extensive than mere conveying, or carrying or moving incidental to one's own use of the drug to warrant a conviction under s. 4(1) for trafficking.
> ... It seems to me that, if I am wrong, every person who has a narcotic in his possession can be held guilty of trafficking, for it is inconceivable that he would not have conveyed or carried it from one place to another, if only from the hand of the supplier to his own person. The inclusion in s. 4(1) of the words "represented or held out by him to be a narcotic" indicate that Parliament had in mind the concept of transaction with someone else. Having regard to the creation of the three separate and distinct offences contained in ss. 3(1) and 4(1) and (2) Parliament could not, I think, have intended that proof of transporting in the mere dictionary sense of conveying or carrying from one place to another and without more should be sufficient to establish the crime of trafficking.[35]

---

[33] *Ibid.*, at 40-41.
[34] (1981), 22 C.R. (2d) 46 (Que. S.P.).
[35] *Ibid.*, at 52.

Similar reasoning was adopted by the Newfoundland Court of Appeal in *R. v. Greene*, where Furlong C.J. stated:

> Transport as I read it in this case must be read to mean that the drug was being carried from one point to another with the intention of futhering the distribution or giving it to another person.[36]

(iii) *Administering*

While the words "sell, give, send, deliver and distribute" have been given their ordinary dictionary meaning, the word "administer" has been given a specialized legal meaning. The Concise Oxford Dictionary of Current English defines "administer" as follows:

> . . . present (oath *to*); furnish, give, (thing, *to*); apply (remedies *to*) . . . .[37]

The Saskatchewan Court of Appeal in *R. v. Tan*[38] has held that the word "administer," as used in the Narcotic Control Act, does not include prescribing a drug to someone. The court stated:

> We conclude in the light of the language of the Act and regulations passed thereunder that the meaning to be given to the word "administer" is the more limited meaning of "to apply, as medicine" or "to give, remedially", rather "than to make drugs available by giving a prescription".
>
> . . . .
>
> In our opinion, a narcotic is not "administered" until it enters the intended recipient's system parenterally or otherwise.[39]

(iv) *Manufacturing*

If a trafficking charge is based on manufacturing, the Crown must show that the drugs were manufactured for use by someone other than the accused. Thus, in *R. v. Kerner*,[40] Mossop Co. Ct. J. acquitted the accused on charges of trafficking in cannabis resin because the Crown had failed to show that the accused, when chemically converting marijuana into hashish, was manufacturing the drug other than for his personal use.

---

[36] (1976), 33 C.C.C. (2d) 251 at 255 (Nfld. C.A.).
[37] (Oxford: Clarendon Press, 1982), p. 13.
[38] (1984), 15 C.C.C. (3d) 303 (Sask. C.A.).
[39] *Ibid.*, at 306-307.
[40] (1980), 4 W.C.B. 374 (Ont. Co. Ct.).

(v) *Holding out*

An accused does not actually have to traffic in a specific narcotic to be convicted of trafficking. Holding out or representing a substance as a narcotic falls under the definition of "trafficking" set out in the Narcotic Control Act. Accordingly, if an accused represents that sugar is cocaine, the accused can be charged with trafficking in a substance held out to be cocaine and will, if a court concludes that the representation was made, be convicted under section 4(1) of the Narcotic Control Act, which provides:

> No person shall traffic in a narcotic or any substance represented or held out by the person to be a narcotic.

In *R. v. Masters*,[41] His Honour Judge Honsberger of the Ontario County Court explained the elements of the offence of holding out a substance to be a narcotic:

> The offence is trafficking in a substance, either a narcotic or a substance held out to be a narcotic. It is a single offence which may be done in one of two ways, either in a narcotic or in a substance represented or held out to be a narcotic. The *mens rea* is the holding out or representation.
>
> . . . .
>
> . . . The Crown need not prove what in fact the substance was, on a charge such as here. There is evidence that there was a substance offered and held out to be a narcotic.
>
> I further conclude that it is not an element in this offence that the Crown is required to prove that the accused made a fraudulent misrepresentation in that, in fact, he knew it was not a narcotic while holding it out so to be.
> The offence is trafficking.[42]

(b) Specific Defences

(i) *Agent of the purchaser*

While it is an offence to be in illegal possession of a narcotic, it is not an offence to purchase a narcotic under the Narcotic Control Act. Thus, if an accused is charged with trafficking under the Narcotic Control Act, the accused will have a defence to the charge if the evidence indicates that he or she simply purchased the drug for another without engaging in any of the acts which constitute trafficking, such as transporting and delivering a narcotic. The defence will only succeed where it can be shown that the accused intended only to aid the purchaser and not the seller. Thus, a simple introduction of

---

[41] (1973), 12 C.C.C. (2d) 573 (Ont. Co. Ct.), affirmed (1974), 15 C.C.C. (2d) 142 (Ont. C.A.).
[42] *Ibid.*, (Ont. Co. Ct.), at 575-576.

a buyer to a seller accompanied by a passive acquiescence in the subsequent transaction does not warrant a conviction.[43]

(ii) Entrapment

Several Canadian courts have accepted that entrapment forms a defence to trafficking charges. In *R. v. Haukness*,[44] Cronin, a British Columbia Provincial Court judge, acquitted the accused of trafficking in marijuana because he had only sold the marijuana to an undercover police officer after the officer had made several requests that the accused supply him with marijuana. Cronin Prov. J. acquitted the accused because of the officer's persistent request for the drug. His Honour defined entrapment as:

> Now as to what constitutes entrapment. First of all, what is entrapment? The best definition that I can find of entrapment is that entrapment is the act of officers or agents of the government in inducing a person to commit a crime not contemplated by him, that is, by that person, for the purposes of instituting a criminal prosecution against him.[45]

In *R. v. Rippey*,[46] a Nova Scotia County judge acquitted an accused of trafficking in narcotics contrary to section 4(1) of the Narcotic Control Act. In the *Rippey* case, McLellan Co. Ct. J. stated that in determining whether the facts in a case supported a defence of entrapment a court should consider whether the accused committed the offence "as a result of calculated inveigling and persistent importuning."[47] In this case, the evidence indicated that the accused was not prepared to sell marijuana and would not have done so had it not been for the insistence of the police officer. In acquitting the accused McLellan Co. Ct. J. stated:

> Since other evidence indicates that the accused had only a couple of dollars on him that evening after this transaction I am prepared to make findings, first, that the accused had no prior intention of committing the offence of trafficking or dealing in marijuana when he arrived in the Town of Windsor on the night of these events. And secondly, I make a specific finding that the accused was induced to commit the alleged offence by the "calculated inveigling and persistent importuning" of Constable Webb. I reached these conclusions the more readily because, after having observed the accused on the stand, considering his manner of testifying, his age and physical size, it seems to me that the accused was an unsophisticated youth, with no prior experience in drug transactions and indeed a very strictly limited experience with the use of marijuana. I accept his explanation that he committed the alleged offence because Constable Webb had become a pain to him and it seems to me that he felt the easiest and simplest way of get-

---

[43] *R. v. Rodriguez*, [1978] 6 W.W.R. 667 (B.C.C.A.); *R. v. Schartner* (1977), 38 C.C.C. (2d) 89 (B.C.C.A.).
[44] [1976] 5 W.W.R. 420 (B.C. Prov. Ct.).
[45] *Ibid.*, at 429.
[46] (1981), 65 C.C.C. (2d) 158 (N.S. Co. Ct.).
[47] *Ibid.*, at 166.

ting rid of Webb was to accommodate Webb as indeed Webb had requested of him. The fact that he had no cash resources on his person that night seems to me to be highly relevant to his claimed intention not to traffic in marijuana when he went to Windsor on the night in question. His naiveté in the ways of the drug sub-culture is, I think, amply supported by the fact that he put his own money (five dollars) to further his plan of getting rid of Webb and he had no intention of prof-iting in any way from the deal.[48]

In *R. v. Baxter*,[49] the Quebec Court of Appeal ordered a new trial for an accused who had been convicted by a jury after the trial judge instructed the jury that the defence of entrapment did not exist in Canadian law. The accused had been convicted of trafficking in cocaine. An undercover police officer had asked a 17-year-old, emotionally disturbed youth to obtain drugs for him on 40 different occasions. The officer, who was working as a doorman in a bar which the accused frequented, had on occasion allowed the accused to enter the bar without paying a cover charge and had offered him alcoholic bever-ages. The accused was not a trafficker of cocaine and in ordering a new trial Nolan J.A. stated that it was possible for a jury to conclude that the accused had been entrapped by the police officer. In *R. v. Amato*,[50] a majority of Supreme Court of Canada, in a five to four decision, concluded that the defence of entrapment does exist in Canada.

3. POSSESSION FOR THE PURPOSE OF TRAFFICKING

Section 4(2) of the Narcotic Control Act provides:

No person shall have in his possession any narcotic for the purpose of trafficking.

(a) Elements of the Offence

Possession for the purpose of trafficking is an offence which is distinct-ly different from the offence of trafficking under the Narcotic Control Act. In *R. v. Blais*,[51] Wilson J., of the Manitoba Queen's Bench, explained the differ-ences:

. . . the charge under s. 4(2) of the Act of possession for the purpose of traffick-ing is something quite different from a simple charge of trafficking only, under s. 4(1). In the latter, the case against the accused relates to, and must emerge from what he is shown to have done as a completed act. The charge under s. 4(2)

---

[48] *Ibid.*, at 166-167.
[49] (1983), 9 C.C.C. (3d) 555 (Que. C.A.).
[50] (1982), 69 C.C.C. (2d) 31 (S.C.C.).
[51] (1974), 19 C.C.C. (2d) 262 (Man. Q.B.).

depends upon a demonstration of what the accused means to do, his "purpose" in possessing the drug, something which in the absence of a declared intent is a matter of inference (but not mere speculation) from what has gone before, *e.g.*, the bulk quantities involved, or the activities of the accused in relation to the drugs of which he now has, or earlier had, possession.[52]

In determining whether the accused has possession of a drug for the purposes of trafficking, a court will consider factors such as the quantity of drugs which the accused was found to have in his or her possession and the manner in which the drug was packaged. Many of the factors which a court considers in determining whether an accused had possession for the purpose of trafficking have been set out in the Ontario Court of Appeal's decision in *R. v. Oakes*[53] by Martin J.A.:

> In cases where narcotics are possessed for the purpose of trafficking, the quantity is usually such as to indicate that the possession of the drug is not for personal use. Frequently . . . the drugs are packaged in such a way as to indicate that they are intended to be distributed. Commonly, where substantial quantities of a narcotic are found in the possession of an accused other *indicia* of trafficking are also found, such as packing material, bags, scales and records; such evidence is, of course, sometimes supplemented by surveillance, including electronic surveillance.[54]

Frequently, an accused will be found to be in possession of such a large quantity of drugs that the only logical inference is that the accused had possession of the drugs for the purpose of trafficking. Thus, in *R. v. MacPhee*,[55] a British Columbia County Court judge convicted an accused of possession of marijuana for the purpose of trafficking after it was established that the accused had possession of 35 pounds of marijuana. The court stated that, given the large quantities of drugs found in the accused's possession, the only reasonable conclusion was that the accused had possession of the drugs for the purpose of trafficking. Similarly, in *R. v. Barsikhian*,[56] the Quebec Court of Appeal upheld an accused's conviction on a charge of possession of heroin for the purpose of trafficking, concluding that the large quantities of drugs found in the accused's possession, coupled with a finding of a scale to weigh drugs, led to an inference that the accused had possession of the drugs for the purpose of trafficking.

In some cases there will be expert evidence which indicates that the quantity of drugs found is inconsistent with personal use. In one such case, *R. v. Dudar*, a Manitoba County Court judge convicted an accused of possession of a narcotic for the purpose of trafficking, having heard expert evidence that the four ounces of hash oil found in the accused's possession was of a suffi-

---

[52] *Ibid.*, at 272.
[53] (1983), 2 C.C.C. (3d) 339 (Ont. C.A.).
[54] *Ibid.*, at 363.
[55] (1985), 16 W.C.B. 77 (B.C. Co. Ct.).
[56] (1984), 12 W.C.B. 153 (Que. C.A.).

ciently large quantity to be inconsistent with personal use.[57] There was also evidence that the quality of the hash oil was high and the accused was found in possession of a substantial quantity of cash. Also, the accused had possession of packaging containers, which suggested that these containers would have been used to package the hash oil.

(b) Aiding and Abetting

A person who assists someone charged with possession of a narcotic for the purpose of trafficking may be convicted of possession for the purpose of trafficking. A person who assists another person in carrying out an unlawful activity may, in certain circumstances, become a party to the offence being carried out so that the person assisting will be as guilty of the offence being committed as the person who actually commits it. Section 21 of the Criminal Code provides:

21. (1) Every one is a party to an offence who

(*a*) actually commits it,
(*b*) does or omits to do anything for the purpose of aiding any person to commit it; or
(*c*) abets any person in committing it.

(2) Where two or more persons form an intention in common to carry out an unlawful purpose and to assist each other therein and any one of them, in carrying out the common purpose, commits an offence, each of them who knew or ought to have known that the commission of the offence would be a probable consequence of carrying out the common purpose is a party to that offence.

R. v. Ryckman,[58] a decision of the Ontario Court of Appeal, presents an interesting example of aiding and abetting. Several accused were charged with possession of narcotics for the purpose of trafficking, contrary to section 4(2) of the Narcotic Control Act. The three accused had been hired to cut marijuana by one, Philbrick, who owned a farm. The accused were acquitted, but the Crown successfully appealed the accused persons' acquittal. The trial judge found that the three accused harvested the growing crop and placed it in plastic bags knowing that what they were harvesting was marijuana. The trial judge stated that while the accused assisted Philbrick in his possession of marijuana for the purpose of trafficking, that one could not conclude that the accused persons had intended to assist Philbrick in trafficking. In allowing the appeal, the Ontario Court of Appeal stated that the accused had aided and abetted Philbrick "in the offence of possession of marijuana for the purpose of trafficking."

---

[57] (1984), 27 Man. R. (2d) 154 (Man. Co. Ct.).
[58] (1981), 64 C.C.C. (2d) 192 (Ont. C.A.).

(c) Specific Defences

(i) *Personal use*

If an accused is charged with possession of a narcotic for the purpose of trafficking, the Crown must establish that the accused not only had possession of the narcotic but also that it was for the purpose of trafficking. Therefore, if a court concludes that an accused possessed a narcotic for personal use, rather than for trafficking, the accused will be acquitted of possession for the purpose of trafficking and convicted of simple possession of a narcotic. In many cases, an accused charged with possession of a narcotic for the purpose of trafficking has had possession of such a large quantity of drugs that the defence of personal use has not been accepted by the court.

(ii) *Entrapment*

Someone who has been entrapped by a police officer will have a defence to a charge of possession of a narcotic for the purpose of trafficking. The essential features of this defence were examined in the section dealing with trafficking.

4. IMPORTING A NARCOTIC

The Narcotic Control Act makes it an offence to import or export a narcotic. Section 5 of the Act provides:

5. (1) Except as authorized by this Act or the regulations, no person shall import into Canada or export from Canada any narcotic.

(2) Every person who contravenes subsection (1) is guilty of an indictable offence and liable to imprisonment for life but not less than seven years.

(a) Elements of the Offence

(i) *What constitutes "importing"*

The Narcotic Control Act does not define importing or exporting. The Supreme Court of Canada has stated that the word "importing" in the Narcotic Control Act should be given its dictionary meaning. In *Bell v. R.*,[59]

---

[59] (1983), 8 C.C.C. (3d) 97 (S.C.C.).

Dickson J. stated that "courts have generally held there is no ambiguity or equivocation in the phrase 'import into Canada' as used in the *Narcotic Control Act* and that it should be given its ordinary and natural meaning."[60] Dickson J. stated that the issue before the court was "whether the act of importing a narcotic terminates upon the narcotic crossing the border into Canada or whether the act of importing carries on until the narcotic reaches the intended final destination within Canada."[61]

In the *Bell* case, footstools which were shipped from Jamaica to the accused in Quebec were examined by the R.C.M.P. in Toronto and were found to contain 6.7 lbs. of marijuana. The footstools were shipped to Quebec and held at the R.C.M.P. headquarters there. The accused was acquitted at trial on the ground that he could not be convicted as a result of acts committed after the narcotic crossed the border, as the offence was completed once that had happened. On appeal, the Quebec Court of Appeal ordered a new trial and the accused appealed that decision to the Supreme Court of Canada. Dickson J. set out the elements of importing a narcotic under the Narcotic Control Act, saying:

> To "actually commit" importing, an accused must bring in, or cause to be brought in, to Canada, goods from a foreign country; this, by definition, necessitates crossing the Canadian border. Someone who becomes involved only after the border crossing, however, may be aiding and abetting a person bringing the goods from outside Canada to a given destination inside Canada.[62]

McIntyre J., who gave the majority judgment in *Bell*, said "import" should be given its ordinary meaning and that the offence was complete when the goods entered the country. He said that it was not necessary to show the accused was at the point of entry because he could make arrangements for entry while he was far away. Some earlier decisions had held that importing was a continuing offence so that the offence continued after the border crossing. McIntyre J. repudiated this view while making it clear that if a person arranged the importation or assisted in it, the person would be guilty of an offence. Thus, a person may be guilty of the offence because activities subsequent to actual importation make it clear that that person participated in or planned the importation. In *R. v. Miller*,[63] the British Columbia Court of Appeal held that the offence of importing marijuana was not complete upon the crossing of the border, but only when a vessel reached its destination and was unloaded.

---

[60] *Ibid.*, at 101.
[61] *Ibid.*, at 98.
[62] *Ibid.*, at 103.
[63] (1984) 12 C.C.C. (3d) 54 (B.C.C.A.).

(ii) *Mens rea*

The Supreme Court of Canada has held that *mens rea* is an essential element of an importing charge. In *Cloutier v. R.*,[64] the accused was charged with importing marijuana. The accused had stored marijuana in furniture which he took to his brother's house and which subsequently was imported. Pratte J. held that the Crown must prove that the accused had *mens rea*, saying:

> *Mens rea* is an essential aspect of the crime attributed to the accused. The prosecution cannot therefore be content with proving only the importation of the dresser; this occurred in normal circumstances which did not suggest that it contained a foreign substance. The prosecution also had to establish beyond a reasonable doubt that, to the accused's knowledge, this dresser contained a narcotic when it was imported. . . .[65]

The *mens rea* involved has also been commented on by the Nova Scotia Court of Appeal in *R. v. Salvador.*[66] MacDonald J.A. set out the elements of the offence of importing a narcotic, saying that:

> 1. The *actus reus* of the offence is the act *simpliciter* of voluntarily (by which I mean an act or conduct flowing from the exercise of a free will) bringing narcotics into Canada from abroad.
>
> 2. The *mens rea* of the offence is to be found in the basic intent to . . . bring narcotics into Canada from abroad.[67]

The *mens rea* may be established by showing that the accused knew the substance in question was a narcotic, although it was not the form of narcotic he believed it to be. Accordingly, a person may be convicted of importing if he intended to import cannabis and actually imported hashish.

(iii) *Aiding and abetting*

In *R. v. Hijazi*,[68] an accused who helped to secure the release of narcotics from a bonded warehouse after they had been brought into Canada was a party to the offence of importing and convicted of importing a narcotic, even though his or her only involvement in the offence took place after the narcotics had been imported into Canada.

---

[64] (1979), 48 C.C.C. (2d) 1 (S.C.C.).
[65] *Ibid.*, at 30.
[66] (1981), 59 C.C.C. (2d) 521 (N.S.C.A.).
[67] *Ibid.*, at 540.
[68] (1974), 20 C.C.C. (2d) 183 (Ont. C.A.).

(b) Specific Defences

(i) *Entrapment*

The entrapment offence, which was discussed earlier, may also apply to a charge of importing or exporting a narcotic.

(ii) *Licence*

Someone who has a licence to import or export narcotics, or otherwise deal with narcotics, will not be guilty of an offence under the Narcotic Control Act. Section 20 of the Narcotic Control Act provides:

20. The Governor in Council may make regulations

(*a*) providing for the issue of licences for the importation, export, sale, manufacture, production or distribution of narcotics and for the cultivation of opium poppy or marihuana;

. . . .

5. CULTIVATION OF OPIUM POPPY OR MARIJUANA

Section 6 of the Narcotic Control Act provides:

6. (1) No person shall cultivate opium poppy or marihuana except under the authority of, and in accordance with, a licence issued to the person under the regulations.

(2) Every person who contravenes subsection (1) is guilty of an indictable offence and is liable to imprisonment for a term not exceeding seven years.

(3) The Minister may cause to be destroyed any growing plant of opium poppy or marihuana cultivated otherwise than under authority of and in accordance with a licence issued under the regulations.

(a) What Constitutes "Cultivation"

In *R. v. Busby*,[69] the Yukon Territory Court of Appeal applied the ordinary dictionary definition of the word "cultivation" in dismissing the accused's appeal from his conviction for cultivating marijuana. In applying the ordinary dictionary definition to the term "cultivation," the court rejected the accused's argument that for there to be cultivation the Crown must establish that "there is evidence of some overt act by the accused which proves an

---

[69] (1972), 7 C.C.C. (2d) 234 (Y.T.C.A.).

assistance by him to the actual growing of the plants."[70] In upholding the accused's conviction, the court applied the Oxford English Dictionary definition of "cultivation":

> To bestow labour and attention upon land in order for the raising of crops, to till, to improve and render fertile by husbandry.

The evidence was that marijuana plants had been growing in the accused's basement. The court noted that marijuana plant material had been found in the accused's bedroom and marijuana seeds in a liquid form were found in the basement. At trial, the magistrate concluded that "the plants were germinated from seed and grew into plants due to the efforts of the accused Busby."[71] The evidence that the plants had germinated from seed due to the accused's efforts was sufficient to convict the accused of cultivation of marijuana. The definition of the word "cultivate" which was adopted by the Yukon Territories Court of Appeal in *R. v. Busby* has also been adopted by several courts in other jurisdictions: *R. v. Munce; R. v. Champagne.*[72]

The Ontario Court of Appeal has held that the word "cultivate" is limited to growing a plant and does not include processing of a plant. In *R. v. Gauvreau,*[73] Blair J.A. stated:

> All the definitions are alike in restricting the meaning of the word "cultivate" to activities associated with the growing of plants. They clearly exclude the processing of a plant after harvest, whether by curing, drying or other means.[74]

The courts have held that someone may cultivate marijuana without having possession of it. In *R. v. Powell,*[75] the British Columbia Court of Appeal held that possession was not an included offence in cultivation under the Narcotic Control Act. Esson J.A. said that: ". . . one can bestow labour and attention upon land in order to raise a crop without being in possession of the crop."[76]

(b) Specific Defence

Someone who is in possession of a licence to grow opium poppy or marijuana will have a defence to a charge of cultivating opium poppy or marijuana.

---

[70] *Ibid.,* at 237.
[71] *Ibid.,* at 236-237.
[72] (1974), 15 C.C.C. (2d) 326 (Ont. Co. Ct.); (1970), 2 C.C.C. 273 (B.C.C.A.).
[73] (1982), 65 C.C.C. (2d) 316 (Ont. C.A.).
[74] *Ibid.,* at 320.
[75] (1983), 9 C.C.C. (3d) 442 (B.C.C.A.).
[76] *Ibid.,* at 445.

6. FOOD AND DRUGS ACT OFFENCES

The Food and Drugs Act makes it illegal to possess a restricted drug and to traffic in a controlled drug. Restricted drugs include lysergic acid diethylamide (LSD) and methylenedioxy-amphetamine (MDA) while controlled drugs include drugs such as amphetamine, barbituric acid, methaqualone. The Food and Drugs Act states that a controlled drug means those substances which are listed in schedule "G" of the Act and provides that a restricted drug includes those substances listed in schedule "H" of the Act.

(a) Controlled Drugs

The provisions dealing with controlled drugs are set out in sections 38, 38.1 and 39 of the Food and Drugs Act. Section 38.1 provides:

38.1 (1) No person shall, at any time, seek or obtain a controlled drug or a prescription for a controlled drug from a practitioner unless that person discloses to the practitioner particulars of every controlled drug or prescription for a controlled drug issued to that person by a different practitioner within the preceding thirty days.

(2) Every person who contravenes subsection (1)

(*a*) is guilty of an indictable offence and is liable to a fine not exceeding five thousand dollars or to imprisonment for a term not exceeding three years; or

(*b*) is guilty of an offence punishable on summary conviction and is liable

(i) for a first offence, to a fine not exceeding one thousand dollars or to imprisonment for a term not exceeding six months, and

(ii) for a subsequent offence, to a fine not exceeding two thousand dollars or to imprisonment for a term not exceeding one year.

(3) No summary conviction proceedings in respect of an offence under this section shall be instituted at any time within but not later than one year from the time when the subject-matter of the proceedings arose.

Section 39 of the Food and Drugs Act makes it an offence to traffic in a controlled drug. This section provides:

39. (1) No person shall traffic in a controlled drug or any substance represented or held out by the person to be a controlled drug.

(2) No person shall have in his possession any controlled drug for the purpose of trafficking.

(3) Every person who contravenes subsection (1) or (2) is guilty of an offence and liable

(*a*) on summary conviction, to imprisonment for a term not exceeding eighteen months; or

(*b*) on conviction on indictment, to imprisonment for a term not exceeding ten years.

(b) Restricted Drugs

Offences dealing with possession of a restricted drug are set out in sections 47 and 48 of the Food and Drugs Act. Section 47 provides:

47. (1) Except as authorized by this Part or the regulations, no person shall have a restricted drug in his possession.

(2) Every person who contravenes subsection (1) is guilty of an offence and liable

(*a*) on summary conviction for a first offence, to a fine not exceeding one thousand dollars or to imprisonment for a term not exceeding six months, or to both and, for a subsequent offence, to a fine of two thousand dollars or to imprisonment for a term not exceeding one year or to both; or

(*b*) on conviction on indictment, to a fine not exceeding five thousand dollars or to imprisonment for a term not exceeding three years or to both.

Section 48, which makes it an offence to possess a restricted drug for the purpose of trafficking, states:

48. (1) No person shall traffic in a restricted drug or any substance represented or held out by the person to be a restricted drug.

(2) No person shall have in possession any restricted drug for the purpose of trafficking.

(3) Every person who contravenes subsection (1) or (2) is guilty of an offence and liable

(*a*) on summary conviction, to imprisonment for a term not exceeding eighteen months; or

(*b*) on conviction on indictment, to imprisonment for a term not exceeding ten years.

It is not an offence to possess a controlled drug if the drug has been prescribed by a physician. Section 38.1 of the Food and Drugs Act provides that a person who obtains a controlled drug must tell his or her physician that a similar drug was obtained from a different physician. This requirement ensures that the use of such drugs is supervised by a physician who has knowledge of the drug usage of the patient.

(c) Meaning of "Traffic"

The definition of "traffic" contained in the Food and Drugs Act is different than the definition of "traffic" in the Narcotic Control Act. The word "traffic" in the Narcotic Control Act is defined as:

"traffic" means

(*a*) to manufacture, sell, administer, transport, send, deliver or distribute, or

(*b*) to offer to do anything referred to in paragraph (*a*) otherwise than under the authority of this Act or the regulations.

In the Food and Drugs Act the word "traffic" is defined as follows:

... to manufacture, sell, export from or import into Canada, transport or deliver, otherwise than under the authority of this Part or the regulations.

The Food and Drugs Act definition of the word "traffic" is narrower than the definition found in the Narcotic Control Act and this has caused several courts to interpret the word "traffic" under the Food and Drugs Act differently than it has been interpreted under the Narcotic Control Act. *R. v. Jimmo*,[77] a Quebec Court of Appeal decision, illustrates the differences between the two definitions. In the *Jimmo* case, the accused was charged under the Food and Drugs Act with illegally being in possession of a restricted drug for the purpose of trafficking. The evidence, which established that the accused had possession of LSD, indicated that the accused had delivered some of the LSD to his girlfriend who had split the cost of the drug with the accused. The accused was convicted at trial and appealed to the Quebec Court of Appeal. In acquitting the accused, Owen J.A. dealt with the differences between trafficking under the relevant statutes:

I disagree with the proposition that when one person, with joint funds, buys a restricted drug for consumption, he is guilty of trafficking under the *Food and Drugs Act*. According to s. 33 of the *Food and Drugs Act* "traffic" means "to manufacture, sell, export from or import into Canada, transport or deliver . . .". It should be noted that this definition is more restrictive than under the *Narcotic Control Act* . . . where "traffic means "(a) to manufacture, sell, give, administer, transfer, send, deliver or distribute . . .".

In his cross-examination of the accused the counsel for the Crown placed emphasis on having the accused admit that he gave . . . or allowed his companion to take the tablets of LSD. In my opinion, there was no "delivery" by the accused to his companion in the sense of "manufacture, sell, export, import, transfer or deliver". These words must be read together to determine the meaning of the statute.

If a person passes a box of chocolates or a box of cigarettes and someone takes one it is true that there is delivery in the literal sense, the possession passes from one person to the other. However, this is not delivery in the sense of a statute providing that it is an offence to manufacture, sell, export, import, transport or deliver restricted drugs.[78]

The Quebec Court of Appeal's decision in *Jimmo* has been followed by the Saskatchewan Court of Appeal in *R. v. Rogalsky*.[79] In the *Rogalsky* case, the trial judge decided that the word "deliver" in the Food and Drugs Act did not cover the situation where someone offered to share a drug with someone else. Hall J.A. stated:

---

[77] (1973), 16 C.C.C. (2d) 396 (Que. C.A.).
[78] *Ibid.*, at 397-398.
[79] (1975), 23 C.C.C. (2d) 399 (Sask. C.A.).

It is significant that while to offer to give or deliver is included in the definition of trafficking under the *Narcotic Control Act*, it is not included under the *Food and Drugs Act*. It must be assumed, therefore, that Parliament did not intend that merely offering a restricted drug to another, or being prepared to so offer, would constitute trafficking under the *Food and Drugs Act*.[80]

The *Jimmo* case has also been applied by the Alberta Court of Queen's Bench in *R. v. Johnston*.[81]

The differences between trafficking as defined in the Food and Drugs Act and the Narcotic Control Act have not been universally accepted, as in *R. v. Kopach*[82] the Alberta Court of Appeal decided that the word "deliver" as used in the Food and Drugs Act in defining "traffic" should be given its ordinary dictionary meaning as being to give or distribute to someone else. A number of other appellate courts have followed the *Kopach* case so the law is still uncertain on this point.[83]

(d) Specific Defences

Most of the defences to charges under the Narcotic Control Act are applicable to offences under the Food and Drugs Act.

Section 45(1) of the Food and Drugs Act authorizes the Federal Cabinet to make regulations providing for the issue of licences to import, manufacture or otherwise sell controlled drugs. Accordingly, someone who had a licence to sell a controlled drug may have a defence to a charge of trafficking in a controlled drug. Such defences are essential for those who are engaged in the distribution of drugs for proper purposes because the legislation is drawn so broadly that it could apply to a sale by a druggist.

7. EFFECT OF THE CHARTER

The Charter of Rights and Freedoms[84] has had a great impact on the prosecution and defence of drug offences. The Supreme Court of Canada's decision in *R. v. Oakes*[85] illustrates the profound impact which the Charter of Rights has had in this area. Prior to the *Oakes* decision, under the Narcotic Control Act, once someone was found to have possession of a large quantity of narcotics the accused had to establish that he or she was not in possession

---

80 *Ibid.*, at 402.
81 (1979), 52 C.C.C. (2d) 57 (Alta. Q.B.).
82 (1980), 53 C.C.C. (2d) 300 (Alta. C.A.).
83 *R. v. Pottie* (1979), 46 C.C.C. (2d) 321 (N.S.C.A.); *R. v. Gill* (1982), Registry No. 810048, B.C.C.A.
84 Being Part I of the Constitution Act, 1982 [en. by the Canada Act (U.K.), c. 11, s. 1].
85 (1986), 50 C.R. (3d) 1 (S.C.C.).

of a narcotic for the purpose of trafficking. Section 8 of the Narcotic Control Act provides that once a court finds that the accused was in possession of a narcotic, contrary to section 3 of the Act, the accused,

. . . .

. . . shall be given an opportunity of establishing that he was not in possession of the narcotic for the purpose of trafficking and, thereafter, the prosecutor shall be given an opportunity of adducing evidence to establish the contrary.

. . . .

(*a*) if the accused establishes that he was not in possession of the narcotic for the purpose of trafficking, the accused shall be acquitted of the offence as charged but shall be convicted of an offence under section 3 [possession of a narcotic] . . .

Similar provisions are found in section 49 of the Food and Drugs Act. Before the Charter came into effect, section 8 of the Narcotic Control Act had been used to force the accused to prove his or her innocence, once a court found that the accused was in possession of a large quantity of narcotics. This section, however, has now been declared unconstitutional by the Supreme Court of Canada in *R. v. Oakes*. Chief Justice Dickson decided that section 8 of the Narcotic Control Act,

violates s. 11(*d*) of the Charter [which states that anyone charged with a criminal offence has the right to be presumed innocent until proven guilty] by requiring the accused to prove on a balance of probabilities that he was not in possession of the narcotic for the purpose of trafficking.[86]

The significance of *Oakes* is that the Crown will now be forced to prove all elements of the offence beyond a reasonable doubt and will no longer be able to rely upon the statutory presumptions in the drug legislation which reverse the burden of proof.

---

[86] *Ibid.*, at 27.

12

Defences

1. INTRODUCTION

The term "defence" may have several meanings in criminal law. A defence, in its broadest sense, is any claim which, if accepted, would lead to an acquittal. Thus, defence in this sense could include a claim that the Crown had failed to prove the commission of the *actus reus*, or the presence of *mens rea*. Used in a narrower sense, the term may be limited to a claim for an acquittal which requires the accused to discharge some evidentiary burden. For example, if a matter such as provocation has not been put in issue by the evidence for the Crown, then the accused must introduce relevant and credible evidence which does place the matter in issue.

Section 7(3) of the Criminal Code[1] provides that every rule or principle of the common law which renders any circumstance a justification or excuse for an act or defence to a charge, continues in force and applies in respect of proceedings for any offence created by federal legislation. Some provinces have a similar provision in respect of provincial offences. Such justifications or excuses constitute the type of defences which lead to an acquittal, even though what appears to be a criminal act has been committed, because public policy determines that in such circumstances a person should not be convicted. An example of such a defence is when an act has been committed under duress, about which Mr. Justice McIntyre, giving the judgment for the Supreme Court of Canada in *Bergstrom v. R.*, said:

> The defence . . . can become effective to protect an accused when it can be shown that the accused has, in fact, actually committed the offence. Where it applies, the commission of the offence is excused.[2]

Accordingly, defences such as duress need only be considered once the case has otherwise been proved beyond a reasonable doubt. If the Crown has failed to make out its case, it will not be necessary, in theory at least, to adduce

---

[1] R.S.C. 1985, c. C-46.
[2] (1981), 59 C.C.C. (2d) 481 at 484 (S.C.C.).

the defence evidence. In practice, an accused will, in most cases, advance all the defences open to him, unless for some reason adducing defence evidence would be contrary to his interest. The facts necessary to raise some defences, such as duress, may also justify the conclusion that the Crown has failed to prove an essential element of its case. For instance, if a person is forced to participate in the commission of a crime, the trier of fact may well conclude that the person lacked the necessary *mens rea* and that, accordingly, the prosecution has failed to prove one of the essential elements of the offence.[3]

Section 7(3) of the Code speaks of justifications and excuses. Considerable attention has been paid by a number of legal writers to the difference between an excuse and a justification.[4] The question of the exact difference between a justification and an excuse has not been settled and it would not be useful to examine the question which has been the topic of much legal analysis. Rather, it is sufficient to appreciate that the word "defence" covers a number of different situations and concepts which will become manifest when the various defences are considered. It should be appreciated that the onus of proof remains on the Crown throughout. The only burden on the accused, in the case of defences such as duress or provocation, is to adduce some evidence to put the defence in issue. The accused may either call evidence putting the defence in issue or do so by the cross-examination of prosecution witnesses. Once the defence has been put in issue the Crown must then destroy that defence, if it is to succeed, so as to remove any reasonable doubt of the accused's guilt.[5]

2. DURESS

Section 17 of the Code provides:

A person who commits an offence under compulsion by threats of immediate death or bodily harm from a person who is present when the offence is committed is excused for committing the offence if the person believes that the threats will be carried out and if the person is not a party to a conspiracy or association whereby the person is subject to compulsion, but this section does not apply where the offence that is committed is high treason or treason, murder, piracy, attempted murder, sexual assault, sexual assault with a weapon, threats to a third party or causing bodily harm, aggravated sexual assault, forcible abduction, hostage taking, robbery, assault with a weapon or causing bodily harm, aggravated assault, unlawfully causing bodily harm, arson or an offence or an offence under sections 280 to 283 (abduction and detention of young persons).

---

[3] A.W. Mewett and M. Manning, *Criminal Law*, 2nd ed. (Toronto: Butterworths, 1985) at p. 340.
[4] G. Fletcher, "The Individualization of Excusing Conditions", (1974) 47 S. Cal. L. Rev. 1269. D. Stuart, *Canadian Criminal Law* (Toronto: Carswell, 1982) at p. 376 et seq.
[5] *Woolmington v. D.P.P.*, [1935] A.C. 462 (H.L.).

A very large number of offences are excluded which makes the Canadian law much more restrictive in this respect than the laws of other nations. For example, under English common law the only excluded offences are murder and some forms of treason.[6] In *R. v. Paquette*,[7] the Supreme Court of Canada held that section 17 applied only to actual perpetrators of crimes and not to other parties to the offence.

Duress can remove the *mens rea* element where the *mens rea* required is a desire to achieve certain consequences and not mere knowledge that they will follow or recklessness as to whether they will or will not follow. In *R. v. Steane*,[8] Steane was acquitted on a charge of acting "with intent to assist the enemy" because he was acting under duress and, accordingly, did not have the necessary intent.

Duress will not, however, eliminate the *mens rea* element where all that is required is that the accused knew of the consequences of the act. The Supreme Court of Canada, in *R. v. Carker*,[9] upheld a conviction of an accused charged with wilfully damaging government property. The accused, while locked in his cell, was threatened that if he did not join in a disturbance by smashing the toilet fixtures he would be beaten as soon as his fellow convicts got to him. The court held that as section 386 [429] of the Code provided that one is deemed wilfully to have caused an act if he does any act, knowing that the act will probably cause the occurrence of the event and being reckless whether the event occurs or not, Carker had the requisite *mens rea* as only knowledge was required. In that case the defence of compulsion was not available, as the threats were not of immediate death or bodily harm.

It is not clear whether the threat may be to harm a third person where the defence is raised under section 17. It has been held that where the common law defence of duress was available, a threat to a child was sufficient to cause duress.[10] It would be reasonable to apply the same approach to section 17.

Under section 17, the accused must believe that the threats will be carried out. Accordingly, the question is not what a reasonable man would have believed in the circumstances, but what the accused actually did believe, although the reasonableness of the belief may be relevant to whether his evidence is worthy of belief. In *R. v. Smith*,[11] a defence of duress was allowed in an impaired driving charge after the court was convinced that a woman believed that she could avoid a beating by her enraged husband only if she drove a car. In *R. v. Bergstrom*,[12] the Manitoba Court of Appeal indicated that

---

[6] *R. v. Steane*, [1947] 1 K.B. 997 (C.A.); *D.P.P. for Northern Ireland v. Lynch*, [1975] A.C. 653 (H.L.).

[7] (1979), 45 C.C.C. (2d) 575 (S.C.C.).

[8] *Supra*, note 6.

[9] [1967] 2 C.C.C. 190 (S.C.C.).

[10] *R. v. Morrison* (1980), 54 C.C.C. (2d) 447 (Ont. Dist. Ct.).

[11] (1977), 40 C.R.N.S. 390 (B.C. Prov. Ct.).

[12] (1980), 13 C.R. (3d) 342 (Man. C.A.).

the defence was not available to someone who had an obviously safe avenue of escape before committing the prohibited act. This factor may obviously have an influence on whether a jury believes the evidence as to duress, but it should not change the standard under section 17 to one of whether the belief was both honest and reasonable.

The appropriate standard would appear to be that set out in *R. v. Falkenberg*, wherein Judge Lyon stated:

> It seems clear to me that the rationale behind this section is to provide a defence where there are such threats under such circumstances that an accused person honestly believes that he has no other alternative but to commit the offence or suffer immediate death or grievous bodily harm without the opportunity of relief from such a proposed attack.[13]

The defence will not be open to a person who is a party to a conspiracy or association by which he is subject to compulsion. Thus, if an accused joined in a conspiracy to rob a bank and was later forced to accompany his co-conspirators, the defence would not be available if the conspiracy still existed.

3. MENTAL DISORDER

(a) General

16. (1) No person is criminally responsible for an act committed or an omission made while suffering from a mental disorder that rendered the person incapable of appreciating the nature and quality of the act or omission or of knowing that it was wrong.

(2) Every person is presumed not to suffer from a mental disorder so as to be exempt from criminal responsibility by virtue of subsection (1), until the contrary is proved on the balance of probabilities.

(3) The burden of proof that an accused was suffering from a mental disorder so as to be exempt from criminal responsibility is on the party that raises the issue.

The new provisions in section 16, which were enacted in 1991, are substantially the same as the previous section 16, except for wording which replaces the term "insane" with the term "not criminally responsible" and replaces the term "state of natural imbecility or has disease of the mind" with the term "mental disorder." Since "mental disorder" is defined in section 2 of the Criminal Code as "disease of the mind," many of the cases decided under the old insanity provision will still be relevant to the new provision. Where a jury or judge finds that an accused committed an act or omission at the time

---

[13] (1973), 13 C.C.C. (2d) 562 at 567 (Ont. Co. Ct.).

he was suffering from a mental disorder so as to be exempt from criminal responsibility under section 16(1) of the Code, the jury or judge shall find that the accused is not criminally responsible for the act or omission on account of mental disorder.

Insanity is frequently referred to as a defence, but as Martin J.A. stated in *R. v. Simpson*:

> The fact is, that although insanity is frequently referred to as a "defence", an accused who is insane lacks capacity to commit the offence, in the same way that a child under the age of seven years is incapable of committing an offence.[14]

The issue of insanity may be raised both by the Crown and by the defence. Although section 16 states that if a person is found to have been suffering from a mental disorder at the time of the commission of the offence, he shall not be criminally responsible, section 672.54 provides that in certain circumstances the person may be detained indefinitely. This section states:

> **672.54** Where a court or Review Board makes a disposition pursuant to subsection 672.45(2) or section 672.47, it shall, taking into consideration the need to protect the public from dangerous persons, the mental condition of the accused, the reintegration of the accused into society and the other needs of the accused, make one of the following dispositions that is the least onerous and least restrictive to the accused:
> (*a*) where a verdict of not criminally responsible on account of mental disorder has been rendered in respect of the accused and, in the opinion of the court or Review Board, the accused is not a significant threat to the safety of the public, by order, direct that the accused be discharged absolutely;
> (*b*) by order, direct that the accused be discharged subject to such conditions as the court or Review Board considers appropriate; or
> (*c*) by order, direct that the accused be detained in custody in a hospital, subject to such conditions as the court or Review Board considers appropriate. 1991, c. 43, s. 4.

Accordingly, where an accused believes that there is a valid defence to the charge he is likely to plead not guilty and not rely on a section 16 defence. Furthermore, it is certainly difficult to conduct a defence on the basis that the accused did not commit the offence, but at the same time assert that if he did he was insane at the time.

Section 16 is, in large part, based on rules formulated by English judges in 1843 which became known as the "M'Naghten Rules." There has been great controversy over the years about these rules because psychiatrists believe that they have little relationship to medical knowledge, while lawyers assert that the discipline of psychiatry is based on a very inexact science, which really does not permit one to form conclusions as to the exact state of a person's mind at a particular point in time.

---

[14] (1977), 35 C.C.C. (2d) 337 at 360 (Ont. C.A.).

(b) Disease of the Mind

In *Cooper v. R.*,[15] Dickson J. of the Supreme Court of Canada, defined disease of the mind as:

> In summary, one might say that, in a legal sense, "disease of the mind" embraces any illness, disorder or abnormal condition which impairs the human mind and its functioning, excluding, however, self-induced states caused by alcohol or drugs, as well as transitory mental states such as hysteria or concussion.[16]

In *R. v. Rabey*, Mr. Justice Martin, of the Ontario Court of Appeal, held that it is a question of law for the judge to decide whether a particular condition is a disease of the mind and then it is for the jury to determine whether the accused did have such a disease.[17] In *R. v. Simpson*, Mr. Justice Martin held that it was proper to ask a psychiatrist whether the condition was a disease of the mind, but such an opinion would not decide the legal question.[18]

The definition of disease of the mind given by Dickson J. in *Cooper v. R.* [19] excludes self-induced states caused by alcohol or drugs, as well as transitory mental states such as hysteria or concussion. A reading of the definition may indicate that the use of alcohol or drugs which has an effect on the mind will negate the defence of insanity in all cases. However, this is not the case.

In *D.P.P. v. Beard*, a House of Lords decision, Lord Birkenhead suggested that there were three degrees of drunkenness.[20] A person could be sufficiently drunk that his passions were inflamed, which would be irrelevant to liability. He might, however, have a degree of drunkenness which affected his capacity to form a specific intent, with the result that he would have a defence. In other cases, a person might have a degree of drunkenness which had reached such an extreme stage as to amount to a disease of the mind. Hence, in *Revelle v. R.*, Martin J.A. held that when brain damage could be shown, which contributed to a disease of the mind, the defence of insanity could be raised, notwithstanding that other factors, including drunkenness, contributed to the respondent's condition.[21] It is certainly possible that there may be an abnormal condition of the human mind which is exacerbated by drunkenness, or even caused by the repeated use of alcohol.

In *R. v. Hilton*, the Ontario Court of Appeal held that the defence of insanity was available to an accused who was suffering from a disease of the mind due to ingestion of drugs.[22] As Dickson J. did not purport to overrule

---

[15] (1980), 13 C.R. (3d) 97 (S.C.C.).
[16] *Ibid.*, at 117.
[17] (1977), 37 C.C.C. (2d) 461 (Ont. C.A.), affirmed (1980), 15 C.R. (3d) 225 (S.C.C.).
[18] *Supra*, note 14.
[19] *Supra*, note 15.
[20] [1920] A.C. 479 (H.L.).
[21] (1979), 21 C.R. (3d) 161 at 162 (Ont. C.A.), affirmed (1980), 21 C.R. (3d) 161 (S.C.C.).
[22] (1977), 34 C.C.C. (2d) 206 (Ont. C.A.).

such cases, it appears that where the evidence establishes that the accused has an abnormal mental condition which has impaired the mind the defence may be raised, although the brain damage was caused by the ingestion of drugs or alcohol. The distinction is illustrated by the decision of the English Court of Appeal in *R. v. Quick*; *R. v. Paddison*, where the court stated:

> Our task has been to decide what the law means now by the words 'disease of the mind'. In our judgment the fundamental concept is of a malfunctioning of the mind caused by disease. A malfunctioning of the mind of transitory effect caused by the application to the body of some external factor such as violence, drugs, including anaesthetics, alcohol and hypnotic influences cannot fairly be said to be due to disease.[23]

A distinction may be made between drunkenness affecting the mind, which is transitory in its nature, and an impairment of the mind which is internal to the accused and, presumably, will exist whether or not the accused is drunk or under the influence of drugs. In *R. v. Rabey*,[24] Martin J.A., in a judgment which was subsequently approved by the Supreme Court of Canada, said that the distinction to be drawn

> . . . as between a malfunctioning of the mind arising from some cause that is primarily internal to the accused, having its source in a psychological or emotional make-up, or in some organic pathology, as opposed to a malfunctioning of the mind, which is the transient effect produced by some specific external factor, such as, for example, concussion.[25]

The distinction appears to rest on whether the malfunctioning of the mind, which may be induced by alcohol or drugs, is merely transitory in its nature, or whether the effect of the use of such substances has led to some malfunctioning of the mind, which, although it may have been caused by these substances, is of a permanent nature or, at least, is of a nature which cannot be described as transitory.

The same conclusion seems appropriate about a transitory mental state, such as hysteria, which may be caused by some malfunction of the mind. A transitory mental state may relieve one of criminal responsibility. This will be seen later when the defence of automatism is discussed; where an accused is in a dissociative state at the time of the offence the accused may be acquitted since the existence of such a state may deny the conscious act necessary to constitute the *actus reus*. In *R. v. Rabey*, the accused was charged with causing bodily harm with intent to wound and defended on the ground that he was in a dissociative state because of a severe emotional shock. Martin J.A., in distinguishing between non-insane automatism and insanity, said:

---

[23] [1973] 3 All E.R. 347 at 356 (C.A.).
[24] *Supra*, note 17.
[25] *Supra*, note 17 (Ont. C.A.), at 477-478.

334 / Fundamentals of the Criminal Justice System

... the distinction to be drawn is between a malfunctioning of the mind arising from some cause that is primarily internal to the accused, having its source in a psychological or emotional make-up, or in some organic pathology, as opposed to a malfunctioning of the mind which is the transient effect produced by some specific external factor such as, for example, concussion. Any malfunctioning of the mind, or mental disorder having its source primarily in some subjective condition or weakness internal to the accused (where fully understood or not), may be a "disease of the mind" if it prevents the accused from knowing what he is doing, but transient disturbances of consciousness due to certain specific external factors do not fall within the concept of disease of the mind.[26]

As this judgment was affirmed by the Supreme Court of Canada it appears that a malfunctioning of the mind arising from some cause primarily internal to the accused may be a disease of the mind, even if its effect is temporary in nature. Thus, in *R. v. O'Brien*[27] the New Brunswick Court of Appeal held that the issue of insanity should have been left to the jury when there was evidence that an accused was not conscious of what she was doing due to an epileptic condition. The evidence was that the assault committed by the accused was committed while she was in an epileptic fit during which she would automatically perform acts of which she was totally unconscious and of which she afterwards had no memory. The fit was temporary in its nature, while epilepsy was a condition internal to the accused.

(c) Incapable of Appreciating the Nature and Quality of an Act or Omission

The defence may be established if the disease of the mind affects the mind to an extent that renders a person incapable of appreciating the nature and quality of an act. This element was considered in a report of the Royal Commission on the Law of Insanity as a Defence in Criminal Cases, known as the "McRuer Report," where it was said that mere knowledge of the nature and quality of the act was not the true test to be applied, but that,

The true test . . . is, was the accused at the very time of the offence — not before or after but at the moment of the offence — by reason of disease of the mind, unable fully to appreciate not only the nature of the act, but the natural consequences that would flow from it? In other words, was the accused person by reason of disease of the mind deprived of the mental capacity to foresee and measure the consequences of the act?[28]

In *Cooper v. R.*, Mr. Justice Dickson, speaking for the majority of the

---

[26] *Supra*, note 17 (Ont. C.A.), at 477-478.
[27] [1966] 3 C.C.C. 288 (N.B.C.A.).
[28] Report of the Royal Commission on the Law of Insanity as a Defence in Criminal Cases (Hull, F. Cloutier, 1955), p. 13.

Supreme Court, adopted this test but omitted the word "fully." [29] His Lordship said that the test of appreciation embraces "[e]motional, as well as intellectual, awareness of the significance of the conduct."[30] Mr. Justice Dickson said that there had to be a real understanding of the nature, character and consequence of the act at the time of its commission in the sense that there had to be "an ability to perceive the consequences, impact, and results of a physical act."[31] In *R. v. Barnier*,[32] Mr. Justice Estey said that appreciating would include knowing, but that knowing might not include appreciating. He said:

> The verb "know" has a positive connotation requiring a bare awareness, the act of receiving information without more. The act of appreciating, on the other hand, is a second stage in a mental process requiring the analysis of knowledge or experience in one manner or another.[33]

A person may appreciate the nature and quality of the act, although he may lack any feeling of remorse or guilt for what he has done. Thus, in *R. v. Simpson*, Martin J.A. stated:

> . . . I do not think the exemption provided by the section extends to one who has the necessary understanding of the nature, character and consequences of the act, but merely lacks appropriate feelings for the victim or lacks feelings of remorse or guilt for what he has done, even though such lack of feeling stems from "disease of the mind."[34]

The result is that a defence of insanity may succeed where a person had knowledge of what was done, but did not appreciate the nature and quality of the act. Thus, in *O.*, a woman was acquitted on the ground of insanity, although she admitted to a neighbour that she had killed her three children, but had no appreciation of what she had done and wanted to come back to care for them.[35] A person may not appreciate the nature and quality of an act, although he knows that he is actually committing an act, such as firing a revolver into the brain of another, and that this will cause death. Some delusions may result in an accused regarding an act in an entirely different character than a reasonable person would. In *R. v. Swain*, an accused was found insane where, although he knew that cutting his wife with a knife would draw blood, he believed he was saving the members of his family, not injuring them, because he suffered from a delusion.[36]

---

[29] *Supra*, note 15.
[30] *Supra*, note 15, at 118.
[31] *Supra*, note 15, at 120.
[32] (1980), 51 C.C.C. (2d) 193 (S.C.C.).
[33] *Ibid.*, at 203.
[34] (1977), 35 C.C.C. (2d) 337 at 355 (Ont. C.A.).
[35] (1959), 3 C.L.Q. 151 (Ont. H.C.).
[36] (1986), 50 C.R. (3d) 97 (Ont. C.A.).

(d) Incapable of Knowing that an Act or Omission is Wrong

The defence may also succeed where there is a disease of the mind which renders the accused incapable of knowing that an act or omission is wrong. In *Schwartz v. R.*, the Supreme Court of Canada considered whether the word "wrong" meant simply that an act was contrary to law or whether it meant wrong in the eyes of society.[37] A bare majority of the court held that wrong means legally wrong. Martland J., who gave the majority judgment, considered it was inappropriate to acquit an insane person who knew that his act was illegal, but considered it morally justifiable when a sane person would not be acquitted in similar circumstances. He was also of the view that an interpretation based on moral wrong-doing would require a subjective test of insanity. Mr. Justice Dickson, speaking for four of the nine judges who dissented, held that wrong meant wrong by the judgment of society, saying:

> The argument is sometimes advanced that a moral test favours the amoral offender and that the most favoured will be he who had rid himself of all moral compunction. This argument overlooks the factor of disease of the mind. If, as a result of disease of the mind, the offender has lost completely the ability to make moral distinctions and acts under an insane delusion, it can well be said that he should not be criminally accountable.[38]

In *R. v. Chaulk*, the Supreme Court of Canada overruled its previous decision in *Schwartz*, holding that the term "wrong" as used in the predecessor to section 16 of the Code meant morally wrong. Lamer C.J.C., writing for a majority of the court, stated that:

> A person may well be aware that an act is contrary to law but, by reason of "natural imbecility" or disease of the mind, is at the same time incapable of knowing that the act is morally wrong in the circumstances according to the moral standards of society. This would be the case, for example, if the person suffered from a disease of the mind to such a degree as to know that it is legally wrong to kill but, as described by Dickson J. in *Schwartz*, kills "in the belief that it is in response to a divine order and therefore not morally wrong." . . .[39]

In *Chaulk*, Lamer C.J.C. made it clear that what constitutes "moral wrong" is not to be judged by the subjective view of the offender, but rather by the standards that society regards as wrong.

In *R. v. Oommen*,[40] a case decided subsequent to the amendment of section 16 of the Criminal Code, the Supreme Court of Canada held that the phrase "knowing that an act or omission is wrong" extends to the accused's ability to rationally apply knowledge of right and wrong and concluded that

---

[37] (1976), 29 C.C.C. (2d) 1 (S.C.C.).
[38] *Ibid.*, at 22.
[39] (1990), 2 C.R. (4th) 1 at 42-43 (S.C.C.).
[40] *R. v. Oommen* (1994), 91 C.C.C. (3d) 8 at 15 (S.C.C.).

the act in question is one which he ought not to do. In this case, although the accused knew that it was wrong to kill, he believed as a result of a psychiatric illusion that the deceased was about to kill him. Accordingly, he shot her while she was sleeping on his apartment floor. The accused believed that his enemies had commissioned the deceased to kill him and on the night of the killing was convinced that members of the conspiracy had surrounded his apartment building with the intention of moving in on him and killing him.

(e) Specific Delusions

The "specific delusions" defence has little practical application. The McRuer Report recommended that the section be dropped from the Code because the wording of the subsection described a person who could not exist. The medical experts relied upon by McRuer had given their opinion that no one who had "specific delusions" could be "in other respects sane."[41]

(f) Burden of Proof

Section 16(3) of the Criminal Code states:

The burden of proof that an accused was suffering from a mental disorder so as to be exempt from criminal responsibility is on the party that raises the issue.

Before section 16 was amended in 1991, the accused had the burden of proving that he was insane at the time of the commission of the offence. Section 16(4) of the Code provided:

Everyone shall, until the contrary is proved, be presumed to be and to have been sane.

Under the old section, the accused was required to establish insanity on the balance of probabilities. In *Chaulk*, the Supreme Court of Canada held that the presumption of sanity in section 16(4) of the old legislation violated the presumption of innocence in the Charter but found that the violation was a reasonable limitation under section 1. The court held that requiring the accused to prove insanity on the balance of probabilities was a justifiable limitation on the presumption of innocence as the reversal of onus avoided placing a virtually impossible burden on the Crown to prove the accused's insanity.[42] Despite the court's ruling, Parliament has done away with the presump-

---

[41] *Supra*, note 28, at 36.
[42] *Supra*, note 39, at 33.

tion in the new legislation and has provided that the burden of proving that the accused was suffering from a mental disorder rests upon the party raising the issue.[43] In most cases, evidence that the accused was suffering from a mental disorder at the time of the offence will be led by the accused rather than the Crown. Accordingly, the accused will usually bear the burden of leading some evidence to show that he was suffering from a mental disorder.

4. AUTOMATISM

(a) General

The Criminal Code does not specify that an action must be voluntary to warrant punishment. Yet, our courts have concluded that it is not appropriate to convict a person in the absence of a voluntary act. In *Rabey v. R.*, Mr. Justice Dickson said, "A defence that the act is involuntary entitles the accused to a complete and unqualified acquittal."[44] Oliver Wendell Holmes, in his work on the common law, said,

> The reason for requiring an act is, that an act implies a choice and that it is felt to be impolite and unjust to make a man answerable for harm, unless he might have chosen otherwise.[45]

Our courts have adopted this view, sometimes holding that an involuntary act negates the necessary *mens rea*, while in other cases concluding that an involuntary act cannot constitute an *actus reus*.

The defence of automatism is based on this concept. In *Rabey*, Ritchie J. defined "automatism" as:

> ... a term used to describe unconscious, involuntary behaviour, the state of a person who, though capable of action, is not conscious of what he is doing. It means an unconscious, involuntary act, where the mind does not go with what is being done.[46]

In *Rabey*, Dickson J. (as he then was) gave a useful explanation of automatism stating:

> Although the word "automatism" made its way but lately to the legal state, it is basic principle that absence of volition in respect of the act involved is always a defence to a crime. A defence that the act is involuntary entitles the accused to a

---

[43] S.C. 1991, c. 43, s. 2.
[44] (1980), 15 C.R. (3d) 225 at 235 (S.C.C.).
[45] O.W. Holmes, *The Common Law* (Boston: Little, Brown & Co., 1881), at p. 54.
[46] (1980), 15 C.R. (3d) 225 at 232 (S.C.C.).

complete and unqualified acquittal. That the defence of automatism exists as a middle ground between criminal responsibility and legal insanity is beyond question. Although spoken as a defence, in the sense that it is raised by the accused, the Crown always bears the burden of proving a voluntary act.[47]

The result of the adoption of this view is that our courts have acquitted in a number of cases where the element of voluntariness was lacking. In *R. v. Butler*,[48] the accused was acquitted of having care or control of a motor vehicle while impaired when his drinking companions carried him to the car in an inebriated condition. In *R. v. Minor*,[49] the Saskatchewan Court of Appeal recognized the defence and ordered a new trial because the trial judge had failed to do so when the evidence in a motor manslaughter case was that the accused was in an unconscious condition and did not know what he was doing as a result of being injured in a fight which had taken place during a wedding reception. In that case, the court treated the defence as one which would negate *mens rea*.

In *R. v. King*,[50] the Supreme Court of Canada considered whether a person who had been given a drug by a dentist could be convicted of impaired driving when there was evidence that the drug could have induced a state of amnesia, accompanied by a period when the accused might not know what was happening. Ritchie J., in the majority judgment of the Supreme Court of Canada, said that if the impairment had been brought about without any act of the accused's own will, then the offence had not been committed. In a later case, *R. v. O'Brien*,[51] Ritchie J. said that non-insane automatism is a defence which goes to the absence of intent. If the defence is limited to the question of intent, then it would only be applicable in cases where *mens rea* is a requirement. However, it seems more logical to conclude, as some courts have, that automatism is a defence applicable in all cases, since if the element of voluntariness is absent, then the *actus reus* cannot be the result of a willing mind at liberty to make a definite choice or decision, which Mr. Justice Dickson has said is a necessary element of crime.

(b) Burden of Proof

The burden of proving the presence of *actus reus* is on the Crown, so that the Crown must not only prove the commission of the act, but also that it was a conscious act. Ordinarily, this burden will be discharged by showing that the

---

[47] *Ibid.*, at 235 (S.C.C.).
[48] [1939], 4 D.L.R. 592 (Alta. C.A.).
[49] (1955), 112 C.C.C. 29 (Sask. C.A.).
[50] [1962] S.C.R. 746.
[51] [1966] 3 C.C.C. 288 (N.B.C.A.).

accused did, in fact, commit the act, leading to the inference that the accused acted consciously. But, if evidence is adduced which places the element of voluntariness at issue, then a conviction may only be entered if the Crown satisfies the trier of fact beyond a reasonable doubt on this issue. There must be some evidence in the record which establishes that the accused was in a state of automatism. The accused must either raise the issue through cross-examination of Crown witnesses or lead evidence to show that he was in an automatistic state when the crime was committed. If the accused has laid the proper evidentiary foundation, the trial judge must consider whether the accused's condition is, in law, non-insane automatism. If the judge decides that there is sufficient evidence to leave with the jury, the jury will be asked to answer the factual question of whether the accused was suffering from automatism at the time the crime was committed. Once a defence has been left with the jury, the Crown always has the onus of proving that the accused acted voluntarily and, accordingly, the Crown must prove the absence of automatism beyond a reasonable doubt.

Since the mere assertion by the accused that he was in a state of automatism when he committed the crime will not be sufficient evidence to support leaving the defence with the jury, in most cases an expert witness will be called who will testify that the accused committed the offence while in a state of automatism. In *R. v. Parks*,[52] the accused was acquitted on charges of first and second degree murder and attempted murder after a jury found that he was acting in a state of automatism when he killed his mother-in-law with a kitchen knife and seriously injured his father-in-law. The accused, whose family had a history of sleepwalking, presented the defence of automatism, stating that at the time the offences took place he was sleepwalking. The accused was at the home of his parents-in-law when the attack took place. Immediately after the attack took place, the accused went to the police station, driving his own car and told the police:

> I just killed someone with my bare hands; oh my God, I just killed someone; I've just killed two people; my God I've just killed two people with my hand; my God I've just killed two people; I've just killed my mother and father-in-law. I stabbed and beat them to death. It's all my fault.[53]

At trial, the accused called five physicians who testified with respect to his sleep disorders. All five medical doctors agreed that the accused was in fact sleepwalking when he committed the acts with which he was charged. The accused's acquittal was appealed by the Crown to the Ontario Court of Appeal which affirmed the trial judgment, holding that the trial judge had properly put the defence of automatism rather than the offence of insanity to the jury. The Crown appealed to the Supreme Court of Canada. The issue before the Supreme Court of Canada was whether the Ontario Court of

---

[52] (1992), 15 C.R. (4th) 289 (S.C.C.).
[53] *Ibid.*, at 308-309.

Appeal erred in law in holding that the condition of sleepwalking should be classified as non-insane automatism, resulting in an acquittal instead of being classified as a "disease of the mind" (insane automatism) which would result in a verdict of not guilty by reason of insanity. The Supreme Court held that for the defence of insanity to have been put to the jury there would have had to have been evidence showing that sleepwalking was the cause of the accused's state of mind. While the court did not rule out that sleepwalking could never be a disease of the mind, the court held that the expert evidence in this case did not establish that sleepwalking was the cause of the accused's state of mind.[54]

(c) Relation to Other Defences

In many cases, the evidence of automatism might also justify a defence based on drunkenness or insanity. The question of how the evidence is to be classified becomes a very important one because if the defence of automatism could succeed, then an accused would be acquitted; whereas drunkenness may only reduce the gravity of the offence, while insanity may result in an accused being confined by a Provincial Review Board. The issue of whether the evidence justifies a finding of automatism, drunkenness or insanity has been held to be a question of law which is decided by the court. This results in some limitation of the defence of automatism because the courts have not permitted it to be used as a means of escaping liability easily. Accordingly, they have held that a person who takes drugs or alcohol voluntarily, and knowingly, cannot be allowed to take advantage of the defence of automatism. In that case, the only defence open to the accused is that of drunkenness, which will result, if it succeeds, in ameliorating the gravity of the offence, but will not result in an acquittal. The approach of the courts has also been to limit the defence of automatism in cases where the evidence is consistent with insanity. Thus, in *R. v. Hartridge*, Culliton C.J.S. stated:

> Where the possibility of an unconscious act depends on, and only on, the existence of a defect of reason from a disease of the mind within the M'Naghten Rules, the defence to be put to the jury is one of insanity and no other.[55]

Accordingly, the defence will not succeed where there is legal insanity, self-induced drunkenness or negligence leading, for example, to the driving of a car after having been warned that a prescribed drug may affect one's capacity to drive.

---

[54] *Ibid.*, at 304-305.
[55] [1967] 1 C.C.C. 346 at 366 (Sask. C.A.).

5. INTOXICATION

(a) General

As discussed earlier, it is a basic principle that absence of volition in respect of an act is a defence to a crime. Accordingly, one might have thought that if a person was sufficiently intoxicated that he was not conscious of what he was doing, he would be treated as one who lacked capacity. However, our courts have not applied this apparent logic and where the intoxication is self-induced they have been unwilling to exempt intoxicated persons of responsibility. The result is that the law relating to intoxication suffers from a certain lack of logic as severe intoxication can clearly lead to significant mental incapacity and in certain circumstances the incapacity would be equivalent to the incapacity which, apart form the exception for drunkenness, would form the basis for a defence of insanity.

As early as the sixteenth century, the Exchequer Court held, in *Reniger v. Fogossa*, that even if a person killed another when he was so drunk that he had no understanding or memory he should not be acquitted as his ignorance was "occasioned by his own act and folly."[56] Accordingly, the courts will only conclude that there has been no proof of *actus reus* in the sense that the act was not voluntary where the intoxication is involuntary. Thus if a person was forcibly injected with a drug and in a drugged condition committed a crime, he could be acquitted if the jury was convinced that his action was involuntary. In *R. v. King*, a case involving impaired driving, Mr. Justice Ritchie held:

> If the driver's lack of appreciation when he undertook to drive was induced by voluntary consumption of alcohol or of a drug which he knew or had any reasonable ground for believing might cause him to be impaired, then he cannot, of course, avoid the consequences of the impairment which results by saying that he did not intend to get into such a condition, but if the impairment has been brought about without any act of his own will, then, in my view, the offence created by s. 233 cannot be said to have been committed.[57]

In that case, King was acquitted because his impairment was as a result of an injection of sodium pentothal administered by a dentist and he was able to show that he was unaware of its likely effects.

(b) Voluntary Intoxication and Specific Intent

In the case of voluntary intoxication, our courts have been greatly influ-

---

[56] 75 English 53 Reports (K.B.D.), 1 Plowden 1, at 31 (Exch. Ct.).
[57] *Supra*, note 50, at 763.

enced by Lord Birkenhead's decision in *D.P.P. v. Beard.* In that case Lord Birkenhead established three rules:

> 1. . . . insanity, whether produced by drunkenness or otherwise, is a defence to the crime charged. . . If actual insanity in fact supervenes, as the result of alcoholic excess, it furnishes as complete an answer to a criminal charge as insanity induced by any other cause.
>
> . . . .
>
> 2. That evidence of drunkenness which renders the accused incapable of forming the specific intent essential to constitute the crime should be taken into consideration with the other facts proved in order to determine whether or not he had this intent.
>
> 3. That evidence of drunkenness falling short of a proved incapacity in the accused to form the intent necessary to constitute the crime and merely establishing that his mind was affected by drink so that he more readily gave way to some violent passion, does not rebut the presumption that a man intends the natural consequences of his acts.[58]

Although the *Beard* rules have been criticized in the work of the Law Reform Commission, the Supreme Court of Canada has followed them in large part.[59]

As seen earlier, when insanity was discussed, our courts have been very reluctant to accept the defence of insanity based on alcoholism unless it is found that there has been an actual mental disease which may have been caused by repeated use of alcohol. In *R. v. Lipman,*[60] a decision by the English Court of Appeal, Lipman, an addict of LSD, had killed a woman by shoving several inches of sheet down her throat when he was hallucinating. Despite this evidence, he was convicted of manslaughter.

The effect of the second rule is that voluntary intoxication will only be a defence to offences which require a "specific intent." This rule has been severely criticized by the distinguished lawyer, A.D. Gold, on the ground that it imposes, in the case of offences which are not specific intent offences, liability whether or not the *mens rea* was present even though it may be quite clear that because of intoxication the requisite *mens rea* was lacking.[61]

In *R. v. George,* Mr. Justice Fauteux stated:

> In considering the question of *mens rea,* a distinction is to be made between (i) intention as applied to acts considered in relation to their purposes and (ii) intention as applied to acts considered apart from their purposes.[62]

---

[58] *Supra,* note 20, at 501-502.

[59] *R. v. George,* [1960] S.C.R. 871; *R. v. Perrault,* [1971] S.C.R. 196.

[60] [1970] 1 Q.B. 152 (C.A.).

[61] A.D. Gold, "An Untrimmed Beard: The Law of Intoxication as a Defence to a Criminal Charge" (1977) 19 C.L.Q. 34.

[62] [1960] S.C.R. 871 at 877.

A general intent attending the commission of an act is, in some cases, the only intent required to constitute the crime, such as assault, while, in others, there must be in addition to that general intent, a specific intent attending the purpose for the commission of the act.

In *R. v. Bernard*, McIntyre J. explained the difference between a general and specific intent offence stating:

> The general intent offence is one in which the only intent involved relates solely to the performance of the act in question, with no further ulterior intent or purpose. . . . A specific intent offence is one which involves the performance of the actus reus, coupled with an intent or purpose going beyond the mere performance of the questioned act.[63]

The application of this principle has not always been clear. British Columbia courts held that rape was a general intent offence, while Ontario courts held that the offence was a specific intent offence. The result was that voluntary intoxication could be a defence to rape in Ontario, but not in British Columbia.[64] When the Supreme Court of Canada was called upon to resolve this difference in *Leary v. R.*, Mr. Justice Pigeon, giving the majority judgment, held that rape was a general intent offence and, accordingly, the defence of drunkenness had no application.

The result has been that a number of offences, such as breaking and entering with intent, theft, and assault with intent to wound, are offences of specific intent, while common assault, indecent assault, sexual assault, and assault causing bodily harm have been held to be crimes of general intent. The approach by the courts generally has been to find that specific intent is required when the Code specifically mentions a specific intent, but that otherwise offences are generally ones of general intent. Nevertheless, although murder is not defined as one requiring specific intent, our courts have so concluded with the result that drunkenness can reduce the offence to one of manslaughter.

Under the *Beard* rule it could be argued that if the accused had a capacity to form the intent, then the Crown should succeed without actually proving that he had the necessary intent. However, in *R. v. Otis*, the Ontario Court of Appeal held that it was necessary to determine whether the accused actually had the intent.[65] Evidence of intoxication capable of depriving the accused of the capacity to form such an intent in its view had to be taken into account with all other evidence to determine whether the accused actually had the intent. In *R. v. Dees*, Mr. Justice Arnup stated:

> An accused person may have the capacity without the requisite specific intent. The ultimate question must always be: did the accused have the requisite intent?

---

[63] (1988), 67 C.R. (3d) 113 at 139 (S.C.C.).

[64] *R. v. Boucher*, [1963] 2 C.C.C. 241 (B.C.C.A.); cf. *R. v. Vandervoort* (1961), 130 C.C.C. 158 (Ont. C.A.).

[65] (1978), 39 C.C.C. (2d) 304 (Ont. C.A.).

Of course, if he lacked the capacity to form that intent, then he did not have the intent, but the converse proposition does not follow, i.e., it does not follow that because he had the capacity he also had the specific intent.[66]

(c) Critique of Law

The law has been severely criticized. Mr. Justice Dickson, in dissenting in *Leary v. R.*, concluded, what now must be obvious to the reader, that it is very difficult to distinguish between specific intention and general intention.[67] In his view it seems illogical that drunkenness can absolve in respect of graver crimes, but not in respect of the lesser. Thus, intent in respect of murder can be negatived by drunkenness, but not the intent for assault. He stated

> When an accused, in answer to a criminal charge, says that he was so sodden as to be virtually an automaton, incapable of knowing what he was about, his defence is not drunkenness but an absence of voluntariness caused by excessive drinking.[68]

Dickson J. stated that "the question is then whether the act was voluntary." Likewise, in his view, when the offence includes a mental element which must be proven by the Crown, such as intention or recklessness, the accused should be able to argue that upon all of the evidence the Crown has failed to prove the required mental element. His Lordship said that the law should take no note of the cause which led to the accused's incapacity. Dickson J. said that it is usually recognized that the general effect of alcohol is to remove inhibitions and induce self-confidence and maybe aggressiveness. If the accused was intoxicated at the time of the offence, and it is proved that he did the act intentionally or recklessly, it should be irrelevant that, were it not for the drinking, he would not have committed the offence.

In such circumstances, the intent or recklessness constituting the required mental element exists, and the fact that by reason of intoxication the accused's judgment was clouded so that he more easily gave way to his instinctual drives, should avail him nothing. Mr. Justice Dickson rejected the view that one who voluntarily ingests a drug or alcohol is necessarily acting sufficiently recklessly to support a criminal conviction. It was his view that recklessness imports foresight and cannot exist in general terms but must refer to the consequences of a particular act. He stated:

> But to say that everyone who gets drunk is thereby reckless and thereby account-

---

[66] (1978), 40 C.C.C. (2d) 58 at 66 (Ont. C.A.).

[67] (1977), 33 C.C.C. (2d) 473 at 478 (S.C.C.); *D.P.P. v. Majewski*, [1976] 2 All E.R. 142 at 167-168 (H.L.).

[68] *Ibid.*, at 492.

able is to use the word "reckless" in a non-legal sense and, in effect, in the case of an intoxicated offender, to convert any crime into one of absolute or strict liability.[69]

(d) Recent Case Law and Possible Statutory Reform

In *R. v. Bernard*, the majority of the Supreme Court of Canada held that the rule that self-induced intoxication was not a defence to a crime of general intent did not violate section 7 or 11(*d*) of the Charter. Mr. Justice McIntyre J. (Beetz J. concurring) held that the common law rule was justified on the ground that persons who became voluntarily intoxicated and thereby deprived themselves of self-control, leading to the commission of a crime, were not morally innocent, but were indeed criminally blameworthy.[70] Wilson J. and L'Heureux-Dubé J. agreed for different reasons. Wilson and L'Heureux-Dubé JJ. held that evidence of intoxication would be relevant to the trier of fact (i.e. judge or jury) in general intent offences where the evidence of extreme intoxication is such that the accused was in a state akin to insanity or automatism.[71]

In 1994, the Supreme Court of Canada considered whether drunkenness can be a defence to crimes of general intent in cases where an accused is so intoxicated that his condition resembles automatism or mental disorder as defined in section 16 of the Criminal Code. In *R. v. Daviault*,[72] the Supreme Court of Canada held that the common law rule that voluntary intoxication is no defence to general intent offences violates sections 7 and 11(*d*) of the Charter. Cory J., writing for the majority of the court, noted that the common law rule prevented the accused from being acquitted in cases where there is a reasonable doubt as to his capacity to form the minimal mental element required for a general intent offence as a result of his extreme intoxication. Cory J. noted that in such cases the intentional act of the accused in becoming voluntarily intoxicated is substituted for the mental element of the offence. In *Daviault*, Cory J. held that the consumption of alcohol cannot lead automatically to the conclusion that the accused possessed the required mental element to commit a crime. Cory J. held that the *mens rea* for a crime "is so well recognized that to eliminate that mental element, an integral part of the crime, would be to deprive an accused of fundamental justice."[73]

Cory J. also held that a strict application of the *Leary* rule that intoxication is no defence to general intent offences could in certain cases result in an infringement of the presumption of innocence under section 11(*d*) of the

---

[69] *Ibid.*
[70] (1988), 67 C.R. (3d) 113 at 151-152 (S.C.C.).
[71] *Ibid.*, at 157.
[72] (1994), 33 C.R. (4th) 165 (S.C.C.).
[73] *Ibid.*, at 190.

Charter. The majority of the court stated that the presumption of innocence would be infringed in cases where an accused who was in an extreme state of intoxication tantamount to automatism or mental illness would have to be found guilty, although there was a reasonable doubt as to the voluntary nature of the act committed by the accused. Cory J. held that "the mental element of voluntariness is a fundamental aspect of the crime which cannot be taken away by a judicially developed policy."[74] Cory J. found that it is unlikely that someone could intend to become so intoxicated that they would reach a state of insanity or automatism.

The majority of the Supreme Court of Canada have anticipated the criticism that the flood gates will be opened by permitting an accused to raise the defence of drunkenness to general intent offences where the accused is in a state akin to automatism or insanity. Cory J. stated:

> Given the minimal nature of the mental element required for crimes of general intent, even those who are significantly drunk will usually be able to form the requisite mens rea and will be found to have acted voluntarily. In reality it is those who can demonstrate that they were in such an extreme degree of intoxication that they were in a state akin to automatism or insanity that might expect to raise a reasonable doubt as to their ability to form the minimal mental element required for a general intent offence. Neither an insane person nor one in a state of automatism is capable of forming the minimum intent required for a general intent offence. Similarly, as the words themselves imply, "drunkenness akin to insanity or automatism" describes a person so severely intoxicated that he is incapable of forming even the minimal intent required of a general intent offence. The phrase refers to a person so drunk that he is an automaton. As such he may be capable of voluntary acts such as moving his arms and legs but is quite incapable of forming the most basic or simple intent required to perform the act prohibited by a general intent offence.[75]

Cory J. held that the accused bears the burden of establishing extreme intoxication akin to automatism or insanity, saying that the accused must establish the defence based on a balance of probabilities.

Cory J. stated that there will be rare occasions when the evidence supports such an extreme level of intoxication that the accused can be said to have been incapable of forming the minimum intent required to commit a general intent offence. The facts in *Daviault* are unusual and support Cory J.'s conclusion that there will be few cases where an accused can be said to be incapable of forming the minimum mens rea required to commit a general intent offence. In *Daviault*, the accused was convicted of sexually assaulting a 65-year-old woman who was partially paralyzed and confined to a wheelchair. The evidence led at trial established that the accused, who was a chronic alcoholic, had consumed seven or eight beers during the day and about 35 ounces of brandy on the evening when the assault took place. Expert evidence

---

[74] *Ibid.*
[75] *Ibid.*, at 196-197.

led at trial established that the accused's blood alcohol level, which would have been between 400 and 600 milligrams per 100 millilitres of blood, would cause death or a coma in an ordinary person.[76]

6. PROVOCATION

(a) General

Provocation provides a partial defence to murder in that it reduces murder to manslaughter. The partial defence is established by section 232 of the Criminal Code:

> **232.** (1) Culpable homicide that otherwise would be murder may be reduced to manslaughter if the person who committed it did so in the heat of passion caused by sudden provocation.
> (2) A wrongful act or insult that is of such a nature as to be sufficient to deprive an ordinary person of the power of self-control is provocation for the purposes of this section if the accused acted on it on the sudden and before there was time for his passion to cool.
> (3) For purposes of this section the questions
> > (a) whether a particular wrongful act or insult amounted to provocation, and
> > (b) whether the accused was deprived of the power of self-control by the provocation that he alleges he received,
> are questions of fact, but no one shall be deemed to have given provocation to another by doing anything that he had a legal right to do, or by doing anything that the accused incited him to do in order to provide the accused with an excuse for causing death or bodily harm to any human being.
> (4) Culpable homicide that otherwise would be murder is not necessarily manslaughter by reason only that it was committed by a person who was being arrested illegally, but the fact that the illegality of the arrest was known to the accused may be evidence of provocation for the purpose of this section.

In *R. v. Hill*, Chief Justice Brian Dickson, who delivered the judgment of the court, stated:

> The defence of provocation appears to have first developed in the early 1800's. Tindal C.J. in *R. v. Hayward* (1833), 6 C. & P. 157 at 159, 172 E.R. 1188, told the jury that the defence of provocation was derived from the law's "compassion to human infirmity". It acknowledged that all human beings are subject to uncontrollable outbursts of passion and anger which may lead them to do violent acts. In such instances, the law would lessen the severity of criminal liability.

> Nevertheless, not all acts done in the heat of passion were to be subject to the doc-

---

[76] *Ibid.*, at 200.

trine of provocation. By the middle of the 19th Century, it became clear that the provoking act had to be sufficient to excite an ordinary or reasonable person under the circumstances. As Keating J. stated in *R. v. Welsh* (1869), 11 Cox C.C. 336 at 338:

> The law is, that there must exist such an amount of provocation as would be excited by the circumstances in the mind of a reasonable man, and so as to lead the jury to ascribe the act to the influence of that passion.[77]

In *Hill*, Chief Justice Dickson stated that section 215(1) and (2) [232(1), (2)] of the Criminal Code leads to three questions which a court must answer:

1. Would an ordinary person be deprived of self-control by the act or insult?

2. Did the accused in fact act in response to those "provocative" acts; in short was he or she provoked by them whether or not an ordinary person would have been?

3. Was the accused's response on the sudden and before there was time for his or her passion to cool?

In answering these successive questions, the first, or "ordinary person", test is clearly determined by objective standards. The second . . . test, as to the laws of self-control by the accused, is determined, like any other question of fact as revealed by the evidence, from the surrounding facts. The third test, as to whether the response was sudden and before passions cooled, is again a question of fact.[78]

(b) Objective Test

An act or insult which would not provoke an ordinary person will not meet the objective test set out under section 232 of the Criminal Code. In *Hill*, Dickson J. stated that if there was no objective test of provocation, a well-tempered individual would not be able to rely on provocation as a partial defence to murder while someone who had an excessively violent temper could claim the benefit of the defence. His Lordship said that the law must apply a reasonable standard in determining whether the accused's actions in the circumstances of the case were reasonable as measured by objective criteria. Chief Justice Dickson noted that the objective standard encourages non-violent behaviour and ensures that people conform to the reasonable expectations of society. The tests are not completely objective in that having considered whether an ordinary person would have reacted to the insult or actions in the way that the accused did, a jury then considers whether the acts or insult caused the accused to be provoked and thus acted in the heat of passion. The second part of the test is subjective because it takes into account the particular state and psychological makeup of the accused.

Before dealing with the subjective test, jurors must measure the

---

[77] (1985), 51 C.R. (3d) 97 at 107-108 (S.C.C.).
[78] *Ibid.*, at 104.

accused's actions against objective criteria. In *Hill*, Chief Justice Dickson said that there was considerable Supreme Court of Canada authority to the effect that the particular psychological temperament and makeup of the accused was not to be considered when jurors were determining whether an ordinary person would have acted in the manner in which the accused acted. The accused, who was 16 years of age, was acquitted of first degree murder, but convicted of second degree murder. On appeal, the accused argued that the trial judge had erred by not instructing the jury that an ordinary person within the meaning of section 215 [232] of the Criminal Code was an "ordinary person of the same age and sex as the accused." The Court of Appeal held that the trial judge should have told jurors that they should consider whether the wrongful act or insult was sufficient to deprive an ordinary person of the same age and sex as the accused of his power of self-control. The court overturned the conviction and ordered a new trial on the second degree murder charge.

Hill testified that he had been the victim of unexpected homosexual advances by the victim when he was sleeping on a couch in the victim's apartment. Hill testified that he picked up a hatchet and swung at the victim in an attempt to scare him after being pursued to the bathroom. He said that the hatchet struck the victim on the head and that he then ran from the apartment but returned a short while later. When he re-entered the apartment the victim threatened to kill him. Then Hill got two kitchen knives and stabbed the victim to death. The Supreme Court of Canada held that the trial judge had not erred in instructing the jury as to the objective test to be applied, as it was not necessary to specifically instruct a jury that an ordinary person is deemed to be of the same age and sex as the accused. Chief Justice Dickson was not unmindful of the importance of age, saying:

> For a jury to assess what an ordinary person would have done if subjected to the same circumstances as the accused, the young age of an accused will be an important contextual consideration.[79]

His Lordship held that a jury, when considering the ordinary person test in section 215 [232] of the Code, would naturally apply certain characteristics to the "ordinary person" and did not need to be instructed as to what these characteristics were.

In *Hill*, Chief Justice Dickson stated that in considering whether an ordinary person would be provoked by the act or insult, jurors could consider the age or racial characteristics of the person alleged to have been provoked. In defining the parameters of the objective test, His Lordship stated:

> I think it clear that there is a widespread agreement that the ordinary or reasonable person has a normal temperament and level of self-control. It follows that the ordinary person is not exceptionally excitable, pugnacious or in a state of drunkenness.

---

[79] *Ibid.*, at 114.

In terms of other characteristics of the ordinary person, it seems to me that the "collective good sense" of the jury will naturally lead it to ascribe to the ordinary person any general characteristics relevant to the provocation in question. For example, if the provocation is a racial slur, the jury will think of an ordinary person with the racial background that forms the substance of the insult. To this extent, particular characteristics will be ascribed to the ordinary person. Indeed, it will be impossible to conceptualize a sexless or ageless ordinary person. Features such as sex, age, or race do not detract from a person"s characterization as ordinary. Thus, particular characteristics that are not peculiar or idiosyncratic can be ascribed to an ordinary person without subverting the logic of the objective test of provocation. As Lord Diplock wrote in Camplin . . .

> . . . the "reasonable man" has never been confined to the adult male. It means an ordinary person of either sex, not exceptionally excitable or pugnacious, but possessed of such powers of self control as everyone is entitled to expect that his fellow citizens will exercise in society as it is today.

> . . . the central criterion is the relevance of the particular feature to the provocation in question. With this in mind, I think it is fair to conclude that age will be a relevant consideration when we are dealing with a young accused person.[80]

Chief Justice Dickson believed that jurors had sufficient common sense to place the ordinary person test in the context of the case which they were considering. It is unfortunate that the court did not specifically require that a jury should be so directed, rather than leaving the matter to the judgment of a jury.

(c) Subjective Test

After considering the objective test and determining whether an ordinary person can be provoked by the act or insult, the judge or jury must consider whether the accused before the court was actually provoked by the act or insult. In *Hill*, Chief Justice Dickson characterized the second branch of the test as being a "subjective" test, saying that his test involves an assessment of what actually occurred in the mind of the accused."[81] When considering the subjective test, jurors must consider "whether the accused reacted to the provocation on the sudden and before there was time for his passion to cool."[82] His Lordship stated that in determining whether the accused had been provoked by the act or insult, jurors could consider the accused's mental state and psychological temperament. In other words, the second branch of the provocation test permits a judge or jury to consider characteristics which are peculiar to the accused.

---

[80] *Ibid.*
[81] *Ibid.*, at 115.
[82] *Ibid.*

In a jury trial, a trial judge will have to determine as a matter of law whether there is sufficient evidence of provocation to put the issue before a jury. In *Parnerkar v. R.*, Fateux C.J.C., who delivered the judgment of the Supreme Court of Canada, stated:

> If, then, the record is denuded of any evidence potentially enabling a reasonable jury acting judicially to find a wrongful act or insult of the nature and effect set forth in s. 203(3)(a) and (b) [s. 215], it is then, as a matter of law, within the area exclusively reserved to the trial Judge to so decide and his duty to refrain from putting the defence of provocation to the jury.[83]

The issue as to whether the particular act or insult constitutes provocation for the purpose of section 232 of the Code is a factual question as is made clear by section 232(3) of the Code. Section 232(3) of the Code states that no one can be deemed to have been provoked by an act which a person had a legal right to do. This section also provides that whether an accused incited the victim to do an act in order to provide an excuse for causing death or bodily harm, the act or insult as the case may be will not be deemed to be provocative. In addition, section 232(4) of the Code provides that the person who has been arrested illegally cannot claim provocation in circumstances where that person committed a culpable homicide. However, the section does allow a person to claim provocation in circumstances where the illegal nature of the arrest was known to the person making the arrest. Subsections 232(2) and (4) of the Criminal Code have not given rise to many cases. While these sections limit the circumstances under which provocation may be used as a defence, the main limitation to the provocation defence is that provocation is not a defence generally; the defence only applies to reduce murder to manslaughter.[84]

The Supreme Court of Canada held in *R. v. Squire*[85] that a trial judge does not have a duty to put a defence to a jury if there is no evidence in support of it or from which it may reasonably be inferred. If it can be said that no jury acting judicially on the evidence could find an insult sufficient to deprive an ordinary person of self control, the defence of provocation need not be left to the jury.

7. CONSENT

(a) General

In general, consent is a defence to a criminal offence. Thus, someone who is charged with the use of a stolen credit card will have a valid defence

---

[83] (1973), 10 C.C.C. (2d) 253 at 256 (S.C.C.).
[84] *Parnerkar v. R.*; *ibid.*; *R. v. Cunningham*, [1959] 1 Q.B. 288.
[85] [1977] 2 S.C.R. 13.

to the charge if there is evidence which indicates that the person using the card had the cardholder's consent. While the defence of consent applies to property defences, such as possession of stolen property and theft, the defence has also been applied to legitimize sexual acts between consenting adults which would otherwise be criminal. In Don Stuart's *Canadian Criminal Law: A Treatise* 2nd ed., the author states:

> The general principle, to which there are exceptions, that the true consent of the victim is always a defence to criminal responsibility is a fundamental principle of the criminal law.[86]

In some cases, the law vitiates the consent given on the basis that the person who consented to the act in question was not sufficiently mature to properly give an informed consent. Thus, for example, someone under 14 years of age cannot validly consent to sexual intercourse. Also, a person under 18 years of age cannot validly consent to an act of prostitution or participate in a pornographic film. One cannot consent to certain acts as a matter of public policy. Thus, section 14 of the Criminal Code abrogates consent to the infliction of death. It states:

> **14.** No person is entitled to consent to have death inflicted on him, and such consent does not affect the criminal responsibility of any person by whom death may be inflicted on the person by whom consent is given.

(b) As Defence to Assault

Consent is most frequently used as a defence to a charge of assault. Two people can consent to engage in a fist fight provided that they do not consent to inflict more than minor hurt or trivial bodily harm upon one another. In England, the courts have held that it is against public policy for consent to be a defence where bodily harm is inflicted as a result of a fight. In *R. v. Donovan*, a case decided in 1934, the English Court of Criminal Appeal stated:

> As a general rule, although it is a rule to which there are well-established exceptions, it is an unlawful act to beat another person with such a degree of violence that the infliction of bodily harm is a probable consequence, and, when such an act is proved, consent is immaterial.[87]

More recently, in 1980, the English Court of Appeal in *Attorney General's Reference (No. 6 of 1980)*[88] held that when two persons fight other

---

[86] Don Stuart, *Canadian Criminal Law: A Treatise*, 2nd ed. (Toronto: Carswell, 1987) at p. 469.
[87] [1934] All E.R. Rep. 207 at 210 (C.C.A.).
[88] [1981] 2 All E.R. 1057 at 1059 (C.A.).

than in the course of sport it cannot be a defence to an assault charge that the complainant consented to fight. The court held that consent is no defence when "actual bodily harm is intended and/or caused," saying that it was against the public interest that persons should cause each other bodily harm for no good reason.

In Canada, provincial courts of appeal have taken inconsistent positions with respect to whether one could consent to the infliction of more than minor bodily harm. Some provincial appellate courts dealt with the issue of consent simply on the basis of whether the bodily harm which was inflicted exceeded the consent which was given. In *R. v. MacTavish*, a case in which a boy received a broken nose from kicks landed by the other in a school yard fight, the New Brunswick Court of Appeal held that while the boy had consented to a "fair fight," he had not consented to having his "head kicked in."[89] In *R. v. Dix*,[90] the Ontario Court of Appeal overturned the accused's conviction for assault causing bodily harm on the ground that the trial judge erred in not considering whether the complainant could have consented to the force applied. The accused and the complainant had engaged in a fight following a bar room argument after one of the parties had challenged the other to go out and settle the matter.

In *R. v. Setrum*,[91] the Saskatchewan Court of Appeal applied the *Dix* case in allowing the accused's appeal of a manslaughter conviction. The court, which ordered a new trial, made it clear that proof of a lack of consent to an assault is an essential element which the Crown must prove in order to obtain a conviction.

More recently, in *R. v. McIntosh*,[92] the Nova Scotia Court of Appeal held that as it was not in the public interest that people should attempt to cause each other actual bodily harm, most fights would be unlawful irrespective of consent. In *McIntosh*, the issue was whether a participant in a fist fight could lawfully consent to the intentional infliction of bodily harm upon himself.

Although there has been disagreement amongst provincial appellate courts as to whether persons engaged in a fist fight can lawfully consent to the infliction of bodily harm, the courts have not been willing to allow the defence of consent to prevail where weapons are involved. The Alberta Court of Appeal's decision in *R. v. Carriere*[93] is typical of the approach taken by the appellate courts where weapons are involved.

In *Carriere*, the Alberta Court of Appeal held that consent to being stabbed is not a defence to a charge of aggravated assault under section 245.2(1) [268(1)] of the Criminal Code.[94] The accused and another woman

[89] *R. v. MacTavish* (1972), 20 C.R.N.S. 235 at 237 (N.B.C.A.).
[90] (1972), 10 C.C.C. (2d) 324 (Ont. C.A.).
[91] (1976), 32 C.C.C. (2d) 109 (Sask. C.A.).
[92] (1991), 64 C.C.C. (3d) 294 (N.S.C.A.).
[93] (1987), 56 C.R. (3d) 257 (Alta. C.A.).
[94] *Ibid.*, at 264.

had a fist fight in the lobby of a Calgary hotel. The fight was stopped by hotel employees, but was continued outside in the parking lot. The victim, who pulled a knife on the accused, was stabbed by the accused after the accused accosted the victim with her own knife. When the case was heard by the Court of Appeal, the Crown admitted the facts indicating that the complainant consented to the knife fight in that she was armed with a knife and had started the fight. The accused testified at trial and she was asked the following:

> You say that someone slipped you a knife. What happened after someone slipped you a knife? . . . I said, "So you want to knife it, do you?" and then I just opened my blade and that's when we went at it.[95]

Laycraft C.J.A. held that it was against public policy for a court to hold that consent to being stabbed was a defence to a charge of aggravated assault. His Lordship stated:

> I have . . . no doubt of the answer which the law must reach in a fight with knives where the charge is under one of the assault sections. One cannot consent to be stabbed. The public policy of the law intervenes to nullify the apparent consent of each of the combatants. Each committed an assault on the other. With the infliction of stab wound, the appellant was guilty of aggravated assault. I would dismiss her appeal and affirm the conviction.[96]

8. SELF-DEFENCE

(a) General

Self-defence is perhaps the most widely known defence in criminal law. It is common knowledge that someone who is attacked is entitled to use force to repel the attack. Most people are aware that self-defence is a defence to a charge of murder. However, few people realize that the defence exists only as defined in the Criminal Code. A person who claims self-defence as justification for committing an offence will have to fall within the criteria set out in the Criminal Code. Someone who does not meet the criteria set out in sections 34, 35 or 37 of the Criminal Code will not be able to rely on the justification of self-defence. Section 34 deals with an unprovoked assault. Section 35 provides that someone who provokes an assault is justified in using force to defend against an assault which is intended to cause death or grievous bodily harm. Section 37 authorizes the use of force to protect oneself or someone under one's protection from being assaulted; thus, a parent could use force to protect his or her child from being assaulted.

---

[95] *Ibid.*, at 259.
[96] *Ibid.*, at 269.

Section 34 of the Criminal Code justifies the use of force to protect oneself from an unprovoked assault.

34. (1) Every one who is unlawfully assaulted without having provoked the assault is justified in repelling force by force if the force he uses is not intended to cause death or grievous bodily harm and is no more than is necessary to enable him to defend himself.

(2) Every one who is unlawfully assaulted and who causes death or grievous bodily harm in repelling the assault is justified if

(a) he causes it under reasonable apprehension of death or grievous bodily harm from the violence with which the assault was originally made or with which the assailant pursues his purposes; and

(b) he believes, on reasonable grounds, that he cannot otherwise preserve himself from death or grievous bodily harm.

In *Brisson v. R.*, Dickson J., as he then was, said:

Section 34(1) may be invoked only if there is no intention to cause death or grievous harm and no more force than is necessary is used. Section 34(2) is invoked where death or grievous harm has resulted but: (i) the accused reasonably apprehended his own death or grievous harm; and (ii) he believed on reasonable grounds that he had no other means of avoiding his own death or grievous harm. Section 34(1) affords justification in circumstances where the force used was not intended to cause death or grievous harm and is not excessive. Section 34(2) affords justification where there was an intention to cause death but under circumstances where objectively it was reasonable that the person accused believed he was going to be killed and subjectively he did so believe. Section 34(2) obviously provides for acquittal, despite the fact that the accused means to cause death or bodily harm that he knows is likely to cause death.[97]

In *R. v. Martin*, the Quebec Court of Appeal stated:

This does not mean, of course, that the provisions of s. 34(1) are automatically excluded where death has resulted. Obviously there are cases where death or bodily harm are not intended by a person defending himself and where death does occur. Where there is an issue as to whether or not the accused intended to cause death or serious bodily harm the jury should be carefully instructed as to the differences between the two situations in s. 34(1) or s. 34(2) and as to the different requirements for each . . . .[98]

Someone who accidentally causes death or grievous bodily harm having been a victim of an unprovoked assault would fall within the scope of section 34(1). Such a person would not have used force intended "to cause death or grievous bodily harm." Furthermore, if the accused is too intoxicated to form the intent to kill or cause grievous bodily harm, or for any other reason did not have the intent to kill or cause grievous bodily harm, then section 34(2) cannot apply.

---

[97] (1982), 29 C.R. (3d) 289 at 342 (S.C.C.).

[98] (1985), 47 C.R. (3d) 342 at 349 (Que. C.A.).

Section 34(1) presupposes that the person defending against an unprovoked assault used no more force "than is necessary to enable him to defend
himself." The wording introduces a proportionality test and a judge or jury
will have to decide on the facts whether the person being assaulted was justified in using the force which he used. However, the courts have held that a
person defending himself against an unprovoked assault is not required to
measure the force used with a nicety. Support for this proposition is found in
R. v. Baxter, a decision of the Ontario Court of Appeal. Martin J.A., who
delivered the judgment of the court, stated:

> Under s. 34(2) a person who is unlawfully assaulted is justified even if he inten-
> tionally kills or intentionally causes bodily harm to his assailant subject to the
> conditions specified in that subsection.
>
> . . .
>
> . . . in deciding whether the force used by the accused was more than was neces-
> sary in self-defence under both s. 34(1) and (2) the jury must bear in mind that a
> person defending himself against an attack, reasonably apprehended, cannot be
> expected to weigh to a nicety, the exact measure of necessary defensive action . . ."[99]

Section 34(2) of the Code is the appropriate provision in circumstances where
the accused, having been unlawfully assaulted, caused death or grievous bodily harm with the intention of causing death or grievous bodily harm. In this
regard, His Lordship stated:

> Where there is an issue as to whether the accused intended to cause death or
> grievous bodily harm the trial Judge, notwithstanding death or grievous bodily
> harm has resulted, should instruct the jury with respect to the provisions of
> s. 34(1) and then proceed to s. 34(2) as the applicable provision, in the event that
> the jury is satisfied that the accused intended to cause death or grievous bodily
> harm.[100]

In *Reilly v. R.*, the Supreme Court of Canada examined the subjective and
objective standards applicable in section 34(2) stating:

> Section 34(2) places in issue the accused's state of mind at the time he caused
> death. The subsection can afford protection to the accused only if he apprehended
> death or grievous bodily harm from the assault he was repelling and if he believed
> he could not preserve himself from death or grievous bodily harm otherwise than
> by the force he used. Nevertheless his apprehension must be a *reasonable* one and
> his belief *must be based upon reasonable and probable grounds*. The subsection
> requires that the jury consider, and be guided by, what they decide on the
> evidence was the accused's appreciation of the situation and his belief as to the
> reaction it required, so long as there exists an objectively verifiable basis for his
> perception.

Since s. 34(2) places in issue the accused's perception of the attack upon him and

---

[99] (1975), 27 C.C.C. (2d) 96 at 110-111 (Ont. C.A.).
[100] *Ibid.*, at 111.

the response required to meet it, the accused may still be found to have acted in self-defence even if he was mistaken in his perception. Reasonable and probable grounds must still exist for this mistaken perception, in the sense that the mistake must have been one which an ordinary man using ordinary care could have made in the same circumstances.[101]

The defence of honest mistake of fact exists for section 34(1) as well as for section 34(2) of the Code.[102]

In *R. v. Lavallee*,[103] the Supreme Court of Canada held for the first time that under section 34(2) the accused may lead expert evidence of "battered wife syndrome." In this case, the accused, who shot her common-law husband in the back of the head as he left the room, had successfully invoked a defence of self-defence and had been acquitted by a jury. Evidence led at trial established that the accused had been repeatedly physically abused by her common-law husband and that the accused told the police that just before the killing the deceased had told her that "if I didn't kill him first he would kill me. . . . He told me he was gonna kill me when everyone left."[104]

In *Lavallee*, the Supreme Court of Canada held that where there is evidence that an accused is in a battering relationship, expert testimony can assist the fact finder in determining whether the accused had a "reasonable apprehension of death when she acted by explaining the heightened sensitivity of the battered woman to her partner's acts."[105]

Prior to *Lavallee*, the Supreme Court of Canada in *Reilly* and the Ontario Court of Appeal in *Baxter* had held that under section 34(2)(a) the accused must apprehend imminent danger when he or she repels an assault. It is now clear from the Supreme Court's judgment in Lavallee that, at least in the context of "battered wife syndrome," self-defence under section 34(2) can be invoked where the accused acts to prevent assault. In *Lavallee*, Wilson J., writing for a majority of the court, stated that the requirement that a battered woman wait until an assault is actually underway before defending herself under section 34(2) of the Code would be equivalent to sentencing her to "murder by installment."[106]

In 1994, the Supreme Court of Canada again affirmed the *Lavallee* judgment. In *R. v. Pétel*, Lamer C.J.C. stated:

> There is thus no formal requirement that the danger be imminent. Imminence is only one of the factors which the jury should weigh in determining whether the accused had a reasonable apprehension of danger and a reasonable belief that she could not extricate herself otherwise than by killing the attacker.[107]

---

[101] (1984), 42 C.R. (3d) 154 at 162 (S.C.C.).
[102] *Supra*, note 9.
[103] (1990), 76 C.R. (3d) 329 (S.C.C.).
[104] *Ibid.*, at 335.
[105] *Ibid.*, at 352.
[106] *Ibid.*, at 353.
[107] (1994), 87 C.C.C. (3d) 97 at 104 (S.C.C.).

(b) Not Intending to Cause Death or Grievous Bodily Harm

Section 35 of the Criminal Code is available to an accused who has assaulted someone or provoked an assault in circumstances where the accused did not intend to cause death or grievous bodily harm. Section 35 states:

> **35.** Every one who has without justification assaulted another but did not commence the assault with intent to cause death or grievous bodily harm, or has without justification provoked an assault on himself by another, may justify the use of force subsequent to the assault if
>
> (*a*) he uses the force
>
>   (i) under reasonable apprehension of death or grievous bodily harm from the violence of the person whom he has assaulted or provoked, and
>
>   (ii) in the belief, on reasonable grounds, that it is necessary in order to preserve himself from death or grievous bodily harm;
>
> (*b*) he did not, at any time before the necessity of preserving himself from death or grievous bodily harm arose, endeavour to cause death or grievous bodily harm; and
>
> (*c*) he declined further conflict and quitted or retreated from it as far as it was feasible to do so before the necessity of preserving himself from death or bodily harm arose.

In *R. v. Merson*, the British Columbia Court of Appeal held that section 35 applied to a situation in which an accused assaulted a person whose death he or she subsequently caused or provoked an assault by that person. In order to fall within the section, the accused must not have intended to cause death or grievous bodily harm when the deceased was assaulted or provoked to assault the accused. In *Merson*, Taggart J.A., giving the judgment of the British Columbia Court of Appeal, distinguished section 34 and section 35, saying:

> Unlike s. 34, s. 35 is available to an accused notwithstanding the fact that he initiates the conflict by assaulting, or by provoking an assault by, the other combatant. It is, of course, necessary that there be an absence of intent on the part of the accused to cause death or grievous bodily harm to the other combatant. Here the respondent said he had no such intent. If those requirements are met then the accused may ". . . justify the use of force subsequent to the assault. . . .", if he meets the requirements of paras. (a), (b) and (c) . . . . It is during the "further conflict" that the accused must, if it is feasible to do so, decline further conflict and retreat from it before the necessity of preserving himself from death or grievous bodily harm arises.[108]

The "further conflict" is the conflict generated by the initial assault or provocation.

Section 37 of the Criminal Code justifies the use of force in protecting oneself or someone who is under one's protection, such as a child, from being assaulted:

---

[108] (1983), 4 C.C.C. (3d) 251 at 266-267 (B.C.C.A.).

37. (1) Every one is justified in using force to defend himself or any one under his protection from assault, if he uses no more force than is necessary to prevent the assault or the repetition of it.

(2) Nothing in this section shall be deemed to justify the wilful infliction of any hurt or mischief that is excessive, having regard to the nature of the assault that the force used was intended to prevent.

Section 37 of the Criminal Code, unlike section 34(2), requires that the force used in defending oneself or someone under one's protection against an assault be proportional to the force used by the assailant. The courts have held that where section 34(2) and section 37(1) are both put before a jury, the trial judge must make it clear that section 34(2) contemplates that excessive force will be used in defending against the assault whereas section 37 requires that the force used not be excessive. The failure to clearly differentiate between the two sections may result in a new trial being granted.[109]

In *R. v. Nelson*, Morden A.C.J.O, writing for the Ontario Court of Appeal, stated:

> In my respectful view, the diminished intelligence of an accused, depending upon the nature and extent of impairment . . . is a factor which should properly be taken into account in the application of s. 34(2). I do not think that *Reilly* mandates otherwise. Richie J., in holding that an intoxicated person could not have a reasonable apprehension and a belief based on reasonable and probable grounds, said that: "[a] reasonable man is a man in full possession of his faculties". A person with diminished intelligence may well be in full possession of his or her faculties. The difficulty is that these faculties are, through no fault of his or her own, diminished. In this regard, such a person may be in a position similar to that of the accused in *Lavallee* in that his or her apprehension and belief could not be fairly measured against the perceptions of an "ordinary man."[110]

In *Nelson*, the Ontario Court of Appeal held that the issue under section 34(2) is what the accused reasonably apprehended and believed. The court stated that in determining what the accused reasonably apprehended and believed, evidence relating to the accused's intellectual capabilities is of central importance. The court stated that where the accused has an intellectual impairment, which takes him out of the "broad band of normal adult intellectual capacity," such an impairment should be taken into account when applying section 34(2) of the Criminal Code.[111]

The reasoning of the Ontario Court of Appeal in *Nelson* is supported by the Supreme Court of Canada's decision in *R. v. Pétel*.

---

[109] *R. v. Mulder* (1978), 40 C.C.C. (2d) 1 at 5 (Ont. C.A.).
[110] (1992), 13 C.R. (4th) 359 at 379-380 (Ont. C.A.).
[111] *Ibid.*, at 382.

9. DEFENCE OF PROPERTY

Section 38 of the Criminal Code gives someone who is in possession of movable property the authority to defend it from a trespasser. This section states:

38. (1) Every one who is in peaceable possession of personal property, and every one lawfully assisting him, is justified

(*a*) in preventing a trespasser from taking it, or

(*b*) in taking it from a trespasser who has taken it, if he does not strike or cause bodily harm to the trespasser.

(2) Where a person who is in peaceable possession of personal property lays hands on it, a trespasser who persists in attempting to keep it or take it from him or from any one lawfully assisting him shall be deemed to commit an assault without justification or provocation.

Section 39 of the Criminal Code is also relevant:

39. (1) Every one who is in peaceable possession of personal property under a claim of right, and every one acting under his authority is protected from criminal responsibility for defending that possession, even against a person entitled by law to possession of it, if he uses no more force than is necessary.

(2) Every one who is in peaceable possession of personal property, but does not claim it as of right or does not act under the authority of a person who claims it as of right, is not justified or protected from criminal responsibility for defending his possession against a person who is entitled by law to possession of it.

In *R. v. Weare*,[112] the Nova Scotia Court of Appeal held that sections 38 and 39 of the Criminal Code permit someone to use force to defend movable property. In *Weare*, an employee of a credit care company which held a mortgage on the accused's personal property went to collect the property from the accused. The representative of the credit card company showed up at the accused's residence with the deputy sheriff. The evidence indicated that the accused had gone into personal bankruptcy and that a trustee in bankruptcy had been appointed before the representative of the credit card company came to collect the property. The accused ordered the company representative off his property. The sheriff did not produce identification and did not show the accused a copy of a court order allowing the credit card company interim possession of the property. When the credit card company representative and the sheriff did not leave, the accused came out onto his front porch carrying a rifle. The Nova Scotia Court of Appeal refused to overturn the decision acquitting the accused. Morrison J.A., writing for the court, noted that section 38(1) of the Code provides for a defence of movable property, saying that under that section the proper test to be applied is "whether or not an accused used more force than he, on reasonable grounds, believed was necessary."[113]

---

[112] (1983), 4 C.C.C. (3d) 494 (N.S.C.A.).
[113] *Ibid.*, at 499.

Morrison J.A. held that the same test should apply to an accused relying on section 39(1) of the Criminal Code.

> If the court found that Weare had reasonable grounds to believe they were trespassers then it seems to me that s. 38(1) of the Criminal Code would apply and the respondent, Weare, would be justified in preventing a trespasser from taking his moveable goods by ordering him off the property as long as he did not strike or cause bodily harm to the trespasser. In pointing the rifle after he came out on the verandah in his weakened condition [the accused had had a serious bowel operation] it seems to me that the respondent used no more force than was necessary and could also rely upon the provisions of s. 39(1) of the Criminal Code.[114]

A person with a claim of right includes people who are in possession of property with some right, although the lawful title may be in someone else. Thus, a person holding under a conditional sale agreement would have such a claim, although the vendor might have a right to repossess it. A person may only defend possession of property if he has such a right.

10. DEFENCE OF DWELLING

The Criminal Code authorizes a person to use force to protect his or her residence from being broken into. Section 40 of the Code states:

> **40.** Every one who is in peaceable possession of a dwelling-house, and every one lawfully assisting him or acting under his authority, is justified in using as much force as is necessary to prevent any person from forcibly breaking into or forcibly entering the dwelling-house without lawful authority.

In *R. v. Clark*,[115] the Alberta Court of Appeal refused to overturn the accused's manslaughter conviction, holding that the trial judge did not err in instructing jurors as to the defence of property. In *Clark*, McGillivray C.J.A. held that someone defending his or her property against a trespasser can use reasonable force to evict the trespasser, but "is not entitled to kill a trespasser in the absence of some threat to his person."[116] In *Clark*, the court noted that the difference between sections 34, 40 and 41 of the Criminal Code was that the Criminal Code did not require someone who was acting under the authority of those latter sections in defending his or her property to retreat before applying force to remove the trespasser from the property. He held that someone who kills a trespasser must rely upon section 34 of the Code, as such a killing cannot be justified as a response to a forcible entry, but must be justi-

---

[114] *Ibid.*, at 503.
[115] (1983), 5 C.C.C. (3d) 264 (Alta. C.A.).
[116] *Ibid.*, at 271.

fied as self-defence. The court stated that in such a situation the person using force must meet the requirement of self-defence under section 34 of the Code. The Criminal Code authorizes a person to use reasonable force in defence of his or her real property. Section 41 of the Criminal Code deals with the defence of a dwelling-house as well as real property, such as land:

> **41.** (1) Every one who is in peaceable possession of a dwelling-house or real property, and every one lawfully assisting him or acting under his authority, is justified in using force to prevent any person from trespassing on the dwelling-house or real property, or to remove a trespasser therefrom, if he uses no more force than is necessary.
>
> (2) A trespasser who resists an attempt by a person who is in peaceable possession of a dwelling-house or real property, or a person lawfully assisting him or acting under his authority to prevent his entry or to remove him, shall be deemed to commit an assault without justification or provocation.

In *R. v. Antley*,[117] the Ontario Court of Appeal allowed an accused's appeal from his conviction of assault causing bodily harm contrary to the Criminal Code. The court held that an accused was entitled, by virtue of section 41 of the Criminal Code, to use reasonable force to remove a trespasser who had refused to leave his property. The complainant had threatened the accused while standing in his living room. There was evidence that the accused, who was a much smaller man than the complainant, tried to push the complainant away with a stick and then, fearing for his safety, struck the complainant with the stick. Roach J.A. held that someone who was on his own property is not required to retreat before using reasonable force in protecting himself against a threatened attack. In other words, the accused did not have to wait until he was struck first before using force to protect himself from a perceived attack. It was also held that a person cannot be expected to measure the amount of force necessary to a "nicety."

Section 41 is not restricted to homeowners. In *R. v. Dillabough*,[118] the Ontario Court of Appeal held that a boarder may use reasonable force in removing a trespasser from the premises. In *R. v. Spencer*,[119] Mr. Justice Berger held that a tenant in an apartment building is not in possession of the common hallway of the building and therefore cannot rely on section 41 of the Criminal Code. Berger J. stated that "the landlord did not grant possession of the common hallway to his tenant."[120]

In *R. v. Alkadri*, the Alberta Court of Appeal dealt with the limits of section 41(2) of the Criminal Code. In *Alkadri*, Kerans J.A. stated:

> When s. 41(2) is invoked, the jury must be charged to consider not only whether the deceased resisted an attempt to eject him but also whether the attempt was

---

[117] [1964] 2 C.C.C. 142 (Ont. C.A.).
[118] (1975), 28 C.C.C. (2d) 482 (Ont. C.A.).
[119] (1977), 38 C.C.C. (2d) 303 (B.C.S.C.).
[120] *Ibid.*, at 304.

lawful. The accused cannot invoke the section if he used unnecessary force which provoked the deceased. . . .[121]

Section 41 will not justify shooting at a trespasser or the infliction of serious injury; if these are to be justified it must be done under section 34 as self-defence. The use of a weapon to prevent a trespass cannot be justified unless in self-defence.[122] The police may be trespassers. Thus, the Supreme Court of Canada, in *Colet v. R.*,[123] held that an accused who attacked police officers who had come to the accused's property to search for firearms was justified. The officers held a warrant authorizing them to seize firearms, but did not have a search warrant. The court held that police are not justified in entering private property unless they announce their presence and demonstrate their right to enter by stating a lawful reason for their entry.

11. ALIBI

The defence of alibi is raised by evidence that the accused was not present when the alleged offence was committed. The defence will succeed when the accused satisfies the judge or jury that he actually was present or raises a reasonable doubt that he was present. The onus is not on the accused to establish that he was not present, but rather is on the Crown to prove that he was at the scene of a crime.

In *R. v. Miller*,[124] Martin J.A. said that the accused's evidence alone might satisfy the jury as to an alibi, but Mr. Justice Galliher stated that an alibi must be proved by evidence other than that of the accused, and his view was shared by the other judge who heard the appeal. However, whether evidence by an accused that he was not present when a crime was committed may not be termed an alibi, it is certainly open to the trier of fact to believe such evidence and acquit the accused. In *Lizotte v. R.*,[125] Cartwright J. said that the proper approach to alibi evidence was that the trier of fact should, even if the alibi has not been proved, acquit the accused if the evidence in support of it raised a reasonable doubt of the guilt of the accused.

Some difference appears in the case law whether the trier of fact should look at the evidence of alibi alone and give the accused the benefit of any doubt on that issue, or whether it is more appropriate to consider all the evidence, including the evidence of alibi, and give the accused the benefit of any

---

[121] (1986), 29 C.C.C. (3d) 467 at 471 (Alta. C.A.).
[122] *R. v. Baxter* (1975), 27 C.C.C. (2d) 97 (Ont. C.A.); *R. v. Figueira* (1981), 63 C.C.C. (2d) 409 (Ont. C.A.).
[123] (1980), 57 C.C.C. (2d) 105 (S.C.C.).
[124] (1923), 40 C.C.C. 130 (B.C.C.A.).
[125] (1950), 99 C.C.C. 113 (S.C.C.).

doubt which arises on the whole of the case. The matter cannot be considered to have been definitively settled, although it would certainly appear that if, after considering the evidence of alibi, the trier of fact has a reasonable doubt the doubt should be resolved in favour of the accused.

If the defence of alibi is raised, then not much weight will be given to it unless the accused testifies. It has also been held that the defence should be raised at the earliest possible moment and that if it is not, the jury may take this into account in weighing the evidence.[126]

12. ACCIDENT

Sometimes an accused will have a defence if the crime with which he was charged is caused by accident. An accident will not in all cases constitute a defence. Under section 229(*b*) a person may be convicted of murder if he engages in an act that he knows is likely to cause death and being reckless whether death ensues or not, causes death by accident. Ordinarily a person is held to intend the natural consequences of his intentional act, but he is not taken to intend his accidental acts.

In *R. v. Hughes*,[127] the accused entered a shop intending to rob the shop. The family of the victim was sitting in a room at the rear separated by a half door with curtains. Hughes fired a shot through the partition of the door and a second one through the curtains wounding the victim. A struggle ensued and Hughes shot and killed the victim. The Supreme Court of Canada ordered a new trial, holding that the trial judge did not deal with the possibility that the jury could find that the pistol had been discharged accidentally. Duff C.J.C. stated that the trial judge should have told the jury that they ought to find a verdict of manslaughter if they thought the pistol was not discharged by the voluntary act of Hughes and that he did not anticipate and ought not to have anticipated that his conduct might bring about a struggle in which somebody's death might be caused.

In *Woolmington v. D.P.P.*,[128] a man was accused of killing his wife and gave evidence that the death occurred as a result of his shifting the gun from his shoulder across his chest. He said that the gun went off without any intention on his part. The House of Lords stated that the presumption that a man intends the natural consequences of his acts could not mean that the accused must satisfy the jury that he did not have such an intention. Rather, the jury must be instructed that it would consider all the evidence and that if it had a reasonable doubt on the matter the accused was entitled to be acquitted.

---

[126] *Russell v. R.* (1936), 67 C.C.C. 28 (S.C.C.).
[127] (1942), 78 C.C.C. 257 (S.C.C.).
[128] [1935] A.C. 462 (H.L.).

In *R. v. Tennant*, the Ontario Court of Appeal overturned the conviction of the accused for murder and ordered a new trial. The court held:

> The jury should have . . . been told that if they had a reasonable doubt that the gun was discharged accidentally and if they were not satisfied beyond a reasonable doubt that the appellant Naccarato procured and used the gun for an unlawful object and knew or ought to have known that his use of the gun in the circumstances was likely to cause death, they must acquit him of murder. They must then consider whether or not he was guilty of manslaughter. When death is accidentally caused by the commission of an unlawful act which any reasonable person would inevitably realize must subject another person to, at least, the risk of some harm resulting therefrom, albeit not serious harm, that is manslaughter.[129]

The court held that the jurors should have been instructed

> . . . that if they were satisfied that the accused was engaged in a lawful purpose or had a reasonable doubt in this regard and his death was caused by the accidental discharge of the pistol, then, in the absence of proof of criminal negligence, accident was a complete defence.[130]

The court held that a person could be convicted of murder under section 229(c) if the jury was satisfied that an accused procured and used a firearm for the unlawful purpose of assaulting the deceased and if the accused knew, or ought to have known, that his conduct was likely to bring about a situation in which someone might be killed.

13. CHARTER DEFENCES

(a) General

The Charter has broadened the defences which are available to someone charged with a criminal offence. Legislation which violates the fundamental rights set out in the Charter, such as the presumption of innocence or the right to be tried in accordance with principles of fundamental justice, can be struck down as contravening the Charter. The Supreme Court of Canada held, in *R. v. Big M Drug Mart Ltd.*,[131] that an accused cannot be convicted of an offence where the statute creating the offence is unconstitutional. Thus, an accused who is subjected to an unreasonable search may be able to have such evidence excluded at his or her trial. Whether the evidence is excluded will depend on whether a judge concludes that the admission of the evidence would bring the administration of justice into disrepute. Before the Charter came into effect,

---

[129] (1975), 31 C.R.N.S. 1 at 19 (Ont. C.A.).
[130] *Ibid.*
[131] (1985), 18 C.C.C. (3d) 385 (S.C.C.).

the Supreme Court of Canada held that a trial judge had no discretion to exclude evidence on the basis that its admission would bring the administration of justice into disrepute. The admission of evidence has been discussed elsewhere in this book, particularly Chapter 5, A Person's Rights and Obligations Under the Criminal Law. For purposes of this chapter, it is sufficient to note that the Charter's protections have, in many cases, led to an accused being acquitted after evidence obtained in a manner which contravened the Charter was not admitted.

The Charter's protection against being deprived of one's life, liberty and security of the person except in accordance with principles of fundamental justice had also had a profound effect on the right of Parliament to make criminal law. Section 7 of the Charter states:

> **7.** Everyone has the right to life, liberty and security of the person and the right not to be deprived thereof except in accordance with the principles of fundamental justice.

When section 7 was first drafted, politicians and high-ranking civil servants believed that the section only guaranteed procedural fairness. There was widespread opinion that section 7 only protected such rights as the accused's right to be represented by a lawyer, the right to have notice of the charges laid and a full opportunity to present one's case and cross-examine witnesses. The then federal Minister of Justice, The Honourable Jean Chrétien, and many provincial Attorneys General espoused the view that section 7 would be limited to procedural fairness and could never be used to challenge the content of legislation. In *Reference Re Section 94(2) of the Motor Vehicle Act*, the Supreme Court of Canada held that section 7 was not confined to procedural protection and can be used to review the content of the legislation.[132] The Supreme Court's ruling is of enormous significance because it means that section 7 can be used to strike down legislation which unfairly deprives an accused of his right to life, liberty and security of the person.

---

[132] (1986), 23 C.C.C. (3d) 289 (S.C.C.).

13

The Trial

1. THE ADVERSARY SYSTEM AND THE ROLE OF JUDGES

The Canadian legal system is based upon what is known as the adversary system of justice. Under the adversarial system of justice lawyers, as advocates, attempt to convince the impartial arbitrator who judges the case that the relief sought should be granted. In a criminal case the defence lawyer attempts to convince the judge that his or her client should be acquitted, while the Crown prosecutor attempts to show that the accused's guilt has been proven beyond a reasonable doubt. The principal features of the adversarial model have been described by Evans J.A. in *Phillips v. Ford Motor Co. of Can.*, where His Lordship stated:

> Our mode of trial procedure is based upon the adversary system in which the contestants seek to establish through relevant supporting evidence, before an impartial trier of facts, those events or happenings which form the bases of their allegations. This procedure assumes that the litigants, assisted by their counsel, will fully and diligently present all the material facts which have evidentiary value in support of their respective positions and that these disputed facts will receive from a trial judge a dispassionate and impartial consideration in order to arrive at the truth of the matters in controversy. A trial is not intended to be a scientific exploration with the presiding judge assuming the role of a research director; it is a forum established for the purpose of providing justice for the litigants. Undoubtedly a Court must be concerned with truth, in the sense that it accepts as true certain sworn evidence and rejects other testimony as unworthy of belief, but it can not embark upon a quest for the "scientific" or "technological" truth when such an adventure does violence to the primary function of the Court, which has always been to do justice, according to law.[1]

The adversarial system of justice is completely different than the inquisitorial system of justice which exists in much of Europe, including France and

---

[1] [1971] 2 O.R. 637 at 657 (Ont. C.A.).

Italy, where a trial judge plays an active role in investigating the matters before the court.

Many people believe that the principal function of a court is to seek the truth. But while a court attempts to determine the truth of what occurred, a civil or criminal trial must, of necessity, be an approximation of the truth. A court is not concerned with truth in the abstract. A court attempts to arrive at the truth within the context of an adversarial system of justice where strict rules are applied as to what evidence is admissible and what evidence is not admissible. Mr. Justice Haines, of the Supreme Court of Ontario, has noted that the adversarial system of justice is mainly concerned with proving one's case in accordance with accepted rules of evidence applied in a court of law. In this regard, His Lordship noted that a trial is not an open-ended search for the truth, saying:

> A trial is not a faithful reconstruction of the events as if recorded on some giant television screen. It is an historical recall of that part of the events in which witnesses which may be found and presented in an intensely adversary system where the object is quantum of proof.[2]

The adversary system of justice is not without its critics and some commentators believe that the truth can be a casualty under such a system of justice. Proponents of the adversary system of justice argue that it is the best system because it recognizes that truth should not be secured at the cost of the accused's fundamental rights, such as the presumption of innocence and the right against self-incrimination. They also argue what while it is often impossible to attain the absolute truth about events which happened some time ago, a just result is best secured by having each party present the evidence supporting its position.

2. THE PRESUMPTION OF INNOCENCE

In Canada, Britain and the United States, the accused is presumed innocent until proven guilty. The presumption of innocence is the cornerstone of our criminal law. In a criminal trial, the onus is on the prosecution to prove the accused's guilt beyond a reasonable doubt. Generally speaking, the prosecution bears the burden of establishing every element of the offence and there is no duty upon the accused to prove anything.

There are several offences in the Criminal Code[3] where Parliament has provided that the onus is on the accused to prove that he or she did not have the intent to commit the offence presumed by the section. Section 349 is an example of a section which places such an onus on the accused.

---

[2] *R. v. Lalonde* (1971), 15 C.R.N.S. 1 at 4 (Ont. H.C.).
[3] R.S.C. 1985, c. C-46.

349. (1) Every one who without lawful excuse, the proof of which lies on him, enters or is in a dwelling-house with intent to commit an indictable offence therein is guilty of an indictable offence and liable to imprisonment for a term not exceeding ten years.

(2) For the purposes of proceedings under this section, evidence that an accused, without lawful excuse, entered or was in a dwelling-house is, in the absence of any evidence to the contrary, proof that he entered or was in the dwelling-house with intent to commit an indictable offence therein.

The effect of this section is that the Crown does not have to prove that the accused intended to commit the offence. Once the accused is found in a dwelling-house, the onus shifts to the accused to establish that he or she did not have the intent to commit an indictable offence. This section is an example of the statutory exceptions which place an evidential burden on the accused because the onus is normally on the Crown to establish all the essential ingredients of an offence, such as that the accused acted with a particular intent.

The presumption of innocence has now been entrenched in the Canadian Charter of Rights and Freedoms,[4] which means that it is now part of the supreme law of Canada. Section 11(*d*) of the Charter provides that:

11. Any person charged with an offence has the right

. . . .

(*d*) to be presumed innocent until proven guilty according to law in a fair and public hearing by an independent and impartial tribunal. . . .

The entrenchment of the presumpton of innocence in the Charter of Rights has called in to question legislation which forces the accused to prove his or her innocence. Thus, the reverse onus provision in the Narcotic Control Act[5] has already been struck down by the Supreme Court of Canada.

3. REASONABLE DOUBT

(a) Defined

The term "reasonable doubt" has been defined in many cases. However, the definition given in *R. v. Sears*,[6] a 1947 decision of the Ontario Court of Appeal, remains an excellent definition of the term. In *R. v. Sears*, Mr. Justice Roach said that reasonable doubt means:

---

[4] Being Part I of the Constitution Act, 1982 [en. by the Canada Act, 1982 (U.K.), c. 11, s. 1].

[5] R.S.C. 1985, c. N-1.

[6] [1948] O.R. 9 (Ont. C.A.).

By reasonable doubt as to a person's guilt is meant that real doubt — real as distinguished from illusory — which an honest juror has after considering all the circumstances of the case and as a result of which he is unable to say: "I am morally certain of his guilt". Moral certainty does not mean absolute certainty. Absolute, that is demonstrable, certainty is generally impossible and juries might well be told that in discharging their serious responsibility their consciences need not be racked and tortured because of the fact that absolute certainty is impossible. . . . . if, after applying themselves to the best of their ability, they are, in a criminal trial, morally certain of the guilt of the accused, then it is their duty to return a verdict of guilty. It might even turn out later that they were wrong but they need not be mentally tormented by that possibility, provided that they presently use their best judgment and are presently morally certain of the prisoner's guilt.

It is the necessity for such moral certainty that prevents a jury in a criminal trial from testing the guilt of the accused by that standard of doubt which would influence them in their ordinary daily affairs. In our daily affairs we constantly act on probabilities and seldom on moral certainty. It is rudimentary that a jury can never convict simply because they conclude that the prisoner is probably guilty. They must be able to say: "he really is guilty; of that I am morally certain." In the process of making decisions in our daily affairs, we resolve doubts that confront us by considering the whole balance of probabilities. By way of example, a doubt that would be insufficient to deter us from a particular business decision, the wisdom of which is gauged by the balance of probabilities, is something considerably removed from the doubt that would deter us where moral certainty is to be the gauge.[7]

(b) Explaining Reasonable Doubt

In *Linney v. R.*,[8] the Supreme Court of Canada held that there is no one formula for explaining legal principles, such as reasonable doubt, saying that one explanation may be as good as another depending upon the understanding which was conveyed to a jury. The court held that an appeal court should consider the meaning which would have been conveyed to a jury. Having said that there may be more than one way of explaining reasonable doubt, Dickson J. stated:

The Court must be satisfied that the jury would understand the onus was on the Crown to prove each issue or negative each defence beyond a reasonable doubt. They must realize that the reasonable doubt doctrine is always engaged; that it is not displaced in respect of the defences. They must be clear in their minds that, if they have reasonable doubt on any issue, they have the duty to allow the accused to succeed on that issue.[9]

The degree of proof required in a criminal case may be contrasted with the proof required in a civil case. Civil cases are decided upon a balance of

---

[7] *Ibid.*, at 14.
[8] (1977), 32 C.C.C. (2d) 294 (S.C.C.).
[9] *Ibid.*, at 297.

probabilities and the plaintiff is not required to prove his or her case beyond a reasonable doubt. The burden of proof in a civil case has been explained by Lord Denning, a famous British judge, in *Miller v. Minister of Pensions.*[10] His Lordship defined the standard as follows:

> That degree is well settled. It must carry a reasonable degree of probability, but not so high as is required in a criminal case. If the evidence is such that the tribunal can say: 'We think it more probable than not,' the burden is discharged, but if the probabilities are equal, it is not.'[11]

4. "GUILT" IN FACT AND "GUILT" IN LAW

A public opinion sampling of criminal defence lawyers would probably reveal that the most frequently asked question by members of the public is: "How can you defend someone whom you know to be guilty?" The question reveals a curiosity about the criminal justice system and a profound ignorance of the workings of the system. The question presupposes that a lawyer who defends a client he or she believes has committed a prohibited act is acting unethically. The question assumes that only those persons who are factually innocent — that is to say, they did not commit the prohibited act — are entitled to a defence. The general public can be forgiven for believing that a defence lawyer who defends someone whom he or she knows to be "guilty," in the sense most people understand the word, is acting improperly. After all, the public's view of defence attorneys has been distorted by television which shows defence lawyers only defending those clients who are innocent of any wrong-doing. Typically, television shows portray defence lawyers as white knights in shining armour: people who rescue innocent defendants who have been wrongfully accused of committing a crime. In the time-honoured tradition of television courtroom dramas, the "real" guilty party spontaneously confesses his or her guilt having undergone strenuous questioning from the defence.

Television's portrayal of criminal defence work bears no resemblance to reality. The vast number of clients who are defended by criminal lawyers in Canada, Britain and the United States are factually "guilty" in the sense that they have committed a prohibited act. The defendant may have committed such an act, but have a good legal defence to the charge. For example, the defendant may have killed someone, but been insane when the killing was committed. In such a case, the defendant, while factually "guilty," will have a defence at law.

Similarly, someone who is charged with first degree murder will, if the

---

[10] [1947] 2 All E.R. 372 (K.B.D.).
[11] *Ibid.*, at 374.

evidence establishes that the accused was, because of drunkenness, incapable of forming the specific intent required to commit first degree murder, have a defence to the first degree murder charge and in the circumstances described above will be found guilty of the lesser offence of manslaughter. In other words, drunkenness is a partial defence to a charge of first degree murder in that it reduces first degree murder to manslaughter.

In Canada, the Charter of Rights has given rise to several defences which were not previously available. Everyone is now protected against unreasonable search and seizure. Accordingly, if a police officer conducts an illegal search for narcotics, and a court decides that the search is unreasonable, the court can exclude the evidence obtained which may result in the accused being acquitted. Thus, although police officers may have found narcotics in the accused's apartment, the accused, although factually "guilty," would have a good legal defence to the charge. Recently, the Supreme Court of Canada overturned an accused's conviction for murder because the accused's right to counsel under the Charter had been infringed. The case, which may have caused consternation in some quarters, illustrates the kinds of legal arguments which defence counsel frequently raise in contesting the legal guilt of their clients. Such defences must be made and upheld if our freedoms are to be preserved.

5. FIRST COURT APPEARANCE

When an accused first appears in court to set a date for trial, the accused will be asked if he or she has retained a lawyer. If the accused has not retained a lawyer, the accused will be given an opportunity to hire a lawyer. In jurisdictions where there is a private legal aid scheme, an accused who cannot afford a lawyer will, if his application to legal aid is accepted, be able to select a lawyer of his or her choice from a list of lawyers who have agreed to participate in the legal aid panel. When an accused first appears in court to set a date, the judge will usually ask the accused whether he or she is applying for legal aid. If the accused is applying for legal aid, the matter will usually be put over for two weeks to set a date. Judges will not allow accused persons to use legal aid as a delaying tactic and, accordingly, will require proof that the accused actually applied for legal aid before granting further adjournments. After an accused has appeared in court on a first appearance, the accused will be asked to bring a letter from his or her lawyer giving trial dates.

When an accused presents the court with a letter from his or her lawyer setting out trial dates, the lawyer has gone on the record as representing the client. This means that the lawyer is committed to act for the client and will, unless his or her name is removed from the record, be obligated to appear at the accused's trial. Thus, lawyers will want to ensure that they are prepared to represent the accused and that their fees are secure before setting a trial date. If an accused cannot get legal aid and cannot agree with a lawyer as to an appropriate fee, the judge will inform the accused that the matter has been marked pre-emptory which means that it will proceed to trial whether or not the accused has a lawyer.

Someone who is charged with an indictable offence must appear in court personally to set a date. However, an accused who is charged with a summary conviction offence may appear by an agent. Thus, a lawyer could set a date for the accused without the accused being present. An accused who is charged with a summary conviction offence may not have to appear at his or her trial and could technically have an agent appear at the trial. Accordingly, a lawyer could appear in the accused's stead. However, the trial judge can order that the accused appear at trial. While it is permissible to send an agent to set a trial date on a summary conviction matter, it would be unwise for someone who is charged with a summary conviction criminal offence not to appear personally for trial.

6. CHOICE OF COURTS

The jurisdiction of the criminal courts to try an accused has been discussed in Chapter 4, A Basic Overview of the Criminal Code. Most criminal offences will be tried in front of a provincial court judge. However, for most serious criminal offences the accused has an election as to the mode of trial. When the accused has an election as to the mode of trial, the clerk of the court will put the election to the accused in the words of section 536(2) of the Criminal Code, asking the accused whether he or she wishes to be tried by a provincial court judge without a jury and without having had a preliminary inquiry; or to have a preliminary inquiry and to be tried by a judge without a jury; or to have a preliminary inquiry and to be tried by a court composed of a judge and a jury. In some courts, the accused may be asked to make an election as to the mode of trial on the first appearance to set a date, but usually the accused will not be asked to elect a mode of trial until the trial date. If an accused appearing before a provincial court judge elects to be tried by a higher court on the date of trial, a preliminary inquiry will be held. If the judge commits the accused for trial, the matter will be set down to set a date in a court of criminal jurisdiction.

(a) Election by Accused

The election as to which court to be tried in is a matter which warrants careful consideration by an accused and his or her lawyer. The election is an important strategic consideration and may make a difference between the accused being acquitted or convicted. Someone who is in custody awaiting trial will usually elect to be tried in provincial court. An accused who elects to be tried by a provincial court judge will come to trial much more quickly than an accused who elects to be tried by a higher court. There are not as many time-consuming matters tried in the provincial courts and the trial lists are much shorter than the lists in the district court or the Supreme Court.

Usually someone who is being tried by a District Court judge or by a Supreme Court judge will want to have a preliminary hearing which will mean that the trial would take considerably longer than if the trial were held in provincial court. If the accused elects to be tried by a judge and jury, it may in a serious case, take half a day to select a jury. Because of the backlog of cases, trials in the higher courts do not always proceed when they are scheduled to proceed. This is particularly true of a jury trial. In short, someone who wishes to expedite his or her trial will usually elect to be tried in provincial court.

(b) Tactical Considerations

If an accused is facing a serious charge, the accused, whether in custody or not, may wish to be tried by a court of criminal jurisdiction — i.e., a County or District Court judge or by judge and jury. Depending upon the seriousness of the charge, the accused may wish to have a preliminary inquiry to obtain adequate disclosure as to the circumstances of the crime. If the accused wishes to test the strength of the Crown's case through rigorous cross-examination, or by forcing the Crown to disclose the essential elements of its case, the accused should elect to have a preliminary inquiry and to be tried by a judge other than a provincial court judge.

7. THE PRELIMINARY INQUIRY AND COMMITTAL FOR TRIAL

At the preliminary inquiry, the Crown will be forced to present sufficient evidence to have the accused committed for trial. This does not mean that the Crown attorney must call every witness who can give evidence against the accused. Rather, the Crown must present sufficient evidence to establish a *prima facie* case. The courts have held that it is improper for a judge to weigh the evidence at a preliminary inquiry — that is, make findings as to the guilt or innocence of the accused. Accordingly, the preliminary inquiry affords the accused the opportunity to test the strengths and weaknesses of the Crown's case against the accused through cross-examination without running the risk of being convicted of an offence. If a Crown witness gives contradictory evidence at trial the witness may be faced with the evidence given at the preliminary inquiry, and the judge or jury made aware of the contradiction in the testimony of the witness. The accused rarely testifies at a preliminary inquiry. The accused's testimony would serve little purpose since the judge cannot weigh the evidence.

The test for committing someone to stand trial following a preliminary inquiry has been set out in the *United States of America v. Sheppard*,[12] a decision of the Supreme Court of Canada. In the *Sheppard* case Ritchie J. stated that the test for committal is as follows:

> I agree that the duty imposed upon a "Justice" under s. 475(1) is the same as that which governs a trial judge sitting with a jury in deciding whether the evidence is "sufficient" to justify him in withdrawing the case from the jury and this is to be determined according to whether or not there is any evidence upon which a reasonable jury properly instructed could return a verdict of guilty. The "justice", in accordance with this principle, is, in my opinion, required to commit an accused person for trial in any case in which there is admissible evidence which could, if it were believed, result in a conviction.[13]

The test for committal set down in the *Sheppard* case is not a very strict test and most preliminary inquiries result in the accused being committed for trial. The fact that the accused has been committed for trial does not mean that the accused will be convicted. A judge presiding over a preliminary inquiry usually only hears part of the case because usually the defence does not call any evidence, and is not in a position to assess the evidence and determine the guilt or innocence of the accused.

Where the accused has previously obtained disclosure as to the evidence which would be given at the preliminary inquiry, the accused may wish to dispense with the inquiry. In such circumstances, the accused would waive the preliminary inquiry and consent to a committal for trial. The statutory authority for consenting to a committal for trial is found in section 549 of the Criminal Code, which provides:

> **549.** (1) Notwithstanding any other provision of this Act, the justice may, at any stage of a preliminary inquiry, with the consent of the accused and the prosecutor, order the accused to stand trial in the court having criminal jurisdiction, without taking or recording any evidence or further evidence.
>
> (2) Where an accused is ordered to stand trial under subsection (1), the justice shall endorse on the information a statement of the consent of the accused and the prosecutor, and the accused shall thereafter be dealt with in all respects as if ordered to stand trial under section 548.

In some cases, it may be to the advantage of the accused to waive the preliminary hearing because the prosecution will not have the advantage of seeing how its witnesses testify. In a case where the only evidence linking the accused to the crime is weak eyewitness identification the accused may be better served if the preliminary hearing is waived so that the prosecution is not

---

[12] (1976), 34 C.R.N.S. 207 (S.C.C.).
[13] *Ibid.*, at 211.

given an opportunity to shore up the weaknesses in its case. However, it is advisable to have a preliminary hearing where the charge is particularly serious, such as a murder charge.

8. TRIAL BY JUDGE ALONE OR TRIAL BY JURY

An accused who has an election as to the mode of trial may not wish to be tried by a provincial court judge. If the accused wishes to be tried by a higher court, the accused will elect to be tried by a judge and jury or a judge sitting alone. There are few principles which guide the accused in making such an election. The election will depend upon the facts involved in the particular case. Lawyers and social scientists believe that many juries are not dispassionate when an accused is charged with a particularly heinous offence, such as a sexual assault involving a child. In a case involving the sexual assault of a child, defence counsel will want the accused to be tried by a judge sitting alone.

In other cases, a jury may not be dispassionate because of the sympathy they feel for the accused. Such was the case in *R. v. Stafford*,[14] a famous Nova Scotia case, where the accused Jean Stafford was acquitted by a jury of murdering her husband on the grounds that she had acted in self-defence. In this case, the jury heard evidence that the accused, Jean Stafford, had been brutally beaten by her common-law husband, Billie Stafford, until the night when the accused shot and killed her husband. There was no evidence which would justify a verdict of self-defence. The evidence presented at trial indicated that Mrs. Stafford shot her husband when he was passed out behind the wheel of his pick-up truck. This evidence was completely inconsistent with the law of self-defence under the Criminal Code and the jury's verdict was no doubt brought about by the sympathy which they had for the accused, Jean Stafford. The jury's verdict did not stand and was overturned on an appeal by the Crown to the Nova Scotia Court of Appeal, which held that the trial judge had erred in leaving self-defence with the jury. The court ordered a new trial and Mrs. Stafford pleaded guilty to manslaughter. She was sentenced to six months' imprisonment with two years' probation.

Juries are often sympathetic to accused persons who have been charged with committing criminal offences which many members of the public believe are victimless crimes. This is particularly true in cases where large segments of the public believe that the activity which forms the subject matter of the charge should be decriminalized. Historically, many juries were reluctant to convict consenting adults of morals offences such as gross indecency, believing that sexual acts which consenting adults committed in private should not form the

---

[14] (1983), 37 C.R. (3d) 198 (N.S.C.A.).

basis of a criminal charge. More recently, juries have been reluctant to convict doctors who perform illegal abortions. Many members of the public do not view the providing of abortion on demand as a criminal offence and refuse to apply the law as given under the Criminal Code. The classic case in this regard is the *Morgentaler* case: juries on four different occasions have refused to convict Dr. Henry Morgentaler of performing an illegal abortion under section 251 [287] of the Criminal Code.[15]

9. TRIAL BY JURY

(a) Historical Background

Trial by jury, which is one of the most cherished features of our legal system, came to the colonies of Prince Edward Island, Nova Scotia and New Brunswick as part of the common law of England. The right to trial by jury in criminal and civil cases did not exist in Ontario and Quebec until 1791 when Ontario and Quebec were divided into the provinces of Upper and Lower Canada.

The rationale for the jury system has been eloquently stated by an English judge, Lord Devlin, who expressed his admiration for the jury system as follows:

> Each jury is a little parliament. The jury sense is the parliamentary sense. I cannot see the one dying and the other surviving. The first object of any tyrant in Whitehall would be to make Parliament utterly subservient to his will; and the next to overthrow or diminish trial by jury, for no tyrant could afford to leave a subject's freedom in the hands of twelve of his countrymen. So that trial by jury is more than an instrument of justice and more than one wheel of the constitution: it is the lamp that shows that freedom lives.[16]

Lord Devlin believed that jurors provided a counterbalance to judges who were appointed by the government in power. In Lord Devlin's view, juries could not be counted on as frequently as judges to do the government's bidding. In this regard, His Lordship stated:

> Judges are appointed by the executive and I do not know of any better way of appointing them. Our history has shown that the executive has found it much easier to find judges who will do what it wants than it has to find amenable juries. Blackstone, whose time was not so far removed from that of the Stuarts thought of

---

[15] See (1973), 14 C.C.C. (2d) 459 (Que. Q.B.); (1976), 33 C.R.N.S. 244 (Que. C.A.); (1985), 48 C.R. (3d) 1 (Ont. C.A.). See also D. Stuart's Annotation to *R. v. Morgentaler* 48 C.R. (3d) 1, at 5.

[16] As cited in R.E. Salhany, *The Origin of Rights* (Toronto: Carswell, 1986), p. 111.

the jury as a safeguard against "the violence and partiality of judges appointed by the Crown."

Commenting on that in 1784, Mr. Justice Willes said: "I am sure no danger of this sort is to be apprehended from the judges of the present age: but in our determinations it will be prudent to look forward into futurity." Although in 1956 we may claim that "futurity" has not yet arrived, it still remains prudent to look forward into it.[17]

Lord Devlin also stated that the jury system was important because juries protected people against laws which were not fair:

It [i.e., trial by jury] gives protection against laws which the ordinary man may regard as harsh and oppressive. I do not mean by that no more than that it is a protection against tyranny. It is that: but it is also an insurance that the criminal law will conform to the ordinary man's idea of what is fair and just. If it does not, the jury will not be a party to its enforcement. They have in the past used their power of acquittal to defeat the full operation of laws which they thought to be too hard. I dare say that the cases in which a jury defies the law are very rare. Juries do not deliberately marshall legal considerations on one side and broader considerations of justice and mercy on the other and bring them into conflict on the field of conscience. Their minds are not trained to the making of an orderly separation and opposition; they are more likely to allow one set of considerations to act upon the other in such a way as to confuse the issues. One way or the other they are prone to give effect to their repugnance to a law by refusing to convict under it, and no one can say them nay. The small body of men, who under modern conditions constitute the effective body of legislators, have to bear this in mind. It affects the character of the laws they make, for it is no use making laws which will not be enforced. They may put it down to the perversity of juries, though for my part I think that if there is a law which the juryman constantly shows by his verdicts that he dislikes, it is worth examining the law to see if there is something wrong with it rather than with the juryman. . . . The ordinary member of Parliament participates in law-making by helping with the deails, but in all matters of principle he is obedient — subject to his conscience — to the party whip, which is the executive. The executive knows that in dealing with the liberty of the subject it must not do anything which would seriously disturb the conscience of the average member of Parliament or of the average juryman. I know of no other real checks that exist today upon the power of the executive.[18]

(b) Criticism of Trial by Jury

While most citizens regard trial by jury as being an essential component of the democratic system, trial by jury is not universally accepted. Some commentators have argued that a jury comprised of laymen is not qualified to make findings of fact in criminal or civil cases. Many critics of the jury system believe that juries do not have the ability to understand complex legal issues. In

---

[17] *Ibid.*
[18] *Ibid.*, 111-112.

this regard, a well-known critic of the jury system, Dean E.N. Griswold, of the Harvard Law School, stated in 1963 in his dean's report that:

> The jury trial is the apotheosis of the amateur. Why should anyone think that 12 persons brought in from the street, selected in various ways, for their lack of general ability, should have any special capacity for deciding controversies between persons.[19]

An American judge, Jerome Frank, has expressed similar sentiments towards juries, saying:

> While the jury can contribute nothing of value so far as the law is concerned, it has infinite capacity for mischief, for twelve men can easily misunderstand more law in a minute than the judge can explain in an hour.[20]

(c) Right to be Tried by Jury

(i) *General*

Despite the fact that trial by jury is regarded as one of the essential cornerstones of our legal system, there is not a universal right in Canada to be tried by a jury comprised of one's peers. Thus, someone who is charged with a summary conviction offence has no right to elect to be tried by a judge and jury and will be tried by a provincial court judge sitting alone. A provincial court judge has absolute jurisdiction under section 553 of the Criminal Code to try an accused who is charged with one of the indictable offences set out in that section. Section 553 deals with matters such as obtaining money or property by false pretenses, theft, keeping gaming or betting houses where the offence does not involve property exceeding $5,000 and offences such as driving while disqualified. Section 553 offences are the less serious indictable offences, as the maximum imprisonment for committing such offences does not exceed two years. Also, people who are serving in the military will, if they are charged with military offences, be tried by a military court rather than by a judge and jury. Furthermore, an accused who is being tried as a young offender does not have the right to be tried by a jury of his peers. Thus, a young offender who is charged with a very serious crime, such as first degree murder, will not have the right to be tried by a judge and jury.

(ii) *Charter guarantee*

The right to be tried by a jury is guaranteed by the Charter. Section 11(*f*) of the Charter states:

---

[19] As cited in Hans & Vidmar, *Judging the Jury* (New York: Plenum Press, 1986) p. 114.
[20] *Ibid.*, p. 15.

11. Any person charged with an offence has the right

. . . .

(f) except in the case of an offence under military law tried before a military tribunal, to the benefit of trial by jury where the maximum punishment for the offence is imprisonment for five years or a more severe punishment. . .

(iii) Limitations on right

Section 598 of the Criminal Code provides that an accused who fails to appear without lawful excuse may lose his right to be tried by a jury. In *R. v. Bryant*,[21] the Ontario Court of Appeal held that section 526.1 [598] contravened section 11(f) of the Charter and was not a reasonable limitation which could be justified under section 1 of the Charter. In so holding, Blair J.A., who wrote one of the concurring opinions, stated that section 526.1 [598] could not be justified on the basis of administrative convenience. In holding that the legislation cannot be justified as a reasonable limitation, His Lordship stated:

> Section 526.1 must, of course, be viewed in a much wider context. The sanction it imposes on absconding accused is part of the legislative scheme described above which was designed to overcome the abuse of the judicial system and other administrative problems arising from the *Bail Reform Act*. In my view, this may be taken to be a valid legislative purpose. In this case, the Crown must establish that the denial of jury trial to absconding accused is necessary for the attainment of that purpose. In my opinion, it has failed to do so.
>
> . . . there is no evidence in this case that the proper operation of the *Bail Reform Act* and the attainment of its objectives is dependent upon section 526.1. This section, therefore, cannot be justified as a reasonable limit on the right to trial by jury under s. 1 of the Charter.[22]

The Ontario Court of Appeal's ruling in *Bryant* conflicts with the Alberta Court of Appeal's ruling in *R. v. Crate*[23] holding that section 526.1 [598] of the Criminal Code did not infringe section 11(f) of the Charter. The Alberta Court concluded that an accused who failed to appear should be deemed to have elected trial by a judge and that the section was a reasonable limitation. The reasoning is not persuasive.

The Ontario Court of Appeal has held that young persons tried under the Young Offenders Act[24] are not entitled to be tried by a jury. In *R. v. R.L.*, the Court held that section 11(f) of the Charter did not apply to the Young Offenders Act because the maximum imprisonment for crimes committed

---

[21] (1984), 16 C.C.C. (3d) 408 (Ont. C.A.).
[22] *Ibid.*, at 425-426.
[23] (1983), 7 C.C.C. (3d) 127 (Alta. C.A.).
[24] R.S.C. 1985, c. Y-1.

under it is not five years or more.[25] Section 20(1)(*k*) of the Young Offenders Act provides that a young person who commits an offence which would carry a maximum penalty of life imprisonment under the Criminal Code is not liable to receive more than three years' imprisonment under the Young Offenders Act. Section 20(1)(*k*.1) was subsequently added to provide for a maximum disposition of five years less a day, consisting of a commital to custody not exceeding three years and a placement under conditional supervision. In *R. v. R.L.*, Morden J.A., who delivered the judgment of the court, held that section 11(*f*) did not apply to someone who has been tried as a young offender. In so holding, His Lordship stated:

> . . . It seems reasonably plain to me that the right to a jury trial conferred by this provision turns on what is at stake for the person charged. If the maximum punishment for the offence for which he or she could be liable is not "imprisonment for five years or a more severe punishment", then the person charged has no right under section 11(*f*).[26]

Bill C-37, which received Royal Assent on June 26, 1995, but is not yet proclaimed, replaces section 20(1)(*k*.1), increasing the maximum disposition to 10 years. It remains to be seen whether the increased penalty will affect a young person's right to be tried by a jury.

(iv) *When mandatory*

Certain Criminal Code offences make it mandatory for an accused to be tried by a judge and jury. For example, someone who is charged with murder, treason, piracy or one of the other offences listed in section 469 of the Criminal Code, does not have an election and must be tried by a judge and jury unless the Attorney General of the province consents to the accused being tried by judge alone. Section 469 of the Criminal Code covers the following offences:

1. Treason
2. Murder
3. Alarming her Majesty
4. Intimidating Parliament or a Legislature
5. Inciting to mutiny
6. Seditious offences
7. Piracy
8. Piratical acts
9. Bribery by the holder of a judicial office
10. Being an accessory after the fact to offences of murder, high treason or treason
11. Conspiring to commit any of the above offences

---

[25] (1986), 52 C.R. (3d) 209 (Ont. C.A.).
[26] *Ibid.*, at 215.

12. Attempting to commit any of the offences mentioned in 1 to 7

Section 473 of the Criminal Code provides that an accused who is charged with a section 469 offence may, with the consent of the Attorney General, be tried by a judge of a superior court of criminal jurisdiction sitting without a jury. Section 473 states that:

> **473.** (1) Notwithstanding anything in this Act, an accused charged with an offence listed in section 469 may, with the consent of the accused and the Attorney General, be tried without a jury by a judge of a superior court of criminal jurisdiction.
>
> (2) Notwithstanding anything in this Act, where the consent of an accused and the Attorney General is given in accordance with subsection (1), such consent shall not be withdrawn unless both the accused and the Attorney General agree to the withdrawal.

Having regard to the serious offences listed in section 469, it would be rare for an accused who is charged with a section 469 offence to obtain the Attorney General's consent to be tried by a judge sitting alone.

The Attorney General of a province may, in certain circumstances, override an accused's election to be tried by a judge sitting alone and require an accused to be tried by a judge and jury. Section 568 of the Criminal Code provides:

> **568.** The Attorney General may, notwithstanding that an accused elects under section 536 or re-elects under section 561 to be tried by a judge or provincial court judge, as the case may be, require the accused to be tried by a court composed of a judge and jury, unless the alleged offence is one that is punishable with imprisonment for five years or less, and where the Attorney General so requires, a judge or provincial court judge has no jurisdiction to try the accused under this Part and a preliminary inquiry shall be held prior to the requirement by the Attorney General that the accused be tried by a court composed of a judge and jury.

(d) Qualifications of Jurors

The Criminal Code does not set out what qualifications someone must have in order to serve as a juror, but does state that the provinces may determine whether a person is qualified to sit on a jury. Accordingly, as the individual provinces are free to set their own guidelines, the qualifications may vary from province to province. However, most provinces prohibit someone who has been convicted of a serious criminal offence from serving on a jury. In some districts in the Province of Quebec a sheriff is required by law to provide a jury panel comprised of jurors one half of whom speak English and one half of whom speak French. Section 626 of the Criminal Code provides that:

> **626.** (1) A person who is qualified as a juror according to, and summoned as a juror in accordance with, the laws of a province is qualified to serve as a juror in criminal proceedings in that province.
>
> (2) Notwithstanding any law of a province referred to in subsection (1), no

person may be disqualified, exempted or excused from serving as a juror in criminal proceedings on the grounds of his or her sex.

The National Defence Act[27] excludes members of the armed forces from jury duty.

In Canada, unlike many states in the United States, a jury's verdict must be unanimous. If a jury after careful consideration cannot agree on its verdict, the judge has the power under section 653 of the Criminal Code to discharge the jury and direct that a new jury be empanelled. Alternatively, the judge may adjourn the court on such conditions as is required. When a jury cannot agree on a verdict, the case must start all over again with another jury.

10. ARRAIGNMENT AND PLEA

(a) Arraigning the Accused

Before the accused is asked to plead to the charge, the accused will be arraigned. In other words, the clerk of the court will read the charges as set out in the information or indictment before the accused is called upon to plead to the charge. The following example illustrates the procedure which is followed in arraigning the accused.

> CLERK OF THE COURT: Donald A. MacIntosh, you are charged that on or about the 29th day of July, 1989, at the Municipality of Metropolitan Toronto in the Judicial District of York, you unlawfully did commit an assault on John Smith, and caused bodily harm to the said John Smith, contrary to the Criminal Code, section 266, paragraph (*b*)
>
> How does the Crown elect to proceed on this charge?
>
> THE CROWN: Summarily.
>
> CLERK OF THE COURT: How do you plead to this charge, guilty or not guilty?
>
> THE ACCUSED: Not guilty.

If the accused is committed for trial after a preliminary inquiry is held, the accused will be arraigned before the court which will try the case. Once the accused has been arraigned at trial and pleaded to the charge, the Crown will then call its first witness.

(b) Entering a Plea

The decision as to whether to plead guilty is made by the accused after

---

[27] R.S.C. 1985, c. N-5.

discussion with his lawyer upon the considerations discussed earlier. But the decision must be the accused's. Thus, if the defence counsel enters a plea for her client, the trial judge will ask the accused whether the accused adopts the statements of his lawyer.

(c) Effect of Guilty Plea

If an accused enters a guilty plea, the accused is admitting all the essential elements of the offence. If the facts as read out by the Crown are not substantially correct and the accused appears to have a defence, the judge will not accept the guilty plea. It is not uncommon for an accused who is not represented by a lawyer to tell a judge that he or she is pleading guilty with an explanation. An accused cannot plead guilty with an explanation. An accused must either plead guilty or not guilty. By pleading guilty, the accused is admitting that the facts stated in the Crown brief are substantially correct. If an accused has some explanation for having committed a crime, this explanation, assuming that it does not provide a defence to the charge, should be dealt with when counsel makes submissions as to what sentence the accused should receive.

(d) Objections Before Plea

If defence counsel has an objection to the wording of the charge and believes that the information or indictment should be quashed, counsel must object to the wording of the charge before the accused enters a plea. Furthermore, if defence counsel believes that the section of the Criminal Code under which the accused is charged is unconstitutional, any motion to quash the information or indictment should be made before the accused pleads to the charge.

11. EVIDENCE

(a) Relevant Evidence

The purpose of a criminal trial is not to decide whether the accused is innocent, but rather a trial is held to determine whether the accused is guilty of the offence charged. Accordingly, where an accused is acquitted, this does not mean that the trial judge or the jury is satisfied that the accused is innocent. In a criminal trial, the burden is upon the prosecution to prove the accused's guilt beyond a reasonable doubt in accordance with evidence which is acceptable to the court. Not all evidence is admissible and there are strict rules which govern the type of evidence which can be admitted in a trial. Evidence which is not relevant to the charge before the court is not admissible. Sir James Steven, the author of Canada's first Criminal Code, which still forms the basis of the present day Criminal Code, stated in his book, *A Digest of the Law of Evidence* (1876), that:

> The great bulk of the law of Evidence consists of negative rules declaring what, as the expression runs, is not evidence. The doctrine that all facts in issue and relevant to the issue, and no others, may be proved, is the unexpressed principle which forms the centre of and gives unity to all these express negative rules.[28]

Mr. Justice Pratte, of the Supreme Court of Canada, has explained what it means for evidence to be relevant in a criminal case, saying in *Cloutier v. R.*:

> For one fact to be relevant to another, there must be a connection or nexus between the two which makes it possible to infer the existence of one from the existence of the other. One fact is not relevant to another if it does not have real probative value with respect to the latter.[29]

A judgment of the Ontario Court of Appeal, *R. v. Birmingham*,[30] provides a good example of what type of evidence the courts consider relevant. In this case, the accused was convicted of criminal negligence in the operation of a motor vehicle. The accused appealed his conviction to the Court of Appeal which held that evidence which indicated that a small quantity of drugs had been found in the accused's car should not have been admitted at trial because it was not relevant to the criminal negligence charge. *Birmingham* illustrates that evidence which is admissible must be relevant to the issues before the court. Evidence which simply establishes that the accused is a bad person or evidence which is highly prejudicial to the accused and has no relevance to the charge will not be admitted.

(b) Hearsay Evidence

Probably the most important rule of evidence law is that evidence which is considered to be hearsay is not admissible in a court of law. The hearsay rule, which has been a feature of the common law since the 15th century, has been explained by Mr. Justice Dixon of the Supreme Court of Canada in *R. v. O'Brien* as follows:

---

[28] Sir James Steven, *A Digest of the Law of Evidence* (1876), cited in P.K. McWilliams, *Canadian Criminal Evidence* (Aurora: Canada Law Book, 1984) p. 30.
[29] (1979), 48 C.C.C. (3d) 1 at 28 (S.C.C.).
[30] (1976), 34 C.C.C. (2d) 386 (Ont. C.A.).

... evidence of a statement made to a witness by a person who is not himself called as a witness is hearsay and inadmissible when the object of the evidence is to establish the truth of what is contained in the statement; it is not hearsay and is admissible when it is proposed to establish by the evidence, not the truth of the statement but the fact that it was made.[31]

The hearsay rule applies to written statements as well as to oral statements. Thus, the Crown may not introduce evidence by a person that someone told him that he had seen the accused strike someone to prove that fact. Such evidence could be used only to show that the statement was made.

While there are many reasons as to why hearsay evidence is not admissible, probably the main reason why hearsay is not admissible is that the courts believe that the accused should have the opportunity of cross-examining a witness who gives evidence as to the truth of his or her evidence. If hearsay was admitted, an accused could be convicted on evidence which could not be effectively tested.

If there was no rule against hearsay, the witness could represent that someone else's statement, as told to the witness, was the correct version of the facts when in fact, the statement may have been totally false or the witness giving evidence in court may have misunderstood what he or she was told. Although there are some limited exceptions to the hearsay rule, generally judges will not allow hearsay evidence to be admitted as they regard such evidence as not being trustworthy.

(c) Disclosures by the Accused

While the accused may testify, the accused has an absolute right not to say anything at his trial. The accused's right to remain silent, which is also referred to as his freedom from self-incrimination, is guaranteed by section 11(c) of the Charter of Rights, which provides:

Any person charged with an offence has the right

. . . .

(c) not to be compelled to be a witness in proceedings against that person in respect of the offence. . . .

The Canada Evidence Act[32] prohibits a Crown attorney from commenting on the accused's failure to testify. Section 4(6) of the Canada Evidence Act states:

(6) The failure of the person charged, or of the wife or husband of such person,

---

[31] (1977), 35 C.C.C. (2d) 209 at 211 (S.C.C.).
[32] R.S.C. 1985, c. C-5.

to testify shall not be made the subject of comment by the judge or by counsel for the prosecution.

However, there is no rule prohibiting defence counsel from telling the jury that the accused is not obliged to testify. The accused's right to silence extends from the moment that he is questioned or arrested. Someone who is questioned by the police about a criminal matter has a right to remain silent and can refuse to answer any questions. There are many justifications for an accused's right to remain silent. The rationale for the rule has been eloquently stated in *Wigmore on Evidence*. The famous legal author concluded that the rule had two purposes which were:

> The first is to remove the right to an answer in the hard cores of instances where compulsion might lead to inhumanity, the principal inhumanity being abusive tactics by a zealous questioner. . . .
>
> The second is to comply with the prevailing ethic that the individual is sovereign and that proper rules of battle between government and individual require that the individual not be bothered for less than good reason and not be conscripted by his opponent to defeat himself. . . .[33]

The reasoning behind the right to remain silent has also been eloquently expressed by the then dean of Harvard Law School, Erwin Griswold, in his book, *The Fifth Amendment Today*. Dean Griswold states:

> I would like to venture the suggestion that the privilege against self-incrimination is one of the great landmarks in man's struggle to make himself civilized. As I have already pointed out, the establishment of the privilege is closely linked historically with the abolition of torture. But torture was once used by honest and conscientious public servants as a means of obtaining information about crimes which would not otherwise be disclosed. We want none of that today, I am sure. For a very similar reason we do not make even the most hardened criminal sign his own death warrant, or dig his own grave, or pull a lever which springs the trap on which he stands. We have through the course of history developed a considerable feeling for the dignity and intrinsic importance of the individual man. Even the evil man is a human being.[34]

The right to remain silent, which is a feature of the Canadian, British and American common law legal systems, does not exist in countries such as Italy which operate under the inquisitorial system. Thus, an accused who is charged with committing an offence in Italy is forced to testify at his trial and can be questioned about the offence by the presiding judge. The privilege against self-incrimination is not without its critics, as is evident from the acid comments of the well-known 19th century political philosopher, Jeremy Bentham:

---

[33] *Wigmore on Evidence*, Vol. 8 (McNaughton Revision) (Little, Brown & Company) p. 2251 *et seq.*

[34] E. Griswold, *The Fifth Amendment Today* (Cambridge, Mass., 1955).

One of the most pernicious and irrational rules that ever found its way into the human mind. . . . If all criminals of every class had assembled and framed a system after their own wishes, is not this rule the very first that they would have established for their security? Innocence never takes advantage of it; innocence claims the right of speaking as guilt invokes the privilege of silence.[35]

The United States Supreme Court held, in *Carter v. Kentucky,*[36] that a criminal defendant has the right to insist that a trial judge instruct a jury that they cannot conclude that the defendant is guilty because the defendant has not testified at his trial. The Supreme Court stated that this jury instruction is an important part of the defendant's protection against self-incrimination. In Canada, there is no obligation upon the trial judge to instruct a jury that they cannot draw an inference of guilt from the accused's failure to testify. Although the Crown prosecutor and the trial judge are prohibited from commenting on the accused's failure to testify, there is nothing which prevents a jury from considering this factor in its deliberations.

(d) Criminal Record of Accused

In Canada and the United States, if the accused does not testify at his or her trial, the jury will not be told that the accused has a criminal record. This rule ensures that the accused is tried on the basis of evidence presented before the court and is not convicted because of evidence which would tend to show that he or she is a bad person. The reasons behind the principle have been stated as follows:

> The judicial experience has been that it is fairer to try a man on the facts of the particular case than to allow the prosecution to try him on his whole life. A rule of policy based on fairness has therefore emerged that the prosecution may not, in general, introduce any evidence of the bad character of an accused simply to show that he is the sort of person likely to have committed the offence. The rule was succinctly expressed by the Privy Council in *Makin et al. v. A.-G. New South Wales,* [1894] A.C. 57 at p. 65, where the Lord Chancellor said:

> > It is undoubtedly not competent for the prosecution to adduce evidence tending to shew that the accused has been guilty of criminal acts other than those covered by the indictment, for the purpose of leading to the conclusion that the acccused is a person likely from his criminal conduct or character to have committed the offence for which he is being tried.

In *Koufis v. The King* (1941), 76 C.C.C. 161 at p. 170, [1941] 3 D.L.R. 657, [1941] S.C.R. 481, Taschereau J. said:

---

[35] R.E. Salhany, *supra*, note 16, at p. 99.
[36] 450 U.S. 288 (1981).

When an accused is tried before the Criminal Courts, he has to answer the specific charge mentioned in the indictment for which he is standing on trial, "and the evidence must be limited to matters relating to the transaction which forms the subject of the indictment" (*Maxwell v. Director of Public Prosecutions*, [1935] A.C. 309). Otherwise, "the real issue may be distracted from the minds of the jury," and an atmosphere of guilt may be created which would indeed prejudice the accused.

In *R. v. Scopelliti* (1981), 63 C.C.C. (2d) 481 at 493, 34 O.R. (2d) 524 (Ont. C.A.), the rule was expressed by Mr. Justice Martin as follows:

> The law prohibits the prosecution from introducing evidence for the purpose of showing that the *accused* is a person who by reason of his criminal character (disposition) is likely to have committed the crime charged, on policy grounds, not because of lack of relevance.

and at p. 496:

> Evidence of prior acts of bad conduct of an accused which has no probative value other than to permit an inference that the *accused* is a person who by reason of his criminal conduct or character is likely to have committed the offence charged is excluded by a rule of policy.

In *Morris v. The Queen* (S.C.C. — unreported — judgment pronounced on October 13, 1983) [since reported 7 C.C.C. (3d) 97, 1 D.L.R. (4th) 385, 36 C.R. (3d) 1], the court unanimously agreed with the following statement by Mr. Justice Lamer of the exclusionary rule under discussion, namely [at p. 106],

> . . . the fact that the accused is the sort of person who would be likely to have committed the offence, though relevant, is not admissible. As a result, evidence adduced *solely* for the purpose of proving disposition is itself inadmissible, or, to put it otherwise, evidence the sole relevancy of which to the crime committed is through proof of disposition, is inadmissible.[37]

However, when the accused testifies, the accused may be questioned as to the existence of a criminal record. If the accused denies the existence of a criminal record, the Crown may prove that the accused has such a record. In a jury trial, where the accused has admitted the existence of a criminal record, the trial judge will instruct the jury as to the limited use which can be made of the criminal record. The criminal record cannot be used to draw an inference that the accused is the sort of person who is likely to have committed the offence. The jury must be instructed that a criminal record can only be used to assess the accused's credibility or truthfulness and cannot be used to assess the guilt or innocence of the accused. The law in Canada may be contrasted with the law in England where an accused who testifies may not be questioned as to previous criminal convictions. It is highly unlikely that most juries understand the narrow use which can be made of a criminal record; it is naive

---

[37] *R. v. Gottschall* (1983), 10 C.C.C. (3d) 447 at 463-464 (N.S.C.A.).

to believe that juries once being informed of the existence of a record will use it for the narrow purpose of determining credibility.

(e) Full Answer and Defence

The Criminal Code guarantees that an accused has the right to make full answer and defence. Section 650(3) of the Criminal Code states:

(3) An accused is entitled, after the close of the case for the prosecution, to make full answer and defence personally or by counsel.

The purpose of section 650(3) has been considered by Mr. Justice Kelley in *R. v. Sproule*, a decision of the Ontario Court of Appeal:

The fundamental requirements embodied in s. 577(3) [650(3)] entitling an accused to make full answer and defence after the close of the case for the prosecution, require that the trial court permit an accused to introduce any evidence upon which the accused proposes to found a defence. Of course, an accused is restricted in that the evidence he intends to produce must be relevant and not subject to rejection on any recognized legal grounds. . . . To fail to accord an accused person the right to adduce admissible evidence is an interference with or circumvention of the purpose of the trial.[38]

In this case, the Ontario Court of Appeal ordered a new trial because the trial judge failed to allow the accused to introduce evidence that the accused was in a state of automatism. Such evidence, if accepted, would have provided the accused with a defence to the charge of non-capital murder.

12. TRIAL PROCEDURE

(a) Joint Trials

Where two people are charged with jointly participating in committing an offence the prosecution will attempt to have both the accused jointly tried. Thus, if the accused were alleged to have jointly assaulted someone, the Crown would want to have both tried on the same information or indictment as the evidence against each accused would be interrelated. The Canadian position as to joint trials has been stated by Mr. Justice Wurtele in *R. v. Weir (No. 4)* wherein His Lordship said:

When several persons are indicted jointly, the Crown always has the option to try them either together or separately; but the defendants cannot demand as a matter of right to be tried separately.

---

[38] (1975), 30 C.R.N.S. 56 at 62 (Ont. C.A.).

Upon good ground being shown, however, for a severence, the presiding judge may, in his discretion, grant them separate trials.

The general rule is that persons jointly indicted should be jointly tried; but when in any particular instance this would work an injustice to any of such joint defendants the presiding judge should on due cause being shown permit a severence and allow separate trials.[39]

Section 567 of the Criminal Code authorizes the trial judge to require that persons jointly charged be tried by a court comprised of a judge and jury. This section provides:

567. Notwithstanding any other provision of this Part, where two or more persons are charged with the same offence, unless all of them elect or re-elect or are deemed to have elected, as the case may be, the same mode of trial, the justice, provincial court judge or judge

(*a*) may decline to record any election, re-election or deemed election for trial by a provincial court judge or a judge without a jury; and

(*b*) if he declines to do so, shall hold a preliminary inquiry unless a preliminary inquiry has been held prior to the election, re-election or deemed election.

A judge may order that the co-accused be tried separately where justice requires a separate trial take place. In determining whether justice requires that a separate trial take place, the trial judge will consider factors such as whether the defendants have antagonistic defences, and whether a confession has been made by one defendant which would prejudice the other defendant in the mind of a jury. In some cases, the defendant may have a defence to the charge before the court if he or she is able to subpoena the co-defendant as a witness. In such cases, the judge will order that both accused be tried separately because a co-defendant cannot be forced to testify.

(b) Before Judge Alone

If the trial is held before a judge alone, after the accused has entered a plea to the charge before the court, Crown counsel will present its evidence. Afterwards, the accused will have an opportunity to call evidence. The Crown will call such witnesses as it believes essential to prove that the accused committed the offence.

When a witness takes the stand, the witness will be handed the Bible and asked to swear under oath that he or she will tell the truth. If the witness objects to taking the oath on religious grounds, the witness will be asked to solemnly affirm to tell the truth. Once the witness has taken an oath or affirmed to tell the truth, the party calling the witness will question the witness about events relevant to the charge. The questioning of one's witness is

---

[39] (1899), 3 C.C.C. 351 at 352 (Que. Q.B.).

referred to as direct examination, or examination-in-chief. In attempting to prove the case against the accused beyond a reasonable doubt, the Crown has a discretion as to which witnesses to call. However, the Crown must not exercise an oblique motive in calling witnesses. In other words, a Crown prosecutor should not refuse to call a witness because the witness' testimony would be favourable to the accused.

Crown counsel will structure the examination-in-chief to comply with the rules of evidence. Thus, for example, hearsay will not generally be admissible and the Crown must refrain from asking the witness leading questions in direct examination. A leading question is a question which suggests the answer to the witness. If, for example, in direct examination Crown counsel suggested to the witness, "You saw the accused, Donald MacIntosh, shoot the victim in the head, didn't you?" this would be a leading question, which would be inadmissible. If Crown counsel is not asking questions which the trial judge believes are relevant, the trial judge may decide to question the witness.

After the Crown prosecutor has finished his examination-in-chief, counsel for the accused is given an opportunity to cross-examine the witness. At this stage the witness will be cross-questioned as to the evidence which he or she has given in examination-in-chief. The cross-examiner will attempt to show that the witness' testimomy is not reliable or, if this is not possible, bring out evidence which is favourable to the accused. Skillful cross-examination is an art and a criminal case can be won because of the cross-examiner's skillful questioning, or lost because the cross-examiner has committed a stupid blunder. In cross-examining the witness, the cross-examiner must be careful not to ask the witness questions which simply reinforce the witness' testimony given in examination-in-chief. There is no rule that a witness must be cross-examined and if defence counsel decides that the witness' testimony has not really hurt the accused, counsel should avoid cross-examining that witness. If there is more than one accused, the order of cross-examination usually proceeds according to the order of the names on the indictment. When the witness has been cross-examined, the Crown can re-examine the witness on matters which arose during cross-examination. Re-examination cannot be used to raise new matters but only to clarify issues that were raised during cross-examination.

At the close of the Crown's case, defence counsel may make a motion for a non-suit. When defence counsel asks the judge to grant a motion for a non-suit, counsel is either suggesting that the Crown has failed to establish an essential element of the offence, or is arguing that there is no evidence by which a trial judge could convict the accused. If there is no case to answer, the judge will dismiss the case. If the motion is refused, the judge will ask the defence whether it intends to call any evidence. The defence may call evidence or, alternatively, elect not to call evidence and argue that the Crown has not proven its case beyond a reasonable doubt. If the defence elects to call witnesses, such witnesses will be examined-in-chief by defence counsel, after which Crown counsel will have an opportunity to cross-examine the witnesses called. After Crown counsel cross-examines the witness, defence counsel will have an opportunity to re-examine the witness. Defence counsel is bound by the rules of evidence discussed earlier. Once the Crown has presented its witnesses and the defence has presented its case, the trial judge will rule as to whether the Crown has proven its case beyond a reasonable doubt.

(c) Jury Trials

When an accused is being tried by a judge and jury, the presiding judge will inform the jurors of their function after which Crown counsel will give his or her opening address. In the opening address to the jury the Crown will outline the facts in the case and summarize for the jury the evidence which the Crown expects to call. Neither Crown counsel nor defence counsel are allowed to express an opinion as to the guilt or innocence of the accused. If counsel expresses such an opinion, this will constitute grounds for an appellate court to order a new trial. Once the Crown finishes its opening address, the Crown will call its first witness. The Crown will attempt to prove its case in the examination-in-chief. In attempting to prove its case, the Crown must comply with the rules of evidence discussed earlier in this chapter. After the Crown prosecutor has finished his or her examination-in-chief, counsel for the accused will cross-examine the witness. The witness may then be re-examined by Crown counsel. At the close of the Crown's case, defence counsel may make a motion for a directed verdict. (A directed verdict is the same as a non-suit which was discussed earlier.) If the trial judge refuses the motion for a directed verdict, the trial judge will ask the defence whether it intends to call any evidence.

After the Crown has closed its case, defence counsel will be given an opportunity of addressing the jury. In the opening address to the jury, defence counsel will usually remind the jury that jurors must arrive at a verdict only after carefully considering all the evidence. If defence counsel is planning to call the accused as a witness, counsel will usually indicate this to the jury when making the opening address. Defence counsel's opening address may, depending on the facts in the case, contain a summary of the type of evidence which the defence intends to call.

Defence counsel is not obliged to give an opening address to a jury and some defence lawyers believe that the defence counsel do not make sufficient use of the opening jury address.

When the defence opens its case, it will call witnesses who will give evidence which is favourable to the accused. Like the Crown, the defence has a discretion as to which witnesses to call. There is no obligation on the defence to call witnesses who do not assist the accused's case. The defence may decide not to call witnesses and simply rely on the weaknesses in the Crown's case. If the defence decides not to call any evidence, counsel will argue in his or her closing jury address that the Crown's case is so weak that the defence is not required to answer it. If the defence is calling the accused to the stand the accused should testify before other witnesses so that no suggestion can be made that the accused changed his or her testimony to conform with previous testimony.

If the defence calls no witnesses the defence will address the jury last. However, if the accused testifies or the defence calls other witnesses to testify on the accused's behalf, Crown counsel will be entitled to address the jury last. In addressing the jury, counsel will summarize the evidence presented with a view to persuading the jury that the evidence supports a conviction or acquittal. Crown counsel will be arguing that there is sufficient evidence to convict, while defence counsel will argue that the case has not been proven beyond a reasonable doubt.

After both counsel have addressed the jury, the trial judge will instruct the jurors as to the relevant law. The trial judge will explain the meaning of terms, such as the presumption of innocence and reasonable doubt, and deal with the specific law governing the offence. The trial judge will usually tell the jury that they are the judge of the facts while he or she is the judge of the law. Jurors are to take the law as given by the trial judge; the judge will summarize the evidence of the witnesses and apply the law to the evidence. The judge's summary of the law and evidence is referred to as the judge's charge to the jury. While crown counsel and defence counsel may discuss some legal principles with the jury, the jury will take the law as given by the trial judge.

After the trial judge has completed his charge to the jury, the jurors will retire to consider their verdict. The jury conducts the deliberations in private and jurors are prohibited from discussing their verdict publicly. When the jury has retired to consider its verdict, defence counsel and Crown counsel will voice any objections they have to the wording of the judge's charge. The trial judge may, depending upon the lawyers' objections, re-instruct the jury as to a portion of the charge. If jurors are unclear as to what the judge said, they will ask to have the judge's charge re-read. It is not uncommon for jurors to ask to have the evidence of one or more witnesses re-read to them.

When the jury retires to consider its verdict the jurors will elect a foreman who will act as the spokesperson for the jury. When the jury has reached a verdict, the foreman will inform the judge as to the verdict and the verdict will be read in open court. In Canada, unlike some states in the United States, jurors must be unanimous. If jurors cannot agree as to the verdict, the Crown will have to decide whether to re-try the accused before another jury.

14

Sentencing

1. PRINCIPLES OF SENTENCING

Historically, retribution was thought to be one of the principal aims of sentencing. Sir James Stevens, who was the author of Canada's first Criminal Code, has written in his history of the criminal law in England that criminals should be hated and the punishments imposed upon criminals should reflect society's hatred for them. Sir James Stevens also stated that one of the primary principles of sentencing was the principle of deterrence. In Sir James Stevens' view sentences should be imposed to deter like-minded individuals from committing offences similar to those committed by the offender before the court. It was Stevens' view that in order to act as a deterrent a sentence must instill fear in like-minded individuals who were considering committing an offence similar to the offence for which the offender was being sentenced.[1] While deterrence is still a principal component of the sentencing philosophy, as the centuries have passed retribution has faded into insignificance and is, for the most part, no longer considered to be a legitimate sentencing principle.

In *R. v. Roberts*, Mr. Justice MacKay of the Ontario Court of Appeal stated:

> At one time punishment was regarded in the light of vengeance or retribution against the wrongdoer and offenders were sentenced to be hanged for comparatively minor offences. This was an outgrowth of the old Biblical concept expressed in the words "eye for eye and tooth for tooth". Retributive justice has faded into comparative insignificance in the present-day administration of criminal justice.[2]

While retribution has faded "into comparative insignificance" as a sentencing principle, this was not something which happened overnight. For many years the Criminal Code appeared to reflect Sir James Stevens' philosophy that

---

[1] Sir James Stevens, *History of Criminal Law* (1883) Vol. 2, pp. 80-83.
[2] [1963] 1 O.R. 280 at 294 (C.A.).

society must seek vengeance against criminals. The Criminal Code contained a number of offences which made an offender liable to be whipped upon conviction. Today, the Criminal Code[3] does not contain any sections which provide for whipping or other corporal punishment upon conviction. The community has come to expect more out of the sentencing process than simple retribution. While there is no doubt that the protection of the public remains the principal aim of sentencing,[4] the sentencing process is also concerned with the rehabilitation and reform of the offender.

In sentencing an offender judges strive to impose sentences which fit the crime. There are a few offences in the Criminal Code which require a judge to impose a mandatory sentence of imprisonment. Where a judge is required to impose a mandatory sentence, there is no room for judicial discretion and the principle of making the punishment fit the crime does not really come into play. Murder is an example of an offence where a minimum sentence is prescribed. Section 235 of the Criminal Code states:

235. (1) Every one who commits first degree murder or second degree murder is guilty of an indictable offence and shall be sentenced to imprisonment for life.

(2) For the purposes of Part XXIII the sentence of imprisonment for life prescribed by this section is a minimum punishment.

Section 85 of the Criminal Code, which deals with the use of a firearm during the commission of an indictable offence, is an example of another section which creates a minimum punishment. Section 85(1) states:

85. (1) Every one who uses a firearm

(*a*) while committing or attempting to commit an indictable offence, or
(*b*) during his flight after committing or attempting to commit an indictable offence,

whether or not he causes or means to cause bodily harm to any person as a result thereof, is guilty of an indictable offence and liable to imprisonment

(*c*) in the case of a first offence, except as provided in paragraph (*d*), for not more than fourteen years and not less than one year, and
(*d*) in the case of a second or subsequent offence, or in the case of a first offence committed by a person who, prior to January 1, 1978, was convicted of an indictable offence or an attempt to commit an indictable offence, in the course of which or during his flight after the commission or attempted commission of which he used a firearm, for not more than fourteen years and not less than three years.

Section 717 of the Code states that judges are to be given a large measure of discretion in sentencing offenders and creates a presumption against minimum sentences. Section 717 states:

---

[3] R.S.C. 1985, c. C-46.
[4] *R. v. Grady* (1971), 5 N.S.R. (2d) 264 (C.A.); *R. v. Morrissette* (1970), 12 C.R.N.S. 392 (Sask. C.A.).

717. (1) Where an enactment prescribes different degrees or kinds of punishment in respect of an offence, the punishment to be imposed is, subject to the limitations prescribed in the enactment, in the discretion of the court that convicts a person who commits the offence.

(2) Where an enactment prescribes a punishment in respect of an offence, the punishment to be imposed is, subject to the limitations prescribed in the enactment, in the discretion of the court that convicts a person who commits the offence, but no punishment is a minimum punishment unless it is declared to be a minimum punishment.

. . . .

Where the Criminal Code does not provide for a minimum sentence, judges will have a large measure of discretion in determining what sentence the accused should receive. A starting point for determining what sentence an accused should receive is the section which creates the offence. Most sections in the Code provide for a penalty upon conviction. Where a minimum sentence is not prescribed, the penalty section usually states that the accused, upon conviction, is liable to receive up to X number of years' imprisonment. The length of imprisonment which an accused is likely to receive will depend upon whether the offence is an indictable or summary conviction offence, the seriousness of the offence committed and the penalty which is prescribed in the particular section creating the offence. If an offence is punishable by summary conviction, an accused, upon conviction, is liable to receive up to six months' imprisonment. This means that an accused can be sentenced to a variety of penalties ranging from an absolute discharge, to up to six months' imprisonment. If the offence is an indictable offence, it will be necessary to consult the section creating the offence to determine what penalty is prescribed by law.

Section 334 of the Criminal Code sets out the punishment for theft, distinguishing between thefts of $5,000 and more, and lesser thefts. If the Crown elects to proceed by way of summary conviction, the accused will be liable to receive up to six months' imprisonment. If an accused steals something which has a value exceeding $5,000, because the offence is an indictable offence by virtue of section 334, the accused will be liable to be imprisoned for up to two years. The use of the phrase "liable to imprisonment" does not mean that a judge is bound to imprison an accused. Where no minimum penalty is prescribed by the Criminal Code, a judge is free to impose a sentence which he or she thinks protects the public and fits the crime of which the accused is charged. A sentencing judge could give the accused an absolute discharge, which means that the accused would not have a criminal record, suspend the passing of sentence, fine the accused, place the accused on probation or imprison the accused for a period not exceeding two years. A judge may combine two different sentencing alternatives. Thus, for example, a judge may impose a suspended sentence with probation, or impose a period of incarceration to be followed by a period of probation. Whether a court grants an accused an absolute discharge, fines the accused, imposes a period of probation or imprisons the accused will depend upon what sentence the trial judge believes is appropriate. He will consider the need to protect society and the individual circumstances surrounding the commission of the offence including what punishment is mostly likely to result in rehabilitation of the offender.

Section 737(1) of the Criminal Code sets out some of the factors which judges consider. This section states:

> **737.** (1) Where an accused is convicted of an offence, the court may, having regard to the age and character of the accused, the nature of the offence and the circumstances surrounding its commission,
>
> (*a*) in the case of an offence other than one for which a minimum punishment is prescribed by law, suspend the passing of sentence and direct that the accused be released on the conditions prescribed in a probation order;
>
> (*b*) in addition to fining the accused or sentencing him to imprisonment, whether in default of payment of a fine or otherwise, for a term not exceeding two years, direct that the accused comply with the conditions prescribed in a probation order; or
>
> (*c*) where it imposes a sentence of imprisonment on the accused, whether in default of payment of a fine or otherwise, that does not exceed ninety days, order that the sentence be served intermittently at such times as are specific in the order and direct that the accused, at all times when he is not in confinement pursuant to such order, comply with the conditions prescribed in a probation order.

Many of the factors which courts take into consideration in determining an appropriate sentence have been set out in *R. v. Bruce*, a 1982 decision of the Prince Edward Island Court of Appeal.[5] In *Bruce*, MacDonald J., who delivered the judgment of the court, stated:

> Numerous cases have set forth the principles to be considered when imposing sentence. These principles are: (1) protection of the public; (2) deterrence; (3) reformation and rehabilitation of the offender; and (4) punishment. . . .
>
> Although the principles that I have listed are in no particular order and may have some overlapping considerations, there is no doubt that the protection of society must be considered as the primary function to be achieved in sentencing.
>
> In determining how the principles of sentencing are to be applied to the circumstances of a particular case, various factors have been set forth for a court to take into consideration. These factors relate to the particular circumstances of each case, and would include: the amount of premeditation; the circumstances as to the commission of the crime; the gravity of the crime; the attitude of the offender after the crime; the accused's previous criminal record; the age, mode of life and character of the accused; mitigating and other circumstances; incidence of crime in the jurisdiction; recommendations for mercy; and the customary sentence for similar offences. . . .[6]

The principles set out in *Bruce* have been employed by numerous courts across the country.[7]

---

[5] (1982), 39 C.R. (3d) 247 (P.E.I.C.A.).

[6] *Ibid.*, at 250-251.

[7] *Quebec (A.G.) v. Rubio* (1984), 39 C.R. (3d) 67 (Que. S.C.); *R. v. Morrissette, supra,* note 4; *R. v. Grady, supra,* note 4; *R. v. Iwaniw; R. v. Overton* (1959), 32 C.R. 389 (Man. C.A.).

The factors listed above are not exhaustive and other factors, such as renunciation of the offence, will come into play. A more detailed discussion of the general principles considered in sentencing may be found in books which deal specifically with sentencing, such as Clayton C. Ruby's book on sentencing.[8]

2. FACTORS IN SENTENCING

(a) Mitigating Circumstances

(i) *Guilty plea*

While a judge must consider the protection of the public, a sentencing judge cannot ignore individual factors which contributed to the crime in determining what constitutes a fit sentence and must consider the accused as an individual. In determining what is an appropriate sentence for the crime, a judge will consider mitigating circumstances which would lessen the sentence that otherwise would be imposed. If an accused pleads guilty to the charge before the court, the guilty plea is considered to be a mitigating factor which lessens the sentence. In *R. v. Layte*, His Honour Judge Salhany, an Ontario County Court judge, explained the rationale for a guilty plea being a mitigating factor on sentencing, saying:

> It is a fundamental concept of our system of justice that a person accused of a crime is entitled to demand that the Crown prove his guilt by a fair and impartial trial. There is nothing that the court should ever do to whittle down or undercut that fundamental principle. At the same time, it would be unrealistic not to recognize that if everyone demanded a full and complete trial our system of justice would come to an abrupt halt. It is for that reason that those who are guilty, and wish to so plead, should be given special consideration when they appear before the court. There are many reasons for this. One is that the state is saved a considerable expense. Another is that witnesses are spared the inconvenience and the expense and occasionally the trauma of a trial. Another is that a plea of guilty is an indication and demonstation of the accused's remorse.[9]

In *R. v. Johnston*, the Ontario Court of Appeal recognized that a guilty plea is a mitigating factor which lessens the sentence which the accused would otherwise receive.[10] While a guilty plea is a mitigating factor, an accused who is not guilty should not plead guilty in order to receive a lighter sentence.

---

[8] C.C. Ruby, *Sentencing*, 3rd ed. (Toronto: Butterworths, 1987), pp. 1-15.
[9] *R. v. Layte* (1983), 38 C.R. (3d) 204 at 206 (Ont. Co. Ct.).
[10] January 6, 1977, Ont. C.A.

Before accepting a guilty plea, the court must be sure that the accused admits all the elements of the offence of which he or she is charged. A defence lawyer is duty bound to advise an accused to plead not guilty in circumstances where the client informs the lawyer that he did not commit the offence or the lawyer believes that the client has a good defence to the charge. While a guilty plea is a mitigating factor which a court takes into consideration when imposing the sentence, a plea of not guilty is not an aggravating factor which increases the sentence imposed.[11]

(ii) First or youthful offender

If an offender is a first offender or is a youthful offender this will be considered a mitigating factor in sentencing. Generally, first offenders are not sentenced to a period of imprisonment or, if they are sentenced to a jail term, the period of incarceration is not as great as it would be for an offender who is not a youthful offender. In *R. v. Stein*, the Ontario Court of Appeal dealt with the principles that should be applied when sentencing a youthful offender.[12] In *Stein*, the accused pleaded guilty to 13 counts of obtaining property under false pretenses. The accused, who had made restitution before trial, was sentenced to a period of incarceration. The accused appealed her sentence to the Ontario Court of Appeal. Allowing the appeal, Martin J.A., who delivered the judgment of the court, set out the principles which must be applied when dealing with a youthful offender, saying:

> It is the view of the Court that the sentence imposed upon the appellant does reflect an error in principle. In our view, before imposing a custodial sentence upon a first offender the sentencing Court should explore the other dispositions which are open to him and only impose a custodial sentence where the circumstances are such, or the offence is of such gravity that no other sentence is appropriate. In our view, this offence does not fall within the category of offences where a custodial sentence is the only appropriate sentence to be imposed upon a first offender, nor are there other circumstances which require the imposition of a custodial sentence.[13]

The Alberta Court of Appeal has also held that, in general, a youthful first offender should not be sentenced to a period of imprisonment. Thus, in *R. v. Beacon*, Sinclair J.A., who delivered the judgment of the court, said:

> Custodial sentences are generally avoided in the case of young first offenders. A Court's first impression is to ask whether a suspended sentence, with probation, would not be a suitable sentence for the offender, and for the offence. . . .

---

[11] *R. v. Kozy* (1990), 80 C.R. (3d) 59 at 64 (Ont.C.A.).

[12] (1974), 15 C.C.C. (2d) 376 (Ont. C.A.).

[13] *Ibid.*, at 377.

Should a term of imprisonment be thought fit, the fact that a youthful first offender is involved is an element to be considered in determining the length of the sentence, for in most of such cases it is usually undesirable that a first sentence of immediate imprisonment should be very long.[14]

(iii) *Old age*

Old age is also a mitigating factor which the court will consider in sentencing an accused. In *R. v. Kalsta*, the accused, Kalsta, was convicted of manslaughter and sentenced to six months' imprisonment and placed on probation for two years.[15] The accused, who was 77 years of age, stabbed a man to death with a hunting knife after he had knocked on the accused's apartment door. The Ontario Court of Appeal held that the trial judge had not erred in imposing a sentence of six months' imprisonment and two years' probation. In holding that the sentencing was proper, the Ontario Court of Appeal took into consideration the accused's age and special medical problems. A Crown psychiatrist had given evidence that the accused was suffering from arteriosclerosis and had a rigid personality structure. The evidence indicated that on the night in question the accused had consumed some alcohol. Medical evidence indicated that someone who had the accused's medical problems would, having consumed alcohol, not be able to form the intent to commit murder.

(iv) *Illness*

In passing sentence a court will consider any physical or mental disorders which contributed to the commission of the offence. Thus, for example, if an accused suffers from a mental illness, such as schizophrenia, and commits a crime, then the accused's mental illness would be a mitigating factor which would lessen the sentence that would otherwise be imposed. Appellate courts have held that the primary consideration in passing sentence is the protection of the public from the offender who is being sentenced. However, the protection of the public is not the only consideration. When an offender is suffering from a mental or physical illness which contributed to the commission of the offence, this is a proper factor to be considered in the mitigation of the sentence.

(v) *Drug or alcohol addiction*

An offender's addiction to drugs or alcohol can be, in certain cases, a

---

[14] (1976), 31 C.C.C. (2d) 56 at 59 (Alta. C.A.).
[15] (1977), 20 C.L.Q. 21 (Ont. C.A.).

mitigating circumstance which will be considered by the trial judge before passing sentence. The extent to which the accused's drug addiction or addiction to alcohol will be a mitigating factor will depend on the circumstances involved in each particular case. Thus, for example, an accused who is breaking and entering residential premises in order to support a drug habit will, upon conviction, be punished for breaking and entering which is a serious charge, but consideration will also be given to the circumstances motivating the accused to commit the offence. In such a case, the court may, as part of the sentence, impose a period of probation with strict conditions that the accused seek treatment for his or her drug addiction at a recognized treatment centre.

(vi) *Delay*

Delay in bringing an accused to trial is a mitigating factor to be considered on sentencing. In *R. v. Therrault*, the Quebec Court of Appeal held that a sentence that would otherwise be imposed was mitigated by the fact that the accused's case had been adjourned 33 times in six years.[16] In this case, there was evidence that the accused's heart condition had worsened as a direct result of the continual court appearances.

The courts have also held that delay in arresting the accused is a factor to be considered in the mitigation of sentence. In *R. v. Simon*, the accused appealed against the sentences imposed in respect of his conviction on two charges of breaking and entering and one charge of assault.[17] The sentence imposed in respect of the assault charge was not overturned. However, the Ontario Court of Appeal held that the sentence imposed in respect of the breaking and entering charges was excessive. In so holding, the court took into consideration the fact that the accused was not brought to trial for two and a half years after the offence occurred. The court noted that although the offence took place in October, 1971, the accused was not arrested or brought to trial for two and a half years although he remained in the vicinity where the offence took place. The court also noted that the accused spent several months in custody in 1973 but was released and did not come to trial until March, 1974. With respect to all the circumstances, particularly having regard to the unexplained delay, the court stated that "it was wrong to bring him back and impose a very severe sentence for these offences after so much time had elapsed."[18]

(vii) *Life expectancy*

If an accused is ill and his life expectancy reduced, this could be a mitigating factor which would lessen the sentence normally imposed. In *R. v.*

---

[16] (1979), 22 C.L.Q. 163 (Que. C.A.).
[17] (1975), 25 C.C.C. (2d) 159 (Ont. C.A.).
[18] *Ibid.*, at 160.

Zabor, the Ontario Court of Appeal reduced an accused's two-year sentence on a perjury conviction to three years' probation because of the accused's physical illness.[19] In *Zabor*, the accused was 57 years of age, had a stroke and had cancer. Reducing the two-year sentence imposed at trial, the Court of Appeal took into consideration the fact that the accused was not expected to live for more than five years.

(viii) *Cooperation with police*

Cooperation with the police is considered to be a proper mitigating factor which a judge may consider on sentencing. The cooperation may range from an accused informing the police of offences which he has committed which he has not been arrested for, to an accused acting as an informant and providing police officers with information concerning the activities of fellow criminals.[20] However, if an accused confesses to a crime when he is caught red-handed, his confession is not to be given as much credit as if he spontaneously confesses to having committed crimes which the police do not know about.[21]

(ix) *Time spent in custody*

Time spent in custody is a mitigating factor which lessens the sentence an accused would otherwise receive. Section 721(3) of the Code states:

> (3) In determining the sentence to be imposed on a person convicted of an offence, a justice, provincial court judge or judge may take into account any time spent in custody by the person as a result of the offence.

While a court will consider time spent in custody as a mitigating factor, the courts have generally held that there is no precise formula for determining the amount of custodial time which an accused should be given credit for. In *R. v. Meilleur*, the accused was sentenced to a period of four years' imprisonment upon his conviction for manslaughter.[22] The trial judge stated that he was reducing the seven and a half year sentence to four years because of the time which the accused had spent in custody. The Crown's appeal to the Ontario Court of Appeal was allowed and the sentence was varied from four to six years. In allowing the appeal, Martin J.A. stated that the trial judge had erred in using a mathematical formula to calculate the sentence which should be imposed.

---

[19] (1984), 9 W.C.B. 32 (Ont. C.A.).

[20] *R. v. Stein, supra,* note 12.

[21] *R. v. Sullivan* (1978), 15 Nfld. & P.E.I.R. 271 (Nfld. C.A.).

[22] (1981), 6 W.C.B. 184 (Ont. C.A.).

The Alberta Court of Appeal has stated that while time spent in custody before sentencing is a factor which a trial judge should consider in sentencing the accused, there is no precise formula for determining the amount of time which an accused should be given credit for.[23]

(x) Mistake of law

While mistake of law is not a defence to a criminal charge, it is a mitigating factor which may be considered on sentencing.[24] A person who acts on wrong legal advice will be treated more leniently.[25] Honest action is not treated as severely as deliberate disregard of the law.

(b) Aggravating Factors

(i) Generally

The manner in which the offence was committed can be an aggravating factor which will increase the sentence imposed. If the crime is premeditated, the accused's premeditation in committing the offence will be an aggravating factor. If an accused has been convicted of committing a violent offence, the viciousness of the assault will be considered an aggravating factor. The sentencing principles which courts have applied in such cases have been set out in *R. v. Lévesque*, a decision of the Quebec Superior Court.[26] In *Lévesque*, the court quoted Halsbury, saying that:

> The Court, in fixing a punishment for any particular crime, will take into consideration the nature of the offence, the circumstances in which it was committed, the degree of deliberation shown by the offender, the provocation which he has received, if the crime is one of violence, the antecedents of the prisoner up to the time of sentence, his age and character . . .[27]

In *Lévesque*, the accused was sentenced to concurrent sentences of three years for kidnapping and six years for rape. The accused had threatened the 19-year-old complainant with a knife and he and his two co-accused subsequently raped the complainant. In sentencing the accused, the court stated that there were several aggravating factors which must be considered in imposing sentence. The aggravating factors were that the accused was the ring-leader of

---

[23] *R. v. Regan* (1975), 24 C.C.C. (2d) 225 (Alta. C.A.).
[24] *R. v. Everton*, (1980), 22 C.L.Q. 294 (Man. C.A.).
[25] *R. v. Whitehouse* (1972), 8 C.P.R. (2d) 96 (Alta. Dist. Ct.).
[26] (1980), 19 C.R. (3d) 43 (Que. S.C.).
[27] *Ibid.*, at 49.

the group, the accused presented a false alibi to the court, and refused to identify his two co-accused.

In *R. v. Bradbury*, the Ontario Court of Appeal dismissed a sentence appeal where an accused had been convicted of wounding with intent to maim or disfigure, contrary to section 244 of the *Criminal Code*.[28] In *Bradbury*, the accused had been sentenced to 14 years' imprisonment. Dismissing the appeal, Kelly J.A., who wrote the judgment of the court, stated that the trial judge's sentence was not excessive having regard to all the circumstances, including the fact that the young girl wounded was the victim of an unprovoked knife attack.

In *R. v. Thompson*, the Ontario Court of Appeal considered the place where the offence occurred to be an aggravating factor.[29] The Crown appealed from the accused's sentence on a charge of breaking and entering a dwelling-house and committing an indecent assault while in that dwelling-house. The accused had broken into a dwelling-house and indecently assaulted the complainant who was three months pregnant at the time of the assault. Upon conviction, the accused was given a suspended sentence and probation. The Court of Appeal altered the sentence to imprisonment for a period of two years less one day. Brooke J.A. considered the invasion of a private home to be an aggravating factor which must be considered in determining what constitutes a fit sentence. In imposing the sentence, Brooke J.A. stated that "[t]he fitness of the sentence must reflect the need for protection and the complete repudiation by the public of such conduct."[30]

In *R. v. Campbell*, the British Columbia Court of Appeal held that the trial judge had erred in giving an armed robber a suspended sentence with two years' probation and 200 hours' of community work.[31] The Court of Appeal allowed the Crown's appeal and varied the sentence to seven years' imprisonment with two years' probation. The accused, who was 25 years of age, had robbed a theatre with a rifle. The accused wore a stocking mask during the hold-up and fled after obtaining $700 from the theatre. The accused was subsequently apprehended and entered a guilty plea to a charge of armed robbery. When the accused was sentenced, the Criminal Code stated that someone who was convicted of armed robbery was liable to receive a sentence of 14 years' imprisonment. The trial judge held that the accused's expression of remorse was a mitigating factor to be considered on sentencing, as was the psychiatric evidence that the offence committed was out of character for the accused. In overturning the trial judge's decision, Nemetz C.J.B.C. stated:

> I am in respectful agreement with Howland C.J.O. [writing in *R. v. Ouillet*, an unreported judgment of the Ontario Court of Appeal] that the principles of reha-

---

[28] (1973), 14 C.C.C. (2d) 139 (Ont. C.A.).
[29] (1974), 20 C.C.C. (2d) 100 (Ont. C.A.).
[30] *Ibid.*, at 103.
[31] *R. v. Campbell* (1982), 26 C.R. (3d) 279 (B.C.C.A.).

bilitation and individual deterrence should always be taken into consideration where young offenders are involved; nevertheless, where a serious offence involving violence has been committed, general deterrence then becomes the prime consideration.

In this case the respondent committed the crime of armed robbery with a loaded rifle. In view of the seriousness of the crime, general deterrence should have been the prime consideration to have been considered by the judge. That would have necessitated a term of imprisonment which would not only punish the offender but would warn others of society's abhorrence of crimes of violence which usually result in either injuries or death to innocent victims.

Aside from the general deterrence, I must also consider the question of the safety of the public in acts of violence of this kind. Were I the sentencing judge, I think that I would have imposed a heavy sentence on this person.[32]

(ii) *Use of violence*

The use of violence is an aggravating factor. In *R. v. Gonidis*,[33] the Ontario Court of Appeal allowed a Crown appeal from the sentences imposed upon the three accused who were convicted of robbery. The accused were sentenced to six months' imprisonment to be followed by two years' probation. Arnup J.A. stated:

It has been frequently held by this Court that in general young offenders should not be given long sentences of incarceration where some other appropriate sentence can be imposed, but rather that a short, sharp sentence and fairly lengthy period of probation should be imposed.

The principle does not apply to serious crime or where violence is involved.

. . . .

In the present case the trial Judge, while stating the general principle applicable to youthful first offenders, overlooked the corollary to that principle, that different considerations apply in serious crimes of violence, particularly where careful planning is evident.

When we turn to the facts of this case, we find that the respondent Stevenson was the first instigator, who made a suggestion that the three respondents should, on some occasion, be in a hold-up. McCullough, who had already encountered difficulties with the law, ought to have been conscious of the necessity of behaving himself; he was on probation. Gonidis, in the true sense, was in a position of trust. He was the "inside man" whose detailed knowledge of the premises and leadership in the planning of the enterprise was essential to its success.

---

[32] *Ibid.*, at 282.
[33] (1981), 57 C.C.C. (2d) 90 (Ont. C.A.).

In our view, an appropriate sentence in all the circumstances of this case would certainly have not been less than 18 months' incarceration, and a sentence imposed by a trial Judge of two years less a day could not have been seriously criticized in this Court.

We have had regard to the facts urged in mitigation. These young men, when apprehended, immediately confessed to their participation. They made, or arranged to be made, restitution for the loss to McDonald's. They pleaded guilty at their trial. They have lived an exemplary life since their original arrests and, during their period of custody, have behaved in a manner which leads to no criticism whatever by the custodial authorities of their conduct while incarcerated. Nevertheless, giving full weight to this, we regard the sentence of the trial Judge as quite inadequate and, taking into consideration all of the mitigating factors, we nevertheless think that this appeal must be allowed and the sentence in each case increased to one of 15 months.[34]

(iii) *Premeditation*

Careful planning and premeditation of an offence is an aggravating factor which increases the sentence that would otherwise be imposed. In *R. v. Bengert (No. 14)*, the British Columbia Supreme Court considered the substantial degree of planning and deliberation involved in sentencing nine accused persons for conspiracy to traffic in cocaine. In imposing substantial terms of imprisonment, Berger J. stated:

> Character evidence has been submitted on behalf of all of the accused, and reference has been made to the difficulties which many of the accused have encountered in various aspects of life, and to their family ties and obligations. But this is of no consequence in a case where there is planned, deliberate and continuing criminal activity extending, in the case of Robertson and Zamai, over a period of a year or more, and so also in the case of Bengert, Ponak, Ferron and Jeffries. I do not think that in the case of these accused such evidence can extenuate, though it may in the case of Perry and Layman, who were on a lower echelon and whose participation extended over a period of six months.[35]

In *R. v. Pearce*, the Ontario Court of Appeal upheld a trial judge's sentence of six years for conspiracy to traffic in speed.[36] In upholding the sentence imposed, Jessup J.A. noted that the accused had been distributing speed for two years and also noted that the accused's distribution scheme was a sophisticated, well-planned endeavour.

---

[34] *Ibid.*, at 94-96.
[35] (1979), 15 C.R. (3d) 97 at 111-112 (B.C.S.C.).
[36] (1974), 16 C.C.C. (2d) 369 (Ont. C.A.).

(iv) *Prevalence of the offence in the community*

The prevalence of a crime in a community is a factor which a court considers in imposing sentence. In *R. v. Johnas: R. v. Cardinal*, the Alberta Court of Appeal considered the prevalence of a particular offence in a community to be an aggravating factor which increased the sentence imposed.[37] In so holding, the court stated:

> ... The Court must recognize that some offences require that the aim of rehabilitation be subordinated to the principle of deterrence. We are of the opinion that the prevalence of robberies together with the seriousness of violence or threats of violence have put robberies in the category of cases where the emphasis must be on deterrence to the individual and to others.[38]

In *Johnas*, the Alberta Court of Appeal adopted the reasoning of the Nova Scotia Court of Appeal in *R. v. Mitchell* where that court stated that "the prevalence of a particular offence in a particular area is a relevant factor to be taken into account in the sentencing process."[39]

(v) *Breach of trust*

If an accused who is in a position of trust commits an offence, the breach of trust will be an aggravating factor. Persons such as bank managers, police officers, lawyers and others occupy positions of trust and will, in general, receive stiffer penalties where there is evidence that such persons have abused their position of trust.

In *R. v. McEachern*, the Ontario Court of Appeal allowed the Crown's appeal from the sentence imposed, holding that the trial judge gave insufficient consideration to the accused's breach of trust.[40] The 34-year-old accused pleaded guilty to theft from a bank where he was the assistant manager. The accused had signed official bank cheques totalling $87,000 which he used to purchase a marina and a house in his wife's name. The funds which the accused used came from customer term deposits which were held by the bank. The accused was given a suspended sentence with three years' probation and 200 hours community service. In allowing the Crown's appeal, Howland C.J.O, who delivered the judgment of the Ontario Court of Appeal, stated:

> As an assistant manager of a bank, the respondent was in a position of trust. It has long been established that the most important principle in sentencing a person

---

[37] (1982), 2 C.C.C. (3d) 490 (Alta. C.A.).
[38] *Ibid.*, at 494.
[39] (1981), 23 C.R. (3d) 1 at 3 (N.S.C.A.).
[40] (1978), 7 C.R. (3d) S-8 (Ont. C.A.).

who holds a position of trust is that of general deterrence. The offences were serious and involved a large sum of money. They were concealed by the respondent until they were detected by the bank.

In our opinion, the gravity of the offences called for the imposition of a custodial term and there were no exceptional circumstances which would justify a lesser punishment. The trial judge placed too much emphasis on restitution and on community service work as an alternative to imprisonment and did not attach sufficient importance to general deterrence. The public interest requires that it be made very clear to one and all that, in the absence of exceptional circumstances, a person holding a position of trust who steals from his employer must expect a term of imprisonment. The restitution and community service work ordered by the trial judge were not an adequate punishment in the circumstances of the present case.

Accordingly, leave to appeal is granted and the appeal is allowed. The sentence will be varied to a term of 18 months' imprisonment.[41]

In *R. v. Scherer*, the Ontario Court of Appeal stated that in cases involving a breach of trust by a lawyer, the primary consideration is general deterrence and "societal denunciation."[42] In *Scherer*, the court noted that the accused's scheme for defrauding the public was persistent and, in some cases, resulted in clients being victimized for their entire life savings. A sentence of seven years was imposed on the accused who misappropriated $2 million.

A person who is in a position of trust and sexually abuses his or her victim will almost certainly be sentenced to a period of imprisonment. In *R. v. Belanger*, the Ontario Court of Appeal considered the English case of *R. v. Taylor* which stated that a person who abuses his or her position of trust for sexual gratification should, upon conviction for one of the sexual offences set out in the Criminal Code, receive a sentence "somewhere near the maximum allowed by law . . .."[43]

(vi) *Previous criminal record*

A previous criminal record can be an aggravating factor which will increase the accused's sentence. The existence of a substantial criminal record may indicate that the accused is a poor candidate for rehabilitation. This will certainly be the case if the accused has a number of recent convictions for offences similar to the offence which the trial judge is dealing with. If an accused's record consists of mainly unrelated offences, the record will be given less consideration by the court and will not be as damaging as it otherwise would be. If the record is an old record and there is a significant time period between convictions, the record will not be given as much emphasis as a recent criminal record.

---

[41] *Ibid.*, at S-9, S-10.
[42] (1984), 42 C.R. (3d) 376 (Ont. C.A.).
[43] (1979), 46 C.C.C. (2d) 266 at 268 (Ont. C.A.).

(vii) *The victim*

The courts have held that the principles of general and individual deterrence are to be more readily applied when the victim is a child, elderly person, or some other person whom a court considers warrants special protection. In *R. v. Cudmore*, the Ontario Court of Appeal allowed the Crown's appeal from the sentence imposed upon a father who had been convicted of assault causing bodily harm.[44] The accused had aided his wife in assaulting his 4-year-old daughter. When the little girl was brought into the hospital she was pale, unconscious and covered with bruises from head to toe. Evidence lead at trial indicated that there was a danger the girl could become an epileptic. After considering a pre-sentence report, His Honour Judge Dodds, a Provincial Court judge, suspended the accused's sentence and placed him on three years' probation. In allowing the Crown's appeal Schroeder J.A. stated:

> The learned Provincial Judge suspended sentence and put the accused on probation because, in his opinion, the injuries were in large part inflicted upon this little girl by one Jean Harding with whom the accused was living as his wife. Nevertheless, the accused was present and permitted these grave injuries to be inflicted upon this defenceless little child. There was also evidence of his active participation in the assault. Little children are entitled to look for protection to their parents or to those to whose care they are entrusted, and brutality of the kind involved in the present case cannot and will not be tolerated. In the light of the injuries inflicted upon this unfortunate child the sentence imposed is entirely inadequate. Deterrence and the protection of those who cannot protect themselves is the important factor to be considered here.

> It is our conclusion that the appropriate sentence in the present case is a term of imprisonment for one year. It is further ordered that the respondent be placed on probation thereafter for a period of three years on the same terms and conditions as those laid down by the learned Provincial Judge.[45]

The courts will emphasize general and individual deterrence in sentencing someone who preys upon elderly people or who takes advantage of the aged. In *R. v. Riordan*, the accused was convicted of defrauding elderly people by fraudulently selling hearing aids that were used rather than new.[46] In sentencing the accused to six months' imprisonment, the trial judge stated:

> In this particular case I propose to give a great deal of consideration to the matter of deterrence because I consider that the action of this man preying on the disabilities of aged persons, or persons suffering with a hearing loss, ought to be punished severely.[47]

---

[44] (1972), 5 C.C.C. (2d) 536 (Ont. C.A.).
[45] *Ibid.*, at 538.
[46] (1974), 15 C.C.C. (2d) 219 (N.S.C.A.).
[47] *Ibid.*, at 222.

On appeal to the Nova Scotia Court of Appeal, the accused's sentence was reduced, but the Nova Scotia Court of Appeal did not take issue with the trial judge's ruling that persons who prey upon the elderly must be deterred from doing so in the future.

3. TYPES OF SENTENCES

(a) Conditional or Absolute Discharge

In sentencing an accused where no minimum penalty is prescribed by law, the judge has the option of giving the accused an absolute or conditional discharge. If an accused pleads guilty or is found guilty of committing a criminal offence and a judge gives the accused an absolute discharge, a conviction will not be registered and the accused will not have a criminal record. If a judge gives an accused a conditional discharge, the accused will not have a criminal record if the accused complies with the conditions set out in a probation order. The authority for granting an absolute or conditional discharge is found in section 736(1) of the Criminal Code, which states:

> **736.** (1) Where an accused, other than a corporation, pleads guilty to or is found guilty of an offence, other than an offence for which a minimum punishment is prescribed by law or an offence punishable, in the proceedings commenced against him, by imprisonment for fourteen years or for life, the court before which he appears may, if it considers it to be in the best interests of the accused and not contrary to the public interest, instead of convicting the accused, by order direct that the accused be discharged absolutely or on the conditions prescribed in a probation order.

A discharge must be in the best interests of the accused and not contrary to the public interest. In *R. v. Sanchez-Pino*, the Ontario Court of Appeal dealt with what constitutes the best interests of the accused.[48] Arnup J.A., speaking for the court, said:

> The granting of some form of discharge must be "in the best interests of the accused". I take this to mean that the deterrence of the offender himself was not a relevant consideration, in the circumstances, except to the extent required by conditions in a probation order. Nor is his rehabilitation through correctional or treatment centres, except to the same extent. Normally he will be a person of good character, or at least of such character that the entry of a conviction against him may have significant repercussions.[49]

In assessing whether it is against the public interest that an accused be

---

[48] (1973), 11 C.C.C. (2d) 53 (Ont. C.A.).
[49] *Ibid.*, at 59.

given an absolute or conditional discharge for the offence committed, a trial judge will consider a myriad of factors including the seriousness of the offence, the type of offence committed, the premeditation, if any, involved, and individual factors relating to the character of the accused. Certain offences are so serious that a judge would be loath to grant an absolute or conditional discharge. If an accused is convicted of a particularly brutal assault it is unlikely that a trial judge would grant an absolute or a conditional discharge. If an accused has committed a well-planned and highly sophisticated fraud, it is likely that the principles of general and specific deterrence would dictate that a discharge not be given. Similarly, in cases involving a breach of trust where the primary consideration is the deterrence of the accused and like-minded individuals, a discharge would usually be considered inappropriate.

The general rule governing an absolute or conditional discharge is that the discharge is not available where Parliament has prescribed a minimum penalty for the commission of an offence. This rule, which is set out in section 736(1) of the Code, is subject to an exception for impaired driving offences. Someone who is convicted of operating a motor vehicle, vessel or aircraft or having the care or control of a motor vehicle, vessel or aircraft while his ability to operate the vehicle, vessel or aircraft is impaired by alcohol or a drug can obtain a conditional discharge under section 255(5) of the Criminal Code. Also, someone who is charged with operating a motor vehicle, vessel or aircraft having consumed alcohol in such a quantity that his or her blood-alcohol content exceeds 80 mg of alcohol in 100 ml of blood can receive a conditional discharge under section 255(5) of the Code.

(b) Fine

An accused who is sentenced for a particular offence can be fined instead of being placed on probation or given some other penalty. A fine is available where there is no minimum sentence prescribed by law or where an accused is convicted of an offence punishable by five years or less imprisonment. A fine may also be coupled with another disposition, such as imprisonment or probation. Section 718 states:

> **718.** (1) An accused who is convicted of an indictable offence punishable with imprisonment for five years or less may be fined in addition to or in lieu of any other punishment that is authorized, but an accused shall not be fined in lieu of imprisonment where the offence of which he is convicted is punishable by a minimum term of imprisonment.
>
> (2) An accused who is convicted of an indictable offence punishable with imprisonment for more than five years may be fined in addition to, but not in lieu of, any other punishment that is authorized.
>
> . . . .

For summary convictions offences the relevant provision which authorizes a judge to impose a fine is section 787(1) of the Code, which states:

787. (1) Except where otherwise provided by law, every one who is convicted of an offence punishable on summary conviction is liable to a fine of not more than two thousand dollars or to imprisonment for six months or to both.

If a judge imposes a fine and the fine is not paid, the accused who is in default of payment of the fine may be sentenced to imprisonment. The provisions which deal with imprisonment in default of payment of a fine may be found in sections 718(3) and 787(2) of the Code. In imposing a fine, a trial judge should not order that the fine be paid immediately unless there is evidence that the accused has sufficient funds to pay the fine forthwith or waives the time, or there are special reasons to order immediate payment. If an accused requires time to pay the fine, defence counsel should request that the trial judge allow the accused time to pay the fine imposed by the court.

(c) Suspended Sentence

A judge may give an accused a suspended sentence with probation. The effect of a suspended sentence is that the accused is not sentenced, but rather the sentence is suspended and the accused is placed on probation for a period prescribed by the court. If the accused complies with the conditions of the probation order, including a condition that he or she is to keep the peace and be of good behaviour, the accused will not be sentenced. However, if the accused fails to comply with the probation order, the accused may be brought before the judge who originally suspended the sentence and sentenced on the original charge. In addition, the accused may be charged with breach of probation which is a separate offence under the Criminal Code.[50] If a court wishes to suspend sentence, the suspension of sentence must be coupled with an order placing the accused on probation. The authority for suspending a sentence is found in section 737(1) of the Code, which states:

737. (1) Where an accused is convicted of an offence, the court may, having regard to the age and character of the accused, the nature of the offence and the circumstances surrounding its commission,
  (*a*) in the case of an offence other than one for which a minimum punishment is prescribed by law, suspend the passing of sentence and direct that the accused be released on the conditions prescribed in a probation order;

. . . .

If an accused is convicted and fined or imprisoned, a fine or imprisonment cannot be coupled with a suspended sentence. A suspended sentence can only be combined with probation.

---

[50] Criminal Code, s. 740.

(d) Probation

A probation order may be combined with a suspended sentence, a conditional discharge, a fine, or a judge may order that an accused be sentenced to a term of imprisonment to be followed by a period of probation. If a judge imposes a period of probation following imprisonment, the probation order will take effect when the accused is released from prison.[51]

Every probation order which is issued must meet the mandatory terms set out in section 737(2) of the Criminal Code which requires that the accused keep the peace and be of good behaviour and appear before the court when required to do so. The section also states that a judge has the discretion to include conditions in a probation order requiring the accused to:

> (a) report to and be under the supervision of a probation officer or other person designated by the court;
> (b) provide for the support of his spouse or any other dependants who he is liable to support;
> (c) abstain from the consumption of alcohol either absolutely or on such terms as the court may specify;
> (d) abstain from owning, possessing or carrying a weapon;
> (e) make restitution or reparation to any person aggrieved or injured by the commission of the offence for the actual loss or damage sustained by that person as a result thereof;
> (f) remain within the jurisdiction of the court and notify the court or the probation officer or other person designated under paragraph (a) of any change in his address or his employment or occupation;
> (g) make reasonable efforts to find and maintain suitable employment; and
> (h) comply with such other reasonable conditions as the court considers desirable for securing the good conduct of the accused and for preventing a repetition by him of the same offence or the commission of other offences.

In imposing one or more of the conditions quoted above, the trial judge will consider the nature of the offence committed and any individual circumstances which caused the accused to commit the offence. If the offence was committed because of a drug or alcohol abuse problem, a trial judge will probably make it a condition of the accused's probation that he or she abstain from the use of alcohol or drugs. If the accused used a gun or other weapon to commit the offence, the trial judge will make it a term of the probation that the accused is not to be in possession of a firearm. If a probation order is coupled with a fine, suspended sentence, or conditional discharge, the order will come into effect upon the date when the order is made. Before imposing a probation order a judge must ensure that the terms of the order are brought to the attention of the accused and that a copy of the order is given to the accused. The accused must also be informed of the consequences of failure to comply with the terms of a probation order.

---

[51] *R. v. Constant* (1978), 40 C.C.C. (2d) 329 (Man. C.A.).

A judge who wishes to avoid sentencing an accused to a term of imprisonment can use a probation order to maintain some control over the accused. A probationary order may shorten the term of imprisonment which an accused would otherwise receive. Thus, if a judge believes that the crime for which the accused is being sentenced warrants imprisonment, the judge may combine a term of imprisonment with probation. Imprisonment coupled with probation will usually result in the accused serving less time in prison than if she or he had been sentenced to a term of imprisonment without probation. The Criminal Code provides that a probation order shall not last for more than three years from the date when the order came into effect.[52]

(e) Community Service Order

A judge may decide, as a term of probation, to impose a community service order. If a judge imposes a community service order as part of a term of probation, the accused will be ordered to perform some specified work for the community. Thus, an accused may be ordered to do some work for a church or assist senior citizens at an old age home. The authority for authorizing a community serivce order is found in section 737(2)(*h*) of the Code which gives the judge the discretion to make it a term of the accused's probation that the accused "comply with such other reasonable conditions as the court considers desirable for securing the good conduct of the accused and for preventing a repetition by him of the same offence or the commission of other offences."

(f) Restitution

A judge has the power under the Criminal Code to make it a condition of the accused's probation that the accused compensate the victim for his or her loss. Such compensation is normally called restitution. Section 737(2)(*e*) of the Criminal Code gives a judge the power to order that the accused "make restitution or reparation to any person aggrieved or injured by the commission of the offence for the actual loss or damage sustained by that person as a result thereof." If a judge orders that an accused make restitution as a term of a probation order, the judge will determine the amount of money which is to be paid to the victim. There are cases which hold that before considering a restitution order, a judge must determine whether the accused has the financial means to pay the required restitution.[53]

A judge may order that a victim be compensated without making restitution a term of a probation order. Where an accused has caused damage to a

---

[52] Criminal Code, s. 738(2)(*b*).

[53] *R. v. Hudson* (1981), 65 C.C.C. (2d) 171 (Ont. C.A.); *R. v. Wilcox* (1988), 43 C.C.C. (3d) 432 (N.W.T.S.C.); *R. v. Dashner* (1974), 15 C.C.C. (2d) 139 (B.C.C.A.).

victim's property, an accused can be ordered to compensate the victim for loss or damage to the property suffered when the offence was committed. Section 725(1) of the Criminal Code authorizes a court to order that the accused pay monetary compensation to the victim for loss or damage to the victim's property. If the accused does not pay the moneys required forthwith, the person seeking compensation may obtain a civil judgment against the accused by filing the compensation order with the Superior Court of the province where the accused was tried.[54]

The Criminal Code provides for compensation to an innocent purchaser of stolen property where the purchaser has unknowingly purchased such property from an accused who was subsequently tried for an offence under the Code. In such circumstances, a court may, after restoring the property to its rightful owner, order that the accused compensate the innocent purchaser for the sum of money which the purchaser paid for the stolen property.

(g) Imprisonment

(i) *Intermittent sentence*

A judge has the power under the Criminal Code to impose an intermittent sentence. An intermittent sentence allows the accused to serve the sentence at night or on the weekends. An accused will not be eligible for an intermittent sentence unless the accused is sentenced to a term of imprisonment which does not exceed 90 days. An intermittent sentence is usually imposed where the accused is attending school or is gainfully employed and a term of imprisonment would result in the loss of the school year or employment, as the case may be. There are certain offences which are so serious that a judge would not consider imposing an intermittent sentence. Under section 737(1)(c) of the Criminal Code a judge has the power to combine an intermittent sentence with a period of probation. There is a difference between the British Columbia and Ontario appellate courts as to whether probation may be ordered to continue after completion of sentence. The British Columbia court has held that it cannot be imposed, while the Ontario court has held that it can be imposed.[55]

(ii) *Length of sentence*

The offender starts serving his sentence from the time it is imposed. If an accused is sentenced to two years less a day, the accused will serve the sen-

---

[54] Criminal Code, s. 726.
[55] *R. v. Thomas* (No. 2) (1980), 53 C.C.C. (2d) 285 (B.C.C.A.); *R. v. Weber* (1980), 52 C.C.C. (2d) 468 (Ont. C.A.).

tence in a provincial reformatory, while if an accused is sentenced to a period of imprisonment exceeding two years less a day, the sentence will be served in a penitentiary. Whether an accused serves his or her sentence in a provincial reformatory or is sentenced to a penitentiary term depends upon several factors, not the least of which is the seriousness of the offence. In determining whether an accused goes to the penitentiary or not, a trial judge will consider the offence committed, the seriousness of the offence, any criminal record of the accused, and the principles of general and specific deterrence. The trial judge will also consider any relevant sentencing cases which set down guidelines from the higher courts.

(iii) *Consecutive and concurrent sentences*

When an accused has been charged with several offences which really arise out of the same criminal activity, the accused should be given a concurrent sentence. In *R. v. Turland*, the English Court of Appeal said that "it is a well-established principle that consecutive sentences should not be passed for offences which are all part of one incident . . .".[56] The principle expressed in *Turland* was adopted by the Quebec Court of Appeal in *Valade v. R.*[57] In that case, the accused was convicted of having unlawful possession of a revolver for a purpose dangerous to the public peace and pleaded guilty to being in unlawful possession of a 38 calibre firearm without holding a valid permit. The accused was also convicted of covering his face with the intent to commit an indictable offence contrary to the Criminal Code. The accused was sentenced to a term of five years' imprisonment on the first charge, six months on the second charge and seven years on the third charge. The sentences were all to be served consecutively. The accused appealed against the sentences imposed, arguing that such sentences were excessive because they arose out of the same venture. The Quebec Court of Appeal modified the sentences imposed and made them concurrent which meant that he served them at the same time. In making the sentences concurrent to one another, the court noted that the charges really arose out of a single incident.

In *R. v. Auerswald*, the Ontario Court of Appeal allowed the accused's appeal from the sentence imposed after he was convicted of two charges of unlawfully having possession of a restricted weapon contrary to the Criminal Code.[58] At trial, the accused entered a guilty plea to both charges and was sentenced to nine months' imprisonment on each charge with the sentences to run consecutively. In allowing the accused's appeal from sentence, Martin J.A., speaking for the Court of Appeal, held that the trial judge erred in not imposing concurrent sentences rather than consecutive sentences because the pos-

---

[56] [1968] Crim. L.R. 281 at 282 (C.A.).
[57] (1970), 15 C.R.N.S. 42 (Que. C.A.).
[58] (1976), 28 C.C.C. (2d) 177 (Ont. C.A.).

session of two pistols consisted of part of the same transaction. Where an accused is convicted of more than one offence and the transactions do not really arise out of the same matter a judge may decide that the principle of concurrent sentencing is not appropriate and give a consecutive sentence.

Section 717(4)(c) of the Criminal Code states:

(4) Where an accused

. . . .

(c) is convicted of more offences than one before the same court at the same sittings, and

. . . .

(ii) terms of imprisonment for the respective offences are imposed,

. . . .

the court that convicts the accused may direct that the terms of imprisonment shall be served one after the other.

The Supreme Court of Canada has held that this section empowers a judge to order that a sentence be served consecutively to or after a sentence that she or he has previously imposed or is imposing. However, a judge's powers are limited and a judge cannot order that the accused's sentence be made consecutive to a sentence of another trial judge in another case then before the courts. However, if the sentence has already been imposed by the other judge at the time when the accused is being sentenced, the sentence may be made consecutive to the earlier sentence under section 717(4)(a). In imposing consecutive sentences, the court must ensure that the sentences are not excessive.

The courts have held that in imposing consecutive sentences it is proper for a trial judge to consider whether the sentences as a whole are excessively long. This principle is referred to as the totality principle. The totality principle is that sentences imposed should not, in the aggregate, be more than would be appropriate for the crimes for which the accused has been sentenced. The sentence imposed may be in the range of sentences which are appropriate for the type of crime which the accused has committed, but excessive because the total number of years exceeds the sentence which is appropriate when the accused is being sentenced for more than one offence at the same time.

4. RECENT DEVELOPMENTS

In July, 1995, Bill C-41[59] received Royal Assent. It replaces Part XXIII of the Criminal Code, making significant changes in the Code's sentencing

---

[59] S.C. 1995, c. 22. At the time of publication, this Act was not yet proclaimed in force.

provisions. Sections 718, 718.1 and 718.2 set out the purpose and principles of sentencing. Where a crime is committed by a person abusing a position of trust or authority, or is motivated by hate, it will be considered an aggravating factor for the purposes of sentencing. New section 717 provides for the use of "alternative measures" to deal with adult offenders, but only if they are not inconsistent with the protection of society, and certain conditions are met. "Alternative measures" are defined under section 716 as being measures other than judicial proceedings under the Criminal Code.

Under section 742.1, where a judge imposes a sentence of incarceration of less than two years, the judge may suspend the operation of the sentence and substitute a "conditional sentence", prescribing certain compulsory conditions such as reporting to a supervisor. As a result, the offender would serve the sentence in the community and may also be ordered to abstain from owning or possessing a weapon, and to perform community service work.

The penalty for breach of a probation order (section 733) is increased to a maximum of 18 months where the Crown proceeds summarily, or 10 years where the Crown proceeds by indictment.

Before imposing a fine, a court must be satisfied that an offender can pay. Provinces and the federal government are permitted to impose certain penalties, e.g., refusal of permits or licences, until the fine is paid. Incarceration is a last resort; rather, civil enforcement of fines is provided. If incarceration is deemed necessary, its length is determined by a formula based on the provincial hourly minimum wage.

Section 722 allows a court to consider a victim impact statement for the purpose of determining sentence. "Victims", which includes spouses and relatives of the deceased, are permitted to make representations at hearings held to determine whether the period of the parole ineligibility for first or second degree murder should be changed (section 745.6).

15

Young Offenders

1. YOUNG OFFENDERS ACT

(a) Background

Young people have always been given special treatment under the criminal law because it has been considered that their lack of maturity called for special treatment. Section 13 of the Criminal Code[1] provides that "No person shall be convicted of an offence in respect of an act or omission on his part while he was under the age of twelve years." Someone who is 12 years of age or more and under 18 years of age who commits a criminal offence will not be tried as an adult, but rather will be tried as a young offender under the Young Offenders Act.[2] A person being tried under the Young Offenders Act will have special benefits and protections which are not available to an adult offender and will not be treated as severely as an adult offender who is convicted of a similar offence. Thus, an adult who is convicted of first degree murder under the Criminal Code may be sentenced to life imprisonment, whereas a young offender convicted of first degree murder will, by virtue of section 20(1)(k.1) of the Young Offenders Act, be sentenced to a disposition not exceeding five years less a day. Bill C-37 increases the maximum disposition to 10 years.

The philosophy of the Young Offenders Act is that young people who commit criminal offences should not be held as accountable as adults who commit similar offences. This philosophy is expressed in section 3 of the Act which states:

---

[1] R.S.C. 1985, c. C-46.

[2] R.S.C. 1985, c. Y-1. Bill C-37, An Act to amend the Young Offenders Act and the Criminal Code, S.C. 1995, c. 19, received Royal Assent June 26, 1995. At time of publication, this Act (hereafter Bill C-37) was not yet proclaimed in force. Changes made by Bill C-37 will be referred to throughout this chapter.

3. (1) It is hereby recognized and declared that
(a) while young persons should not in all instances be held accountable in the same manner or suffer the same consequences for their behaviour as adults, young persons who commit offences should nonetheless bear responsibility for their contraventions;

. . . .

(f) in the application of this Act, the rights and freedoms of young persons include a right to the least possible interference with freedom that is consistent with the protection of society, having regard to the needs of young persons and the interest of their families;

. . . .

Bill C-37 adds a paragraph emphasizing the long-term protection of society by identifying and responding to "children and young persons at risk of committing offending behaviour in the future."

The legislation provides that young persons have special needs and require guidance and assistance and that they should have special guarantees of their rights and freedoms. The direction in section 3 of the Act that a young person is entitled to the least possible interference with freedom that is consistent with the protection of society may mean that in certain cases a young offender will not be prosecuted for a criminal offence. In this regard, section 4(1) of the Young Offenders Act provides:

4. (1) Alternative measures may be used to deal with a young person alleged to have committed an offence instead of judicial proceedings under this Act only if

(*a*) the measures are part of a program of alternative measures authorized by the Attorney General or his delegate or authorized by a person, or a person within a class of persons, designated by the Lieutenant Governor in Council of a province;
(*b*) the person who is considering whether to use such measures is satisfied that they would be appropriate having regard to the needs of the young person and the interests of society;
(*c*) the young person, having been informed of the alternative measures, fully and freely consents to participate therein;
(*d*) the young person has, before consenting to participate in the alternative measures, been advised of his right to be represented by counsel and been given a reasonable opportunity to consult with counsel;
(*e*) the young person accepts responsibility for the act or omission that forms the basis of the offence that he is alleged to have committed;
(*f*) there is, in the opinion of the Attorney General or his agent, sufficient evidence to proceed with the prosecution of the offence; and
(*g*) the prosecution of the offence is not in any way barred at law.

Under the Young Offenders Act, a young person may not be sentenced to a disposition in excess of five years less a day when the offence committed is one which would call for life imprisonment under the Criminal Code (increased to a maximum of 10 years for first degree murder and seven years for second degree murder by Bill C-37) or in excess of two years for an offence for which an adult may be sentenced to something less than life imprisonment. Thus, a young person charged with sexual assault causing bodily harm under section 272 of the Criminal Code would, under the Young Offenders Act, if convicted, be liable to receive a maximum penalty of two years in jail; an adult if convicted would be liable to receive a maximum penalty of 14 years in jail.

The Act does not create criminal offences. Rather, it provides a procedure by which criminal offences committed by young people shall be tried, provides for the penalties or treatment to be applied and provides for the protection of privacy of young persons by prohibiting reports of the proceedings, and even in certain cases permitting young persons involved in the proceedings to be excluded from the court, if information presented to the court could be seriously injurious or prejudicial to them.

(b) Distinguished from the Juvenile Delinquents Act

(i) *Generally*

The Young Offenders Act, which was proclaimed on April 2, 1984, is markedly different than its predecessor, the Juvenile Delinquents Act,[3] which covered provincial offences and offences such as contributing to juvenile delinquency. Under the Juvenile Delinquents Act a "juvenile delinquent" was defined as follows:

> "juvenile delinquent" means any child who violates any provision of the Criminal Code or of any federal or provincial statute, or of any by-law or ordinance of any municipality, or who is guilty of sexual immorality or any similar form of vice, or who is liable by reason of any other act to be committed to an industrial school or juvenile reformatory under any federal or provincial statute;[4]

Now that the Young Offenders Act has replaced the Juvenile Delinquents Act, someone who is charged under the Young Offenders Act may only be prosecuted for Criminal Code offences or for breaching a regulation or by-law made pursuant to federal legislation, other than ordinances applicable to the Yukon or Northwest Territories.[5] The restrictive scope of the Young Offenders Act means that it is now up to the provinces to deal with matters such as truancy. Prior to the Young Offenders Act (the Act), someone who was under seven years of age could not be charged with a criminal offence. The minimum age for being charged with a criminal offence has now been raised from seven to 12 years of age so that someone who is under 12 years of age cannot be charged with a criminal offence. However, the provinces can pass legisla-

---

[3] R.S.C. 1970, c. J-3.
[4] *Ibid.*, s. 2.
[5] Young Offenders Act, s. 2.

tion covering provincial offences so that a child under the age of 12 who commits a provincial offence formerly covered by the Juvenile Delinquents Act may not escape the responsibility for his or her actions.

Under the Act, the Crown prosecutor is not required to prove that the accused who appears before a youth court judge is 12 years of age and under 18 years of age, as the Act permits a youth court to make an assumption as to the age of the youth appearing. Section 2(1) of the Act states that a young person means:

> . . . a person who is or, in the absence of evidence to the contrary, appears to be twelve years of age or more, but under eighteen years of age and, where the context requires, includes any person who is charged under this Act with having committed an offence while he was a young person or is found guilty of an offence under this Act;

The Young Offenders Act represents a radical shift in philosophy from the Juvenile Delinquents Act which treated young people who committed criminal offences as juvenile delinquents rather than as offenders. Section 3(2) of the Juvenile Delinquents Act provided that:

> (2) Where a child is adjudged to have committed a delinquency he shall be dealt with, not as an offender, but as one in a condition of delinquency and therefore requiring help and guidance and proper supervision.

It is significant that one could be found to be a juvenile delinquent under the Juvenile Delinquents Act without ever having committed a criminal offence, as the definition of juvenile delinquent made no mention of the word offence. Section 2 of that Act provided that juvenile delinquent included a child "who is guilty of sexual immorality or any similar form of vice." The philosophy behind the Juvenile Delinquents Act as set out in section 2 of that Act may be contrasted with the declaration of principles contained in section 3 of the Young Offenders Act, which provides that young people must be responsible for their contraventions.

The Young Offenders Act is a recognition by Parliament that the special concerns of the young offender must be balanced with society's need to be protected against illegal activity. Section 3(1)(b) of the Act provides:

> (b) society must, although it has the responsibility to take reasonable measures to prevent criminal conduct by young persons, be afforded the necessary protection from illegal behaviour;

(ii) *Sentencing*

The difference in philosophy between the Young Offenders Act and the Juvenile Delinquents Act as expressed in the general principles set out in section 3(1) of the Young Offenders Act is perhaps best reflected by the different sentencing procedures under the two Acts. Under the Juvenile Delinquents Act someone found to be a juvenile delinquent was subject to be placed indefinitely in a foster home, to be made a ward of the Children's Aid Society for an indefinite period or to be committed to an industrial school for an indefinite period. Also a court had the power to fine a juvenile or place the juvenile on probation. In addition, the court could give the juvenile a suspended sentence for a period of time which was in the discretion of the court. Once a young person was found to be a juvenile delinquent and sentenced, the courts could, until the youngster reached 21 years of age, have the young person brought into court to be further sentenced or released, as the case may be, if, in the opinion of the court, the action taken would be in both the child's and the community's best interest. The result was that a juvenile delinquent could be detained longer than an adult offender who committed a similar offence.

The sentences which were given under the Juvenile Delinquents Act were in keeping with the act's philosophy that juvenile delinquents required "help and guidance and proper supervision." This philosophy may be contrasted with the explicit philosophy of the Young Offenders Act which treats young persons who commit crimes as offenders rather than as delinquents. A young person who is sentenced under the Young Offenders Act will not be imprisoned for an indefinite period of time, or placed on probation indefinitely, as there are definite time limits. Thus, for example, a young person on probation under the Act cannot be placed on probation for a period exceeding two years, regardless of whether the young person has reformed or not.

A judge sentencing a young offender has a broader range of sentencing options than were available to a juvenile court judge. A young offender may be given an absolute discharge — which means that he or she will not have a criminal record — or, if sentenced to a period of incarceration, the youth court judge has the option of ordering that the sentence be served intermittently — e.g., on the weekend.[6] A judge may order that a young person convicted of having committed a criminal offence pay a fine of up to $1,000. This may be contrasted with the Juvenile Delinquents Act where the maximum fine that a judge could impose was $25.

Under the Act, judges also have been given specific power to make young offenders pay compensation to the person or persons whose property they destroyed, and, in the case of personal injury, the young person can be compelled to compensate the victim for any injuries which the victim received. A young person who is in receipt of stolen property can be ordered to return such property to the victim, and, where someone has innocently purchased stolen property, the young person who stole the property can be ordered to pay a sum of money to the innocent purchaser of the stolen property.[7] The broader range of sentencing options available to a youth court judge

---

[6] Young Offenders Act, s. 20(1)(*k*).
[7] Young Offenders Act, s. 20(1)(*e*).

means that young offenders will be held more accountable for their actions than young persons who were sentenced as juvenile delinquents. This is reflected by provisions such as the restitution provision and the provision authorizing the judge to award compensation to victims of crime.

The difference in philosophy between the Young Offenders Act and the Juvenile Delinquents Act is further reflected by the fact that a person who commits a crime under the Young Offenders Act is referred to as a young person, whereas a person governed by the Juvenile Delinquents Act was, throughout the Act, referred to as a child. The use of the word young person in the Young Offenders Act reflects the intention of Parliament that young persons who are charged with committing criminal offences bear a higher degree of responsibility than that imposed by the Juvenile Delinquents Act.

2. YOUTH COURT

(a) Jurisdiction

The Young Offenders Act provides that a youth court is the only court which has jurisdiction to deal with young offenders. Someone who is over 12 and under 18 years of age will be tried by a court which has been designated as a youth court by the legislature of a province.[8] In most provinces this means that a young offender will be tried by a family court judge.

(i) *Exceptions to its exclusive jurisdiction*

The youth court does not have exclusive jurisdiction to try a young person who is a member of the armed forces and young persons who commit minor criminal offences while employed by the armed forces will usually be tried by a military tribunal.[9] Also, section 16 of the Act authorizes a youth court to order that a young offender who has reached 14 years be tried as an adult in ordinary court; such an offender will be subject to the penalties the Criminal Code provides for adult offenders. Section 16(1) states that on application by the Crown or the young person or his counsel "[a youth court shall] after affording both parties and the parents of the young person an opportunity to be heard, determine, in accordance with subsection (1.1), whether the young person should be proceeded against in ordinary court."

---

[8] Young Offenders Act, s. 2.

[9] G.P. Johnstone, B.A. Ferns and J.C. Pearson, "The Child and Young Persons and the Criminal Process" in *Criminal Procedure, 1983-84*, R.J. Carter and David Watt, eds. (Toronto: Carswell, 1984), p. 302.

(1.1) In making the determination referred to in subsection (1), the youth court shall consider the interest of society, which includes the objectives of affording protection to the public and rehabilitation of the young person, and determine whether those objectives can be reconciled by the youth remaining under the jurisdiction of the youth court, and if the court is of the opinion that those objectives cannot be so reconciled, protection of the public shall be paramount and the court shall order that the young person be proceeded against in ordinary court in accordance with the law ordinarily applicable to an adult charged with the offence.

Before section 16(1.1) was passed by Parliament, the Supreme Court of Canada held that the Act does not require that all factors be given equal weight, but only that each be considered.[10] The addition of section 16(1.1) means that where protection of the public collides with rehabilitation of the young person, protection of the public will be the pre-eminent factor in determining whether the young person should be tried as an adult.[11]

Section 16(2) sets out the criteria which a court is to consider in determining whether a young offender should be tried as an adult:

(2) In considering an application under subsection (1) in respect of a young person, a youth court shall take into account

(*a*) the seriousness of the alleged offence and the circumstances in which it was allegedly committed;

(*b*) the age, maturity, character and background of the young person and any record or summary of previous findings of delinquency under the Juvenile Delinquents Act . . . or previous findings of guilt under this Act or any other Act of Parliament or any regulation made thereunder;

(*c*) the adequacy of this Act, and the adequacy of the *Criminal Code* or other Act of Parliament that would apply in respect of the young person if an order were made under subsection (1) to meet the circumstances of the case;

(*d*) the availability of treatment or correctional resources;

(*e*) any representations made to the court by or on behalf of the young person or by the Attorney General or his agent; and

(*f*) any other factors that the court considers relevant.

A young person who is charged with one of the more minor indictable offences set out in section 553 of the Criminal Code cannot be tried in an adult court and must be tried by a youth court judge. The courts have held that in deciding whether a young person should be tried in adult court, a judge should have regard to only those factors set out in section 16 and that, accordingly, the fact that a young person is charged with murder will not automatically mean that the charge should be heard in adult court.

---

[10] *R. v. M. (S.H.)* (1989), 71 C.R. (3d) 257 at 305 (S.C.C.).
[11] *R. v. C. (D.)* (1993), 85 C.C.C. (3d) 547 (Ont. C.A.), leave to appeal to S.C.C. refused (1994), 86 C.C.C. (3d) vii (note) (S.C.C.).

(ii) *Limitation period*

The Act does not state that a young person must be prosecuted for a criminal offence within so many months after the offence occurred. Section 5(2) does state that a young person cannot be prosecuted after the time for prosecution stipulated in the statute creating the offence expires. Thus, where a young person is charged with a Criminal Code offence, the time when the offence must be prosecuted will depend upon the provisions of the Criminal Code. The Criminal Code provides a six-month limitation period for summary conviction offences and, accordingly, someone who is prosecuted for shoplifting must be prosecuted within six months from when the offence occurred. Generally speaking, there is no time limit for prosecuting someone who has committed an indictable offence under the Criminal Code. Accordingly, a young offender who commits an indictable offence, such as murder, may be prosecuted years after the offence took place.

(iii) *Young offender turned adult*

If a young offender becomes an adult in the midst of his or her trial, the youth court judge trying the young offender will continue to have jurisdiction to hear the case. Section 5(3) of the Young Offenders Act provides: "Proceedings commenced under this Act against a young person may be continued, after he becomes an adult, in all respects as if he remained a young person."

(b) Young Offender's Rights

Throughout this book we have seen that an accused who is detained or arrested by the police has, upon detention or arrest, certain rights under the Charter of Rights and Freedoms.[12] A young person who is detained or arrested by the police has rights under the Act as well as the Charter of Rights and in fact has greater rights than an adult offender who is detained or arrested in similar circumstances.

(i) *Right to counsel*

The Act provides that a young person who is detained or arrested must be advised of his or her right to retain a lawyer. The right to retain a lawyer is guaranteed by section 11 of the Young Offenders Act which provides:

---

[12] Being Part I of the Constitution Act, 1982 [en. by the Canada Act, 1982 (U.K.), c. 11, s. 1].

11. (1) A young person has the right to retain and instruct counsel without delay, and to exercise that right personally, at any stage of proceedings against the young person and prior to and during any consideration of whether, instead of commencing or continuing judicial proceedings against the young person under this Act, to use alternative measures to deal with the young person.

(2) Every young person who is arrested or detained shall, forthwith on his arrest or detention, be advised by the arresting officer or the officer in charge, as the case may be, of his right to be represented by counsel and shall be given an opportunity to obtain counsel.

. . . .

A young person who is released upon a promise to appear, appearance notice, or is given a summons to appear in court, will be told that he or she has the right to retain and instruct counsel. Section 11(9) of the Young Offenders Act provides:

(9) A statement that a young person has the right to be represented by counsel shall be included in
(*a*) any appearance notice or summons issued to the young person;
(*b*) any warrant to arrest the young person;
(*c*) any promise to appear given by the young person;
(*d*) any recognizance entered into before an officer in charge by the young person;
(*e*) any notice given to the young person in relation to any proceedings held pursuant to subsection 26.1(1), 26.2(1) or 26.6(1); or
(*f*) any notice of a review of a disposition given to the young person.

The requirement that a summons, appearance notice, recognizance or a warrant contain a statement as to a young person's right to contact a lawyer is unique to young offenders; there is no such requirement for adult offenders.

(ii) *Right to legal aid*

In the United States, everyone who is charged with a serious criminal offence has a guaranteed right to legal representation; thus, someone who cannot afford to hire a lawyer is entitled to be represented by a court-appointed attorney. The United States Supreme Court held, in *Argersinger v. Hamlin,*[13] that an accused person has the right to have the services of a court-appointed attorney in all cases where the accused is liable to be imprisoned if convicted of the offence charged. The American law differs markedly from Canadian law, as in Canada generally someone who is charged with a criminal offence has no absolute right to legal assistance paid for by the state. The young offender is the exception to this general rule. Subsection 11(3) requires every presiding judge or official in any proceeding under the Act to advise the

---

[13] (1972), 407 U.S. 25, 92 S.Ct. 2006.

young offender of his or her right to counsel and afford the young offender an opportunity to obtain one.

Section 11(3) of the Act provides that young people are entitled to legal representation at the following proceedings:

1. At a judicial interim release hearing or bail hearing.
2. At a hearing to determine whether the young person should be tried in an adult court.
3. At the trial itself.
4. Where submissions are made by the Attorney General or his representative as to the length of imprisonment and the conditions that should apply on release.
5. At a review of the disposition held before a youth court or a review board under the Act.
6. Bill C-37 adds paragraph (*e*): "at a review of the level of custody pursuant to subsection 28.1(1)."

Young offenders have been guaranteed the right to government-funded legal assistance; a young offender who cannot afford to hire a lawyer can make an application to a youth court judge to have a lawyer appointed to defend him or her. Section 11(4) of the Act authorizes a youth court judge to appoint a lawyer to represent a young offender:

> (4) Where a young person at his trial or at a hearing or review referred to in subsection (3) wishes to obtain counsel but is unable to do so, the youth court before which the hearing, trial or review is held or the review board before which the review is held
> (*a*) shall, where there is a legal aid or assistance program available in the province where the hearing, trial or review is held, refer the young person to that program for the appointment of counsel; or
> (*b*) where no legal aid or assistance program is available or the young person is unable to obtain counsel through such a program, may, and on the request of the young person shall, direct that the young person be represented by counsel.

The Young Offenders Act guarantees that a young person will be represented by a lawyer when the court is considering whether the young person is a proper candidate for the alternative measures program. It will be recalled that the alternative measures program usually involves community service or special education.[14]

---

[14] A.W. Mackay, *Education Law in Canada* (Toronto: Emond-Montgomery, 1984), p. 226.

(iii) *Independent counsel*

The Act provides that a young person is entitled to be represented by a lawyer other than the lawyer appointed by the young person's family. In this regard, section 11(8) of the Act states:

> (8) In any case where it appears to a youth court judge or a justice that the interests of a young person and his parents are in conflict or that it would be in the best interest of the young person to be represented by his own counsel, the judge or justice shall ensure that the young person is represented by counsel independent of his parents.

(c) Procedure

(i) *Appearance in court*

The Act makes it mandatory that a justice of the peace or a judge, as the case may be, inform the young person of the charge which he or she is facing when the young person first appears in youth court. Section 12(1) of the Young Offenders Act states:

> **12.** (1) Where a young person against whom an information is laid first appears before a youth court judge or a justice, the judge or justice shall
> (*a*) cause the information to be read to him; and
> (*b*) where the young person is not represented by counsel, inform him of his right to be so represented.
> (2) A young person may waive the requirement under paragraph (1)(*a*) where the young person is represented by counsel.

Bill C-37 adds paragraph 12(1)(*c*) which provides that if the young person is one referred to in subsection 16(1.01), he shall be informed that proceedings will be in ordinary court unless an application is made to have the young person proceeded against in youth court, and an order is made to that effect. The young person identified in new subsection 16(1.01) is one alleged to have committed first or second degree murder, attempt to commit murder, manslaughter, or aggravated sexual assault and was 16 or 17 years old at the time of the alleged offence.

Thus, when a young person appears in court to set a date, or appears for a bail hearing, the charge must be read to him or her unless the young person's counsel indicates to the court that the young person is familiar with the charges and does not need to have the information read. Failure on the part of the justice of the peace or a judge to read the information setting out the charge to the young offender when the young offender first appears in court may deprive the court of jurisdiction to hear the case.[15]

---

[15] *H. v. R.* (1985), 21 C.C.C. (3d) 396 (B.C.S.C.).

(ii) *Bail hearings and pre-disposition detention*

While a young person will be tried before a youth court judge, a justice of the peace does have the power to conduct bail hearings and issue processes, such as notice to a parent. Section 6 of the Young Offenders Act states:

> **6.** Any proceeding that may be carried out before a justice under the *Criminal Code*, other than a plea, a trial or an adjudication, may be carried out before such justice in respect of an offence alleged to have been committed by a young person, and any process that may be issued by a justice under the *Criminal Code* may be issued by such justice in respect of an offence alleged to have been committed by a young person.

Although, generally speaking, a justice of the peace has the power to conduct a bail hearing, section 8 of the Young Offenders Act provides that a justice of the peace does not have the power to release a young person against whom proceedings are commenced under the Act where the person is charged with certain specified offences, such as murder (see section 522 of the Code).

A young person arrested or detained prior to a disposition shall be detained in a place of temporary detention. The Act provides that young persons are not to be detained in the same facilities as adult offenders. Section 7(2) of the Act provides:

> (2) A young person referred to in subsection (1) shall be held separate and apart from any adult who is detained or held in custody unless a youth court judge or a justice is satisfied that
> (*a*) the young person cannot, having regard to his own safety or the safety of others, be detained in a place of detention for young persons; or
> (*b*) no place of detention for young persons is available within a reasonable distance.

The Act states that where a youth court judge or justice is satisfied that a responsible person is prepared to take care of and control over a young person, the young person may be released into the care and custody of that person instead of being detained, if the young person consents. The responsible person would usually be a parent; the young person could be released into the custody of someone other than a parent. Section 7.1(1) of the Act provides:

> (1) Where a youth court judge or a justice is satisfied that
> (*a*) a young person who has been arrested would, but for this subsection, be detained in custody,
> (*b*) a responsible person is willing and able to take care of and exercise control over the young person, and
> (*c*) the young person is willing to be placed in the care of that person,
> the young person may be placed in the care of that person instead of being detained in custody.

(iii) *Notification of parents*

If a young person is arrested and detained in custody, the police must notify the young person's parents that the young person has been arrested and is detained in custody. If the police are unable to contact the young person's parents, notice may be given to an adult relative who is known to the young person. The notice must contain the following:

1. The name of the person in respect of whom the notice is given.
2. A statement of the offence with which the young person is charged.
3. The time and place where the young person is to appear in court.
4. An indication that the young person is entitled to be represented by a lawyer.

Failure to give notice under the Act will not mean that a judge will not have jurisdiction or authority to hear the case. However, section 9(9) of the Young Offenders Act states:

> (9) Failure to give notice under subsection (2) in accordance with this section in any case renders invalid any subsequent proceedings under this Act relating to the case unless
> (a) a parent of the young person against whom proceedings are held attends court with the young person; or
> (b) a youth court judge or a justice before whom proceedings are held against the young person
> > (i) adjourns the proceedings and orders that the notice be given in such manner and to such persons as the judge or justice directs, or
> > (ii) dispenses with the notice where the judge or justice is of the opinion that, having regard to the circumstances, the notice may be dispensed with.

Section 10 of the Young Offenders Act authorizes a judge to dispense with notice, if, in the opinion of the judge, notice to a parent or other relatives should not be required.

Under the Act a parent can be ordered to attend at his or her son's trial. Section 10(1)of the Act provides:

> **10.** (1) Where a parent does not attend proceedings before a youth court in respect of a young person, the court may, if in its opinion the presence of the parent is necessary or in the best interest of the young person, by order in writing require the parent to attend at any stage of the proceedings.

If a parent fails, without reasonable excuse, to attend court after being ordered to do so by the youth court judge, the parent can be charged with contempt of court.

(iv) *Admissibility of statements*

The Act contains detailed requirements which must be fulfilled before a young person's confession may be used at trial. Subsections 56(2) and (3) of the Young Offenders Act provide:

(2) No oral or written statement given by a young person to a police officer or other person who is, in law, a person in authority[16] is admissible against the young person unless
    (*a*) the statement was voluntary;
    (*b*) the person to whom the statement was given has, before the statement was made, clearly explained to the young person, in language appropriate to his age and understanding, that
        (i) the young person is under no obligation to give a statement,
        (ii) any statement given by him may be used as evidence in proceedings against him,
        (iii) the young person has the right to consult another person in accordance with paragraph (*c*), and
        (iv) any statement made by the young person is required to be made in the presence of the person consulted, unless the young person desires otherwise;
    (*c*) the young person has, before the statement was made, been given a reasonable opportunity to consult with counsel or a parent, or in the absence of a parent, an adult relative, or in the absence of a parent, an adult relative, or . . . any other appropriate adult chosen by the young person; and
    (*d*) where the young person consults any person pursuant to paragraph (*c*), the young person has been given a reasonable opportunity to make the statement in the presence of that person.
(3) The requirements set out in paragraphs (2)(*b*), (*c*) and (*d*) do not apply in respect of oral statements where they are made spontaneously by the young person to a peace officer or another person in authority before that person has had a reasonable opportunity to comply with those requirements.

Section 56(3) of the Young Offenders Act covers a situation where a young person suddenly and unexpectedly makes a statement admitting his or her guilt to a police officer or another person in authority before the officer has had an opportunity to fulfill the detailed requirements of section 56(2). Sometimes an accused who is caught red-handed will suddenly confess his or her guilt to a police officer; if section 56(3) were not in the Act, any spontaneous oral statement made to a police officer would not be admissible given the strict requirements governing the admissibility of confessions set out in section 56(2).

---

[16] Bill C-37 inserts at this point: "on the arrest or detention of the young person or in circumstances where the peace officer or other person has reasonable grounds for believing that the young person has committed an offence".

3. DISPOSITIONS

(a) Generally

Under the Act, what are normally called sentences are called dispositions. The penalties which a young person is liable to receive upon conviction are set out in section 20 of the Act. A youth court judge has the power to impose one or more of the following dispositions, which are not inconsistent with each other:

1. Grant an absolute discharge, or, pursuant to Bill C-37, the judge may order a conditional discharge.

2. Impose up to a $1,000 fine.

3. Order that the young person compensate the victim for loss or damage to property or for loss of income or support. The young person can also be ordered to pay monetary compensation for personal injury arising from the commission of the offence.

4. Order that the young person return stolen property.

5. Where a young person has been ordered to restore property to its original owner, the young person can be ordered to pay a monetary sum to the person who purchased stolen property from the young offender not realizing that such property was stolen.

6. Order the young person to perform such personal services as may be required to compensate the victim for "any loss, damage or injury suffered by that person in respect of which an order may be made."

7. Order a young person to perform community service on such terms and conditions as are imposed by the court.

8. Place the young person on probation for a period not to exceed two years.

9. Sentence the young person to a term of imprisonment to be served continuously or intermittently as a judge may direct for a period not exceeding two years from the date of committal or "where the young person is found guilty of an offence for which the punishment provided by the Criminal Code or any other Act of Parliament is imprisonment for life" order the young person to serve a sentence of five years less a day that shall consist of three years imprisonment and conditional supervision in the community. Bill C-37 increases the maximum disposition to 10 years.

10. "Make any order of prohibition, seizure or forfeiture that may be imposed under any Act of Parliament or any regulation made thereunder where an accused is found guilty or convicted of that offence."

11. "Impose on the young person such other reasonable and ancillary conditions as it deems advisable and in the best interest of the young person and the public."

The Act states that where a judge imposes more than one disposition on a young offender, the dispositions shall, where they are imposed in respect of the same offence, not exceed two years. Despite this general rule, a judge has the power to impose a longer disposition where the young person is convicted of an offence such as murder, which would normally carry a penalty of life imprisonment, if the young person was prosecuted under the Criminal Code. As the Act provides that a judge may make "any order of prohibition, seizure or forfeiture that may be imposed under any Act of Parliament," a youth court judge would, for example, have the power to order that a young person convicted of possession of a dangerous weapon not have in his or her possession any weapon for a period not exceeding two years. Section 20(4) of the Act provides that, where a young person is sentenced in respect of different offences, the combined length of the dispositions shall not exceed three years. The Young Offenders Act also states that a young person may not receive a greater punishment than an adult offender would receive in similar circumstances. Section 20(7) of the Act states that:

> (7) No disposition shall be made in respect of a young person under this section that results in a punishment that is greater than the maximum punishment that would be applicable to an adult who has committed the same offence.

Under the Juvenile Delinquents Act it was not uncommon for a young person found to be a juvenile delinquent to serve more time in a foster home or a group home than an adult sentenced for the same crime in the adult system. The paternalistic philosophy of the Juvenile Delinquents Act was discussed earlier in this chapter. The Young Offenders Act has done away with the indefinite sentences which were a product of the Juvenile Delinquents Act.

The youth court must consider the ability of the young person to pay any fine which the court may decide to impose. A youth court judge cannot order that a young person perform a community service order unless the judge concludes that the young person is a suitable candidate and the organization or person for whom the service is to be performed has agreed. This provision, which is contained in section 21(9) of the Act, ensures that an unwilling organization will not be forced to work with a young offender. In *R. v. D.*, the Nova Scotia Court of Appeal held that a youth court could not impose a suspended sentence.[17] The British Columbia Court of Appeal in *R. v. W.G.* held that a young offender could not be directed where to live.[18] If a sentence has been imposed, a sentence for a later offence must not increase the time served to more than three years.

---

[17] (1985), 18 C.C.C. (3d) 476 (N.S.C.A.).
[18] (1985), 23 C.C.C. (3d) 93 (B.C.C.A.).

(b) Secure Custody

When a young person is sentenced to a period of imprisonment, the court must specify whether the sentence is to be one of open custody or secure custody. Open custody as defined in section 24.1 of the Act means custody in:

> (*a*) a community residential centre, group home, child care institution, or a forest or wilderness camp, or
> (*b*) any other like place or facility
> designated by the Lieutenant Governor in Council of a province [the cabinet] or his delegate as a place of open custody for the purposes of this Act, and includes a place or facility within a class of such places or facilities so designated;
> "secure custody" means custody in a place or facility designated by the Lieutenant Governor in Council of a province for the secure containment or restraint of young persons, and includes a place or facility within a class of such places or facilities so designated.

The rules dealing with secure custody are set out in section 24.1(3) of the Act. In general, no young person under 14 years of age may be committed to secure custody. This general rule is subject to a number of exceptions:

1. A young person under 14 may be committed to secure custody where the offence is an offence, such as murder, for which an adult would be sentenced to life imprisonment.

2. The offence committed is one for which an adult would be sentenced to 5 years or more and the young person has previously been convicted of committing such an offence.

3. The offence involves a prison breach or escaping from lawful custody or being at large without lawful excuse.

4. The offence involves an attempt to commit any of the offences mentioned in paragraph 3.

A young offender over 14 may be placed in secure custody where the young offender commits offences similar to those described in the previous paragraph (see section 24.1(3)).[19]

The Act states that the youth court judge shall not commit a young person to custody unless the judge concludes that the committal is "necessary for the protection of society." The Act states that in determining whether a committal to custody is "necessary for the protection of society" the judge shall consider the following factors:

1. The seriousness of the offence.
2. The circumstances in which the offence was committed.
3. The needs and circumstances of the young person.

The Act directs a youth court judge to consider a pre-disposition report before committing a young person to custody. Such a report includes the result of an interview with the offender, where possible the parents, the victim, and factors relevant to possible rehabilitation. The court may with the consent of the young person and prosecutor dispense with the pre-disposition report.

(c) Reasons for Sentence

The Young Offenders Act makes it mandatory for a youth court judge to state his or her reasons for disposition or sentence. Section 20(6) of the Act provides:

> (6) Where a youth court makes a disposition under this section, it shall state its reasons therefor in the record of the case and shall

---

[19] Bill C-37 restates the factors to be considered in deciding whether a young person should be placed in open or secure custody in this way:

> (4) In deciding whether a young person shall be placed in open custody or secure custody, the youth court or the provincial director shall take into account the following factors:
>
> (a) that a young person should be placed in a level of custody involving the least degree of containment and restraint, having regard to
>
> (i) the seriousness of the offence in respect of which the young person was committed to custody and the circumstances in which that offence was committed,
> (ii) the needs and circumstances of the young person, including proximity to family, school, employment and support services,
> (iii) the safety of other young persons in custody, and
> (iv) the interests of society;
>
> (b) that the level of custody should allow for the best possible match of programs to the young person's needs and behaviour, having regard to the findings of any assessment in respect of the young person;
>
> (c) the likelihood of escape if the young person is placed in open custody; and
>
> (d) the recommendations, if any, of the youth court or the provincial director, as the case may be.

(*a*) provide or cause to be provided a copy of the disposition, and
(*b*) on request, provide or cause to be provided a transcript or copy of the reasons for the disposition
to the young person in respect of whom the disposition was made, the young person's counsel and parents, the provincial director, where the provincial director has an interest in the disposition, the prosecutor and, in the case of a custodial disposition made under paragraph (1)(*k*) or (*k*.1), the review board, if a review board has been established or designated.

(d) Review of Disposition

The Act provides that where a young person has been sentenced to a custodial period exceeding one year, the sentence shall be reviewed by a youth court judge after one year. The Act directs the youth court to consider a progress report on the young person's performance while in custody before reviewing a young person's disposition. Upon reviewing the young person's disposition, a youth court judge has the power to confirm the disposition or direct that the young person be transferred to open custody, or release the young person and place him on probation.

After serving six months in custody, a young person may request that the youth court review the disposition imposed. A review may be brought at an earlier time if the young person has obtained the permission of a youth court judge to bring the review. The grounds for bringing the review are as follows:

1. The young person has made sufficient progress to justify a change in disposition.
2. There has been a material change in the circumstances which led to the young person being committed into custody.
3. On the ground that new services or programs are available that were not available at the time of the disposition.
4. Such other grounds as the court considers appropriate.
5. Bill C-37 adds a fifth: "on the ground that the opportunities for rehabilitation are now greater in the community."

4. POLICE RECORDS

Great care is taken of records to protect young people, and to shield their identity. The youth court records are segregated from other records and only released to those with a legitimate interest. Section 41 of the Act deals with the rights of police to keep records of such offences:

41. (1) A record of any offence of which a young person has been found guilty under this Act may be kept in such central repository as the Commissioner of the Royal Canadian Mounted Police may, from time to time, designate for the purpose of keeping criminal history files or records on offenders or keeping records for the identification of offenders.

(2) Where a young person is found guilty of an offence under this Act, the police force responsible for the investigation of the offence shall provide a record of the offence . . . for inclusion in any central repository designated pursuant to subsection (1).[20]

These records are subject to similar restrictions as court records. Section 43 permits government departments to maintain records of such offences, but the records may only be made available to the restricted class of persons who may have access to court records. Young persons may be fingerprinted. Section 45 of the Act deals with non-disclosure and destruction of police records:

45. (1) Subject to sections 45.1 and 45.2, records kept pursuant to sections 40 to 43 may not be made available for inspection under section 44.1 or 44.2 in the following circumstances:

(*a*) where the young person to whom the record relates is charged with the offence to which the record relates and is acquitted otherwise than by reason of a verdict of not criminally responsible on account of mental disorder, on the expiration of two months after the expiration of the time allowed for the taking of an appeal or, where an appeal is taken, on the expiration of three months after all proceedings in respect of the appeal have been completed;

(*b*) where the charge against the young person is dismissed for any reason other than acquittal or withdrawn, on the expiration of one year after the dismissal or withdrawal;

(*c*) where the charge against the young person is stayed, with no proceedings being taken against the young person for a period of one year, on the expiration of the one year;

---

[20] Bill C-37 replaces section 41 with the following:

41. (1) A record of any offence that a young person has been charged with having committed may, where the offence is an offence in respect of which an adult may be subjected to any measurement, process or operation referred to in the *Identification of Criminals Act*, be kept in such central repository as the Commissioner of the Royal Canadian Mounted Police may, from time to time, designate for the purpose of keeping criminal history files or records on offenders or keeping records for the identification of offenders.

(2) Where a young person is charged with having committed an offence referred to in subsection (1), the police force responsible for the investigation of the offence may provide a record of the offence, including the original or a copy of any fingerprints, palmprints or photographs and any other measurement, process or operation referred to in the *Identification of Criminals Act* taken of, or applied in respect of, the young person by or on behalf of the police force, for inclusion in any central repository designated pursuant to subsection (1).

(3) Where a young person is found guilty of an offence referred to in subsection (1), the police force responsible for the investigation of the offence shall provide a record of the offence, including the original or a copy of any fingerprints, palmprints or photographs and any other measurement, process or operation referred to in the *Identification of Criminals Act* taken of, or applied in respect of, the young person by or on behalf of the police force, for inclusion, in any central repository designated pursuant to subsection (1).

(*d*) where alternative measures are used to deal with the young person, on the expiration of two years after the young person consents to participate in the alternative measures in accordance with paragraph 4(1)(*c*);

(*e*) where the young person is found guilty of the offence and it is a summary conviction offence, on the expiration of five years after the young person is found guilty; and

(*f*) where the young person is found guilty of the offence and it is an indictable offence, on the expiration of five years after all dispositions made in respect of that offence and all dispositions made in respect of any other indictable offence of which the young person may have been found guilty after he was found guilty of that offence but prior to the expiration of the five year period have been completed.

(2) Any record kept pursuant to section 41 shall be destroyed forthwith when the circumstances set out in subsection (1) are realized in respect of that record.[21]

(3) Any record kept pursuant to sections 40 to 43 may, in the discretion of

---

[21] Bill C-37 replaces paragraphs 45(1)(*e*) and (*f*), and subsection 45(2) with the following:

(*d*.1) where the young person is found guilty of the offence and the disposition is an absolute discharge, on the expiration of one year after the young person is found guilty;

(*d*.2) where the young person is found guilty of the offence and the disposition is a conditional discharge, on the expiration of three years after the young person is found guilty;

(*e*) subject to paragraph (*g*), where the young person is found guilty of the offence and it is a summary conviction offence, on the expiration of three years after all dispositions made in respect of that offence;

(*f*) subject to paragraph (*g*), where the young person is found guilty of the offence and it is an indictable offence, on the expiration of five years after all dispositions made in respect of that offence; and

(*g*) where, before the expiration of the period referred to in paragraph (*e*) or (*f*), the young person is, as a young person, found guilty of

(i) a subsequent summary conviction offence, on the expiration of three years after all dispositions made in respect of that offence have been completed, and

(ii) a subsequent indictable offence, five years after all dispositions made in respect of that offence have been completed.

(2) Subject to subsections (2.1) and (2.2), when the circumstances set out in subsection (1) are realized in respect of any record kept pursuant to section 41, the record shall be destroyed forthwith.

(2.1) Where a special records repository has been established pursuant to subsection 45.02(1), all records in the central repository referred to in subsection 41(1) that relate to a conviction for first degree murder or second degree murder within the meaning of section 231 of the *Criminal Code* or an offence referred to in the schedule shall, when the circumstances set out in subsection (1) are realized in respect of the records, be transferred to that special records repository.

(2.2) Where a special fingerprints repository has been established pursuant to subsection 45.03(1), all fingerprints and any information necessary to identify the person to whom the fingerprints belong that are in the central repository referred to in subsection 41(1) shall, when the circumstances set out in subsection (1) are realized in respect of the records, be transferred to that special fingerprints repository.

(2.3) For the purposes of subsection (2), "destroy", in respect of a record, means

(*a*) to shred, burn or otherwise physically destroy the record, in the case of a record other than a record in electronic form; and

(*b*) to delete, write over or otherwise render the record inaccessible, in the case of a record in electronic form.

the person or body keeping the record, be destroyed at any time before or after the circumstances set out in subsection (1) are realized in respect of that record.

(4) A young person shall be deemed not to have committed any offence to which a record kept pursuant to sections 40 to 43 relates when the circumstances set out in paragraphs (1)(*d*), (*e*) or (*f*) are realized in respect of that record.

(5) For the purposes of paragraphs (1)(*e*) and (*f*), where no election is made in respect of an offence that may be prosecuted by indictment or proceeded with by way of summary conviction, the Attorney General or his agent shall be deemed to have elected to proceed with the offence as an offence punishable on summary conviction.

(6) This section applies, with such modifications as the circumstances require, in respect of records relating to the offence of delinquency under the *Juvenile Delinquents Act*, chapter J-3 of the Revised Statutes of Canada, 1970, as it read immediately prior to April 2, 1984.

The Young Offenders Act is increasingly coming under attack from victims' rights groups and other community organizations. While the philosophy behind the Act is sound, there is no doubt that the Act is in need of some fine-tuning. Much of the furor against the Act is really directed towards the sentencing provisions. A young person who is convicted of first degree murder will be sentenced to a term of five years' imprisonment less a day (section 20(1)(*k*.1)). It will be recalled that a person who is convicted of first or second degree murder will be imprisoned for a period not to exceed three years followed by a two year period of conditional supervision in the community. Under Bill C-37 the disposition has been increased to a maximum of 10 years. The public concern about some of the sentencing provisions is not misplaced. Someone who is convicted of first degree murder should be liable to receive more than three years' imprisonment under the Act. The three-year period of imprisonment for first degree murder does not take sufficient account of the principles of general and specific deterrence and is not in keeping with the primary goal of sentencing, which is the protection of the public. However, the principle behind the Young Offenders Act is a valid one and young offenders should continue to be treated more leniently than adults who commit similar offences.

Glossary

A Person in Authority. A person who the accused believes has authority over him or over the criminal proceedings so as to be able to influence the accused in making a statement.

Abet. To encourage someone to commit a crime.

Absolute Liability. The term is used to describe those offences where proof that the accused committed the prohibited act is sufficient for conviction.

Accused. The defendant in a criminal case.

Actus Reus. This is a latin expression which refers to an act. Generally every crime involves an act (*actus reus*) and a mental element (*mens rea*).

Adversary System. Under the adversarial system two opposing parties attempt to establish their case through relevant evidence presented before a judge. Each side presents evidence which is favourable to its case. The judge does not act as an investigator, but rather as an impartial arbitrator.

Aid. To assist someone in the commission of a criminal offence.

Appeal. The procedure in which a lower court case is brought to a higher court. One can appeal on questions of law or mixed fact and law.

Appellant. The person who appeals a decision to a higher court.

Arrest. The process whereby a person is seized or touched with a view to his detention. Mere words of arrest are not sufficient to constitute an arrest unless the person being placed under arrest voluntarily accompanies the arresting officer.

Assault. In criminal law, an assault is defined as the intentional application of force to another person without that person's consent. The Criminal Code gives a broad definition of the word assault. The Criminal Code states that in certain circumstances a threat to apply force to someone can constitute an assault (s. 265(1)).

Balance of Probabilities. The standard of proof which applies in civil cases. Is it more probable than not that something happened? In some cases, an accused is required to establish a defence on the balance of probabilities — i.e., insanity and entrapment.

Civil Law. The term is used to distinguish private law, which cover areas such as tort, property and contract law, from criminal law, which deals with the rights and responsibilities of the individual vis-a-vis the state. (The word civil can also be used to refer to the Civil Code of Quebec which codifies private areas of law such as wills, estates and real property.)

Co-accused. Someone who is jointly charged with the accused as part of the same information or indictment.

Common Law. Case law which is often referred to as judge-made law. Common law is different from statute law, which refers to legislation passed by Parliament or the legislature of a province.

Complainant. This term is used to describe the person who is the alleged victim of a criminal offence.

Confession. Refers to a written or oral statement in which the accused admits his guilt or admits some fact which could assist the Crown in proving his guilt. A confession must be freely and voluntarily made.

Credibility. Is the witness a believable witness? Does his or her evidence have the ring of truth to it? In considering whether a particular witness is credible, a judge or jury will look at the demeanour of the witness in the witness box.

Cross-examination. Refers to the process whereby a lawyer attempts to elicit favourable testimony from an opposing witness or attempts to weaken the testimony of a witness.

Culpable. Blameworthy, as in culpable homicide.

Direct Evidence. Evidence which indicates what a person saw or heard, etc. The evidence differs from circumstantial evidence in that direct evidence does not require the judge or jury to draw a series of inferences.

Direct Examination. The questioning of a witness by the party calling the witness is referred to as direct examination.

Directed Verdict. A motion made by the accused, at the close of the Crown's case, in which the accused argues that (1) there is no evidence upon which a properly instructed jury could convict the accused, or (2) the Crown has failed to prove an essential element of the offence. If the judge grants the motion, the judge will instruct the jury to render a not guilty verdict.

Election. The procedure whereby the accused has the right to decide whether to be tried before a provincial court judge or a County or District court judge sitting alone or a judge and jury.

Entrenched. The legal rights and freedoms contained in the Charter of Rights and Freedoms are called entrenched rights. The word entrenched refers to rights which have been given specific constitutional protection by inclu sion in the Charter of Rights. Such rights may be distinguished from rights created by ordinary statute which can be taken away by Parliament or the legislature of a province at any time.

Free and Voluntary. The principal test for determining whether a confession given by the accused is admissible in a court of law. The confession must not have been obtained by fear of prejudice or hope of advantage held out by someone in authority.

Hearsay. Hearsay evidence consists of a statement — oral or written — made by a witness in court which relies on something said or done by a person, who is not himself giving evidence. The statement which is being quoted is only hearsay if the party introducing the statement is using the statement to prove that the contents of the statement are true.

Hybrid Offence. Is an offence which may be prosecuted by indictment or summary conviction at the option of the Crown attorney. This offence is also known as a dual procedure offence or electable offence.

Included Offence. A lesser offence which is an offence which is included in the offence with which the accused is charged. An accused may be acquitted of the more serious offence, but convicted of the lesser included offence (s. 662(1) of the Criminal Code).

Indictable Offence. The Criminal Code classifies offences as being indictable, summary conviction, or hybrid offences. Indictable offences are the most serious offences in the Criminal Code carrying penalties ranging from 2 years imprisonment to life imprisonment. Thus, for example, an accused who is convicted of assault causing bodily harm is liable to receive up to 10 years' imprisonment. First-degree murder, which carries a mandatory penalty of life imprisonment, is an indictable offence.

Indictment. The document which sets out the charge against the accused. The indictment is the formal charging document which is used for indictable offences. The indictment is signed by the Attorney General or a Crown attorney acting as the agent of the Attorney General.

Information. A written accusation given before a justice of the peace in which the informant states that an unknown person, or the person named in the information, has committed an offence. The information is sworn under oath. In the search warrant context, the information is a statement sworn under oath before a justice of the peace alleging that the informant has reasonable and probable grounds to believe that there is, in a building, receptacle or place, something which will provide evidence with regard to the commission of a criminal offence. The information must be on oath in Form 1 of the Criminal Code.

Intra Vires. A latin expression used to describe the constitutional authority which Parliament or the Legislature of a province has to legislate in a certain field. Criminal law falls under federal jurisdiction and thus one can say that it is *intra vires* federal jurisdiction.

Mandatory Presumption. A presumption that must be drawn upon proof of certain facts.

Mens Rea. A Latin term which refers to the mental element which the Crown must prove in order to obtain a conviction. Literally translated, the term means "guilty mind". If the offence requires proof of *mens rea*, the Crown must show intent or recklessness on the part of the accused. *Mens rea* offences are often referred to as true criminal offences because such offences necessitate proof that the accused acted with a particular intent.

Peace Officer. The term, which is defined in section 2 of the Criminal Code, includes a mayor, warden, reeve, as well as a police officer and sheriff. A peace officer has certain arrest powers. (For the full definition, see s. 2 of the Criminal Code and Chapter 6, The Role of the Police.)

Permissive Presumption. A presumption that may be drawn but does not have to be drawn. The presumption can be a presumption of fact or law. The presumption that a man intends the natural consequences of his acts is a factual presumption which a judge or jury may or may not draw.

Planned and Deliberate. The Crown has to prove that a first degree murder was planned and deliberate.

Precedent. A case which is binding on a lower court so that the lower court must follow the principle of law set down by the higher court. The doctrine only applies if the facts in the case being decided are the same or similar to the facts in the precedent-setting case.

Preliminary Inquiry. A hearing in which a justice of the peace or judge (usually a judge) determines whether there is evidence of probable guilt which is sufficient to commit the accused to stand trial.

Prescribed by Law. The phrase, prescribed by law, is used in section 1 of the Charter. The Supreme Court of Canada has held that the phrase refers to a limit which is imposed by statute or is part of judge-made common law.

Pre-sentence Report. A report which tells the judge something about the offender's personal history. The report usually contains information about the accused's family background, educational and employment history. The report is prepared by a probation officer. Under the Young Offenders Act, a pre-sentence report is called a pre-disposition report.

Presumption of Innocence. The accused is presumed innocent until the trier of fact finds, after considering all of the evidence, that the Crown has proven the accused's guilt beyond a reasonable doubt.

***Prima Facie* Case.** The Crown must lead evidence to prove all of the essential elements of the offence so that a jury may convict. The jury does not have to convict once a *prima facie* case has been proved. If the Crown fails to prove a *prima facie* case, the defence can ask the judge to dismiss the case.

Promise to Appear. A document which sets out the name of the accused and the offence with which he is charged. The document, which is signed by the accused, also sets out the time and place of the court appearance.

Provocation. A partial defence which reduces murder to the included offence of manslaughter. The defence only applies to a first-degree murder charge.

Ratio Decidendi. This term is used to describe the reason for a court's decision.

Real Evidence. Evidence which can be observed by a judge or jury. This evidence usually consists of physical evidence such as objects found in the accused's possession.

Reasonable and Probable Grounds. The term is used in connection with certain arrest provisions of the Criminal Code. Some sections of the Criminal Code state that an arrest must be based on reasonable and probable grounds. To justify an arrest the facts must be such as to create a reasonable suspicion in the mind of a reasonable man. An arrest which is based on suspicion alone cannot be said to have been made on reasonable and probable grounds.

Reasonable Doubt. A real doubt as distinguished from a fanciful doubt. The trier of fact must be morally certain of the accused's guilt. Moral certainty has been held to be something less than absolute certainty.

Recognizance. A form which acknowledges that the person signing the form owes a debt to the crown in the event that the accused breaches certain conditions of his release.

Relevant Evidence. Evidence which logically proves or tends to prove a fact which is in issue in the case. While evidence must be relevant to be admissible, not all relevant evidence is admissible.

Reverse Onus Clause. A clause which relieves the Crown from establishing one of the essential elements of the offence by placing the burden of proof on the accused. Such a clause forces the accused to disprove the presumed essential element.

Rule of Law. Is a doctrine inherited from England. The doctrine, which lies at the heart of our legal system, holds that all men are subject to the law. In short, no man is above the law.

Search. Examining a place or person's premises for objects which will provide evidence of a criminal offence. The term can also refer to a personal search of an accused.

Search Warrant. An order signed by a justice of the peace which gives the person named in the warrant the authority to search the place specified in the warrant for evidence of a criminal offence.

Stare Decisis. To stand by decided matters.

Strict Liability. An offence which does not require proof of intent before the accused may be convicted. The offence is different from an absolute liability offence as the defences of due diligence and honest mistake of fact can be invoked by the accused. Public welfare offences, such as pollution, usually fall into this category.

Summons. A summons refers to a document which orders the accused to appear at the time and place specified in the summons to respond to the charge stated in the summons. The summons, which is signed by a justice of the peace, is a court order.

Voir Dire. A hearing within a trial to determine whether a statement or confession given by the accused is admissible in evidence.

Would Bring the Administration of Justice into Disrepute. The test for excluding evidence which violates a Charter right under section 24(2) of the Charter. Would the evidence obtained as a result of the Charter violation bring the administration of justice into disrepute? The French version of the test reads "could" and the Supreme Court of Canada has held that an accused is entitled to the benefit of the French version so that the word "would" should be read as "could".

Index